NASAL VOWEL EVOLUTION IN ROMANCE

Nasal Vowel Evolution in Romance

RODNEY SAMPSON

OXFORD
UNIVERSITY PRESS

OXFORD
UNIVERSITY PRESS

Great Clarendon Street, Oxford OX2 6DP

Oxford University Press is a department of the University of Oxford.
It furthers the University's objective of excellence in research, scholarship,
and education by publishing worldwide in

Oxford New York

Athens Auckland Bangkok Bogotá Buenos Aires Calcutta
Cape Town Chennai Dar es Salaam Delhi Florence Hong Kong Istanbul
Karachi Kuala Lumpur Madrid Melbourne Mexico City Mumbai
Nairobi Paris São Paulo Singapore Taipei Tokyo Toronto Warsaw
with associated companies in Berlin Ibadan

Oxford is a registered trade mark of Oxford Univeristy Press
in the UK and in certain other countries

Published in the United States
by Oxford University Press Inc., New York

© Rodney Sampson 1999

The moral rights of the author have been asserted

Database right Oxford University Press (maker)

First published 1999

British Library Cataloguing in Publication Data

Data available

Library of Congress Cataloging in Publication Data
Nasal vowel evolution in Romance/Rodney Sampson.
Includes bibliographical references.
1. Romance languages – Vowels.   2. Romance languages – Nasality.
I. Title.
PC91.S25   1999   440'.0415–dc21   98-55421

ISBN 0-19-823848-7

1 3 5 7 9 10 8 6 4 2

Typeset in Minion
by J&L Composition Ltd, Filey, North Yorkshire
Printed in Great Britain
on acid-free paper by
Biddles Ltd, Guildford and King's Lynn

Preface

Je n'entrerai pas dans la discussion aride et embrouillée de l'histoire des voyelles nasales.

Gaston Paris (1878: 125)

The present work addresses an aspect of historical Romance phonology which has so far lacked a general comparative treatment of any substance. Accounts of the fortunes of nasal vowels in individual Romance languages are of course not in short supply. French in particular has long exercised the curiosity of linguists, so much so that already in the 1870s the eminent French linguist Gaston Paris could sound a little weary of the subject of nasal vowel development in his native language. (It may be added that any weariness was short-lived and he engaged in lively polemical discussion on the topic on a number of later occasions.) But French is just one Romance variety amongst many which have experienced high levels of vowel nasalization, although the way in which its nasal vowels have evolved is by no means representative of what has happened elsewhere. It is hoped that the systematic comparative review which has been undertaken will help to correct this 'gallocentrism' and provide a more balanced view of nasal vowel evolution across Romance.

It is something of a truism that social and cultural factors are of no less importance in determining patterns of language change than internal structural forces. In recognition of this, attention has been paid throughout our coverage to the nature and possible impact of extralinguistic determinants on nasal vowel evolution. Also, the treatment of each branch of Romance has been prefaced with a brief outline of the external linguistic history of the area concerned in order to set the internal developments in an appropriate perspective.

A further aim of this study is to make a modest contribution to the wider phonological debate on the universals of vowel nasality. Since the 1960s, a substantial amount of work has been carried out on the characteristics and effects of vowel nasalization. In the main, the data used have been synchronic in nature, for understandable reasons, but the probative value of diachronic material has always been recognized. With its long and well-attested history, Romance is uniquely placed to add to that material, and it is hoped that the present work will prove of some interest to general phonologists who wish to know more of the diversity and complexity of nasal vowel evolution in Romance beyond the familiar developments found in French.

Finally, it is a pleasure to be able to express my gratitude to those who have assisted in the preparation of this study. Ralph Penny, Mark Tatham, John Charles Smith, and Mair Parry were generous and patient enough to read draft sections of the text and made many helpful comments. I am very grateful to John Hajek for kindly providing me with a copy of his excellent thesis, a revised version of which has just recently been published. The observations and suggestions made by the anonymous readers of Oxford University Press have been of great benefit and led to considerable improvement of the text. To all I extend my deepest thanks, and of course none can bear any responsibility for whatever shortcomings remain in the present work. However, my heaviest debt of gratitude goes to my long-suffering wife, Bodil, who has at all times provided solace and encouragement. Tusind tak min skat.

R. S.

Bristol
Easter 1998

Contents

List of Figures

List of Maps

Abbreviations

AIS	Jaberg, K. and Jud, J. 1928–41. *Sprach- und Sachatlas Italiens und der Südschweiz.* 8 vols. Zofingen: Ringier.
ALAL	Potte, J.-C. (ed.). 1975–87. *Atlas linguistique et ethnographique de l'Auvergne et du Limousin.* 2 vols. Paris: CNRS.
ALB	Taverdet, G. (ed.). 1975–88. *Atlas linguistique et ethnographique de Bourgogne.* 4 vols. Paris: CNRS.
ALCat	Griera, A. (ed.). 1923–64. *Atlas lingüístic de Catalunya.* 8 vols. Barcelona: Instituto Internacional de Cultura Románica.
ALCB	Bourcelot, H. (ed.). 1966–78. *Atlas linguistique et ethnographique de la Champagne et de la Brie.* 3 vols. Paris: CNRS.
ALEA	Alvar, M. (ed.). 1961–73. *Atlas lingüístico y etnográfico de Andalucía.* 6 vols. Granada: Univ. of Granada–CSIC.
ALEANR	Alvar, M., et al. (eds.). 1979–83. *Atlas lingüístico y etnográfico de Aragón, Navarra y Rioja.* 12 vols. Madrid: CSIC.
ALEIC	Bottiglioni, G. (ed.). 1933–42. *Atlante linguistico etnografico italiano della Corsica.* 10 vols. Pisa: L'Italia dialettale.
ALF	Gilliéron, J. (ed.). 1902–10. *Atlas linguistique de la France.* Paris: Champion.
ALG	Séguy, J. (ed.). 1954–73. *Atlas linguistique de la Gascogne.* 6 vols. Toulouse–Paris: CNRS.
ALGa	Instituo da Lingua Galega. 1990– . *Atlas lingüístico galego.* Santiago de Compostela: ILG.
ALI	Massobrio, L. (ed.). 1995– . *Atlante linguistico italiano.* Rome: Istituto Poligrafico e Zecca dello Stato.
ALIFO	Simoni-Aurembou, M.-R. (ed.). 1973–8. *Atlas linguistique et ethnographique de l'Ile-de-France et de l'Orléanais.* 2 vols. Paris: CNRS.
ALJA	Martin, J.-B., and Tuaillon, G. (eds.). 1971–8. *Atlas linguistique et ethnographique du Jura et des Alpes du Nord.* 3 vols. Paris: CNRS.
ALLoc	Ravier, X. (ed.). 1978–86. *Atlas linguistique et ethnographique du Languedoc Occidental.* 3 vols. Paris: CNRS.
ALLor	Boisgontier, J. (ed.). 1981–6. *Atlas linguistique et ethnographique du Languedoc Oriental.* 3 vols. Paris: CNRS.
ALN	Brasseur. P. (ed.). 1980–4. *Atlas linguistique et ethnographique normand.* 2 vols. Paris: CNRS.

ALP	Bouvier, J. C., and Martel, C. (eds.). 1975–86. *Atlas linguistique et ethnographique de la Provence*. 3 vols. Paris: CNRS.
ALPI	*Atlas lingüístico de la Península Ibérica*. Madrid: CSIC, 1962.
ALPic	Carton, F., and Lebègue, M. (eds.). 1989. *Atlas linguistique et ethnographique picard*. Paris: CNRS.
ALR	*Atlasul lingvistic român*. Serie nouă. 7 vols. Bucharest: Ed. Acad., 1956–72.
ALW	*Atlas linguistique de la Wallonie*. Liège: Vaillant-Carmanne, 1953.
ASLEF	Pellegrini, G. B. (ed.). 1972–84. *Atlante storico-linguidtico-etnografico friulano*. 5 vols. Padua: Univ. of Padua.
CIL	*Corpus Inscriptionum Latinarum*. 16 vols. Berlin: Reimer, 1862– .
CLE	Buecheler, F. (ed.). 1895–1926. *Carmina Latina Epigraphica*. 3 vols. Leipzig: Teubner.
CTM	Hedfors, H. (ed.). 1932. *Compositiones ad tingenda musiva*. Uppsala: Almqvist and Wiksell.
DCECH	Corominas, J., and Pascual, J. A. 1980–91. *Diccionario crítico etimológico castellano e hispánico*. 6 vols. Madrid: Gredos.
DECLC	Coromines, J. (ed.). 1980–91. *Diccionari etimològic i complementari de la llengua catalana*. 9 vols. Barcelona: Curial.
DOP	Migliorini, B., Tagliavini, C., Fiorelli, P. 1981. *Dizionario d'ortografia e di pronunzia*. New ed. Turin: ERI–Ed. RAI.
FEW	Wartburg, W. von. (ed.). 1922– . *Französisches etymologisches Wörterbuch*. 25 vols. Leipzig–Basel: Klopp–Zbinden.
HLF	Brunot, F., and Bruneau, C. 1905–72. *Histoire de la langue française des origines à 1900*. 13 vols. Paris: A. Colin.
K.	Keil, H. (ed.). 1857–80. *Grammatici Latini*. 7 vols. Leipzig: Teubner.
REW	Meyer-Lübke, W. 1935 [repr. 1968]. *Romanisches etymologisches Wörterbuch*. 3rd ed. Heidelberg: Carl Winter.
Ronjat, i, ii	Ronjat, J. 1930–41. *Grammaire istorique des parlers provençaux modernes*. 4 vols. [I. *Fonétique* (Vowels) (1930), II. *Fonétique* (Consonants) (1932)], Montpellier: Société des Langues Romanes.
TDR	Rusu, V. (ed.). 1984. *Tratat de dialectologie românească*. Craiova: Scrisul Românesc.
Thurot, i, ii	Thurot, C. 1881. *De la prononciation française depuis le commencement du XVIe siècle*. 2 vols. Paris: 1881. Repr. Geneva: Slatkine, 1966.

abl.	ablative
acc.	accusative
c.	circa
Cat.	Catalan
CL	Classical Latin
d.	died

dat.	dative
Engad.	Engadinese (Rheto-Romance)
f.	feminine
Fr.	French
gen.	genitive
Germ.	Germanic
It.	Italian
l.	line
m.	masculine
mod.	modern
n.	neuter
nom.	nominative
OCS	Old Church Slavonic
OFr.	Old French
past part.	past participle
pl.	plural
Port.	Portuguese
pres. part.	present participle
Rom.	Romanian
sg.	singular
Span.	Spanish
St.	standard
*	unattested reconstruction
**	non-occurring form in a known language
>	develops through time into
<	has developed through time from
[ ]	phonetic transcription
/ /	phonemic transcription

1

Nasal Vowels and Vowel Nasalization: Preliminaries

Vowel nasalization is a process which has operated widely in Romance. Amongst the standard varieties,[1] French and Portuguese have been particularly affected and they have developed a series of independent nasal vowel phonemes. Romance is consequently well represented in the modest set of present-day European languages possessing nasal vowel phonemes (others include Polish, Albanian, Irish, Gaelic, and Breton). In the remaining standard varieties of Romance, nasalization has not led to the creation of nasal vowel phonemes, but in many cases it has exercised a considerable influence on patterns of vowel evolution. A similar picture emerges when non-standard varieties of Romance are considered; vowel nasalization has had a widespread impact, and in some cases it has been great enough to result in the creation of nasal vowel phonemes. The different varieties of Romance thus provide a rich quarry for the investigation of nasal vowels and their evolution.

As we shall see, the details of vowel nasalization vary a good deal across Romance. Yet such has been the cultural prestige of French that this language has been the focus of particular attention in explorations into the nature and characteristics of vowel nasalization, and it was widely believed to provide the classic example of how this phenomenon operates. Indeed, some linguists continue to subscribe to this belief. Nonetheless, patterns of evolution in other Romance varieties are not infrequently at some variance with the 'classic' French-based pattern of evolution. For example, exceptions can be found in Portuguese, Gascon, and various northern Italian dialects to the allegedly universal tendency for high nasal vowels to lower, a tendency postulated largely on the evidence of French. In addition, the very facts from French itself can readily be seen to have arisen from exceptional circumstances rather than from some general guiding principle of change.

In the following chapters of this work, we will be systematically exploring the patterns of vowel nasalization across the standard and non-standard varieties of Romance. To facilitate matters, our treatment is divided into sub-sections corresponding to the broad geographical-linguistic divisions customarily made by Romanists, Ibero-Romance, Gallo-Romance, and so on. In the light of the data which emerge, the concluding chapter will distil the general characteristics of vowel nasalization in Romance and identify certain areas where controversy remains.

Our focus will be firmly on developments in Romance. However, to set the data into their proper context it will be helpful initially to consider briefly the general nature of nasality and its relationship to vowels.

1.1. The Phonetics of Nasality

Phoneticians recognize three resonance chambers in the supra-glottal vocal tract. Two are closely related and effectively form a horn-shaped continuum. These are the pharyngeal cavity and the oral cavity. Above this pairing of cavities lie the nasal cavities. These have the nostrils as their front entrance and at the rear end there are two openings, the *choanae*, each of which is approximately 3 cm² in cross-section. The choanae open into the top section of the pharynx, the *naso-pharynx*. The nasal cavities themselves are divided, often asymmetrically, into two parts by a vertical central wall, the *septum*, the front section of which forms the central wall dividing the nostrils. The internal configuration of the nasal cavities is a complex one, for bony downward-flanging processes project from the side walls and create three nearly horizontal passages in each of the two halves. There is however no mobile organ within the nasal cavities, so that it is not possible for speakers to vary the volume and shape of this chamber at will and thereby bring about different resonance effects.

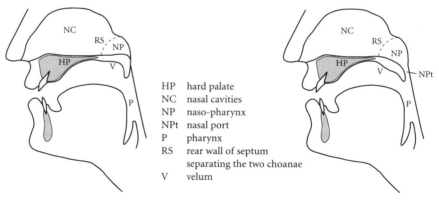

HP   hard palate
NC   nasal cavities
NP   naso-pharynx
NPt nasal port
P   pharynx
RS   rear wall of septum
     separating the two choanae
V   velum

Sagittal section of the vocal tract
during the articulation of an oral vowel

Sagittal section of the vocal tract
during the articulation of a nasal vowel

FIG. 1.   Vocal tract during oral and nasal vowel production

Predictably, the dimensions of these cavities vary somewhat between individuals, depending upon their age, sex, and physiological make-up. However, phoneticians generally work on the assumption that the average adult has a vocal tract (glottis to lips) of some 17–17.5 cm in length (Fant 1960: 61; Lieberman and Blumstein 1988: 37). The mean distance from uvula to the outlet at the nostrils is reckoned to be about 12 cm and from the choanae to the outlet of the nostrils about 8 cm. The naso-pharynx, from uvula to choanae, may be taken to measure approximately 4 cm therefore, with the whole pharynx extending over about 12 cm. Against these figures which, it should be emphasized, represent just averages between different speakers, we may set the dimensions of the electrical analog constructed by House and Stevens (1956) to simulate the acoustic properties of the vocal tract. Here, an overall length of 17 cm was adopted and the analog of the nasal tract was connected at a point 8 cm from the glottis counterpart.

Mention may also be made of four small cavities which lead off the nasal cavities. These are two pairs of sinuses, the *sinus maxillares* which are set in the bone on either side of the nasal cavities, and the *sinus frontales* which are located in the bone of the forehead above the nasal cavities. Each of the sinuses is linked with the nasal cavities, and serves to modify the complex nature of nasal resonance in speech.

When an egressive pulmonic airstream is set up (this being the only linguistically relevant type for Romance[2] and hence the only type with which we shall be concerned), it may be expelled from the body in one of three ways. Most commonly, in Romance and other languages, the airstream escapes via the oral-pharyngeal cavity alone. Where this happens, oral speech sounds are produced. However, it is possible for the nasal cavities to be involved, as a result of the airstream escaping either partly or wholly via them. The former occurs when there is free passage for the airstream through the oral cavity but also access to the nasal cavities, so that the airflow passes out simultaneously through both channels. The vowels of the French words *an* and *on* have such an articulation. The latter is found when there is access to the nasal cavities but passage through the oral cavity is blocked by a total obstruction. The result here is an exclusively nasal channel for the airstream to escape through during the articulation of the speech-sound, as in [m] and [n].

We will not formally distinguish between sound types in which the airstream is channelled partially as opposed to totally through the nasal cavities, but will simply describe as 'nasal' any sound type in whose production the nasal cavities participate. Some phoneticians do make such a distinction, describing as 'nasal' those sounds with an exclusively nasal airflow and as 'nasalized' those with simultaneous oral and nasal airflow. However, as the term 'nasalized' will be much used by us in a historical sense to indicate sound types whose articulation has changed in the course of time from oral to partly or wholly nasal, it will be safer not to use it as well with a synchronic value. Synchronically, therefore, only 'nasal' will be used.

Access for the airstream to the nasal cavities is controlled by the position of the *velum*. This organ forms the rear part of the palate and is made up of muscle tissue. Thanks to its muscular composition, the velum is flexible and can be raised or lowered under the control of the speaker. When the velum is lowered, either as a result of a controlled gesture by the speaker or because it is in its neutral position of rest, it hangs down and leaves free the opening bounded by the rear of the velum and the side and rear walls of the upper pharynx, the *nasal port*, so that the airstream has access to the nasal cavities. The maximal cross-sectional area of the nasal port is variable. On the basis of the findings of Björk (1961: 40) with Swedish speakers, Reenen (1982a: 64) calculates that the area can be between 120 mm^2 and 310 mm^2, and he suggests (p. 117) an average figure of the order of 200 mm^2 might be postulated for adult males.[3]   Alternatively, the velum can be raised, to varying degrees, up towards the side and rear walls of the upper pharynx, thereby partly or totally closing the nasal port. According to Guth (1975: 28), the smallest cross-sectional area of the nasal port yielding perceptible nasality is about 30 mm^2.[4] This observation is of interest too in that it reveals that some airflow through the nasal cavities may occur without nasality being perceived by the hearer. Indeed, even for the production of oral plosive consonants, it has been found that there may be a certain amount of nasal port opening.[5] Thus, the velum acts as a readily governable, if sometimes leaky, valve which allows the nasal cavities to be brought into play as a secondary resonance chamber alongside the primary oral-pharyngeal cavity. And, all other things being equal, the greater the opening of the nasal port during a vowel's articulation, the more intense will be the nasal resonance accompanying it.

The variability of nasal port opening is invested with especial significance by Reenen for the production of nasality in vowels. He postulates a so-called 'N%' factor (i.e. a nasality factor), calculated on the basis of the ratio between nasal port opening and oral cavity opening, each of these being computed according to their cross-sectional area.[6]   Purely oral vowels would have a 0% value and nasal consonants with full oral closure a 100% value. Vowel nasality is then viewed as a dynamic phenomenon 'produced with an increase in N% from (almost) zero to about 75' (1982a: 118). Since a ratio is involved here, the implication is that the degree of nasal port opening required to give rise to a comparable level of perceived nasality in vowels of different height (hence with different degrees of oral constriction) will vary. High vowels will need less nasal port opening, low vowels more, for the hypothesized N% ratio to be satisfied. The experimental evidence for this claim is not strong however. If we assume that there is a correlation between velum height and nasal port opening, then some confirming data are available, e.g. in the study of English and Hindi by

Henderson (1984).[7] However, other cross-linguistic investigations of vowel nasality report that degrees of nasal port opening do not systematically vary in proportion with vowel height (Clumeck 1976; Al-Bamerni 1983 cited in Hajek 1997: § 5.2.2), so that Reenen's N% ratio cannot represent a general characterization of vowel nasality in language.

A further variable factor in this context is the precise timing of the adjustments to nasal port opening. Although the velum is a relatively slow-moving organ of speech, increases or decreases in the degree of port opening may be effected at different speeds and may be initiated at different stages during the articulation span of the vowel. As a result the exact nature of the 'nasal profiling' of a nasal vowel may vary a good deal.

Physically, the movements of the velum are controlled by various muscles which work in a cooperative way (cf. Laver 1991: 101–2). Raising is achieved mainly by the action of two muscles, the *levator veli palatini* and the *superior pharyngeal constrictor*. The former of these, which connects the front surface of the velum with the base of the skull, raises and retracts the velum about 2 cm all in all in an average adult; the latter, which primarily serves to propel food down towards the oesophagus, may also when contracted raise the velum. A further muscle, the *tensor palatini*, also acts to spread and tense the velum as it is raised. Lowering is effected by two muscles, assisted to some extent as well by the relaxation of the raising muscles and by gravity. On the one hand, there is the *palatoglossus* which runs down from the under-surface of the velum, splitting to form the anterior pillars of the fauces in front of the tonsils and then passing into the tongue, to give this muscle an almost circular, sphincter-like character. It can raise the back of the tongue as well as lower the velum. On the other hand, the *palatopharyngeus* is a long, slender muscle connecting the velum and the posterior edge of the thyroid cartilage and the side wall of the pharynx. When innervated, it is notable that this causes the larynx to be pulled up slightly unless the musculature surrounding the larynx is braced (cf. Laver 1980: 74).

Interestingly, although individual speakers have the same set of muscles, they do not necessarily operate them in an identical way to achieve given gestures during the production of speech. Thus, the palatoglossus may not be activated by some speakers to cause velum lowering or the superior pharyngeal constrictor to cause raising. Indeed, Benguerel et al. (1977: 166) discovered that with the French speakers they investigated there was innervation of the palatoglossus for nasal vowel articulation but not for nasal consonants, suggesting that different anatomical strategies may routinely be used by a single speaker to achieve the 'same' effect.[8] Finally, it appears that for the closing of the nasal port there is generally some fronting of the posterior pharyngeal wall (Hardcastle 1976; Henderson 1984; Lieberman and Blumstein 1988).

1.1.1. ACOUSTIC CHARACTERISTICS

Acoustically, vowels arise as a result of resonance in the oral-pharyngeal cavity. The energy source for the resonance is glottal excitation caused by the periodic vibration of the vocal cords. Associated with each vowel type are a number of formants, or resonance bands, which are located at specific frequencies and can vary in amplitude. Thus, the values for the French vowel /a/ as reported by Lonchamp (1979) were: F_1 660 Hz, F_2 1,350 Hz, F_3 2,380 Hz, where F_1 indicates the lowest formant and so on. The different resonance effects and, consequently, different formant values found with individual vowel types are determined by the size and shape of the air chamber in the oral-pharyngeal cavity. The configuration of the air chamber can readily be modified, principally as a result of movement of the tongue (raising/lowering, fronting/retracting) but also through lip and jaw movement. For instance, raising the tongue height correlates well with a decrease in the frequency of the F_1 and vice versa. Also, retraction of the tongue body correlates quite well with a decrease in the F_2 frequency.

The nasal cavities represent what acousticians term a shunting side-chamber in relation to the oral-pharyngeal cavity. The addition of this side-chamber during vowel articulation complicates the pattern of resonance a good deal. It has the effect of adding not only new resonances but also associated anti-resonances, these often being referred to as poles and zeros, respectively. The zeros or anti-resonances serve to damp or cancel any resonance energy which happens to lie in the vicinity of their frequency. When the nasal port is closed, some sound can propagate into the nasal cavities, but as the cavities are then sealed off, the associated poles and zeros coincide in frequency and they cancel each other out. When however the nasal port is open and there is nasal coupling, the associated poles and zeros created in the nasal cavities become differentiated in frequency. The greater the level of nasal coupling, i.e. the greater the opening of the nasal port, the more the pole and zero pairs of the nasal cavities are separated in frequency. Now, the poles and zeros yielded by resonance in the nasal cavities interact with the formants arising in the oral-pharyngeal cavity (no anti-resonances or zeros are created in the oral-pharyngeal cavity, it may be noted). The result is a complex overall acoustic output in which the components from the different but inter-connected cavities cannot readily be distinguished. Nasal vowels are, acoustically, not just oral vowels plus a clearly identifiable super-imposition of acoustic energy attributable to added bands of nasal resonance. As Guth (1975: 317) observes, 'on peut ajouter à une voyelle orale tous les formants que l'on veut: on n'obtient jamais par ce moyen de voyelle nasale.'

In addition, further modifying the acoustic effect of nasal resonance are the sinuses, which act in their turn as side-chambers. According to Lindqvist and Sundberg (1976), these yield particular resonance frequencies between 200 and

2,000 Hz which alter the resonance pattern. However, Feng (1987: 33–45) is a little more circumspect and claims that their main contribution is generally to modify the overall wave structure rather than to add a component or components of specific frequency.

What then are the acoustic characteristics of nasal vowels? Extensive investigation of this question has taken place over the past four decades through the analysis of natural speech signals especially by sound spectrography and also on the basis of data from mechanical or electrical analogs of the vocal tract, underpinned by the predictions of acoustic theory. However, the results have proved diverse and at times even conflicting. In Figure 2, some of the findings and proposals are summarized. It may be noted that mention of a 'new formant' implies that the presence of a formant which is not found in the counterpart oral vowel and which has an amplitude significantly affecting the spectral structure of the vowel. The 'bandwidth' of a formant is the spread of frequencies over which it extends.

Some points of agreement exist in these different characterizations. The main signs of added nasality in a vowel are generally found to be spectral modifications in the lower frequencies, particularly in the vicinity of the first oral formant. A recognizable nasal formant, which is also a major hallmark (the *nasal murmur*) of nasal consonants, is identified as usually occurring at about 250 Hz. A zero has also been observed to interact with the F_1, reducing its amplitude and increasing its bandwidth so that the spread of the acoustic energy of the F_1 may result in its splitting into two linked bands. Modifications at higher frequencies have also been noted, with additional formants appearing along with changes in amplitude, frequency, and bandwidth in the oral formants. These changes, which appear to be less significant, give rise to a more diffuse distribution of spectral energy with less intense energy peaks.

Despite these common points however, a good deal of uncertainty and variation can be seen in these descriptions of the acoustic properties of vowel nasality. The reasons for this are diverse. Differences in the degree of methodological adequacy shown by the investigators may play a part. Also, in experiments where natural speech signals were used the obvious possibility exists of variation in the anatomical or physiological make-up of the subjects investigated. The very asymmetry of the two halves of the nasal cavities, common in humans, may well mean that a complex and variable blend of differing resonance effects will be yielded by those two halves, as Fant (1960: 141) notes. In addition, the sometimes large variations between individuals as to the dimensions of their nasal passages and the degree of mucous obstruction in their nasal cavities at any given moment will give rise to differing acoustic effects. Furthermore, the degree of nasal coupling used can readily vary between speakers and indeed from vowel type to vowel type within one and the same speaker.[9] Finally and perhaps most significantly, vowel nasality can show significant variation in the way it is

Joos (1948)	Anti-resonance c.900 Hz; new formant c.1,000 Hz; tendency for additional formants to be created.
Durand (1953)	New characteristic formant c.7,500 Hz.
Delattre (1954)	Extreme weakening of F1; additional formant c.250 Hz (= NF1); additional formant c.2,000 Hz (= NF2).
Hockett (1955)	F3 is raised; often an additional band of resonance just above F1.
House and Stevens (1956/1957)	Weakening of F1 + increase of its bandwidth; raising of centre frequency of F1; reduction of overall energy of vowel; various 'secondary' effects.
Jakobson and Halle (1956)	'Spreading the available energy over wider frequency regions by a reduction in the intensity of certain (primarily the first) formants and introduction of additional (nasal) formants'.
Hattori, Yakamoto, and Fujimura (1958)	Reinforcement of intensity c.250 Hz; weakening of intensity c.500 Hz; comparatively weak and diffuse components in between formants.
Fant (1960)	Intensity reduction of F1; fairly fixed nasal formants at (especially) 250, and 1,000, 2,000, 3,000, 4,000 Hz; increased formant bandwith.
Lafon (1961)	Filtering out of much low-level intensity; additional intensity at 3,500–4,000 Hz.
Schwartz (1968)	Reduction in intensity of F1; zeros at various frequencies (variable values however); additional energy at (variable) frequencies; frequency shifts in formants.
Debrock (1974)	Additional formant (variable between 700–2,170 Hz); substantial weakening of F1 not found; some evidence of low NF1 (150–250 Hz).
Guth (1975)	Slight loss of intensity in F1; loss of intensity in F2; F3 tends to spread in bandwidth and split; additional formant c.1,000 Hz; zero c.2,500 Hz; resonance bands below 2,500 Hz, c.3,000 Hz, 3,500 Hz.
Ohala (1975)	Upward shifted F1 'in theory'; lowered F1 amplitude; increased bandwidth of all formants; additional nasal resonance c.250–350 Hz.
Halle and Stevens (1979)	Lowest spectral peak is split or broadened in bandwidth.
Reenen (1982a)	Change in formant structure through time.
Hawkins and Stevens (1985)	Usually a shift in frequency and increase in bandwidth in F1; more inconsistent changes at higher frequencies, frequency shifts of higher formants, change in amplitude of spectral peaks, appearance of additional peaks.
Lieberman and Blumstein (1988)	Reduction in spectral prominence of F1 by widening the bandwidth or creating an additional peak nearby.

Fig. 2.   Proposed acoustic correlates of nasality

physically realized from language to language, making any universally valid statement of its acoustic properties very problematic. There can therefore be no straightforward and invariant acoustic correlate to vowel nasality. In view of this, while the recourse to speech analogs and theoretical prediction in exploring and modelling the acoustic properties of vowel nasality is both understandable and indispensable, the results obtained ultimately have to be interpreted in the light of the facts of actual speech from individual languages.

1.1.2. PERCEPTUAL CORRELATES

As we have seen, rather complex acoustic modifications occur when nasality is added to vowel articulations. Now, since these complex signals are what the hearer is confronted with and has to interpret, a number of questions suggest themselves. What are the perceptual cues which enable the hearer to perceive a vowel as being nasal? Do these cues vary for different vowel types? Does the presence of the relevant cues have any other perceptual effect apart from that of signalling the presence of nasality in the vowel? And an overarching consideration relating to each of these questions is the extent to which the perception of vowel nasality is conditioned by the hearer's linguistic background.

Looking at the three questions in turn, we find that what seem to be the main cues for nasality tie up with certain acoustic characteristics previously noted. A vowel is readily perceived as nasal if the prominence in the area of F_1 is reduced and the bandwidth widened. Indeed, already in the 1950s it was shown by Delattre (1954 [1966]) with the help of an early speech synthesizer that nasality may be signalled merely by reducing the intensity of the F_1 of an oral vowel. Later, the same scholar confirmed this, noting that for the vowel [ɛ] a reduction of the F_1 by 12 decibels resulted in its being perceived by native French speakers as [ɛ̃] (1968: 65). The study of Hawkins and Stevens (1985), using synthetic speech data presented to speakers of Gujerati, Hindi, Bengali, and English, found that these basic cues for the perception of nasality (reduced prominence and widening of bandwidth in F_1 area) are apparently language-independent, since speakers from these different linguistic backgrounds agreed well over the cut-off point between oral and nasal in the test material. However, in real language situations the cut-off point may well vary depending on the structure of the speaker's language. Thus, the vowel of English *shan't* could have comparable physical cues for nasality as the vowel of French *chante*, but the former may still be perceived as 'oral' because an oral vowel is what is expected by an English hearer.

In addition, attention has been called to certain other physical characteristics which may need to be present if the cues for nasality are to be perceived. One is the progressive increase of the level of nasal coupling and hence acoustic nasality during the articulation of the vowel segment. This is briefly noted by Hattori, Yakamoto, and Fujimura (1958: 274) for French, but Reenen (1982a) lays considerable importance on this dynamic property, viewing it as a crucial cue in the acoustic signal for the perception of nasality in a vowel, irrespective, it seems, of which language is involved. Some striking evidence for this comes in an experiment reported by Linthorst (1973: 88–9). Three French words *même*, *dais*, *baie* were recorded and their vowels spliced out and added in various combinations to the initial consonants of the test words. If we indicate the partly nasal vowel of the first word as [E] and the oral vowel of the other two as [ɛ], then it was found that whilst the nine French listeners almost invariably perceived the vowel glide [ɛE] as a nasal vowel, other possibilities including [E] and [EE] (i.e. long [E]) were overwhelmingly perceived as oral. However, it remains to be demonstrated whether the same perceptual cue for identifying vowel nasality is used by speakers of all other languages, especially those in which nasal vowels do not share the dynamic profile of French.

Further observations have also been made by various phoneticians touching on the duration of nasal vowels. It has been noted by Delattre (1965) and following him Entenman (1976) that nasal vowels are typically longer than their oral counterparts. For French, which has been by far the most investigated language in this connection, greater durations are reported for nasal vowels as compared with their nearest oral counterparts, especially in blocked syllables. Using three informants, Delattre and Monnot (1981) found that nasal vowels were on average 42% longer than that of their oral counterparts, and some further confirmation comes from the studies by Brichler-Labaeye (1970) and O'Shaughnessy (1981) who use, respectively, radiocinematographic and spectrographic data, although with only one informant in each case and just a small number of tokens. Delattre and Monnot (1981) also conducted an experiment into the perceptual significance of duration for the recognition of vowel nasality by French speakers. A synthesized simulation of *l'aide* was generated and its vowel was manipulated by lowering the intensity of the first formant so as to give the impression of 'half nasality' to a French hearer, hence making it interpretable as *l'aide* or *l'Inde*. Nine versions of it were then taken each with a different vowel duration, from 10 to 26 csecs in gradations of 2 csecs. In a test using these synthesized versions, the nine French-speaking subjects uniformly perceived the token with minimal vowel duration as oral and the one with maximal duration as nasal. The crossover point was about 18 csecs.[10] In view of the more indeterminate character of the acoustic signal in nasal vowels, a tendency for greater duration in their articulation is understandable in order to facilitate their identification, and consequently the presence of levels of duration higher than the average for all vowel types might well be perceived as a cue for nasality. However, it is significant that this and the other observations made on the association between duration and the perception of vowel nasality are founded on the basis of data from French. In fact, experiments exposing listeners of not only French but also other linguistic backgrounds to the same test material reveal significant differences in the extent to which added duration acts as a cue for nasal vowel recognition. Indeed, this was the case with the Anglophone subjects who also took Delattre and Monnot's perception test. Francophones appear to expect the use of relatively greater duration in nasal vowels, but for speakers of Portuguese (another language in which nasality is distinctive in vowels) this is less true (cf. Stevens, Fant, and Hawkins 1987). It may well be therefore that added duration and progressive increase in nasal coupling both act as perceptual cues for vowel nasality in a language-specific rather than a general way.

A final comment is needed in answer to our first question. We have so far assumed that, perceptually, nasality arises as a result of resonance phenomena of some sort emanating from the nasal cavity. However, phoneticians have found that a 'nasal effect' can in fact be produced in the vocal tract without the intervention of the nasal cavities. As has been seen, important acoustic correlates of perceived nasality are damping and the greater diffusion of spectral energy, and it has been shown that this can be achieved by other cavities being formed by the muscular systems of the lower and upper pharynx and acting as side-chambers (cf. Laver 1980: 84–7). Vowels occurring adjacent to sounds accompanied by a high airflow may also take on a perceptually nasal quality. The explanation for the phenomenon appears to be that, acoustically, the airflow causes lowering of the amplitude of the first formant of the vowel and increases its bandwidth, both of these yielding the perceptual effect of nasality (Matisoff 1975; Ohala 1987: 220–1). Such instances of nasality are not typical, in the sense that nasal vowels usually are produced in speech through the participation of the nasal cavities. However, it is significant that a nasal percept can be produced without these cavities being involved. This suggests an avenue whereby what were originally physiologically non-nasal articulations may be perceived as nasal and consequently a nasal pronunciation could be taken to be the target intended. The result might then be that through imitation some speakers would deliberately adopt a physiologically nasal articulation for the vowel concerned (cf. 1.3 below). In view of this and the possibility noted earlier of 'oral' sounds actually having some nasal airflow during their articulation, perceptual considerations can be seen to play at least as important a role as articulatory factors in determining when and where vowel nasality is present.

Turning to the question of whether perception cues for nasality vary markedly from vowel type to vowel type, there is no indisputable evidence of such variation. But there is certainly some evidence for believing that varying levels of the relevant cues may be needed before nasality is perceived in different vowel types. The investigations of House and Stevens (1956) and House (1957) using synthetic speech generated by an electrical analog suggested this rather clearly, when it was found that the American subjects used in the experiment required about three times the level of synthetic nasality to perceive the low vowel [a] as nasal, as compared with the high vowels [i] and [u]. This may be explained in part as the result of low (oral) vowels in American English tending to be articulated with some degree of nasality, so that they require a considerable amount of extra nasality to be present before they are perceived as truly nasal. But a number of other phoneticians have also noted that the degree of opening of the nasal port, and hence the level of acoustic nasality, does not in general need to be so great for high vowels as for low vowels to yield perceptual nasality (Fant 1960: 156; Reenen 1982a: 115; Feng 1987: 75). Experimental data from French further confirm this difference between distinct vowel types. Benguerel and Lafargue (1981) discovered that the limen between perceptually oral and nasal vowels was different as between [a] vs. [ã] and [ɛ̃] vs. [o], [õ] vs. [o]. As with House and Stevens, the low vowel [a] was found to require a higher level of nasality before being perceived as nasal.

Finally, a good deal of attention has been paid in recent years to the secondary perceptual effects which may arise when nasality is superimposed on vowels. One such effect is the tendency for the nasality to obscure the basic oral quality of the vowels. The reason for this is that, as already noted, the addition of nasal coupling causes the first peak of spectral prominence, F_1, which is critical for vowel quality identification, to lose in intensity and spread in bandwidth. As a result, the differences between neighbouring but distinct vowel types can be masked to some extent, such that there is a greater possibility amongst hearers for associating and equating originally different nasal vowel types.

The significance of such possible perceptual confusion is of course considerable for helping to explain historical cases of vowel merger between nasal vowels. The phenomenon here has been the subject of a number of experimental investigations. Bond (1976) reports on a perception test using American English speakers judging vowels excerpted from the frames [h _ d] and [N _ N] (where 'N' indicates a nasal consonant of some sort). Much greater difficulty was experienced in discriminating between the contextually nasalized vowels occurring in the latter frame, and notable was the consistent failure to distinguish the short front vowels [æ], [ɪ], and [e] appearing in this frame whereas in the former frame the three vowels were readily distinguished. Wright (1980, 1986) confirms the lesser degree of perceptual distinctness between nasal vowels, though once again the data used are based on experimentation with English speakers only so that the effects observed may be language-specific. In view of the available experimental evidence, he is led to speculate on what he calls the 'truncated cone hypothesis'. According to this, the addition of nasality to vowels provides a new dimension for expanding the potential phonetic range of vowels, like a new vertical dimension rising from the oral two-dimensional base of the cone. However, the perceptual space decreases as one proceeds along this new dimension just as cross-sections of a cone decrease in area as one goes higher. But the perceptual cone is truncated, since nasality even at its most intense level does not mask all oral contrasts in vowels.

Another observed effect of added nasality concerns perceived vowel height. The claim here, which is clearly related to what has just been discussed, is that when nasality is superimposed on a vowel, the hearer may perceive a change in its original tongue height. Wright (1975) reports on a perception test involving twelve American subjects in which all the test vowels, when nasalized, were judged to be accompanied by lowering except for the vowels [æ] and [ɔ] which were perceived to have raised and [ɑ] which remained constant. This finding, with high vowels perceptually lowering and a majority of low vowels perceptually raising, is in line with the results of the experiment described by Bond (1976). More recently, Wright (1986) gives an account of a more rigorous perception test the results of which are entirely consistent with those already found previously. The main additional item of information is that vowels may be perceived as somewhat more centralized when they receive nasality (in line with the 'truncated cone hypothesis').

These findings, which are particularly suggestive in respect of the history of nasal vowels in French, are explicable if we recognize that the perception of height in a nasal vowel is not exclusively determined by the frequency of the F_1, the first oral formant. When other spectral energy occurs in the vicinity of the F_1, a sort of perceptual 'averaging out' seems to take place with the result that the location of the final centre of perceptual gravity may lie at a frequency intermediate between the F_1 and the other bands of energy (nasal formants and zeros, and also F_2 for back vowels). It will be the relative intensity of these bands which determines the precise frequency level perceived. This phenomenon, which has come to be known as 'spectral integration', was noted already by Delattre et al. (1952) with oral back vowels, where F_1 and F_2 are the bands concerned, these being fairly close to one another in frequency. But it may well apply to all nasal vowels, since the nasal formants are located near enough to the crucial F_1 to be able to interact with it perceptually. Spectral integration can occur between formants up to approximately 425 Hz apart. Now, acoustic studies of spectra of oral vowels and their nasal counterparts, using either synthetic speech (e.g. House and Stevens 1956) or natural speech (e.g. Beddor 1983: 131–60), show that, when nasality is added to high vowels, additional spectral energy appears at a higher frequency than the original oral F_1. In consequence, the new centre of gravity for the crucial low frequency peak of prominence would be drawn upwards in frequency, hence causing a perceptual lowering of the vowel. Conversely, for low vowels, a centre of gravity lower in frequency than the original F_1 generally emerges, yielding a perceptually raised vowel.

The significance of this deviation on the perception of nasal vowels is potentially very great. The implication would appear to be that users, and more especially young learners, of a language containing vowels with high-level nasality may take the perceived tongue height of a given nasal vowel as the target height, and thus come to produce originally high nasal vowels with a lower tongue position and low nasal vowels with a higher tongue position (Ohala 1981; Beddor, Krakow, and Goldstein 1986; Beddor 1991). However, it is important to remember that this physical-perceptually based tendency is no more than a tendency. For otherwise all languages in which nasal vowels have been in existence for a reasonable period of time would have them bunched in the mid area of the vowel space—which is far from being the case. Other forces therefore must clearly be working against this tendency. Nonetheless, it remains present in the background, discreetly acting as a force for guiding phonetic and phonological change.

1.2.   Phonological Aspects of Vowel Nasality

Phonologically, the presence of nasality in vowels may be ascribed a variety of interpretations. These will ultimately depend both upon the way in which it operates within the sound pattern of the language concerned and also upon the theoretical stance of the linguist. Five broad modes of interpretation can be distinguished: *generic, universal phonetic, allophonic, phonemic*, and *phonological*.

First, we have the case where all vowels are articulated with some degree of nasality. This happens most notably amongst speakers of any language who for pathological reasons 'talk through their nose' (rhinolalia). However, the presence of significant levels of nasality may be characteristic of the usual pronunciation of vowels by all speakers of certain language varieties. For instance, in some forms of Cockney English, perceptible nasality may be heard accompanying all or almost all theoretically oral vowel types, whether or not they are adjacent to nasal consonants (cf. Wells 1982: 318), as in *he* [ə̃ĩ], *bought* [bõ̃ʔ], etc.[11] In such cases of vowel nasality, which may be called *generic*, the presence of the nasality is automatic. For this reason, it is not ascribed any phonological significance.

Much more normally however, if a language possesses nasal vowels, it will also possess oral vowels. It is in this circumstance that the nasality of the nasal vowels may receive varying phonological interpretations. The most widespread pattern in language is for nasal vowels to occur only in specific and predictable phonetic contexts. A familiar instance, which appears to be of universal validity, concerns vowels occurring adjacent to nasal consonants. Here, there is a tendency in normal speech for co-articulation to take place so that at least the part of the vowel adjacent to the nasal consonant would be accompanied by some degree of nasality, even though the precise degree of phonetic nasality present may vary somewhat according to the nature of the vowel itself and the precise nature of the context. In such cases as this, the nasality of the vowel may be said to be *universal phonetic* and it can in principle be described by means of a phonetic rule of conditioned nasalization.

However, a problem presents itself here. This is that different languages (and, of course, different varieties within individual languages) can and do display a good deal of variation in the relative intensity of such conditioned nasality and also its profiling. By 'profiling' we mean the scope of nasality (the presence over all or just part of the vowel segment) and its gradience (the rate and extent of increase or decrease in levels of nasality over the span of the vowel). In Canadian French, anticipatory nasalizing of a vowel preceding a nasal consonant, as in *bonne*, is evidently more intense than in European French and its scope is greater in that the onset of increasing nasality comes earlier during the vowel's articulation (cf. Reenen 1982a: 85–6). Similarly, in certain varieties of Andalusian Spanish the vowel found immediately preceding a nasal consonant belonging to the same syllable is much more strongly nasal than in other varieties of Peninsular Spanish, e.g. Canary Islands *porrón* [po'rõŋ] 'earthenware jug' (Alvar 1959).

The variability in the precise phonetic realization of conditioned nasality in vowels clearly indicates that the use of a single, language-general statement or rule of allophonic nasalization would be insufficient to handle the facts appropriately. One solution would be systematically to describe the exact nature of conditioned vowel nasality separately for each language. But, more recently, there have been various attempts to establish formal categorical distinctions in this connection. Solé (1992, 1995), for instance, proposes a distinction between general or universal phonetic nasality, on the one hand, and 'phonologized conditioned' nasality, on the other. The former would imply the presence of low levels of nasality in the vowel concerned and graded shifts in nasality over the vowel's duration in line with general patterns of coarticulation, while the latter would be recognized in those cases where a given language systematically uses high levels of conditioned nasality in vowels or departs from the neutral, graded pattern of timing the increases or decreases in nasality over the vowel's duration. Another proposal of a similar type but in a rather different theoretical setting is made by Cohn (1988, 1990, 1993). On the basis of measurements of nasal airflows, she notes a significant difference in the nasality of ostensibly 'oral' French vowels depending upon the context in which they appear. Where an 'oral' vowel precedes a nasal segment, as for instance with the [e] of *Léon* [leõ], the vowel has a low-level, plateau-like nasal profiling for most of its duration until its final stages, but where an 'oral' vowel follows a nasal segment, as with the [e] of *nez* [ne], no such plateau-like profiling is found but instead the vowel shows a steady and gradual decrease of nasality. To characterize this difference, systematically distinct specifications are proposed: the [e] of *Léon* would be phonologically [− nasal] indicating an oral target articulation with the rise in nasality in the final stage specified by universal phonetic rules; on the other hand, the [e] of *nez* would be phonologically unspecified for nasality as [o nasal] indicating that there is no target for nasality, and consequently graded cline-like effects are found. In this framework, the language-specific phonologized nasality identified by Solé would be handled by [o nasal] specification.

It will also be appropriate for us to distinguish between types of conditioned vowel nasality. In addition to the universal phonetic nasality proceeding from the general tendency for co-articulation to occur in speech, we recognize the category of *allophonic* or *high-level allophonic* nasality to characterize vowels in which the presence of enhanced levels of nasality is phonologized, i.e. adopted by speakers as an intended property of the realization of those vowels.

A final, and somewhat different, instance of conditioned nasality can also be noted. In the cases considered so far, the nasality can be seen to be conditioned by the phonetic environment in which the vowel appears. But the nasality of a vowel may be conditioned by grammatical factors, notably the presence of a grammatical boundary of some sort. Duraffour (1932: 19–22) reports one example of such grammatically conditioned nasality in certain Franco-Provençal dialects. Here, unstressed vowels occurring in phrase-final position become nasal, as in [ẽ 'revõ] 'an oak tree' but [lo'revo dy 'bwaː] 'the oak in the wood'. Though the nature of the conditioning factor is no longer purely phonetic, the presence of vowel nasality is once again clearly predictable and hence is allied to the more familiar types of allophonic nasality just considered.

More significant from a phonological point of view are those cases where the nasality of a vowel cannot be attributed to its immediate phonetic or grammatical environment. This happens most strikingly when a nasal vowel appears in a context in which non-nasal vowels may also occur. Thus, in such pairs of French words as *pente* : *pâte* and *feinte* : *fête*, the corresponding nasal and oral vowels [ɑ̃]:[ɑ] and [ɛ̃]:[ɛ] appear in identical contexts. The nasality in the first item of each pair is clearly not predictable from the phonetic or grammatical context alone, therefore, and in recognition of this, phonologists would interpret the nasality in these modern French vowels as being *phonemic* or distinctive. The vowels /ɑ̃/, /ɑ/ and /ɛ̃/, /ɛ/ would thus be viewed as separate phonemes. The target realization of such nasal vowel phonemes may of course show some variability from language to language in respect of the degree and profiling of the nasality. Thus, according to Reenen (1982*a*: 74–7), the nasality of the nasal vowel phonemes of Parisian French is typically more intense and has an earlier onset than that of the nasal vowels of Canadian French.

A rather different circumstance in which vowel nasality can be phonemic may also be mentioned, although it has little relevance for the Romance languages. Unlike the cases just indicated, where the nasality is associated with a single vowel segment appearing within a simple lexical item, nasality may occur distinctively as a feature spread over sequences of segments. Two types may be distinguished. On the one hand, nasality may operate at a lexical level, serving to distinguish individual morphemes. Thus, in Desano, a language of Amazonia, there are items such as [wai] 'fish' and [wãĩ] 'name' which are distinguished in essence by, respectively, the absence and presence of nasality throughout the entire morpheme (cf. Kaye 1971). Rather than treat each segment of these and other morphemes of the language as being distinctively nasal or non-nasal, a more economical and revealing analysis would result if nasality were seen as a distinctively exploitable feature capable of overlaying the morpheme as a whole, such that the morphemes cited might be represented as /wai/ [− nasal] and /wai/ [+ nasal], respectively. In the other type, nasality is used as a morphological marker which may apply to and grammatically modify lexical items in a language. Thus, in Terena, another native language of Brazil, nasality is used as the marker of 1st person singular and extends from the first segment of the word so marked through to the final segment, unless its action is blocked by the presence of a supraglottal obstruent; e.g. ['ajo] 'his brother' vs. ['ãj̃õ] 'my brother', ['owoku] 'his house' vs. ['õw̃õgu] 'my house' (Bendor-Samuel 1970: 216). In this case as with the preceding one, the consensus amongst phonologists is to treat the nasality as a special phonological unit, a prosody or suprasegmental phoneme or autosegment, accompanying and overlaying the individual segmental phonemes. Such nasal prosodies do not appear to have figured significantly within Romance, but Lunt (1973: 138) does speculate on the possibility that European Portuguese with its tendency to display assimilatory allophonic nasalization may in time develop a lexical-type nasal prosody.

Finally, for some, though not all, phonologists, a further interpretational distinction is made, which relates to the crucial question of the predictability of nasality in a vowel. Adherents of 'classical' phonemic theory have usually assumed that predictability here means predictability on the basis essentially of phenomena present in the immediate phonetic context in which the relevant vowel occurs, along the lines of our discussion of French *pente : pâte, feinte : fête*. In this approach, the assumption is that the description is founded solely on phonetic material supplemented by knowledge of the location of grammatical boundaries. However, with the rise of generative phonology in the 1960s, a rather different perspective became established whereby the phonologist's task was seen to be to describe the pronunciation of sentences whose syntax and meaning are already known. Accordingly, a full range of grammatical and lexical information could be utilized in arriving at phonological descriptions. The effect of this was that it was no longer necessary automatically to interpret nasal vowels as phonemes if their nasality was unpredictable from their environment. Now, they could be treated as oral vowels provided their nasality was predictable on the basis of grammatical or lexical considerations, and thereby greater descriptive simplicity could be achieved. Thus, the French word *don* contains a nasal vowel, whose nasality is distinctive and hence phonemic for some phonologists, as its presence cannot be predicted in this context on phonetic grounds alone (cf. *dos* which presents an oral vowel in the same context). However, if grammatical and lexical information is available, *don* can be related to the verb *donner*, such that *don* and the stem of *donner* may be given the same 'underlying form' |don|. Then, to account for the nasal vowel of the form [dõ], various rules within the phonological description would specify that where |don| occurs before a word-boundary or a consonant, the vowel preceding the nasal consonant is nasalized and subsequently the nasal consonant is deleted (cf. Schane 1968).

In this way, nasal vowels can be interpreted at a more abstract level as sequences of oral vowel + nasal consonant. Indeed, some early generative phonologists suggested that nasal vowels should always be so described, cf. Harms (1968: 36). But views have been somewhat tempered in this connection as phonological descriptions of individual languages have sometimes indicated the preferability of having underlying nasal vowels in certain cases. Thus, Szabo (1973) showed that in Haitian Creole French it would be impossible to arrive at a satisfactory analysis without recognizing nasal vowels in underlying forms, and some phonologists, such as Tranel (1981), have argued for the desirability of postulating nasal vowel phonemes for standard French, the very language for which some of the most striking attempts were made to eliminate nasal vowels as phonemes. Nevertheless, a general assumption amongst 'classical' generative phonologists has continued to be that surface nasal vowel phonemes may be interpreted at an underlying level as sequences of oral vowel + nasal consonant which are converted by appropriate rules to nasal vowel segments.

In more recent years, a further development in generative phonology has been the adoption of a non-linear approach to description. This provides a more flexible way of handling types of material that were less satisfactorily covered by the 'classical' generative technique of operating with linear sequences of segments. The new tiered approach works well for cases where nasality acts as a prosody spreading over whole morphemes, cf. the cases of Desano and Terena mentioned above. As far as nasal vowels like those of French are concerned, the general (though not universal) assumption amongst non-linear phonologists is that these are often best interpreted as sequences of oral vowel + nasal element of some sort. Surface nasal vowels would result from rules associating the nasality of the second element of such sequences with the preceding vowel segment.

As we have seen, the possibility of having nasal vowels in underlying forms is not excluded by practitioners of classical or non-linear generative phonology, but it is much less widely countenanced than in classical phonemic descriptions.

In those cases where it might be proposed, as in Haitian Creole French, we can say that nasality would be a *phonological* feature of the vowel in the language concerned.

For our purposes, however, it will not be practicable or appropriate to use systematically the full range of theoretical distinctions outlined above. Generic nasality does not appear to be a relevant descriptive category in any Romance variety and universal phonetic nasality may be assumed to have operated as a default throughout the history of Romance. Regarding phonological nasality, the decision to recognize this category for a given vowel type is at the best of times somewhat controversial and, more importantly, it can only be justified on the basis of a thorough investigation of the language in question, this being something which of course cannot be undertaken in most instances of non-contemporary language states. Accordingly, we may dispense with it. This leaves the two classification types of vowel nasality which will be of central importance: (high-level) allophonic nasality and phonemic nasality. Henceforth, then, attention will focus on cases where conditioned vowel nasality has been heightened significantly, albeit with variations of degree and profiling, and cases where surface conditioning has been eliminated leading to the possibility of oral : nasal vowel contrasts.

1.2.1. FUNCTIONS OF NASALITY

Discussions of nasality in phonology have focused primarily on its paradigmatic or distinctive role in language. However, a number of other functions can be identified which nasality can perform.

Nasality in a normally oral vowel may be seen to have a *demarcative* function. One possibility is that it may indicate the end of a grammatical unit. Various examples of this have been reported from Romance. As noted above (1.2), nasality regularly accompanies an unstressed vowel occurring at the end of a phonetic phrase in certain varieties of Franco-Provençal (Duraffour 1932: 19–22). Similarly, Robe (1960: 36) reports that in the Spanish of rural Panama nasal vowels occur as variants of vowel + [ɾ] or [l] in phrase-final position, e.g. *vamos a ver* [bamohaˈβeɾ] or [bamohˈβẽ], the latter realization being characteristic of allegro speech. In some Picard dialects, high vowels (original or secondary) have been nasalized when they are in absolute word-final position (Flutre 1977: 41, 55).

Outside the domain of phonology proper, the use of nasality may be bound up with various *sociolinguistic* functions. Speakers may adopt a nasal pronunciation in specific situations to express an attitude. In the Cayuvava language of Bolivia, for example, the use of heavily nasalized vowels evidently serves to indicate deference or respect to one's interlocutor (Laver 1980: 4). As well as this 'situational' use, nasality may also have a 'sociolectal' function, marking an individual's membership of some social grouping. In Brazilian Portuguese, the degree of nasality present in the stressed syllable of such words as *cama* can have clear social implications. The presence of higher levels of nasality is taken as a sign of less educated speech, while the use of low levels of nasality is a mark of cultivation (Tlaskal 1980: 566).[12]

In the Portuguese example, it is noteworthy that nasality cannot operate as a distinctive feature in the contexts concerned (the oral/nasal contrast in vowels does not apply before nasal consonants). It is in cases such as this where nasality is a non-distinctive feature that sociolinguistically significant variations in its intensity are more likely to be found occurring. The possibility of exploiting nasality for socially relevant purposes has doubtless been made use of at different times and places throughout the history of Romance.

1.2.2.   THE FEATURE [NASAL]

In formal specifications, the feature [nasal] will be needed to characterize the sound systems of all Romance varieties and probably most if not all varieties of human language. However, definitions of [nasal] have varied somewhat amongst phonologists down the years. In the first major presentation of features, that of Jakobson and Halle (1956), both acoustic and articulatory criteria were invoked: *Nasal/oral (nasalized/non-nasalized)*: acoustic—spreading the available energy over wider (vs. narrower) frequency regions by a reduction in the intensity of certain (primarily the first) formants and introduction of additional (nasal) formants; articulatory—mouth resonator supplemented by the nose cavity vs. the exclusion of the nasal resonator' (1956: 31).

But subsequently there has been a clear tendency to adopt articulatory criteria only as the basis of feature definitions. This is seen in the much-quoted characterization of [nasal] provided by Chomsky and Halle (1968: 316): 'Nasal sounds are produced with a lowered velum which allows the air to escape through the nose; nonnasal sounds are produced with a raised velum so that the air from the lungs can escape only through the mouth.'

However, the appropriate representation of nasality in a given segment using the feature [nasal] does raise some problems. One obvious problem relates to the treatment of different degrees of nasality. In the feature presentations considered above, [nasal] is viewed as a binary feature such that segments will be interpreted categorically as being either [+ nasal] or [− nasal]. But, as we have seen, the degree of nasality in vowels, whether perceptual or articulatory, can readily be varied at the phonetic level. To express this correctly, the feature [nasal] will clearly need to be multi-valued or scalar in phonetic descriptions. In order to resolve the conflict here, features such as [nasal] are required to operate in principle in two different ways: at the more abstract phonological or classificatory level, they are typically taken to be binary, but at a phonetic level they are scalar and variable values may be assigned to them. As a result, a given vowel could be [− nasal] phonologically, but [3 nasal] phonetically where the coefficient '3' would indicate some point on a predetermined sliding scale of nasality. Unfortunately, as rather less attention has been paid to the details of phonetic features, the question of how many values or coefficients should be identified for scalar phonetic features like [nasal] still remains to be resolved. The possibility of the 'same' feature operating on a binary or scalar scale, depending on the level of analysis, and the way in which the interface between features at the two levels operates raise significant theoretical issues which continue to be a source of controversy.

We may return to the general assumption that phonologically the feature [nasal] is binary. Though this is the standard view, it is worthwhile noting that there is some limited evidence to suggest that nasality may be multi-valued at the phonological level as well. In Chinantec, which is spoken in the Oaxaca region of Mexico, variable vowel nasality has been claimed to operate distinctively such that a systematic three-way opposition exists between non-nasal, partly nasal, and heavily nasal vowels, as in [ha] 'so, such', [hã] '(he) spreads open', and [hã̃] 'foam, froth' (Ladefoged 1971: 34–5). However, more recently it has been found that the apparent three-way contrast here is more accurately described as being non-nasal vowel vs. mixed oral-nasal contour vowel vs. nasal vowel (Ladefoged and Maddieson 1990: 104–5, 1996: 299–300). If this is the case, the feature [nasal] can remain uniformly binary at the phonological level. Certainly, there is no reported evidence from Romance languages which is at odds with this assumption.

Finally, a common view of phonological features has been that the relevant distinctive property which relates to each feature characterizes the whole of the segment with which it is associated. Thus, if a segment is phonologically [+ nasal], the implication is that nasality will be present throughout the (idealized) articulation of that segment. However, there may well be instances where certain segments, most obviously nasal consonants, have nasality associated with only a specific part of their articulation, namely the onset or the coda. Instead of appealing to further features such as [pre-nasal] or [post-nasal] to characterize such complex segments, Anderson (1975) proposed the idea that the feature structure within a segment need not be fixed throughout the segment but may change. Thus, a pre-nasalized consonant could be specified as [+ nasal/− nasal]. As far as nasal vowels are concerned, there seem to be few clear cases of the use of feature-structure changing at a phonological level such that pre-nasalized or post-nasalized vowels would contrast with nasal vowels, although Chinantec (seen above) may be an instance. However, as we have seen, at a phonetic level there is ample evidence of nasality showing very varied profiling in vowels suggesting the need for a detailed and flexible means of representation. Diagrammatically or numerically specified feature values have been proposed, cf. Reenen (1982a) and section 1.1 above, but no consensus has emerged on this question.

1.2.3.   NASALITY IN RELATION TO OTHER FEATURES IN VOWELS

In principle, the presence and the degree of nasality accompanying the production of a vowel can be controlled independently of other articulatory activity. Thus, the French words *eau* and *on* are pronounced without and with nasality, respectively, while other articulatory activity is effectively the same. We might therefore expect that the appearance of nasality in a vowel would not have any implications for other features of pronunciation of that vowel. However, there is evidence to suggest that nasality may interract with other vowel features.

The most discussed case has been the relationship between nasality and *vowel height*. Perceptual studies considered above (cf. 1.1.2) indicate that the addition of nasal resonance can have a broadly centralizing effect, causing high and high mid vowels to be perceived as having a lower tongue height whereas low vowels may be perceived as having a more elevated tongue height (Wright 1980). This is particularly likely with vowels in which nasality is unconditioned. However, the link between nasality and vowel height is by no means simple and direct, as the conflicting results from experiments on vowel perception bear out.

Diachronically, the interrelations between nasalization and vowel height are equally controversial. The classic case is that of French, where originally high vowels have indeed developed to become low-mid, as in Old French [fin] > Modern French [fɛ̃] *fin*. But it is likely that special factors have operated here so that French may provide only limited support for any claim that vowel nasalization and lowering are directly connected (see 4.3.3).

Also, if nasality had the effect on vowel height that is claimed, languages which developed nasal vowel phonemes would be expected to lose the high and high-mid types and have exclusively low-mid vowels. However, cross-linguistic surveys of languages with nasal vowels offer limited support in this respect. For instance, in the survey by Ruhlen (1978) there are 71 languages in which vowel nasality is phonemic but only 19 of these are reported to be lacking one or more of the high nasal vowels which structural considerations would lead us to expect (and indeed French counted for 2 of the 19, under the headings of Parisian French and Canadian French). The findings of Crothers (1978) are even more unsupportive. On the basis of a review of 50 languages containing phonemic nasal vowels, he is led to propose the following universal: 'If a nasal vowel system is smaller than the corresponding basic vowel system, it is most often a *mid* vowel that is missing from the nasal vowel system' (emphasis added). On the other hand, the survey of Beddor (1983, 1993) found that of 75 languages investigated there was some evidence of lowering in 39 of them. Here, patterns of allophonic or morphophonemic variation provided the source of data; for example, items like French *fine* [fin] vs. *fin* [fɛ̃] 'fine (f. sg./m. sg.)' were taken to indicate the lowering effect of nasality. However, the rather broad nature of the criteria used meant that almost the same number of languages were also found to display vowel raising allegedly due to nasal influence.

In view of these findings, perhaps the most that can safely be said on the relationship between nasality and vowel height is that the presence of high levels of nasality does undoubtedly have a masking effect on the acoustic signal and this allied to spectral integration (cf. 1.1.2 above) can lead to perceptual reinterpretations or 'mistakes' on the part of the hearer in respect of vowel height. But language-specific circumstances, such as phonological patterning and the speaker-hearer's knowledge of his/her language, can readily 'correct' such mistakes.

There are three other features of vowel production with which nasality may interract. These are *length*, *lip rounding*, and the *front–back* axis of tongue position. Regarding the first of these, it has been suggested that associated with nasality in a vowel may be extra length. This would suggest two things. First, synchronically, nasal vowels will typically be phonetically longer than their oral counterparts and, in languages with a phonological length distinction in oral but not nasal vowels, nasal vowel phonemes will be aligned with the long oral vowels. Second, diachronically, nasalization will operate more readily on long vowels.

Synchronically, there is rather limited supporting evidence. As we have noted, Delattre and Monnot (1981) demonstrate on the basis of experimental evidence that not only are nasal vowels systematically longer than their oral counterparts in all contexts, but also their greater duration is used by French speakers as a recognitional cue. However, in other languages the findings are less clear (cf. 1.1.2). Phonologically, the picture is even more equivocal. French again offers positive data since the nasal vowels clearly align themselves phonologically with the oral vowels /ɑ o ø/ in that they all show regular lengthening in final blocked syllables (as against the other oral vowels which are only lengthened in final syllables by specific blocking consonants, notably /ʀ/). But the evidence from cross-linguistic surveys does not bear out the expectation that, in languages showing a length contrast for oral but not nasal vowels, the nasal vowels phonemes are consistently identified with the long oral vowels. In the extensive study by Maddieson (1984), 4 languages are reported (out of 317 covered) which systematically use length distinctively in oral vowels and neutralize the distinction in nasal vowels. Of these, 2 are cited as having long nasal vowels and 2 as having short nasal vowels. A further point is that if length were directly associated with the presence of nasality in vowels, the distinctive use of length in nasal vowels might be expected to be rare if not unknown. Yet, 9 languages are reported by Maddieson as having a length distinction for nasal vowels. None of the languages concerned is Romance, but the case of standard French of the seventeenth and eighteenth centuries may be mentioned for inclusion, since distinctive long and short oral and nasal vowels clearly existed then (cf. 4.3.9). Significantly, all the languages concerned here also have a length distinction in oral vowels; no language is presented in which length is distinctive for nasal vowels but not for oral vowels. The presence of distinctive length in nasal vowels thus appears to be dependent on its presence in oral vowels, and there is a tendency for it to undergo neutralization.

Diachronically, there is some evidence of a link between vowel length and nasality. In the history of the Teke sub-group of Bantu languages, Hombert (1986) discerned a clear tendency for long vowels to be affected by nasalization prior to short vowels. Also, Hajek (1997: § 4.1.2) identifies a direct connection between length and nasalization in the evolution of nasal vowels of North Italian dialects, noting that in oxytons it is only long vowels which have nasalized whereas short vowels are not susceptible to nasalization unless they first undergo lengthening. This leads to the claim that 'vowels must always be phonologically long *before* they can be nasalized'. However, in other areas of Romance the evidence is less obviously supportive (see also 13.3). Some correlation between added length and nasality does therefore appear to exist, which perceptual considerations would lead us to expect (cf. 1.1.2 above). But how strong the correlation is and the extent to which it can be overridden by other constraints within individual languages remain unclear.

The links between nasality and lip rounding and nasality and backness are a good deal more uncertain. As regards the former, it is notable that whilst back rounded nasal vowels occur widely, front rounded nasal vowels appear very rarely as phonemes. Of the 71 languages with oral/nasal vowel contrasts listed by Maddieson (1984), 3 possess the oral vowel /y/, but none of these have a corresponding nasal vowel /ỹ/. Only one highly dubious case of a language containing /ø̃/ is cited, while French stands alone with /œ̃/. It is unclear whether the results here are merely unrepresentative or whether the presence of nasality poses particular difficulties for hearers in discriminating between rounded and unrounded front vowels. If the latter were the case, the more recent tendency in standard French for /œ̃/ to merge with /ɛ̃/ to leave just the vowel /ɛ̃/ would become more understandable. Yet, in French dialects /ỹ/ and /ø̃/ do appear as phonemes just as in dialects of North Italy (cf. 5.2 and 10.7). The relative rarity of nasal front rounded vowel phonemes may therefore just reflect the fact that both nasal vowel phonemes and front rounded vowel phonemes are minority phenomena, and consequently the combination of the two is likely to be statistically rarer. At all events, current evidence does not suggest any genuine correlation between nasality and lip rounding.

The link between nasality and backness is equally uncertain. Diachronic evidence in particular has been cited in support of such a link, notably from French and from Chinese dialects. This allegedly points to the more ready adoption of enhanced nasality in front vowels of a given height (Chen 1973*a*, 1973*b*; Ruhlen 1978). The French evidence is based on the changing patterns of assonance in medieval verse, a key point being that nasalized and oral mid front vowels cease to assonate at an earlier stage than nasalized and oral mid back vowels. However, the assumption that this was due to nasalization affecting front vowels prior to back vowels has been called into question and other factors have been identified which might explain the facts (cf. 4.2.3). Also the available synchronic data from other languages are somewhat indeterminate in this connection, in that nasal vowel systems do not appear to be preponderantly weighted in favour of front vowels. It may therefore be safest to assume no special association between nasality and the front–back dimension in vowels.

1.3.   The Dynamics of Vowel Nasalization

Where vowel nasalization has occurred, it owes itself usually to the effect of assimilation. Typically, nasal vowels arise from sequences made up of oral vowel + adjacent nasal consonant, and by assimilation with the nasal consonant the possibly very low original level of nasality already present in the vowel as a result of co-articulation (i.e. universal phonetic nasality) is stepped up until the vowel is perceived as nasal rather than oral (i.e allophonic nasality). The cognitive status of the vowel is thus changed as the presence of high-level nasality now forms part of its target articulation.

Subsequently, phonemically nasal vowels may be created. This comes about when the adjacent nasal consonant is deleted, so that the nasality of the vowel ceases to be predictable from the adjacent nasal consonant and instead becomes distinctive. For the creation of nasal vowel phonemes, two successive processes are thus involved which can be represented in the following way:

$$VN > \tilde{V}N > \tilde{V}$$

(where '$\tilde{V}$' = a vowel with high-level allophonic nasality, and 'N' = a nasal consonant)

An important aspect of the development here concerns the *direction* of the nasal assimilation. In our schematic illustration above, the nasal consonant follows the vowel segment, such that the assimilation is of the *regressive* type. However, the same stepping up of nasality in a vowel can be caused by a preceding nasal consonant, via *progressive* assimilation. But in this instance the crucial second stage, the deletion of the conditioning nasal consonant, does not usually take place, although very occasional cases of this have been reported. For instance, in the New Caledonian language Hienghene, post-nasalized sonorants are reported to have given rise to nasal vowel phonemes via the stages CNV > CNṼ > CṼ (Hagège and Haudricourt 1978: 203). In Romance, there do not appear to have been any directly comparable cases. Instead, the context type NV has generally developed at most to NṼ, thereby just increasing the stock of of vowels displaying strong allophonic nasality. However, where such progressive nasalization is not uniformly implemented, it may give rise to phonemic contrasts, as in MĀTRES > (Portuguese) *mães* 'mothers' vs. MĂGIS > *mais* 'more'. It may also be noted that, in the history of Romance at least, vowel nasalization by progressive assimilation occurs a good deal less frequently than with the regressive type.

Turning back to the much more common regressive type of nasalization, we should recognize that although the neat two-staged statement VN > ṼN > Ṽ usefully summarizes the principal phases, it gives only a rather crude and idealized description of the actual physical events which take place. In reality, the first stage is frequently not carried through in a simple and uniform way. Constraints of various types may operate so that the change occurs in a gradual way. These relate to (*a*) the quality of the conditioning nasal consonant, (*b*) the quality of the vowel undergoing nasalization, (*c*) the duration of the vowel undergoing nasalization, (*d*) the degree of stress accompanying the syllable containing the vowel, (*e*) the syllabic relationship between the vowel and the conditioning nasal consonant, and (*f*) the quality of the consonantal segment (if any) following the conditioning nasal consonant. As we shall see, all of these parameters need to be considered when describing the way in which vowel nasalization has operated across the different varieties of Romance, although only a subset of these parameters may be relevant in the implementation of nasalization in individual varieties.

The second stage of the process frequently involves a gradual and complex series of changes as well. These involve the weakening of the nasal consonant, culminating in its loss as it is absorbed into the preceding vowel. However, full nasal consonant loss may be confined to certain phonological contexts only and may also entail various modifications in the quality of the nasal consonant before it finally disappears.

Lastly, the question needs to be raised whether nasal vowels only ever arise from the effect of assimilation from an adjacent nasal consonant or whether they can be created 'spontaneously', i.e. without an overt nasal conditioning factor being present.   In his influential pioneering study on the universals of nasals, Ferguson (1966: 59) concluded from the rather limited evidence provided by the history of a small number of mainly Indo-European languages that 'NVs [i.e. nasal vowels], apart from borrowings and analogical formations, always result from the loss of a PNC [i.e. primary nasal consonant].' Here

Ferguson is discussing the rise of nasal vowel phonemes, but the key point at issue is whether nasality can only arise in a vowel when a conditioning nasal consonant is present (irrespective of whether or not the consonant is deleted later on). While such a claim is true in the overwhelming majority of cases, there do appear to be some rare instances where nasal vowels have arisen from earlier oral vowels without there being nasal consonant loss beforehand. One apparent case, however, needs to be set aside at the outset. This arises when, prior to the operation of vowel nasalization, nasal epenthesis occurs so that a nasal consonant is inserted within a word for some reason. If vowel nasalization then comes to operate in the language, it will of course also apply to the words which have undergone epenthesis. Examples of nasal epenthesis in Romance are not rare (cf. Balcke 1912; Malkiel 1990), and in those varieties which have experienced vowel nasalization it has also been triggered by an epenthetic nasal consonant, e.g. *grincer, cingler* 'to sail', *grimper, lamper* 'to swallow down', *lambeau* (< Old Fr. *grisser, sigler, gripper, laper*, Frankish **labba*). The vowel nasalization in such cases is thus in reality directly conditioned.

Various types of vowel nasalization may be distinguished where no discernible nasal segment has acted as a conditioning factor. Already, we have noted the use of nasal vowels for sociolinguistic reasons, the nasality being added to express some stylistic or affective value. Also, examples from Romance languages were cited where oral vowels have been nasalized for structural and communicative reasons, namely to indicate grammatical boundaries of some sort (1.2.1 above). Lastly, it has been found that oral vowels may be nasalized apparently spontaneously without any nasal consonant being in the vicinity (cf. 1.1.2). Sundry examples of this phenomenon figure in the general literature. Typically they come from more 'exotic' languages of the Americas and Asia, where the significant factor is the presence next to the vowel of a consonant with a high airflow. This may be a glide, a glottal or pharyngeal consonant, or a consonant with aspiration or high-flow friction (e.g. [s]). The explanation for the phenomenon appears to be that, acoustically, the airflow causes lowering of the amplitude of the first formant of the vowel and increases its bandwidth, both of these yielding the perceptual effect of nasality (Matisoff 1975; Ohala 1987: 220–1). Rarely, and more uncertainly, the presence of length alone has been alleged to be a possible catalyst for spontaneous nasalization, as in some Eastern Algonquian languages of the north-eastern United States (Whalen and Beddor 1989).

Examples of the last type of spontaneous nasalization do not abound in Romance, but something similar is indicated in dialects of Andalusia and also for the local speech of Florence.[13] In both cases it has been caused by the presence of an adjacent consonant with a high airflow. In the dialect of Cabra, spoken near Cordoba in southern Spain, the *jota* is realized as a glottal fricative and especially between vowels it nasalizes the vowels which surround it, as in [la'βĩhã] *clavija* 'plug, peg', [se'rõhõ] *cerrojo* 'bolt' (Zamora Vicente 1967: 323). The Florentine case concerns especially the usage of younger urban speakers. In casual styles, vowels adjacent to the glottal fricative which results from a weakened original plosive are realized nasal, as in ['kwellẽ'hõse] *quelle cose* 'those things' and [ik'ke vu 'fãhẽ] *che fate?* 'what are you doing?' (Giannelli and Savoia 1978: 50).

1.3.1. DENASALIZATION

After the creation of phonemically nasal vowels, it is not uncommon to find the opposite process of denasalization setting in. Since nasal vowels represent special and complex vowel types, they may be seen as inherently less stable so that a tendency to eliminate them is understandable (Ruhlen 1978: 228–9). As far as Romance is concerned, a general trend for denasalization to occur after unconditioned nasal vowels have arisen was identified over a century ago by the eminent Romanist Meyer-Lübke (1890: § 389). However, it is clearly no more than a trend as nasal vowel phonemes have shown resistance to elimination in many Romance varieties.

Looking more closely at denasalization, we find that it may apply equally to phonemically nasal vowels and to allophonically nasal vowels. When it does apply, the scope of its implementation may vary. For instance, it may just affect those nasal vowels which appear in specific phonological contexts, as in French during the sixteenth and seventeenth centuries. Only nasal vowels which preceded a nasal consonant belonging to the following syllable were denasalized, as in *fi-nir*, while nasal vowels in other contexts remained unaffected, as in *fin*.

As to the actual process of denasalization, it may operate simultaneously to all types of nasal vowel or be staged so that certain vowel types are modified earlier than others. Where the latter is the case, the pattern of staging may resemble in reverse that previously seen for vowel nasalization, as claimed by Pope (1952: § 440) for French, although claims have also been made that staged denasalization operates on vowels in the same order as staged nasalization, e.g. by Chen (1972*a*: 163) and (1975: 107–10) on the basis of Chinese data.[14]

Finally, the phonetic outcome of denasalization may also be varied, particularly when phonemically nasal vowels are involved. On the one hand, the result may be just an oral vowel; on the other hand, the nasal vowel may be restructured into a sequence of oral vowel + nasal consonant. As we shall see, both possibilities are to be found in Romance. In the latter case, the precise quality of the nasal consonant may well vary, depending on syllabic position and/or the the phonetic environment (notably, the quality of the preceding vowel).

1.3.2. CAUSATION

Much heat but, arguably, rather less light has been generated in discussions about the causation of sound change. The more fanciful ideas of scholars of earlier times who appealed to the influence of geographical conditions, climate, or assumed racial characteristics have been abandoned. But in their place there is still no coherent and generally accepted view of why sounds change. In fact, a number of linguists have despaired of discovering the causes, such as Bloomfield (1935: 385), Postal (1968: 283), G. Sampson (1980: 25). Perhaps the most pessimistic expression of this view is provided by Lass (1980: 75) who writes 'we don't have a clue as to what (if anything) causes or constrains linguistic change'.

Lass is led to this extreme assessment because he directly equates explanation with *prediction*, in the sense that we can only claim to be able to explain the causes of sound change if we can establish scientific laws that would enable us to predict accurately when and how individual sound changes will take place. However, this represents a very strong concept of 'explanation' which is typical for the fields of physics and chemistry but is less often invoked for other areas of science, including the social sciences. Here, a probabilistic conception of explanation is more often adopted (Hempel 1965). By this the investigator identifies various testable facts and principles relevant to the field of enquiry, noting their distribution and statistical frequency, and (s)he then uses these as a basis for deciding what, on the balance of probabilities, is the most likely explanation for the specific phenomena in question.

As far as historical linguistics is concerned, this means that when an explanation is sought for a specific sound change, it will be reached in the light of our knowledge of factors which have come into play in shaping observed sound changes, particularly those changes which are well documented. On the basis of a number of case studies it becomes possible to identify tentatively circumstances where change is feasible and the likely paths which individual changes will follow, linguistically and sociolinguistically, as and when they get underway. Some of the determining factors will relate to the physical properties of speech-sounds, others to structural characteristics of the language system to which the sounds belong, and still others to known sociolinguistic patterns and tendencies operating within the community before and during the period when the sound change took place (cf. McMahon 1994).

It appears that all these different types of factor, and doubtless others beside, have been influential in shaping nasal vowel evolution in the various forms of Romance. Where relevant evidence is at hand to suggest the likely action of some recognizable type(s) of factor, we shall attempt to explore the circumstances. Some new shafts of light may thereby be shed on certain developments. However, all too often a statement of the likely path of implementation of a specific change is the most that can realistically be attempted.

NOTES

1. The term 'variety' is used as a neutral label to designate any linguistic system used by a speech-community. It therefore incorporates both 'language' and 'dialect'.
2. Exceptionally, another type of airstream may occasionally be used by speakers. A much-cited example is French *oui* which may be heard articulated with an *ingressive* pulmonic airstream. According to Léon (1992: 52), such a pronunciation is typical of women and seems to suggest hesitation or uncertainty. The airstream is only used for affective or paralinguistic purposes, however.
3. Some notable discrepancies do however exist in the figures presented by phoneticians. Thus, Ohala (1975: 292) claims that with nasal consonants the velopharyngeal opening can reach up to 600 mm^2, i.e. almost double the figure of Reenen.
4. We may note the observation that for acoustic excitation of the air to take place in the nasal cavities, the nasal port opening will normally be greater than about 20 mm^2 (Krakow and Huffman 1993: 54). Acoustic excitation in the nasal cavities is normally a precondition to the perception of nasality, but of course it is not the case that hearers will necessarily perceive nasality at low levels of excitation. This figure and that of Guth therefore are not incompatible.
5. Bell-Berti (1993: 68) reports that a velic opening of up to a maximum of 20 mm^2 is compatible with the production of oral consonants including plosives.
6. The precise formula used in determining the value of N% is:

$$N\% = \frac{N}{MC + N} \times 100$$

where N = nasal coupling and MC = mouth coupling (Reenen 1982*a*: 51).
7. Investigation of English and Hindi subjects revealed that 'the higher the vowel, the higher the velum' (Henderson 1984: 68), this being true for both allophonic and phonemic nasal vowels. (Vowel nasality is phonemic in Hindi, whereas in English it is allophonic; see below 1.2.)
8. In terms of 'Action Theory', there would be differences in the organization or 'coordinative structures' used in the way the musculature is marshalled for producing these two types of nasal speech-sound (Nolan 1982).
9. Cf. the conclusion of Krakow and Huffman (1993: 43), 'the spectral variations due to vowel identity and speaker characteristics are numerous enough that a single description of the spectral properties of nasalized vowels as a whole must necessarily be worded in very general terms, along the lines of House and Stevens's conclusion that nasalization results in a general flattening of the vowel spectrum.'
10. These results may be set against the claim made by Guth (1975: 28) that nasality needs to be present for at least 4 csecs in French nasal vowels for it to be perceptible. No data are provided in support of this claim however.
11. The perceptibility of such nasality is of course determined to some extent by the background of the hearer. A fellow Cockney speaker may well not perceive the nasality unless specific attention is called to it, for example by a linguist.
12. This evaluation may well be bound up with the greater prestige of European Portuguese, which has lower levels of nasality in such forms.

13. Outside the field of European Romance proper, we may note a further case with the Afro-Hispanic creole known as *bozal*, cf. Lipski (1992).

14. Elsewhere, Chen (1973*b*: 914) appears to contradict his own claim when stating in respect of the evolution of Chinese dialects that 'denasalization pursued exactly the opposite direction [to that of nasalization]: it progressed from the high to the low vowels' and he writes of the 'mirror picture of nasalization and denasalization of Chinese dialects'.

2

Vowel Nasalization in Romance

2.1. Incidence of Vowel Nasality in Present-Day Romance

Nasal vowels are found widely across Romance (see Map 1). Although two varieties in particular have tended to monopolize attention in discussions of nasal vowels in Romance, namely French and Portuguese, these are far from being the only forms of Romance in which significant levels of nasality have developed in vowels. In fact, varieties from almost all areas of *Romania*[1] have been affected. Some have nasal vowel phonemes just as French and Portuguese, others present just high levels of allophonic nasality. At the present time, the following Romance varieties show one or other form of vowel nasality:

Galician-Portuguese
Andalusian Spanish
Gallo-Romance
Some varieties of Rheto-Romance
Many North Italian dialects (including Gallo-Italian dialects transplanted to Sicily)
Varieties of Corsican (especially in north-west)
Varieties of Sardinian (especially in centre and south)
Romanian

In earlier times, it seems that vowel nasalization took place in other varieties as well but that traces of this have been camouflaged by subsequent denasalization. Some North Italian dialects, e.g. that of Bergamo, offer examples of this, and so perhaps does Catalan though this is less certain.

The process by which nasal vowels were created was by no means uniform across Romance. In the following chapters, we explore the sometimes delicate patterns of vowel nasalization found in each of the different forms of Romance. However, despite the manifest local differences, a number of common characteristics can be identified. These will be brought out in the course of our coverage by means of cross-referencing and they are also recapitulated in the final chapter.

2.2.   Nasalizing Contexts

In general, the process of vowel nasalization is seen as typically falling into two successive stages (see 1.3). First, a vowel is nasalized by a following nasal consonant, to give an allophonically nasal vowel. Then, the conditioning nasal consonant may be deleted, leaving a phonemically nasal vowel. The process may be summarized in the following way:

$$VN > \tilde{V}N$$
$$\tilde{V}N > \tilde{V}$$

(where 'V' indicates an oral vowel, '$\tilde{V}$' a nasal vowel, and 'N' a nasal consonant)

Both stages can be complex in the way they are carried through with various formal and sociolinguistic factors affecting the implementation process. Such factors have certainly been at work in Romance. Here, the relevant socio-linguistic factors have been highly diverse and often capricious, so that they have to be dealt with on a largely individual basis. However, formal factors lend themselves more readily to classification. To take due account of the varied data provided by Romance, a rather more complex framework of classification is required than that provided by the simple schema just presented. A sufficiently detailed yet practical basis for handling the data systematically is achieved if three distinct context-types are recognized to cover the major sorts of environ-ment in which vowel nasalization has occurred. These will be referred to as 'nasalizing contexts'. Three such contexts will be used:

context (i): this is representable as /VNC/, where the vowel precedes a nasal consonant which is followed by another consonant; for example, the stressed vowel of TĚMPUS 'time'. This context-type is well represented in Latin and throughout the history of Romance. Using a terminological shorthand, we will call items such as TĚMPUS 'context (i) forms', and a comparable shorthand will be used for the two other context-types.

context (ii): this is representable as /VN#/, where the vowel precedes a word-final nasal consonant. The Latin of the Classical period presents many examples of this context-type. On the one hand, there were numerous word-forms containing word-final nasal -M (e.g. DĪCAM 'I will say', MŪRUM 'wall (acc. sg.)', SĔPTEM 'seven'), particularly because -M served as an inflexional marker for both verbs and nominals, as in our two first examples. On the other hand, Classical Latin also had a number of words ending in -N (e.g. NŌMEN 'name (nom. sg.)', NŌN 'not'), although these were much less numerous, being largely confined to certain case-forms of a small subset of nouns and to a limited number of invariable function words.

Now, despite the substantial presence of items satisfying context (ii) in Classical Latin, very few continued as context (ii) forms in the post-Classical period. In almost all the relevant word-forms which continued in use into Romance, the crucial original word-final nasal was deleted in Imperial times (see 3.2). A limited source of replenishment for this context-type came from Latin forms containing the 3rd plural verb ending -NT in Classical Latin, such as DŪRANT 'they last'. These lost their final -T in some, though by no means all, areas of the Empire during the post-Classical period to emerge as new context (ii) forms. For example, -T was evidently soon lost in Portuguese, as in *duram*, but not French which still had *durent* [dyrənt] in the thirteenth century. However, by far the greatest proportion of context (ii) forms which appeared in early Romance (and which will be of concern to us) came into being as a result of *apocope*. This brought about the deletion of final unstressed vowels, and of particular concern are those cases in which vowels were lost after a nasal consonant, for example in BĚNE 'well' > ['bɛn(e)] > [bɛn] or in PĀNEM 'bread' > ['pane] > ['pan(e)] > [pan] (where, after the early loss of the final -M, apocope has likewise taken place). Apocope was a widespread phenomenon already in the early medieval period, although the precise circumstances under which it operated varied regionally and chronologically. It affected in differing degrees all areas of Western Romance (i.e. those areas to the north and west of the 'La Spezia–Rimini' line in northern Italy), but it had little or no early impact on central and southern Italy, Sardinia, and Romania although some of the latter areas have been subject to apocope in more recent times.

For our purposes, only those forms which contained a word-final nasal in early Romance will be viewed as 'context (ii) forms'. Thus, forms such as [bɛn] and [pan] are particularly implicated, although, for certain varieties of Romance, other types of form may also be involved (e.g. forms originally in -NT which lost the final plosive). In this way, our classificational framework will take as its basic point of reference a chronological period in Romance situated in the early part of the Middle Ages after apocope has applied. As a result, nasalizing context-type (ii) will not figure significantly in the discussion of those varieties of Romance which were largely untouched by apocope at this stage.

context (iii): this is representable as /VNV/, where the vowel precedes an intervocalic nasal consonant; for example, the stressed vowel of LŪNA 'moon'. This context-type is found widely in Latin and throughout the history of Romance.

The most obvious distinguishing factor operating between the three context-types relates to the nature of the segment which follows the conditioning nasal consonant, respectively (oral) consonant, zero, and vowel. However, an important syllabic distinction is also involved. In contexts (i) and (ii), the nasal consonant is *tautosyllabic* with the preceding vowel, i.e. it belongs to the same syllable as the vowel and forms the syllable coda, as in TĔM-PUS and very obviously [pan]. On the other hand, in context (iii) the nasal consonant is *heterosyllabic* with the preceding vowel, i.e. it belongs to a different syllable from that of the vowel and forms the onset of the following syllable, as in LŪ-NA. The process of vowel nasalization has often been significantly affected by whether the conditioning nasal is tautosyllabic or heterosyllabic, reflecting the importance of the syllable as a structural unit in the diachronic and synchronic phonological patterning of Romance. We have therefore incorporated this syllabic distinction in our classificational framework.

The proposed framework provides a viable working basis for handling the data of Romance and will be systematically exploited in the following chapters. However, two final comments may usefully be made. First, the question of the interpretation of *geminate* nasals within the framework needs to be considered. Two types appeared in Classical Latin, MM and NN, for example in SŬMMA 'summit' and CĂNNA 'reed'. In addition, during the later Empire period a further type of geminate nasal developed in many areas, namely the palatal [ɲɲ] as in ['viɲɲa] 'vineyard' (< VĪNEA). Like all the other geminates in Latin, the nasal types were only able to appear in intervocalic position. Now, at first sight, forms like SŬMMA might seem to fit in with nasalizing context (iii) in view of the fact that they both contained a conditioning nasal which was intervocalic. However, it is clear that all geminates in Latin were ambisyllabic, i.e. they straddled syllable boundaries, with part of the geminate forming a syllable coda to the preceding vowel while the remainder formed the onset of the following syllable, as in SŬM-MA. As (part of) the geminate formed a nasal coda, vowels which preceded geminates resembled those vowels occurring in context (i) forms like ŬM-BRA, and they have normally evolved in the same way. In view of this, the 'C' element which figured in our earlier specification for context (i), /VNC/, may be taken to cover both oral and nasal consonants so that geminate nasals would represent a special instance of 'NC'.

Our other remark relates to the possibility of *variation* in the type of nasalizing context occurring within an individual word-form. In many cases, the nasalizing context-type found in a Latin form has not changed in the passage of that form into modern Romance. Thus, the initial vowel of CANTĀRE appears in nasalizing context-type (i), and in the reflex of this word in Portuguese, Romanian, Occitan, etc. the initial vowel continues to be in the same context-type. However, it can happen that, under certain circumstances, a vowel changes its context-type. This may take place either synchronically or, more obviously, diachronically. Synchronically, variability can result from the effect of *linking*. In Romance, within closely-knit word groups there is a tendency for the final consonant of a word to link up with a following word-initial vowel so that they belong together in the same syllable, as in modern French *belle île* [bɛ-lil]. This linking arrangement, often referred to as 'enchaînement', can also affect word-final nasal consonants, so that a context (ii) form may emerge in some environments with a context (iii) syllable structure. For example, when group-final or preceding a word which was consonant-initial, Old French *un* 'a, one (m. sg.)' had a context (ii) structure, namely [ỹn], but when followed by a vowel-initial word in the same group, as in *un os* 'a bone', it occupies context (iii), as [ỹ-nɔs]. The possibility of individual words satisfying different nasalizing context-types, depending on their environment, has led on occasions to complex patterns of evolution, as conflicting forces relating to the distinct syllable structures have interacted.

Diachronically, sound change may have the effect of modifying the context-type in which a vowel appears. In fact, this possibility became apparent in our discussion above on nasalizing context (ii), since the overwhelming majority of cases of context (ii) in Romance arose from earlier non-apocopated forms in Latin which originally would have fallen under context (iii). Thus, although [bɛn] is a context (ii) form, it derives from earlier ['bɛne] which would be a context (iii) form. As already noted, our decision has been to describe the reflexes of apocopated forms like [bɛn] < BĔNE as context (ii) forms rather than context (iii) forms in those Romance varieties which experienced apocope, such as French, Spanish, and Portuguese.

In the later medieval period onward, rather predictably there have been a number of more localized developments which have resulted in changes in the nasalizing context-type occupied by a given vowel. Examples are:

context (i)   > (ii)   (DĔNTEM >)   dent   >   den   'tooth'   (Catalan)
context (i)   > (iii) (FŬNDA >)   'fonda > 'fonə 'sling'   (Catalan)
context (iii) > (ii)   (LŪNA >)   'lynə   >   lyn   'moon'   (French)

However, while recognizing the clear possibility that vowels may switch context-types, we will take as our basic point of reference the situation in early Romance. Accordingly, an item such as French *lune* will continue to be referred to as a context (iii) form despite its more recent realization in the standard language as [lyn]. Where there is any risk of confusion, explanation of the circumstances will be provided.

2.3.   Sources of Knowledge

An extensive range of materials is available to shed light on the incidence of nasal vowels in modern times. There are numerous detailed descriptions of individual varieties of Romance, standard and non-standard. Also, during this century linguistic atlases have been compiled which cover almost all parts of the Romance area. The pioneering work was the *ALF* (*Atlas Linguistique de la France*), published between 1902 and 1910, which has remained an important research tool for French dialectology, and comparable ventures were sub-sequently undertaken for other Romance areas, notably the *AIS* (1928–41) for Italy, including Sardinia and southern Switzerland, and the *ALR* (1956–72) for Romania. More recently, a number of more detailed atlases focusing upon linguistic usage in individual regions have also been compiled (further details: Holtus (1990) for French; Caragiu Marioțeanu (1989) for Romanian), and the long-awaited publication of the richly documented *ALI* (*Atlante linguistico italiano*) has recently begun (1995–). Nonetheless, the picture is not a complete one as some areas are less well served, the Iberian peninsula in particular. The abortive pan-peninsular *ALPI* yielded just one volume, which appeared in 1962, although substantial regional atlases are available: we may mention the *ALCat* (1923–64) for Catalan, the *ALEA* (1961–73) for Andalusia, and the *ALGa* (1990–), in course of publication for Galicia. Portugal still awaits proper coverage.

For earlier stages of Romance, our knowledge is of course much less certain. Sometimes there is documentary evidence to provide indications of the likely presence of vowel nasality. A special case is provided by the works of gram-marians describing the language of their time. We have a number of such writings about Latin by Roman grammarians (collected in Keil 1857–80, abbre-viated henceforth as K.). For Romance, Occitan is the first variety to receive attention at the turn of the twelfth–thirteenth centuries, in the *Razos de trobar* of Raimon Vidal de Besalú, and several other studies of Occitan appear over the next 150 years (Schlieben-Lange 1991). However, it is not until the sixteenth century that a body of systematic descriptions for other varieties of Romance becomes available, and for certain types of Romance we must wait even longer. The earliest grammar of any consequence for Romanian dates from 1780 (Turculeț 1989) and for Rheto-Romance the nineteenth century (Kramer 1989). Such grammatical works are of variable quality and reliability but none-theless they offer invaluable information.

In addition, valuable evidence may be provided by earlier literary and non-literary texts. Romance is fortunate in being richly attested, but even so the textual record is quite uneven. A substantial number of non-standard varieties have little or nothing in the way of written historical records, and some standard varieties too are poorly documented for their earlier stages. A striking case is that of Romanian for which the first extant running text of known date goes back only to the early sixteenth century.

Where textual materials are available, the appropriate evaluation of the data which they contain often poses problems however. As far as nasal vowels are concerned, it is clear that the use of a graphy consisting of a vowel followed by a nasal consonant does not by itself shed any light on whether the vowel was phonemically nasal or (weakly or strongly) allophonically nasal, as is demon-strated by comparing the pronunciation of the present-day item spelt *pan* in French and Spanish, [pã] vs. [pan], respectively. Similarly, the widespread practice among medieval scribes of using a tilde ' ˜ ' over a vowel is ambiguous as to levels of vowel nasality. Often the tilde served as no more than a conventional abbreviation for indicating the presence of a following nasal consonant, this being its function in medieval Latin texts where its use had first developed.[2] However, in certain Romance areas, scribes began to use the tilde as a sign of vowel nasality too. This ambiguity means that it is by no means self-evident what value the tilde has in a particular text and usually any decision on the likely value can only be tentatively made in the light of our general knowledge about the patterns of linguistic evolution in the area concerned. Thus, in areas where vowel nasalization has had little discernible impact, the probability is that the tilde indicated just the presence of following nasal consonant. For instance, in lines 18–19 of the Spanish epic poem *Cantar de Mio Cid* (MS mid-fourteenth century) which read:

> Plorãdo delos oios tãto auyen el dolor
> Delas ſus bocas todos diziã una RAZÕ

we may assume that the tilde is unlikely to be a sign of strong vowel nasality, since Spanish appears to have experienced minimal vowel nasalization. However, the status of the tilde in medieval French texts is more equivocal in view of the known occurrence of vowel nasalization in the history of the language. Its appearance where there is no nasal consonant following is inconclusive in respect of vowel nasalization, as in <biẽ> for *bien* in the mid-twelfth-century manuscript of the *Chanson de Roland*, l. 135 (Samaran and Laborde 1933). But where it is found in conjunction with a following nasal consonant, as in early thirteenth-century graphies like <fontãine>, the presence of high-level vowel nasality may be more plausibly inferred (Beaulieux 1967: 57). The substitution of a nasal consonant for the tilde led to the adoption of a double nasal graphy, as in <donne> (< DŌNAT), which appears in thirteenth-century texts and becomes more common during the fourteenth and fifteenth centuries. This graphy has also been widely taken to indicate the likely presence of vowel nasality.[3]

Tantalizing problems are also posed by graphies in which an etymologically inappropriate nasal consonant is used, as in <tenpo> to indicate the reflex of Latin TĔMPUS 'time', and by graphies where the original nasal consonant is omitted, as in <tep> another reflex for the same item (both these graphies are to be found in medieval texts from northern Italy). Does the use of the 'wrong' nasal consonant or the absence of any nasal consonant at all imply the weakening or even the deletion of that consonant and possible associated high-level vowel nasalization? This may be the case, but an interpretation of the likely value of a given graphy can only be tentatively arrived at after close attention has been paid to the frequency and distribution of the graphy and also to the orthographical conventions operative at the time and place when the text at issue was written down. The uncertainty in interpretation becomes even greater in Romance texts written in non-roman script. For instance, the earliest Romanian texts are almost all written in the Cyrillic alphabet in which there is a symbol ' ↑ ', seemingly indicating the presence of nasality. However the precise value of the symbol, which can have a vocalic or consonantal value depending on context, has occasioned a deal of debate and is still not entirely resolved (cf. Avram 1964: 575–611).

In texts written in verse, evidence can be gleaned from observing rhyme or assonance patterns. Perhaps the best known example of such a source of evidence is the medieval assonating poems of northern France which have been the subject of close attention in attempts to determine the likely path of vowel nasalization in early French (cf. 4.2.3). However, 'bad' or approximate assonances and rhymes are used on occasions by poets, and these may prompt inappropriate conclusions on contemporary language patterns. Also, prevailing poetic conventions and the exigences imposed by verse writing because of metrical constraints can shape usage so that a misleading impression may be given of linguistic circumstances at the time of the composition of a given work. Careful statistical and philological examination is therefore needed when exploiting the evidence provided by verse texts.

To back up the information provided by written documentation, the established techniques of comparative and internal reconstruction can be exploited, underpinned by the findings of linguistic theory. Even so, inferring the possible presence of vowel nasality is problematic, and there is little doubt that at various stages in the history of Romance many cases of substantial vowel nasalization have occurred which remain undetectable to us. However, two formal indicators can be recognized which may be taken to point to the likely operation of vowel nasalization and these we will be regularly making use of.

First, if a given vowel-type evolves differently in a nasalizing context from the way it evolves in other types of phonological context, this may be taken to reflect the likely influence of heightened vowel nasalization. The different evolution may take two forms. Either the allophones of a given vowel occurring in a nasalizing context may adopt a new quality which is distinct from the other allophones of that vowel and all other vowels, or more normally the allophones may come to be assigned to another vowel phoneme so that there is a phonemic merger in nasalizing contexts. The latter is commonly found in Romance with the mid vowels /ɛ/: /e/ and /ɔ/: /o/ in context (i) forms.

Second, as heightened vowel nasality is often associated with some weakening of the conditioning nasal, we may assume that especially in contexts where nasal consonants have been systematically deleted, the preceding vowel may well have been subject to significant nasalization, even if subsequent events have resulted in the vowel being denasalized. Another, but less extreme, case of nasal consonant weakening may be found. This is manifested in the neutralization of contrasts between conditioning nasals, especially in our context-type (ii). Where this occurs, the possibility of increased levels of allophonic vowel nasality having developed may be inferred.

Having established our classificational framework and certain basic methodological assumptions, we may explore the main features of nasal vowel evolution from Latin into Romance.

NOTES

1. We use the term *Romania* (italicized) to designate that area of the former Roman Empire in which languages deriving from Latin have continued to be spoken. Also included are areas where a Latin-based language was used until recent times, notably Dalmatia. The use of italics is to prevent possible confusion with the name of the sovereign state of Romania, in which a Latin-based language continues to be used (see Chapter 12).
2. The tilde derives from a superscript N placed over the preceding letter symbol. Subsequently, it was also sometimes used as an abbreviatory device to represent non-nasal sounds. For example <q̃> is found in texts from various areas to represent *que*.
3. The medieval practice of using the tilde over a vowel as an abbreviatory device to indicate a following nasal consonant was continued in printed works also. In Spanish, the grammar by Nebrija appearing in 1492 contains forms such as <perderiã, pronũciaciõ>, and in France, Henri Estienne's *Traicté de la conformité du langage François avec le Grec* (published in Paris in 1565) likewise contains forms such as <lãgue, quãd, cõdamneriõs>, where in this instance the tilde happens to coincide with the presence of vowel nasality. The use of the tilde is found in some printed works into the seventeenth century.

3

The Latin Background

3.1. Introduction

Our starting point for tracing the history of vowel nasalization lies in the ancestor of the various Romance languages and dialects, Latin. Clearly, knowledge of the pronunciation of a language form which is no longer used by native speakers can never be complete, so that any conclusions drawn on the characteristics of Latin speech must be somewhat tentative. As regards more delicate features of pronunciation, such as vowel nasality, for which no special written symbolization existed, the tentativeness must be even greater. However, from the information which is available there are some indications to suggest that vowels may well have been significantly affected by nasality at various stages of the history of Latin.

First, evidence can be drawn from texts which become available in substantial quantities from the third century BC onwards. There are also direct descriptions of the language by contemporary grammarians, although the information which they yield is at times frustratingly imprecise and misleading. Further data of a rather different nature are also forthcoming from the Romance languages themselves. Using the techniques of linguistic reconstruction, we can exploit the substantial quantity of information which we have of these from the later Middle Ages onward to shed light on the nature and distribution of unattested or fitfully attested pronunciation features in Roman times. The same techniques can also be pressed into service to glean information on pre-literary Latin, using as a basis attested Latin material and relevant items of data from other related languages. However, the dating and localization of the reconstructed forms are necessarily rather uncertain.

The information provided by these different sources, duly evaluated in the light of the general principles established by theroretical linguistics, makes it possible to infer likely pronunciation patterns in Latin. However, a point which it is easy to overlook is that like any other language Latin must have been characterized by internal variation. Although the grammarian Quintilian, writing in the later first century AD, claims that Latin differed from Greek in that it was not dialectalized (*Inst. Or.* 1. 5. 29), we have to assume that, with the rise and expansion of the Roman Empire, the Latin language did in fact undergo considerable development and diversification, chronologically, regionally, and socially. The norm variety, Classical Latin, which had crystallized out by the beginning of the first century BC and remained thereafter as a relatively static model of prestige linguistic usage for succeeding centuries, was doubtless therefore just one variety among many. Since its mastery implied considerable education, it was doubtless only ever acquired by a small minority of Romans. Indeed, the Latin-speaking world could scarcely have failed to be to some degree polylectal. At the death of Augustus in AD 14, for example, the estimated population for Italy was 6 million and for the other predominantly Latin-speaking provinces of the West it was some 20 million (Pulgram 1958: 309).[1] These were scattered over a vast geographical area and displayed wide social and ethnic diversity. If we add to this the likelihood that even at the height of the Empire literacy levels never reached 10% (Harris 1989: 272), the inevitable conclusion is that there must have been substantial variation in the linguistic habits of Latin speakers.

With regard to pronunciation, we know that significant accent differences existed even at the period of the greatest regional and social cohesion. Thus, Cicero (106–43 BC) remarks specifically on differences of intonation and sound quality as the distinguishing features of the orators of Cisalpine Gaul (*Brutus* 46. 171) and elsewhere censures the 'thick and foreign' quality of the speech of the then fashionable Cordovan poets (*Pro Archia* 10. 26). And later, when Roman emperors were of provincial origin, even they too could be found with non-standard accents. The Spaniard Hadrian (117–38) is recorded in the late fourth-century *Historia Augusta* as being the object of derision in the senate for his uneducated accent 'agrestius pronuntians' (*Vita Hadriani* 3. 1), while Septimius Severus (193–211), a native of North Africa, is described elsewhere in the same historical work as sounding rather African right into old age 'Afrum quiddam usque ad senectutem sonans' (*Vita Severi* 19. 9). Both emperors were of good social pedigree, it may be noted, Hadrian of senatorial background and Severus from an equestrian family with senatorial connections.

The implication of this for us is that there is every reason for believing that in the history of Latin significant vowel nasality, allophonic and perhaps even phonemic, may well have been found at different times, in different places, and with different sociolinguistic significance. Unfortunately, we can only have glimpses of the undoubtedly enormous variation which existed.

3.2.   Vowel Nasality in Latin

It is generally assumed that in Classical Latin there were no nasal vowel phonemes (cf. Brandenstein 1951; Mariner Bigorra 1962; Muljacic 1965; Vincent 1989). However, there are grounds for believing that strongly nasal vowels arose at various stages in the history of Latin including the Golden Age period and that phonemically nasal vowels may even have become established in some varieties of Latin. This is indicated by the fact that certain phonological changes have operated which seem to imply heightened vowel nasality. All the changes involve the weakening and sometimes the deletion of nasal consonants appearing in syllable-coda position.

3.2.1. MID-VOWEL RAISING

During the pre-literary period, short mid vowels [e o] were raised to [i u] in context (i) forms, i.e. forms like ŬNGUIS 'nail' where the vowel preceded a non-final coda nasal consonant. Such raising of mid vowels, which is rare in non-nasal contexts, may be attributed to the nasality of the context and this in turn suggests increased nasality in the vowel concerned. The assumption is therefore that, for some time at least, enhanced levels of allophonic nasality appeared in vowels in context (i) forms.

The implementation of this change was evidently complex. It seems to have begun with mid vowels preceding [ŋ], then affected vowels preceding [m], before finally applying to vowels before [n]. The evidence for this lies primarily in the number of exceptions to the raising action of the different context types. Only two forms failed to show raising before [ŋ] in the standard language, LŎNGUS 'long' and the rare verb TŎNGERE 'to know'. In contrast, a fair number of forms have not been affected when [m] is the raising consonant, particularly those containing original [e], for example MĔMBRUM, TĔMPUS 'limb, time'. Raising before [n] probably began just prior to the literary period but never established itself in the Roman variety of Latin that gave the standard language, hence CĔNTUM, PĔNDO, PŎNDUS 'hundred, I hang, weight'.

Chronologically, it appears that raising began to take place at a time when the Latin-speaking community was small and hence linguistically fairly homogeneous. Even so, there was some variation in the extent to which raising was implemented. In some non-standard varieties, raising before [ŋ] was generalized to include the item LŎNGUS 'long' as is indicated by the inscriptional forms LUN<GUM> (*CIL* vi. 12 1353 Rome), LUNGO (*CIL* xi. 6671a, on a marble pillar of uncertain provenance but possibly from Tuscany). Standard Italian *lungo* 'long' evidently goes back to this variant (cf. 10.2.2). Also, raising before [n] is attested, particularly with /o/. In the writings of Ennius (239–169 BC), we have the form FRUNDES (= CL FRŎNDES 'fronds') (*Annales*, 241), while Lucilius (d. *c.*102 BC) has DETUNDETE (= CL DETŎNDETE 'cut off (pl.)!') (l. 622) and DUPUNDI (= CL DUPŎNDII 'the sum of two asses (gen. sg.)') (l. 1237 of the Loeb edition). Significantly, neither poet was from

Rome; Ennius was a native of Calabria and Lucilius was born in Campania. After these early attestations, there is a steady stream of evidence pointing to the vitality of the non-standard realization of Classical short /o/ as /u/ in many parts of the Empire. Suggestive inscriptional forms are: CUNTRA 'against' (*CIL* v. 1732 Cisalpine Gaul), FRUNTE or FRUTE 'forehead' (*CIL* vi. 28440 Rome; *CIL* x. 4936, 8249 S. Italy), and at Pompeii DIPUNDIUM (*CIL* iv. 1679) beside DUPUDIU (*CIL* iv. 5123). Roman grammarians also call attention to this feature of pronunciation, cf. the second-century Velius Longus (K. 7.49.15), the fourth-century Charisius (K. 1.130.29). However, the sixth-century Priscian (K. 2.26.25) sees such a pronunciation as archaic.

Parallel examples of non-standard raising of short /e/ are also found in inscriptions: VIOLINTIA 'violence' (*CIL* xiii. 2386 Gaul), CALINDAS 'Calends' (*CIL* x. 7776 S. Italy), BENEMERINTI 'worthy' (*CIL* vi. 28448 Rome).

Possibly related to this general development is the raising of long /eː/ in context (i) forms, as in PRINDERE (*CTM* 135 Italy 6th c.), VINDEDIT (*CIL* iii. 14305 Dalmatia), cf. CL PRĒNDERE 'to take', VĒNDIDIT 'sold (3rd sg.)'. In this context, the vowel in fact became short over most of *Romania* in accordance with the new syllabically determined arrangement of having only short vowels in blocked syllables. In practice, the only nasal consonant implicated in the raising is the coronal [n], and the number of lexical items potentially affected is small. This type of raising appears to date mainly from the later Empire period and to have been rather localized.[2]

In those cases where raising has been generalized to mid vowels preceding [n], the implication is that higher levels of vowel nasality may have been found in the Latin of the areas concerned. But it is unclear how widespread the incidence of such generalized mid-vowel raising was across the Empire. Although some scholars have been prompted to recognize a universal tendency for one or both of the Latin short mid vowels to raise systematically before medial coda nasals (cf. Löfstedt 1961: 31), the evidence is not compelling. Certainly, some regions have very few examples of inscriptions showing the presumed tendency. Carnoy cites just one case of /e/ raising for Spain, SENTINTIAM 'judgement' (*CIL* ii. 1963), from a first-century AD official inscription found near Malaga, but he questions its fidelity. In his corpus of Christian inscriptions, Gaeng (1968: 43–6, 76–9) finds very little evidence of raising in Spain and Gaul, though there are a number of cases attested in Italy. From the more peripheral areas of the Empire too, such as Africa and Britain, the inscriptional cases of raising are comparatively scant (cf. Omeltchenko 1977: 79–83, 115–18).[3] The evidence provided by the Romance languages is obscured by the fact that considerable overall restructuring of the vowel system was taking place in Late Latin, and this interacted with any potential vowel raising (cf. 3.3). However, it is apparent that some varieties of Ibero-Romance, notably

Castilian, have not experienced raising, and there is no evidence of raising in most Central and Southern Italian dialects or in Dalmatian.

Assuming a link between vowel raising and nasality, the fluctuating evidence of vowel raising suggests that levels of vowel nasality in mid vowels in context (i) forms may have varied a good deal from region to region and from period to period. In the educated variety of Rome, which came to form the basis of the Classical language, presumably levels were becoming less intense by the beginning of the literary period, hence the widespread failure of vowels to raise before tautosyllabic [n]. Subsequently, certain regional forms of Latin had similarly reduced levels of nasality in this context. However, other regions evidently had higher levels of nasality and hence a more generalized pattern of raising, as in parts of northern Italy.

Two other developments occurring in Latin are equally indicative of possible vowel nasalization. These are the general move to neutralize contrasts between syllable-coda nasals, and the deletion of certain syllable-coda nasal consonants. Both involve the undermining of syllable-coda nasal consonants which is often associated with vowel nasalization.

3.2.2. NEUTRALIZATION OF SYLLABLE-CODA NASAL CONSONANTS

During the pre-literary period, nasals preceding oral sonorants and plosives underwent modifications which led to the neutralization of contrasts between them. The main lines of development were the following:

(a) *before oral sonorants*: /n/ underwent total assimilation whilst /m/ came to be followed by an epenthetic oral bilabial consonant:

-NL- > -LL-	*CORON-LA	>	CORŌLLA	'crown'
-NR- > -RR-	*CON-RAPIO	>	CORRĬPIO	'I seize'
-ML- > -MPL-	*EXEM-LOM	>	EXĔMPLUM	'example'
-MR- > -MBR-	*UMRA	>	ŬMBRA	'shade'

(b) *before oral plosives*: /n/ became homorganic whereas /m/ either developed an epenthetic glide (this development also applied with the sequence /ms/) or it became homorganic:

-NP- > -MP-	*IN-PIGER	>	ĬMPIGER	'energetic'
-NB- > -MB-	*IN-BELLIS	>	IMBĔLLIS	'peaceful'
-MC- > -NC-	*PRIM-CEPS	>	PRĪNCEPS	'chief'
-MT- > -MPT-	*EM-TOM	>	ĔMPTUM	'bought (n. sg.)'
-MD- > -ND-	*QUAM-DO	>	QUĂNDO	'when'
-MS- > -MPS-	*SUM-SI	>	SŬMPSI	'I took up'

The sequences -NT- -ND- and -NC- -NG- [nt nd ŋk ŋg] are not affected, since the nasal consonant was already homorganic.

Later, neutralization also came to operate on coda nasal consonants preceding another nasal consonant. Contrasts were still possible in this context in the norm pronunciation of the Classical period, e.g. ĂMNI 'river (dat. sg.)' vs. ĀNNI 'years (nom. pl.)' vs. ĂGNI 'lambs (nom. pl.)'.[4] However, neutralization may have already been carried through in certain non-standard varieties of the time and certainly became more widespread in the later Empire, usually through assimilation, cf. inscriptional forms such as DANNO (*CLE* 1339, 19); ALONNUS (*CIL* iii. 2240); INTERANNIENSIS (*CIL* ii. 509, 510, 511). However, cases of epenthesis are also found with the sequence -MN- in later codices, perhaps caused by hypercharacterization, DAMPNUM SOMPNUS (cf. Väänänen 1967: 64; Sommer 1977: 176).

The move towards the neutralization of syllable-coda nasals affected certain word-final nasals too, especially in grammatical words functioning effectively as prefixes within phonetic phrases. Here, assimilation of the nasal to the initial consonant of the following word was usual. Pompeiian inscriptions show IM BALNEUM (*CIL* iv. 2410) and TAN DURUM (*CIL* iv. 1895), and the letters from Claudius Terentianus writing in the first quarter of the second century AD have IM BIA (= VIA), IM MENSEM (Adams 1977: 23). Cicero twice notes the unfortunate phonetic similarity of CUM NOS and CUM NOBIS to the word CŬNNUS (*Ep. ad Fam.* ix. xxii. 2; *Orator*, 154), suggesting that even in the standard variety assimilation was normal. This conclusion is confirmed by the second-century grammarian Velius Longus who states that the M of the phrase ETIAM NUNC 'is pronounced more with an *n* than an *m*' (K. 7.78.18).

In all these cases showing neutralization, the coda element which remains has a reduced phonological status. In feature terms it would just be [− syllabic, + nasal]. This being so, the use of <M> for <N> indifferently to indicate the coda nasal even within morphemes is understandable; e.g. already in the *Lex Iulia Municipalis* of 45 BC (*CIL* i. 593 Rome) SENTEMTIAM (ll. 125, 132) and SENTENTIAM (ll. 96, 107) both appear and TUEMDAM, TUENDAM occur in the same line (l. 46). The diminished phonological status of such nasals and their sometimes capricious representation both suggest the possibility of phonetic weakening which would be compatible with the assumption of heightened nasalization of the preceding vowel.

3.2.3. DELETION OF SYLLABLE-CODA NASAL CONSONANTS

When nasals occurred preceding a fricative or in word-final position, they experienced greater weakening and ultimately deletion.

3.2.3.1.   Deletion in Pre-Consonantal Position

Nasals showed weakness from earliest times when preceding *fricatives*, doubt-less because the nasal tended to assimilate to the following consonant to become a nasal fricative, a rather unstable consonant type. We may note that comparable pre-fricative weakening and deletion of nasal consonants has also occurred in many types of Romance later on (cf. 4.2.5, 6.2.1.1, 7.4.1.2, 8.2.4, 9.2, 10.4.3.3, 11.2.2).

Many cases of nasal + fricative sequences arose across morpheme boundaries, typically involving the attachment of the prefixes IN- or CON- to stems beginning with a fricative. In word forms of this type, there was considerable tension between the phonological tendency to weaken and delete the nasal consonant and the morphological tendency to preserve the nasal of the prefix intact by analogy with the many other forms in IN- and CON- where the nasal was not threatened. There is evidence that the phonological tendency made a good deal of headway in Roman times, but subsequently in Romance the morphological tendency has come to predominate. As speakers evidently became increasingly aware (however dimly) of the presence of prefixal elements, they restructured the relevant word-forms accordingly by restoring the coda nasal consonant, as in I(N)-SIGNĂRE (> Fr. *enseigner*, Sp. *enseñar*, It. *insegnare*).

We may examine the change a little more closely. The sequence NS is of special interest because it is the only nasal + fricative sequence which occurred widely within morphemes rather than just across morpheme boundaries. Already in the pre-literary period, deletion of the nasal had taken place at the end of words, e.g. LŬPŎNS > LŬPŌS 'wolves (acc. pl.)', the preceding vowel undergoing compensatory lengthening.[5] The nasal consonant in medial -NS- experienced the same weakening in the pre-Classical period until by the Golden Age it had evidently ceased to be pronounced by most speakers. Varro (*Ling. Lat.* 108) mentions this in the first century BC, and the grammarian Velius Longus (K. 7.79.1) informs us that even Cicero did not pronounce the N in FORENSIA 'public matters', MEGALENSIA 'name of a festival to Cybele', and the proper name HORTENSIA. From early times, inscriptions regularly omit the nasal, as in COSOL CESOR (= CL CŌNSUL CĒNSOR) in the third century BC epitaph on the tomb of L. Cornelius Scipio (*CIL* i. 8). Sub-sequently, however, official inscriptions tend to restore the graphy N, although numerous cases continue be found in less formal inscriptions of its omission: SPOSA (*CIL* vi. 10013 Rome), MESA (*CIL* ii. 563, 21 Spain), and especially forms of the word CO(N)SUL. Romance also points to the general deletion of the nasal consonant in -NS- within morphemes, as in MĒNSA 'table' > Sp., Port. *mesa*, Rom. *masă*; Fr. *moise*; SPŌNSA 'betrothed (f.), bride' > Sp., Port. *esposa*, It. *sposa*, Fr. *épouse*.[6]

Parallel weakening of the nasal in -NF- is indicated by inscriptions, cf. COFECI (*CIL* i. 560) and IFERI (*CIL* vi. 19873) for Classical CONFĒCI 'I completed' and ĪNFERI 'the dead, nether world' as well as by comments by contemporary writers. Cicero (*Orator*, 159) explicitly notes that the first letter (i.e. vowel) is short in words such as INDŎCTUS 'untrained', COMPŌSUIT 'he composed', CONCRĔPUIT 'it creaked', but long where N was followed by S or F, e.g. INSĀNUS 'mad', INFĒLIX 'unhappy', CONSUĒVIT 'he became accustomed', CONFĒCIT 'he composed'. The tell-tale vowel lengthening suggests comparable weakening of the nasal and vowel nasalization in both cases.

The Romance languages, however, provide less clear evidence on nasal weakening in the sequence /nf/. The modern forms Fr. *enfant, enfer*, Sp. *enfermo* indicate neither deletion nor vowel lengthening, although Engadinish *uffant* 'child' does show deletion. However, forms with weakened nasals appear more widely in medieval texts, e.g. Old Spanish *i(f)ante* 'royal child' (cf. 7.4.1.2), Old Occitan *efan* 'child'. This once again suggests that there has been a Romance tendency to restore the prefixal IN- and CON- (or, more precisely, the phonetically evolved forms of these) wherever they are identified.

Before the fricative /h/, parallel nasal consonant weakening does not appear to occur. Suggestively, Cicero (loc. cit.) specifically cites the word INHUMĀNUS 'savage' as having a short initial vowel, just like INDŎCTUS. However, as /h/ was probably only pronounced by more educated speakers in the Golden Age and ever more rarely thereafter, the apparent anomaly here is not significant.[7]

It therefore appears that before fricatives, especially /s/, considerable weakening of nasals occurred from early times. Associated with this was lengthening and probably nasalization of the preceding vowel. The weakening process was a protracted one, however, probably delayed by the conservative influence of grammarians and officialdom. There seems every reason to expect that in the Golden Age a fair range of pronunciations existed for the written sequence vowel + NS, with varying degrees of nasality in the vowel and varying degrees of consonant deletion from partial (educated style) to total.

In certain non-standard varieties, there is some evidence of weakening and perhaps even occasional deletion of nasals before *plosives*. Väänänen (1966: 67–8) notes numerous instances from Pompeii, e.g. PRICIPIS 'leader (gen. sg.)' (*CIL* iv. 1945), SIICUDO (= SECŬNDO) 'second (abl. sg.)' (*CIL* iv. 8270), POPIIIANIS (= POMPEIĀNIS) 'for those of Pompeii' (*CIL* iv. 1121), and Carnoy (1906: 171–3) cites examples from Spain. Cases of hypercorrection are likewise to be found SCIANTIS (= SCIĀTIS) 'you (pl.) know (pres. subj.)' (*CIL* ix. 5860). This tendency has left no direct trace in the Romance languages however.

3.2.3.2. *Deletion in Word-Final Position*

Word-final nasal consonants are also subject to deletion. Final -M in words of more than one syllable was evidently weakened from earliest times, as in the third-century BC inscription on the tomb of L. Cornelius Scipio: DUONORO OPTUMO FUISE VIRO (= CL BONŌRUM ŎPTIMUM FUĬSSE VĬRUM) 'to have been the best of good men' (*CIL* i. 9). And although as a result of learned reaction official inscriptions from the later second-century BC onward tend to indicate final -M, in popular inscriptions final -M is commonly omitted in all regions of the Empire and at all periods. Grammarians too mention the weakness of final -M. In the first century AD, Quintilian says of this nasal that when it occurs before a word beginning with a vowel (e.g. in QUANTUM ERAT), 'even though it is written, it is hardly pronounced' (*Inst. Or.* IX. iv. 40). The Romance languages uniformly confirm the deletion of word-final -M, the only anomaly concerning monosyllables. Here, a nasal consonant segment was generally retained in items which often carried sentential stress, QUĒM 'whom' > Sp. *quien*, Rom. *cine*; RĔM 'thing (acc. sg.)' > Fr. *rien*, but lost in items usually sententially unstressed, IĂM 'already' > Sp. *ya*, OFr. *ja*. TAM 'so' and CUM 'with' develop as prefixal elements, although some inscriptional evidence suggests independent word status, cf. CU AMEICEIS 'with friends' (*CIL* i. 1702).

Word-final -N became relatively rare in the pre-literary period with its disappearance from the nominative singular form of nouns with -ŌN- stems, *LEŌN > LĔŌ 'lion'. It survived after short vowels in nominative/accusative singular forms of neuter nouns, e.g. NŌMEN 'name', and in a small set of monosyllabic forms notably the nouns RĒN 'kidney', SPLĒN 'spleen', LIĒN 'spleen', and the negative adverb NŌN. Inscriptional evidence suggests that in certain varieties of Latin at least there was a trend towards deletion particularly before vowels, NO IICO (= NŌN ĔGO 'not I') from Pompeii (*CIL* iv. 4133). A few Romance languages show signs of the retention of -N, e.g. Sardinian dialects such as Nuorese *numen*, *semen*, *non* (Pittau 1972), but generally it has been lost except in the single item NŌN.

3.2.4. VOWEL NASALITY IN LATIN RECONSIDERED

Many scholars have concluded that after syllable-coda nasal consonants were deleted long nasal vowels appeared in Latin (Allen 1978: 28, 30; Bassols de Climent 1981: 190; Kent 1945: 58; Niedermann 1953: 113; Palmer 1954: 224; and Sommer 1977: 221). However, as noted earlier, few have wished to accept that these nasal vowels would have given rise to surface contrasts with oral vowels and hence would have been phonemic, as in DĒSUM 'I am lacking' vs.

DĒNSUM 'dense (n. sg. nom./acc.), RŎTĂ 'wheel (nom. sg.)' vs. RŎTĂM 'wheel (acc. sg.)' etc.). Maniet (1975: 152) indeed explicitly denies phonemic status to the nasal vowels deriving from word-final vowel + M sequences, describing them instead as combinatory variants with demarcative function. Nonetheless, the evidence for surface contrasts between nasal and oral vowels is strong and it suggests that at certain periods and in certain styles of speech nasal vowel phonemes may well have arisen.[8] However, these vowels failed to become fully established, perhaps in part due to their limited distribution.

Whereas phonemic vowel nasality only gained limited acceptance, it is likely that the use of high-level allophonic nasality developed in many varieties of Latin at various periods. But how directly the broad nasalizing tendencies detectable in Latin times relate to later Romance developments found in specific areas such as France and Portugal is uncertain. Unfortunately, the lack of solid evidence of regional usage in the Empire and early medieval periods prevents continuity in the use of high-level vowel nasality from being identified reliably. For this reason, our treatment of vowel nasalization in individual Romance varieties will at most make tentative references to nasalizing trends in Latin.

3.3.   Nasalization and Other Sound Changes

In the Empire period, further changes got underway which were to have an effect on the incidence of vowel nasalization and on vowel patterns.

First, the range of nasal consonants came to be extended in late Latin with the appearance of the palatal phoneme /ɲ/ which became established in all parts of the Roman Empire except Sardinia and parts of southern Italy. It developed from -NJ- and, except in Romanian, from -GN-, but it only appeared in intervocalic position, where it was always geminate. As Latin geminates lay across syllable boundaries, occupying the coda and onset positions of successive syllables, this new phoneme provided a further source of nasalizing context (i), e.g. SĔNIOR > ['seɲ-ɲor].

In the vowel system itself, the major development in the Empire period was the emergence of a system based solely on quality. In the majority of areas, northern and central Italy, Dalmatia, Rhetia, Gaul, and Spain, a stressed vowel system with seven members /i e ɛ a ɔ o u/ gradually arose. In the development of this new arrangement, the earlier tendency for the short mid nasalized vowels to raise (cf. 3.2.1 above) was partly reversed. For, when Ĕ and Ŏ underwent raising, they presumably gave vowels which were identified with the existing short high vowels, Ĭ and Ŭ respectively. However, the effect of the restructuring of the vowel system in the areas concerned was to identify original short Ĭ with long Ē and short Ŭ with long Ō, and for these to emerge as high mid /e/ and /o/ respectively. When there was no previous raising of Ĕ and Ŏ, they developed into the low-mid vowels /ɛ/ and /ɔ/. From the viewpoint of early Romance, therefore, the mid-vowel raising which occurred in pre-literary Latin resulted in the neutralization of mid-vowel contrasts with /e o/ appearing in the forms affected. As we shall see, comparable cases of neutralization between mid vowels in nasalizing contexts can be observed in the history of many Romance varieties.

NOTES

1. These figures are not universally accepted. For instance, Christ (1984: 270) puts forward the following estimates: Italy 13 million, other Latin-speaking provinces 14 million.

2. For instance, Löfstedt (1961: 35–6) found that the graphy <I> as against <E> is used for the verb VĒNDERE in the majority of cases in the seventh-century *Codice Diplomatico Langobardo* from northern Italy. Stotz (1996: 18) describes forms such as <PRINDERE> as especially characteristic of northern Italy. In Merovingian documents, the use of <I> is even more consistent in this lexical item, but this may well be due to the general scribal tendency to represent original long /eː/ by means of the graphy <I> in all types of context (cf. Vielliard 1927: 5–10).

3. The Balkans is also included amongst the areas covered by Omeltchenko. However, rather more cases of raising are reported by Mihăescu (1978), indicating that vowel nasality may have been more intense in this region during the Empire, cf. 12.2.1.

4. The contrasting pre-nasal nasals here had in fact arisen overwhelmingly from oral plosives through another instance of assimilation in the pre-literary period: e.g. *SOP-NOS > SŎMNUS 'sleep', *AT-NOS > ĂNNUS 'year', *LEG-NOM > LĬGNUM 'wood'. In the norm pronunciation of the Classical period the graphy <GN> as in LĬGNUM probably had the value [ŋn], cf. Allen (1978: 23–5); Sturtevant (1968: 155); Traina (1953: 60–1).

5. Paradigmatic pressure kept the nasal element in nominative singular forms like ĀMANS 'loving (pres. part.)' and FRŌNS 'foliage', where the nasal was motivated by its appearance in the stem used for all the other inflected forms AMANT-, FROND-.

6. One notable exception is the word PENSĀRE > Sp., Port. *pensar*, Fr. *penser*, It. *pensare*, with the value 'to think' in all cases. Often explained without more ado as a semi-learned form, it probably arose from the lexical exploitation of pronunciation differences in this word in different varieties and styles of Latin. The more informal popular pronunciation [peːˈsaːre] was assigned the original concrete value 'to weigh' (> *pesar, peser, pesare*) while the more conservative and educated pronunciation [peːnˈsaːre] indicated the metaphorical value 'to think'. Such polymorphism, with different values being mapped separately onto variant pronunciations, finds a parallel in English *courtesy* and *curtsy*.

7. Allen (1978: 66–7) postulates a further case of nasal consonant weakening before a fricative in the sequences NCT and NX. It is claimed that the [k] became the fricative

[χ] which, before disappearing, triggered the weakening of the preceding nasal. This in turn caused characteristic compensatory lengthening in the vowel which preceded. Thus, QUĪNTUS 'fifth' allegedly developed as ['kwiŋktos] > ['kwiŋχtos] > ['kwĩːχtos] > ['kwĩːtos] > ['kwiːntus]. The assumption is that after [χ] was lost, the pre-plosive nasal vowel [ĩː] which arose was subsequently reconstituted as an oral vowel + [n]. The numerous cases of apparently exceptional forms such as SĀNCTUS, CĪNCTUS, with [k] preserved and with long stressed vowels, are explained as having had their [k] element maintained or restored as a result of paradigmatic analogy (here with SANCĪRE 'to make sacred', CĪNGERE 'to gird').

8. A similar view is adopted by Safarewicz who recognizes distinctively nasal vowels in Latin, which he claims survived down to the second century AD when they denasalized and merged with their oral counterparts (1974: 176, 185–7).

4

Gallo-Romance I: French

4.1. Introduction

No Romance language has received as much attention in the investigation of vowel nasalization as French. It is therefore appropriate that the first area of Romance to be considered in our review should be Gallo-Romance within which the French language fits. In fact, the patterns of vowel nasalization which emerge vary a good deal from region to region. It will therefore be helpful to divide the coverage of Gallo-Romance into three sections. In this chapter, the focus of attention falls on northern French, and more specifically on the developments which have occurred in the variety which became the standard language. In the following chapter, general patterns of vowel nasalization in non-standard northern varieties are examined, and in Chapter 6 the major developments in southern varieties of Gallo-Romance are considered.

4.1.1. HISTORICAL BACKGROUND

Following the break-up of the Roman Empire, the political and hence linguistic patterns of Gaul underwent substantial change. The Germanic-speaking Franks conquered most of Gaul in the late fifth and sixth centuries, but their main area of settlement and power base was centred in the north, above the River Loire, and it was here that Frankish influence was especially intense. To the south, the Frankish presence was fairly restricted and the established Roman culture was able to continue with some degree of independence (James 1982).

This split was to have linguistic consequences. In the north, a more innovative and individual variety of Romance developed out of what had been a more peripheral form of Latin. The dialects of this northern form of Gallo-Romance are collectively known as the *langue d'oïl* (*oïl* was the form of the affirmative particle which developed characteristically in these dialects; it corresponds to modern standard French *oui*). In the south, a more conservative form of Romance is found which in many respects has greater affinities to the Romance found south of the Pyrenees and the Alps. The group of dialects here collectively form the *langue d'oc* (*oc* being the corresponding form of the affirmative particle common to these dialects). The rather different effect of nasalization on vowel evolution in the two areas provides one instance of this linguistic division.

The separate identity of north and south was to remain until the thirteen century. Then, as a result of direct military and political action (notably the Albigensian Crusade 1209–29), the monarchy, which was by now based in Paris, asserted its titular authority over the south. A long, gradual process of integration thus began. Linguistically, this led to the growing adoption of northern speech habits in the south for prestige and practical reasons. *Langue d'oc* varieties steadily lost ground and in many areas came to be confined to rural communities (see also 6.1.1).

Meanwhile, in the north the development of an increasingly centralized political state had a familiar consequence: one dialect was elevated to the status of standard language. The dialect of the *langue d'oïl* concerned was Francien, the dialect of the Ile-de-France with Paris at its centre. Already by the end of the twelfth century there are indications that Parisian usage is beginning to be identified as some sort of norm. It is this variety, and particularly the cultivated form of it, which has come to form the basis of standard French today, and from the twelfth century onward it has exercised an ever-growing influence on other Gallo-Romance varieties (Lodge 1993).

Tracing the patterns of vowel nasalization in the standard variety of French will form a major part of this chapter. However, it is important to recall that the linguistic patterns found in this variety by no means correspond exactly to those found in other varieties, be they of the *langue d'oc* or the *langue d'oïl*. Familiar and 'natural' though the standard French treatment of nasal vowels seems to be (especially to some French linguists), we might well have had a very different picture of nasal vowel evolution if some other area than the Ile-de-France had become the political and hence linguistic centre of the country.

4.1.2. VOWEL NASALITY IN MODERN STANDARD FRENCH

The impact of vowel nasalization has been considerable throughout the *langue d'oïl* area. In the standard language as well as in non-standard varieties, it has given rise to unconditioned nasal vowels which can form surface contrasts with oral vowels. In standard French, there are four such nasal vowel types in formal and conservative usage [$\tilde{\epsilon}$ $\tilde{a}$ $\tilde{œ}$ $\tilde{ɔ}$], as in *bain, banc, un, bon* [b$\tilde{\epsilon}$ b$\tilde{a}$ $\tilde{œ}$ b$\tilde{ɔ}$] 'bath, bench, a (m. sg.), good (m. sg.)' which contrast with *baie, bas, oeufs, beau* 'bay, low (m. sg./pl.), eggs, beautiful (m. sg.)'. Amongst many speakers today, however, only three nasal vowel types occur [$\tilde{\epsilon}$ $\tilde{a}$ $\tilde{ɔ}$]. Phonetically, it may be noted that the traditional transcriptions given here for the nasal vowels are somewhat imprecise. The vowel represented by [$\tilde{\epsilon}$] is typically realized as [$\tilde{æ}$], [$\tilde{ɔ}$] usually has a tongue position which is roughly midway between cardinal 6 and 7 and consequently is sometimes transcribed [õ] instead, and [ɑ̃] is commonly very retracted and slightly raised and is also accompanied in the speech of Parisians by slight lip rounding. Indeed, it has been claimed that the difference between the vowels of *on* and *an* is carried principally by the degree of lip rounding which accompanies them, the vowel of *on* having intense rounding ('surlabialisation') as against the limited rounding ('labialisation') of *an* (Zerling 1984).

The reduced range of nasal vowels as compared to the range of oral vowels (4 vs. 12) is notable, as is the absence of any high nasal vowels. The nasal vowels have a wide distribution. They appear in final and non-final syllables, although they are not normally found preceding nasal consonants except across grammatical boundaries. Statistically, they occur in the decreasing order of frequency [ɑ̃ ɔ̃ ɛ̃ œ̃] and in frequency lists covering all French vowels only the vowel [ɑ̃] figures in the top half (Akamatsu 1967; Hug 1979: 27).

Much has been written on the phonological interpretation of the nasal vowels of French. Amongst structuralist linguists, the nasal vowels have consistently been considered to be distinct phonemes (cf. Gougenheim 1935; Malmberg 1969; Rothe 1972). A rather different view was adopted by most early generative phonologists who interpreted them at an underlying level as sequences of two systematic phonemes /VN/, i.e. (oral) vowel + nasal, so that no nasal vowel phonemes as such were recognized (cf. Schane 1968; Dell 1973). Some generativists however argued for the need to postulate underlying nasal vowel phonemes (e.g. Tranel 1981). More recently, non-linear phonology with its use of separate tiers of representation has given rise to more nuanced descriptions. Depending upon the circumstances, surface nasal vowels may be described as deriving from underlying nasal vowels or from sequences of oral vowel + nasal element, but in the latter case the nasal element is 'floating' and may either link with the preceding vowel to give a nasal vowel or be attached to a following vowel to form a (consonantal) syllable onset, i.e. in liaison forms (cf. Plénat 1987; Encrevé 1988; Tranel 1992; Scullen 1994). Our interpretation however will be of a very 'surface' kind, as was noted in the opening chapter. Where a nasal vowel occurs without an overt conditioning factor and forms surface contrasts with oral vowels, it will be termed a phoneme.

4.2.   Vowel Nasalization in Standard French: General Considerations

4.2.1.   BACKGROUND DEVELOPMENTS

Underlying the vowel systems of all varieties of Gallo-Romance (G-R) is the same seven–type arrangement as that forming the basis of Ibero-Romance, Rheto-Romance, and north and central Italo-Romance. This was:

As was the case in the other Romance areas mentioned, G-R neutralized contrasts between mid vowels in unstressed syllables, leaving just the high-mid vowels /e o/ in that context.

A further important feature of early G-R in the *langue d'oïl* area is that in stressed syllables vowel length came to vary according to syllable structure. The pattern was that in free syllables the vowel was lengthened, while it remained unchanged in blocked syllables. Thus:

(free)   VĒNA   > ['ve-na]   > (early G-R) ['veː-na] 'vein'
(blocked) VĒNDAS > ['ven-das] > (early G-R) ['ven-das] 'you sell (subj.)'

This syllabically conditioned vowel length differentiation also arose in Italo-Romance and Rheto-Romance, but there is no evidence that it developed in the *langue d'oc* area in the south or in areas of the east–west periphery of Romance, the Iberian Peninsula and Romania (Lausberg 1963: § 163; Weinrich 1969: 177, 179).

G-R also experienced wide-ranging apocope in the pre-literary period (i.e. the period prior to the mid-ninth century when for the first time texts appear which were written using a vernacular or non-Latinizing orthography). Apocope affected all final vowels except −A which developed to [−ə]. However, it operated at a later stage than vowel lengthening in free syllables. Long vowels could therefore appear in blocked syllables in apocopated forms, e.g. VĪNUM > ['viːnu] > [viːn] .

4.2.2. THE NASALIZING CONTEXT

Vowel nasalization has typically occurred as a result of *regressive* assimilation from some nasal consonant. All types of nasal consonant have exercised this influence. Cases of *progressive* nasalization are occasionally found in the varieties of *langue d'oïl*, particularly in those of the east (cf. 4.2.5 (*a*)). Where examples appear in the history of Francien, they probably owe themselves to influence from these eastern dialects.

Vowels underwent regressive nasalization under the influence of heterosyllabic as well as tautosyllabic nasal consonants. Thus:

QUĪNTA > (OFr.) ['kĩntə], VĪNUM > (OFr.) [vĩn], FĪNA > (OFr.) ['fĩnə]

Looking more closely at the nasalizing contexts, types (i) and (iii) had been inherited in substantial numbers from Latin, e.g. VĒNDAS CANTĀRE and VĒNA LŪNA, respectively. As a result of apocope, the small set of context (ii) forms, such as NŌN RĔM, were added to in large numbers. Thus, in the ninth-century text *Eulalia* we have examples such as *christiien, nom* < CHRISTIĀN(UM) NŌM(EN).

4.2.2.1. Vowels in Later Context (iii) Forms

In one special set of words, there is some uncertainty as to whether vowel nasalization occurred. It concerns the forms in which a vowel came to appear before a nasal consonant as a result of the deletion of an intervening oral consonant. Thus,

ĂSINUM > ['az(e)nu] > (early OFr.) ['a(z)nə] > [aːnə] *âne* 'donkey'
RĔTINA > ['rɛd(e)na] > (early OFr.) ['rɛ(ð)nə] > [rɛːnə] *rêne* 'rein'

The syllable-final consonants [z ð] here were probably lost before or during the twelfth century and this change normally resulted in the lengthening of the preceding vowel. The loss of the oral consonant now meant that the vowel which had preceded it was followed directly by a nasal consonant, thereby apparently creating new instances of context (iii) forms. Various scholars have assumed that vowel nasalization did affect the vowels of these forms, e.g. Fouché (1969: 357, 359) and Rochet (1976: 69 n. 207). However, it is not clear that these vowels did nasalize in the same way as vowels had done in original context (iii) forms such as VĒNA. Morin (1994: 37–8, 64) in particular presents some persuasive evidence to suggest that vowel nasalization very probably did not take place.[1]

If Morin's view is accurate, there are some important implications. First, the rule of vowel nasalization affecting context (iii) forms must have ceased to be productive after the eleventh century. The alternative explanation would be that the long vowels of forms like *âne* exceptionally resisted nasalization: such a case would provide a striking counterexample to the apparent pattern of vowel nasalization in North Italy (Hajek 1997). Secondly, from the twelfth century onward Old French presumably had a phonemic contrast between oral and nasal vowels specifically preceding nasal consonants, for example between [aːnə] *âne* and [dʒə'ānə] *Jeanne*.

4.2.3. IMPLEMENTATION OF VOWEL NASALIZATION

The process by which early French vowels were nasalized and the chronology of this process have been subjects of long-running debate amongst historians of the language. At the centre of the debate has been the relevance of vowel height in determining the implementation of nasalization, although to a lesser extent the relevance of the front–back dimension has also been at issue. (Other potential differentiating factors such as vowel length, which plays an important role in shaping patterns of vowel nasalization in northern Italian dialects (cf. 10.4.3.1), appear to have been of less significance in French and have not received much attention.) As regards the impact of height and the front–back dimension on vowel nasalization, two main schools of thought exist. On the one hand, there are those who believe that they were of decisive importance and led to nasalization taking place as a phased development, beginning first with the low vowels *a* and *ai* and then spreading progressively to the other vowels in the following chronological order, *e* and *ei* > *o* > *i* > *u* (= [y]) in a process lasting several centuries. Nasalization thus affected low vowels before high vowels and front vowels before back vowels.[2] Adherents of this view include Paris and Pannier (1872: 82), Paris (1898: 300), Pope (1952: §§ 434, 441), Straka (1955: 253–5), Fouché (1969: 356–7), Price (1971: 83), Posner (1971: 190), and Ruhlen (1979: 30–1). Some differences exist in the proposed chronology of nasalization, but the consensus is that nasalization got underway about the tenth century and was completed by the thirteenth or fourteenth century.

On the other hand, there is an almost equally long tradition which denies the significance of vowel height or the front–back dimension in the implementation of vowel nasalization. According to this tradition, nasalization operated as a single-stage development such that all vowels appearing in an appropriate nasalizing context were affected simultaneously. Adherents of this view include Suchier (1893: 118), Rheinfelder (1968: §§ 184–5), Rochet (1976: 55), Entenman (1976: 144, 206), Matte (1982: 121–2), and Reenen (1985: 44). Rather variable chronologies have been proposed for nasalization by these scholars, but none are later than approximately AD 1000.

A minority of scholars have opted for a compromise view by proposing that all vowel types probably did nasalize at the same time, but that high vowels were less strongly nasalized than low ones and hence were slower to be influenced in their evolution by nasality, cf. Uschakoff (1897) and, more recently, Wüest (1979: 280).

Underpinning the 'phased' view of nasalization is the evidence provided by assonance in early French texts. (Assonance operated as a simple form of rhyme and grouped together lines of verse whose final words had a stressed syllable containing the same vowel; modern French examples of assonating words would be *rêve, aile* and *mèche*. It was widely used in verse works from the tenth century to the early thirteenth century, when rhyme progressively supplanted it; cf. Lote 1949; Elwert 1965.) The key piece of evidence which is adduced is that assonance between vowels in an oral context and those in a nasalizing context becomes rare at an earlier stage for low vowels than for high vowels. Thus, already in the tenth-century text *St. Leger*, forms ending with the sequences written as *aN* and *aiN* do not appear in assonance with forms ending in the sequences *aC* and *aiC* (where *N* indicates a nasal consonant and *C* an oral consonant), and in the eleventh century text *St. Alexis* there is non-assonance also between the sequences *eN* and *eiN* and their counterparts *eC* and *eiC*. However, *oN* assonates with *oC* until the second half of the twelfth century, whereas *iN* assonates with *iC* and *uN* with *uC* quite regularly in verse until well into the thirteenth century. This diverging pattern of assonance is taken to reflect the earlier implementation of nasalization in low vowels. However, it is far from clear whether such a conclusion is justified. Nasalization may have operated more or less simultaneously on all types of vowel but in the period up to the late thirteenth century the resultant high-level nasality may only have caused a significant change in the tongue position of low vowels so that it was these vowels alone which could no longer assonate readily. Other considerations have also been advanced to call the 'phased' view of nasalization into question. For example, already in the twelfth century it appears that there was a statistically significant tendency for assonance to group together instances of the high vowels /i/ or /y/ which occurred in a nasalizing context, suggesting that these high vowels too had undergone conditioned nasalization (cf. Reenen 1985, 1987; and Hajek 1993). The question of the process of implementation thus remains controversial, the problem being that the available data are compatible with both views. Indeed, it is not easy to see what empirical facts could help us to choose between the two competing views, as Morin (1994: 33) notes, even if the 'simultaneous' view might appear more persuasive on the grounds that individual speakers of Old French would perhaps be more likely to generalize high-level allophonic nasality to the target articulation of all types of vowel rather than just using it with certain types. If the 'simultaneous' view is accepted, then the assumption must be that heightened vowel nasalization had been implemented by the tenth century at the latest.

In fact, looking more specifically at the chronology of vowel nasalization, we find certain pieces of evidence which suggest that vowels with raised levels of allophonic nasality may already have been present well before the tenth century, the date which figures as the starting point for nasalization in many traditional presentations.

(*a*) Already in the earliest examples of French verse, where assonance rather than rhyme is used, the contrasts between mid vowels, /e/ vs. /ɛ/ and /o/ vs. /ɔ/, have clearly been neutralized before the nasal coda consonant of context (i) forms, whereas before oral consonants there is no such neutralization. This difference of treatment points to the early action of vowel nasalization. Neutralization only affected the stressed vowels of context-type (i), which had not undergone syllabically conditioned lengthening. It did not affect the vowels of context-type (ii).

(*b*) Metaphonic diphthongization of low-mid vowels through the action of a following palatal consonant (e.g. FŎLIA > OFr. *fueille* 'leaf') has not regularly occurred when [ɲ] followed, e.g. LŎNGE CŎGNITUM > OFr. *loin cointe* 'afar' 'familiar, elegant' rather than **luein cueinte, cf. Old Occ. *luenh cuende*. However, with the front vowel /ɛ/ there has been diphthongization in INGĔNIUM > OFr. *engin* 'strategem' (via *engiein like LĔCTUM > *lieit > OFr. *lit* 'bed'). The implication is that /ɔ/ was nasalized strongly enough for it to be raised in this context to /o/ and hence avoid diphthongization. As metaphonic diphthongization is a change of some antiquity, the heightened nasalization of /ɔ/ by a following [ɲ] was evidently a fairly early development. This change also suggests that nasalization affected back vowels before front vowels (cf. above).

(*c*) Also relating to context (i) forms, there is scribal evidence in Merovingian documents which indicates nasal coda weakening, e.g. *volomtate, adinplire* (noted long ago by d'Arbois de Jubainville 1872: 325), and also possible shifts in quality for vowels in nasalizing contexts, such as *spunte, sumpnus* (cf. Latin SPŎNTE SŎMNUS) in the eighth-century Reichenau Glossary. If these graphies do reflect nasal weakening and quality shifts, then they also point to the likely presence of heightened vowel nasality.

(*d*) In the ninth-century poem *Eulalia* the much-discussed form *maent* (< MĂNET) 'she remains' is found. Comparison with other words appearing in the same text with original stressed free /a/, e.g. *spede* and *chieef* (< SPĀTA CĂPUT) 'sword, head', indicates that already by the ninth century some pre-nasal vowels had diverged phonetically from their oral counterparts. A plausible way of accounting for such divergence would be to attribute it to the presence of heightened nasality.

All these pieces of data betray the likely influence of nasalization and suggest the existence of significantly nasalized vowels well back into the pre-literary period. The vowels concerned were still conditioned variants of oral vowel phonemes, but evidently their nasality was already strong enough to disturb the regular patterns of vowel change. Entering the literary period, levels of nasality in these vowels were stepped up and this was to lead them to evolve in further special ways. However, as we have seen (4.2.2.1), it may be that the productivity of the process of heightened vowel nasalization came to an end during the eleventh century, at least in context (iii) forms.

4.2.4. FATE OF THE CONDITIONING NASAL CONSONANT

Directly bound up with vowel nasalization in French is the presence of a conditioning nasal consonant which follows the vowel concerned. This consonant was to undergo two important changes in syllable-coda position in the period up to the sixteenth century. First, in contexts where contrast was possible between nasal consonants, neutralization progressively took place implying some diminution in the articulatory strength of these consonants. Second, coda nasals as a class experienced weakening until they were lost in all contexts by the end of the sixteenth century even in the most conservative styles of speech.

Looking more closely at these two syllable-coda developments in contexts (i) and (ii) in turn, we find that already by the beginning of the literary period (mid-ninth century) the contrast between coda nasals in context (i) forms like *rompre chanter* [rõmprə tʃãnteːr] had doubtless long since gone. Nasals here were homorganic with the following oral consonant, just as they had been in Latin. Where the palatal nasal /ɲ/ came to appear before another consonant, it was restructured through linearization to [ĩn] early on, perhaps already by the ninth century: IŬNCTUM > ['dʒõɲt(u)] > (early OFr.) [dʒõĩnt] 'joined (past part.)'; CŎGNITUM > ['kɔɲɲ(e)tu] > (early OFr.) ['kõĩntə] 'familiar, elegant'.

In context (ii) forms, apocope had led to a range of distinctive nasal consonants appearing in coda position by the outset of the literary period:

-m	FĀMEM	>	fãĩm 'hunger'	DĂMNUM	>	dãm	'loss'
-n	PĀNEM	>	pãĩn 'bread'	PĂNNUM	>	pãn	'cloth'
-ɲ	BĂ(L)NEUM	>	bãɲ 'bath'				

However, already in the eleventh century the first steps toward neutralization of these coda nasals as [-n] were underway. Final [-m] was beginning to merge with [-n], cf. the spellings *Dinan* for *Dinam* (1065), *Brion* for *Brium* (1096) cited by Pope (1952: § 435). Inflected forms of words which ended in [-m] may have promoted this change. Thus, the plural of *nom* 'name' would be [nõns] where the stem-final nasal was realized as [n] by the rule of homorganicity already noted above. A tendency to generalize the plural form of the stem [nõn-] to the singular also would be understandable, since it would simplify the grammar of French by eliminating a paradigmatic alternation. A little later final [-ɲ] started to be restructured to [-ĩn] as in context (i) forms. Certainly from the thirteenth century there are cases of words originally ending in [-n] rhyming with those which had formerly ended in [-ɲ]; for example, *plain* (< PLĀNUM): *plain* (< [plãɲ] < PLĂNGO), both of which are presumably [plãĩn], appear in Rutebeuf's *Poèmes concernant l'Université de Paris* (poem 3, 41–2).[3]

Despite neutralization and weakening, word-final nasals appear to have remained in existence into the sixteenth century, when the earliest descriptions of the French language by grammarians become available. The phonetic nature of this disappearing consonant is commented upon by several writers of the time. One of the most perceptive of these, Théodore Bèze (1519–1605), who was brought up and educated in Paris, noted that word-final 'm' and 'n' were 'half sounds' (1584: 32). Making clear that the tongue tip does not make any contact with the 'roots of the upper teeth', he compares the sound made with that of Greek ν, i.e. /n/, preceding velar consonants (κ γ χ). The value indicated is thus presumably either a velar nasal [ŋ] or some sort of nasal constrictive perceptually akin to it. The comments of the grammarians Spalt and Duez, writing for a German audience in the first half of the seventeenth century, appear to point to a value [ŋ], although in a somewhat impressionistic fashion. Both writers equate final nasals in French with German 'ng', Spalt for instance representing *renom* as 'almost renong' (Thurot, ii. 423–4). However, the similarity between this observation and the way many English speakers perceive and reproduce the nasal vowels of modern French, *très bon* becoming 'tray bong', is suggestive. The fact that such English speakers 'hear' a velar [ŋ] does not of course mean that there really is such a consonant at the end of words like *bon*. Similarly, there may well have been no [ŋ] in the French pronunciation when Spalt and Duez were writing and they were merely offering a rather crude approximation. The most that can be said is that before disappearing altogether in the standard variety, the word-final nasal underwent major weakening, though it is far from clear that it actually passed via the stage [ŋ] with a full velar closure. It may only have been in the early seventeenth century that total deletion of word-final nasals became general amongst the most conservative of educated speakers.

There was a good deal of regional variation in the way the word-final nasals were realized. Palsgrave, an Englishman writing in 1530, and Claude de Sainliens, who became naturalized English and wrote *The French Littleton* in 1576 under the name of Claudius Holyband, both make clear that final 'm' and 'n' are pronounced at the end of words and that their value is [n]. However, the Norman pronunciation provided the basis for both descriptions. Later in the century, Bèze was in fact to note that speakers from Normandy engaged in what he judged to be hypercorrection, by pronouncing final 'n' with a full [n] (1584: 32).

As regards coda nasals in context (i) forms such as *danser*, the first clear indication that the nasal consonant has been entirely lost in the standard language leaving just an unconditioned nasal vowel seems to be that of Dangeau (1694: 15–19). However, grammarians seldom talked explicitly of the pronunciation of medial coda nasals. In view of the parallelism of development of medial and final coda nasals, it seems likely that deletion became general by the early seventeenth century in medial position too.

Once again, regional variation doubtless existed in the realization of such coda nasals. On the basis of the evidence from non-literary documents where scribes have omitted the nasal consonant, Morin (1994: 39) claims that nasals may have been deleted by as early as the end of the thirteenth century in the more innovatory eastern dialects. However, the evidence is not conclusive.

As long as coda nasals were still pronounced medially and finally, nasal vowel phonemes as such would not have existed. The changes which transformed the pronunciation of nasal vowels in the medieval period therefore operated upon what were still nasal allophones of oral vowel phonemes.

Finally, the conditioning nasal consonants found in context (iii) forms have been preserved without neutralization. The loss of final [-ə] which was only completed by the end of the seventeenth century in the spoken usage of the educated (Fouché 1969: 524) has not undermined the contrasts between these nasals when they have become word-final, *dîme:dîne:digne*.

4.2.5. ISOLATED EARLY CASES OF UNCONDITIONED NASAL VOWELS

Nasal vowels not followed by a conditioning nasal consonant only occurred systematically in the standard language after the sixteenth century. However, there are special cases where nasal vowels may have appeared already in the medieval period without being accompanied by a following nasal consonant.

(*a*) In eastern, northern, and north-western areas of the *langue d'oïl*, high vowels preceded by a nasal consonant frequently underwent progressive nasalization. Examples are found already in twelfth-century texts especially from the eastern dialect area, *amin* 'friend' < AMĪCUM, *connin* 'rabbit' < CUNĪCU-LUM, *nun* 'none' < NŪLLUM, *munt* 'much, very' < MŬLTUM.[4] In the first two items, we might attribute the vowel nasalization in the stressed syllable in part to the spreading of nasality which was already present in the initial syllable. However, the last two items arise solely from progressive assimilation. Pronunciations such as these were sporadically adopted into Parisian usage; thus, Richelet admits *connin* in his 1680 dictionary and observes, 'on prononce *connin*, quoiqu'on écrive quelquefois ce mot par une *l* finale' (Thurot, ii. 195).

The precise phonetic value of the final syllable in these forms is uncertain: was *amin* realized as [ãmĩ] or rather as [ãmĩn] with adaptation of the final nasal vowel to the general pattern of having a nasal consonant following nasal vowels? If the former were the case, the nasal vowel would arguably be unconditioned, since a nasal consonant evidently did not regularly nasalize a following high vowel. Furthermore, occasional items such as *ainsin* 'thus' (< ANTIUS-SĪC) extended the scope of this type of forward-spreading nasalization to words where no nasal consonant immediately preceded the final vowel.

(*b*) Reenen (1982*b*) identifies a specific context where nasal coda deletion apparently occurred in medieval times, namely preceding the sibilants [s] and [z] or the fricative [f], as in *penser, onze*, and *enfant*. Already by the end of the thirteenth century, the nasal may have been lost here. Evidence for this comes

from the use of graphies like <consseil> <presensse> in non-literary documents. The use of the <ss> graphy for [s] implies that the sibilant in such forms
was actually intervocalic and hence a single <s> risked suggesting a value [z]
(cf. parallel scribal practices in Castilian, section 7.4.1.2, and in Portuguese,
section 8.2.4).[5] Forms with this graphy appear in growing numbers in the later
thirteenth century over all the *langue d'oïl* area with the exception of Normandy
and the far north and north-east, indicating the wider usage of unconditioned
nasal vowels in this context. However, it seems likely that such vowels, phonologically isolated as they were, would have continued to be interpreted by
speakers of the period as sequences of oral vowel phoneme + nasal consonant,
just as American speakers of today interpret [kæ:t] *can't* as /kænt/ rather than
recognizing a distinctive nasal vowel phoneme (Malécot 1960). Nonetheless,
such a development would be a significant one, in that it results in the
appearance of substantial numbers of unconditioned nasal vowels.

(c) During the Middle Ages, there is some evidence from verse that in certain
varieties of French the conditioning coda nasal consonant following high vowels
may have been very weak and possibly even deleted, resulting in the appearance
of unconditioned nasal vowels. The evidence lies in rhymes between the oral
and nasal high vowels, [y]:[ỹ], [u]:[ũ], and especially [i]:[ĩ]. Examples are
princes: crevices (Guiot de Provins, early thirteenth century), *coissins : assis* (Jean
Renart, early thirteenth century), *Jehan de Meün: respondu* (Honoré Bonet, late
fourteenth century) and *contes: toutes* (Nicole de Margival, early fourteenth
century), cf. Pope (1952: §§ 455, 464) and Marchello-Nizia (1979: 80–1). The use
of such rhymes indicates that the coda nasal consonant was at best weakly
articulated, so that it could be ignored for rhyme purposes. But the nature of
the apparently nasal vowels of forms like *princes* is less clear. They may have
been only weakly nasal so that they were readily identified with oral vowel
counterparts and used in rhyme with them. Or, more plausibly, they may have
been accompanied by high-level nasality, but speakers of the variety of French
used by the poets continued to view nasality as a non-distinctive feature in
vowels, even when there was no overt conditioning factor present, so that oral
and nasal vowels sharing the same lip and tongue positions could still rhyme.
The fact that it is typically high vowels which are involved here is striking (cf.
subsection (a) above). An observation made by theoretical phoneticians seems
relevant in both connections, namely that the higher the tongue position of a
vowel is the smaller the articulatory adjustments which the speaker has to make
in order to bring about perceptual nasality (cf. 1.1). It may be therefore that the
relatively greater articulatory proximity between high oral and nasal vowels,
allied to the as yet phonologically non-distinctive nature of nasality in vowels,
helps to explain occasional cases of interplay.

(d) In the unstressed 3rd person plural verbal inflexion -*ent*, there was early
loss of the nasal consonant in some varieties which may have left an uncondi-

tioned nasal vowel. Dees (1980: map 220) notes the significant use (11% of all cases) of the graphy <-et> in thirteenth-century administrative documents from the eastern area of Vosges. Late thirteenth-century glosses using Hebrew characters and written in the eastern area and Champagne also suggest loss, e.g. *hateret* for *hasterent* (Pope 1952: § 437; Morin 1994: 39). If a pronunciation [-ɔ̃t] resulted, this was evidently short-lived. No trace of a nasal vowel here is to be found in later Parisian usage.[6]

4.3.   Evolution of Nasal Vowels in Standard French

Vowel evolution has been highly complex in the history of French. We have already seen that in the pre-literary period a length difference had arisen with stressed vowels depending on syllable structure: when they appeared in free syllables they were lengthened, whereas in blocked syllables their length remained neutral. Subsequently, all types of long vowel except [iː] and [uː] diphthongized, so that diphthongs were widely found in Old French and, when adjacent to a vocalic segment, these gave rise to triphthongs. Unstressed vowels meanwhile showed a strong tendency to weaken and be deleted, especially in syllables following the stress.

In the period from Old French onwards, a major trend was towards the elimination of diphthongs and triphthongs either by monophthongization or some other strategy.

The evolution of nasal vowels at first runs in tandem with developments affecting oral vowels. However, in the later medieval period the system of nasal vowels begins to take on a dynamic of its own and thereafter it displays quite distinct patterns of evolution.

4.3.1.   NASAL VOWELS IN EARLY OLD FRENCH

In early Old French (tenth–eleventh centuries) there were no nasal vowel phonemes, but corresponding to the system of oral vowel phonemes there appeared a sub-system of nasal vowel allophones which developed in stressed and unstressed syllables alike. It is likely that the following types were found in the *langue d'oïl* area:

ĩ		ỹ/ũ		ỹ̃i/ũ̃i		
ẽ	ə̃	õ	ẽĩ	õĩ	ĩẽ	ỹẽ/ũẽ
		ɔ̃				
	æ̃/ã			æ̃ĩ/ãĩ		

Examples

stressed   *unstressed*

[ī]	vīn vīnt	<	VĪNUM VIGĬNTĪ	tsīŋkæ̃ntə	<*	CĪNQUA(GĬ)NTA
[ē]	vēntə vēnt	<	VĒNDITA VĚNTUM	tēmpɛstə	<	TEMPĚSTA
[æ̃]	tæ̃nt æ̃n	<	TĂNTUM ĂNNUM	tʃæ̃mpæ̃ɲə	<	CAMPĀNIA
[ɔ̃]	æ̃ntɔ̃njə	<	ANTŌNIUM			
[ō]	kōn fōnt mæjzōn	<	CŬNNUM FŌNTEM MANSIŌNEM	bōnteː	<	BONITĀTEM
[ȳ/ū]	ȳmblə/ūmblə ȳn/ūn	<	HŬMILEM ŪNUM	lȳndi/lūndi	<	LŪNAE-DĪEM
[ə̃]	—			prə̃mier	<	PRIMĀRIUM
	—			pɔrtə̃nt	<	PŎRTANT
[ēī]	plēīn pēīnt	<	PLĒNUM PĬNGIT	tsēīntyrə	<	CINCTŪRA
[æ̃ī]	mæ̃īn sæ̃īnt	<	MĂNUM SĂNCTUM	sæ̃īnteː	<	SANCTITĀTEM
[ōī]	pōīnt lōīn	<	PŬNCTUM LŎNGE	pōīntyrə	<	PUNCTŪRA
[ȳī/ūī]	dʒȳīn/dʒūīn	<	IŪNIUM			
[īē]	bīēn tʃīēn	<	BĚNE CĂNEM			
[ȳē/ūē]	bȳēn/būēn kȳēns/kūēns	<	BŎNUM CŎMES			

Some brief notes may be made on these.

(*a*) The sound changes seen in these forms largely mirror oral vowel developments. Two notable divergences exist however. First, in context (i) forms, the
contrast between mid vowels was neutralized early on in favour of a high-mid
value. Hence, VĒNDITA 'sale' and VĚNTUM 'wind' emerge with the same
stressed vowel [ē].

Second, free stressed /a/ retained the early diphthongal quality when in a
nasalizing context and this developed to [æ̃ī], as in [mæ̃in] < MĂNUM 'hand'.
In oral contexts, the diphthong simplified before the mid-ninth century (cf.
spede < SPĀTA 'sword', *Eulalia*, l. 22) to give a long mid front monophthong
whose precise quality is disputed, [eː] or [æː].

(*b*) The low vowel /a/ was partly fronted in many varieties of *langue d'oïl* of
the early medieval period, including Francien which has formed the basis of
standard French. The passage of its long counterpart /aː/ to become a fronting
diphthong and later a mid front vowel provides evidence for this, as does the
ability of original /a/ and long /aː/ to palatalize a preceding velar plosive,
chanter jambe < CANTĀRE GĂMBA 'to sing, leg'. Palatalization affected
all varieties of *langue d'oïl* except those of Picardy and Normandy in the north.
The precise phonetic value of this fronted /a/ in the tenth-eleventh centuries in
the palatalizing dialects is of course uncertain. However, we may suspect that
the nasal allophones would have tended toward [æ̃], such a value being
predicted on theoretical grounds (cf. 1.1). Accordingly, we will use the transcription [æ̃] for this vowel in early Francien. Oral allophones of /a/ may have
been slightly less fronted, [ä]. Such a divergence between the tongue position of
nasal and oral allophones would help to explain the patterns of assonance
found in early French verse of the eleventh-thirteenth centuries.

(c) The development /u/ > /y/ for both oral and nasal allophones spread to northern areas of the *langue d'oïl* relatively late and was never adopted in the far north-east in eastern Wallonia (see below 5.2). In certain areas where the change was slow to apply, increased nasalization had the effect of preventing the fronting of [ũ] to [ỹ], even when oral [u] > [y] took place. This divergent development is characteristic of Franco-Provençal dialects of east central France (see 5.4). We may therefore assume that in the tenth-eleventh centuries a good deal of regional variation existed in the realization of early Gallo-Romance /u/. But as fronting was evidently adopted fairly early on in Francien, we use the transcription [y] for this vowel.

(d) There is no evidence at all that the high-mid back vowel [õ:] occurring in original free syllables diphthongized like its oral counterpart, FLŌREM > [flour] 'flower'.[7] On the other hand, the high-mid front vowel [ẽ:] did diphthongize just like oral [e:], cf. [plẽĩn] < PLĒNUM 'full' and [peil] < PĬLUM 'hair'. Later, the high-mid back vowels (blocked) [õ] and (free) [õ:] raised to become high vowels in many varieties of *langue d'oïl* after the fronting of original /u/ > /y/, and they merged as [ũ] just as other long and short high vowels came to merge in blocked syllables in medieval French. In Francien, it is uncertain whether full raising took place or whether the reflex of these merged nasal vowels was a high type of [õ] (cf. Rochet 1976: 80–2).

(e) The vowel [ɔ̃] appears only in a limited number of loans and learned words, all of them involving context (iii) forms. Laisse 123 of the *Chanson de Roland* (late eleventh-early twelfth centuries) offers the examples *Grandonies, Antonie* which assonate with *force, nostre*, etc.

(f) As regards the length of nasal vowels, these were doubtless of neutral duration in unstressed syllables. In stressed syllables, it is likely that the earlier syllabically determined arrangement was maintained in context (i) and (iii) forms. Thus, nasal vowels in the blocked syllables of context (i) forms were of neutral duration, whereas in the free syllables of context (iii) forms they remained long. There is no evidence that nasalization took place earlier with either the long or neutral-length vowels found in the different context types. In context (ii) forms, vowels had originally been long but it is possible that the process of shortening which has widely affected nasal vowels in this context by the sixteenth century was already beginning to get underway, e.g. VĪNUM > ['vi:nu] > ['vi:n(u)] > [vĩ:n] > [vĩn] 'wine'. However, it is difficult to discover the precise pattern and chronology of this development (see also 4.3.9).

4.3.2. EARLY STRUCTURAL CHANGES

In the later medieval and Renaissance period, a series of changes took place in Francien, the result of which was a system of nasal vowels much reduced in size as compared to its oral counterpart. Our focus will be on stressed nasal vowels. Unstressed nasal vowels are considered in 4.3.8.

4.3.2.1. *Merger of* [ẽ] *and* [æ̃]

The first major development was the gradual merger of the two non-high front nasal vowels. Modern spelling reflects the original vowel quality quite faithfully, as in *tend tant*, both of which are now pronounced [tɑ̃]. However, certain items have the etymologically 'wrong' letter, e.g. *redan* (vs. *dent*), *langue, revanche, bande* < RE-DĔNTEM LĬNGUA REVĬNDICAT (Germ.) binda.

The starting point to the merger appears to lie in the eleventh century with an important change which first got underway in the Picardy area in the north of the *langue d'oïl*. This was the lowering of the short high-mid vowel /e/ < blocked Late Latin /e/) to low-mid /ɛ/ (van den Bussche 1984). The change affected both oral and nasal allophones, so that earlier nasal [ẽ] was lowered to [ɛ̃]. It seems possible that this development represented some sort of response to the progressive fronting of /u/ > /y/, since in many dialects of *langue d'oïl* the appearance of a new high front vowel /y/ beside /i/ has occasioned some articulatory distancing of pre-existing short /e/, either by lowering or retraction (Haudricourt 1947).

The Francien dialect fully adopted this change for its oral allophones only at the end of the twelfth or early thirteenth centuries, judging by textual evidence. The delay here was doubtless due in part to the fact that a merger between two existing phonemes /e/ and /ɛ/ was involved. As no such contrast existed for nasal vowels (there was no previously existing nasal **[ɛ̃]), the lowering of [ẽ] to [ɛ̃] could take place more rapidly.

The only exceptions are cases where [ẽ] was adjacent to a palatal element whose raising influence prevented lowering. These appear in context (iii) forms where [ẽ] preceded the nasal [ɲ], e.g. *enseigne* [ẽsẽɲə] < INSĬGNAT, and also in the diphthong [ĩẽ], e.g. *bien* [bĩẽn] < BĔNE (see below 4.3.2.2).

At the time when [ẽ] lowered to [ɛ̃], the original low vowel /a/ probably had a somewhat fronted pronunciation, as we have seen, and its nasal allophones may well have been realized as [æ̃]. Consequently, when the low-mid vowel [ɛ̃] developed, it came into the orbit of [æ̃] and there was growing interference between the two. This was encouraged by other factors:

(*a*) there was a morphophonemic link, albeit a fairly slender one, due to the merger between the reflexes of the present participle endings -ĔNTEM and -ĂNTEM as -*ant* (Rochet 1974).[8]

(*b*) odd cases of lexical polymorphism had arisen in which the two vowels were associated. A notable example is *talent/talant* both of which co-existed as variants from earliest times (Mombello 1976).

(*c*) more generally, there is the perceptual difficulty in readily discriminating relatively fine quality differences such as that between [ɛ̃] and [æ̃] as a result of the masking effect of nasality (cf. 1.1).

The association and ultimate merger between [ɛ̃] and [æ̃] was a protracted process however. The earliest indications of significant interplay come in the *Chanson de Roland* (earliest MS from *c.*1125–50, but composed late eleventh century–beginning of 12th century). In this work, there are a number of cases of assonance between forms containing these two vowels, e.g. *grant* : *tens* < GRĂNDEM TĔMPUS 'big (sg.), time' (laisse 260). But, as more careful scrutiny has revealed, the facts do not yet suggest identity but rather that there was enough similarity between the two vowels to permit their occasional association through 'poetic licence'. It is significant that a comparable association for assonance purposes can be found in the same work with the oral allophones of /a/ and /ɛ/ as well; cf. *sale* : *damisele* (laisse 274) and *large* : *tere* (laisse 288), even though merger between such oral vowels did not occur in any dialect. Other assonating texts of the twelfth century similarly point to [ɛ̃] and [æ̃] being phonetically close enough for them to be associated but not to their complete merger (Bédier 1927: 278; Rochet 1976: 73–5).

In contrast to the signs of interplay in assonated verse, in rhymed verse the two vowel types were long kept apart. In the first work traditionally described as coming from the Ile-de-France region, *La Vie de St. Thomas*, composed in rhyme in the early 1170s, there is just one case of rhyme between [ɛ̃] and [æ̃]. Over 200 years later, Charles d'Orléans (1394–1465), nephew of Charles VI, still scrupulously distinguished these two vowel types in his poetry. It is of course questionable how far the distinction between the two vowels here reflects a phonetic difference. Their separation in rhyme may arise from the stricter demands made by the conventions of rhyming verse as against the more approximate conventions used for assonance.[9] On the other hand, it is possible that the influence of spelling was of decisive importance. However, the consistency of the separation in rhymed verse points to their still being perceived as distinct vowel types, although doubtless not by all speakers.

Further information is provided by the recent extensive computer-based investigation by Dees (1980, 1987) of graphies used for specific lexical or grammatical items in literary and non-literary Old French texts across the *langue d'oïl* area. Literary texts of the north, especially, and to a lesser extent of the east and south-east of the *langue d'oïl* show widespread use of <a>, particularly in forms where original [ẽ] preceded the labial nasal [m], e.g. *tans* < TĔMPUS 'time' and *ensamble* < INSĪMUL 'together' (Dees 1987: maps 215, 487). Non-literary texts of the thirteenth century confirm this geographical pattern for the outcome of TĔMPUS (Dees 1980: map 195) but seem to indicate that the merger was being more rapidly carried through for the final vowels of *présent couvent serment -ment* (nominal suffix) in the east and south-east in particular (Dees 1980: maps 124, 140, 193, 205). However, such is the variation from one word to another in the use of <a> or <e> graphies that lexical diffusion must also have played a role in the merger alongside the other linguistic and extra-linguistic conditioning factors.

The conclusion to be drawn from all this is that, in the Ile-de-France area from which the standard language developed, the merger of [ɛ̃] and [æ̃] during the later medieval period was doubtless a prolonged development. It may be that the gradual retraction of [æ̃] to [ã] at this time represents a response to the on-going merger, as speakers sought to safeguard the [ɛ̃]/[æ̃] distinction by re-establishing a clearer qualitative distinction between the two vowels. However, the reflex of [ɛ̃] also came to adopt this new target and a low value [ã] eventually became the norm for the reflexes of both nasal vowel types.

It seems that for some speakers at least, the two vowels may have remained distinct until well into the sixteenth century. Influenced by spelling perhaps, a number of grammarians of that century continue to report a slight qualitative difference between the vowels of words such as *dent* and *tant*, the former being slightly less open (Thurot, ii. 430–4; Rochet 1976: 94–7). However, it is significant that almost all these grammarians come from regions where a distinction has continued to be made between the two vowels until the present century (Morin 1994: 68 n. 96). In contrast, the Parisian Bèze (1584: 14) states that the pronunciation of these vowels is the same or at most marginally different (*pronuntiatio recta, vel eadem, vel tenuissimi discriminis, & quod vix auribus percipi possit* 'the correct pronunciation is either the same or minimally different, as [the difference] can scarcely be perceived by the ear'). In the less conservative usage of the mass of Parisians, identity had probably been achieved some centuries earlier. Seventeenth-century grammarians do not indicate any quality difference.

4.3.2.2.   *The Diphthongs* [ĩẽ] *and* [ũẽ]

As original [ẽ] took on a lower point of articulation, this might be expected to have implications for the diphthongs whose peak element was [ẽ]. There were two such diphthongs, [ĩẽ] and [ũẽ] (or [ỹẽ] after the fronting of /u/ to /y/), which had developed from the nasalized variants of stressed free /ɛ/ and stressed free /ɔ/, respectively. These gave the rising diphthongs [jẽ] and [wẽ] / [ɥẽ] in most varieties of *langue d'oïl* by the end of the twelfth century or early thirteeth century.[10] We will examine each briefly.

The Diphthong [jẽ] (< [iẽ])

First, it may be noted that the diphthong [jẽ] as in *bien* [bjẽn] < BĔNE resembled but was nonetheless quite separate from the disyllabic nasal [ĩ-ẽ] which typically occurred in learned words such as *orient, patient, science, escient*. The second element of the latter disyllabic sequence regularly underwent lowering, and the resultant lowered vowel has been preserved to the present day.

In the case of [jẽ], the palatal on-glide [j] seems to have acted as a brake on evolution in many varieties of *langue d'oïl*, giving a wide range of reflexes noted by the grammarians of the sixteenth century; these extend from [jã] and [jẽ], with variable lowering, to [jẽ] and even [jĩ]. The variation is conditioned by linguistic, geographical, and social factors. Linguistically, there is some indeterminacy with words such as *lien, chrétien, ancien* (<LIGĀMEN CHRISTIĀNUM ANTEĀNUM). In these, the [ĩẽ] sequence had originally been disyllabic but it evidently passed to become [jẽ] in many varieties during the later medieval period. In the sixteenth and seventeenth centuries, grammarians continue to be divided over the syllabic status of such -*ien* forms (cf. Thurot, i. 538). Indeed, the authoritative eighteenth-century grammarian Wailly (1786: 407) still describes *lien* as dissyllabic in contrast with monosyllabic *bien, mien*. Geographically, the lowered variants are more generalized in southern areas of the *langue d'oïl*, whereas northern and north-western dialects have widely preserved a closed vowel as the syllable peak.[11] Socially, where competing variants existed, as in Francien, the pattern would be for the lowered one [jã] to enjoy less prestige and be associated with uncouth speech.

In Francien, both non-lowered and lowered variants were evidently found from the end of the thirteenth century. Early signs of a lowered pronunciation come in forms like *Gardian* (varying with *Gardien* in the Parisian Tax Rolls of 1297–8), *Crestiane* and *Marguerite la parisianne* (in documents of 1298 and 1304, respectively). Still earlier attestations of the [jã] pronunciation are widely found in literary and official texts from the Orléans area to the south and also in Anjou, e.g. *lian, viant, reans, paians* (= *lien, vient, riens, païens*) all from the second half of the thirteenth century (cf. Michaëlsson 1934–5).[12] However, it remains uncertain whether the pronunciation [jã] first arose in the south and south-west and spread thence to Paris or whether it developed independently in popular speech in Francien.

At all events, [jã] is attested for Francien down to the sixteenth century and indeed into the seventeenth century.[13] In his description of the emerging norm variety, Palsgrave (1530: 3) certainly claims [jã] to be the normal pronunciation for context (ii) forms like *convient*, which he represents as 'conuiant'. For context (iii) forms like *mienne, tienne, sienne*, he identifies the vowel with that of *femme*, representing them as 'famme', 'mianne', etc., where presumably the vowel has an intended value of [(j)ã]. No sociolinguistic judgement is made on these pronunciations, but by the end of the century Tabourot (1547–90), born in Dijon but educated in Paris, identifies [jã] firmly with popular Parisian speech, and in his *Bigarrures* (1616) he pastiches this feature in a much-quoted sentence, 'Et bian bian, ie varron si monsieur le Doyan qui a tant de moyan, ayme les citoyans, et si, à la coustume des ancians, il leur baillera rian' (= 'Et bien bien, je verrai si M. le Doyen qui a tant de moyen(s) aime les citoyens, et si, à la coutume des anciens, il leur baillera rien').

After the sixteenth century, the use of the pronunciation [jã] progressively recedes to uneducated varieties of the Ile-de-France and provincial speech.[14] The only traces of it today in the standard variety are in the place name Orléans and in the eminently 'popular' word *fiente* (< *FĔMITA) 'animal excrement' and its derivatives.

The Diphthong [ɥẽ/wẽ] (< [ũẽ])

A curious situation presents itself with the diphthong [ɥẽ] (we will only consider this variant, since it is the one found in Francien). In most dialects of the *langue d'oïl*, including Francien, there are scarcely any direct survivors of the vowel, since the forms in which it occurred have by chance been almost entirely eliminated. Thus, the nominals *buen(e), tuen(e), suen(e); cuens, suen* (<SŎNUM 'sound'), *huem* have given way to *bon(ne), tien(ne), sien(ne); comte, son, on/homme* for various independent reasons, while forms of the Old French verbs *so(n)ner, ton(n)er* stressed on the stem vowel, e.g. *suene, tuene* (<SŎNAT TŎNAT 'it sounds, it thunders'), have been replaced analogically by forms built from the unstressed stem, namely *sonn- tonn-* respectively.

However, there are three apparent relics, two place names, *Rouen* and *Etrœungt* (<*ROTŎMAGUM, *STRŎMUUM),[15] and the adjective *jeune* 'young' (<*IŎVENEM <IŬVENEM).[16] The last of these evolved into Early Old French [d͡ʒuevnə] which developed variously in different areas. In Francien, the [v] element was deleted after [ue] had already passed to [ɥe] > [ɥø] > [ø], but it is unclear whether the vowel underwent nasalization when it became pre-nasal (cf. 4.2.2.1). In *Etrœungt*, the nuclear element of the nasal diphthong [ɥẽ] did not undergo lowering, perhaps because of the presence of the high on-glide [ɥ] which preceded it. Instead, the diphthong developed like its oral counterpart to give a front rounded vowel, i.e. [ɥẽ] > [œ̃]. The evolution of *Rouen* reflects a regional development.

As a result of the lowering of [ẽ], the system of nasal vowel monophthongs to which Francien was moving in the thirteenth century would appear to be:

$$\begin{array}{ccccc} \tilde{\imath} & \tilde{y} & & & \tilde{u} \\ & (\tilde{\phi}) & & \tilde{o} & \\ & & \tilde{a} & & \end{array}$$

As we have seen, the vowel [ø̃] was rarely found. The vowel [ã] derives from earlier [ẽ] and [ã]. The two vowels [ũ] and [õ] represent regional and/or sociolinguistic variants of a single back rounded vowel type.

4.3.2.3   Merger and Subsequent Monophthongization of [æ̃ɪ̯] and [ẽɪ̯]

The lowering of [ẽ] and the front realization of nasal /a/ as [æ̃] was to have implications for the two nasal diphthongs [æ̃ɪ̯] and [ẽɪ̯]. As the initial element grew more similar, the possibility clearly existed of the two diphthongs becoming associated and even merging. This in fact happened, earliest in the west and south-west of the *langue d'oïl*. Rhymed and assonated texts from this area already show signs of the merger in the twelfth century, e.g. in the *Roman de Troie* (*c.*1165) which has *novains : pleins* and *peine : prochaine* etc. (ll. 23265–6, 25253–4).[17]

The fact that the merger of the diphthongs [æ̃ɪ̯] and [ẽɪ̯] gained ground first in western and southern areas and was only subsequently adopted in Francien is confirmed by developments in eastern and northern areas of *langue d'oïl*. In the eastern dialects of Lorraine and Burgundy, a strong dissimilatory tendency arose in the twelfth century to change oral and nasal variants of /ei/ to /oi/ (Haudricourt 1948; Remacle 1948: 56). This development spread north into Wallonia and also into Champagne, from where it affected Francien. In Francien, many oral variants were modified but nasal variants were largely resistant, hence [freit] > [froit] > *froid* but [frẽɪ̯n] > *frein* not **froin*.[18] Also, in northern dialects where the fronting of /a/ had not occurred, original [æ̃ɪ̯] has been able to remain separate from [ẽɪ̯] in many areas to this day.[19]

The two nasal diphthongs had probably merged in most forms of Francien as [ẽɪ̯] by the end of the twelveth century (Pope 1952: § 467). Thereafter they shared a common fate, monophthongization.

Already in the twelfth century there are indications of a general levelling of front diphthongs to monophthongs, particularly in texts from the west and south-west of the *langue d'oïl*. In this change, the nasal diphthong [ẽɪ̯] tended towards a pronunciation [ɛ̃] or [ẽ]. The new mid nasal vowel remained distinct from the earlier mid vowel [ẽ] which had already lowered to [ɛ̃] and gradually become a low vowel [ã] (cf. 4.3.2.1). Thus, we may contrast:

PĪNGIT > (early OFr.) [pẽɪ̯nt] > [pẽɪ̯nt] > [pẽnt/pẽnt]   *peint* '(s)he paints'
VĒNDIT > (early OFr.) [vẽnt] > [vẽnt] > [væ̃nt] > [vãnt] *vend* '(s)he sells'

In fact, the appearance of the new mid nasal vowel can only have hastened the generalization of a lower pronunciation [ã] for earlier [ɛ̃] (< [ẽ]) in items like *vend*, since this would help to safeguard the contrast between the two vowel types.

However, some trace of a diphthongal pronunciation continues to be described by grammarians of the sixteenth century. Thus, Meigret writes: 'leur prononciation [i.e. of *saint, pain, main, vain, vrai*] n'èt point aotre qe d'vn *e* clos accompagné d'vn *i* en vne même syllabe tout einsi q'en *teindre feindre*' (Thurot, ii. 482). To what extent spelling influence affected such a conservative pronunciation is uncertain. However, by the seventeenth century a nasal monophthong was recognized as the norm.

4.3.3. LOWERING OF HIGH NASAL VOWELS [ĩ ỹ ũ]

Up to the beginning of the thirteenth century, the high nasal vowel allophones had evolved in a directly comparable way to their oral counterparts. Nasal [ĩ] and [ỹ] evidently had the same tongue positions as oral [i] and [y] all over the *langue d'oïl*, since oral and nasal allophones were able to appear together in assonance. Only the back nasal vowel may have been partly exceptional. Oral [o] < Late Latin blocked /o/, as in [kort] < CŬRTUM 'short (m. sg.)', had begun raising to [u] perhaps by the beginning of the twelfth century in western dialects and this change had probably gained acceptance in central dialects by the end of the twelfth century (Pope 1952: § 184). But whereas nasal [õ] almost certainly underwent parallel raising to [ũ] in the west and north-west (cf. the Norman French loans into English *mount, count, round*, etc. where the present-day diphthong presupposes original high [ũ]), it is possible that in some dialects, including Francien, the raising of [õ] resulted in a very high mid vowel rather than fully high [ũ]. This disparity would explain why after the twelfth century we start to find texts in which forms containing what had been oral and nasal /o/ no longer appear together in assonance. While recognizing possible regional variation between [ũ] and high [õ], we will for convenience simply refer to this vowel as [ũ], such a pronunciation doubtless occurring in the usage of at least some speakers from the Paris region at the end of the twelfth century.

In the later thirteenth century, the first signs become apparent of an important change in the high nasal vowels. They begin to take on a lower tongue height. However, the process is protracted and complex, showing much geographical, chronological, and especially sociolinguistic variation.

The earliest evidence comes with [ĩ]. In texts from various parts of the *langue d'oïl*, but more especially perhaps from the centre and from Burgundy in the south-east, forms such as the following are found:

context (i)	*gindre* (< ʒ(w)ēndrə < IŬNIOR)	Paris 1296
	vainrent (= *vinrent*)	Amiens 1291
context (ii)	*Cochin* (= *Cochein*)	Paris 1296
	plin (= *plein*)	late thirteenth century
context (iii)	*saisene*	Chalon 1299
	Martene Pepene	Beaune 1320

(Philipon 1910: 522; Pope 1952: § 454; Fouché 1969: 361)

There is little evidence of the lowering of [ỹ] until a good deal later. An isolated form *lene* (< LŪNA) is attested *c.*1300 in Burgundy (*FEW*, s.v. *luna*) and *pleume* (< PLŪMA) is found in a 1465 *sottie* (*FEW*, s.v. *pluma*). In the following century, forms such as *heumble eung* appear in 1548 in the Guise Letters written by Marie of Guise, mother of Mary Queen of Scots. As regards the date when lowering of the back nasal vowel [ũ] got underway, the use of the graphy <o> from early times to represent this vowel unfortunately masks quality changes.

Judging from the textual evidence then, the use of a lowered realization for high nasal vowels, especially for [ĩ], may well have been found amongst ordinary Parisians from as early as the end of the thirteenth century. However, amongst educated users there was evidently a resistance to adopting this lowered pronunciation, and it was not until well into the seventeenth century that the norm for original [ĩ], [ỹ], [ũ] was accepted to be mid rather than high for all three vowels.

Having been the first high vowel type to have lower variants attested, [ĩ] was perhaps predictably the first for which a lowered target pronunciation was recognized in the standard language. The majority of grammarians of the sixteenth century clearly indicate that the value [ẽ] is already the norm in Parisian usage, though it is only from the last quarter of the seventeenth century that the predominant view amongst grammarians is that a low-mid value [ɛ̃] represents the norm pronunciation for this vowel (see also 4.3.4 below).

Indications that [œ̃] had been adopted as the norm pronunciation only appear from the mid-seventeenth century onward (Thurot, ii. 542–5). D'Aisy writing in 1674 says, '*Un* a toujours le son confus et l'*u* sonne *eu*', and twenty years later the Parisian Abbé Dangeau (1694: 65) expresses matters even more clearly, '*Notre voyelle un*, qui se prononce dans le mot commun, est plutôt un *eu* nazal qu'un *u* nazal.'

The norm pronunciation for earlier [ũ] is likewise definitively established as a mid vowel [õ] in the seventeenth century. A substantial number of grammarians of this century still indicate [ũ] as the norm, but these are typically people of provincial origin or foreigners.[20] The target value [õ] for 'good' Parisian speakers emerges clearly only in the second half of the century. Dangeau lucidly describes the contemporary pattern, citing [õ] as the standard and associating [ũ] with provincial speech, '*Je sai bien qu'il y a des provinces dans lesquelles on prononce un ou nazal, & où l'on dit boun, au lieu de dire bon*' (1694: 65).

4.3.3.1. *Reasons for Lowering of High Nasal Vowels*

The factors leading to the appearance of the lower variants, and the acceptance of these variants as the norm, have been much discussed. Many historians of the language appeal to simple articulatory considerations, the assumption being that by their very nature high nasal vowels are difficult sounds to produce so that there is a 'natural tendency' for them to lower. French would thus merely have followed the tendency.[21] However, as standard French has always been the classic case used to prove the existence of this alleged tendency, the circularity of such an argument is obvious. In fact, there is little objective evidence that high nasal vowels have a particularly complex articulatory basis which makes them inherently unstable and prone to lower. The preservation of high nasal vowels, allophonic and phonemic, in many varieties of Romance (for instance, Portuguese and many north Italian dialects) provides telling evidence in this respect, as do numerous other non-Romance languages which have developed and maintained high nasal vowels (see 1.2.2).

Rather more plausible as a possible general conditioning factor is the perceptual effect of nasality on vowels, since there is evidence that the presence of nasality in the acoustic signal can lead hearers to perceive high vowels to have a lower point of articulation. This may encourage them to interpret such vowels as being articulatorily non-high and consequently to adopt a non-high target articulation for them (cf. 1.1). However, in view of the maintenance of high nasal vowels elsewhere in Romance, we can at best see this as a background factor which could reinforce some pre-existing tendency in the language. Special circumstances specific to French must have provided the main impetus to cause the lowering of high nasal vowels, just as special circumstances had operated earlier on to bring about the lowering of [ẽ] and its eventual merger with [æ̃].

As we have seen, the high vowel which first showed signs of developing a lowered pronunciation was [ĩ]. A factor which was probably closely bound up with this development was the appearance of lowered realizations of /i/ in other environments. (It will be remembered that nasal vowels remained allophones of oral vowel phonemes throughout the Middle Ages.) As well as appearing as an independent vowel, /i/ figured as the second element in a whole range of diphthongs, namely /ai ɔi oi yi/. Of these, all but /ɔi/ could be found nasal as well as oral. Between the eleventh and the thirteenth centuries, the second element of these diphthongs lowered in Francien and many other varieties of *langue d'oïl*. The changes may be summarized as follows:

ai > ae > aɛ > ɛ	First indicated in Western dialects and completed pre-consonantally during the twelfth–thirteenth centuries in Francien (Pope 1952: § 529)
ɔi > ɔe > ɔɛ > wɛ oi > oe > uɛ > wɛ	Both changes are completed by the later twelfth and thirteenth centuries (Pope 1952: § 519)
yi > ɥi	Completed by the end of the twelfth century

The move towards lowering /i/ in diphthongs may have originated in western dialects, where the diphthong /ei/ was also affected such that [ei > εi > εe > ε], the monophthong being generalized in the west by the mid-twelfth century. Underlying all these changes was an attempt to equalize the height of the two component elements of the various diphthongs. The non-lowering of the final /i/ in /yi/ is therefore understandable. Subsequently, where the two component elements agreed in frontness/ backness, they fused to give a monophthong, and where they differed, a regular pattern consisting of on-glide + vowel nucleus was generalized.

The widespread lowering of /i/ (oral or nasal) when it formed the second element of a diphthong must have affected monophthongal /i/. Lowering in the oral allophones of /i/ would have been inhibited as [eː] and short [e] (found in the second element of the diphthong [je]) already existed, so that unwelcome mergers would be threatened. No such inhibiting factor existed for nasal allophones, since the [ẽ] of early Old French had already lowered to [ɛ̃]. In this way, the lowering of the second element in the diphthongs [ãĩ ẽĩ õĩ] may well have pointed the way to monophthongal [ĩ] developing a variant [ẽ]. And of course the general perceptual considerations mentioned earlier would also have operated to promote this development.

The variant [ẽ] for the high vowel [ĩ] seems to have arisen first in popular speech. Whether it represents a 'native' development in Francien or rather a pronunciation initially brought to the capital by migrants from other areas (for instance the south-east of the *langue d'oïl* where it is frequently attested early on) and rapidly generalized there remains uncertain.

Turning to the vowel [ỹ], we can envisage that phonological pressures of vowel symmetry might encourage the appearance of a lowered variant which would parallel the developments which had occurred with [ĩ] (cf. Rochet 1976: 113–14). Also, the perceptual considerations which have been noted would have come into play encouraging the adoption of a lowered pronunciation [õ]. But beside these general factors a rather more direct influence can be identified, namely the interplay between the vowels /y/ and /ø/ in the Paris region during the later Middle Ages. This arose mainly as a result of dialectal influence, as regional variant pronunciations made their presence felt. Notable was the treatment of the earlier sequence [əy] which usually developed to [yː] in Francien but which emerged as the mid vowel [øː] in many other dialects especially those of the West and North, e.g. MATŪRUM SAP-ŪTUM > [məyr səy] > Francien [myːr syː] vs. regional [møːr søː] ModFr. *mûr su* 'ripe, known (past part.)'. The modern standard forms *feu* [fø] 'late' and *heur* [œːʀ] 'fortune' (as in *bonheur, malheur, heureux*) < FAT-ŪTUM AUGŪRIUM illustrate this variant pronunciation, both these items being borrowings from western and north-western dialects (Pope 1952: § 245).[22] The adoption of [ø] as a variant of [y] for certain lexical items in educated usage dates from the beginning of the fifteenth century at least. This is borne out by the writings of the royal poet Charles d'Orléans, nephew of Charles VI, who used rhymes such as *maleurs*: *ardeurs* (Ballades 111).

Moreover, in some cases Francien /ø/ corresponded to regional pronunciations in /y/. Most notably, the Picard dialect had the high vowel in the reflex of the earlier triphthong [ieu], which developed in Francien to [(j)ø]. For example, VĔTULUM IŎCUM (> OFr. *vieus jeu*) developed into Francien [vjø ʒø] but gave Picard [vjy ʒy] (Gossen 1970: §§ 9, 25). The Parisian grammarian Bèze (1584: 46–7) specifically cites the use of [y] for [ø] here as a characteristic Picard trait, and indeed pronunciations of the type [vjy ʒy] are still current in wide areas of Picardy (Flutre 1977: §86).

A rather fluid variation thus existed between /y/ and /ø/ in Parisian usage of the late medieval and Renaissance period in a substantial number of words, as poets and grammarians used or recommended one or other variant depending on their own regional background. The situation was further complicated by spelling influence. The appearance of numerous words containing the graphy <eu> created more variation, since <eu> could represent both [ø], as in *peu*, and [y], as in *eu* 'had (past part.)' and the usual contemporary spelling *seur* *s(c)eu* etc. for modern *sûr su*. A range of words such as *eunuque, Europe, rheume*, and *teudesque* were involved, all typically acquired from the written page by more educated individuals. (Modern French *gageure* may be compared here; the norm pronunciation has [y] but many speakers use [œ] through spelling influence.) Uncertainty reigned well into the seventeenth century and even beyond, with [ø] or [œ] finally gaining acceptance as the norm except with the two words *rhume* and *tudesque* whose spelling was later changed in consequence (Rosset 1911: 181–5). However, evidence of the fluidity still present at the outset of the seventeenth century even amongst the highest members of society appears in the speech of the child who would become Louis XIII, documented by his physician Héroard. The young dauphin reportedly used [y] in *heurter* [yte], *(il) pleut* [ply], and *déjeuner* [deʒyne], as against [røm] for *rhume* (Ernst 1985: 42–3).

Against this background, the creation of comparable variation with the nasal allophone of /y/ is understandable. The absence of a pre-existing mid nasal vowel [œ̃], except in rare isolated lexical items, also meant that no serious structural obstructions impeded the development of a high-mid variant for [ỹ].

Finally, the back vowel [ũ] would have experienced the same phonological pressures as [ỹ] to develop a lower variant [õ], and the general perceptual considerations already outlined would likewise have operated here too. However, once again other factors can also be identified which may have played a part in promoting a mid-vowel realization for [ũ].

First, from the late twelfth century onward a good deal of variation existed between dialects in the realization of the high back nasal vowel. Certain dialects used a high vowel [ū] and others a very high mid [õ], as we have already noted. Both variants may well have been represented amongst inhabitants of Paris. Such a situation offered some scope for the use of the lower variant to become accepted as a target pronunciation amongst sections of Parisian society which had previously used just [ū]. This would be especially likely if the use of the lower variant came to acquire social prestige for some reason.

A determining factor in promoting the use of [õ] can readily be identified. Its background was the lively controversy which arose in the sixteenth century over the 'correct' pronunciation of a large set of words showing sociolinguistically conditioned variation as between the vowels /u/ and /o ɔ/. On the one hand, the 'ouïstes' advocated pronunciations with the vowel /u/, as in *chouse, giroufle, coulonne, grous*, etc., whilst the 'non-ouïstes' recommended the use of a mid vowel for such items, *chose, girofle, colonne, gros* (Thurot, i. 240–66; Rosset 1911: 67–83; Beaulieux 1967: 276–8). Throughout the sixteenth century, the two realizations co-existed in a complex pattern of variation and it was only in the course of the seventeenth century that one of the variant pronunciations came to be accepted as the norm for each word.

In the items affected by this controversy, the use of /u/ rather than /o ɔ/ was well-established. Geographically, pronunciations with /u/ were evidently widely found throughout the *langue d'oïl*. In the Paris region, they characterized the speech not only of the Court but also of uneducated speakers as well. At the end of the sixteenth century, the common use by courtiers of 'ouïste' forms is shown by the fact that it attracted the attention of Henri Estienne who roundly condemned it.

> Si tant vous aimez le son doux,
> N'estes vous pas bien de grands fous,
> De dire Chouse, au lieu de Chose?
> De dire l'ouse, au lieu de l'ose?
>
> (*Remonstrance aux autres Courtisans*, ll. 41–4)

At the beginning of the following century, the young dauphin is similarly recorded as using 'ouïste' forms, such as *doun* (= *donc*), *boune* (= *bonne*), *moucheu* (= *monsieur*), and *poumi* (= *promis*), such forms being far more commonly found when the vowel is allophonically or phonemically nasal rather than oral (Ernst 1985: 36–7). At the other end of the social scale, 'ouïste' forms are recorded in various *Mazarinades* (mid-seventeenth century), especially the *Agréables conférences de deux paysans de Saint-Ouen et de Montmorency* where examples such as *counesson* (= *connaissons*), *propou* (= *propos*), *noute* (= *notre*) abound (Deloffre 1961).

Yet, despite the geographical and social range of its adherents, the 'ouïste' pattern of usage failed to establish itself as the norm. The result was that for many lexical items the /u/ variant was rejected in the standard language in the course of the seventeenth century. Thereafter, 'usage of [u] for [o] became the province of the illiterate' (Ayres-Bennett 1990: 154).

It seems inevitable that the interplay between /u/ and /o ɔ/ exercised a strong influence on the variation between the nasal vowels [ũ]:[õ] too. 'Non-ouïste' speakers would have been likely to adopt and generalize the lowered vowel [õ]. Furthermore, the growing preference in the norm language for 'non-ouïste' usage would undoubtedly have led to the promotion of [õ] over [ũ].

An additional powerful factor was the influence of spelling. Given that all popular words with a back nasal vowel were spelt with <o>, it is likely that this had an effect on the speech habits of the literate and cultivated classes. Also, as ever more learned words containing orthographic <o> in a nasalizing context entered French (e.g. items in *con-* or *-ition*), cultivated speakers may well have consciously opted for what seemed a more appropriate target pronunciation [õ], in keeping with the new Erasmist principles enunciated in the first half of the sixteenth century whereby each letter should be pronounced and given as far as possible its original value (Buben 1935). This practice with learned words undoubtedly had its effect upon the way popular words were pronounced by the educated classes, encouraging the adoption of [õ] as a norm for 'good' speech.

In summary, a variety of special internal linguistic and sociolinguistic factors can be identified which, in conjunction with more general structural and perceptual tendencies, operated on the individual high nasal vowel allophones and led to the appearance of mid variants for each of them. The latter came to be adopted as the norm by the end of the seventeenth century but only after a lengthy period of competition.[23]

4.3.4. MERGER OF [ẽ] (< [ĩ]) AND [ɛ̃] (< [ẽĩ, æ̃ĩ])

The progressive adoption of a lowered target pronunciation [ẽ] for the high vowel [ĩ] brought this vowel phonetically closer to the existing mid-front vowel [ɛ̃] to which the earlier Old French diphthongs [ãĩ] and [ẽĩ] had been tending (see 4.3.2.3). For some length of time, there was a delicate interplay between these two emerging vowel types before they finally coalesced as [ɛ̃]. Certain speakers may already have pronounced them identically from the fifteenth century, but amongst the more conservative ranks of educated speakers the two vowels were regularly distinguished throughout the sixteenth century and it was not until the 1680s that there was a consensus amongst grammarians that the standard language had just one type of front unrounded nasal vowel in words such as *pin, pain,* and *sein* (Thurot, ii. 484). Among the factors which played a part in prolonging the period over which the merger was implemented, spelling influence was doubtless one of the most important. The fact that the two vowel types were systematically distinguished in writing may be expected to have coloured linguistic habits among literate people consciously wishing to 'speak well'.

Looking more closely at the observations made by grammarians, we find that those of the sixteenth century express differing views (Thurot, ii. 481–95). The Bourbonnais Claude Sainliens, who wrote in England under the name of Claudius Holyband, accepts that the two vowels have merged, 'We sound *ain* as *in*: so instead of *main maintenant demain saint* say *min mintenant demin sint*' (1576: 172). However, Etienne Tabourot (1547–90) from Dijon presents the merger of [ẽ] and [ɛ̃] as a regional feature, characteristic of Parisian usage, 'Autres y a qui prononcent à la parisienne *in* comme *ain*. Exemple, *i'ay beu de bon vain à la pomme de pain*, pour dire *i'ay beu de bon vin à la pomme de pin*' (Thurot, ii. 483). However, the general view amongst Parisian grammarians themselves in the sixteenth century is that in standard usage the two vowel types are distinct, even if the phonetic difference between them is small. Writing in 1582, Henri Estienne describes a complex situation where the two vowels are evidently distinguished but not necessarily on the basis of their historical origin.. He indicates that the words *sainct* and *peindre, feindre, ceindre* were typically pronounced with the vowel of *in*, that is [ẽ], but that the vowel of *pain, vain* was more open. In 1584, Bèze likewise points to there still being some difference between the vowels. He claims however that the realization of *ein* (which is presented as being identical with *ain*) was diphthongal although the initial element corresponding to the orthographic *e* was scarcely detectable. It is not clear what the basis was for the delicate phonetic difference between these vowels—aperture, presence/absence of an on-glide and possibly added duration for [ɛ̃] (< [ẽɪ̃] [æ̃ɪ̃]). Also, spelling may well have had an impact in shaping views here. But whatever the basis was for the distinction between these vowel types, the fact is that educated speakers evidently did perceive them to be different.

In the seventeenth century, Parisians of good education are slowly beginning to accept the merger between the two front unrounded nasal vowels. The adopted daughter of Montaigne, Marie de Jars de Gournay (1566–1645), clearly states in 1626 that the merger is already universal amongst educated speakers of French.[24] However, grammarians continue to defend the distinction until as late as the 1680s.[25] One such, D'Aisy, writing in 1674, not only censures those who merge the two vowels, he also suggestively indicates the occurrence of hyper-corrections, with some speakers 'prononçant mesmes avec affectation *in* pour *èn*, *vain* et *faim* comme *vin* et *fin*' (Thurot, ii. 489). Though he attributes this pronunciation to the 'vice' of provincial influence, it could well mark the final attempt amongst puristic speakers to preserve a moribund distinction. Certainly, within a few years the authoritative Abbé Dangeau, a Parisian, unequivocally states that the final vowels of *certain, dessein,* and *divin* are identical (1694: 76).

The slow-changing views of the grammarians are reflected in the patterns of versification used by the great writers of the seventeenth century. Drawing guidance for pronunciation and spelling from the recognized authorities on good usage, for a long time they avoided rhymes between -*in* and -*ain* /-*ein*. No such rhymes appear in the works of Corneille (1606–84) or Molière (1622–73), and they only become more common after 1665 in the plays of Racine (1639–99), though in the verse of La Fontaine (1621–95) they are general (Straka 1985: 136).

Finally, there is evidence to suggest that the generalization of the merger between [ẽ] and [ɛ̃] may not have affected all varieties of Parisian speech by the end of the seventeenth century. On the one hand, the continual migration of people to Paris from the provinces where the distinction may have been preserved and, on the other hand, residual traces of puristic attempts in the capital to save the former distinction together led to at least some Parisian speakers still making a distinction until as late as the early part of the twentieth century. Bauche (1920: 41 n. 1) claims that '*pain* est plus sourd et plus profond que *pin*. Et les lèvres s'ouvrent plus pour dire *pain* que pour dire *pin*'. This, it is claimed, applies to general Parisian pronunciation and not just to the *langage populaire* of the capital which he is principally describing. Damourette and Pichon (1911: 117 n. 4) likewise reported that the distinction was made by some Parisian speakers through quantity and/or quality differences, 'il peut y avoir une différence de longueur: *pain* et *faim*, par exemple, étant plus longs, et dans certaines bouches plus ouverts, que *pin* et *fin*.' Isolated traces of this distinction linger until well into this century amongst some educated speakers; for instance, the linguist Emile Benveniste (1902–76) claimed that he differentiated between *pin* and *pain* (Martinet 1985: 34). However, this distinction appears now to have been lost amongst users of the norm variety.[26]

4.3.5. THE NEW NASAL VOWEL /ĩ/

In his review of standard French at the end of the seventeenth century, the Abbé Dangeau identifies five types of nasal vowel, all of which are at this stage unconditioned phonemes. Four of these correspond directly with those still found in the conservative variety of the present-day norm pronunciation, namely /ɛ̃ ɑ̃ œ̃ ɔ̃/. The remaining one, which appears as type three on his list, is a high front vowel /ĩ/. His comments on it are the following: 'La troisième voyelle sourde, qui est *in*, s'exprime par *in*; mais dans notre langue, nous n'avons ce son de *in* que dans le commencement des mots, comme dans *ingrat, infidèle*: par-tout ailleurs les lettres *in* ont le son de *en*, seconde voyelle sourde, comme je viens de le dire' (1694: 76).

The nasal vowel indicated here was thus confined to the prefix *in-/im-* found in learned words, and must have arisen at first as a compromise between the

French tendency to nasalize vowels preceding a tautosyllabic nasal consonant and the learned tendency to adopt an 'authentic' pronunciation in words drawn from Latin, i.e. a pronunciation faithfully reflecting the phonetic quality of the original source word. Many speakers adopted a fully native pronunciation for words such as *ingrat* and *impie*, but the use of a high nasal vowel /ĩ/ enjoyed prestige amongst the educated elite. In 1696, the grammarian Hindret in fact reproaches ordinary Parisian speakers for using a mid vowel rather than a high vowel in words containing prefixal *in-/im-*, 'Prononcez donc ces mots *importun, impie, imparfait*, etc. comme vous prononceriez les premières syllabes de *importunus, impius, imperfectus*, sans pourtant faire sonner votre *m*, et non pas comme s'il y avoit *aimportun, aimpie, aimparfait*, comme fait la plûpart de la bourgeoisie de Paris, et même quelques gens au-dessus d'eux, les uns faute de sçavoir le bon usage et les autres manque de l'observer' (Thurot, ii. 504).

In the eighteenth century, the use of the high vowel /ĩ/ progressively loses its prestige and, with it, its currency. It is notable that Giles Vaudelin in the special phonetic script used for his works of 1713 and 1715 does not indicate the existence of this vowel. The Canon Boulliette, writing in 1760, lists various pronunciations for prefixal *in-/im-* including [ĩ] and the mid vowel [ẽ], adding that [ĩ] was still found amongst the best speakers at court, amongst actors and elsewhere, although this was very much a minority pronunciation. However, in the later, revised edition of his *Traité des sons* from 1786, Boulliette declares that 'cette cinquième voyelle nazale est maintenant tombée dans l'oubli' (Thurot, ii. 505–6). An exactly parallel impression is given by the second and third editions of the dictionary of the Marseillais Abbé Féraud, dated 1768 and 1787. In the former, initial *in-* is described as being different from medial and final *in* which is transcribed *ein*, although Féraud's comments here draw on authorities from some decades earlier. However, in the third edition of the dictionary all cases of nasal *in* are transcribed as *ein* including the prefix *in-* (e.g. *ein-komode* for *incommode*). At the end of the century, the abandonment of /ĩ/ is confirmed in the writings of Urbain Domergues, who rather curiously believed that it had been introduced by a fashionable singer, 'Il eut des imitateurs; mais cette mode n'a eu qu'un temps, on est revenu à l'*en* nasal, qui est propre à notre langue' (1797: 128). Henceforth, the norm pronunciation would have a system of no more than four nasal vowels.

4.3.6. PHONETIC QUALITY OF NASAL VOWELS (*c*.1700)

At the end of the seventeenth century, it appears that if no account is taken of the special vowel /ĩ/, a four–way nasal vowel system is gaining general acceptance amongst 'good' speakers. This system is comparable to that still found in conservative usage today. However, the precise quality of the various types of nasal vowel used by 'good' speakers of the time is rather less clear, since the descriptions by contemporary grammarians are quite imprecise in this respect. We confine ourselves therefore to just a few brief comments on this matter.

The vowel /ɛ̃/ evidently had a low-mid articulation in the norm variety. The grammarian D'Aisy (1674) indicates such a value by his use of the transcription 'èn' (rather than 'én'), although he maintains the conservative view that this pronunciation only applies to the vowel resulting from earlier [ãĩ] and [ẽĩ] (as in *pain plein*), whereas the reflex of OFr. [ĩ] (as in *pin*) has in his opinion a different realization, perhaps [ẽ] (Thurot, ii. 479, 489). Amongst grammarians who accept that these vowels have merged, e.g. Mauconduit (1669), it is suggestive that the resulting vowel type is identified with *ain/ein* rather than *in*. Thus, for example, *fin* is represented as *fein* (Thurot, ii. 479). The use of the low-mid value [ɛ̃] for this vowel seems likely therefore.

The rounded front vowel /ø̃/ appears still to have had a high target articulation [ỹ] in the descriptions of the sixteenth-century grammarians, although a high-mid realization was doubtless gaining ground. From the mid-seventeenth century the latter has become the norm. However, a notable development affecting the oral vowel /ø/ takes place in the course of the seventeenth century; a distinct low-mid variant [œ] is created beside [ø], the former appearing in blocked final syllables, as in *oeuf,* and the latter in open final syllables, as in *oeufs.* The earliest grammarian to comment explicitly on the existence of two distinct oral vowels [ø] and [œ] is Dangeau in 1694.[27] A parallel tendency can therefore be envisaged for /ø̃/ to develop a low-mid variant [œ̃], which would also fit in with theoretical predictions based on general acoustic and perceptual considerations (cf. 1.1 above). Nonetheless, it is not clear how far the use of the more open variant [œ̃] had become generalized amongst users of the norm variety by the end of the seventeenth century.

The pronunciation of the low vowel /ã/ is problematic. It is not until the beginning of the eighteenth century that we have the first clear confirmation of the existence of two qualitatively distinct low oral vowels, a front /a/ and a back /ɑ/.[28] The back vowel /ɑ/ had developed from long front [aː], and remained phonetically long when passing to [ɑː]. The nasal vowel /ã/ probably shared in this development, but at the end of the seventeenth century it is not unlikely that there were varying realizations for the vowel, some speakers still using a fronter vowel [ã] in words like *France* and others the retracted pronunciation [ɑ̃]. Certainly, the Parisian Abbé Dangeau implies that he still uses a front pronunciation [ã] when he indicates that the vowel in the initial syllables of *danser* and *danger* differs only in nasality from that of *paroître* (1694: 15–16).

Finally, the exact quality of the mid back vowel /õ/ is unclear. In contexts where it was realized long, e.g. in *monde,* a higher point of articulation [õː] would be expected (as with its oral counterpart [oː] in words like *hôte*). However, the desire to avoid any suggestion of an 'ouïste' pronunciation may have encouraged a more open vowel closer to [ɔ̃] to be used by some speakers. Linguistic and social factors therefore probably resulted in /õ/ having a range of realizations from low-mid to mid.

4.3.7. MORE RECENT DEVELOPMENTS AMONGST NASAL VOWELS

In the ninteenth and twentieth centuries, the nasal vowel system of French has undergone further adaptation. On the one hand, there have been modifications in the size of the system, and, on the other hand, changes have occurred in the target articulation of individual nasal vowels.

4.3.7.1. *Changes in the Size of the Nasal Vowel System*

Three developments are relevant here, each leading to further reductions in the system of nasal vowels.

Merger of /ɛ̃/ and /œ̃/

Already in the early nineteenth century there is evidence of the vowel /œ̃/ losing its lip rounding and coming to be identified with /ɛ̃/. The first known allusion to this merger in Parisian usage appears in the *Petit dictionnaire du peuple* of J.-C.-L.-P. Desgranges (1821) in which the following entry figures: 'KEQU'UN et KEKZAINS pour quelqu'un et quelques-uns, prononciation trop relâchée.' Attention is being focused on the 'negligent' omission of the consonant [l] and the vowel [ə], but it is the spelling of the nasal vowel in the second item which is of particular interest for us. Desgranges suggests that an unrounded realization for the nasal vowel was already enjoying some currency, although it is less clear whether he is censuring this new pronunciation as strongly as the omission of [l] and [ə].

Half a century later, an actor Henri Dupont-Vernon in his *Art de bien dire*, which appeared in various editions between 1879 and 1891, likewise remarked on this pronunciation feature and condemned it unambiguously. Thereafter, the phenomenon evidently became widespread enough to attract the attention of linguists. Rousselot and Laclotte (1903: 44–5) report the use of [ɛ̃] for [œ̃] 'dans beaucoup de provinces et même à Paris, dans certaines classes de la société', while Bauche (1920: 41) notes simply that '*un* (nasal) se prononce toujours *in* en LP [= langage populaire de Paris]. Ainsi, "lundi" se prononce *lindi*'. In the course of the opening decades of this century, numerous other French linguists confirm this development, often in somewhat disparaging terms (Nève de Mévergnies 1984).

Since the early 1900s, the neutralization of the /œ̃/ vs. /ɛ̃/ contrast has steadily gained ground. In his pioneering survey of French pronunciation, André

Martinet (1945) asked his informants whether they pronounced in identical fashion, *brun* and *brin, alum* and *Alain*, and, if they did make a distinction, whether this required a conscious effort. The results from the 409 informants pointed to north and north-west France, and especially Paris, as the areas where this merger was most strongly represented. Also, the merger appeared more widespread amongst Parisian informants born 1901–9 than those born before 1901. However, informants born after 1909 preserved the distinction better, perhaps because of social pressures (Martinet 1945: 148–50).

Later surveys taking up this question point to the growing identification of /œ̃/ and /ɛ̃/ amongst the younger generations of the Paris area and beyond (Reichstein 1960; Deyhime 1967; Léon 1973). The merger is now no longer a feature mainly of the *classes populaires* but is found in the usage of the educated bourgeoisie of Paris. As to the realization of the neutralized vowel, Malécot and Lindsay (1976) found that a vowel of intermediate and variable lip rounding may be used rather than a uniformly unrounded vowel (cf. also Zerling 1984). The conservative pressures of prescriptive education and spelling influence can be seen as partly responsible for this.

The background to the merger of /œ̃/ and /ɛ̃/ is a complex one. Although often considered as a development first arising amongst the 'common people' of Paris, the evidence provided by the *ALF* from the beginning of the twentieth century offers little support for this view. Although urban Paris is not covered by the *ALF*, the surrounding Ile-de-France area is conspicuous for its lack of participation in the merger.[29] Instead, three other areas, in Picardy, the lower Loire Valley, and a zone encompassing north-west Burgundy and southern Champagne, seem independently to have initiated the change. Textual evidence also points to a regional origin for the merger. Examples of the spelling <in> to represent the rounded vowel are found already in the sixteenth century in Poitou and from the seventeenth century in Franche-Comté (Tuaillon 1994). It would seem therefore that we have here a pronunciation feature introduced from the provinces into Paris in the large population migrations to the capital during the nineteenth century.

Subsequently, its acceptance and generalization amongst users of the norm variety have predictably been subject to conflicting social and linguistic forces. On the one hand, certain factors favour the merger. These include the small number of actual words containing /œ̃/[30] and, more significantly, the rarity of words which are distinguished solely by the contrast between /œ̃/ and /ɛ̃/, suggesting that the loss of this contrast would not seriously threaten communication between speakers. On the other hand, acting to block the change have been the powerful influence of the clear spelling distinction between <un> and <in, ain, ein> and, more generally, the pressures of linguistic conservatism. With respect to spelling influence, it is noteworthy that in modern borrowings from English *shunt, punk, funky,* and *jungle* a value [œ̃] is widely and consciously adopted because of the presence of the spelling <un>. A further point of interest is that the move towards merger has been gradual, affecting individual forms at different stages, i.e. lexical diffusion has operated. The process seems to have begun with *un* (article), then spread to *lundi* (with pre-stress /œ̃/) and thereafter to all forms with pre-stress /œ̃/, then on to *un* (numeral) + *quelqu'un, chacun, aucun*, and finally to all forms with stressed /œ̃/ (Nève de Mévergnies 1984: 210–11).[31]

Possible Merger of /ɑ̃/ and /ɔ̃/

If merger can take place between the two front nasal vowels /ɛ̃/ and /œ̃/, we might envisage the possibility that a parallel change could happen with the back nasal vowels /ɑ̃/ and /ɔ̃/ as well. In fact, there are occasional signs of inter-ference between these vowels amongst users of the standard language, although the evidence is patchy and variable.

A key change which seems to open the way for such a merger in the future is the growing use amongst Parisian speakers of a retracted and somewhat rounded pronunciation for /ɑ̃/. Such a realization for this vowel is already indicated in descriptions of the French of Paris at the end of the nineteenth century (Straka 1981: 184). It runs parallel to the rise of a rounded pronunciation for the oral counterpart /ɑ/, a conspicuous feature of Parisian speech especially in the inter-war years (cf. Martinet 1969b: 203). But whereas, more recently, the oral vowel has progressively abandoned any rounding, although Fouché (1959: p. xi) still indicates a rounded articulation as the norm, rounding in the nasal vowel /ɑ̃/ has remained and become more general and an important con-sequence has been some overlap between /ɑ̃/ and /ɔ̃/. Pronunciations of *en France* rather similar to *on fronce* are commonplace on French radio and television. Martinet (1980: 229) reports a snatch of overheard dialogue between two educated Parisian adults where the communicational problems which can arise are well illustrated:

> Man: Tu as dit 'blanc' ou 'blond' ?
> Woman: 'Blanc'.
> Man: Tu articules très mal depuis quelque temps!

Léon (1979: 548) certainly sees the merger as having a social identity, it being a 'tendance actuelle de certain parler chic', and, as has already been noted, Zerling (1984) claims that for some speakers the only real articulatory difference between /ɑ̃/ and /ɔ̃/ now lies in the heightened lip rounding of the latter. A further dimension to this merger is that in a number of types of *français régional* in northern France it has evidently already been accomplished. Thus, in the Haute-Marne *blanc/blond* are both realized as [blɑ̃] and in the area around Lille they both appear as [blɔ̃] (Hawkins 1993: 64), although the precise relationship between these mergers and the situation in the standard language is not entirely clear. It remains to be seen how far and how fast moves will continue amongst standard speakers towards the complete merger of /ɑ̃/ and /ɔ̃/ as some sort of low or low-mid nasal vowel.

Possible Merger of /ɛ̃/ and /ɑ̃/

An even more recent development which has been noted is the interplay between the nasal vowels /ɛ̃/ and /ɑ̃/ (Fonagy 1989: 226–32; Straka 1990: 4). It appears that in the pronunciation of some young Parisians the distinction between *ma main* and *maman*, *teinte* and *tente* may be slight, to the extent that misinterpretation by listeners can result. The evidence presented by Fonagy suggests that the speakers concerned may have adopted a pronunciation where the /ɑ̃/ : /ɔ̃/ merger is being resisted by the use of a vowel /ɑ̃/ with little or no lip rounding and a slightly fronted tongue position, approximating to [ã]. If so, a merger with /ɛ̃/ becomes more readily explicable, especially in the light of the normal realization of /ɛ̃/ as [æ̃] (see also the following section). Again, we must await future developments.

4.3.7.2.   Changes in the Quality of Nasal Vowels

The small number of nasal vowels and the independence which their phonemic status gives them allow speakers a certain amount of freedom of manoeuvre for adopting variable tongue and lip positions. One development has been the marked drift downwards in the target tongue-height of /ɛ̃/ to a value [æ̃], i.e. a vowel very like a nasal version of the English vowel in *cat*. This phonetic adjustment is in line with theoretical predictions from acoustic phoneticians (cf. 1.1).

Another recent change involves the rounding and slight raising of /ɑ̃/, which is threatening the former contrast with /ɔ̃/ as we saw above. The shift of its oral counterpart /ɑ/ doubtless played an important part in causing the change in /ɑ̃/, although such a raising is also in broad accord with acoustic theory (cf. 1.1). Needless to say, internal linguistic and sociolinguistic pressures may reverse both these developments in due course.

4.3.8.   EVOLUTION OF UNSTRESSED NASAL VOWELS

In general, there is a close relationship between the way in which nasal vowels have developed in stressed and unstressed syllables. Thus:

ĩ > ẽ > ɛ̃   *CINQUA(GI)NTA   >   sɛ̃kɑ̃:t   (cf. *CĪNQUE > sĩ:k)
ẽ   MENTĪRE   >   mɑ̃ti:ʀ   (cf. VĔNTUM > vɑ̃)
    ⟩ ã > ɑ̃
æ̃   LANTĔRNA   >   lɑ̃tɛʀn   (cf. TĂNTUM > tɑ̃)

õ > ũ > ɔ̃	MONTĀNEA	>	mɔ̃taɲ	(cf. PŎNTEM > pɔ̃)
ū > ȳ > œ̃	LŪNAE-DĪEM	>	lœ̃di	(cf. ŪNUM > œ̃)
ẽĩ ⟩ ẽĩ > ɛ̃	CINCTŪRA	>	sɛ̃tyːʀ	(cf. PLĒNUM > plɛ̃)
ãĩ	MANU-TENĒRE	>	mɛ̃təniːʀ	(cf. MĂNUM > mɛ̃)
õĩ > wẽ > wɛ̃	LONGITĀNUM	>	lwɛ̃tɛ̃	(cf. PŬNCTUM > pwɛ̃)

(respectively, 'fifty (five), to lie (wind), lantern (so much), mountain (bridge), Monday (one m.), belt (full m. sg.), to maintain (hand), distant (point)')

The gradual change in phrasal stress patterns during the medieval period is significant in explaining the similarity seen in nasal vowel evolution in stressed and unstressed syllables. Word stress came increasingly to be subordinated to group stress, whereby the stressed syllable of the final word of a syntactic group carried the main stress and preceding syllables were given a more uniform level of stress, as is the basic pattern of modern standard French. The result was that inherent intensity differences which had previously existed between stressed and unstressed syllables in individual words decreased and vowels came to develop in a more directly comparable fashion in both types of syllable.

Two particular points of interest present themselves. The first concerns the only vowel which was found exclusively in unstressed syllables, namely [ə]. When preceding a nasal consonant, it too underwent nasalization but its subsequent evolution has been complex.

In post-stress syllables, nasalized [ɔ̃] occurred in 3rd plural verbal inflexions, e.g. PŎRTANT > OFr. ['pɔrtɔ̃nt] 'they carry'. However, it appears to have lost its allophonic nasality by the end of the thirteenth century in at least some northern French varieties (cf. 4.3.10 below). Certainly, it had been denasalized by the time of the earliest descriptions of Parisian usage (sixteenth century).[32]

In pre-stress position, [ɔ̃] could arise in initial or medial syllables preceding a nasal consonant. In medial syllables, as in ORNAMĔNTUM > early OFr. [ɔrnɔ̃mẽnt] 'ornament', nasal [ɔ̃] subsequently evolved as in final syllables and denasalized to [ə]. In initial syllables, [ɔ̃] likewise usually developed via denasalization to [ə], as in FENĔSTRA > fenêtre [fənɛtʀ] 'window' and CANŪTUM > chenu [ʃəny] 'hoary' where the two main sources of earlier [ɔ̃] are seen: /e/ preceding a heterosyllabic nasal and /a/ preceded by a palatal consonant and followed by a heterosyllabic nasal consonant. However, in a group of words containing [ɔ̃] in the former context type the result has been [a] rather than [ə] in the modern standard language. Examples are: faner, faneur, ramer 'to turn hay, haymaker, to row' (< FENĀRE, FEN-ATŌREM, REMĀRE). These probably represent lexically specific restructurings whereby regular [ɔ̃] was adapted for special reasons to [ã] prior to denasalization (Straka 1987).

Where original /e/ in initial syllables preceded a geminate nasal, it did not develop to [ɔ̃] as this change only occurred when /e/ was in a free syllable. Instead, it nasalized to [ẽ] and underwent lowering to [ã]. Thus, GLENNĀRE (Celtic borrowing, attested from the sixth century) > late medieval Fr. [glãner] > *glaner* 'to glean', although a variant based on GLENĀRE also existed to give a form *glener* [glɔ̃ner], attested between the thirteenth and sixteenth centuries; SEMINĀRE > *samer* 'to sow' (attested from the thirteenth century) which co-exists with the form *semer* that prevailed in the norm variety of French; and HINNĪRE > [(h)ãnir] > *hennir* 'to neigh'[33] (Straka 1987: 244–6). This pattern of development is identical to that found in stressed syllables, e.g. VĚNNA > *vanne* 'sluice', PĬNNA > *panne* 'panne (cloth); fat', BĚNNA > *banne* 'wicker basket' (= the northern variant *benne* 'skip, tipper lorry').

The other notable point concerning unstressed nasal vowel evolution is the interplay between [õ] and [ã] which led to sporadic crossing between the two vowels in individual words. Examples are:

[õ] > [ã]	DOMIN-IĀRIUM	>	*danger*	'danger' (beside OFr. *dongier*)
	HŎMO	>	*en*	'one (proclitic subject pronoun)' (beside *on*)
	DŎMINA	>	*dame*	'lady' used as a proclitic honorific (cf. OFr. *danz* < DŎMINUS)
[ã] > [õ]	DAMN-ĀTICUM	>	*dommage*	'damage' (beside OFr. *damage*)

It is striking that the conditioning nasal was [m] in all the forms involved. Its labial articulation may well have been the trigger for the variable assimilatory or dissimilatory influence in relation to lip rounding in the preceding vowel. Other forms attested in Old French, such as *danter* (= modFr. *dompter*) < DOMITĀRE 'to tame' and *danjon* (= modFr. *donjon*) < DOMIN-IŌNEM 'castle keep', suggest that this phenomenon was not unusual. The realization [ã] for the pronoun *on* evidently remained in popular usage in the Paris area until the seventeenth century at least, as in the *Agréables conférences* (1649–51); *l'en di qu'il* . . . (i. 92), *an avet* (i. 96), etc. (Deloffre 1961).

4.3.9. NASAL VOWELS AND LENGTH

Length variations appear to have been present in nasal vowels at all stages of the history of the French language. However, their phonological significance and their incidence have changed in important ways as the language has evolved.

By way of introduction, the circumstances in modern standard French may be outlined. Every nasal vowel type can vary in respect of length, the variation being conditioned by either phonological or stylistic factors. The latter type of factor, seen in emphatic *c'est bien!* [sɛbjẽ:] as against neutral *c'est bien* [sɛbjẽ], is of course extralinguistically determined and hence somewhat unpredictable in its occurrence. For present purposes, it may be noted but set to one side.

The other type of factor yields predictable patterns of length variation in French vowels. Some of these patterns apply systematically to all vowels and not just to nasal vowels. Thus, every vowel is phonetically longer when preceding a voiced consonant than when preceding a voiceless consonant. Also, all other things being equal any vowel will be somewhat longer in a syllable carrying stress than in an unstressed syllable.

However, over and above these general characteristics there are more specific patterns of length variation which affect certain vowel types only. Two major patterns of length variation can be distinguished, each French vowel type following one or other of the two patterns. Both patterns involve the appearance of additional length in a vowel when it is located in the final syllable of a phonetic phrase (or *groupe rythmique*), provided that the syllable is of a certain structure. Final syllables of phonetic phrases, it may be noted, typically carry group stress. The two patterns may be summarized as follows:

1. nasal vowels and the oral vowels /o ɑ ø/: these have additional length when they appear in blocked final syllables;
2. all other oral vowels: these have additional length when they appear in blocked final syllables containing as its blocking consonant either [ʀ] or a voiced fricative, or the sequence [vʀ] (hence *dire* [diːʀ] vs. *dites* [dit], *sage* [saːʒ] vs. *salle* [sal], etc.).

When length variation in French vowels is discussed, it is usually this vowel-specific variation in final syllables which is in question. Also, it is normally only those vowels which take on additional lengthening under this type of conditioning that are said to be 'long' (Fouché 1959: pp. xxxvii-xlii; Tranel 1987: 49–51; Price 1991: 88–91).

Looking more particularly at length variation in the subset of nasal vowels, we can see from the preceding comments that it is phonologically conditioned in a fairly simple way: nasal vowels are long in blocked syllables at the end of phonetic phrases, as in *elle est blonde* [blɔ̃ːd], and of neutral length elsewhere, as in *il est blond* [blɔ̃]. Vowels in syllables not lying at the end of phonetic phrases are of neutral length.

This pattern of length variation however represents a fairly recent creation, which has developed in important ways over the past four centuries. Indeed, even at the beginning of this century a somewhat different arrangement is described by some phoneticians. Rather than a two-way length variation for nasal vowels, three degrees of length are identified. Thus, Passy (1914: 45) describes non-final nasal vowels as 'half-long' and transcribes *(cette) grandeur (-là)* in 'conversational' pronunciation as [grɑ̃ːdœːr]. Similarly, Martinon (1929: 127) presents vowels in final open syllables as neutral (e.g. *long*), vowels in non-final syllables as half-long (e.g. *longer*), and vowels in final blocked syllables as long (e.g. *longue*).[34] The relationship between length and nasal vowels is a volatile one therefore, and some of the details of the changes which have occurred in the history of French are still not well understood. We will merely outline the main lines of development.

In the early medieval period, it seems likely that all vowels, i.e. oral vowels as well as vowels in nasalizing contexts, also varied in length according to syllable structure, but not in the same way as in modern French. In stressed free syllables, e.g. the first syllable of the reflex of LŪNA 'moon', vowels were long and elsewhere they were of neutral length. But in the later medieval period, the originally syllabically conditioned pattern of vowel length variation was evidently abandoned little by little. Variation in vowel length continued to exist but new determining factors came into being. Unfortunately, direct evidence on vowel length is not available until the late sixteenth century, when grammarians like Bèze (1584) and Lanoue (1596) offer valuable descriptions of the contemporary situation in the norm variety. As a result, some uncertainty exists over the chronology of the developments noted.

4.3.9.1. *Context (iii) Forms*

Looking first at length changes affecting vowels in original context (iii) forms, we find that in the later medieval period (when nasality was still only an allophonic feature in vowels except possibly before a nasal consonant, cf. 4.2.2.1) systematic shortening evidently operated. These vowels, which had been long because they were originally in a free stressed syllable, thus emerged short. Evidence for shortening is clearly provided by Lanoue (1596) who indicates that the stressed vowels of forms such as *bonne, donne; hautaine, vaine, veine, laine; chienne, mienne; lime* were all short, even though they had all earlier been long. Bèze (1584) also confirms shortening for the items *voisine, hautaine,* and *bonne*. In context (iii) forms which had formerly had a geminate intervocalic nasal which subsequently simplified early on in the literary period, the previously short vowel remained short, e.g. in *femme* < [fẽm(m)ə] < FĒMINA 'woman', *lame* < [lãm(m)ə] < LĂMINA 'blade', *(il) vanne* < VANN-AT (= CL VANNIT with change of conjugation) '(he) winnows'. Subsequent grammarians confirm the presence of short vowels in forms such as these.

The regular pattern of evolution for these forms was therefore:

$$Ṽ{:}Nə > VNə$$
$$ṼN(N)ə > VNə$$

Independent of the changes just considered, other developments gave rise to *long* vowels in certain words, such as *âne* and *chaîne*, which superficially share the same structure, *vowel + nasal + [ə]*, as the original context (iii) forms. Such long vowels arose as a result of the loss of [ə] adjacent to the vowel and the incorporation by the vowel of its timing slot. Thus:

əṼNə > Ṽ:Nə > V:Nə :   ʃəẽnə > ʃẽːnə > ʃɛːn(ə)   *chaîne*
                                   rəĩnə > rẽːnə > rɛːn(ə)   *reine*

A further source of long vowels in forms resembling context (iii) came as a result of the deletion of syllable-coda [z ð] before a nasal consonant, as in *frêne* < Old Fr. *fresne* 'ash tree', *âne* < Old Fr. *asne* 'donkey', and *rêne* < Old Fr. *redne* 'rein'. However, it appears likely that a nasal vowel did not develop in such forms in the period after the loss of the coda consonant (cf. 4.2.2.1).

4.3.9.2.   *Context (ii) Forms*

In context (ii) forms, the originally long stressed vowels of items such as *vin* [vĩːn] 'wine', *charbon* [(t)ʃarbũːn] 'coal' were still presumably long in Old French. However, by the late sixteenth century when the conditioning nasal consonant had been deleted to leave nasal vowel phonemes (cf. 4.2.4), the nasal vowel itself had undergone shortening in the variety of French which was recognized as the norm.   This is indicated by the comments of Bèze (1584: p. xx) who specifically notes a short value for the final vowel of *voisin*, *hautain* and *maison*. Later grammarians confirm this (Thurot, ii. 609). Thus, the regular pattern of evolution here was:

$$\tilde{V}:N \ \# \ > \ \tilde{V}:(N) \ \# \ > \ \tilde{V} \ \#$$

The generalization of this pronunciation doubtless took a good deal of time. There are indications for instance that a long nasal vowel continued to be used by some speakers in word-final position well into the seventeenth century. Thus, Chiflet (1659: 176) notes a long vowel [ãː] for the items *an*, *tiran*, and *courtisan*, although a short vowel is recommended for *ruban*, *turban*, *écran*, *satan*. It seems probable that the use of [ãː] in the former items reflects an archaic pronunciation still partly alive in the provinces (Chiflet came from Besançon).

4.3.9.3.   *Context (i) Forms*

The pattern of change here has been complex. To clarify the main lines of devlopment, it will be helpful to distinguish two subtypes of this context:

(*a*) context (i) forms where the consonant following the nasal coda has always continued to be pronounced, e.g. *lance* (< LĂNCEA) 'spear';

(*b*) context (i) forms where the consonant following the nasal coda has more recently been lost, e.g. *grand* (< GRĂNDEM) 'big'.

In (*a*) forms, the 'covering' oral consonant has been retained; we may therefore refer to the nasal vowel in such forms as 'covered'. In (*b*) forms, where the covering consonant has later been deleted, the nasal vowel may be said to be 'uncovered'. Uncovered vowels, it will be noted, only appear in word-final position.

In both subtypes, the original stressed vowel was short, so that Old French had *lance* [lãntsə], *vente* [vẽntə] 'sale', *grant* [grãnt], etc. However, when syllable-coda conditioning nasal consonants began to weaken and be deleted in the later medieval period up to and including the sixteenth century, they systematically left behind unconditioned nasal vowels which were long, e.g. *vente* [vã:tə]. The same development appears to have occurred in syllables of comparable structure which were not word-final, as in *danger* [dã:ʒer]. This arrangement has been maintained up to the present day with (*a*) forms. Bèze (1584: 77) clearly indicates the new pattern when he describes the nasal vowels of *endormir, feindre, teindre, bonté, temporel* as long (even if he suggests elsewhere that the nasal coda consonant has not been entirely deleted yet).

A century later, Hindret (1687: 187) reports the same pattern, 'Les penultièmes Syllabes, qui finissent par une *m* ou par une *n* suivie d'une autre consone sont longues', as in *chambre, tomber*, and *prendre*, and in his second edition of 1696 he generalizes the scope of this statement to include all syllables and not just 'penultimate' ones. In the following century, the Abbé d'Olivet (1736: 73) reiterates exactly the same description as a 'Regle sans exception' for nasal vowels, offering examples such as *jambe, jambon, tomber* and *humble*. In these descriptions, it is not clear whether all long nasal vowels were being pronounced with the same duration or whether vowels in final covered syllables were slightly longer than in non-final syllables, as certain phoneticians still noted to be the case at the beginning of this century (see above in this section).

At all events, the pattern for these (*a*) forms is representable as:

$$\tilde{V}NC > \tilde{V}{:}C \ (> \tilde{V}C \text{ recently in non-final syllables})$$

The modification here has generally been viewed as a case of compensatory lengthening whereby the vowel takes up the timing slot left by the deleted nasal consonant $\tilde{V}NC > \tilde{V}{:}C$ (cf. Rochet 1976; Morin 1994). However, an alternative view would be to postulate that the vowel was lengthened prior to nasalization and that the nasal consonant was deleted without modifying vowel length, $VNC > V{:}NC > \tilde{V}{:}NC > \tilde{V}{:}C$, as Hajek (1997) does for comparable developments in North Italian dialects (cf. 10.4.3.1, 13.3). The available facts are compatible with both interpretations.

We may turn now to subtype (*b*), concerning those forms where the nasal vowel became uncovered prior to the seventeenth century. Here, the evolving pattern of pronunciation has been less straightforward. The expected vowel lengthening did initially occur on the loss of the conditioning nasal consonant, but evidently speakers soon became aware of a conflict in the motivation of the vowel length when the covering consonant was being deleted. The problem was that in certain forms vowel length was *phonologically* conditioned (as in *long* or *bond*), but in others it could be seen to have a clear *morphological* basis in that it signalled plural number (as in *bons*).

The conflict was fairly rapidly resolved in favour of the latter where length was identified with plurality. Bèze (1584: 78) certainly indicates the final vowels of *autant* and *haultement* to be long, but already in seventeenth-century descriptions uncovered nasal vowels in non-plural forms are beginning to show some variability in individual words. For instance, Maupas (1625) claims *long* has a long vowel while Oudin (1633) describes it as short (Thurot, ii. 10). Hindret (1687, 1696) even cites the pair *le tĕmps* (singular) vs. *les tēmps* (plural) where the association of length with plurality has analogically created a contrast through shortening the vowel of the singular form despite the presence of an earlier final [-s] (Dagenais 1991: 84). However, the trend towards generalizing a short nasal vowel in non-plural forms takes time to gain ground and the grammarian Buffier, a native of Rouen, shows a system still very much in transition in his 1709 work where he identifies *plomb, flanc, pédant*, and *content* as having short final vowels, but long vowels are recognized for *constant, rond, prompt* (Thurot, ii. 611). Amongst speakers from the capital, usage was doubtless also variable through much of the seventeenth century, but by the early eighteenth century the use of just short vowels in singular forms such as *long, grand, content* was probably well on its way to becoming established as the norm pronunciation. Some evidence for this comes in the transcription of Vaudelin (1713) where the only nasal vowels to be marked as distinctively long appear in plural nominals.[35]

We may look more carefully at the pronunciation of plural forms in nominals. The general trend to eliminate the regular plural marker, final /-s/, which began by the early sixteenth century but was only finally accepted into the norm pronunciation by the mid-seventeenth century (Pope 1952: § 621), did not just affect type (*b*) of context (i) forms. It also involved the plural forms of context (ii) forms, such as *maisons* and *bons*. In these forms, the same pattern of vowel length differences was adopted for indicating number distinctions: the singular form had a short vowel (as we saw above) and the plural form had a long vowel. This arrangement was also found with nominals which ended phonetically in an oral vowel, e.g. *drap* [dra] 'sheet' vs. *draps* [draː] 'sheets'.[36]

In the sixteenth century, the new morphological pattern using vowel length to mark number gained ground. Lanoue (1596) recognizes it for many but not all nominals (Thurot, ii. 622–3), but by the mid-seventeenth century it has evidently been generalized in Parisian usage. Oudin writes in 1633, 'tous les pluriers des masculins se prononcent longs à la fin' and cites amongst his examples various forms with nasal vowels, *pronoms, unions, longs, estangs, plains, soings, bruns*' (Thurot, ii. 624). Hindret (1687: 140) confirms the pattern and Vaudelin (1715) does likewise in his phonetic transcriptions of the French of his time.[37]

As far as nasal vowels are concerned therefore, through the seventeenth century and into the eighteenth century, we may assume that a length contrast was systematically used to indicate the number distinction both in nominals of context type (ii), e.g. *maison* vs. *maisons*, and context type (i), subset (*b*), e.g. *pont* vs. *ponts*.

Further indications of this arrangement are found well into the eighteenth century (Thurot, ii. 625). Wailly (1724–1801) still presents it as the norm in his authoritative grammar *Principes généraux et particuliers de la langue française* which went through eleven editions. Thus, he cites -*ent* as short and -*ein*, -*oin* as 'douteux' in length, while their plurals -*ents*, -*eins*, -*oins*, -*on(d)s* are all unambiguously long (1786: 417, 418, 421). A similar pattern of morphologically conditioned length variation is also presented by Féraud in his 1787 dictionary.

However, in general Parisian usage it seems that the eighteenth century saw a growing move to abandon the length contrast to signal number distinctions. Various possible reasons can be identified for this. The conflicting tendency of certain consonants to lengthen oral vowels in *singular* forms was a relevant factor. Especially involved were final '-s', as in *bas, dos, abus* (cf. Hindret 1687: 140–1), and a little later final [-r].

Furthermore, the fact that vowel length variations were also used to signal gender distinctions, as in *amie* [amiː] vs. *ami* [ami], may have prompted the abandonment. It is striking that to this day French semi-productively distinguishes gender morphologically in nominals, by the phonetic form of the nominal itself (*gros* vs. *grosse*), whereas number is marked almost exclusively by syntactic means, principally the form of the preceding determiner.[38] In any competition between possible ways of exploiting vowel length variation for morphological purposes, it would be understandable that gender distinction has tended to take priority over number distinction.

Some further impetus for shedding length as a number marker may have come from those regional varieties of French in which this distinction had already been lost. One suggestive case is that of the highly influential figure Vaugelas (1585–1650), a native of Chambéry, who explicitly stated that he heard no difference between the noun forms in *un faux tesmoin* and *des faux tesmoins* (1647: 347). Other grammarians, André Chapelain and Thomas Corneille, contested this and said that these noun forms did indeed differ in vowel length (Thurot, ii. 625), but the impact of authoritative provincials like Vaugelas may well have helped to hasten the loss of length distinctions to mark number differences.

By the end of the eighteenth century, it seems that speakers of the norm variety were increasingly adopting the pattern of length variation in nasal vowels which is found today. In the early nineteenth century, there were still doubtless speakers who preserved the earlier status quo, perhaps through conservatism or regional influence. However, these became progressively rarer during the course of the century as the present-day pattern was generalized.

4.3.10. DENASALIZATION OF NASAL VOWELS

In the sixteenth century or possibly the later fifteenth century, a counter-tendency to denasalize nasal vowels began to get underway. Not all nasal vowels were affected, but just those appearing in forms of our context type (iii), where the conditioning nasal consonant formed the onset of the following syllable. Thus, words such as *lune* [lỹ-nə] and *fini* [fĩ-ni] (where '-' indicates a syllable boundary) emerged as [lyn(ə)] and [fini]. The process of denasalization was prolonged. As far as Parisian usage is concerned, it appears that the last stages were not completed until the later eighteenth century.

Denasalization is bound up directly with two other sound changes which were being carried through at the same period of time. These were the deletion of coda nasals, as in *bon, grand,* which was completed by the end of the sixteenth century (cf. 4.2.4), and the deletion of final [-ə] which had probably operated in many forms of speech by the end of the sixteenth century, although [-ə] lingered on in the more conservative *langue cultivée* until the end of the seventeenth century (Fouché 1969: 524). We explore this point when considering the causes of denasalization.

As regards the implementation of this change, it is apparent that nasal vowels did not denasalize in a single uniform development. Instead, nasality was preserved longer in some forms than others. Amongst certain speakers, especially those who came from western areas, the mid back nasal vowel [õ/ɔ̃] evidently remained nasal into the sixteenth century (Morin 1994: 81) and indeed there are traces of this pronunciation still being used by educated speakers as late as the eighteenth century. Also, certain learned words such as *grammaire* preserved vowel nasality until the seventeenth century and even later.

Furthermore, there was undoubtedly a good deal of variation at a socio-linguistic level over how rapidly vowel nasalization was implemented. In the more cultivated styles of French, the adoption of denasalized vowels in the appropriate contexts was evidently generalized more speedily than in the usage of less educated speakers of the capital.

4.3.10.1. *Denasalization in Stressed Syllables*

In the fifteenth century, the following range of nasal vowels existed in context (iii) forms:

$$(\tilde{\imath}N\mathrm{\vartheta}) \qquad (\tilde{y}N\mathrm{\vartheta}) \qquad (\tilde{u}N\mathrm{\vartheta})$$
$$\tilde{e}N\mathrm{\vartheta} \qquad \tilde{\varnothing}N\mathrm{\vartheta} \qquad \tilde{o}N\mathrm{\vartheta}$$
$$\tilde{\varepsilon}N\mathrm{\vartheta}$$
$$\tilde{a}N\mathrm{\vartheta} \quad \tilde{a}{:}N\mathrm{\vartheta}$$

(where 'N' = any nasal consonant)

No reference is made to nasal dipththongs since, by this stage, the second segment of surviving diphthongs had formed the nucleus and this was to develop exactly like its comparable nasal monophthong counterpart. Thus, just as [vẽnə] *veine* developed to [vɛn], so too [vjẽnə] *viennent* gave [vjɛn].

The bracketed items were earlier pronunciations which had been rivalled by the lowered variants on the row immediately below. The latter had probably gained wide acceptance in the speech of the less educated in the Paris area before the end of the fifteenth century, but, in the conservative speech of the educated, high nasal vowels in all contexts were maintained in the sixteenth century and into the seventeenth century (cf. 4.3.3).

As a result of denasalization, these nasal vowels have emerged in the standard language as follows:

FĪNA	>	fĩnə	>	fĩnə/fẽnə	>	fin	*fine*
PLĒNA	>	plẽĩnə	>	plẽnə	>	plɛn	*pleine*
FĒMINA	>	fẽmə	>	fãmə	>	fam	*femme*
ĂNIMA	>	ã(m)mə	>	ã:mə	>	ɑ:m	*âme*
LĂMINA	>	lãmə	>	lãmə	>	lamə	*lame*
HŎMINEM	>	ũmə	>	ũmə/õmə	>	ɔm	*homme*
LŪNA	>	lỹnə	>	lỹnə/lõ̃nə	>	lyn	*lune*

The long vowel [ɑ:] of [ɑ:m] < ĂNIMA *âme* finds counterparts in [flɑ:m] < FLĂMMA 'flame', [ʒɑ:n] < IOHĂNNA *Jeanne*, [dɑ:n] < DĂMNAT *damne* '(he) damns', [kõdɑ:n] < CON-DĂMNAT *condamne* '(he) condemns'. The source of this long vowel has been much debated. Haudricourt (1947) and Martinet (1969*a*) claim that short /a/ in context (iii) forms regularly emerged as a long vowel [ã:] in the later medieval period e.g. in [ã:mə], in contrast to short /e/ which first underwent regular lowering before giving a short nasal vowel [ã] as in [fãmə]. Then, when denasalization occurred, the long nasal vowel became [ɑ:] and the short nasal vowel gave [a]. However, this view has been persuasively contested by Rochet (1976: 97–101) and especially Morin (1994: 52–65). The latter argues that the normal outcome for original short /e/ and /a/ in context (iii) forms was [ã] which denasalized to give [a]. Items with a long

vowel which denasalized as [ɑː] owe their vowel length either to the presence
of a later medieval nasal geminate or cluster which caused vowel lengthening
when it simplified (as in DĂMNAT > *damne*), or to the fusion of two
adjacent vowels (as in IOHĂNNA > Old Fr. [dʒəãnə] > *Jeanne*).[39] More
recently, however, the long vowel which arose in these forms has progressively
been abandoned in favour of /a/. Nowadays the use of the vowel [ɑː] in
pronunciations like [ɑːm] appears somewhat old-fashioned and affected, and
especially amongst younger speakers this vowel has commonly merged with
[a] to give a single low oral vowel, so that [am], [flam], etc. would be
normal.

The use of /a/ in *femme* reflects the fact that by the time of denasalization
the Old French mid nasal vowel [ẽ] had already undergone lowering to [ã].
Other words showing the same development [ẽ > ã > a] include *couenne*,
banne, *vanne*, *panne* 'bacon rind', 'wicker basket', 'sluicegate', 'fat/breakdown'
(< CUTĬNNA, BĔNNA, VĔNNA, PĬNNA) and for unstressed syllables
solennel and the adverbial ending *-emment* (e.g. *ardemment*).

4.3.10.2.   *Quality of Denasalized Vowels*

On undergoing denasalization, the non-high vowels [ẽ ã] of words such as
pleine and *femme*, respectively, preserved their point of articulation and thereafter evolved in the same way as oral [ɛ a]. The three original high nasal vowels
[ĩ ỹ ũ] pose problems however. In view of the lowering seen in *fin*, *un*, and *bon*,
the associated denasalized vowels might have been expected to emerge as [ɛ œ ɔ].
In the event only the back vowel [ɔ] is found (as in *bonne* [bɔn]), the front
vowels have remained high [i y] (as in *fine*, *une* [fin yn]).

Various attempts have been made to explain the absence of lowering in the
front denasalized vowels [i y]. Most commonly, appeal is made to the relative
chronology of lowering and denasalization. The assumption is that the front
vowels [i] and [y] underwent denasalization in context (iii) forms before
lowering occurred (Pope 1952: § 440; Straka 1955: 263 and 1990: 27).[40] However,
this leaves open the question of why the back vowel [ũ] lowered before
denasalizing, unless of course the very existence of [ũ] is denied (cf. Straka
1955: 259).

It seems likely that relative chronology is indeed a major factor in explaining
the facts here. In educated Parisian usage, lowering of high nasal vowels was
evidently slow to be adopted, while denasalization was rapidly accepted. On the
other hand, in less educated usage the converse appears to have been the case:
lower target articulations were adopted more rapidly for high vowels and
denasalization was slow to be implemented. This accounts for the occurrence
of forms such as *epaine*, *origene*, *cuirene* (= *épine*, *origine*, *cuisine*) and *leune*,
eceume, *feume* (= *lune*, *écume*, *fûmes*) in the eminently uncultivated *Agréables*

conférences of the mid-seventeenth century and the negative comments made about such forms as these by grammarians of the seventeenth century.[41]

The use of high vowels [i y] in denasalized forms did eventually gain acceptance in less educated Parisian varieties, but this was a gradual development and almost certainly involved lexical diffusion. Some indication of this is already apparent in the phonetic transcription of Giles Vaudelin (1713, 1715), where it is notable that *lune* and *plume* clearly had [y] but that *une* and its related forms *aucune, quelqu'une* are transcribed with the symbol used for /ø, œ/ (these two vowels are not formally distinguished).[42] The tenacity of the high frequency form [œn] *une* in the face of competition from the standard [yn] is indicated by the dictionary of 'solecisms' by Desgranges (1821), in which may be found the entry *Je n'en ai qu'eune* (adjudged 'une faute'). Even into the twentieth century the pronunciation [œn] for *une* is reported for the *langage populaire* of Paris 'surtout parmi les basses classes' (Bauche 1920: 41). Survivals of [ɛn] where the standard language has [in] are less in evidence, but the popular word *bedaine* (< OFr. *boudine*) may be a relic although it could reflect interference from the suffix *-aine*.

Another factor which played an important role in guiding vowel denasalization was the influence of *spelling*. In denasalized forms containing variable [i]/[e] or [y]/[ø], the presence of the spelling <i> and <u> doubtless guided the choice of educated speakers towards the use of the high variant. For forms with variable [u]/[ɔ], the adoption of the variant [ɔ] rather than [u] finds an explanation in the spelling <o> used both in French and in most Latin source words (cf. Buben 1935: 92). In this instance, the preference for 'non-ouïste' pronunciations would have acted as a further factor (see 4.3.3).

4.3.10.3. *Length of Denasalized Vowels*

Usually, the oral vowels arising from denasalization seem to have emerged with normal length.[43] However, as a result of special factors long denasalized vowels could also be found.

First, a long nasal vowel which had developed from an earlier short vowel as a result of the late simplification of a nasal cluster or geminate preserved its length after denasalization. Thus, [aː] which later velarized to [ɑː] arose in *âme* and *damne* (see above in this section), and similarly a long vowel appeared in *hymne*.

Second, nasal vowels which had been lengthened as a result of absorbing an adjacent segment also remained long. Thus:

əṼ > Ṽː > Vː					
ʃəɛ̃nə	>	ʃɛ̃ːnə	>	ʃɛːn(ə)	*chaîne*
rəĩnə	>	rɛ̃ːnə	>	rɛːn(ə)	*reine*
ʒəãnə	>	ʒãːnə	>	ʒɑːn(ə)	*Jeanne*

Finally, long vowels were adopted in certain *mots savants*: e.g. *amazone*, *diadème, infâme, atome*. However, a long pronunciation tended not to be used for the high vowels [i y] in such words, e.g. *origine, tribune* (cf. Hindret 1687).

More recently, the long denasalized vowels from both sources have been subject to the general moves in French to eliminate inherent length in vowels, thus [ʃɛːn(ə)] > [ʃɛn] *chaîne* just as [mɛːtʀ(ə)] > [mɛtʀ] *maître*.

4.3.10.4.   *Unstressed Syllables*

Denasalization also affected vowels in unstressed syllables, and here it operated in a progressive way. Whilst the process was probably complete for stressed vowels in educated Parisian usage by the mid-seventeenth century, there is evidence that in certain cases unstressed nasal vowels retained their nasality rather longer.

The two vowels [ɑ̃] (< [ã]) and [ɔ̃] were apparently the slowest to undergo full denasalization in Parisian French, especially in words of a popular, everyday character. There is no indication of a nasal pronunciation of the high vowels [ĩ ỹ] or of the mid vowel [ɛ̃][44] surviving the seventeenth century in denasalizing contexts.

Looking first at the low vowel [ɑ̃], we find that grammarians throughout the seventeenth century report as standard the use of this nasal vowel in the pre-stress syllable of such items as *grammaire, condamner* and adverbs in -*amment*, -*emment* (*constamment, ardemment*).[45] One consequence was the near-identity of the words *grammaire* and *grand-mère* (the former had the stressed vowel [ɛ] and the latter had [e]). This is exploited by Molière for comic effect in *Les Femmes savantes* (II. vi. 64–5) which was published in 1672.[46] The use of a nasal vowel in these words continues to be noted by grammarians until well into the eighteenth century, but by the second half of the century the use of an oral vowel has become the norm. Thus, the grammarian Roche (1777) writes: 'On prononçoit *puissant-ment, abondant-ment* et quelques personnes gardent encore cette prononciation' (Thurot, i. 454), and likewise Féraud in the 1787 edition of his influential dictionary remarks more censoriously about *grammaire* 'Plusieurs veulent qu'on prononce *Granmère, Granmérien*: c'est une mauvaise prononciation' and in similar fashion he condemns the use of a nasal vowel in adverbs such as *ardemment, puissamment*.

Thereafter, the preservation of a nasal vowel [ɑ̃] is the sign of rustic or simply 'bad' pronunciation. Desgranges (1821) notes *gran-maire* for *grammaire* as a 'faute' which 'est du langage villageois', whilst *gangner* for *gagner* is just a 'vice de prononciation'. Even so, this phonetic trait continues to be used into the early twentieth century amongst (presumably provincial) speakers of the standard language, as Martinon (1929: 131) indicates, 'Beaucoup de personnes conservent encore, très malencontreusement, le son nasal dans an-*née*, dans *solen-nel* et *solen-nité*, ou dans les adverbes en *-amment* ou *-emment*.' The only items to retain a nasal vowel before a nasal consonant in the norm pronunciation are forms containing the prefix *en-* (*ennoblir*, *enivrer*) and by association *ennui, ennuyer, ennuyeux* where a 'pseudo-prefix' *en-* has been recognized.

The vowel [ɔ̃] was kept in a denasalizing context into the eighteenth century as well. Thus, Restaut (1730) recommends, 'il faut prononcer *hon-neur, don-ner, enton-ner*' (Thurot, ii. 523). However, such a pronunciation appears to have been abandoned earlier than for [ɑ̃] in the norm usage, since later grammarians and lexicographers of that century do not mention the pronunciation, even to censure it.

4.3.10.5. *Causation of Denasalization*

The factors leading to vowel denasalization are rather uncertain. Although we may see this change as just a case of nasal dissimilation, whereby a sequence of nasal vowel + nasal consonant becomes oral vowel + nasal consonant, such an 'explanation' is less than convincing. Numerous varieties of *langue d'oïl*, in Normandy, Picardy, and elsewhere, have preserved the original nasal vowel + nasal consonant sequences to this day, showing that dissimilation is far from being an automatic and inevitable development in such contexts.

Denasalization was evidently carried through first in stressed syllables and it is in this context that we must look for possible initiating factors. An important background consideration is that as a result of two other sound changes of the period, namely the deletion of coda nasals and the deletion of final [-ə], two sorts of word-final sequence containing nasal vowels developed. These were: -Ṽ and -ṼN (where 'V' = any vowel and 'N' = any nasal consonant). Two related forms *plein, pleine* may be used as examples:

	plein	*pleine*
	plɛ̃^{n}	plɛ̃nə
deletion of coda nasals	plɛ̃(^{n})	—
deletion of final shwa	—	plɛ̃n(ə)
	plɛ̃	plɛ̃n

The outcome would thus be conditioned and unconditioned nasal vowels, in *pleine* [plɛ̃n] and *plein* [plɛ̃], respectively. Given that phonetically *oral* vowels did not yet exist before nasal consonants, the possibility would be open to adapt the sequence nasal vowel + nasal consonant to the sequence oral vowel + nasal consonant. One important factor which would encourage this would be the desire to make the gender distinction between the masculine and feminine forms perceptually clearer (cf. Martinet 1969*a*: 144–54).

A further factor may well have been the influence of spelling pronunciation in the wake of the sixteenth-century Erasmist reforms. The norm which established itself for the pronunciation of Latin, and by extension in learned words, was that a vowel preceding a nasal consonant should be oral unless the nasal consonant was in syllable-coda position when the 'French' pattern took over.[47] Amongst growing numbers of educated speakers of the sixteenth century, learned forms like *origine, tribune, sirène* consequently were given oral stressed vowels. This pattern of pronunciation which enjoyed high prestige provided a model which could then be generalized throughout the lexicon, particularly as it allowed easier discrimination of word forms like *plein/pleine*.

As far as denasalization in unstressed syllables is concerned, the new pattern found amongst educated speakers in stressed syllables was rapidly extended to unstressed syllables in learned forms. Subsequently, the generalized use of only oral vowels preceding nasal consonants probably spread along two axes: lexically, from learned to non-learned words and, sociolinguistically, from more educated to less educated speakers of the Parisian area.

4.3.11.   NASAL VOWELS AND LIAISON

A very special problem area concerns forms of our context-type (ii), e.g. *bon, plein*. Usually an unconditioned nasal vowel emerges in such forms in modern French, but in contexts where these forms precede a vowel-initial word with which there is a close syntactic bond, a final nasal consonant appears; e.g. *plein* [plɛ̃] but *plein air* [plɛnɛːʀ]. This phenomenon whereby an otherwise 'silent' final consonant appears as a linking element with a following word is called *liaison*. The circumstances of liaison are complex in modern French, cf. Delattre (1947, 1955, 1956) and Fouché (1959) for standard presentations. Also, the interpretation of liaison has provided a lively field of debate for French and general phonologists in recent years.[48] Our interest however will lie solely in the historical development of liaison.

The background to liaison lies in the more general phenomenon known as *enchaînement*. This refers to the process by which re-syllabification occurs in close-knit phrases containing a word ending in a consonant and a following word beginning with a vowel. The word-final coda consonant links up with the initial vowel of the following word and becomes an onset consonant. Hence, the coda [l] of *mal* becomes an onset consonant in *ma-lorganisé*. This linking process is normal in modern French and indeed it seems to have been found at all times in the history of French.

In Old French, coda nasal consonants were still normally pronounced so that context (ii) forms would have been subject to *enchaînement*. For instance, a phrase like *plein air* would have been syllabified as *plei-nair*. However, when all traces of a coda nasal were finally lost in the sixteenth century, *enchaînement* gave way to liaison since now the non-linking form of context (ii) words such as *plein* had a 'silent' final consonant. The result was a pair of alternating forms:

[plɛ̃] found in pre-consonantal and phrase-final position
[plɛ̃n] a liaison form used in pre-vocalic, phrase-medial position

The subsequent history of the liaison forms has been complex.[49] Broadly, there have been two competing tendencies at work. On the one hand, we have what may be called a 'phonological' tendency whereby the Ṽ-N sequence of the liaison form (where '-' indicates a syllable boundary) shared the same evolution as other Ṽ-N sequences, the vowel regularly undergoing denasalization. Thus, *bon* developed in *bon ami* [bɔ-na-mi] just as it did in *bonheur* [bɔ-nœːʀ]. On the other hand, there has been a 'morphophonemic' tendency to preserve a closer formal link between liaison and non-liaison alternants by maintaining the nasality of the vowel in both alternants, as in *mon ami* [mɔ̃-na-mi] beside *mon sac* [mɔ̃-sak] where *mon* has a nasal vowel in both contexts.

Neither tendency has been totally dominant and this has led to a good deal of variation in the present-day norm pronunciation. Some words in liaison contexts surface with a final oral vowel and others with a final nasal vowel. For example, [plɛnɛːʀ mwajɛnaːʒ] *plein air, Moyen Age* vs. [œ̃nɛːʀ bjɛ̃nɑ̃tɑ̃dy] *un air, bien entendu*.

Historically, the phonological tendency appears to have been gaining ground in the later sixteenth century and the seventeenth century. The earliest comment for Parisian usage comes from Bèze (1584: 32) who himself preferred the morphophonemic tendency and is moved to reproach his fellow citizens for pronouncing the clitic pronoun *en* as [ən] in *il s'en est allé, on m'en a parlé*. A century later, Dangeau (1694: 66) writes that in cases of liaison with words ending in -*n*, 'il ne reste plus rien de la prononciation nazale, & qu'on lit *certain homme*, comme s'il y avoit *certai nhomme*; *mon ami*, comme s'il y avoit *mo nami*.'

Entering the eighteenth century, the morphophonemic tendency begins to gain ground, as the comments of various grammarians attest (Thurot, ii. 557–9). Even so, such influential figures as Féraud (1787) and Domergues (1797) still present the phonological tendency as the standard pattern towards the end of the century. Both grammarians, it may be noted, were from the south of France and their observations suggest that the relative strength of the two competing tendencies may already have varied geographically and given rise to regional differences in the pronunciation of the norm language. The dominance of the phonological tendency in the south has left its legacy in the widespread use of an oral vowel in *un air, mon ami*, etc. amongst present-day speakers from southern France (Tranel 1981: 146).

In the nineteenth century, the tide was clearly flowing in favour of the morphophonemic tendency amongst speakers from Paris and northern France. However, the adoption of nasal vowel + [n] pronunciations in liaison operated in piecemeal fashion, depending on the nature of the vowel, the syntactic class of the word concerned, and its spelling. The social background of the speaker and the social situation in which liaison forms occurred were also significant determinants. A great deal of variation existed therefore even in educated Parisian usage. One example of this concerns the indefinite article *un*. In his highly authoritative dictionary of 1863–73, the lexicographer Emile Littré (1801–81) recommends [yn] in *liaison* (e.g. in *un homme*), although [œ̃n] and [œn] are also mentioned as possible pronunciations. The pronunciation [yn] continued into the early twentieth century. Bruneau (*HLF*, xii. 534 n. 6) records, 'Quand j'étais étudiant à la Sorbonne, vers 1906, le doyen Alfred Croizet, dont la prononciation était citée comme modèle, prononçait: [yn] ami (et non [œ̃n] ami).' (Transcription adapted to IPA) In 1920, Bauche still reports this pronunciation amongst Parisians, associating it specifically with usage in seminaries.[50]

During the present century, the morphophonemic tendency has continued to gain ground, most notably with the possessives *mon, ton, son*. As a result, most *grammatical* words preserve their nasal vowel in liaison contexts in modern standard usage. *Lexical* forms however are more variable in their realization. The present-day arrangement may be summarized as follows (cf. Delattre 1966: 39–48; Fouché 1969: 434–79):

   nasal vowel + liaison [n]:

(determiners)	*un aucun; mon, ton, son*
(adverb)	*bien*
(pronouns)	*on, en; rien*
(adjectives)	*commun*

oral vowel + liaison [n]:

(adjectives)	*bon, -ein (plein* etc.), *-ain (vain* etc.), *-ien (ancien* etc.)
(adverb)	*non*

Within this broad pattern, there continues to be some variability in usage. One case is provided by adjectives ending in [-(j)ɛ̃]. The pattern found with high-frequency items ending in *-ein, -ain, -ien* might seem to suggest that all adjectives ending in [-(j)ɛ̃] follow the phonological tendency. However, the small set of adjectives in *-in* proves exceptional. Although *divin* has an oral vowel in the phrase *divin enfant*, in the other (rare) cases where it is in liaison position there is variation amongst speakers between [divɛ̃n] and [divin]. The form of the adjective *fin* in liaison contexts, e.g. in *fin observateur*, is equally variable. French speakers may be heard using [fɛ̃n] and rarely [fin], but educated users of the standard variety appear increasingly to be favouring [fɛ̃] with no liaison consonant at all.[51]

NOTES

1. Three types of argument are advanced. First, in those regional dialects which have preserved vowel nasality in original context (iii) forms, especially in the Franco-Provençal area, there are consistently oral vowels in these forms, as in [ˈãːna] < LĀNA 'wool' vs. [ˈɔːno] < ĀSINUM 'donkey' in the dialect of Hauteville (Martinet 1956). Secondly, in the phonetic description of the standard variety by Lanoue (1596) an oral value is clearly identified for the vowels of these later context (iii) forms, although a nasal value is indicated for original context (iii) forms like *femme panne* etc. Thirdly, if vowel nasalization had operated after syllable-final [z ð] had been deleted, the absence of lowering in forms such as *même* (< [ˈme(z)mə] < MET-ĪPSIMUM) and *rêne* (< [ˈrɛ(ð)nə]) would be inexplicable, since front mid nasal vowels [ẽ/ɛ̃] regularly underwent lowering, as in VĔNTUM > [vã] *vent* (cf. 4.3.2.1).

2. The claim of a preferential order of nasalization, front vowels before back vowels, would apply only to the *mid* vowels spelt *e* and *o*. It should be recalled that the high vowel spelt *u* was doubtless realized as [y] at the time when nasalization got under-way. It was therefore a front vowel just like *i* so that no front–back implications at all could be drawn from the assumed order of nasalization of these two high vowels.

3. Fouché (1966: 662) claims, albeit without evidence, that [-ɲ] > [-jn] had already occurred as early as the beginning of the eleventh century.

4. Traces of progressive nasalization remain to modern times in a number of varieties of *langue d'oïl*. For *ami*, ALF map 38 indicates the existence of [amẽ], [amɛ̃], etc. with a final nasal vowel at three points in the east/south-east as well at several points in Picardy and in northern Normandy.

5. Reenen (1994) confirms the validity of this interpretation of the value of <ss> by noting the parallel rise of the graphy <rss> in the later thirteenth century, e.g. in <perssonne> for *personne*. Syllable-final /r/ was widely deleted in the later medieval period.

6. In his account of Norman-style pronunciation, Palsgrave (1530: 5) states that all instances of phrase-final *-e(s)* were pronounced as nasal vowels. Yet, rather surprisingly, no such claim is made for the verbal inflexion *-ent*.

7. This has been attributed to the fact that nasal [õː] was raised early to [ũː] before the regular diphthongization of free /o/ occurred (Pope 1952: §§ 164, 426). However, it is not clear why the resulting high vowel would not subsequently have been fronted, since /u/ > /y/ is alleged to have operated chronologically later. Fouché (1969: 368, 377) assumes that diphthongization did occur, but that [õũ] was reduced soon after to [õ]. No explanation is offered for the reduction.

8. Odd signs of coalescence appear in the seventh century in the writings of Bishop Gregory of Tours (d. 536), who uses VADANTE for VADENTE (Bourciez 1956: § 205c). Traces of -ENTEM (giving *-ent*) survive in the south-west and south-east of the *langue d'oïl*, suggestively close to the *langue d'oc* where no such merger occurs.

9. A major contributor to such a convention can readily be identified. This was the influence from Picard literature which enjoyed a considerable reputation throughout northern France until the end of the thirteenth century (Wacker 1916). Significantly,

in Picard dialects [ɛ̃] and non-fronted [ã] have been consistently kept qualitatively distinct.

10. Cf. Pope (1952: §§ 471, 510), Fouché (1969: 379–80). However, there are earlier signs of this change of prominence in nasal/oral *ie* in Western texts such as the *Roland*, e.g. laisse 161 where *irez*, *butét* with [eː] assonate with diphthongal forms including *piet*, *chef*, *laiser*, and even nasal *mien*. Bédier (1927: 291) identifies 20 cases of such assonances in the *Roland* out of a total of 880 relevant lines. He also points out parallel instances in other *chansons de geste*. The possibility that some of these apparent anomalies arise from 'poetic licence' cannot be discounted however.

11. Forms with [jĩ] are still found in this century, notably in the extreme periphery of Normandy. The *ALF* notes [bjĩ] [mjĩ] [r(j)ĩ] [v(j)ĩ] for *bien, mien, rien, (je) viens* throughout north and central Manche (maps 131, 853, 1158, 1361). More recently, Lepelley (1974) reports [bjĩ] [mjĩ] [rjĩ] [vjĩ] with a 'voyelle semi-nasalisée' for the Val de Saire area of Manche. We may note that *lien* surfaces here as [ljã] suggesting an original disyllabic treatment [li-ẽn] of this form, parallel to VĔNTUM > [vã].

12. In fact, the place-name *Orléans* itself, deriving from AURELIĀNIS, shows precisely this lowering. The Parisian form *Orliens* appears in the Tax Rolls of Paris for 1296 (Michaëlsson 1958: 32).

13. Interestingly, the fifteenth-century poet François Villon whose verse was non-traditional and popular in expression shows few signs of using this variant. One rhyme is suggestive, namely *an: ancien: crestien* (*Testament*, stanza 146), but the metre shows the two latter words here to be trisyllabic, i.e. ending in [i-ãn]. These may therefore be variant forms which patterned like *patient* etc., with regular lowering. Whether Villon pronounced forms like *bien, rien* with [jã] remains unknown.

14. Numerous cases of [jã] are to be found in the *Agréables conférences* published between 1649 and 1651 and written in the popular variety of the Ile-de-France region; e.g. *rian* (i. 82), *chian* (iv. 124), *Parisian* (i. 109) in Deloffre (1961). The provincial, if not rustic, overtones of this pronunciation is a source of humour for Molière, e.g. the peasant Pierrot's regular uses of *bian* in Dom Juan. Yet despite the strong negative pressures, traces of the pronunciation still remain in areas surprisingly close to Paris; just to the east in W. Seine-et-Marne and in W. Aube the form [ʃjã] for *chien* is reported for many localities (*ALCB*, map 1030).

15. Cf. Pope (1952: §§ 477, 478). Both localities, it will be seen, lie some way from the Ile-de-France, Rouen in Normandy and Etrœungt in the south-east of the département of Nord.

16. The *FEW*, s.v. *juvenis*, indicates the existence of a form *joene* showing a pre-nasal vowel already in the twelfth century. For Paris, numerous instances of *joenne* appear in the Tax Rolls for 1296 (Michaëlsson 1958).

17. However, in contrast to the numerous cases of rhyme between these nasal diphthongs, oral *ai* and *ei* are found in rhyme on just two occasions in over 25,000 lines of verse (cf. vi. 114 of the edition by L. Constans).

18. Some exceptional forms showing dissimilation to *oin* [wẽ] do appear in modern French, notably *foin, moins* and, with regular denasalization, *avoine* (< FĒNUM MĪNUS AVĒNA). Various explanations have been advanced for these, cf. Fouché

(1969: 376) and, especially, Pope (1952: § 487). The definitive acceptance of these forms was sometimes slow, however. *Foin* and *moins* became established as the norm forms during the seventeenth century, but *aveine* continued in 'good' use until the nineteenth century. Desgranges (1821) describes this pronunciation as affected and he recommends 'a-voi-ne'; fifty years later, Littré in his dictionary says of *aveine* that it 'tombe en désuétude'.

19. Gossen (1970: § 19) claims that in Old Picard the two vowels [ãĩ] and [ẽĩ] merged to give a vowel graphied as <ain>. However, Flutre (1977: §§ 93, 99) reports that whilst in Picardy north of the Somme [ẽĩ] did lower to merge with [ãĩ], south of the Somme the two vowels have remained distinct. The phonetic outcomes today show considerable local variation.

20. Thus, Chiflet (also found with the spelling Chifflet), a native of Besançon, writes, 'Mais si aprés *om* and *on* suit une autre consonne que l'*m* ou l'*n*, *om* & *on* se prononce comme *oun* . . . De plus, aux monosyllabes, *bon*, *don*, . . . Lisez, *boun*, *doun*, &c.' (1659: 186). Yet on the same page he describes the pronunciation *chouse* rather than *chose* as 'une impertinence'. Amongst foreign observers of the language, John Wodroephe (1625) states, 'O changeth its sound being joyned to *m*, *n* or *u* then the french doe sound it as we do the double *oo*: and that generally throughout the whole tongue' and the examples cited are *homme*, *mon*, *comme*, *somme*, *vous* (Thurot, ii. 512).

21. Thus, Pope (1952: § 431) claims that 'it is not quite easy to combine the lowering of the soft palate . . . with the raising of the back or front of the tongue. This fact . . . explains the lowering influence exercised by nasalization on the vowels nasalized.' Straka (1955: 248) baldly states that 'dès qu'une voyelle se nasalise, elle tend aussitôt à s'ouvrir', the alleged explanation for which is that the reduced airflow through the mouth cavity during nasal vowels lowers the air pressure, making the oral muscles, esp. those of the tongue, less tense with the result that the tongue lowers in height. That vowel nasalization and lowering occurred when it did in French, Straka attributes (pp. 273–4) to the general state of physical enfeeblement of the common people of the time. More recently, Wüest (1979: 283) and Matte (1982, 1984) likewise propose ad hoc articulatory-based views.

22. The use of [y] in the stem of *heur-eux* was still widespread in the seventeenth century. Only during the eighteenth century does a mid vowel [ø] (or its low-mid variant [œ]) become recognized as the norm (Thurot, i. 515–16).

23. The *Remarques* of Vaugelas reveal how volatile views on ouïsme could be, 'Il est vray qu'on a fort long-temps prononcé en France l'*o* simple comme s'il y eust un *u* apres, & que c'eust esté la diphtongue *ou*, comme *chouse*, pour *chose*, *foussé*, pour *fossé*. . . . Mais depuis dix ou douze ans, ceux qui parlent bien disent *arroser*, *fossé*, *chose*, sans *u*, & ces deux particulierement, *foussé*, & *chouse*, sont devenus insupportables aux oreilles delicates' (1647: 340).

24. 'Ceux qui disent qu'une partie de la France prononce ces syllabes [sc. those ending in -*ain* and -*in*] diversement ignorent-ils que nous autres purs François devons detordre et redresser, non pas suivre les baragouins? . . . Il n'y a homme, femme, enfant ny pie, au moins d'honneste maison et nourriture en tous ces lieux-là, qui

n'ayt tousiours prononcé ces syllabes d'une tres-constante uniformité' (Thurot, ii. additions et corrections, 74).

25. Cf. Thurot, ii. 484: 'La plupart des auteurs du XVIIe siècle, avant Mourgues, Hindret et Dangeau, ne s'expriment pas autrement que ceux du XVIe: ils disent que *ain* se prononce comme *ein*, et que *ein* diffère, quoique légèrement, de *in*.' Mourgues published his *Traité* in 1685 and the relevant works of Hindret and Dangeau date from 1687 and 1694, respectively.

26. Unfortunately, this aspect of French pronunciation is not explored in the extensive phonetic investigation of Martinet (1945). However, in a recent survey of twenty-six Parisian informants, two (born 1938 and 1966) reportedly claimed to perceive a difference between the vowels of *plinthe* and *plainte*, suggesting a possible residue of the earlier distinction (Hansen 1998: 125).

27. Talking of *E*, he writes: 'Etant joint avec la lettre *u*, il fait la voyelle *eu*, comme dans *Dieu*, dans *feu*; & étant joint avec le même caractère *u*, il a encore le son de la voyelle *eu*, mais un son un peu ouvert, comme dans *bonheur*' (1694: 90).

28. This comes in the *Remarques* (*c*.1709) of the Parisian Nicolas Boindin (1676–1751), cf. Thurot, ii. 570. However, there is at least one earlier reference which suggests the possible existence of quality variation. In C. Plantin and J. Grévin *Dialogues françois pour les jeunes enfans* of 1567, it is said of the vowel *â* in *théâtre* and *âtre* that 'il le faut prononcer ouvertement' (Fouché 1969: 244). Whether a quality difference is being indicated here or just the presence of additional length is unclear. Pope (1932) provides further discussion.

29. Two useful maps based on data from *ALF* 1338, 1351 and 182, 787, 1347, respectively, appear in Straka (1990: 6, 7).

30. Walter (1988: 175) offers an almost exhaustive list of words containing (theoretically) the vowel /œ̃/. It comprises just 60 items and indeed a number of these are lexically related forms; for instance, *emprunt, emprunter, emprunteur, emprunteuse, remprunter* count as five separate entries. Even allowing for odd omissions, most notably *aucun*, the total is very small and certainly the tally of words enjoying any real frequency is highly limited.

31. The results of the recent study by Hansen (1998) on Parisian usage confirm the gradual and incomplete pattern of merger between the two nasal vowels. She found that most speakers still preserve the distinction despite considerable articulatory/perceptual overlapping, and indeed some younger speakers appear to be attempting to reverse the movement towards merger by restoring or heightening the lip rounding in realizations of the nasal /œ̃/.

32. In Normandy, denasalization did not occur until much later. It seems that Norman speakers interpreted the word-final nasal [ɔ̃] marking 3rd person plural as some sort of a demarcative feature indicating a word-boundary, and by analogy all cases of (oral) word-final [-ə] came to be realized nasal. The earliest testimony of this is in Palsgrave (1530: 5) whose description of French is based on Norman usage. Later, Dangeau (1694: 65) confirms the nasal pronunciation of final [-ə] by Normans, as do Boindin and Buffier in the early eighteenth century (Thurot, i. 165–6). There appears to be no trace of this pronunciation nowadays, however.

33. The pronunciation of this word has been affected by spelling influence. The expected

form [aniːʀ] was still indicated as the norm in the nineteenth century, as in the 1835 Académie dictionary and Littré's dictionary (1863–73). Hatzfeld and Darmesteter only cite [aniʀ] in their *Dictionnaire général* (8th edition, 1926). But Martinet and Walter (1973) report just the pronunciations [en(n)iʀ] [ɛn(n)iʀ] for their informants.

34. More recently, Delattre and Monnot (1981) confirm experimentally that, in the modern norm pronunciation, nasal vowels in non-final syllables are of neutral length. Indeed, their statistics indicate that the average duration of non-final nasal vowels is at least 10% less than that of final nasal vowels in free syllables (e.g. in *vaincu* vs. *plein, bonté* vs. *mon*). However, it is noteworthy that nasal vowels are reported to be systematically longer in all contexts than the other vowels which are phonologically comparable with them as far as length is concerned, namely oral /ɑ o ø/. Thus, the duration of the first vowels of *penser, bonté, lyncher* is at least 25% greater than that of the first vowels of *passer, beauté, lécher*. Nasal vowels thus appear to be the most inherently long of all French vowels.

35. Predictably, residues of the earlier lengthening existed beyond the seventeenth century. D'Olivet for instance still contrasts the long vowel of *bond* with the short vowel of *bon* (1736: 95). However, he was a provincial from Salins in the Franche-Comté and Parisians did not always concur with his observations on vowel length. D'Alembert said of him, 'il s'est trompé sur la quantité de quelques syllabes qu'il prononçait à la manière de sa province.'

36. The lengthening caused by the loss of earlier final [-s] here is reminiscent of that found in many dialects of present-day Andalusian Spanish where nominals such as *mesa mesas* 'table, tables' are realized as ['mesa 'mesaː].

37. Having stated that 'Tous les mots terminez en *s* precedez de consones ont toûjours la derniere Syllabe longue' (loc. cit.), Hindret presents various examples including *dents, poincts* containing nasal vowels. Elsewhere, he notes that the final vowel of *content, (le) temps, garçon* is short whilst the final vowel of *(les) temps, (ils) font, sont* is long (Dagenais 1991: 84). Vaudelin (1715) marks as long the final vowels of *artisans, noms,* and *bons,* although perhaps through inadvertence no length marker is included for *nations, enfants,* or *savants* (cf. Walter 1989).

38. This of course applies to the *spoken* language, where there is no pronunciation difference to signal number differences in most nouns, e.g. between *femme* and *femmes* as in *la femme chante* and *les femmes chantent.* The determiner alone assures the number distinction, *la* vs. *les.* Only a few nouns can independently distinguish number, e.g. *oeil* vs. *yeux, cheval* vs. *chevaux.* In the *written* language however the nominal itself can normally indicate number differences

39. The claim by Haudricourt (1947) that short original [ã] lengthened in nasalizing contexts in order to preserve the contrast between it and short [ẽ] when this vowel underwent lowering does fit in with textual evidence from medieval Anglo-Norman dialects (Morin 1994: 55) and also with modern-day Norman dialects, cf. *amende* 'fine' (with a short vowel) vs. *amaonde* 'almond' (with a long diphthongal vowel, probably [ãũ]) in the dialect of Le Havre (cited by Haudricourt 1947: 40) and the data from the Val de Saire presented in section 5.3. However, it is noteworthy that this regional vowel length differentiation was confined to context (i) forms.

40. For a more elaborate (though highly questionable) hypothesis using relative chronology, see Fouché (1969: 384–6).

41. Du Val, writing in 1604, reproaches Parisian *women* for pronouncing *cousaine, raçaine, voisaine* (Thurot, ii. 479). However, Hindret (1687: introd.) describes as provincialisms the pronunciations *voleume, pleume, preune, breune, forteune,* and *fareine, ma cousaine, une medeceine.*

42. To these may be added the popular expression *neune part,* i.e. *nulle part* 'nowhere', which Hindret (1687: introd.) describes as being typical of the 'petite bourgeoisie' of Paris. This first word of the expression is also a derivative of the indefinite article, going back to NEC-ŪNA.

43. This is confirmed by the testimony of sixteenth- and seventeenth-century grammarians. Bèze (1584: 78–9) notes short vowels in *donne, bonne, besongne, hautaine, cuisine, cousine, voisine,* and Lanoue (1596) similarly indicates short vowels for these and other words of parallel structure (see also 4.3.9.). A century later, Hindret (1687: 166–72) identifies short vowels in *lime, deuxiéme, aime, dame, pomme, plume, épine, peine, plaine, panne, bonne, moine, lune,* etc. Curiously, Straka (1955: 263, 1990: 9) claims that denasalized vowels were regularly *long.*

44. As late as the nineteenth century, Desgranges (1821) cites a pronunciation *singneur* for *seigneur,* describing it as 'prononciation de Picards qui parlent sans se gin-ner'.

45. Cf. the Parisian Abbé Dangeau (1694: 75, 89, 100) who clearly indicates a nasal vowel for all these items.

46. The lines read:
    BELISE Veux-tu toute ta vie offenser la grammaire?
    MARTINE Qui parle d'offenser grand'mère ni grand'père?
    Cf. the observation of the grammarian Chiflet (1659: 189–90), 'Mais ne prononcez pas en *é* masculin . . . *breviaire, grammaire, paire.* Autrement les petits escoliers diront; *Ie porte ma grand-mére dans mon sac.*'

47. Subsequently, the use of oral vowel + nasal consonant became established in word-final position also, in unadapted learned forms such as *intérim, requiem, quidam, album, pollen, epsilon* and in other transparent loanwords *djinn, barman/barmen, groom, rhum* (Fouché 1969: 381–90). However, the conflicting pressures at work, Latinising vs. French, are seen in *examen* for which the norm pronunciation was evidently [-ɛn] up to the end of the eighteenth century although [-ɛ̃] is noted by some grammarians as a variant (Thurot, ii. 473–4).

48. Amongst the numerous studies, mention may be made of Malécot (1975), Morin and Kaye (1982), and Tranel (1992). Controversy has surrounded not only the factors determining the occurrence of *liaison,* but also the more theoretical question of whether liaison consonants should figure in the underlying forms of the relevant lexical units or whether they should be introduced by epenthesis.

49. More detailed discussion of this question appears in Thurot, ii. 550–9 and Tranel (1981: 122–56).

50. 'On entend quelques Parisiens dire *une* pour 'un' devant une voyelle: *une homme.* C'est une habitude prise dans les maisons religieuses d'éducation' (1920: 41 n. 41). The episode of the priest in Proust's *Le Temps retrouvé* (Pléiade edn. 1961: 829)

supports the latter claim. On being met coming out of a brothel he remarks, 'Je ne suis pas *une* ange' (emphasis ours).

51. In a recent survey of seven highly educated speakers, three of whom were Parisians, liaison usage was tested for six different adjectives not figuring in the set just cited. These included *fin*. All the adjectives were set in pre-nominal position within noun phrases which were neither semantically nor pragmatically aberrant in any way. The author found that all the informants except one used the liaison form [fɛ̃] for *fin*, and overall in the survey liaison failed to occur in 81% of possible cases.

5

Gallo-Romance II: Non-Standard Varieties of *langue d'oïl*

5.1. Introduction

The impact of nasalization on vowel evolution has been no less profound in non-standard varieties of *langue d'oïl* than it has in the standard language. All varieties have been affected to a considerable degree, but nasalization has modified patterns of vowel evolution in differing ways from one region to another. In this section, we will outline some of the major lines of development which are found.

5.1.1. BACKGROUND DEVELOPMENTS

All varieties appear to show the same early patterns of change. Thus, there is neutralization of mid-vowel contrasts in type (i) contexts, e.g. as between forms like VĒNDO and VĔNTUM. In other types of nasalizing context, vowels evolved at first in the same way as their oral counterparts. Later, phonemically nasal vowels developed very widely throughout the *langue d'oïl* region as a result of the loss of the conditioning nasal consonant. Whether this loss occurred in individual non-standard varieties at an earlier or later stage than in the standard variety, where it was probably completed by the end of the sixteenth century, is often difficult or impossible to establish. Nonetheless, the significant point is that there is a broad comparability between the different *langue d'oïl* varieties over the actual fact that nasal vowels were phonologized. A final common trait has been that the system of nasal vowels has shown a clear and widespread movement to become reduced in size as compared with the oral vowel system. In more peripheral varieties, as many as five qualitatively distinctive nasal vowels have continued to be used, notably in parts of Normandy and Franche-Comté. But, perhaps reflecting inherent tendencies and growing influence from the standard language, the nasal vowel systems of non-standard varieties have shown a marked preference for four or fewer members, with length occasionally being exploited as a further differentiating factor.

Despite these common characteristics, some notable regional variation is apparent in the way individual nasal vowels have developed and consequently in the changing make-up of the nasal vowel system as a whole. It will not be possible to explore details too far here. The frequent lack of textual evidence for the earlier stages of certain regional varieties provides one obstacle. Also, the increasing impact of the standard language on pronunciation patterns over the past century makes it problematic at times to disentangle internal developments from those promoted by influence from standard French. In this connection, the claim by the eminent linguist Albert Dauzat that already by the 1920s the majority of the 'parlers d'oïl' had disappeared is suggestive (cited in the survey of Droixhe and Dutilleul 1990).

Accordingly, some observations of just a general character may be made on the fortunes of vowel nasalization in the non-standard varieties found beyond the Ile-de-France. These take the form principally of a brief enumeration of various broad patterns or trends which have affected large areas of the *langue d'oïl* region, contributing significantly to the varied outcomes encountered. For convenience, we include the Franco-Provençal zone in this review. More specific comments on the varieties of this transitional area between the *langue d'oïl* and the *langue d'oc* appear in section 5.4.

5.2.   Regional Patterns of Nasal Vowel Evolution

Several developments can be identified which have had a considerable influence on nasal vowel evolution amongst the non-standard varieties of *langue d'oïl*, even though they had little or no effect on the variety that was to become the standard language. Perhaps the most significant are the following:

(1)   progressive nasalization;
(2)   spontaneous nasalization;
(3)   non-fronting of [ũ];
(4)   lowering of high nasal vowels;
(5)   modification of [ẽ] > [ɔ̃] and [ẽĩ] > [ɔ̃ĩ];
(6)   denasalization of nasal vowels;
(7)   preservation of contrastive length variation.

5.2.1.   PROGRESSIVE NASALIZATION

Vowel nasalization in Gallo-Romance has typically been regressive, but cases of progressive nasalization are to be found occurring sporadically as a secondary process in various parts of the *langue d'oïl* region. In medieval times there is clear evidence of this happening in the eastern area in particular. Pope (1952: § 429) cites the examples *amin, nanin* < AMĪCUM *NON-ĬLLĪ (= standard Fr. *ami, nenni*) 'friend, no, not at all', to which may be added cases such as *ainsin, nuns, mont* < ANTIUS-SĪC NŪLLUS MŬLTUM (= standard Fr. *ainsi, nul(s), moult*) 'thus, no (m. sg.), very', which appear in the late twelfth-century text *Floovant*, probably composed in Burgundy (Andolf 1941). These examples highlight the fact that progressive nasalization typically affected high stressed vowels.

The habit of using progressive nasalization evidently became more geographically widespread in the later medieval period. It was clearly adopted for certain lexical items in at least some varieties of speech found in the capital (cf. 4.2.5). Odd traces of this phenomenon remained until the seventeenth century, though signs of its regional character are apparent. Ménage, for instance, writing in 1672 identifies the form *ainsin* as provincial and especially used in the south-west, in Maine and Anjou (Thurot, ii. 498).

Subsequently, the use of progressively nasalized vowels has become less widespread geographically. A striking case in point is provided by the reflex of the word AMĪCUM. In medieval times, texts from eastern areas of the *langue d'oïl* region commonly indicate a pronunciation with a final nasal vowel, but nasality has very rarely been maintained to the present period in the final vowel. The forms [ɛːmẽ] and [amẽ] are reported in the *ALF* (map 38) at just two localities (pts. 28 and 38, respectively) in Haute-Marne and as [amẽ] at one locality (pt. 110) in Côtes-d'Or. In other parts of eastern France, forms with oral vowels are recorded, although very commonly with a tell-tale mid vowel [ame amɛ], suggesting earlier nasality.

Elsewhere, there are two areas where progressive nasalization has operated in a significant way. In the south-east, a number of varieties of Franco-Provençal continue to show the effects of generalized progressive nasalization (cf. 5.4 below). In the dialect of Bagnes in Valais for example (see Map 10), the high vowels /i/ and /u/ have regularly been nasalized when following a nasal consonant; e.g. NĪDUM > [nẽĩ] 'nest', NŎSTRUM (> [nustre]) > [nɔ̃trë] 'our (m. sg.)', as against MĪLLE > ['mile] 'thousand' and NŎVEM > [nou] (Bjerrome 1957). Interestingly, the evidence points to progressive nasalization here as being a later change, since it has affected vowels which only emerged as high after a number of independent sound changes had operated.

The other area is Normandy where the high front vowel /i/ has been particularly affected when occurring in the final (i.e. stressed) syllable of words. Thus, in the Val de Saire (Cotentin peninsula), we find [vnẽ amẽ] < VENĪRE AMĪCUM in absolute final position, and pre-consonantally [kmẽːz] < CAMĪSIA 'shirt' (Lepelley 1974). Sporadically, words with no apparent conditioning nasal can participate in this development by analogy, a notable case being [iʃẽ] < ECCE-HĪC 'here'. The other high front vowel /y/ < Ū is not regularly affected, as in [my] < MŪRUM 'wall'. However, analogical pressures have led some forms containing /y/ to undergo progressive nasalization; for instance, the past participle of the verb [vnẽ] < VENĪRE 'to come' is widely found as [vnœ̃] (< VEN-ŪTUM) in the Cotentin peninsula, although in the closely related Jersey dialect it remains [vny] despite the nasalization seen in the infinitive [vnẽ] (Spence 1960).

5.2.2. SPONTANEOUS NASALIZATION

Vowel nasalization in Gallo-Romance has usually been initiated by the assimilatory influence of an adjacent nasal consonant. However, sporadic cases occur where vowels have nasalized without there being an overt conditioning nasal consonant present. Examples appear in parts of Picardy and in the Franco-Provençal zone to the south-east.

In Picardy, numerous varieties of the region of eastern Somme and north-eastern Oise are affected. Spontaneous nasalization has operated exclusively on high vowels [i y u] when they appeared in absolute word-final position. Examples are:

CLĀVEM	> kle	>		kli	> klẽ	'key'
SIFFLĀRE	> sifle	>		sifli	> siflẽ	'to whistle'
SORĪCEM	>			sweri	> swerẽ	'mouse'
SPĪCUM	>			ɛpi	> ɛpẽ	'ear of corn'
PERD-ŪTUM	>			perdy	> perdœ̃	'lost (past part.)'
FŎCUM	> fyɛw	> fiy	> fy	> fœ̃	'fire'
DŎRSUM	> do	>		du	> dõ	'back'
(Germ.) bosk	> bo	>		bu	> bõ	'wood'

(Flutre 1977: 29, 41, 48, 55)

In these forms, after being nasalized the high vowels have subsequently been lowered. However, lowering is not universal amongst high nasal vowels in the area of Picardy concerned. The *ALPic* i reports [esjỹ] 'axle' at two locations and [bɛrbĩ bœrbĩ] 'sheep' at three.[1] A further point of interest is that on the basis of the evidence provided by the *ALPic* i, spontaneous vowel nasalization has been most widespread with /i/, then /y/ and least of all with /u/.

Historically, this is evidently a fairly recent development dating from the eighteenth century at the earliest. Evidence for this assumption comes from the fact that [−i] deriving from raised [−e] has been affected along with original [−i], and the earliest signs of vowel raising from high-mid to high are only forthcoming from the late eighteenth century (Flutre 1977: 48).

The other area showing spontaneous nasalization lies in the Franco-Provençal zone and is geographically a good deal more extensive. Two patterns appear to exist. The first is found in a number of varieties occurring in a region situated between Lake Geneva and Lake Neuchâtel. Here, nasalization affects certain types of vowel when they appear in unstressed syllables. The vowels concerned were originally diphthongs, [ei] or [ou], and they nasalized when the syllable in which they appeared was lexically or phrasally unstressed.[2] Examples are:

Lexically unstressed	*Phrasally unstressed*
CRUCIĀRE > krei'zi > krẽ'zi 'to cross'	PĬLUM NĬGRUM > pei naː > pẽ 'naː (cf. BĔLLUM PĬLUM > bi pei > bi 'paː) 'black hair' ('beautiful hair')
SALTĀRE > ʃou'tɔː > ʃɔ̃'tɔː 'to jump'	NŎVEM CARRŪCAE > nou tsɛru > nɔ̃ tsɛ'ru (cf. INDE HABEO NŎVEM > nẽd e nou > nẽd e 'naː) 'nine ploughs' ('I have nine')

(Burger 1964)

Here, a regular alternation can be seen between nasal phrasally unstressed [pẽ] and [nɔ̃] and oral phrasally stressed [paː] and [naː]. Parallel stressed-based alternations are also found in these dialects but involving oral vowels only.

The second pattern of spontaneous nasalization occurs further west in a part of Dauphiné. Again, unstressed vowels are affected. In this case, however, nasalization operates when unstressed vowels appear at the end of phonetic phrases. Examples from Eydoche (Isère):

ẽ 'revõ	'an oak tree'	vs.	lo'revo dy 'bwaː	'the oak in the wood'
ina ka'valã	'a mare'	vs.	la ka'vala dy vãe'zẽ	'the neighbour's mare'

(Duraffour 1932: 19–20)

Here, the fact that the preceding syllable carries the nuclear stress of the phrase is an important factor. The consequence of this is that the final unstressed vowel may well show a tendency to adopt a 'neutral' articulation, i.e. one with the lowered velum position found when the speaker is at rest. Such nasality also has the effect of serving as a boundary marker, delimiting the end of the phonetic phrase, so its possible exploitation is understandable. Indeed, the development seen here would appear to find some parallel in the pronunciation which Palsgrave (1530: 4) describes for final unstressed *-e* in Norman French, 'sounded almost lyke an *o* and very moche in the noose'.[3] No trace of such a nasal pronunciation has survived in present-day Norman however.

In all the varieties showing spontaneous nasalization, it is noteworthy that there are also nasal vowels arising from the more regular conditioning influence of an adjacent nasal consonant. We may therefore see these cases of spontaneous nasalization as secondary developments exploiting a phenomenon (i.e. intense vowel nasality) which is already well-established.

5.2.3. NON-FRONTING OF [ũ]

The fronting of /u/ > /y/ appears to have operated first in southern and central parts of the *langue d'oïl* region, spreading only gradually to northern and eastern parts (cf. Pope 1952: § 183). It never did reach the far north-east of Wallonia. To this day, RŪGA emerges variously as [rɔw ruw ru] 'street' (*ALW*, i, map 86).

In areas where the fronting of original /u/ was late in being implemented, the move towards a fronted point of articulation was sometimes blocked when a nasal consonant followed. The implication is that, by the time that fronting got under way, vowel nasalization had already operated with sufficient intensity in the dialects concerned to detach the nasal allophone [ũ] from the other (oral) allophones as the latter passed to [ü] and finally to [y]. Thereafter, non-fronted nasal [ũ] tended to merge with the nasalized allophones of /o/ and /ɔ/ to give a high back vowel [ũ] or more usually a high-mid vowel [õ]. Such a merger has occurred in a broad band of territory, in Wallonia in the north-east and in Franco-Provençal in the south-east. Early on, Picardy in the north was evidently affected as well, though later a fronted realization [ỹ] has come to be established for the reflex of [ũ] < nasalized Ū.[4] In dialects of the central east, i.e. of Burgundy, Lorraine, and Franche-Comté, fronting likewise established itself so that only isolated cases of original nasalized [ũ] remaining a back vowel can be found in modern times, e.g. [lũdi] < LŪNAE-DĪEM at a sprinkling of points in Vosges, Haute-Saône, and Doubs; *ALF* 787 (see Map 2).

Where nasal [ũ] remained unfronted, there have been important implications for the subsequent evolution of the system of nasal vowels. In the absence of fronting, a symmetrical system of nasal vowel monophthongs remained:

The non-appearance of a further front vowel **[ỹ] had the effect of allowing the existing front vowels [ĩ] and [ẽ] to preserve their points of articulation undisturbed. In particular, where [ũ] did not front, the mid vowel [ẽ] has widely remained a mid vowel quite distinct in tongue height from the low vowel [ã]. Hence, we still find [dẽ dẽ] and [tẽr tẽr] < DĔNTEM, TĔNERUM 'tooth, tender' vs. [tʃãp ʃãp] < CĂMERA 'room' in almost all varieties of Walloon (*ALW*, i, maps 9, 27, 94).

The situation in Picard dialects is more complex. Original [ẽ] has remained a mid vowel here even though [ũ] has given [ỹ]. This may well reflect the fact that the fronting of [ũ] here occurred relatively late, and the long-standing difference between [ẽ] and [ã] remained resistant to disturbance. Instead, just as in Walloon the vowel [ẽ] came to merge subsequently with the lowered realization of [ĩ], so that VĪNUM and VĒNDIT/VĒNTUM share a common reflex [vẽ].

In a more recent change dating from the seventeenth century onward, there has been a further merger in Picard varieties of the south-west of Nord and, sporadically, in certain varieties of the rest of Nord and in Pas-de-Calais and Somme. Here, the low nasal vowel /ã/ has fronted and raised so that it has coalesced with the mid vowel /ẽ/ or /ɛ̃/ (this vowel varies locally in its realization); cf. Lieu-Saint-Amand [ʃɛ̃kẽt] 'fifty', [vẽ] 'wind', [sɛ̃] 'blood' < *CĪNQUAGĬNTA VĔNTUM SĂNGUINEM (*ALF*, pt. 272; Flutre 1977: 23).

5.2.4.   LOWERING OF HIGH NASAL VOWELS

A pattern of high nasal vowel lowering comparable to that seen in the standard variety is found in many parts of the *langue d'oïl* region, although it is not universal. High nasal vowels have been preserved in a number of peripheral areas, reflecting doubtless a geographically more widespread arrangement in earlier periods which was increasingly undermined by the influence of the standard variety based in the centre of the *langue d'oïl* region.

5.2.4.1.   *Lowering of* [ũ] *and* [ỹ] (< [ũ])

As regards the reflex of original [ũ], in most areas where fronting occurred the resulting nasal allophone [ỹ] has taken on a lower target articulation in context (i) and (ii) forms (i.e. where [ỹ] was followed by a tautosyllabic nasal consonant). The adoption of the lowered pronunciation is formally acknowledged for the standard language towards the end of the seventeenth century (cf. 4.3.3). But a high pronunciation [ỹ] continued to be used for some time in certain areas, and such a pronunciation is still found in modern times in peripheral dialect areas. The slower generalization of a lowered pronunciation of [ỹ] in Normandy is suggested by the observations of the Abbé de Saint-Pierre, who was a native of Lower Normandy. In his treatise on spelling published in 1730, he implies that a high pronunciation was still current in Normandy, although perhaps only as a hypercorrection (cf. the case of [ĩ] discussed below). More generally, the grammarian Dumas writing in 1733 states that 'l'*u* pur ne se trouve jamais nazal que dans la prononciation des Gascons et de certains provinciaus' (Thurot, ii. 545). Since the eighteenth century, the adoption of a lowered pronunciation of [ỹ] has been progressively generalized however. The only exceptions relate to now isolated areas in the east and south-east of the *langue d'oïl* region. For Romance dialects of the Moselle area, Zéliqzon (1924) reports [ĩ] as the general realization, as in [ʃɛkĩ lĩdi] 'each', 'Monday' < *CATA-QUISQUE-ŪNUM, LŪNAE-DIEM (= standard Fr. *chacun, lundi*). In Haute-Saône and northern parts of Doubs, a high rounded vowel [ỹ] is indicated for many dialects by Dondaine (1972: 280–3 and map 38).

Where early [ũ] remained unfronted, there has been regular lowering to [õ]. This is the case in the extreme north-east of our region, namely in eastern Wallonia, where ŪNUM emerges widely as [õ] (art.) or [õk] (numeral) and LŪNAE-DIEM as [lõdi] 'Monday', and also in the extreme south-east, in the Franco-Provençal area ([lõdi], [brõ] < Germ. brūn). Non-lowered forms, such as [lũdi] / [dəlũ] < LUNAE-DIEM/DIEM-LUNAE, are reported in a small number of isolated areas in the Vosges, Haute-Savoie, Doubs, and Valais, i.e. parts of the south-east and the extreme east (*ALF,* map 787 *lundi*).

In areas where [ũ] passed to [ỹ], widespread raising of the mid back vowel [õ] evidently occurred in the *langue d'oïl* region. The result was a new high back vowel [ũ]. The adoption of a lowered, mid realization as the norm for this vowel in the standard variety (cf. 4.3.3) encouraged a comparable development elsewhere in the *langue d'oïl* region, but the use of a high pronunciation [ũ] was still far from rare in the eighteenth century (cf. Dumas 1733) 'Bien des gens prononcent en *oun* la nasale *on* des mots *pont, son, mon, ton,* etc.' (Thurot, ii. 513) but by then it was clearly associated with provincialism (cf. 4.3.3). In modern times, it is reported only in peripheral areas, notably in northern Manche, Normandy [bũ] < BŎNUM (*ALN* 232), and in occasional varieties of Franche-Comté, e.g. Damprichard (Doubs) [bũː ɛˈmũː reːˈzũː] < BŎNUM AD-MŎNTEM RATIŌNEM 'good (m. sg.), uphill, reason' (Grammont 1892–8). In the latter case, it is notable that Dondaine (1972) only reports the appearance of mid nasal vowels in the reflexes of such forms in the Franche-Comté, suggesting that the last traces of an earlier [ũ] may now have been lost.

In context (iii) forms, in the standard language and central varieties of the *langue d'oïl* region a lowered pronunciation has not developed or at least become established. Instead, fronted [ỹ] has typically undergone denasalization to give [y], as in *lune*. However, in the outer ring of territory surrounding the centre a lowered pronunciation has become widely established, with or without subsequent denasalization (see Map 3). Such a distribution points to the adoption of a high tongue position [y] in reflexes of LŪNA, PLŪMA, etc. as being a feature which originated in the centre and then radiated out from its likely source, Paris. Also noteworthy is the fact that a lowered pronunciation [ø] or [œ], rather than [y], has been adopted more widely before /m/ than before /n/, perhaps as a result of a dissimilatory tendency to avoid a sequence of two highly labialized segments. Finally, demonstrating the complexity of competing tendencies in individual dialect areas there are cases where a lowered pronunciation in context (iii) forms has established itself even though a high vowel [ỹ] has been preserved in context (i) and (ii) forms. Thus, in the Romance dialects of the Moselle we find [lœn fɔrtœn] 'moon, fortune' < LŪNA FORTŪNA, where lowering has clearly occurred despite the non-lowering of [ỹ] in other contexts (see examples above). This pattern of evolution is therefore the precise converse of that found in modern standard French, yielding alternations such as [i] (= standard Fr. *un*) vs. [œn] (= standard Fr. *une*) for the indefinite article in the dialects of Messin and Nied (Zéliqzon 1924).

A high back vowel has likewise been widely preserved in non-central varieties as the reflex of [ũ] which developed from nasalized /o/ and /ɔ/ in context (iii) forms. This is particularly true for the west and north-west and the east and south-east of the *langue d'oïl* region. For example: (Normandy) northern Manche, northern Calvados [pũm pum] < PŌMA 'apple' (*ALN* 231) and (Jersey) [pum um dun sun] < PŌMA HŎMINEM DŌNAT SŎNAT (Spence 1960); (Burgundy) [bun parsun] < BŎNA PERSŌNA widely in Nièvre (*ALB*, iii. 1708, 1749).

5.2.4.2. *Lowering of* [ĩ]

Turning to the remaining high vowel [ĩ], we find that this has very generally lowered to become a mid vowel in contexts (i) and (ii). In the standard language, a mid articulation had become established as the norm by the seventeenth century (cf. 4.3.3). But a high realization [ĩ] remained in widespread use, albeit as a 'provincialism'. The Parisian Claude Lancelot, writing in 1663, notes this pronunciation as characteristic of various regions including Normandy (Thurot, ii. 480). The relevant passage runs:

[Dans certaines provinces de France] comme entr'autres la Normandie, . . . gardant autant qu'ils peuvent le son naturel de l'*i*, lors même qu'il est joint avec une *n* qui finit la syllabe, comme en *vin*, *fin*, *devin* (ce qui est très-mauvaise prononciation), ils s'imaginent que ces mots ne peuvent pas rimer avec ceux en *ain* et *ein*, et se fondent même sur cette mauvaise raison, qu'on ne doit pas dire *cousin*, comme si c'étoit *cousain*, parce que c'est très mal prononcer de dire *cousine*, comme si on écrivoit *cousaine*, ne prenant pas garde que dans ce dernier mot l'*n* ne fait rien à la prononciation de l'*i*, parce qu'elle commence une nouvelle syllabe.

The text suggests in fact that Lancelot may well have been talking of a hypercorrect pronunciation style adopted by certain Norman speakers of the standard language. It is unclear to what extent the vowel [ĩ] was still used in the local Norman dialects of the time, but the implication is that by the mid-seventeenth century lowering of [ĩ] in all types of nasalizing context was well underway in most Norman varieties, i.e. in the local dialects and in the *français régional* of Normandy. But as lowering in context type (iii) was by now judged as being definitely sub-standard, the socially aware provincial (and there were many such from Normandy) may well have hypercorrected and substituted [ĩ] for [ẽ] not only in *cousine* but also in *cousin*, spelling influence being a powerful factor too. This finds some parallel in the characteristic use in Normandy of the high back vowel [ũ] in forms like *bonne* (cf. above).

Subsequently, a high articulation has only been preserved in peripheral areas, especially in the far east of the *langue d'oïl* region. In a compact zone incorporating eastern Vosges and northern Franche-Comté, [ĩ] has remained in context (i) and (ii) forms (cf. *ALF* 289, 339, 881, 1411 *cinq, cousin, moulin, voisin*). A high vowel [ĩ] is also noted for the reflex of the context (i) form *CĪNQUE for three points in Brittany (*ALF* 453, 463, 484) and three points in Valais in Switzerland (983, 987, 988) but not for context (ii) forms.

In context (iii) forms, just as [ỹ] lowered in certain outlying areas and has remained a mid vowel, so too [ĩ] has lowered to emerge as [ẽ] or [ɛ̃] which may subsequently denasalize (see Map 3). Finally, we may note that the Romance dialects of the Moselle show the same pattern for the evolution of [ĩ] as for [ỹ] (see above), with lowering in context (iii) but a high vowel in contexts (i) and (ii) directly reversing the standard French arrangement, e.g. [fɛrɛn kɔzɛn] 'flour, female cousin' (= standard Fr. *farine, cousine*) as against [sĩk kɔzĩ] 'five, male cousin' (= standard Fr. *cinq, cousin*) (Zéliqzon 1924).

5.2.5. MODIFICATION OF [ẽ] > [ɔ̃] AND [ẽĩ] > [ɔ̃ĩ]

In western and eastern parts of the *langue d'oïl* area, the Late Latin high-mid front oral vowel /e/ developed in distinct ways in stressed syllables. In blocked syllables, it remained a mid front vowel in the West, although from the twelfth century it tended to lower to a low-mid quality [ɛ] in a change originating in the northern area (cf. 4.3.2.1). In eastern and south-eastern dialects however, it was retracted to become a low-mid back vowel:

$$
\text{blocked} \quad e \;
\begin{cases}
\; e \;>\; \varepsilon & \text{(west/centre)} \\
\; \mathfrak{o} & \text{(east/south-east)}
\end{cases}
$$

In stressed free syllables, two comparable patterns present themselves:

$$
\text{free} \quad e\text{ː} \;>\; ei
\begin{cases}
\; \varepsilon i \;>\; \varepsilon\text{ː} & \text{(west)} \\
\; \mathfrak{o}i & \text{(east)}
\end{cases}
$$

The development [ei] to [ɔi] is attested by the mid-twelfth century, and is clearly bound up directly with the evolution found in blocked syllables.

In the central area of the *langue d'oïl* region, the fate of original /e/ is complex. The change [e] > [ɔ] did not operate, but [ei] > [ɔi] did gain acceptance, notably in the Francien dialect (Haudricourt 1948).

Looking more specifically at the nasalized allophones, we find that the dialects of the east and south-east show a pattern of change in line with that of oral vowels:

free   ẽĩ > ɔ̃ĩ
blocked   (ẽ ɛ̃ via regular merger >)   ẽ > ɔ̃

The vowel [ɔ̃] subsequently gave a short low-mid or low back vowel. Its shortness evidently compromised its nasality, for in certain varieties where structural conditions were appropriate it later denasalized.

As regards the nasal diphthong, the form [ɔ̃ĩ] is already indicated in the Walloon *Poème moral*, which dates from about 1200, where such forms as *poine* < POENA are found (Remacle 1948: 56). In his extensive analysis of Old French literary texts, Dees (1987) finds the graphy <oi> used in 33% of cases for the various forms of *plein* in texts deriving from Franche-Comté in the south-east, whereas other areas almost uniformly offer <ei> or <ai>. The fourteenth-century *Psautier lorrain* offers *moinnes, poinne* < MĬNAS POENA (Pope 1952: § 322, xix).

The geographical incidence of the retraction of the initial element of the diphthong /ei/ appears to have been significantly less for the nasal allophone [ẽĩ] than for the oral [ei]. Central areas have systematically adopted the 'western' solution of levelling for nasal [ẽĩ], although oral [ei] regularly gave [ɔi], hence [plẽ] [pɛn] < PLĒNUM POENA in the standard language. Also, some eastern areas have failed to generalize the retraction of nasal [ẽĩ]. Noting that the forms showing [ẽĩ] > [ɔ̃ĩ] in dialects of Lorraine typically have a labial consonant preceding the nasalized diphthong (cf. the examples above), Meyer-Lübke (1890: § 92) thought it likely that this change may only ever have occurred regularly after a labial consonant. However, in Burgundy the scope of the change evidently included contexts where non-labial consonants preceded, though this may reflect a later generalization of the rule of retraction. Modern forms showing this include [rwẽ] < RĒNES 'small of back', recorded in the *ALF* in a band of territory running from southern Côtes-d'Or and northern Saône-et-Loire across eastwards to south-western Haute-Saône and north-western Doubs (map 1142, pts. 7, 8, 12, 14, 16, 25, 43, 44, 106), and [etwẽ] (< *esteint*) < EXTĬNGUIT '(he/she) extinguishes' (*ALB*, iii. 1459) which is reported for a number of varieties in southern Côtes-d'Or and northern Saône-et-Loire.

The effect of the retraction of [ẽ] in eastern dialects has been considerable. It gave rise to a variety of later developments affecting the mid front and mid back vowels as the nasal vowel system was restructured. A specific instance of such restructuring may be seen in the historical sketch of the dialect of Damprichard appearing in 5.3.2.

5.2.6. DENASALIZATION OF NASAL VOWELS

In central varieties including the standard language, denasalization has uniformly occurred in the conditioned nasal vowels of context (iii) forms (cf. 4.3.10 above), and this pattern has evidently exerted considerable influence on non-central varieties of the *langue d'oïl* region over the past two or three centuries. However, cases are still to be found where high levels of nasality have been preserved in such vowels.

In the south-west and west, conditioned nasal vowels have generally denasalized in Maine, Anjou and Romance-speaking Brittany, but in the areas abutting the Breton-speaking zone nasality has been preserved (*LRL*, v. 1. 624). Likewise, in the more peripheral areas of Normandy, notably in the Cotentin peninsula, western Calvados, and western Seine-Maritime, and also in the north of the *langue d'oïl* region, in Picardy, denasalization has commonly failed to occur. It is notable that Picardy and, especially, Normandy are precisely the areas identified by grammarians of the seventeenth century as standing out in the (typically censured) use of nasal vowels in context (iii) forms in their regional accent (cf. Thurot, ii. esp. 521–4).[5]

In the east and south-east, denasalization has occurred but often only incompletely and with a fair degree of local variation. In many varieties, tongue position has conditioned whether or not a given nasal vowel type has denasalized, and lexical diffusion is also in evidence in the denasalization process. Thus, for example, at the end of the last century the Lorraine dialect of Tannois showed denasalization in SPĪNA > [ɛpɛn] 'thorn' and PŌMA > [pym] 'apple' (with the denasalized vowel reportedly showing considerable shortening of its duration) but not in LŪNA > [lœ̃n] 'moon', POENA > [pwɛ̃n] 'suffering', and LĀNA > [lɛ̃n] 'wool' (Horning 1890).

In varieties where nasal vowels have regularly undergone lowering, the sustained presence of nasality in the vowels of context (iii) forms ensured that these too were lowered and they have usually preserved a lowered tongue position. Hence, in Normandy, such items as PŌMA RADIC-ĪNA LŪNA emerge widely as [põm/pũm raʃɛ̃n lœ̃n] 'apple, root, moon' (cf. *ALN*, maps 231, 532, 537), whilst in Picardy the corresponding forms commonly encountered are [põm/pœ̃m/pɛ̃m raʃɛ̃n/raʃɛ̃ɲ lœ̃n/lɛ̃n] (Flutre 1977: 32, 45, 57). In varieties where the nasal vowels denasalized in more recent times, the lowered tongue position has commonly been preserved, e.g. [lœn raʃɛn] in the Val de Saire (Manche) in Normandy[6] (cf. Lepelley 1974), and in scattered Picard varieties forms such as [pɛm pœm pɔm] are also found (*ALPic*, i, map 265).

In some parts of the *langue d'oïl* area, the process of denasalization has been extended to *unconditioned* nasal vowels as well. In a number of eastern and south-eastern varieties, the vowel [ɔ̃] in particular (deriving from earlier [ẽ]) has denasalized to [ɔ] (Meyer-Lübke 1890: § 91; Haudricourt 1948). This development was perhaps promoted in part by the fact that the vowel was short and hence its nasality was perceptually less secure.

However, in varieties lying on the eastern periphery of the *langue d'oïl*, denasalization has sometimes operated in a more general way on the nasal vowel system. The proximity of the region affected to Germanic-speaking areas where nasal vowels do not occur is suggestive. Mainly on the basis of data drawn from the *ALF*, Lahti (1953) identifies four focal areas of denasalization situated in a sweep of territory running from Liège down to Neuchâtel. These are: north-western Wallonia; south-eastern Wallonia and northern Lorraine; the eastern half of the *département* of Vosges; and a small area in Switzerland close to Neuchâtel. However, denasalization in these areas is not uniform, the data indicating that it has operated preferentially in word-final position or when the vowel concerned preceded a coronal consonant. Also, Lahti concludes that the low vowel /ã/ is more generally susceptible to denasalization than other vowel types.

As far as Wallonia is concerned, the *ALW* provides confirmation of denasalization in the extreme north-west and north-east and especially in the south-east zone (Luxembourg). Thus, from Saint-Vincent [savinsaː] (pt. 18 of the *arrondissement* of Virton) we have [pe sɛd dɛt mɛtʃ] 'bread, ash, tooth, sleeve' with full denasalization. However, there may be a nasal consonantal offglide in some items [rygɛŋ sɛŋk] 'aftermath (= standard Fr. *regain*), five', and in forms originally containing the back vowel [õ] a nasal vowel is still preserved, e.g. [maːzã pɛʃã] 'house, fish'. Denasalization here is therefore still in progress.

Finally, in another peripheral area, the Vendée in the south-west of the *langue d'oïl* region, a rather special case of denasalization is found. In the dialects of this area, three nasal vowels /ẽ ã õ/ have developed, and denasalization has operated on them according to two separate criteria—the nature of the nasal vowel and the phonological environment in which the vowel appears. Thus, only the mid nasal vowel types /ẽ õ/ have been affected, but not the low vowel /ã/. Furthermore, although these mid vowels are denasalized in most environments to become sequences of oral vowel + nasal consonant, they do not undergo denasalization if they are phrasally unstressed (i.e. not phrase-final) and followed by a consonant. Hence: [do van] 'wine' vs. [do vẽ roʒ] 'red wine'; [la mezaŋ] 'the house' vs. [la mezõ blãʃ] 'the white house', as against [tʃẽz ã] 'fifteen years' (Svenson 1959). The vowel-quality alternation is evidently part of a fairly recent development which systematically affects all mid vowels, nasal and oral. The denasalization of previously nasal vowels and the re-establishment of distinct nasal consonants [n] and [ŋ] for the vowels [ẽ] and [õ], respectively, is striking (Morin 1977).

5.2.7. LENGTH

The relationship between length and nasal vowels is a complex one. Unfortunately, descriptions of nasal vowels in *langue d'oïl* varieties of the past and, very frequently, of the present as well do not clearly indicate whether a given vowel was, or is, phonetically or phonemically long. However, at times it is possible to glean reliable information and detect certain patterns of evolution at work.

First, there seem to be no cases where distinctive length variation has arisen in nasal vowels when no such contrast was found with oral vowels. Secondly, where the distinctive use of quantity did arise, it appears generally to have lost ground in favour of quality distinctions. As a result, few instances of dialects with contrasting long/short nasal vowels are to be found today.

One area notable for preserving contrastive vowel length has been Normandy. Many varieties here continue systematically to use vowel length variation for morphological purposes to mark number and gender distinctions, long vowels signalling plurality or feminine gender. For the nasal vowel series, length serves principally to mark the number distinction. Only occasionally does length mark gender, since masculine forms ending in a nasal vowel usually have a feminine counterpart containing a nasal consonant, e.g. [bwõ] vs. [bwon] 'good (m.)/(f.)'. Examples showing distinctive vowel length in nasal vowels may be cited from the dialect of Val de Saire:

Singular	Plural	
rjĩ	rjĩ:	'thing/thing'
pʎẽ	pʎẽ:	'full (m. sg.)/(m. pl.)
vã	vã:	'wind/winds'
mã	mã:	'hand/hands'
bwõ	bwõ:	'good (m. sg.)/(m. pl.)'
ʃikœ̃	bjidzœ̃:	'each one/many people'
		(= St. Fr. *chacun/bien des uns*)
Masculine	*Feminine*	
amẽ	amẽ:	'friend (m. sg.)/(f. sg.)'
		(Lepelley 1974)

The pattern of length variation seen here can be overridden. Occasionally, grammatically singular words are found with a long vowel, especially those deriving from forms with original final /−s/, e.g. [mã:] 'less' < MĬNUS vs. [mã] 'hand' < MĀNUM, and [tã:] 'time' < TĔMPUS vs. [vã ʃã] 'wind, hundred'. Long nasal vowels also appear where originally there had been a verbal inflexional /−t/ irrespective of the number value of the verb form, e.g. [põ:] '(it) lays' < PŌNIT and [sõ:] '(they) are' < SŬNT. Such forms thus create further surface contrasts or near-contrasts unrelated to the number distinction, cf. also [vjĭː] '(he/she) comes' < VĔNIT vs. [bjĭ] 'well' < BĔNE.

5.3. Nasal Vowel Evolution in Selected Non-Standard *langue d'oïl* Dialects

To complement the general presentation of nasal vowel evolution in the *langue d'oïl* region, a brief outline of developments in three non-standard varieties will be given. All varieties are found in peripheral areas, where influence from the prestigious norm language of the centre has been limited until more recent times. They thus provide some insight into other, competing patterns of nasal vowel evolution in the *langue d'oïl* region beside that shown by the standard language.

5.3.1. NORTH-WEST: VAL DE SAIRE (NORMANDY)

The Val de Saire lies in the Cotentin peninsula, in the north-east of the *département* of Manche. The source of data is Lepelley (1974).

Present-day pattern

Nasal vowel system

ẽː ẽ			õː õ
œ̃ː œ̃			
ãː ã	ɑ̃ː ɑ̃		

Oral vowel system

iː i	yː y		uː u
eː e	øː ø		oː o
Eː E	Œː Œ		
ɛː ɛ	œː œ	ɔ	
	aː a	ɑː	

Notes

(*a*) Despite the lack of a series of high vowels, the stock of nasal vowel phonemes is substantial, although it is still much smaller than the set of oral vowels.

(*b*) Contrastive vowel length is found at the lexical level. However, its main role is morphophonemic, additional vowel length serving to indicate plurality or feminine gender in nominals.

(*c*) Nasal monophthongs may be accompanied by glides. The two types with off-glides [ẽᵃ] and [ẽʲ], as in [grẽᵃ] 'big' and [ʃẽʲ] 'six', are evidently interpreted by native speakers as phonemic units. Nasal vowels with on-glides are treated as clusters.

(*d*) /ē/ has the variant [ī] when preceded by the glide [j], as in [bjī] 'well'.

(*e*) For want of more appropriate symbols, the distinctive mid oral vowels are transcribed with small capitals. Of these, the short front vowel /œ/ is of limited distribution; it occurs only before nasal consonants, as in [lœn] 'moon'. In fact, /œ/ is the only front rounded vowel type to be found before nasal consonants, with the sole exception of the feminine singular determiner which contains a high front rounded vowel [yn] 'a', but the corresponding numeral is [jœn] 'one (f.)'.

Evolution of Nasal Vowel Types
The following samples may be cited:

		context (i)		context (ii)		context (iii)	
Late Latin							
i	*CĪNQUE	> ʃēʲ	CAMĪNUM	> kmē	SPĪNA	> epEn
	QUĪNDECIM	> tʃēːz				
e	PRĒNDERE	> prãːr	FĒNUM	> fã	AVĒNA	> avEn
	PĬNGERE	> pēʲr			FĒMINA	> fɔm
ɛ	CĔNTUM	> ʃã	BĔNE	> bjī	MĔUM + -A	> mjen (f. sg.)
a	QUĂNDO	> kēᵃ	FĀMEM	> fã	LĀNA	> lɔn
	GĂMBA	> gēᵃb	CĂNEM	> tʃjī	CĂNNA	> kɔn
ɔ	RESPŎND(E)O	> repõː	BŎNUM	> bwõ	BŎNA	> bwɔn
	LŎNGE	> lwã			HŎMINEM	> ɔ̃m
o	SŬNT	> sõː	CARBŌNEM	> cerbõ	PŌMA	> põm
u	*TŪMBAT	> tœːb	ŪNUM	> jœ̃ (numeral)	LŪNA	> lœn
				> yː (det.)		

Notes
(*a*) Nasalized /u/ fronted to give [ỹ] and then both this vowel and the other high front vowel [ī] underwent lowering in all contexts. The nasalized mid back vowel from /o/ and blocked /ɔ/, after probably raising to become a high vowel [ũ], also underwent lowering.

(*b*) In context (iii) forms, denasalization took place after high vowels had been lowered so that mid vowels have resulted. A weak but noticeable nasal quality is reported in the back vowel [ɔ̃] (< [ũ])

(*c*) Lowered [ẽ] < [ī] has remained distinct from the previously existing nasal mid vowel [ẽ] except in forms like [pēʲr] where the presence of a following palatal caused raising of the stressed vowel. The latter, chronologically earlier type of [ẽ] lowered to [ã], as in [ʃã]. However, it did not merge with the [ã] which already existed, since this had itself lengthened in the context (i) forms in which it appeared and had become a diphthong [ẽᵃ]. Thus, the original three-way distinction is preserved.

(*d*) Original nasalized [ẽ] and [ã] in free syllables appear to have yielded [ẽĩ] [ãĩ], respectively, which then monophthongized and eventually merged as [ɑ̃]. In context (iii) forms, monophthongization and denasalization occurred, but not merger. In context (i) as well there was no merger. Original [ã] evidently acquired extra length to give [ã:] which later developed into a nasal diphthong. Original [ẽ] has lowered to [ã] but remained relatively short; consequently it has never diphthongized. This length distinction is also attested in medieval Anglo-Norman (cf. 4.3.10).

5.3.2. SOUTH-EAST: DAMPRICHARD (FRANCHE-COMTÉ)

Damprichard lies in the far north-east of the *département* of Doubs in the Franche-Comté. The source of our data is the study by Grammont (1892, 1894, 1898).

Late nineteenth-century pattern

Nasal vowel system

$$\begin{array}{ccc} \tilde{\text{ı}}\text{:} & \tilde{\text{y}}\text{:} & \tilde{\text{u}}\text{:} \\ \tilde{\varepsilon}\text{:} \ (\tilde{\varepsilon}) & & \tilde{\text{o}} \end{array}$$

Oral vowel system

$$\begin{array}{cccc} \text{i: i} & \text{y: y} & & \text{u: u} \\ \text{e: e} & \text{ø:} & & \text{o: o} \\ \varepsilon\text{:}\ \varepsilon & & \text{œ} & \text{ɔ: ɔ} \\ & & \text{a: a} \end{array}$$

Notes

(*a*) The nasal vowel system is much reduced compared to the oral vowel system. The length contrast is marginal in the former, and there are fewer qualitative distinctions. The absence of a low nasal vowel type is not characteristic of all dialects of the region. In the dialect of Naisey, situated some 35 miles to the west, both /ã:/ and /ã/ are found as in [tã:] 'so much' and [tã] 'time' (Alex 1965).

(*b*) Nasal vowels are typically realized long. The short vowel /ɛ̃/ appears in isolated lexical items only, notably in [bɛ̃] 'bath' (vs. [pɛ̃:] 'bread'). The other short vowel, namely /õ/, is widely represented however, e.g. [tõ] 'time', [võ] 'winnowing sieve'.

(*c*) Preceding a nasal consonant, only certain types of nasal vowel are found. These are [ĩ: ɛ̃: ỹ:].

Evolution of Nasal Vowel Types
The following samples may be cited:

	context (i)		context (ii)		context (iii)	
Late Latin						
i	*CĪNQUE	> sī:	FĪNUM	> fī:	FĪNA	> fī:n
	QUĪNDECIM	> kī:z			RADICĪNA	> resɛn
e	ĪNDE	> õ	PLĒNUM	> pjũ:	AVĒNA	> avwɔn
					FĒMINA	> fɔn
ɛ	DĔNTEM	> dõ	BĔNE	> bī:		
	TĔMPUS	> tõ	VĔNIT	> vī:		
a	TĂNTUM	> tɛ̃:	FĀMEM	> fɛ̃:	PLĀNA	> pjɛ̃:n
	CĂMPUM	> tʃɛ̃:	CĂNEM	> tʃī:	PĂNNA	> pɔn
			VĂNNUM	> võ		
ɔ	AD-MŎNTEM	> ɛmũ:	BŎNUM	> bũ:	BŎNA	> bwɔn
					HŎMINEM	> ɔm
o	PLŬMBUM	> pjũ:	CARBŌNEM	> tʃɛrbũ:	PŌMA	> pum
u			ŪNUM	> ỹ: (numeral)	PRŪNA	> prỹ:n
				> ī: (det.)		
			brūn	> brỹ:	brūn-a	> brỹ:n

Notes

(*a*) The added length of nasal vowels doubtless arose through compensatory lengthening when the conditioning nasal consonant was deleted. The only exception is the back vowel /õ/. This derives from original high-mid /e/ which retracted to give a mid back vowel, as is regular in eastern dialects. The vowel remained short in context (i) and, like all denasalized vowels, it is short in context (iii). In context (ii) (where the stressed vowel was long), the resulting nasalized vowel evidently preserved its length and merged with the existing long mid back [õ:] vowel deriving from nasalized /o ɔ/ and this later raised to give /ũ:/.

(*b*) The low vowel /a/ in all nasalizing contexts fronted to give [ɛ̃(:)], this being part of a general fronting development which affected oral /a/ also. Subsequently, however, *oral* [ɛ:] < stressed free /a/ lowered again to give [a:] (cf. Dondaine 1972: 227–32, 261–70), but not its nasal counterpart.

(*c*) Exceptionally, /a/ before a geminate nasal did not front but retracted to become a short back vowel [õ] which merged with [õ] < blocked /e/. The development of [bɛ̃] < BĂLNEUM 'bath' is notable. As it stood before a geminate, the stressed vowel remained short but the palatality of the nasal caused the vowel to front.

(*d*) In those context (iii) forms where denasalization has not taken place, analogical influence has probably been at work, e.g. [fī:n] and [brỹ:n] have been remodelled on the basis of their corresponding masculine forms.

5.3.3. NORTH-EAST: OREYE (WALLOON)

Oreye is a village lying 19 km. north-west of Liège in Belgium. The sources used are Warnant (1956) and *ALW*, pt. W13.

Present-day pattern
Nasal vowel system

$$\tilde{\varepsilon}\mathrm{ː}\quad \tilde{œ}\mathrm{ː}\quad \tilde{\mathrm{a}}\mathrm{ː}$$

Nasal vowels are always realized phonetically long. Of these vowels, the front rounded type [œ̃ː] only occurs in two lexical items drawn from standard French, one of which however is of high frequency, namely [dʒœ̃ː] 'June' < IŪNIUM. Even so, it is clear that this variety of Walloon has been moving towards the establishment of a two-way nasal vowel system.

Oral vowel system

iː yː		uː		i y		u
eː øː	oː					
εː				ε œ		ɔ
	aː ɑː				a	

Evolution of Nasal Vowel Types
The following samples may be cited:

	context (i)			context (ii)			context (iii)		
Late Latin									
i	*CĪNQUE	>	sɛɲk	SAPPĪNUM	>	sapɛɲ	COQUĪNA	>	kuhɛn
	QUĪNDECIM	>	kwɛ̃ːs						
e	CĪNGULA	>	sɛ̃ːk	PLĒNUM	>	plɛ̃ː	AVĒNA	>	awɛn
	INSĬMUL	>	ɛsɑ̃ːn				VĒNA	>	voːn
ε	DĔNTEM	>	dɛ̃ː	BĔNE	>	bɛɲ			
	TĔMPUS	>	tɛ̃ː						
a	PLĂNTA	>	plɑ̃ːt	FĀMEM	>	fɛ̃ː	BĂLNEUM	>	baɲ
	blank	>	blɑ̃ː	MĂNUM	>	mɛ̃ː			
ɔ	LŎNGUM	>	lɑ̃ː	BŎNUM	>	bɑ̃ː	BŎNA	>	bɔn
o	ŬNDECIM	>	ɑ̃ːs	PISCIŌNEM	>	pɛhɑ̃ː	PŌMA	>	pɔm
	PŬNCTA	>	pwɛ̃ːt						
u				ŪNUM	>	ɑ̃ːk	LŪNA	>	lœn
							ŪNA	>	œn

Notes

(*a*) As in all northern *langue d'oïl* dialects, original [ẽ] < nasalized blocked /e/ and /ε/ (i.e. in context (i) forms) has not merged with [ã] < nasalized blocked /a/. It remained a front mid vowel with which the high nasal vowel [ĩ] later came to merge when it underwent lowering. The nasalized reflexes of

free /e/ and /a/ in context (ii) forms have also come to provide a further
source of this mid front nasal vowel.

(*b*) Parallel with the simplification of front vowels, the back vowels have
coalesced into just one reflex, /ɑ̃ː/.

(*c*) The nasal allophones of original /u/ have developed differently according
to context type. Before a tautosyllabic nasal consonant, [u] has not fronted, cf.
[ɑ̃ːk] 'one' < ŪNUM and [ʃaskɑ̃ːk] 'each one' < *CATA-QUISQUE-ŪNUM.
But before a heterosyllabic nasal, nasality was evidently less intense and fronting
did take place.

(*d*) Denasalization has occurred in context (iii) forms, but only after lowering
had taken place with originally high nasalized vowels. Denasalization has also
occurred in other context types when the high vowel [i] preceded [n], unless a
continuant followed the nasal. The vowel palatalized the nasal before undergoing regular lowering and later denasalizing.

(*e*) The form [ɛsɑ̃ːn] 'together' < INSĪMUL is doubly noteworthy. The
denasalization of the vowel of the prefix IN- reflects a widespread development
in Walloon dialects going back to medieval times (cf. *ALW*, i, map 34 and
Remacle 1948: 56–8). The quality of the stressed vowel reflects the existence of
variants containing [ẽ] or [æ̃]/[ɑ̃] for this and other items during the medieval
period, cf. 4.3.2.1 above. In medieval literary texts from Picardy and Hainaut,
the graphy <a> is exclusively used for this word (cf. Dees 1987, map 487).
Evidently, the variant with a low vowel [ɑ̃] was generally adopted in the
Walloon dialect, although the variant [ẽ] was adopted for certain lexical items,
e.g. in [tẽ̞ː] 'time' < TĚMPUS.[7]

(*f*) In context (i) and (ii) forms which contained the high vowel [ĩ] (from
nasalized /i/ and nasalized free /ɛ/ via [jẽ] > [jĩ]), the conditioning nasal
consonant underwent regular weakening but at some stage it was palatalized by
the high front preceding vowel. The effect was to strengthen the consonant and
to block its deletion. This in turn triggered the same denasalization as in
context (iii) forms. The only exception came when the nasal consonant was
followed by a continuant consonant. In this context the deletion of the nasal
consonant was hastened and completed at a stage before the palatalization
development got underway. Thus, there emerged [sɛɲk] 'five' but [kwẽ̞ːs]
'fifteen'.

5.4.   Franco-Provençal

To the south-east of the *langue d'oïl* region lies the Franco-Provençal speech
area. This is a dialectal complex forming a transitional zone between the *langue
d'oïl* and the *langue d'oc* areas. There is no standard variety, partly because there
has never been political unity in the zone and partly because the major cities

which might have established a norm variety opted for cultural reasons to go over to the use of standard French as their official language. Already in the thirteenth century, Lyon was adopting French for juridical and administrative purposes and a similar abandonment of the native Romance variety occurred a little later in Geneva, where the use of the original patois was formally forbidden in schools in 1668.

Although the surviving varieties of Franco-Provençal are spoken by fewer than 200,000 people (Martin 1990), they show a great deal of variation. But as far as vowel nasalization is concerned, some common points emerge.

(*a*) Vowel nasalization has been intense in all dialects with the creation of unconditioned nasal vowels in at least some contexts. However, in those cases where the conditioning consonant was deleted, it is unclear at what stage the deletion took place. It seems likely that the original weakening of the conditioning coda nasal and the accompanying heightened vowel nasalization were native developments, but full deletion of the nasal consonant and the consequent creation of nasal vowel phonemes in contexts (i) and (ii) could well have been prompted by influence from French.

(*b*) In context (iii) forms, some dialects show major weakening of original simplex -N- and it may be assumed that this was associated with high-level vowel nasalization. In Franco-Provençal dialects of France, one result of the consonant weakening has been the sporadic appearance of rhotacism, with [r] emerging from what had earlier been a nasal tap [r̃] < [n] (cf. a parallel in Romanian, 12.2.4). Examples are ['snera lra e'pra] 'week, moon, thorn' < SEPTIMĀNA LŪNA SPĪNA in the dialect of Ville-du-Pont (south-eastern Doubs) and [sə'mara 'bora 'lyra e'pira] < SEPTIMĀNA BŎNA LŪNA SPĪNA at Le Rivier d'Allemont in north-eastern Isère (*ALJA*, pts. 1 and 80, respectively) where vowel denasalization has taken place. Comparable rhotacized forms are reported for the dialect of Briançon and nearby villages in northern Hautes-Alpes (Ronjat, ii. § 298). Weakening has led to deletion of the conditioning nasal and the establishment of phonemically nasal vowels in the dialect of Valezan in north-eastern Savoie (*ALJA*, pt. 52), as in ['snãa 'bõa a'vẽa e'pẽa sa'kõẹ] 'week, good (f. sg.), oats, thorn, each one (f. sg.)' < SEPTIMĀNA BŎNA AVĒNA SPĪNA *CATA-QUISQUE-ŪNA.

Across the political border into north-western Italy, parallel cases of weakening and ultimately deletion of -N- with associated vowel nasalization are also found in context (iii) forms, although not usually involving rhotacism (cf. Tuttle 1991: 39 and 10.4.4 below). Full deletion of the conditioning nasal and the presence of nasal vowel phonemes are reported for Prali in the Val Germanasca, an area adjacent to the zone around Briançon which was noted above for weakening of the conditioning nasal (Genre 1992). Further north, in the Val d'Aosta, nasal consonant deletion has occurred in a number of dialects found in a broad sweep of territory extending from the Valtournanche in the north-east across to dialects of the west which abut the French area of north-eastern Savoie where dialects like that of Valezan also show deletion. Thus, in the Valtournanche we have forms such as ['speːa a'veːa 'lãa 'bãa 'brõa] 'thorn, oats, wool, good (f. sg.), brown (f. sg.)' < SPĪNA AVĒNA LĀNA BŎNA brūn-a, where denasalization has later operated on front unrounded vowels (data from Merlo 1934, cited in Tuttle 1991: 40 n. 44). In the western area, the dialect of Maisonasse in Valsavarenche shows ['ɛpẽa a'vẽ͡ja 'lãa 'bõa] < SPĪNA AVĒNA LĀNA BŎNA (data from Walser 1939, cited in Tuttle 1991: 39), and at Rhême-St.-Georges forms such as ['ɛpẽːa 'tsẽːa lãː 'būːɔ] < SPĪNA CATĒNA LĀNA BŎNA are reported (*ALF,* pt. 121). Further north, in Switzerland, comparable weakening leading to deletion of -N- and nasal vowel phoneme creation has not occurred.

(*c*) In the core area of Franco-Provençal, i.e. the Suisse Romande and the adjacent area in France, the fronting of /u/ > /y/ has normally failed to take place in nasalizing contexts (as in north-eastern dialects of the *langue d'oïl*), so that the reflex of Late Latin /u/ in such contexts has remained a back vowel. Furthermore, in almost all cases nasalized [ū] has undergone lowering to merge with the nasalized mid back vowels. In more peripheral Franco-Provençal dialects of Italy and France however, fronting of /u/ did take place in nasalizing contexts (see Map 2).

(*d*) Although vowel nasalization has arisen primarily as a result of regressive assimilation, there are other sources of nasalization in certain dialects. In the Suisse Romande dialect of Bagnes (see below), progressive assimilation has yielded nasal vowels in many lexical items, and in dialects of Ain in France there has been spontaneous nasalization whereby unstressed vowels occurring in absolute final position in phonetic phrases are nasalized (Duraffour 1932, and 5.2 above).

By way of illustration, two varieties of Franco-Provençal may be briefly considered from the wide range of surviving dialects.

5.4.1. BAGNES (VAUD, SUISSE ROMANDE)

The Bagnes valley lies in the south of the Suisse Romande. Its dialects have been studied by Cornu (1877) and again by Bjerrome (1957), thus providing some data for determining the dynamics of the speech of this area.

Present-day pattern

Nasal vowels

$$\tilde{e}^{\bar{\imath}}$$
$$\tilde{\varepsilon} \qquad \tilde{\mathfrak{o}}$$
$$\tilde{a}$$

Oral vowels

iː	yː	uː	ï	ü
eː	øː	oː	ë	ö
ɛː		ɔː		ɔ
	ɑː		a	

Notes

(*a*) Nasal vowels are typically realized with some movement of the tongue during their articulation. Usually, this involves the back of the tongue rising towards the velum and in absolute final position this can yield a weak velar nasal [ŋ] at the end of the articulation. There is no indication as to the length of the nasal vowels.

(*b*) The short high and high-mid oral vowels have a centralized realization.

Evolution of Nasal Vowel Types
The following examples may be taken:

	context (i)		context (ii)		context (iii)	
Late Latin						
i	*CĪNQUE	> ɬẽⁱ	VĪNUM	> vẽⁱ	COQUĪNA	> ku'zïa
			PRĪMUM	> prẽⁱ	PRĪMA	> 'prẽⁱma
e	VĒNDERE	> vẽdre	PLĒNUM	> prẽ	CATĒNA	> 'tseːna
			FĒNUM	> fẽ	FĒMINA	> 'fina
ɛ	TĔMPUS	> tẽ	BĔNE	> bẽⁱ		
	CĔNTUM	> ɬẽ	VĔNIT	> vẽⁱ		
a	QUĂNDO	> kã	FĀMEM	> fã	LĀNA	> 'laːna
	CĂMBA	> tsãba	CĂNEM	> tsẽⁱ	FLĂMMA	> ɬãma
			IOHĂNNEM	> dzjã	VANN-AT	> 'vaːne
ɔ	FRŎNTEM	> frõ	BŎNUM	> bõ	BŎNA	> 'boːna
					HŎMINEM	> 'omo
o	FŬNDUM	> fõ	PULMŌNEM	> pɔr'mõ	CORŌNA	> ku'röna
	ŬNGULA	> 'õla	NŌMEN	> nõ	-ŌNA	> -oːna
u			ŪNUM	> õ	LŪNA	> 'löna
			DIEM-LŪNAE	> dlõ	PLŪMA	> 'plõma

Notes

(*a*) The high back vowel remained unfronted in nasalizing contexts and later underwent lowering to merge with the reflexes of the two mid back vowels which themselves had previously merged. The result is that just one back nasal vowel phoneme remains, /õ/.

(*b*) The nasal vowel /ẽⁱ/ derives from an earlier high vowel /ĩ/ which Cornu (1877) still reported as the only reflex of original /i/ and free /ɛ/ (> /ie/) in nasalizing contexts. The change /ĩ/ > /ẽⁱ/ is thus a recent development which doubtless reflects French influence. A high vowel /ĩ/ is still preserved in some mountain villages of the Bagnes valley (Bjerrome 1957: 48).

(*c*) In context (iii) forms, high vowels preceding intervocalic -N- emerge short but non-high vowels regularly appear long. In both cases, the vowel is oral. The form [ku'röna] < CORŌNA is exceptional, cf. the adjectives [lo'rõ], fem. [lo'roːna] 'lively', [suː'lõ], fem. [suː'loːna] 'drunken'. However, before

/m/ a nasal vowel is usually found, cf. [ˈlẽᶦma ˈɫãma ˈplɔ̃me] < LĪMA FLĂMMA PLŪMAT.

(*d*) Progressive assimilation by a nasal consonant on a following stressed vowel is a common but not a regular development. Examples are [nẽᶦ ˈnɔ̃trë feˈnẽᶦtra droˈmẽᶦ aˈmẽᶦ mɔ̃ ˈmẽᶦgro] < NĪDUM/NŎCTEM, NŎSTRUM, FENĔSTRA, DORMĪRE, AMĪCUM, MŎLLEM, MĀGRUM 'nest/night, our, window, to sleep, friend, wet, thin'. However, these may be compared with [myː ˈmiːre ˈmile mo noː ne: nyː] < MŪRUM, MĀTREM, MĪLLE, MŎTTUM, NĀVEM, NĬGRUM, NŪDUM 'wall, mother, thousand, word, nave, black, naked', where no progressive nasalization has occurred.

5.4.2. DOMPIERRE (SUISSE ROMANDE)

Dompierre lies just to the south of Lake Neuchâtel in the northern part of the Suisse Romande and the vocalism of its dialect was described by Gauchat (1890). Given the similarities between this dialect and that of Bagnes, we may just highlight major points of interest.

(*a*) A three-way nasal vowel system has emerged in this dialect:

$$\tilde{\varepsilon} \qquad \tilde{\mathtt{ɔ}}$$
$$\tilde{\mathrm{a}}$$

In absolute word-final position /ã/ has the value [æ̃] and is so short that the nasality is not easily perceptible. The other nasal vowels are usually realized half-long with a closing off-glide (as with the dialect of Bagnes).

(*b*) Vowel nasalization is regular in context (i) and (ii) forms but in context (iii) the pattern of evolution is more complicated. Nasalization generally occurs before -M(M)-, as in [ˈlẽma ˈçãma ˈpçɔ̃ma] < LĪMA FLĂMMA PLŪMA. But before intervocalic -N-, two developments are found, depending upon the quality of the vowel. All back vowels and the front vowel /i/ give an oral vowel and the originally simplex -N- emerges as a geminate [nn], cf. [ˈtœnna ˈbunna ˈlunna] < TĪNA BŎNA LŪNA. In some words, there has also been a later stress-shift, [ˈkuːzənna ˈkuːrunna ˈfɔrtunna] < COQUĪNA CORŌNA FORTŪNA. With other types of vowel, nasality has been preserved and the nasal consonant has remained simplex, as in [ˈvẽna ˈpçãna] < VĒNA PLĀNA.

(*c*) Unlike at Bagnes, there is no evidence of progressive nasalization.

(*d*) The front vowel /ɛ̃/ derives from /i/, free /e, ɛ/ and /a/ following a palatal in a nasalizing context and also /a/ before palatal /ɲ/, as in [θɛ̃ fɛ̃ pçɛ̃ vɛ̃ tsɛ̃ bɛ̃] < *CĪNQUE, FĪNEM/FĒNUM, PLĒNUM, VĔNIT, CĂNEM, BĂLNEUM. The low vowel /ã/ derives from other cases of /a/ and blocked

/e, ɛ/, as in [tsãba fã vã dã] < CĂMBA, FĀMEM, VIGĬNTI, DĔNTEM. However, when blocked /ɛ/ preceded the nasal /m/ in context (i) forms it developed as if free, presumably as a result of its lengthening through nasalization, hence [tɛ̃ 'mẽbru e'sɛ̃pçu] < TĚMPLUM, MĚMBRUM, EXĚMPLUM. The back vowel /ɔ̃/ derives from all types of original back vowel in nasalizing contexts, as in [pɔ̃ bɔ̃ 'ɔ̃dze pu'mɔ̃ de'lɔ̃] < PŎNTEM, BŎNUM, ŬNDECIM, PULMŌNEM, DIEM-LŪNAE.

NOTES

1. In fact, a good deal of variability in the incidence of nasalization emerges from the *ALPic*. Thus, two of the five locations showing a nasal vowel for 'axle' fail to show a nasal vowel for 'sheep' (maps 81, 181). None of the locations investigated is reported as having a nasal vowel in the reflex of the Germanic loanword bosk, cf. *bois* (map 242). For a map showing the location of the nasalizing area based on *ALPic*, i, map 81, see Carton 1990.

2. The link between nasalization and phrasal stress here may be compared with the phrase-stress conditioned denasalization found in La Vendée (5.2.6 below).

3. For discussion of Palsgrave's description, see Geschiere (1968: esp. 186–8). Also, on the interplay between nasality and 'neutral' vowels, see Avram (1968). See also 4.3.8 and note 32 there.

4. One possible relic form with unfronted /u/ (if it does not reflect influence from Walloon) is [prɔ̃n] < PRŪNA 'plum', which is found almost universally throughout Picardy; cf. Flutre (1977: 57) and *ALPic*, i, map 266.

5. e.g. Lartigaut (1669: 179) writes: 'Danz . . . *pomme, nous sommes, comme, homme* . . . *sonner, banni*, etc., si l'on an prononcèt deus [sc. consonnes nasales], come il et êcrit, on ferèt une prononciation nazarde, et fort dezagréable qui sant le Picar enfermé', while Hindret (1687: 42) suggests that the pronunciation of *bonne* as *bon + ne* is 'comme on le prononce en Normandie', a judgement echoed by the Norman grammarian Buffier (1709); '*bonne, homme* se prononcent *bone, home*, à moins que de vouloir faire une prononciation normande' (Thurot, ii. 552).

6. In this variety, denasalization is apparently more complete with vowels deriving from originally front high vowels. For the reflex of the originally back high vowel [u] a 'semi-nasalized' mid vowel is reported, e.g. in [pɔm] < PŌMA, [tɔn] < TŎNAT.

7. The apparent failure of the stressed vowel to undergo denasalization before the nasal [n] is due to the fact that the final sequence was originally [-ã(ː)l], which is still widely found in varieties of Walloon (cf. *ALW*, i. 34). Denasalization would not therefore be expected. However, at a later stage after denasalization had operated, the final sequence passed to [-ãːn] as a result of the nasal vowel exercising a progressive nasalizing influence on the final consonant.

6

Gallo-Romance III: Occitan

6.1. Introduction

The Gallo-Romance spoken in the southern half of France evolved rather differently from the *langue d'oïl* of the north. The southern varieties, which are collectively known as *langue d'oc* or Occitan (we will normally use the latter term), have certainly experienced vowel nasalization but its effect on their phonetic evolution has generally been rather more limited. The main patterns of nasal vowel development in Occitan are explored in this chapter, but to set these into their proper background some brief general historical comments may usefully be made.

6.1.1. HISTORICAL BACKGROUND

In the period following the break-up of the Roman Empire, the south of France developed socially and politically in partial independence from the north. As a result, its linguistic fortunes were somewhat different from those of the *langue d'oïl* area and in many respects show rather greater affinity with the Catalan speech area to the south. In the later Middle Ages from about 1000 onward, a substantial body of texts appears written in the vernacular. These encompass literary works, most notably the troubadour lyrics of the twelfth–fourteenth centuries, as well as non-literary writings. The works of the troubadours were composed in a rather variable *koine* mainly founded on central dialects, while for administrative purposes a *scripta* evolved, heavily based on centre-south usage and especially that of Toulouse, which enjoyed widespread use from the late twelfth century through to the fifteenth century.

As the south of France was forceably brought under the direct control of the French monarchs of the north from the thirteenth century onward, the influence of the Paris-based norm language began to be felt. Already by the second half of the fourteenth century, northern zones abutting onto the *langue d'oïl* were starting to go over to the use of standard French for administration. Further south, the adoption of standard French for officialdom came in the

sixteenth century, a move consecrated by the celebrated Ordonnance of Villers-
Cotterets (1539) which made all languages other than standard French invalid
for legal use. In literature, by the end of the fifteenth century most southern
writers had abandoned the use of Occitan for their works. Subsequently, the
rise of a progressively centralized state with Paris at its heart was continuously
to reinforce the primacy of the standard language. The result has been the
steady contraction in the use of Occitan, a fate which owes itself in no small
measure to the fact that no undisputed standard variety of Occitan has existed
in modern times around which a challenge to standard French could have been
mounted. Today, the number of native speakers of Occitan is difficult to
estimate accurately but it seems certain to be a good deal less that the 10–12
million claimed by many scholars (cf. Sauzet 1988). Furthermore, all Occitan
speakers are bilingual with standard French (or some form of *français régional*)
and for almost all speakers Occitan is not the first language (Kremnitz 1991: 37).
Also, the use of Occitan is more typical amongst older generations and in rural
areas.

Against this background of political and social fragmentation, it is understandable that considerable dialectal variety has developed. To cover the
linguistic variation, a classification with four broad sub-divisions is generally
used:

(1) North Occitan (Limousin, Auvergne, Dauphiné, and Haute-Provence);
(2) Provençal (Provence);
(3) Languedocien (Centre-South of Occitan area, between Gascony and the
Rhône); and
(4) Gascon (Gascony)

The first three of these groupings form something of a linguistic continuum
with a good deal of overlapping of linguistic features. It will be appropriate
therefore to treat them together. Gascon however has pioneered a number of
special linguistic developments which marked it off in relation to the other
Occitan varieties from early times. As some of these developments directly
involve vowel nasalization, Gascon will be considered separately (6.3).

6.1.2. VOWEL NASALITY IN MODERN OCCITAN

Present-day Occitan offers a rather varied picture as far as vowel nasality is
concerned. In general terms it is apparent that the role played by nasalization in
shaping vowel history has been a good deal smaller in Occitan than in Gallo-
Romance varieties to the north. Nowadays, in Provençal and Languedocien
dialects, nasal vowels may be found but typically the nasality is only allophonic
and is frequently less intense than in dialects of northern France. In North

Occitan and some Gascon dialects, nasal vowel phonemes do appear but even here the exploitation of unconditioned vowel nasalization is a good deal less systematic than in the *langue d'oïl* area in that the range and distribution of nasal vowel phonemes are commonly rather restricted. However, as we shall see, the limited importance of nasality in the vowel systems of modern Occitan may sometimes be due to vowel denasalization in the history of the language rather than just reflecting the muted action of nasalization.

6.2.   History of Vowel Nasalization in Occitan

6.2.1.   DEVELOPMENTS IN THE PRE-LITERARY PERIOD (UP TO ELEVENTH CENTURY)

All varieties of Gallo-Romance including Occitan derive their vowel systems from the familiar seven-type system of Late Latin which underlies all other Western Romance languages: /i e ɛ a ɔ o u/. Just as in the *langue d'oïl*, there was neutralization of mid vowels in unstressed syllables giving just /e o/. Also, apocope took place in the pre-literary period along similar lines to the dialects of north France, with all final unstressed non-low vowels being regularly deleted. Where Occitan differs strikingly from the *langue d'oïl* and Franco-Provençal is in the treatment of vowels in relation to syllable structure. The evidence points to there having been no systematic differentiation in the length of stressed vowels according to whether they were in a free or blocked syllable (Lausberg 1963: § 163; Weinrich 1969: 177, 179). This, together with a rather less innovative pattern of vowel evolution, resulted in a more limited range of vowel types appearing in potentially nasalizing contexts.

All Occitan varieties possessed the three different types of nasalizing context in the early medieval period. Forms showing contexts (i) and (iii) had already existed in Latin (e.g. in GRĂNDEM and LŪNA, respectively), whilst the small number of context (ii) forms in Latin, such as NŌN, had been substantially increased as a result of apocope which deleted all non-low final unstressed vowels, e.g. in the reflexes of BĔNE and VĪNUM. Some degree of nasalization evidently did take place in vowels appearing in these contexts during the pre-literary period, as we shall see.

The available evidence suggests that vowel nasalization in Occitan typically only operated through the action of *regressive* assimilation. However, in parts of Gascony there was evidently significant nasalization by *progressive* assimilation and this was sometimes strong enough to cause changes in vowel height in mid vowels. Ronjat (i., § 107) notes MŎRTEM > [murt] 'death', NŎSTRUM > ['nuste] 'our (m. sg.)' (cf. VŎSTRUM > ['bɔste] 'your (m. sg.)') for south-western Gascony, where /ɔ/ was evidently raised early on to /o/ before this regularly passed to /u/. Also, Rohlfs (1970: §§ 423, 428) notes for dialects of the Pyrenean area and south-western Gascony certain instances of raising with both /ɛ/ and /ɔ/ when a nasal precedes; e.g. (Lescun, Vallée d'Aspe) [mew 'mulo] < MĚLE MŎLA 'honey, large heap' (cf. also *ALG*, map 2084). (See Map 10.)

Looking in more detail at early patterns of development, we may note the following changes which indicate the possible presence of heightened levels of vowel nasality.

6.2.1.1. *Deletion of /n/ Preceding a Fricative*

Sequences of vowel + nasal + fricative appear in Old Occitan texts with the nasal consonant absent; *efant* (*c*.1000), *ifer, cossir, cosel* (1102), *coven, eveja* < INFĂNTEM INFĔRNUM CONSĬDERO CONSĬLIUM CONVĔNIT INVĬDIA 'child (oblique case), hell, I think, advice, it is necessary, desire'. This change affects initial unstressed syllables in particular, since stressed syllables more normally preserve the nasal consonant, as in *enfas* < ĪNFANS 'child (subject case)'. It is possible that in forms where the original nasal consonant was weakened and deleted, nasal vowels were left behind. However there is no reliable evidence for this, and furthermore if nasal vowels did arise, they were evidently soon adapted to become oral vowels. Forms where the nasal consonant was maintained also existed in Old Occitan beside those in which it was deleted, and this variation has left its mark even today. Western and central Occitan dialects tended to show oral vowels reflecting earlier forms which underwent nasal consonant deletion, whilst Eastern dialects generally have forms where the original nasal consonant was maintained and caused later vowel nasalization. Thus, *ALF* map 461 reports a nasal vowel in the opening syllable of the reflex of INFĂNTEM in Provence and dialects of the north exposed to influence from the *langue d'oïl*. Central dialects almost uniformly have an oral initial vowel, as do some western dialects although in many of these the picture is complicated for this item by rivalry from *drolle* and *meinadye*.

6.2.1.2. *Merger of Mid Vowels in Context (i) and (ii) Forms*

Stressed mid vowels in context (i) and (ii) forms (i.e. where a nasal coda consonant is present) underwent widespread neutralization which left just high mid vowels [ẽ õ]. As mid vowel contrasts, /ɛ/ : /e/ and /ɔ/ : /o/, were usually maintained in oral contexts in Occitan, the neutralization may be attributed to the effect of nasality. Thus: VĔNTUM > [vẽn] 'wind' just as VĒNDO > [vẽn] 'I sell', and PŎNTEM > [põn] 'bridge' just as MŬNDUM > [mõn] 'world'.[1]

Neutralization also affected context (ii) forms, as mentioned, such that the stressed vowels of BĔNE and BŎNUM became high-mid in quality, identical to those of FĒNUM and RATIŌNEM, respectively. However, it is not clear whether apocope preceded the introduction of heightened vowel nasalization and consequent vowel raising or not, i.e. whether BĔNE developed as ['bẽne > 'bẽne > bẽn > be] or [bɛn > bɛ̃n > bẽn > be]. The lack of clear examples of context (iii) type forms containing original stressed Ĕ or Ŏ is unfortunate, since these would show whether nasalization and consequent raising required the presence of a tautosyllabic nasal consonant. The nearest available items are verbal forms like VĔNIAT TĔNEAT, where a palatal nasal developed. However, as the palatal nasal was geminate when intervocalic, the stressed vowel here would have been in a blocked syllable in the early medieval period. The reflexes for these forms in literary Old Occitan therefore contain, as might be expected, a high mid vowel ['vẽɲa 'tẽɲa].

The neutralization of pre-nasal mid vowels occurred in the majority of the *langue d'oc*. However, it evidently did not affect the peripheral areas to the east and the west. In Provence and in the area around Nîmes, the mid-vowel contrast between /ɛ/ and /e/ and between /ɔ/ and /o/ was preserved in context (i) and (ii) forms, except when /ɛ ɔ/ appeared in the doubly nasalizing context, namely [m] ___ nasal consonant (e.g. in MOMĔNTUM, AB-MŎNTE), where raising commonly occurred. Examples from the modern-day dialect of Arles are:

[fẽŋ plẽŋ mu'mẽŋ]	<	FĒNUM PLĒNUM MOMĔNTUM
		'hay, full, moment'
[tẽŋ vẽŋ rẽŋ]	<	TĔNET/TĔMPUS VĔNIT/VĔNTUM RĔM
		'he holds/time, he comes/wind, thing'
[kãŋ'sũŋ nũŋ ku'lũŋbo a'mũŋ]	<	CANTIŌNEM NŌMEN COLŬMBA AB-MŎNTE
		'song, name, dove, down(hill)'
[bõŋ frõŋ sõŋ]	<	BŎNUM FRŎNTEM SŎMNUM
		'good, forehead, sleep'

(Coustenoble 1945)

To the west, Gascon dialects of the western Landes have not neutralized /ɛ/ and /e/ in nasalizing contexts (i) and (ii), though they have done so with /ɔ/ and /o/ (Ronjat, i., §§ 93, 106; *ALG* 2078). Conversely, Rohlfs (1970: §§ 423, 428) and *ALG* 2079 indicate certain dialects in the Pyrenean valleys of Luchon and the Haute-Garonne which have neutralized the /ɛ/ : /e/ contrast as [e] but not the /ɔ/ : /o/ contrast. The implication of this patchy neutralization of mid vowels is that the tendency towards nasalization in context (i) and (ii) forms was at best weak in early Gascon and fitfully carried through.

In the area between Gascony and the Rhône, neutralization was widespread, but nonetheless it was not quite universal. Notably, in the varieties spoken in the eastern part of this area, adjacent to the Rhône, /ɔ/ and /o/ did occasionally remain distinct in contexts (i) and (ii).[2]

6.2.1.3. *Deletion of Word-Final /−n/ in Context (ii) Forms*

Apocope of final unstressed non-low vowels took place in pre-literary times in Occitan, and led to the creation of many forms with word-final nasals. Final sequences also developed where the nasal consonant was followed by inflexional /-s/, e.g. *man mans* 'hand, hands' < MĂN(UM) MĂN(O)S. Only paroxytons were affected, since proparoxytons regularly lost their entire final syllable, as in HŎMI(NEM) CĂSSA(NUM) > *(h)ome casse* ['ɔme 'kase] 'man, oak tree'. In apocopated forms which contained a word-final nasal, various changes occurred with the nasal and the preceding vowel .

On becoming final, the nasal consonant deriving from simplex -N- rapidly weakened and even by the time of the first texts it had been deleted altogether in many Occitan dialects (see Map 4). Already in the earliest extant vernacular text written in Romance orthography, the *Boecis* (*c.*1000), there appear forms such as *preso, ta, be* 'prison, so, well' (< PREHENSIŌNEM TĂN(TUM) BĔNE), and in the poems of the earliest known troubadour poet, Count William of Poitou (1071–1127), examples can be found of rhymes between oral vowels and the reflex of vowels which had earlier preceded -N-. Thus, in Poem 6 (*Ben vuelh*) forms such as *pa certa endema* 'bread, certain, day after' (< PĀNEM CERTĀNUM IN-DE-MĀNE) are in rhyme with oxytonic verb forms such as *va aura querra* 'goes, will have, will seek' (< VĀDIT HABERE-HĀBET QUAERERE-HĀBET) and in poem 11 (*Pos de chantar*) *si* and *aizi* 'himself, home' (< SE ASĪLUM) rhyme with *vezi, fi, lati* 'neighbour, end, Latin' (< VICĪNUM FĪNEM LATĪNUM). In such cases, all the rhyming vowels were surely oral, including those which had preceded -N-, so that any nasality which the vowel of forms such as *pa* may have acquired must have been lost fairly rapidly. However, despite the apparent total loss of all trace of final [-n] < -N-, it continued to be represented in other vernacular texts, albeit rather inconsistently, by the graphy <n>, this being referred to as '*n* instable' or '*n* mobile'.

Deletion of the reflex of simplex -N- after apocope was widespread but failed to occur systematically in lateral areas to the east and west. Thus, east of the Rhône and around Nîmes a final nasal consonantal segment was sometimes preserved, usually with some nasalization of the preceding vowel. However, in more northerly dialects of this zone, in Drôme and the Alps, partial deletion of /-n/ < -N- evidently did occur operating preferentially after high vowels /i y u/ and the mid vowel /e/.[3]

To the west, the picture is confused in most Gascon dialects by the action of other rather special factors which affected simplex -N- (cf. below and also 6.3). But in dialects of northern Gironde where these factors did not operate the evidence points to the retention of final /-n/ < -N-. The broad similarity between this area of non-deletion of final /-n/ and the area where neutralization fails to occur between mid vowels in nasalizing contexts (i) and (ii) is note-worthy. It suggests that it was the central block of Occitan dialects which initially experienced raised levels of vowel nasalization in contexts (i) and (ii) and that this development often failed to spread to peripheral areas.

Before the final /-n/ of apocopated forms disappeared, it evidently nasalized the preceding vowel sufficiently strongly to cause changes in its quality.[4] Low and low-mid vowels were particularly affected. Low-mid vowels were raised to high-mid, as we have seen above, and the low vowel /a/ was velarized to [ɑ]. The latter vowel was formally distinguished from [a] by medieval grammarians. Thus, in the grammatical treatise *Donatz Proensals* (*c.*1240), the vowel of *cas pas* 'you fall/case, step' (< CĂDIS/CĀSUS PĂSSUS) is described as '*a* larg' as opposed to the vowel of *cas pas* 'dog, bread' (< CĂNIS PĀNIS) which is referred to as '*a* estreit' (Marshall 1969). Rhymes between the two vowel types were not permitted in verse.

It is impossible to trace the phonetic stages through which /-n/ passed before it disappeared in the central block of Occitan dialects. However, it seems very likely that whatever phonetic path it followed this word-final nasal consonant caused the preceding vowel to nasalize to some degree, but that when the resultant vowel nasality became phonemic after the residue of /-n/ was lost, it was fairly rapidly abandoned in most dialects.

The weakening and deletion of the reflex of simplex -N- after it became word-final contrasts with the fate of other nasal consonants which came to appear in word-final position. Already by the time of the first texts, word-final /-nt/ < -NTEM -NDO had been widely simplified to /-n/, as in GĔNTEM > *gen* 'people', and likewise geminate -NN- which became final through apocope emerged as /-n/ as in ĂNNUM > *an* 'year'. The weakening and widespread deletion of original simplex -N- after it had become word-final through apocope was therefore an early change which allowed other consonant sequences to simplify to give word-final /-n/. All these developments appear to fit in with a broader tendency to reduce word-final consonants.

If at some stage unconditioned nasal vowels came to exist in certain dialects at least, it may be wondered why nasal vowels never went on to gain a firm foothold. The answer is perhaps that they were too structurally isolated. Unconditioned nasal vowels appear to have arisen principally in stressed final syllables only, precisely as a result of the deletion of /-n/. They were thus limited in number and scope, and reinforcements were not forthcoming.

6.2.1.4. *Deletion of Intervocalic -N- in Gascon*

In context (iii) forms such as LŪNA, the nasal consonant has generally been maintained in Occitan and any nasalization of the preceding vowel has been limited. However, in Gascon intervocalic simplex -N- underwent weakening and complete deletion early on leaving behind an unconditioned nasal vowel. This change may be compared with parallel developments in Galician-Portuguese (8.2.4), Alpine dialects of south-eastern France (5.4) and north-western Italy (10.3.1), dialects of Sardinian (11.2.2) and Corsican (11.3.3), and early Romanian (12.2.4).

Deletion is already indicated in early documents from the eleventh century onward. Thus, we have *garias, Aueraed, camiar* 'hens, hazel nut grove, to walk' < GALLĪNAS ABELLAN-ĒTUM CAMINĀRE (Cartulary of Bigorre, eleventh-twelfth centuries) and also place names attested in the eleventh century, Salies, Doat, Castahiet < SALĪNAS DONĀTUM CASTANĒTUM (Bec 1968: 38). Deletion is thus pre-eleventh century but just how ancient it is remains uncertain.[5]

The deletion of intervocalic -N- has been viewed by structuralist linguists as being bound up with the desire to preserve the distinction between simplex and geminate sonorants. Thus, as geminate -NN- tends to simplify to /n/, the original simplex -N- weakens and is finally lost leaving a trace in the nasality of the preceding vowel. The contrast -VNNV- vs. -VNV- therefore becomes /VnV/ vs. /ṼV/; cf. the development of geminate vs. simplex laterals where a length contrast -LL- vs. -L- becomes a quality contrast /-r-/ vs. /-l-/ respectively (Martinet 1955: 273–96; Jungemann 1955: 190–204). Alternatively, we may see the loss of simplex intervocalic -N- as just a special and more localized extension of the more general phenomenon of lenition which affected intervocalic obstruents in western Romance. Both interpretations are compatible with one another. Whatever the motivation for the appearance of vowel nasalization in the original -VNV- sequence, the fact that the conditioning nasal was heterosyllabic in relation to the vowel affected is notable. It suggests that the rise of nasal vowels in context (iii) forms could well reflect a separate development, at first running independent of changes in contexts (i) and (ii) involving coda nasals. Indeed, it seems likely that the weakening of nasal consonants which accompanies the creation of high levels of vowel nasalization took place earlier in context (iii) forms than it did in other context types (cf. Ronjat, ii. § 385; Bec 1968: 40).

The phonetic path of intervocalic -N- prior to its deletion is not clear. One possibility, proposed by Bec (1968: 40), is that it velarized after having nasalized the preceding vowel and then changed its syllabic status to become the coda of the previous syllable. This allows a directly parallel pattern to be postulated for context (iii) forms like LŪNA and context (ii) forms like PĀNEM which apocopated later on:

LŪNA   >   'lū-na   >   'lūŋ-a   >   'lū-a (Old Gascon)
PĀNEM   >   'pã-ne   >   'pãŋ-e   >   pãŋ

However, as there is no evidence for [ŋ] having existed intervocalically and for the arguable syllabification in the second stage of development, an alternative scenario might be the following:

LŪNA   >   'lū-na   >   'lu-^{n}a   >   'lū-$^{(n)}$a   >   'lū-a
PĀNEM   >   'pān   >   pãn   >   pã^{n} >   pã/pãŋ

Here, [^{n}] would represent a weak nasal flap or glide, and the variation in the final stage of the second (context ii) form reflects that fact that locally either an unconditioned nasal vowel may be found following the deletion of [^{n}] or the nasal vowel could be restructured into a sequence of nasal vowel + coda [ŋ] (cf. northern Italian 10.4.4). The choice of [ŋ] would be determined both by its being the most nasal of nasal consonants and also by the fact that it is the only type of nasal consonant not found in word-final position. For whilst [m n ɲ ŋ] are all found medially, only the first three evidently appeared word-finally in early Gascon.

At the beginning of the literary period therefore, Occitan showed three main varieties as far as nasal vowels were concerned. In the central, more prestigious varieties of Languedoc and northern Occitan, only limited allophonic nasalization became established. Vowels in context (i) forms had undergone nasalization sufficient to cause neutralization of mid vowel contrasts but the conditioning nasal remained. In context (ii) forms, the word-final nasal consonant deriving from simplex -N- was deleted, though less uniformly in northern Occitan dialects east of the Rhône, and the nasal vowels which emerged after deletion were rapidly abandoned in favour of oral vowels.

In the dialects of Provence, allophonic nasality in context (i) forms was slight enough not to result in mergers between mid vowels. In context (ii) forms, however, the word-final reflex of simplex -N- underwent major weakening. In some dialects, it was deleted but the resulting nasal vowel was restructured to [Ṽŋ] (cf. 6.2.2.4).

To the west, in Gascony, allophonic nasality in context (i) was of variable intensity and was sufficient to cause neutralization between mid vowels only in dialects closer to Languedoc. Context (iii) provided a source of unconditioned nasal vowels as a result of the weakening and deletion of original intervocalic -N-. This development may have got underway before comparable weakening of the final [n] in context (ii) forms occurred.

6.2.2.   DEVELOPMENTS IN THE LITERARY PERIOD

At the outset of the literary period in Occitan, it seems likely that only Gascon dialects possessed *unconditioned* nasal vowels. These had arisen in context (iii) forms such as LŪNA > ['lũa] as a result of the regular deletion of inter-vocalic -N-. In other dialects, vowel nasalization had taken place to varying degrees though probably it was less intense than in the dialects of the *langue d'oïl*.

The general picture which emerges from subsequent developments is that the exploitation of vowel nasalization has continued to be rather limited. In the great majority of areas, nasal vowels have maintained a level of nasality which is fairly weak and only really perceptible in the latter part of the vowel (Ronjat, ii., § 387). Furthermore, vowel nasality has remained conspicuously allophonic in many parts of the Occitan speech area, more particularly in central and western varieties of Languedocian. This is reflected in the characteristic use of a sequence of vowel + nasal, typically [Ṽŋ], for a standard French nasal vowel in the 'accent méridional'.[6] Phonemically nasal vowels have developed in only a few areas, particularly in northern Occitan and more patchily in the area from the Rhône valley eastward. In the former case, the progressive influence from the *langue d'oïl* has doubtless been an important factor.

We may now briefly review the significant developments relating to vowel nasality which have taken place in Occitan, reserving our coverage of the special case of Gascon to the end (6.3).

6.2.2.1. *Restructuring of Vowel System*

At some stage well into the medieval period, the high vowel /u/ gradually fronted to /y/. The chronology of this change has been much debated and still remains uncertain.[7] However, nasal allophones of /u/ were also affected so that ŪNUM > [ỹ(n)] 'one', (Germ.) brūn > [brỹ(n)] 'brown'.

This change left /o/ free to raise to /u/, which occurred in the thirteenth–fourteenth centuries (Lafont 1991: 4). Again, nasal allophones of /o/ were also affected, as in MŬNDUM > [mõn(t)] > [mũn] 'world' and (Germ.) machi + ŌNEM > [masõ(n)] > [masũn/-ŋ masũ/masu] 'builder'.

In a small zone of the Auvergne, in the Puy-de-Dôme, these changes were reordered, doubtless reflecting the late adoption of /u/ > /y/. By the time the fronting rule began to operate, the original word-final sequence [-õ(n)] in context (ii) forms had already developed [-õ] > [-ũ/-u] and this then underwent fronting: [masũ/masu] > [masỹ/masy]. However, context (i) forms were not affected by this development, since nasal [õ] has typically remained unraised.[8]

6.2.2.2. *Further Retraction of Velarized [ɑ]/[ɑ̃] (< [ã])*

In many Occitan varieties, namely western and central dialects of northern Occitan and adjacent dialects of Languedocian, /a/ in context (ii) forms had velarized in pre-literary times, for instance in [pɑ] < PĀNEM. In certain of these varieties, /a/ was also velarized in other types of nasalizing contexts, more widely with context (i) than with context (iii) forms. This early velarization thus appears to have operated along a parameter in the different context types: (ii) > (i) > (iii).

Subsequently, the velarized [ɑ] or [ɑ̃], oral or nasal, retracted further and rounded to give [ɔ]/[ɔ̃] and often went on to close further to [o]/[õ]. The prior raising of original [õ] to [ũ] facilitated this change. Examples:

context type	(ii)		(i)		(iii)	
Saint-Victor (Ardèche)	PĀNEM	> pɔ̃	QUĀNDO	> kã	GRĀNA	> 'granɔ
Notre-Dame-de-Sanilhac						
(Dordogne)	PĀNEM	> pɔ	QUANDO	> kɔ̃n	GRĀNA	> 'granɔ
Saugues (Haute-Loire)	PĀNEM	> po	CAMPUM	> tsõ	LĀNA	> 'lɔna
	'bread'		'when, field'		'grain, wool'	

(Calvet 1969; Marshall 1984; Nauton 1974)

As to the chronology of this change, examples of the use of the graphy <o> for context (ii) forms have been found in late fourteenth-century Limousin texts, namely *so certos* 'healthy, certain (m. pl.)' < SĀNUM CERTĀNOS (Ronjat, i., § 109). The fifteenth century sees attestations in texts from Poitou and Auvergne, and in the sixteenth century the change is well indicated for Haute-Loire (Pignon 1960: 335; Nauton 1974: 67).

6.2.2.3. *Changes in Tongue Position of Nasal Vowels*

With the presence of increased levels of vowel nasality in Occitan, changes may be looked for in the tongue position and especially in the tongue height of the vowels concerned.

Two early cases have already been noted. First, there was widespread *raising* of low-mid vowels to high-mid position in central dialects of Occitan during the pre-literary period. Second, nasalized [ã] underwent *retraction* in broadly the same dialects.

In the literary period, however, Occitan dialects show few of the striking changes seen in *langue d'oïl* varieties. The retracted low vowel [ɑ̃] raises to become a mid back vowel in some varieties of Languedocian and northern Occitan, as we have seen. However, the raising of original [õ] to [ũ] is part of a general raising of /o/ > /u/.

Where high levels of vowel nasality have arisen and the conditioning nasal coda has been much reduced or wholly deleted, we might perhaps expect signs of vowel lowering as in northern French. However, it is noteworthy that except in those dialects spoken on the borders of the *langue d'oïl* area, there are no indications of such lowering taking place as a result of nasal influence[9] (see

Map 3). As regards mid vowels, in dialect areas where [ẽ] and [ɛ̃] merged as [ẽ] there has been a tendency for a lowered pronunciation [ɛ̃] to be adopted though this may well owe itself less to the effects of nasality than to general syllabic constraints (lowering in blocked syllables) and symmetrical pressures from [ɔ].[10]

6.2.2.4.   *Fate of the Conditioning Nasal Consonant*

Crucial to the creation of nasal vowel phonemes is the deletion of the conditioning nasal consonant. In Occitan, this has often been slow to happen, with the exception of course of word-final -N in context (ii) which was lost in preliterary times (see 6.2.1.3). In many varieties of Occitan in fact, it appears that nasal vowels have at all times continued to be accompanied by a following nasal consonantal segment. However, widespread changes have affected the conditioning nasals, particularly the coda nasals of contexts (i) and (ii), and a number of these changes show the weakening which is suggestive of increased levels of vowel nasalization.

Already at the outset of the literary period, the reflex of simplex -N- in word-final position in context (ii) forms had been weakened and lost in Languedocian and western and central dialects of northern Occitan, and any associated nasalization of the preceding vowel had also been lost (see 6.2.1). However, other types of nasal consonant which also came to appear in word-final position in context (ii) forms in these dialects did not suffer deletion but remained to give a three-way subsystem of word-final nasals:

-n	< -n(n)	< -NN-	ĂNNUM	> ãn			
	-n(t)	< -NT-	INFĂNTEM	> e(m)fãn			
		-ND-	QUĂNDO	> kãn	MŬNDUM	> mõn	
-m	< -m(m)	< -M(M)-	FĂMEM	> fãm	SŬMMUM	> sõm	
	-m(p)	< -MP-/-MB-	CĂMPUM	> kãm	PLŬMBUM	> plõm	
-ɲ	< -ɲ(ɲ)		CŬNEUM	> kõɲ			

(respectively, 'year, child, when, world, hunger, peak, field, lead, wedge')

The velar nasal [ŋ] appears to have been unable to appear word-final in the early literary period. Instead, it was regularly followed in final position by [k], e.g. SĂNGU(IN)EM > [sãŋk] 'blood'.

Subsequently, neutralization has progressively occurred between these word-final coda nasals in a comparable way to what happened in northern French (cf. 4.2.4). In the thirteenth century, rhymes appear in poetry between forms in [-n] and [-ɲ], the common outcome being [-n] (Ronjat, ii., § 389). The palatal [-ɲ] remains only in peripheral areas, namely in Alpine dialects, Gascon, and in the far south adjacent to the Catalan-speaking zone. Similarly, [-m] widely lost its bilabial articulation and came to be realized as [-n]. Once again it is only peripheral varieties in the far east and in Gascony which have preserved final

[-m]. Thus, the pattern of word-final neutralization which was generally implemented may be represented as follows:

In this way, there was now full neutralization between coda nasals in word-final position just as there was word-medially in context (i) forms, since nasal consonants here were homorganic with the consonant which followed. As the neutralization of contrasts between word-final nasals often implies an articulatory weakening which is accompanied by nasalization of the preceding vowel, it seems likely that as the neutralization took place in Occitan, levels of vowel nasality were increased somewhat.

Thereafter, final and medial coda nasals evolved variably from region to region. In Languedocian, medial nasals have generally remained homorganic with the following consonant, whilst in word-final position [-n] appears to have undergone little change in many dialects and levels of vowel nasality have not been stepped up significantly.[11] Thus, in the great mass of central and western Languedocian we find [ra'zīn/rɔ'zīn bēn/vēn ku'dūn] 'grape, wind, quince' < RACĒMUM VĔNTUM COTŌNEUM (*ALLor* 856, 18, 287). Also, in this area the final sequence [-ŋk] has been very retentive, the reflex of SĂNGU(IN)EM still being [sāŋk] in western Hérault, Aveyron, Tarn, Aude, and down into south and south-eastern Gascon. However, in eastern dialects of Languedocian exposed to influence from Provençal the word-final nasal has emerged as [ŋ], giving [razīŋ vēŋ ku'ðūŋ], respectively. Unconditioned nasal vowels are not reported.

In Provence, weakening of coda nasals was evidently more intense. The *ALP* indicates for almost all localities total deletion after [ā] leaving an unconditioned nasal vowel, e.g. [grā 'brāko/'brākœ/'brātʃœ] 'grain, branch' < GRĀNUM BRĂNCA (maps 317, 549). After non-low vowels, either full deletion with an unconditioned nasal vowel or a sequence of nasal vowel + offglide [n] is reported: [karbū/tʃarbū] vs. [karbūⁿ/tʃarbūⁿ] 'coal', [mulī] vs. [mulīⁿ] 'mill'; [vē'ta] vs. [vēⁿ'ta] 'to winnow', [re'fēdre] vs. [re'fēⁿdre] 'to split' etc. < CARBŌNEM MOLĪNUM VENTĀRE RE-FĬNDERE (maps 330, 391, 378, 612). In some dialects, however, there has been restoration of a nasal coda. Coustenoble (1945) notes for Arles the general use of [ŋ] with secondary homorganic co-articulation for pre-consonantal coda nasals and likewise [ŋ] as the generalized realization of the word-final nasal; cf. [āŋ nūŋ tsāŋ pāŋ pɔŋ jõŋ sīŋ; ku'lūŋbo ēŋ'tēŋdʀe 'ūŋglo] 'year, name, field, bread, bridge, far, five; dove, to hear, nail' < ĂNNUM NŌMEN CĂMPUM PĀNEM PŎNTEM LŎNGE *CĪNQUE; COLŬMBA INTĔNDERE ŬNGULA.[12] Such data suggest that the original conditioning nasal underwent major weakening leading to deletion, but that coda restoration has taken place and sequences of nasal vowel + [ŋ] were re-established in a parallel way to what has occurred in many northern Italian dialects (cf. 10.4.3). The use of the velar nasal here as the restored consonant indicates that the coronal off-glide [ⁿ] found in certain dialects (noted above) probably represents a weakened form of the original nasal coda rather than being the result of a double change whereby coda nasals first passed to [ŋ] before strengthening to coronal [ⁿ], as Fagan (1990: 229) has proposed. In Alpine dialects of the far east, however, evolution has been more conservative and coda nasals have widely preserved their identity.[13]

In northern Occitan, considerable weakening of nasal codas has taken place, most notably in dialects lying closer to the *langue d'oïl*. Here, there has usually been total deletion resulting in the creation of unconditioned nasal vowels. Furthermore, other characteristic northern traits have become established, notably lowering of tongue height for high vowels.[14]

South of this transitional belt of northern-influenced dialects, the weakening has been less complete but nonetheless significant. In this way, a complex linguistic picture can present itself in relatively limited areas. For instance, in Drôme, the following pattern in northern and southern dialects is reported for vowels in nasalizing contexts of type (ii) with original simplex -N- (Bouvier 1976: 363–71):

	Northern dialects	*Southern dialects*
high vowels		
i y u	ẽ œ̃ õ	i y u + *coda* [n]
non-high vowels		
ɛ e	ẽ	e + *coda* [n]
ɔ	õ	wõ/wã
a	ã	ã

Here, deletion has failed to occur in southern dialects except after /a/ or /ɔ/. In these southern dialects, maintenance of the coda nasal is associated with very low levels of allophonic vowel nasality (not indicated in our transcription). The intervening central dialects show a variable picture, but typically final /-n/ has been deleted and a final oral vowel has emerged.

In context (i) forms, a residue of the nasal coda is preserved everywhere after original high vowels [ĩ ũ ỹ] although in northern dialects of Drôme the nasal off-glide is marginal. In central and southern dialects, vowel nasality is at best slight and may be minimal. After original [ẽ ã], northern dialects have deleted the nasal coda completely, while the other dialects have nasal vowel + (homorganic) nasal consonant (Bouvier 1976: 371–3).

Further west, in Limousin, there is again variation, although vowel nasalization has made considerable progress. In context (i) forms where the consonant following the original coda nasal has continued to be pronounced (i.e. where the nasal consonant is 'covered'), the nasal has been deleted in the majority of the localities investigated by the *ALAL* leaving behind an unconditioned nasal vowel. In the other localities, it remains as a weak off-glide to the preceding nasalized vowel and homorganic with the following consonant. Word-finally, the coda nasal has generally been deleted leaving an unconditioned nasal vowel.

However, in an area of Dordogne which lies on the border zone between south-western Limousin and north-western Languedocian, there has been some recharacterization of coda nasals. Here, covered nasal codas have been weakened but usually maintained, especially before non-continuants. In word-final position, however, certain dialects have restored a weak labial consonantal segment [-m] after the nasal vowel, as in [frũm bũm dẽm bjẽm blãm] 'forehead, good, tooth, well, white' < FRŎNTEM BŎNUM DĔNTEM BĔNE blank. This phenomenon, noted in the *ALF* 135, 614, etc. and reported by Ronjat (ii., § 387) for the dialect of Mussidan, doubtless reflects a localized attempt to preserve or re-establish Languedocian-style conditioned nasal vowels in place of the northern Occitan unconditioned types. In the same zone, a more typically Languedocian pattern is described by Marshall (1984) for the dialect of Notre-Dame-de-Sanilhac, spoken just south of Périgueux. Here, coda nasals are maintained medially and are neutralized as [-n] word-finally. The vowels which precede the undeleted word-final nasals are only lightly nasalized. Thus:

VĔNTUM	>	vẽn	'wind'	VĒNDERE	>	'vẽndrɛ	'to sell'
LŎNGE	>	lwẽn	'far'	ŬNGULA	>	'ũŋglɔ	'nail'
RACĒMUM	>	rɔ'zĩn	'grape'	CĂMERA	>	'sɔ̃mbrɔ	'room'
(Germ.) blank	>	blɔ̃n	'white'				
LŎNGUM	>	lũn	'long'				

To sum up, the picture is of no more than a rather slow drift towards establishing unconditioned nasal vowels through the weakening and eventual deletion of nasal codas. Moves in this direction have been more rapid in areas directly influenced by the *langue d'oïl* and in the eastern part of the Occitan zone. Vowel quality also appears to have played an important role in the rate of implementation of vowel nasalization. On the basis of his analysis of dialects of the Auvergne, Ronjat, ii., § 387 claims that back vowels [u o a] are more resistant to nasalization than front vowels. The evidence from Drôme considered above, however, suggests rather that non-low vowels are more resistant than low vowels [a ɔ]. Even in this small area of Romance therefore patterns of evolution are far from uniform.

6.3.   Gascon

Already by the time of the earliest Occitan texts Gascon had taken on a highly distinctive phonetic form. In his celebrated *Descort,* the troubadour Raimbaut de Vaqueiras (*c.*1155–*c.*1207) clearly equates Gascon with Italian, French, and Portuguese as languages quite distinct from Occitan. A similar observation is found in the fourteenth-century *Leys d'Amors,* a treatise compiled in Toulouse by Guilhem Molinier for the guidance of participants in the poetry competition known as the *Jocs Florals* which first took place in 1324. This contains the remark, 'We call a foreign language such languages as French, English, Spanish, *Gascon,* Lombard' (emphasis added).

One feature which served to mark Gascon off was the deletion of intervocalic -N- in context (iii) forms such as LŪNA and the creation thereby of unconditioned nasal vowels. As we have seen (6.2.1.4), this change had occurred in the pre-literary period and it affected all the Gascon territory except the northern part of Gironde (see Map 4). At the outset of the literary period therefore, Gascon dialects might be expected to go on to develop a well-integrated system of nasal vowel phonemes. However, this has not happened.

In context (ii) forms, apocope led to a range of nasal consonants appearing in word-final position. Unlike in many other Occitan areas, there was no strong move towards neutralizing these coda nasals. Even today, it is only in a few dialects on the eastern periphery of Gascony that total neutralization has occurred. In the Gascon area proper, anything up to four distinct nasal consonants may appear in word-final position, the maximum total being found in dialects of the Landes.[15] For example, in the dialect of St.-Sever (ALG pt. 675 O) in southern Landes the following forms are found:

-m	PRĪMUM	>	prim	'thin'
-n	HOC-ĂNNO	>	eŋgwan	'this year'
-ɲ	CŬNEUM	>	kuɲ	'wedge'
-ŋ	SĂNGUEM	>	saŋ	'blood'

Word-final [-m] (< -M(M)- and -MP- -MB-) and word-final palatal [-ɲ] (< -GN- -NJ-) have been preserved in all dialects except those spoken in a compact area in western and southern Gers and down into northern Hautes-Pyrénées where [-ɲ] has passed to [-j], for example in [kuj luj baj] < CŬNEUM LŎNGE BĂLNEUM (*ALG* 136, 798, 939). The alveolar nasal [-n] (< -NN- and -NT- -ND-) shows no signs of weakening, except in more peripheral dialects in eastern Gascony exposed to Languedocian influence where it emerges as [-ŋ] The lack of any apparent weakening of note in coda nasals suggests that vowel nasalization in context (ii) forms in Gascon may have been rather limited.

In context (i) forms, i.e. where the conditioning nasal consonant was followed by a covering consonant, the nasal consonant has uniformly been retained and the preceding vowel has consequently never become more than allophonically nasal.

The general lack of vowel nasalization caused by coda nasals highlights the peculiar nature of context (iii) nasalization. The creation of nasal vowel phonemes in this context would appear not to represent part of a general trend towards vowel nasalization but rather a separate and independent phenomenon arising from special circumstances concerning intervocalic simplex -N-.

As regards the subsequent fate of the unconditioned nasal vowels in context (iii) forms, their isolated nature meant that there has been widespread adaptation so as to integrate them within the rest of the vowel system. In unstressed syllables, the nasal vowel has generally become oral transferring its nasality to the following (stressed) vowel which has then been restructured as nasal vowel + nasal coda consonant if a non-continuant consonant follows, as in IENIPERUM > ['ʒĩmbre/'jẽmbru] 'juniper'. Where a continuant consonant followed the stressed vowel, denasalization has usually occurred as in GENŬCULUM > [ʒuʎ/juʎ] 'knee' and GENĔSTA > ['jestœ] 'broom', although rare examples of maintenance of nasality can be found in conservative dialects. For instance, (G)RAN-ŬCULA gives [gri'ãwʎœ] 'frog' in the dialect of Artix but more generally it emerges as ['grawʎœ 'grjawʎœ] (ALG, maps 166, 1239, 165, 41, respectively).

Stressed unconditioned nasal vowels in final syllables (i.e. in apocopated forms) have evolved variously. Mostly, there is restructuring as nasal vowel + [-ŋ],[16] but an oral vowel emerges in parts of south-eastern Basses-Pyrénées and south-western and western Hautes-Pyrénées. Nowadays unconditioned nasal vowels remain only in a compact zone in northern Basses-Pyrénées. Thus, in different varieties of Gascon PĀNEM VĪNUM may appear as [pa pã pãŋ bi bĩ bĩŋ] 'bread, wine'.

Stressed unconditioned nasal vowels in non-final syllables have undergone widespread denasalization. However, they are preserved in the area of northern Basses-Pyrénées just noted. Examples may be cited from the dialect of Artix (ALG, pt. 685; also = ALF, pt. 685) which lies centrally in this area:

Nasal vowel system /ĩ ỹ ũ ẽ ã/

VĪNUM	>	bĩ	skīna	>	es'kĩœ
CATA-ŪNUM	>	ka'ðỹ	LŪNA	>	'lỹœ
MANSIŌNEM	>	majzũ			
PLĒNUM	>	plẽ	PLĒNA	>	'plẽœ
PĀNEM	>	pã	LĀNA	>	lã

(respectively, 'wine, backbone, each (m. sg.), moon, house, full (m. sg.), full (f. sg.), bread, wool')

Word-final nasal coda system [-m -n -ɲ]

-n	(< -NN-, -NT-, -ND-)	HŎC ĂNNO	> awãn	FŎNTEM	> hũn	ŬNDE	> ũn
-m	(< -M(M)-, -MP-, -MB-)	SŬMMUM	> sũm	PRĪMUM	> prĩm	CĂMPUM	> kãm
-ɲ	(< -ɲɲ-)	PŪGNUM	> pũɲ	LŎNGE	> lwẽɲ	BĂLNEUM	> bãɲ
(-ŋ	(< -NC- -NG-)	SĂNGUEM	> sãŋk	IŬNCUM	> jũŋk)		

(respectively, 'this year, fountain, where, peak, first, field, fist, far, bath, blood, reed')

Here, the case of [lã] < LĀNA (cf. RĀNA > [a'rã]) is of interest in that the quality of the vowel exactly matches that of the reflex of PĀNEM. In dialects where [pãŋ] appears for the latter, we also find [lãŋ] for the former. This suggests that the contraction in [lã] < ['lãa] had been completed at a stage when the reflex of PĀNEM was still [pã]. The final vocalic element of these forms was then identified and subsequently evolved in identical fashion, either remaining an unconditioned nasal vowel or being restructured into a sequence of nasal vowel + [ŋ].

Finally, it is noteworthy that where -N- deletion left behind a stressed high nasal vowel in context (iii) forms, there was no creation of a glide between the nasal vowel and the following vowel as in Portuguese (cf. 8.3.13). Thus, in contrast to Portuguese *vizinha farinha* 'neighbour (f.), flour' < VICĪNA FARĪNA, Gascon dialects have [be'zĩœ ha'rĩœ] or denasalized [be'ziœ ha'riœ].

NOTES

1. The high mid quality of the nasalized vowels here is indicated by the description provided by contemporary grammarians, as 'estreit' as opposed to 'larg'. Thus, in the *Donatz Proensals* of Uc Faidit, dated c.1240, *sens fens temps ensems* 'you sense, you split, time, together' (< SĔNTIS FĪNDIS TĔMPUS INSĬMUL) are all described as having 'e estreit', just as *avers pels secs* 'possession, hair, dry' (< HABĒRE+-S PĬLUS SĬCCUS) are said to have 'e estreit'. In contrast, *cers fers cels becs* 'stag, iron, sky, beak' (< CĔRVUS FĔRRUM+-S CAELUM+-S BĔCCUS) are presented as examples of forms with 'e larg'.

2. For instance, in the dialect of Saugues (Haute-Loire) the stressed vowels of TĔMPUS and VĒNDERE merge as a very high mid vowel [tẽ bẽdre] 'time, to sell', whereas the stressed vowels of FRŎNTEM BŎNUM yield different results from those of ROTŬNDUM and SAPŌNEM, respectively [frõ bwõ] 'forehead, good' and [rũ sa'bũ] 'round, soap' (Nauton 1974).

3. Ronjat, ii. § 385 offers a detailed cline of /-n/ deletion in these dialects, which runs from cases where high vowels precede (most common pattern) to where low vowels precede (least common pattern). For Drôme, Bouvier (1976: 363–71) provides an excellent discussion of complex local variation, concluding that preservation of a nasal element was characteristic of northern and southern dialects of that *département* but that central dialects showed a marked tendency to delete the nasal.

4. This may be compared with the parallel deletion of final simplex /-n/ in Catalan, which left no discernible trace at all on the preceding vowel (cf. 7.3.1.3).

5. Some scholars set it as far back as the seventh century, e.g. Ravier (1991: 87) who cites Dinguirard (1979: 39) who follows Bec (1968: 40). It is argued that as intervocalic /n/ is lost in Germanic loans (e.g. skīna) deletion of the nasal consonant presumably post-dates the sixth century. But deletion must pre-date syncope in proparoxytons (eighth century?), *EX-DIS-IEIŪNAT > [ez'dezua] where /n/ was lost before the preceding vowel was syncopated. The latter claim is problematic, however, so that deletion may in fact date from after the seventh century.

6. Cf. the phonological review of varieties of *français régional* by Walter (1982), in which the southern speakers investigated uniformly used an 'appendice consonantique nasal' following a nasal vowel. In the usage of the subject from Tarn who was more closely analysed, the 'appendice' was realized as [ŋ] phrase-finally, and when medial and pre-consonantal it was homorganic with the following consonant (p. 187). See also the comparable findings of Taylor (1996) for Aix-en-Provence.

7. Ronjat, i., § 72 proposes the tenth-thirteenth centuries on the basis of considerations of relative chronology. Other linguists, such as Anglade (1921: 82–4) and Meyer-Lübke (1920: § 234), see this change as operating rather earlier, whereas still others claim a later dating, e.g. Richter (1934: § 174A, B) who in her extensive study of Gallo-Romance sound changes sets this development to as late as the fourteenth century for Occitan, a dating which is arguable for some dialects at least. Later scholars are hesitant over specifying the chronology of the fronting of /u/.

8. *ALF* 791 (MAÇON) identifies three points with fronting in northern Puy-de-Dôme. *ALAL* 888 (CHAUSSONS) reports [-y] at 9 of the 17 localities surveyed in Puy-de-Dôme, these being situated in the central core of the *département*. For context (i) forms, maps 586 (FRONT) and 868 (FOND) of *ALAL* show the common reflexes to be [frõ] and [fõ], respectively.

9. One apparent example of lowering comes in the dialect of Arles where [ỹ] > [ø̃], as in CATA-ŪNUM > [ka'dø̃ŋ] 'each', brūn > [bʀø̃ŋ] 'brown'. However, this is merely part of a general change whereby /y/ has lowered to /ø/, cf. [pø:ʀ nøl] 'pure', 'none' < PŪRUM NŪLLUM (Coustenoble 1945).

10. Cf. the dialect of Saint-Victor (N. Ardèche): ['ɛflɔ plɛ̃ vɛ̃] 'I inflate, full, wind' < ĪNFLO PLĒNUM VĔNTUM, where [ɛ̃] forms a counterpart to [ɔ̃] in a nasal vowel phoneme system /ĩ ỹ ũ ɛ̃ ɔ̃/ (Calvet 1969).

11. In his detailed study of the dialect of Aniane (Hérault), Zaun (1917: 28) pointed out that vowel nasality was only readily detectable either instrumentally or perceptually in vowels lying between nasal consonants and, strikingly, with high vowels which preceded a nasal consonant, especially [u] and less conspicuously [i].

12. Low-level phonetic features noted in this Provençal variety are: (1) vowels preceding nasals are always partly nasalized, nasality being more intense amongst less educated speakers; (2) vowels are normally long when stressed and in paroxytons but are always short when they precede [ŋ]; (3) [ŋ] is lengthened when in a stressed non-final syllable and when following the mid front vowels [e ɛ ø]; (4) when preceding [ŋ], the front vowels [e ɛ ø] have a shwa off-glide (Coustenoble 1945: §§ 249, 250, 251, 255, 385, 403).

13. Thus, in the dialect of Pragelas (Pragelato) spoken just inside the Italian border about 70 km. due west from Turin, the following forms are reported: [maŋ fɔːm bɔːn saŋk kamp grant] 'hand, hunger, bath, blood, field, big' < MĂNUM FĂMEM BĂ(L)NEUM SĂNGU(IN)EM CĂMPUM GRĂNDEM (Ronjat, i., § 68).

14. Earlier this century, Ronjat, ii., § 387 wrote, 'Je n'ai entendu de voy[elles] nasales du tipe fr[ançais] qu'à Saint-Jean-Soleimieux et environs, dans la région ambertoise et dans la région Ceissat-Royat-Volvic-Riom-Aigueperse-Chateldon.' These areas are in northern Auvergne and reflect the establishment of standard French in Clermont from the seventeenth century. The increasing pace of penetration from northern French has pushed the limit of the use of 'northern style' nasal vowels rather further south today.

15. Cf. *ALG* 2176 for an excellent overview of nasal coda systems in Gascony.

16. Other types of restructuring also appear sporadically. In some dialects of the Landes, [-ɲ] appears after front nasal vowels, e.g. PLĒNUM > [plẽɲ plœ̃ɲ] 'full (m. sg.)' and, on all the coastal zone, with later denasalization [plej plœj] (*ALG* 1085). This development is evidently independent of the restructuring of [-n] found in a small Pyrenean zone centred around Ariège on the south-east border of the Gascon speech-area, where [-n] (< -NN- -NT- -ND-) regularly gives [-ɲ] irrespective of the quality of the preceding vowel, e.g. [aɲ suɲ beɲ] 'year, they are, well' <ĂNNUM SŬNT BĔNE (Bec 1968: 57–61). A further development is seen in the Pyrenean dialect of the Val d'Aran, where the reflex of original [-n] becomes [-m] if it follows a back rounded vowel which is itself preceded by another labial segment, e.g. PAVŌNEM > [pa'om] 'capercaillie', IBŌNEM > *Bom* (place name), as against RATIŌNEM > [ara'zoŋ] (Coromines 1990: § 27b). (Cf. a comparable development in Alpine dialects of north-west Italy, 10.4.4.2)

7

Ibero-Romance I: Catalan and Spanish

7.1. Introduction

The incidence and effects of vowel nasalization have been far from uniform in the three major linguistic areas of the Iberian Peninsula. In the west, Galician-Portuguese has experienced considerable influence from nasalization. The effect of nasalization has been most intensely felt in Portugal and nasal vowel phonemes have developed in almost all varieties of Portuguese. Nasalization also operated significantly on vowel evolution in Galician but nasality has proved less tenacious. Today, phonemically nasal vowels have been preserved in only one relic area of Galician, although high levels of allophonic nasality are found in all varieties.

In the centre of the Peninsula, the evolution of vowels in Castilian Spanish has in contrast been almost entirely unaffected by the influence of nasality. And in the east, in Catalan, there is at best marginal evidence that at one stage unconditioned nasal vowels may have existed, at least in some varieties. Otherwise, nasalization has exercised no appreciable effect on patterns of vowel development, just as in Castilian Spanish. An interestingly varied picture thus emerges, which will be explored further in the present chapter and in Chapter 8.

7.1.1. HISTORICAL BACKGROUND

Unlike in other major linguistic areas of Romance, such as France and Italy, many of today's varieties of Ibero-Romance do not represent the outcome of direct and unbroken evolution from Latin in the areas where they are now established. Rather, they represent the result of varieties from the north which were carried at a later stage to the centre and south. The explanation for this lies in the Islamic invasion of Arabs and Moors in 711. By the end of that decade, all the south and centre had been conquered so that about three-quarters of the peninsula fell under Islamic control. The early Romance varieties which had previously been used in the occupied area, the so-called Mozarabic dialects, continued in existence during the following centuries, although they were increasingly influenced by Arabic. Meanwhile, in the mountainous strip of northern Spain which remained under Christian control after 711, political and geographical factors served to heighten the existing dialectal variation, predictably on a West–East axis. A complex linguistic pattern thus began to emerge in the peninsula during the ninth and tenth centuries.

From the eleventh century, the Christian north began on the process of reconquering Islamic Spain. This was very largely carried through by the middle of the thirteenth century, although the final stage was only completed in 1492 with the conquest of the Kingdom of Granada. The *reconquista* was the work of three political forces, Portugal, Castile, and Aragon-Catalonia. It had the effect of bringing their northern linguistic patterns southward, thereby overlaying and ultimately extinguishing Mozarabic varieties which were still in use.[1] As a result, a special linguistic situation arose with comparatively little dialectal variation, at least on a North–South axis, since only a select few of the varieties from just a fraction of the peninsula, the northern periphery, had been projected at a later stage over the peninsula as a whole.

7.2.   History of Vowel Nasalization in Ibero-Romance

In our review of vowel nasalization in Ibero-Romance, we will use the familiar three-way division whose historical basis is clear from the preceding comments. In the present chapter, we consider the main developments occurring in the east and centre of the peninsula, where the effects of vowel nasalization are relatively slight. The more complex pattern of change in the Galician-Portuguese area in the west is explored in the following chapter. However, certain background features of development common to all varieties of Ibero-Romance may be briefly noted here.

7.2.1.   GENERAL BACKGROUND DEVELOPMENTS

The stressed vowel system underlying all varieties of Ibero-Romance was the seven-way arrangement /i e ɛ a ɔ o u/ which had developed widely in Romance, for instance in Gallo-Romance and most of Italo-Romance. In unstressed syllables, mid vowel contrasts were neutralized and a five-way system appeared /i e a o u/, again just as in France and most of Italy. However, there is no indication in any Ibero-Romance variety that stressed vowels came to vary significantly in length depending on the structure of the syllable in which

they occurred, unlike in northern France and Italo-Romance where such variation did arise (cf. 4.2.1, 10.2.1).

7.3.   Catalan

In the Catalan area of the eastern peninsula, the impact of nasalization on vowel
evolution has been limited. Despite the proximity of this area to southern
Gallo-Romance and the sustained socio-political links which existed between
the two areas, Catalan shows few signs of having adopted the patterns of high-
level vowel nasalization seen north of the Pyrenees. Certainly, there are no
present-day varieties with unconditioned nasal vowels, but raised levels of
allophonic vowel nasality are reported to occur in certain contexts. This is
the case when vowels precede a nasal consonant and nasality is particularly
notable when they are located between nasal consonants, e.g. [i] in *caminar* and
[u] in *mundo* (Recasens i Vives 1991).

Catalan is not marked by great dialectal variation, although dialect divisions
can be identified. The basic one is between western and eastern varieties, and
each of these can in turn be subdivided into different sub-groups, the western
variety into Valencian, Andorran, etc. and the eastern into Roussillon dialects,
Balearic, etc. (Veny 1991). The standard variety is of the eastern type and is
based especially on the usage of Barcelona.

7.3.1.   HISTORY OF VOWEL NASALIZATION

7.3.1.1.   *Background Developments*

Early developments which are also common to all Ibero-Romance varieties have
been noted (7.2.1). Further to these was *apocope*, which operated on all final
unstressed vowels except /-a/ in much the same way as in Gallo-Romance. The
effect of this was to establish a substantial range of forms with word-final nasal
consonants, i.e. context (ii) forms. It may be noted that apocope operated with
decreasing intensity from east to west in the peninsula. Its wider incidence in
Catalan thus served to differentiate this variety somewhat from Castilian and
Galician-Portuguese where apocope applied on a much lesser scale. In addition
to the newly evolved context (ii) forms, Catalan had also inherited from Latin
many forms displaying nasalizing contexts (i) and (iii), so that all types of
nasalizing context were well represented, probably as early as the ninth century
(see below, 7.3.1.3).

7.3.1.2.   *Implementation of Vowel Nasalization*

As we have noted, significant levels of vowel nasality are confined at the present time to special contexts in Catalan, and historically vowel nasalization appears to have been of limited importance also, except in context (ii) forms. Indicative of the restricted impact of vowel nasalization has been the parallel evolution of vowels in nasalizing contexts and in oral contexts. As a result the neutralization of contrasts between the mid vowels /e/ : /ɛ/ and /o/ : /ɔ/ specifically in nasalizing contexts, which is widely found in other Romance varieties experiencing vowel nasalization, is notably lacking in Catalan (cf. Castilian 7.4.1.2). For example, the following context (i) forms containing mid vowels may be cited from the standard language:

PRĒNDERE	>	*pendre*	[ˈpɛndrə]	'to take'	vs. INCĒNDERE	>	*encendre* [ənˈsendrə] 'to light'
cf. CAPĬLLUM	>	*cabell*	[kəˈβɛʎ]	'hair'	vs. PĔLLEM	>	*pell* [peʎ] 'skin'
ROTŬNDA	>	*rodona*	[ruˈðonə]	'round (f. sg.)'	vs. RESPŎNDERE	>	*respondre* [rəsˈpɔndrə] 'to answer'
cf. MŬSCA	>	*mosca*	[ˈmoskə]	'fly'	vs. CŎSTA	>	*costa* [ˈkɔstə] 'coast'[2]

It may be noted that the 'flip-flop' evolution of mid vowels seen in the forms containing front mid vowels, namely Late Latin /e/ > /ɛ/ and Late Latin /ɛ/ > /e/, reflects the regular pattern found in Catalan both in oral and nasalizing contexts.

However, occasional cases are found of partial neutralization between mid vowels, which may reflect the effect of vowel nasalization at earlier periods. These relate to context (i) forms in particular. The first concerns a set of items where high vowels have developed when high-mid vowels would be expected. The change evidently dates from the pre-literary period (i.e. before the thirteenth century), since it is indicated in the earliest texts, and it may well be of considerable antiquity in view of the regularity of its application across Catalan dialects and its appearance elsewhere in the peninsula (cf. 7.4.1.2 and 8.2.3) and also in parts of Italy (10.2.2). Examples are:

PĬNCTAT	>	*pinta*	[ˈpintə]	'he paints'	PŬNCTUM	>	*punt*	[pun]	'point'
TĬNCTUM	>	*tint*	[tin]	'dye'	IŬNCTUM	>	*junt*	[ʒun]	'together'
CĬNCTA	>	*cinta*	[ˈsintə]	'belt'	ŬNGULA	>	*ungla*	[ˈuŋglə]	'nail'
TĬNEA	>	*tinya*	[ˈtiɲə]	'ringworm'	CŬNEUM	>	*cuny*	[kuɲ]	'wedge'

In these cases, there has been a raising effect which may have operated after the stressed vowels had regularly passed to [e] [o], or else it may have blocked Ĭ and Ŭ from lowering at all. The latter possibility in fact seems more likely on the basis of the comparison between CŬNEUM > *cuny* as against COTŌNEUM > *codony* 'quince' and CICŌNIA > *cigonya* 'stork'. For convenience however we will use the term 'raising' to cover the phenomenon seen in the examples above.

The development here took place in two types of context. First, it occurred before a sequence of [ŋ] + (velar) consonant which was followed by another consonant. Where there was no following consonant, there has been no raising: TRŬNCUM > *tronc* [troŋ] 'trunk', IŬNCUM > *jonc* [ʒoŋ] 'reed'; LĬNGUA > *llengua* ['ʎeŋgwə] 'language', (Germ.) -ĬNG > [-eŋ] (e.g. *sorrenc* 'sandy'). Amongst these items, however, it is clear that those containing stressed [e] must have undergone some influence to block the expected lowering [e] > [ɛ], and this influence could well be nasalization. In fact, some inconsistency is apparent in the pattern of change from item to item, perhaps reflecting varying levels of allophonic nasalization regionally. Thus, VĬNCULUM > *vincle* ['biŋklə] 'link' but SĬNGULOS > *sengles* ['seŋgləs] 'one each'.

Raising also operated before the original sequence -NJ-, cf. *tinya* and *cuny* above, but not before the original -GN- sequence, e.g. LĬGNUM > *lleny* [ʎeɲ] 'wood'. This suggests that the sequence -NJ- exercised a raising effect at some stage prior to its merger with the sequence -GN- as [ɲɲ].[3] In view of developments such as CONSĬLIUM > *consell* [kun'seʎ] 'advice' where the stressed vowel has not been raised by -LJ- to become high, it is apparent that the raising effect of -NJ- cannot be attributed to palatality alone.

In all the items where raising has taken place, the implication is that it owes itself largely or wholly to the effect of heightened vowel nasality.[4] However, the vowel nasalization here was evidently never associated with weakening of the conditioning nasal consonant.

Sporadic cases of neutralization in context (i) forms are also found, this time affecting mid vowels only and subject to dialectal variation. Many varieties of Catalan including the standard language show raising of original /ɔ/ > /o/ in a fair number of items, e.g. FRŎNTEM > [fron], LŎNGUM > [ʎoŋ], and CŎMPUTAT > ['komtə] 'forehead, long (m. sg.), he counts', although the original low mid vowel is usually preserved in FŎNTEM > [fɔn] and PŎNTEM > [pɔn] 'fountain, bridge'. In mountain dialects of the north-west, there is evidence of neutralization affecting the front vowels /e/ and /ɛ/, as in the dialect of Cardós in the Vall Ferrera where [e] is the uniform reflex; MĬNTA > ['menta] 'mint', PRĒNDERE > ['penɾe] 'to take', INCĔNDERE > [an'senɾe] 'to light', DĔNTEM > [den] 'tooth'. Yet their back counterparts /o/ and /ɔ/ have continued to be distinguished: FŬNDA > '[fona] 'sling' but FŎNTEM > [fɔn] (Coromines 1976: ii. 29–67). Both these parallel developments appear to owe themselves to the effect of vowel nasalization. Their chronology is uncertain.

7.3.1.3. *Fate of the Conditioning Nasal Consonant*

In nasalizing context types (i) and (iii), the nasal consonant has regularly been preserved. But in forms containing context type (ii), significant change has occurred. These forms arose as a result of apocope, which applied much more widely in Catalan than elsewhere in Ibero-Romance. All final unstressed vowels were affected except the low vowel /-a/, such that Catalan in this respect is closely akin to Gallo-Romance. As to the chronology of apocope in Catalan, there is already some evidence of apocopated forms in Latin documents of the early ninth century and possibly the change goes back to the eighth century (Rasico 1982: 114).

Simplex -N- in Apocopated Forms

Following apocope, the reflex of simplex -N- which now became absolute word-final soon weakened and was deleted, as in western Occitan dialects (see Map 4). Deletion took place whether word-final [-n] occurred after the main stressed vowel, as in PĀNEM > [pa(n)] *pa* 'bread', or after an unstressed vowel, as in ŎRPHANUM > ['ɔrfan(u)] > ['ɔrfə(n)] *orfe* 'orphan'. However, if [n] was not in absolute word-final position because it was followed by inflexional [-s], the weakening process was partially obstructed. In forms where [n] was preceded by the main stressed vowel, no weakening occurred and the nasal consonant has been maintained in all dialects; hence, PĀNES > *pans* [pans] 'loaves' beside the singular *pa* [pa], and VĔNIS > *vens* [bens] 'you come' beside VĔNIT > *ve* [be] 'he comes'. But if the preceding vowel was unstressed, weakening and deletion of [n] occurred: *orfes* ['ɔrfəs] 'orphans', *homes* ['ɔməs] 'men' < ŎRPHANOS, HŎMINES.

As regards the chronology of the weakening and deletion of final [-n], attested forms such as *vi* < VĪNUM (doc. 1036), *moltó* < MULTŌNEM (doc. 1042) suggest that deletion of the nasal coda had taken place by the eleventh century, while attestations involving proper names seem to set it even further back. The personal name *Guimera* which probably corresponds to modern *Guimerà* < (Germ.) 'Wigmarane'[5] is found in a document of 931, and the place name *Vià* in Cerdenya appears in 983 as *Auida* < AVITIĀNUM (Rasico 1982: 226, 1986). Thus, deletion of final [-n] was evidently operating already in the tenth century in some varieties, though it may well not have been carried through until the end of the following century in all varieties. Certainly, by the time of the earliest vernacular texts in Catalan, the beginning of the thirteenth century, the deletion is a fait accompli.

Some uncertainty attaches to the phonetic circumstances associated with the deletion of final [-n]. Did deletion lead to the appearance of unconditioned nasal vowels, the path of development being [-Vn] > [-Ṽ(n)] > [-Ṽ] (> [-V]) as some scholars believe (e.g. Duarte i Montserrat and Alcina i Keith 1984: i. 206), or was the development [-Vn] > [-V] without notable intervening vowel nasalization and unconditioned nasal vowels? Also, by what phonetic stages did the alveolar nasal coda [-n] itself undergo deletion—via the velarization of the nasal [-n] > [-ŋ] > [-Ø] or simply [-n] > [-Ø]? As to the first question, it has been argued that the absence of any trace of unconditioned nasal vowels in contemporary varieties of Catalan casts some doubt on whether -N deletion did indeed leave behind unconditioned nasal vowels (Rasico 1985: 53). However, in other Romance areas where context (ii) forms have lost word final [-n] < -N- and have emerged with an oral word-final vowel, there is strong evidence for believing that these forms had first developed an unconditioned nasal vowel which later denasalized; cf. the dialects of the neighbouring Occitan area (6.2.2.2) and northern Italian dialects spoken in eastern Lombardy (10.5.2). It seems reasonable therefore to hypothesize that a similar pattern of change may well have occurred in Catalan too. Some support for this hypothesis also comes from an attested development during the later Middle Ages in the conservative dialect area of the diocese of Girona where a pronunciation with final [-ŋ] appeared in context (ii) forms.[6] This seems to represent the result of a restoration, by which a nasal vowel is restructured into a sequence of vowel + [ŋ] paralleling directly comparable restructurings in northern Italy (10.4.4.2).[7] If this interpretation is valid, the existence of unconditioned nasal vowels is indicated.

However, in most varieties of Catalan any unconditioned nasal vowels which arose in context (ii) forms were evidently soon subject to denasalization. Already in the earliest vernacular verse, the thirteenth century *L'Epístola farcida de sant Esteve*, there appear rhymes such as *fo* : *do* < FŬIT DŌNUM 'was (3rd sg. pret.), gift' (ll. 15–16), suggesting that any quality difference between the two vowels was felt to be non-distinctive. The lack of evidence of any quality change in the low vowel /a/ in forms where final -N was deleted is also notable. Whereas in the neighbouring Occitan area the deletion of final -N was accompanied by velarization of the low vowel /a/ which was presumably associated with the high-level nasality of the vowel (cf. 6.2.1.3), in Catalan there was no such development and the vowel of forms like *pa* < PĀNEM 'bread' was rapidly identified with the vowel of items like *va* < VĀDIT '(he) goes'. Thus, it seems that nasality in the stressed vowels of the reflexes of PĀNEM DŌNUM etc. in Catalan had no significant effect on vowel quality before denasalization took place.

As to the phonetic stages followed by [-n] as it was deleted, there is no evidence that velarization occurred prior to loss. Nothing prevents the assumption that final [-n] remained coronal before it disappeared, [-n > ⁻ⁿ > -Ø].

Other Word-Final Nasals in Apocopated Forms

The deletion of original simplex -N- which had become final through apocope (e.g. in PĀNEM > [pa]) did not presage a general weakening of coda nasals in Catalan. Instead, all other types of word-final nasal were consistently preserved, and indeed further types were developed to yield a range of four distinctive nasals [-m -n -ɲ -ŋ] which became established in Catalan during the later medieval period. This arrangement has been maintained to the present-day and may be represented as follows:

-M(M)- -MB- -MP-	> -m	[fum som ʎom kam]	<	FŪMUM 'smoke', SŬMMUM 'superficial', LŬMBUM 'back', CĂMPUM 'field'
-ND- -N-	> -n	[gran ben]	<	GRĂNDEM 'big', VĔNTUM 'wind'
-NN- -ɲɲ-	> -ɲ	[puɲ aɲ]	<	PŪGNUM 'fist', ĂNNUM 'year'
-ŋk- (< -ŋk- -ŋg-)	> -ŋ	[baŋ saŋ]	<	(Germ.) bank 'bench', SĂNGUEM 'blood'

The parallel may be noted between Catalan and certain Gascon and northern Italian dialects in respect of the preservation of word-final nasals other than -N- after apocope (cf. 6.3, 10.4.4).

It appears that there were several stages in the establishment of the various word-final nasals in Catalan and these may be briefly traced. First, apocope gave rise to two types [-m] < -M(M)- and [-ɲ] < -NN- -ɲɲ-.

Then, two further types [-n] and [-ŋ] were added as a result of independent sound changes. The first of these arose from the effect of progressive assimilation which occurred regularly in *sonorant + voiced non-velar plosive* clusters to give geminate sonorants, e.g. -ND- > -nn- (but not in LŎNGA > [ʎoŋgə] *llonga* 'long (f. sg.)'). These geminates soon simplified and if they were followed by a final vowel subject to apocope, the resulting simplex sonorant became word-final. With nasal + voiced plosive clusters, we find -MB- > -mm- > -m and -ND- > -nn- > -n. The former change would have added to existing cases of [-m], whereas the latter introduced a new type of word-final nasal [-n], as in *gran*. A three-way system of word-final nasals thus emerged [-m -n -ɲ].

As to chronology, progressive assimilation of -MB- > [-mm-], -ND- > [-nn-] (and -LD- > [-ll-]) seems to date from at least the early ninth century; cf. *coma* < CUMBA attested 815, *Palomera* < PALUMBĀRIA att. 839 and *geronnense* < GERUNDĒNSEM att. 881, *sponna* < SPŎNDA 'edge' att. 890 (Rasico 1981). The new coronal geminate consonants which resulted evolved differently from their earlier counterparts inherited from Latin, cf. *espona* 'edge' (< SPŎNDA) vs. *canya* 'reed' (< CĂNNA). We may therefore assume that they arose after the original Latin geminates had undergone modification through palatalization (or in some dialects simplification).

A later medieval development led to the appearance of the fourth type of word-final nasal, [-ŋ]. As part of a general move to simplify consonant clusters in Catalan, the final segment of word-final *nasal + non-continuant consonant* sequences was deleted, as in:

CĂMPUM	>	[kamp]	>	[kam]	*camp*	'field'
DĔNTEM	>	[dent]	>	[den]	*dent*	'tooth'
*CĪNQUE	>	[siŋk]	>	[siŋ]	*cinc*	'five'

The first stages of this change involved the deletion of non-continuant consonants when they were both preceded and followed by consonants. An early attested example is *estachamens* < (Germ.) stakka + -MĔNT(O)S 'palissades', dated 1075. The earliest known examples of the deletion of final non-continuant consonants date from the thirteenth century, *pagamen* < PACA-MĔNTUM (1247), *veramen* < VERA-MĔNTE (late thirteenth century). However, it was not until the fifteenth century that the development became generalized in Catalan. The considerable delay in generalization is borne out by its absence in the Catalan variety spoken in Alguer (Alghero) in Sardinia which was populated by Catalans from 1354 (Blasco Ferrer 1984a). As well as representing an extension of the rule simplifying consonant clusters, this change may owe itself in part to morphophonemic factors. Deletion of word-final non-continuants would serve to eliminate alternations found in a substantial set of nominals by generalizing the stem found in plural forms to the singular. Thus:

(sg.) [kamp] / (pl.) [kam+s] > (sg.) [kam] / (pl.) [kam+s]
(sg.) [dent] / (pl.) [den+s] > (sg.) [den] / (pl.) [den+s]
(sg.) [blaŋk] / (pl.) [blaŋ+s] > (sg.) [blaŋ] / (pl.) [blaŋ+s]

The phonological effect of the change was not only to establish [-ŋ] in Catalan as a new type of possible word-final nasal coda but also to increase the frequency of occurrence of existing word-final nasals. In this way, the four-way set of contrasting nasals in word-final position is well represented. Of particular note is the maintenance of the contrast before the plural marker [-s] as in [kams bens aŋs baɲs] 'fields, winds, years, benches'. The typical Romance arrangement of only permitting homorganic sequences of nasal + oral consonant is thus strikingly overruled.

7.3.1.4. *Possible Reasons for the Lack of Vowel Nasalization in Catalan*

The failure of vowel nasalization to occur in a significant way in Catalan is striking, especially in view of its geographical and historical links with the Occitan zone where nasalization has been widespread. Two possible factors appear to have contributed to this.

The series of sound changes just considered may have played a part. These served to expand the range and incidence of contrasting nasal coda consonants in the language and in so doing strengthened their status. This might well have had important consequences for any possible moves towards vowel nasalization (Sampson 1993). Although it is the case that other Romance varieties, such as the dialect of Milan in northern Italy, have developed nasal vowel phonemes despite the preservation of contrasting word-final nasals (see 10.4.4), the situation in Catalan was different in that a full set of contrasting nasals arose in other contexts as well as word-finally, notably pre-consonantally preceding inflexional /-s/.

In addition to this structural consideration, factors of a socio-political nature have probably also been important. In particular, it is surely not without importance that the period from the fourteenth century on saw increasing contacts westward with Castile, where vowel nasalization has been of only marginal significance, rather than northward towards southern France.

7.4.   Spanish

In the central area of the peninsula, nasality appears to have exerted a very limited influence indeed on vowel evolution. In the standard variety of today, which is based on educated usage and especially that of the capital Madrid, there are no nasal vowel phonemes but in certain contexts vowels may display fairly high levels of conditioned nasality. Significant nasality is reported to accompany the articulation of vowels when they are both preceded and followed by a nasal consonant, as in *mano* ['mãno] 'hand' and *nunca* ['nũŋka] 'never', or when they are word-initial and preceded by a pause and followed by a coda nasal consonant, as in *enfermo* [ẽm'fermo] 'ill' and *ánfora* ['ãmfora] 'amphora' (Navarro Tomás 1968: § 38; Quilis 1992: 55). However, detailed experimental investigation of vowel nasality is still lacking.

Beyond the standard variety, it is notable that despite the enormous territorial expansion of Castilian in the later Middle Ages, the degree of dialectal variation has remained fairly limited. As far as vowel nasalization is concerned, it has operated more intensely in the varieties which became established in the south of the Peninsula, in Andalusia, as a result of the southward expansion of Castile in the *reconquista*. Here, it has given rise to high-level allophonic vowel nasality and occasionally even unconditioned nasal vowels.

7.4.1.   HISTORY OF VOWEL NASALIZATION

7.4.1.1.   *Background Developments*

Early developments affecting all types of Ibero-Romance are indicated in 7.2.1. In addition, Castilian underwent apocope but only on a limited scale. After some variability, it came to operate regularly just with words ending in /-e/ provided that it was preceded by no more than one coronal consonant.[8] Typically, it applied to paroxytons. Where it has applied to originally proparoxyton forms such as in IŬVENEM > ['xoβen] 'young' and MĂRGINEM > ['marxen] 'margin', learned influence may have been involved preserving the medial unstressed vowel from syncope, which usually operated before apocope (Pensado 1984: 237). Also, it may be noted that the 1st sg. perf. marker /-e/ < -Ī in strong paroxytonic verb forms has avoided elimination for morphological reasons even when it followed a single coronal consonant, cf. VĒNĪ > ['bine] 'I came'. In fact, the expected deletion did take place, as thirteenth-century texts clearly reveal, but subsequently there was systematic restoration of final /-e/.[9]

As a result of apocope, a new set of context (ii) forms developed with word-final [-n] < simplex -N- adding to the small handful of items inherited from Latin, such as NŌN and [kjen] < QUĔM 'who', and the 3rd plural verb-forms with [-n] < -NT, as in SŬNT > [son] 'they are', NĔGANT > ['njeɣan] 'they deny', etc. These complemented the wide range of forms containing nasalizing contexts (i) and (iii) which Castilian had inherited from Latin.

7.4.1.2.   *Implementation of Vowel Nasalization*

There is little evidence of nasalization operating in a significant way on vowel evolution in the medieval period. One characteristic sign of nasalization is the neutralization of mid vowels in nasalizing contexts and this has not occurred in Spanish. Thus:

VĒNDIT	>	*vende*	['bende]	'he sells'	vs.	TĔNDA	>	*tienda* ['tjenda] 'shop'
ROTŬNDUM	>	*redondo*	[re'ðondo]	'round (m. sg.)'	vs.	PŎNTEM	>	*puente* ['pwente] 'bridge'
VĔNĪ (> ['beni])	>	*ven*	[ben]	'come! (sg.)'	vs.	BĔNE	>	*bien* [bjen] 'well'
RATIŌNEM	>	*razón*	[ra'θon]	'reason'	vs.	—		
SĪNUM	>	*seno*	['seno]	'bosom'	vs.	CAENUM	>	*cieno* ['θjeno] 'mud'
CORŌNA	>	*corona*	[ko'rona]	'crown'	vs.	BŎNA	>	*buena* ['bwena] 'good (f. sg.)'

where original low-mid /ɛ ɔ/ have undergone regular diphthongization.[10] An alternative interpretation of the data is also possible. This is that diphthongization had already systematically operated before any significant vowel nasalization occurred, so that by the time vowels began to experience any heightened nasalization there were only two types of mid vowel remaining in Castilian [o] and [e] (with on-gliding congeners [je] and [we] or its earlier realization [wo]). In that case, vowel nasalization would not have left readily discernible traces in mid-vowel quality modifications. However, such a view would pre-suppose an unexpectedly early date for the completion of diphthongization. It would also in part conflict with comparative data from Romanian where a similar original mid-vowel contrast between [e] and [ɛ] existed, although there was no comparable back mid vowel contrast. Here, [ɛ] also diphthongized but it was pre-dated by nasalization in context (i) forms (cf. 12.2.3).

Two special cases exist, however, where nasalization may have operated in a limited way in context (i) forms. First, in words originally containing initial CONF- and INF- the nasal was evidently deleted in popular speech during the medieval period. Indeed, this may reflect a continuation of a known phonetic phenomenon in certain varieties of Latin (cf. 3.2). Examples attested in medieval texts include: [11]

INFĂNTEM	>	i(f)fante	'royal child'
*CON-FECTĀRE	>	cohechar	'to suborn'
CONFŬNDERE	>	cofonder / cohonder	'to confound, destroy'
CONFĪCIA	>	cofita / cohita	'grouping of adjacent buildings'

Cases of /n/ deletion in the sequence -N'F- arising from syncope are also found, e.g. BENEFACTŌRIA > benfectria (attested eleventh century) > befetria (thirteenth century) > behetría (fourteenth century) 'township whose citizens elect their ruler' (Catalán 1989: esp. 277–93).

Subsequently, there has however been widespread remodelling with the restoration of coda /n/ in forms seen to contain prefixal CON- or IN-. But whether the earlier deletion of coda /n/ yielded a nasal vowel in these forms is difficult to establish. Evidence from Italo-Romance and Sardinian suggests that consonantal assimilation alone may have been involved, so that the development was -Vnf- > -Vff- > -Vf- (> -Vh-), cf. Hajek (1997: § 6.4.1.1) and 11.2.2. At all events, nasality has left no discernible trace at all subsequently.

The second case concerns the raising of /e o/ to become high vowels before certain nasal + consonant groups. Examples are:

CĬNGULA	>	cincha	'saddle strap'	ŬNGULA	>	uña	'nail'
PĬNCTARE	>	pintar	'to paint'	PŬNCTUM	>	punto	'point'
TĬNEA	>	tiña	'ringworm'	CŬNEA	>	cuña	'wedge'

(the last two items contain the group -NJ- discussed below)

The raising here is similar to that in other Ibero-Romance varieties (cf. 7.3.1.2 and 8.2.3) and is also reminiscent of developments found in standard Italian (cf. 10.2.2). As in these other forms of Romance, raising is subject to strong constraints so that it occurs in two basic types of context only. The first is before a cluster originally made up of [ŋ] + velar + consonant, as in ŬNG(U)LA PŬNCTUM. In forms where there was originally no consonant following the sequence [ŋ] + velar consonant, raising did not take place: tronco, hongo, vence, abolengo / realengo < TRŬNCUM FŬNGUM VĬNCIT (Germ.) -ĬNG 'trunk, mushroom, he conquers, belonging to one's ancestors → ancestry/belonging to the crown → royal patrimony'.

Raising also occurs in another type of context, namely before the original sequence -NJ-, as in tiña and cuña. There are variable outcomes with

-ŌNIUM/-A suggesting some intra-dialectal fluctuation (cf. TERR-ŌNIUM > *terruño* 'clod' but CICŌNIA > *cigüeña* 'stork'). Before the original -GN-sequence, however, raising is not regular, e.g. LĬGNUM > *leño*.[12] This suggests that the sequence -NJ- must have caused vowel raising at some stage prior to its merger with the sequence -GN- as [ɲɲ].

In those items where vowel raising has taken place, the implication is that it owes itself to the effect of heightened nasality. However, there was no associated weakening of the coda nasal.

7.4.1.3. *Fate of the Conditioning Nasal Consonant*

In context types (i) and (iii), the nasal consonant has undergone no significant change. As regards context (ii) forms, apocope in early Castilian only resulted in one nasal consonant being able to occur word-finally, namely the coronal [-n] < -N- or -NN- (PĀNEM > *pan*, IOHĂNNEM > *Juan*). In fact, a constraint developed in the language permitting [-n] as the sole word-final nasal, hence QUĔM > *quien* [kjen]. Even today in standard Castilian pronunciation, this constraint operates with loanwords or neologisms containing word-final -*m* such that it is regularly realized as [n], e.g. *álbum* ['alβun] (Navarro Tomás 1968: § 86). But apart from this development, the final [-n] of standard Spanish has shown no conspicuous signs of weakening and fostering vowel nasalization.

7.4.2. DEVELOPMENTS IN REGIONAL VARIETIES OF SPANISH

In more recent times, there has been a significant tendency to weaken word-final [-n] in context (ii) forms in certain parts of the Castilian speech area in the peninsula, notably in Andalusia and Extremadura in the south and south-west and also in the north-west in the area exposed to influence from Galician-Portuguese (see Map 5). In these areas, the degree of weakening of the word-final nasal is variable as is the level of nasality in the preceding vowel. In contemporary dialects of Andalusia in particular, a spectrum of realizations can be found for underlying word-final vowel + /N/ sequences, including [-Ṽn] [-Ṽŋ] [-Ṽⁿ] [-Ṽ] and even denasalized [-V].[13] In single dialects, there can be variation between individual linguistic items. Thus, in the dialect of Almogia (Malaga), forms such as [kaβe'θõŋ kata'βõ] 'fathead, carpenter's square' are found with [-Ṽŋ] and [-Ṽ] apparently varying from one lexical item to another. Furthermore, denasalization in 3rd plural verb forms is usual, as in *no sé lo que harán* [no θe lo ke ha'ra] 'I don't know what they will do', with the result that there is syncretism between 3rd singular and 3rd plural forms (Lorenz-Gonzalez 1985: 76–9).

Against such a variable background, it is difficult to establish whether any area is preferentially adopting and generalizing the unconditioned nasal vowel variant. Comparison of the data of the 1930s presented in the *ALPI* (maps 11 and 53 *aguijón* and *crin*) and the more recent materials of the *ALEA* do however point to the generalization of [-ŋ], often very weakly present, at the expense of [-n] which appeared widely in Eastern Andalusia in the *ALPI*. But wholly unconditioned nasal vowels are still only sporadically indicated. Where the velar nasal [-ŋ] appears in a given dialect, it has often been assumed that it reflects a simple weakening of an earlier coronal [-n]. However, comparative evidence from northern Italian dialects suggests that the velar nasal may instead represent the result of restoration [-Ṽ] > [-Ṽŋ] (10.4.4.2). But for some dialects at least the process which has operated may have been substitution of [-ŋ] for [-n] rather than restoration as the presumably more prestigious use of final [-ŋ] in certain dialects has been adopted and become geographically more widespread in Andalusia. A further noteworthy point is that in those cases where an unconditioned nasal vowel is reported, it is described as being phonetically of normal duration. The deletion of final [-n] thus does not seem regularly to leave behind a quantitative trace in Andalusian.

The origins of this weakening of [-n] in context (ii) forms are uncertain. In Andalusia, it may represent an independent development of regional Castilian bound up with the general move to unblock syllables, or its starting point might lie more particularly in the speech patterns brought by immigrants from the Asturo-Leonese region in the north-west during the *reconquista* (Penny 1991*b*). This north-west zone of course lies next to the cradle of the Galician-Portuguese area, where vowel nasalization developed early on.

A final development concerning vowel nasalization may be noted. In certain varieties of Andalusia, unconditioned nasal vowels have sometimes arisen as a result of *spontaneous* nasalization. Underlying this phenomenon is the widely reported tendency in Andalusian varieties for the glottal fricative [h] corresponding to standard Castilian [x] to be accompanied by nasality in relaxed styles of speech. (The phonetic basis for this is discussed in 1.3) Where this happens, the nasality readily spreads to adjacent vowels. An example is provided by the dialect of Cabra (near Cordoba) which has such forms as [laˈβĩhã seˈrõhõ] corresponding to standard *clavija* 'plug, peg', *cerrojo* 'bolt'.[14] Further to the west, similar outcomes are reported for the speech of Cadiz, e.g. [meˈhõ] for *mejor* 'better' and, with noteworthy aspiration of syllable-initial [s], [aˈhĩ] for *así* 'thus' (Payán Sotomayor 1988: 76–7). In these and other comparable forms, we may presume the vowel preceding [h] is also somewhat nasalized.

NOTES

1. Our knowledge of the sound system, and particularly the vowel system, of the different varieties of Mozarabic is far from complete. However, no clear evidence is at hand for believing that vowel nasalization ever reached significant proportions (cf. Galmés de Fuentes 1983).

2. Comparable separation between mid vowels is found in other nasalizing contexts. Thus, for context (ii): PLĒNUM > ple [plɛ] 'full (m. sg.)', RATIŌNEM > raó [ra'o] 'reason' vs. TĚNET > te [te] 'he holds', BŎNUM > bo [bɔ] 'good (m. sg.)'; and for context (iii): CATĒNA > cadena [ka'ðɛnə] 'chain', CORŌNA > corona [ku'ɾonə] 'crown' vs. VĚN-ENT > vénen ['benən] 'they come', BŎNA > bona ['bɔnə] 'good (f. sg.)'.

3. The item PŪGNUM > puny 'fist' is clearly problematic here. However, it may go back to a variant PŪGNUM with a long vowel (cf. the parallel case of puño in Castilian, 7.4.1.2, and of pugno in Italo-Romance, 10.2.2).

4. An alternative interpretation of the facts here is possible based on the fate of the original consonant following [ŋ]. We might claim that raising only occurred when that consonant was adapted to become palatal or coronal, whereas in sequences where the structure [ŋ] + velar was preserved there was no raising. The phonetic rationale of such an interpretation, however, would be difficult to understand. Also, the existence of forms such as vèncer 'to conquer' < VĬNCERE and estrènyer 'to tighten' < STRĬNGERE, where the predicted raising does not occur, would pose problems. So too would forms like vincle where non-predicted raising has taken place.

5. Alternatively, the historical base-form may be the nominative 'Wigmara' (with penultimate stress), in which case this item would provide no useful information in the present connection. However the graphy <e> used for the penultimate vowel of the Catalan form suggests the characteristic weakening of unstressed [a] > [ə], which would confirm that the historical ancestor of the form is indeed the oblique 'Wigmarane'.

6. One trace of this is in the word fenc [fɛŋ] < FĒNUM 'hay' which has been adopted into the standard language from the north-eastern area. The adoption of fenc may be explained as a response to the threatened homonymic clash between the native form of the word for 'hay' and [fɛ] < FĬDEM 'faith', and/or as a reflection of the importance for forage production of the north-east, the wettest area of Catalonia, cf. DECLC, s.v. fenc.

7. Such an explanation seems preferable to claiming that [ŋ] arose here from an attempt to preserve the word-final nasal of context (ii) forms. Allegedly, speakers reinforced the vanishing nasal of forms like pa(n), realizing it with a velar articulation because velar coda consonants were widely found elsewhere in the language (cf. Rasico 1982: 228).

8. The history of the apocope of word-final /-e/ in Castilian is complex (cf. Lapesa 1951, 1975; Lloyd 1987: 208–9, 322; Penny 1991a: 49–50). Apocope appears to have got underway in the tenth century and involved final /-e/ (< original final /-e/ and /-i/) when it followed simplex coronal consonants. In the first half of the thirteenth century, texts point to the scope of apocope widening to affect almost all cases of

final /-e/. French influence from growing political and cultural contacts from the eleventh century on may well have promoted this, and Arabic and Hebrew influence from bilinguals in southern Spain may also have been relevant. However, from the later thirteenth century a trend began to restore the earlier status quo (deletion only after simplex coronals), which probably reflected the general pattern of usage of the mass of Castilian speakers. From the second half of the fourteenth century, this pattern has effectively become established as the norm and has remained so to the present day.

9. In the substantial body of thirteenth-century texts emanating from the royal scriptorium of Alfonso X, the reflex of VĒNĪ 'I came' appears on 24 occasions, twice as *vin* and everywhere else as *uin*. Strikingly, there are no cases at all of *uine/vine* with a restored final /-e/, indicating that restoration was still far from general at this period. Our data are drawn from Kasten and Nitti (1978).

10. Occasional exceptions do occur which involve the back vowel /ɔ/. These include MŎNTEM > *monte* 'mountain' (rather than **muente, cf. *fuente* 'fountain' < FŎNTEM as well as *puente* above), HŎMINEM > *hombre* 'man' (but diphthongizing forms *uamne, uemne, huembre* are attested in medieval texts), CŎMITEM > *conde* 'count' (beside the well-attested medieval form *cuende*), and the verbal forms CŎMPARAT > *compra* '(s)he buys', ABSCŎNDIT > Old Sp. *asconde* '(s)he hides' (mod. Sp. *esconde*), and RESPŎNDET > *responde* '(s)he answers' ; cf. relevant entries of *DCECH*. The reason for the lack of diphthongization in these words is unclear, but the sporadic raising influence of nasalization has been proposed as a factor, particularly for the nominal forms (Menéndez Pidal 1940: § 13. 4; *DCECH*, s.v. *monte*).

11. The phonetic/phonological value of the graphy <f> and <h> used in later medieval Castilian for the element deriving from Latin -F- has been much discussed. More recently, Penny (1990) has argued persuasively that in the thirteenth and fourteenth centuries the graphy <f> probably indicated /h/ in most popular words and /f/ in certain borrowings whilst <h> had no phonetic value. Only from the later fifteenth century onward did <f> come systematically to indicate /f/ whereas <h> served to indicate either zero or /h/ (which was later lost in standard Castilian). At the time when the deletion of /n/ in the cases at present under consideration began to take place, the reflex of of Latin -F- may already have been /h/ or it may still have been at the postulated earlier stage of /ɸ/.

12. In this context, the item PŪGNUM > *puño* 'fist' appears anomalous. As already noted for *puny* in Catalan (7.3.1.2 and n. 3 above), the form here may go back to a variant PŪGNUM with a long vowel.

13. Cf. the observations on word-final -*n* in Andalusia by Villena Ponsoda (1987: 15 n. 46): 'Por lo que se refiere a /N/, su realización es bastante constante, aunque sean conocidos los procesos de posteriorización [ŋ] y ulterior pérdida (incluso acompañada de la desaparición de la nasalización vocálica previamente condicionada, sobre todo en el verbo)' and also Fernández-Sevilla (1980: esp. 487–93). See below for some comment on the 'posteriorización' identified here.

14. The following description is given of the circumstances in Cabra: 'es muy corriente oír una aspiración nasalizada en cualquier otra circunstancia [sin vecindad de

nasales], especialmente en aquellos casos en que la sonoridad es más acusada y la articulación más netamente aspirada y relajada, esto es, entre vocales. En estos casos, la nasalización se propaga también a las vocales vecinas' (Rodriguez Castellano and Palacio 1948, cited in Zamora Vicente 1967: 323 n. 35).

8

Ibero-Romance II: Galician-Portuguese

8.1. Introduction

Portuguese is one of the two standard Romance varieties in which nasal vowels appear as independent phonemes (the other case being standard French, cf. Ch. 4). Already in early medieval times there is clear evidence of vowel nasalization operating and its effect has not only been to give rise to unconditioned nasal vowels but also to deflect the pattern of evolution in vowels where nasality has remained allophonic.

In the closely related varieties of Galicia however, a somewhat different picture emerges. As Galician shared a similar development to Portuguese up to the thirteenth century, it too experienced vowel nasalization sufficient to play an important role in shaping early vowel evolution. However, nasal vowels have not subsequently established themselves as phonemes except in one isolated relic area on the border between the Galician and Leonese domains in the east, namely in the Ancares region (cf. 8.4.5). Elsewhere, nasality now operates as a purely allophonic feature in vowels although high levels of nasality may be found in vowels in certain contexts.

8.1.1. HISTORICAL BACKGROUND

The different fate of vowel nasality in Portuguese and Galician appears to owe itself mainly to divergent political and social circumstances. In 1095, Galicia was divided into two parts by its ruler Alfonso VI of Castile. The southern part, which lay to the south of the Minho, was given to Henry of Burgundy by the king as a dowry for his daughter. This formed the County of Portugal. In 1112 Henry died, and in 1128 his son, Afonso Henriques, defeated the forces of his mother Teresa, thereby securing possession of the County of Portugal for himself. A major victory by Afonso Henriques over the Muslims in 1139 and further military and political expansion led Alfonso VII of Castile to recognize the County as the independent Kingdom of Portugal by 1143. The reconquest of large tracts of land from the Moors in the following few decades, including Lisbon in 1147 and Evora in 1165, was to give the new kingdom a more southerly centre of political gravity. Portugal was now quite separate from the rest of Galicia to the north. The process of reconquest was completed during the thirteenth century. The last major gain came with the capture of Faro in 1249, and the modern borders of Portugal were established definitively with the treaty signed with Castile in 1267.

Meanwhile, Galicia remained part of the Kingdom of León (which had temporarily regained its independence from Castile). When León was definitively incorporated into the Kingdom of Castile in the first half of the thirteenth century, the political orientation of Galicia necessarily became increasingly eastward-looking and separate from that of Portugal.

The linguistic consequences of these differing political trajectories were considerable. For Portugal, the southern expansion brought the central zone between Coimbra and Lisbon (the capital from the mid-thirteenth century on) into political and cultural prominence. Here a faster-evolving linguistic variety developed, fostered in part by the interplay between the language patterns of northern colonists and Mozarabs. This was to form the basis of the standard language. Meanwhile, the varieties of the north, in Galicia and, to a lesser extent, in Minho and Trás-os-Montes, evolved more slowly and from the fourteenth century they began to drift apart from their more innovating central and southern counterparts. It is known that already in the sixteenth century Galician was beginning to appear rustic and even comic to users of the norm variety of Portuguese (cf. Teyssier 1980: 49). A major contributory factor to this negative view of Galician was doubtless its progressive loss of social status. For it ceased to enjoy currency as a literary language from the sixteenth century and survived in Galicia itself in an increasingly diglossic situation as the 'low' language beside the 'high' language, Castilian, though recent moves to restore its status and extend its use have arrested and even reversed the decline.

The growing gulf between northern varieties of Galician-Portuguese and those of the centre-south from the twelfth–thirteenth centuries onward is reflected in their different treatments of vowel nasalization. Accordingly, separate coverage will be given to the history of vowel nasalization in the two linguistic blocks over this period: central-southern Portuguese (including the standard variety) will be considered in section 8.3 and Galician and northern Portuguese in section 8.4

8.1.2. VOWEL NASALITY IN STANDARD PORTUGUESE

The *língua padrão*, or standard variety, of Portuguese is based on the usage of educated speakers from the central area between Lisbon and Coimbra. Here, five unconditioned nasal monophthongs and four nasal off-gliding diphthongs appear. These are: /ĩ ẽ ɐ̃ õ ũ/ and /ẽw̃ ẽj õj ũj/, as in *sim, penso, lã, dom, um* 'yes, I think, wool, gift, a (m. sg.)' and *mão, bem, põe, muito* 'hand, well, (he) puts, very', respectively. Nasality in these vowels is typically incremental, moving from low to high level over the vowel's duration. When pre-consonantal and, less commonly, in final position too, nasal vowels may be followed by a consonantal off-glide whose quality is determined by the nature of the following consonant or (if final) by the quality of the vowel. The off-glide is particularly in evidence before plosives, taking the form of a nasal consonant with oral occlusion and variable duration (as in *campo* ['kẽ^{m}p^u] or ['kɐmp^u] 'field', where degree of vowel nasality and prominence of nasal consonant are reciprocally related). Before an intervocalic nasal (as in *cama*), vowels are more weakly nasal, particularly in European Portuguese, as against Brazilian Portuguese where levels of nasality are more comparable to those found in nasal vowels in other contexts (Almeida 1976; Lacerda and Head 1966). We will use the nasal symbol [~] for such nasal vowels, although the nasality is weak.

The set of five nasal vowel phonemes stands beside the larger stock of oral vowel phonemes /i e ɛ a ɐ ɔ o u/, where there is a contrast between low-mid vs. high-mid vowels in both the front and back series, this contrast being neutralized with nasal vowels. The oral vowel /ɐ/ has a limited distribution in stressed syllables, but it is able to form surface contrasts with the other vowels including the closely related /a/, as in *ceia* 'supper' vs. *saia* 'skirt'. With regard to dipththongs, the nasal series is also more limited than its oral counterpart, the range of oral diphthongs running into double figures.

A good deal of discussion has surrounded the phonological status of these nasal vowels, many scholars arguing that their proper interpretation is as sequences of oral vowel + nasal consonant /VN/ rather than as nasal vowel phonemes /Ṽ/.[1] However, there is no doubt that surface contrasts exist between nasal and oral vowels, as in *sim* 'yes' vs. *si* 'oneself' and *dom* 'gift' vs. *dou* 'I give'. Also, it is significant that even in those cases where a nasal vowel is usually followed by some sort of nasal consonant segment which would seem to suggest that the vowel's nasality is merely allophonic (e.g. in *campo, canto, branco*), some native speakers are apparently not aware of the presence of the nasal consonant segment. For such speakers, the nasal vowels of both *sim* and *campo* evidently have 'psychological reality' as phonemes.[2] Accordingly, it will not be inappropriate if for convenience we make reference to nasal vowel 'phonemes' in the coming discussion to indicate nasal vowels not followed by a fully articulated and readily perceived nasal consonant.

Some brief general remarks may be made on the patterning and distribution of these nasal vowels in the contemporary standard language. First, the system of five nasal monophthongs is smaller than that of the oral monophthongs which contains eight members. This arises from the lack of mid-vowel contrasts comparable to that between oral /e ɛ/ and /o ɔ/; Portuguese has just the mid nasal vowels /ẽ õ/. These are realized with variable height. They generally appear with a high-mid tongue position, but in certain contexts a low-mid tongue position is found. The latter is limited to cases where the vowel is followed by a heterosyllabic nasal and hence the nasality is allophonic, namely (*a*) in verb forms subject to the action of metaphony, e.g. *come* ['kɔ̃mə] 'he eats' and *teme* ['tɛ̃mə] 'he fears' and (*b*) in certain lexical items typically of recent learned origin, e.g. *cone* ['kɔ̃nə] 'cone' and *arsénico* [ɐɾ'sɛ̃niku] 'arsenic' (Parkinson 1982). A further point of interest in the light of developments in French is the presence of the high nasal vowels /ĩ/ and /ũ/, which have shown no sign of lowering.

The system of nasal monophthongs, though smaller than the oral system, is not subject to the processes of neutralization in syllables preceding the main stressed syllable which oral vowels undergo. Thus, *cinzel, vencer, lançar, monsão, punção* 'chisel, to conquer, to throw, monsoon, puncture' have as their initial vowel [ĩ ẽ ẽ õ ũ], respectively, with no neutralization between mid and high vowels. In contrast, the opposition between mid and high oral vowels in the same context is regularly neutralized. For example, the three mid or high back vowels [ɔ o u], which appear stressed in *moro, choro, duro* 'I dwell, I weep, I last', undergo neutralization when in pre-stress syllables, such that the initial vowel of the infinitives *morar, chorar,* and *durar* emerges uniformly as [u]. The absence of neutralization in unstressed vowels is not unique to nasal vowels, however. It is also found with diphthongs and sequences of vowel + syllable-coda /l/, this fact providing one of the principal reasons for interpreting nasal vowels phonologically as sequences of some sort.

Amongst the nasal diphthongs, /ũj̃/ is extremely rarely found, occurring effectively in just one item *muito* and its inflexional variants (*muitos, muita(s)*).[3] For some speakers this diphthong may in fact be realized as a rising diphthong [wĩ].

The three other nasal diphthongs are more widely represented, but they are nonetheless restricted in their distribution. They typically occur at the end of words, as in *porém* [pu'ɾẽj̃] 'however'. In inflecting words, they are stem-final. In nominals, they may be followed by the plural marker *-s* /-ʃ/, as in *mão/mão-s* [mɐ̃w̃(ʃ)] 'hand(s)'. Also, certain affective suffixes, notably *-zinh(-o/-a)* and *-zit(-o/-a)*, may be found after a nasal diphthong as in *mãozinha* 'little hand', *cãozinho,* 'little dog' and *liçãozita* 'little lesson'. In such forms, the stem-final diphthong inflects regularly for plurality; hence *mão-zinh-as* 'little hands', *cãe-zinh-os,* 'little dogs' and *liçõe-zit-as* 'little lessons' with the same stem as in *mão-s* 'hands', *cãe-s* 'dogs', and *liçõe-s* 'lessons'.[4] In verbs, only two diphthongs /ẽj̃ õj̃/ appear stem-final and these are confined to the verbs *ter* 'to have', *vir* 'to come', and *pôr* 'to put' and their derivatives, as in the 2nd singular present tense indicative forms *tens vens pões* [tẽj̃ vẽj̃ʃ põj̃ʃ]. Nasal diphthongs also figure in word-final inflectional or derivational morphemes, e.g. the derivational suffix

-ão for nominals (*mulherão* 'big woman', *chorão* 'crybaby') and the 3rd person plural marker for verbs *-am*. Finally, it may be noted that the diphthong [ẽj̃] is in complementary distribution with the nasal monophthong [ẽ].

When stems ending in one of these nasal diphthongs are developed by suffixes other than the affective ones already mentioned, the diphthong is replaced by a nasal monophthong or an oral vowel with or without a following nasal consonant, e.g. *irmão* 'brother' → *irmandade* 'brotherhood', *virgem* 'virgin' → *virginal* 'virginal', → *perdão* 'pardon' *perdoar* 'to pardon'. The nasal diphthongs thus act in a real sense as word boundary markers. The only apparent exceptions concern forms containing derivational suffixes, as in *mãozinha* 'little hand'.

Finally, when a word ending with a nasal vowel is immediately followed by a vowel-initial word, there is no comparable phenomenon in standard Portuguese to French *liaison*. Thus, *bom apetite, lã azul, comum acordo* are all realized phonetically with sequences of nasal vowel + oral vowel without any intervening nasal consonantal segment.

8.2.   History of Vowel Nasalization

8.2.1.   BACKGROUND DEVELOPMENTS

Galician-Portuguese underwent a number of early developments which affected all types of Ibero-Romance. These are discussed in 7.2.1. In addition, Galician-Portuguese was affected by apocope. Apocope probably only began operating rather late in the west of the peninsula, to judge from its limited incidence and the equally modest action in Galician-Portuguese of the related process of syncope. In fact, just final [-e] is regularly affected by apocope, and normally only when it is preceded by a simplex coronal consonant; cf. *mouil, aduzer, barō* < MŌBILE ADDŪCERE BARŌNEM, which appear in the will of Afonso II (1214), the earliest substantial extant text written in reformed (i.e. vernacular Portuguese rather than latinizing) orthography. The sole anomaly concerns the geminate coronal -NN- which is also implicated in apocope, as in *João* < IOHĂNNEM (see 8.2.2 below). Despite the restricted scope of its action, apocope nevertheless did lead to a substantial number of words developing a word-final coronal nasal, for example *fin, ben* (mod. Port. *fim* 'end', *bem* 'well') < FĪNEM BĔNE.

8.2.2.   THE NASALIZING CONTEXT

Vowel nasalization has normally occurred as a result of regressive assimilation from a conditioning nasal consonant. Cases of progressive nasalization are also found (cf. 8.2.5) but they are much rarer and subject to special constraints which point to their secondary status compared to regressive nasalization.

All three of the basic nasalizing contexts of Romance are represented in early medieval Galician-Portuguese. Forms containing context types (i) and (iii) had been inherited in large numbers from Latin, as in VĔNTUM QUĀNDO and LŪNA GRĀNUM, respectively. Context type (ii) also came to be well represented. From the outset there was a small group of Latin forms with an original word-final nasal, such as NŌN and QUĔM > [ken] (where the expected modification of final -M > [n] in monosyllables has occurred and also regular vowel-adjustment [ɛ] > [e], as explained below). To these were added 3rd plural verb-forms which arose as a result of the simplification of -NT > [-n], as in SŬNT > [son] 'they are' and GŬSTANT > ['gostan] 'they taste', and also the set of items containing vowel + (N)NEM which were affected by apocope, e.g. FĪNEM IOHĂNNEM. The occurrence of apocope after geminate -NN- is notable, this being the only non-simplex coronal consonant implicated in the development, cf. *pele* < PĔLLEM 'skin', *torre* < TŬRREM 'tower', *tosse* < TŬSSEM 'cough'.

8.2.3. IMPLEMENTATION OF VOWEL NASALIZATION

It is not known at what stage Galician-Portuguese first developed the high-level nasalization which is indicated from the time of the earliest surviving vernacular texts, the beginning of the thirteenth century. However, there are indications that nasalization had operated on certain vowels well back into the pre-literary period. Particularly revealing is the neutralization of contrasts between mid vowels in nasalizing contexts (i) and (ii), the outcome being a high-mid articulation. Thus:

TĔNDIT   >   ['tɛnde]   >   ['tẽnde] just as   ['vẽnde]   <   VĒNDIT (mod. Port. *tende, vende*)
PŎNTEM   >   ['pɔnte]   >   ['põnte] just as   ['õnde]   <   ŬNDE (mod. Port. *ponte, onde*)

(respectively, 'he tends, he sells, bridge, where')

VĔNIT   >   ['vɛne]   >   ['vẽn(e)] 'he comes' just as   ['ven(i)] < *VĒNĪ (by umlaut) < VĒNĪ 'come!' (mod. Port. both *vem*)

The neutralization here would seem to date from the pre-literary period, since a five-way system of nasal vowels [ĩ ẽ ã õ ũ] is already in place at the outset of the literary period and forms the basis for subsequent nasal vowel evolution in all varieties of Portuguese. Dating is problematic however as the use of <e> and <o> in medieval spelling is indeterminate as to the quality of mid vowels. However, it is noteworthy that the parallel neutralization of mid-vowel contrasts which occurred in the strongly nasalizing area of northern Gallo-Romance clearly dated from before the eleventh century (4.3.1). In

Galicia, there was the same move towards neutralization, but subsequently as a result of special developments the restoration of low-mid vowels /ɛ ɔ/ in certain forms has re-established a mid-vowel contrast in nasalizing contexts (see below 8.4.4.1).

A further and more specific change of note has been the fate of original Ĭ and Ŭ in certain environments containing a nasal consonant. These vowels would normally emerge as high-mid vowels /e o/, but high vowels are found instead which are presumably attributable to the presence of nasality. In these cases, there has either been a raising effect which operated after the stressed vowels had passed to high-mid [e o], or else Ĭ and Ŭ may have been blocked from lowering. Whatever the circumstances, for convenience we will use the term 'raising' to cover the phenomenon as in the treatment of parallel developments seen in Catalan and Castilian (cf. 7.3.1.2, 7.4.1.2). Raising typically occurs in the environment / __ ŋ + k,g + consonant, i.e. where the vowel precedes a velar [ŋ] plus a sequence of consonants. Examples are:

VĬNCULUM   > *brinco* 'ear-ring'   LĬNGUA   > *língua* 'tongue'
ŬNGULA   > *unha* 'nail'   NŬMQUAM > *nunca* 'never'

Less regularly, [ŋ] followed by just one consonant may cause raising, as in DOMĬNICUM > *domingo* 'Sunday', IŬNCUM > *junco* 'reed'.

The palatal nasal [ɲ] < -NJ- may also raise high-mid vowels but in a limited way only. The back vowel [o] has been more susceptible to raising than its front counterpart, though apparently this change occurs preferentially when a nasal or, occasionally, a velar consonant precedes. Thus:

TESTIMŌNIUM   > *testemunho*   'evidence'
QUAERIMŌNIA   > *caramunha*   'lament'
CŬNEA   > *cunha*   'wedge'

but contrary examples without raising are also found: RISŌNEUM > *risonho* 'cheerful', CICŌNIA > *cegonha* 'stork'. The weaker tendency for raising to take place with [e] is indicated by forms such as STAMĬNEA > *estamenha* 'woollen cloth' and SĬNGULOS > *senhos* 'each'.

Nasalizing context type (iii), however, is of particular importance. At first, vowels in this context evidently underwent nasalization through regressive assimilation, as is suggested by the characteristic neutralization of the contrast between stressed mid-vowels which occurred in other nasalizing contexts as well, e.g. BŎNA > ['bɔna] > ['bõna] and CORŌNA > [ko'rõna] where earlier [õ] and [õ] have merged as [õ]. However, in the pre-literary period intervocalic [n] underwent deletion in a development whose background is considered in the following section (8.2.4). The result was that unconditioned nasal vowels arose in Galician-Portuguese by the beginning of the literary period. However, these vowels had a limited distribution as they appeared exclusively in pre-vocalic position, e.g. in ['lũa] < LŬNA.

8.2.4. FATE OF THE CONDITIONING NASAL CONSONANT

Conditioning nasal consonants in Galician-Portuguese have had varied fortunes. In context types (i) and (ii), the broad pattern has been one of progressive weakening and erosion. The process went faster in context (ii) forms where final [-n] had weakened and probably been deleted already by the early stages of the literary period. Thereafter various developments took place depending upon the quality of the preceding vowel (8.3.1.1). Apocope also occurred after the reflex of original -NN-. This is an exceptional development since the weakening process of the final nasal affected the reflexes of original simplex -N- and geminate -NN- identically, indicating that after apocope had taken place the reflex of geminate -NN- rapidly merged with its simplex counterpart:

PĀNEM   > 'pan(e)   > pãn   > pãw̃   > pão 'bread'
IOHĂNNEM > d͡ʒo'ann(e) > d͡ʒo'ãn > d͡ʒo'ãw̃ > João 'John'

It will be recalled that apocope only occurred in words where final [-e] was preceded by coronal consonants, so that -N- and -NN- are the only types of nasal consonant found in this context type.

In context (i) forms, the nasal consonant was rather more retentive. Nonetheless, more recently it too gradually weakened, and especially before continuant consonants (i.e. fricatives and sonorants) it has either given a nasal off-glide of some sort whose precise quality is principally governed by the nature of the following consonant or it has disappeared altogether. Before non-continuant consonants, it may show a brief closure homorganic with the point of articulation of the following consonant but here too articulatory weakening has meant that just a simple nasal glide may be found in present-day Portuguese.[5] The historical interpretation of these elements following a nasal vowel and preceding an oral consonant is unclear. Where a segment of some sort is present, it might represent a residue of the original coda nasal. Alternatively, as Fagan (1988) proposes, such a segment could just be the result of epenthesis after unconditioned nasal vowels arose in recent times, in a development ṼNC > ṼC > ṼG̃C (where [G̃] indicates a nasal glide of some sort). Either view is compatible with the historical evidence.

However, in some varieties of Galician-Portuguese at least, there is some evidence to suggest that the deletion process may have already been taking place in the pre-literary and early literary period in certain contexts, namely where the nasal consonant specifically preceded a fricative consonant (cf. parallel cases in Spanish 7.4.1.2 and French 4.2.5). The appearance of graphies such as *comsselho*, for instance in the thirteenth–fourteenth-century *Livro de linhagens*, does suggest by the use of <ss> that the preceding nasal consonant may have been deleted, since the scribe presumably wishes to convey that the fricative is voiceless [s] rather than voiced [z]. The simple graphy <s> would unambiguously do so only if the nasal consonant were still pronounced, hence the use of <ss> suggests that the nasal consonant may have been phonetically weak or even non-existent. However, forms with the graphy <s> are also found, for instance in the late thirteenth-century *Cancioneiro de Ajuda*, which regularly has *consello* (Carter 1941), though this may just reflect conservative Latin-based spelling. Graphies pointing to the deletion of a nasal consonant before the labiodental fricative /f/ are reported: the form *iffante* (< INFĂNTEM) is noted from the thirteenth century onward by Machado (1977: s.v. *infante*), while Nunes (1960: 135) cites instances of medieval forms such as *cofonder, cofortar, cofujom* (< CONFŬNDERE CONFORTĀRE CONFUSIŌNEM) and *iferno* (INFĔRNUM).[6] It is unclear however whether such forms (assuming that they represent authentic graphies) indicate an oral or an unconditioned nasal vowel in the opening syllable.

The appropriate interpretation of such orthographic evidence is contentious, and a detailed study of the data is required before safe conclusions can be drawn. In this connection, it is unfortunate that we do not have at our disposal a Portuguese counterpart to the massive computer-based statistical studies on patterns of spelling usage in medieval texts provided by Dees (1980, 1987) for French. However, even if full nasal coda deletion did occur before a fricative in these items in some varieties at least, it is not clear whether it was necessarily associated with vowel nasalization (cf. 7.4.1.2).

In context (iii) forms, intervocalic [n] < simplex Latin -N- experienced progressive weakening in the pre-literary period, accompanied by heavy nasalization of the preceding vowel. The weakening resulted in the deletion of [n] by the time of the earliest Portuguese texts (beginning of the thirteenth century). Simplex -N- is the only nasal consonant to have undergone deletion in this context type; cf. the following derivations:

	MĂNUM	>	'manu	>	'mãnu	>	'mão	>	*mão*	'hand'
but	ĂNNUM	>	'annu	>	'ãn(n)u	>	'ãno	>	*ano*	'year'
	RĀMUM	>	'ramu	>	'rãmu	>	'rãmo	>	*ramo*	'branch'
	BĂLNEUM	>	'baɲɲu	>	'bãɲ(ɲ)u	>	'bãɲo	>	*banho*	'bath'

The weakening and deletion of intervocalic [n] parallels the development of intervocalic [l] > [Ø]. Both changes clearly pre-date moves to simplify the original Latin geminates -NN- and -LL-, the simplification of these geminates forming part of a general development affecting all the original Latin geminates -PP-, -TT-, etc. The original simplex consonants -N- and -L- underwent deletion in the pre-literary period. The reflex of simplex -L- disappeared without trace by the time of the earliest surviving vernacular texts (early thirteenth century), whereas the nasal -N- left behind a nasal trace in the preceding vowel; thus, MĂLUM > ['mao] > *mau* 'bad (m. sg.)' vs. MĂNUM > ['mão] > *mão* 'hand'.

The deletion of simplex -N- in context (iii) forms gave rise to unconditioned nasal vowels. These had previously been unknown in the language, and it is likely that their appearance in a substantial number of words, in both unstressed and stressed syllables, was significant in promoting the development of further cases of unconditioned nasal vowels through the deletion of conditioning nasal consonants in other contexts.

Nothing certain is known of the phonetic stages by which simplex -N- was deleted. Certainly, there is no evidence for assuming that the process led to [n] first velarizing to [ŋ] before it finally disappeared. For want of indications to the contrary we may assume that the likely stages of evolution were: [n > ⁿ > Ø].[7]

There is some dispute over the proposed dating of the deletion of intervocalic [n] < -N-. Carballo Calero (1968: 31) attributes it to the beginning of the ninth century, while Teyssier (1980: 18) suggests it took place in the eleventh century and possibly extended into the early twelfth century. Most scholars however have tended to opt for the tenth century (Entwistle 1962: 288; Sletsjøe 1959: 199; Williams 1962: § 78). The forms cited by Sletsjøe from early documents written in traditional (i.e. latinizing) orthography and dating from the pre-literary period include the following: *moimenta* < MONIMĚNTA 'monuments' (mid-tenth century), the proper name *mendiz* < MENĚNDICI (A.D. 933), and *elemosias* < ELEEMŌSINAS 'alms' (A.D. 882). Few cases with [-n-] deletion following the stressed vowel are cited, suggesting perhaps that deletion may have been carried through earlier where the stressed vowel was not immediately preceding. However, in the eleventh century the attestations become more frequent. The evidence is therefore far from clear but the available data indicate that possible deletion of [-n-] may have occurred in some parts of the Galician-Portuguese speech area and in certain linguistic contexts from the ninth century, but that the development evidently required a deal of time to be carried through and become generalized as an accepted feature of 'good' usage and be systematically reflected in the emerging written language.[8]

Finally, there is evidence to suggest that the deletion of intervocalic [n] was a development which originated in the northern part of the Galician-Portuguese dialect area and that it was not native to the southern varieties which emerged as Mozarabic dialects after the Islamic conquest of the eighth century. It was probably only introduced into these dialects when they were later overlaid by the northern varieties brought with the reconquest. The original preservation of intervocalic [n] in southern dialects is revealed by place names such as *Molino* and *Fontanas* (< MOLĪNUM FONTĀNAS) in the Alentejo, and also by local words found in dialects of the Algarve, for example *trena* 'plait' (< TRĬNA) and the derived forms *canito, donina, maçanera, romanera* which correspond to standard Portuguese *cãozinho, doninha, macieira, romãzeira* (cf. Maia 1975: 40–3, 75).

8.2.5. PROGRESSIVE NASALIZATION

A further, though limited, stock of forms with nasal vowels came as a result of progessive assimilation. Initial /m/ and less commonly initial /n/ nasalized a following vowel, particularly when the vowel was high and stressed. Thus, MĬHĪ > [mĩ] > *mim* '(to) me', MĔA > ['mĩa] > *minha* 'my (f. sg.)', NĪDUM > ['nĩo] > *ninho* 'nest'.[9]

The appearance and diffusion of such nasalized forms and their integration within the standard language have been slow and fitful processes extending over many centuries. A fully nasal realization of the stressed vowel in the reflexes of MĔA and NĪDUM, for instance, was evidently accepted in educated usage already by the beginning of the literary period, so that the vowels in these forms have shared the fortunes of [ĩ] arising from the deletion of intervocalic [n]. Thus, just as [ĩ] in ['vĩo] < VĪNUM) 'wine' has been restructured to [iɲ] to give ['viɲu] *vinho*, so too has Old Port. ['nĩo] given ['niɲu] *ninho*.

However, it was to take longer for other words with similar progressively nasalized vowels to gain acceptance. *Mãe* < MĀTREM 'mother'[10] was widely pronounced with a non-nasal vowel, and in Galicia and varieties of N. Trás-os-Montes this is still the case. In literary works, the spellings *may mai* appear until the sixteenth century, suggesting that the variant with a nasal vowel only became fully established in the standard language comparatively late. Similarly, *muito* < MŬLTUM 'much, very' is realized with an oral vowel to this day in Galicia, and in the *Orthografia* of Duarte Nunes de Lião (1576) the stressed diphthong of this word is still explicitly identified with that of the word *ruivo* 'red-haired', while Camões still rhymes *muito* with *fruito*.

In other lexical items, a similar co-existence of variants has not resulted in the variant with the nasal vowel entering the standard language. Thus, a nasalized variant ['mẽɐ] of *mesa* < MĒNSA 'table', recorded already in the sixteenth century, is still found in southern varieties, as is [mẽʃ] for *mes* (Vasconcellos 1970: 76). Grammarians of the seventeenth and eighteenth centuries cite further cases of forms with progressive vowel nasalization, which formerly enjoyed some currency. Such forms, which are regularly adjudged 'popular' and are once again associated with regional usage of southern Portugal, include *(a)menxa* 'plum' < DAMASCĒNA, *menxer* 'to move' < MĬSCERE, *menxiricar* 'to gossip' < MISCER-ICĀRE (= standard Port. *ameixa, meixer, mexericar*). All are noted by Carmelo in 1767 (Pereira dos Santos 1958: 103).

8.3.   Nasal Vowel Evolution in Standard Portuguese and Centre-South Dialects

At the outset of the literary period (thirteenth century), all varieties of Galician-Portuguese had developed (or were in the process of developing) a set of five unconditioned nasal vowels /ĩ ẽ ã õ ũ/ which had arisen in original context (iii) forms, e.g. ['lũa 'mão] < LŪNA MĂNUM. In context type (i), we may assume that vowels were typically strongly nasalized but that nasality here was allophonic only, being conditioned by a still present adjacent nasal consonant, e.g. ['vẽndo] < VĒNDO. In context (ii), the presence of strong vowel nasality may also be supposed, but the situation with the conditioning nasal consonant is less clear. By the early thirteenth century, it may have lost its occlusion and full consonantal status, or it may have still been realized, by some speakers at least, as a weakly stopped nasal, in which case vowel nasality would remain clearly allophonic. The likely fate of this nasal is taken up below (8.3.1.1).

8.3.1.   DEVELOPMENTS IN THE PERIOD UP TO THE SIXTEENTH CENTURY

In the period of the later Middle Ages and into the sixteenth century, the system of nasal vowels underwent some major developments. The incidence of nasal vowel phonemes was increased, various qualitative adjustments occurred with individual types of nasal vowel leading sometimes to mergers, and in special circumstances nasal vowels were denasalized.

8.3.1.1.   *Loss of the Conditioning Nasal Consonant in Context (ii) Forms and its Aftermath*

In context (ii) forms, the final nasal segment which had arisen through the action of apocope was progressively weakened and eventually deleted leaving behind an unconditioned nasal vowel. Phonetically, it seems likely that such vowels would have had slightly greater duration than other vowels. Although this cannot be confirmed from the available textual evidence, recent experimental investigation has shown that nasal vowels are phonetically longer than their oral counterparts in Portuguese (Moraes and Wetzels 1992) and it has also been found experimentally that stressed vowels in oxytons are typically a little longer than in non-oxytonic forms (cf. 10.4.3.1). We may therefore hypothesize that the unconditioned nasal vowels of context (ii) displayed added duration. This would help to explain the development of nasal off-glides in these vowels, such a phenomenon being more common with vowels which are phonetically of greater duration.

After the deletion of the final nasal consonant and the establishment of unconditioned nasal vowels, the high vowels evolved differently from the non-high types. The high nasal vowels [ĩ ũ] may have developed off-glides but if they did so the off-glides were evidently reabsorbed, leaving a monophthong.[11] Thus:

FĪNEM   > fĩn > fĩ[12] > *fim* 'end'
(proclitic) ŪNUM > ũn > ũ > *um* 'a (m. sg.)'

After the remaining (non-high) vowel types, an off-glide developed which remained with the result that three types of off-gliding nasal diphthongs were created:

BĚNE   > bẽn   > bẽ   > bẽj̃>   *bem*   'well'
CĂNEM   > kãn   > kã   > kãw̃   > *cão*   'dog'
RATIŌNEM   > ra'dzõn > rɐ'zõ   > rɐ'zõw̃ > *razão* 'reason'
IŬVENEM   > 'dʒovẽn > 'dʒovẽ > 'dʒovẽj̃ > *jovem* 'young'

The path of change between the second and fourth stages of evolution in these forms has been the subject of debate. One view, which we adopt, has been that the conditioning nasal was fully deleted so that a final unconditioned vowel emerged, and that subsequently an off-gliding diphthong was created, the pattern being that after front vowels a front off-glide [j̃] developed and after back vowels the back glide [w̃] was formed. Any glide which came into being after high vowels would have been absorbed (Nobiling 1903; Lipski 1973; Sampson 1983).

An alternative view has been to assume that the nasal consonant did not undergo deletion but weakened to give an off-glide agreeing in frontness/backness with the preceding nasal vowel. This is proposed by Carvalho (1989a) who claims that off-glide creation was preceded by velarization of the conditioning nasal: [bẽn > bẽŋ > bẽj̃], [ra'dzõn > ra'dzõŋ > rɐ'zõw̃], etc. The appeal to an intermediate velar stage is motivated to a large degree by developments in Galician where forms such as *ben* [bẽŋ] appear (cf. 8.4.4 below). However, there seems good reason for assuming that there was full deletion of the conditioning nasal followed by off-gliding of the nasal vowel and that the appearance of the Galician forms in [ŋ] represents the result of later restructuring of nasal vowels [Ṽ > Ṽŋ], parallel to that found elsewhere in Romance (cf. Occitan 6.2.2.4, and northern Italian dialects 10.4.4.2).

The result of the changes seen here was that the stock of unconditioned nasal vowels already present in context (iii) forms was considerably expanded. They might be found now in stressed and unstressed syllables, in initial, medial, and final position within words. However, there is no clear evidence to suggest that unconditioned nasal vowels could systematically appear before (oral) consonants, except perhaps before fricatives (8.2.4). Thus, it seems that nasal vowels typically remained allophonic in context (i) forms .

There is a further aspect of this development in context (ii) forms. As we have seen, the result has been the appearance of off-gliding nasal diphthongs. Now, these were novelties in the language and of very limited distribution. They could occur only in absolute word-final position or stem-final followed by inflexional /-s/ which acts as a marker for {2nd person singular} in verbs and {plural} in nominals. Thus, such nasal diphthongs seem already to be acquiring the demarcative function of word-boundary or stem-boundary marker which their modern-day counterparts still have today (cf. 8.1.2).

As regards textual evidence for the changes noted here, words originally containing final [-Vn] are spelt in thirteenth century documents as <-Ṽ> <-Vn> and sometimes <-Vm>. The appropriate interpretation of the last of these three graphies is problematic. Its appearance is taken by Carvalho (1989a) to be an indicator of the appearance of a vocalized form [-w̃] deriving from velar [-ŋ] < word-final [-n] (see above); its generalization to contexts following front nasal vowels would presumably be due to analogy. Other explanations for the graphy are possible however, not least the influence of Latin, since -M was with a few exceptions the only word-final nasal found in standard Latin spelling. But whatever the explanation, the appearance of this non-etymological graphy does seem to point to the loss of the coronal quality of the original nasal. If we accept that word-final [n] was deleted, the graphy implies that deletion had occurred by the end of the thirteenth century.

8.3.1.2. *Raising and Centralization of* [ã]

During the later medieval period, the low nasal vowel [ã] underwent raising to take on a low-mid central point of articulation [ɛ̃]. This development introduced [ɛ̃] into all context types, as in:

context (i)   CĂMPUM   > 'kɛ̃mpo > *campo*
context (ii)   CĂNEM   > kɛ̃w̃   > *cão*
context (iii) RĀMUM   > 'rɛ̃mo   > *ramo*

It is difficult to establish a more precise chronology for this change on the basis of philological evidence, since the vowel is represented as <ã, an, am> in available texts with no indication of shifts in vowel height.

Raising did not occur, however, in dialects of Minho in the north-west of Portugal or in Galician. In Minho, velarization to [ɑ̃] occurred instead, and in Galician the vowel [ã] has generally remained low and central, with velarization occurring only when a velar consonant follows or when the velar nasal [ŋ] precedes, as in ['uŋɑ̃ kɑ̃ŋ] < ŪNA CĂNEM, but ['ãntes] < ĂNTE-S (cf. Alvarez, Regueira, and Monteagudo 1986: 19). It is possible that the lack of raising in Galician is connected with the relatively reduced level of vowel nasality found there from the later medieval period. Philological evidence of velarization in the Minho region appears from the fourteenth century, with the graphy <-om> for forms with original -ANE (Vasconcellos 1928: 411). Xove (1988) draws certain inferences from the different treatment of original [ã] in north-western dialects of Portuguese (velarization) and in north-eastern dialects (raising and centralization). Seeing that a raised vowel [ẽ] is widely found in central and southern dialects of Portugal, he concludes that this difference was already established in the period before the reconquest and that it was predominantly the north-eastern speech patterns which were carried to and implanted in the reconquered territories south of the Tagus.[13]   If this view is correct, it would suggest that raising [ã] > [ẽ] was carried through in north-eastern areas by the thirteenth century.

The raising of [ẽ] created a notable dialectal rift in Galician-Portuguese from later medieval times. However, the different fates of [ã] (raising vs. velarization) initially had little phonological significance, in that the structure of the nasal vowel system in all dialects remained basically unchanged.

8.3.1.3. *Restructuring of Hiatus Sequences Containing a Nasal Vowel*

In context (iii) forms such as LŪNA, the loss of intervocalic -N- with the consequent nasalization of the preceding vowel had resulted in the appearance of a wide range of sequences with the form [ṼV]. At the outset of the literary period the two vowels of such sequences belonged to separate syllables, and the main word-stress could fall on the first or the second or on neither of the component vowels, as in:

LŪNA	>	['lũ-ɐ]	'Ṽ-V
MANŬCULUM	>	[mẽ-'o-ʎo]	Ṽ-'V
ŎRPHANUM	>	['ɔr-fẽ-o]	Ṽ-V

(where the dash indicates a syllable boundary)

The reverse pattern [V-Ṽ] also existed, although here the nasality of the nasal vowel element was only allophonic. This pattern had almost always arisen from the loss of an intervocalic (oral) consonant preceding a vowel in context (i) forms, e.g. CALĔNTEM > [kɐ'ẽnte] 'hot', PALŬMBUM > [pɐ'õmbo] 'pigeon'. Vowel contraction, which operated widely in hiatus sequences, reduced the majority of such sequences to a single nasal vowel segment. But this had no effect on the quality of the nasal vowel which developed in exactly the same way here as it did when not preceded by a vowel (cf. CALĔNTEM > [kɐ'ẽnte] > ['kẽntə] *quente* just as DĔNTEM > ['dẽntə] *dente* 'tooth'). The evolution of nasal vowels in [V-Ṽ] sequences thus poses few problems. However, the picture is a good deal more complex for nasal vowel evolution in sequences of the [Ṽ-V] type.

Moves to eliminate the hiatus present in disyllabic vowel sequences got underway in the fourteenth century. In [Ṽ-V] sequences, these moves were carried through in a variable way dependent on where the main word-stress lay in relation to the component vowels, the height of the nasal vowel element, and the nature and degree of the difference of tongue position (if any) between the nasal vowel and the following oral vowel. As a result, original nasal vowels have sometimes been modified in quality or remodelled. The main lines of development are the following.

(a) [Ṽ-V] *sequences where* [Ṽ] *carries the main word-stress*

In sequences of vowels of identical tongue position, the vowels have coalesced to give a single nasal vowel. Thus,

	ẽ-e	>	ẽ	TĔNES	>	'tẽ-es	>	tẽs	'you (sg.) have'
(ã-a >)	ẽ-ɐ	>	ẽ	LĀNA	>	'lẽ-ɐ	>	lẽ	'wool'
	õ-o	>	õ	BŎNUM	>	'bõ-o	>	bõ	'good (m. sg.)'

Coalescence also occurred when a high vowel [ĩ ũ] was followed by a mid vowel, which agreed with it in frontness/backness.[14]

ĩ-e	>	ĩ	FĪNES	>	'fĩ-es	>	'fĩ-is	>	fĩs	'ends'
ũ-o	>	ũ	IEIŪNUM	>	ʒə'ʒũ-o	>	ʒə'ʒũ-u	>	ʒə'ʒũ	'fasting'

Analogy affected the subsequent evolution of coalesced [ẽ]. In all the forms where it occurred, such as [tẽs], [vẽs] < VĔNIS and [bẽs] < BĔNE-S, it was stem-final and followed by inflexional -s. This stem-final [ẽ] was evidently adapted to [ẽj̃] by analogy with the vowel in the related uninflected form. Hence, by analogy with [tẽj̃] < TĔNET and [vẽj̃] < VĔNIT, the forms [tẽs] and [vẽs] became [tẽj̃s] and [vẽj̃s], and similarly the singular form [bẽj̃] < BĔNE caused the plural [bẽs] to be adapted to [bẽj̃s].[15]

In sequences of vowels with different tongue positions where coalescence was not possible, a twofold pattern of evolution can be detected which is guided principally by whether the second vowel of the [Ṽ-V] sequence was lower or higher than the first, namely:

if the second vowel is lower   Ṽ-V > V-(C)V
if the second vowel is higher   Ṽ-V > Ṽ-G̃

Thus, with a lower second vowel, a bisyllabic sequence typically remained and the hiatus was commonly resolved by epenthesis of a consonantal segment. The nasal vowel also regularly underwent denasalization. When the second vowel was higher, it was raised, desyllabified and nasalized to form the off-glide of a nasal diphthong. Sequences of vowels of equal height, namely [ẽ-o] and [õ-e],

give differing results. Somewhat predictably, this complex pattern of development is only carried through in a gradual way extending over many centuries.
The details of individual changes may be outlined.

(i) [Ṽ-V] *sequences where the second* [V] *is lower*
Where the first vowel is [ĩ], there has been restructuring by epenthesis of a
palatal nasal [ɲ] probably arising via the stage [j̃]:

ĩ-V > ĩ-j̃V > iɲV VĪNUM   > 'vĩ-o   > 'vĩ-j̃o   > 'viɲo (> 'viɲu) *vinho* 'wine'
            GALLĪNA > gɐ'lĩ-ɐ > gɐ'lĩ-j̃ɐ > gɐ'liɲɐ   *galinha* 'hen'

This change also applied to two other cases where [ĩ] had arisen: (*a*) from
progressive nasalization, such as *minha, ninho* 'my (f. sg.), nest' whose evolution has been ['miɲɐ] < ['mĩ-ɐ] < [mi-a] < MĔA and ['niɲo] < ['nĩ-o]
< NĪDUM; (*b*) from nasal spreading where nasality has extended from an
adjacent nasal vowel to a previously oral [i], as in *vinha* 'he was coming (imperf.
indic.)' ['viɲɐ] < ['vĩ-ɐ] < [ṽe'i-ɐ] < VENĪ(E)BAT and similarly *tinha* 'he
had (imperf. indic.)'. As regards the chronology of the change, there are
indications of its presence already in the thirteenth-century Galician *Cantigas
de Santa Maria* and also in non-literary Galician documents. Its starting place
therefore may well lie in Galicia and northern Portugal before it spread southward to central and southern Portugal from the fourteenth century onward
(Cintra 1984: 274–83). Interestingly, the fourteenth-century *Cancioneiros* show
no clear evidence of the change, but this may reflect either conservative poetic
traditions or perhaps the slow acceptance of the new pronunciation in the more
prestigious social circles of Portugal. At all events, the change has certainly been
carried through by the beginning of the sixteenth century even amongst the
most conservative speakers, as is clear from rhymes such as *sardinha: vinha*
< SARDĪNA VĪNEA 'sardine, vineyard' in the *Cancioneiro Geral* of 1516
(poem 75, ll. 28–9) where there is identity between the original palatal nasal
inherited from Latin and the new epenthetic one.

The other high vowel [ũ] has a more complex history. It figured in two
sequences [ũ-e(s)] and [ũ-ɐ] (it will be recalled that [ũ-o] underwent coalescence to [ũ], cf. supra). The various patterns of evolution may be summarized:

	ũ	COMMŪNES	> ko'mũ-es	(> ku'mũʃ)	*comuns*	'common (m. pl.)'
ũ-V >	umV	ŪNA	> 'ũ-ɐ	> 'umɐ	*uma*	'a (f. sg.)'
	uV	LŪNA	> 'lũ-ɐ	> 'luɐ	*lua*	'moon'

The sequence [ũ-e] was rarely found, but the evolution of the form
COMMŪNES > *comuns* points to coalescence.[16] Such a development, it
may be noted, runs counter to the general pattern of evolution of [Ṽ-V]
sequences where the second [V] is lower. The sequence [ũ-ɐ] underwent two
patterns of development. In grammatical forms developing from ŪNA(S) and
its derivatives, e.g. ALICŪNA(S), it underwent epenthesis and emerged in the

standard language as ['umɐ] giving *uma, alguma*, etc. The appearance of the bilabial nasal [m] as the epenthetic consonant is clearly determined by the labial quality of the nasal vowel [ũ]. These epenthetic forms only became generalized in the eighteenth century however. Before then, the forms *hūa, algūa* are typically found, suggesting that the introduction of [m] was slow to gain ground.[17] The other pattern of development, with denasalization and no epenthesis, occurred in fully lexical items, notably in LŪNA > *lua* 'moon', where a two-syllable sequence emerges identical to that found in purely oral forms (e.g. RŪGA > ['ruɐ] *rua* 'street'). The graphy *lūa*, suggesting a preserved nasal vowel, survives until the end of the sixteenth century, while *lua* appears as a graphy from the fifteenth century (Machado 1977: s.v. *lua*).

Finally, we may consider sequences where there was a mid nasal vowel initially, namely [õ-ɐ ẽ-ɐ], and also one sequence [ẽ-o] where the component vowels are of the same height. (The other such sequence [õ-e] develops differently and is considered separately below.) The following examples show the various paths of change:

õ-ɐ   >   o-ɐ   CORŌNA   >   ko'rõ-ɐ   >   *coroa*   'crown'
ẽ-ɐ   >   e-ɐ   >   ejɐ   >   ɐjɐ   CĒNA   >   'ts͡ẽ-ɐ   >   *ceia*   'supper'
ẽ-o   >   e-o   >   ejo   >   ɐju   PLĒNUM   >   't͡ʃẽ-o   >   *cheio*   'full (m. sg.)'

The mid nasal vowel [ẽ] thus at first just lost its nasality without any epenthetic consonant appearing. Denasalization was completed during the fifteenth century, so that the resulting sequences became identical with existing oral sequences [e-o] and [e-ɐ], as is shown by rhymes such as *chea: candea* (< PLĒNA CANDĒLA) in the *Cancioneiro Geral* (poem 30, ll. 49–50). In the sixteenth century, there is evidence of the appearance of epenthetic [j] to separate the vowels. However, the modern-day forms *cheio, ceia, candeia*, etc. do not become definitively established in the written language until the ninteenth century (Teyssier 1980: 56).

(ii) [Ṽ-V] *sequences where the second* [V] *is higher*
Sequences beginning with the vowels [ɛ̃] and [õ] are concerned here. The low nasal vowel [ɛ̃] figured in two sequences [ɛ̃-o] and [ɛ̃-e]. In both of these, the second element was raised, nasalized, and desyllabified to give off-gliding nasal diphthongs. The creation of these new diphthongs was completed by the end of the fifteenth century. Examples are:

ɛ̃-o   >   ɛ̃w̃   MĂNUM   >   'mɛ̃-o   >   mɛ̃w̃   *mão*   'hand'
ɛ̃-e   >   ɛ̃j   CĀNES   >   'kɛ̃-es   >   kɛ̃js   (> kɛ̃jʃ)   *cães*   'dogs'

The first diphthong [ɛ̃w̃] became identical with the diphthong which had developed in context (ii) forms like [pɛ̃w̃] < [pã] < PĀNEM 'bread'. This point is explored below (8.3.1.4).

õ-e > õj̃ LEŌNES > le'õ-es > li'õj̃s (> lj̃õj̃ ʃ) leões 'lions'
        PŌNIS   > 'põ-es > põj̃s (> põj̃ ʃ) pões 'you (sg.) put'

The new diphthong was probably well on the way to becoming established by the end of the fifteenth century. A further and rather special source of the [õj̃] diphthong was the final sequence -(I)TŪDINEM (e.g. MULTITŪDINEM, MANSITŪDINEM). This sometimes gave [-'dũe] in early texts, e.g. fourteenth-century *muytedũe* (Machado 1977: s.v. *multidão*), but generally the reflex appears as -*dõe* or -*do(o)m*. To explain the outcome [õj̃], one approach has been to postulate the existence in Latin of a variant form for this final sequence, -(I)TŬDINEM with a short stressed vowel Ŭ (cf. Williams 1962: § 124, 4C). More plausibly perhaps, we might see here an early adaptation of the comparatively isolated sequence [-ũe] to the much more frequent [-õe] which subsequently passed by regular sound change to [õj̃] (cf. Shaffer 1981).

The result of the developments in the sequences [ẽ-e] and [õ-e] was the creation of two entirely new nasal diphthongs, [ẽj̃] and [õj̃] in late medieval Portuguese. These added to the nasal diphthongs [õw̃] and [ẽj̃] which had already arisen in the language in context (ii) forms.

(*b*) [Ṽ-V] *sequences where* [Ṽ] *does not carry the main word-stress*
Three possibilities exist which may be represented as follows:

' -Ṽ-V   where the main word-stress falls on a preceding syllable
Ṽ-'V   where the main word-stress falls on the second [V]
Ṽ-V-'   where the main word-stress falls on a following syllable

In the first case, the development was broadly similar to that seen with sequences in which the nasal vowel [Ṽ] carried the main word-stress. Thus, by the end of the fifteenth century there was denasalization with the sequences [ẽ-o] and [ẽ-ɐ], while the second segment of [ẽ-o] and [ẽ-e] developed into an off-glide, and simple coalescence occurred with [ẽ-ẽ].[18] Thus:

GĔMINUM	> 'dʒɛmẽ-o	> 'ʒɛmju	*gémeo*	'twin'
FĒMINA	> 'femẽ-ɐ	> 'femjɐ	*fêmea*	'woman'
ŎRPHANUM	> 'ɔrfẽ-o	> 'ɔrfẽw̃	*orfão*	'orphan (m. sg.)'
HŎMINES	> 'ɔmẽ-es	> 'ɔmẽj̃s (> ɔmẽj̃ ʃ)	*homens*	'men'
ŎRPHANA	> 'ɔrfẽ-ɐ	> 'ɔrfẽ	*orfã*	'orphan (f. sg.)'

In sequences of the second type [Ṽ-'V], the tendency has been for denasalization to operate. Thereafter, the hiatus has generally been resolved by the sixteenth century through desyllabification of the unstressed segment or by coalescence. Thus:

ẽ-'V	MINŪTUM	> mẽ'udo	> 'mjuðu *miudo*	'tiny'	(desyllabification)
	FENĒSTRA	> frẽ'ɛstɐ	> 'frɛʃtɐ *fresta*	'skylight'	(coalescence)

ẽ-'V	CANĪNUM	>	kẽĩo	>	kɐ'iɲu	*cainho*	'doglike'	
	(Germ.) gan + -ĀTUM	>	gẽ'ado	>	'gaðu	*gado*	'cattle'	(coalescence)
	MANŬCULUM	>	mẽ'oʎo	>	'mɔʎu	*molho*	'bundle'	(coalescence)
õ-'V	MONĒTA		>	mõ'edɐ	>	mu'ɛðɐ	*moeda*	'coin'

Lastly, in [Ṽ-V] sequences occurring before the main-stressed syllable, the nasal vowel has normally undergone denasalization. Thus:

VANITĀTEM	>	vẽ-idade	>	vaj'ðað/vɐj'ðað	*vaidade*	'vanity'
GENERATIŌNEM	>	dʒẽ-erɐ'(t)sõn	>	ʒɛrə'sẽw̃	*geração*	'generation'
SANATĪVUM	>	sẽ-ɐ'dio	>	sa'ðiu	*sadio*	'healthy'

In these forms the unstressed sequence has either undergone contraction resulting in a 'full' or non-reduced unstressed vowel (as in *geração* and *sadio*)[19] or has given a diphthong (as in *vaidade*). In the latter item, there are two outcomes: the variant with [ɐ] owes its vowel nucleus to the regular development of unstressed [a]>[ɐ]; in the other variant, after denasalization operated, the diphthong [ɐj] which arose was presumably remodelled in line with the initial unstressed [aj] found in *faisão, paixão*, etc.

In rare cases however, some trace of the nasality of the original nasal vowel [Ṽ] of these sequences has been preserved. The pattern is that the nasality of the unstressed vowel has spread forward to the main-stressed vowel and subsequently there has been coalescence between the unstressed and stressed vowels or, in the absence of coalescence, denasalization of the unstressed vowel. This development took place almost exclusively when the receiving main-stressed vowel was high and followed by a coronal stop of some sort. Examples amongst verbal forms are:

VEN-ĪTUM	> vẽ'ido	> vi'ĩdo	> 'vĩndu	*vindo* 'came (past part.)'
FINĪTUM	> fĩ'ido	> fi'ĩdo	> (Old Pt.) 'fĩndo	*findo* 'finished (past part.)'

Also, exceptionally with a high-mid vowel there is TENĒTIS > tẽ'edes > 'tẽndes *tendes* 'you have (2nd pl.)', which may be due to the effect of paradigmatic analogy from other inflexional forms containing a stressed nasal vowel, *tem* and *tens,* and also to the possible influence of the verb *vir* 'to come', in which the corresponding forms are *vem, vens* and *vindes.*[20] Non-verbal items include: MANŬCEA > [mẽ'utsɐ] > [mɐ'ũ(t)sɐ] *maunça* 'small handful', PANĪCIUM > [pẽitso] > [pɐĩ(t)su] *painço* 'Italian millet'. Odd examples involving non-high vowels occur here also, most notably BENEDĬCTUM > [bẽ-e(d)eto] > ['bẽntu] *bento* 'blessed' where the analogical influence of *bem* is readily detectable and *ANETHULUM > [ẽ'edro] > ['ẽndru] *endro* 'dill' which seems to show some learned influence. All these cases of spreading involve adjacent vowel segments; for cases of spreading across intervening consonants see 8.3.1.5.

8.3.1.4. *The Evolving Nasal Diphthongs*

Following the resolution of vocalic hiatus during the fifteenth century a total of five off-gliding nasal diphthongs were found, as represented in Figure 3. Examples of the diphthongs were:

[ẽj̃]	[bẽj̃]	<	BĚNE,	[vẽj̃]	<	VĚNIT
[õj̃]	[rɐ'zõj̃s]	<	RATIŌNES,	[põj̃s]	<	PŌNIS
[ɛ̃j̃]	[kɛ̃j̃s]	<	CÁNES			
[õw̃]	[rɐ'zõw̃]	<	RATIŌNEM			
[ɐ̃w̃]	[kɐ̃w̃]	<	CÁNEM,	[mɐ̃w̃]	<	MĂNUM

Of these diphthongs, [ɐ̃w̃] is of particular interest. It had arisen from two distinct sources, [ɐ̃-o] < -ANUM and [-ɐ̃] < -AN(N)EM, which by chance had merged. Now, in the course of the fifteenth century it became involved in a further merger with another nasal diphthong, namely [õw̃]. This diphthong evidently widened first to [ɔ̃w̃] before the first element was centralized to [ɐ̃]; thus, [rɐ'zõw̃] > [rɐ'zɔ̃w̃] > [rɐ'zɐ̃w̃] *razão*. The change was carried through in the standard language during the fifteenth century. Confirming evidence is provided by rhymes in the poems of the *Cancioneiro Geral* of 1516 (Costa Pimpão and Dias 1973). Numerous cases appear where forms which earlier ended in [ɐ̃w̃] and [õw̃] appear in rhyme together. Thus, in poem 75 (ll. 106, 108–9) by the fifteenth-century poet Alvaro de Brito we have *Joham* and *irmão* (< IOHÁNNEM GERMĀNUM) rhyming with *sam* (< SŬNT), where the diphthongal result from all three originally distinct sources is clearly treated as identical.

The details of the merger of the three final vowels [-ã], [-õ], and [-ão] of thirteenth-century Portuguese as [-ɐ̃w̃] and the precise factors which it brought are still uncertain and hence controversial. Some scholars appeal to analogy as the principal cause (Williams 1962: § 157; Tilander 1959), while others invoke various phonetic or phonological factors (Nobiling 1903; Inês Louro 1952; Sampson 1983; Lorenzo 1988; Carvalho 1989*a* Martins 1995; Parkinson 1997). The lack of substantial, unambiguous evidence in surviving texts of the

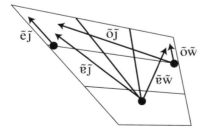

FIG. 3   Nasal diphthongs in Portuguese at the beginning of the fifteenth century

thirteenth and fourteenth centuries is unfortunate, and the problematic nature of the question has been added to by philologists sometimes misinterpreting such fleeting pieces of data as are available (cf. Parkinson 1993). Our account above is therefore tentative. We may summarize the proposed pattern of diphthongal merger in the following way:

			early fifteenth century		*early sixteenth century*		*example*	
ẽ	>	ẽw̃	>	ẽw̃	>	ẽw̃	cão	<	CĂNEM
ẽ-o	>	ẽ-o				mão	<	MĂNUM
õ	>	õw̃	>	ɔ̃w̃		razão	<	RATIŌNEM

As a result of this complex merger, at the outset of the sixteenth century it is likely that most speakers of the standard language had the four nasal diphthongs [ẽj̃], [õj̃], [ẽj̃], and [ẽw̃] represented in Figure 4.

The four nasal diphthongs of sixteenth-century Portuguese are not, however, identical with the four nasal diphthongs found in the modern standard language. On the one hand, two of the diphthongs of the sixteenth century, [ẽj̃] and [ẽj̃], have merged in more recent times, and, on the other hand, the present-day diphthong [ũj̃] had not as yet come into existence, at least not in 'good' speech. These two developments are considered in sections 8.3.2.2 and 8.3.2.3.

8.3.1.5. *Sporadic Changes*

In a small but not insignificant number of words, the evolution of nasal vowels has been anomalous. Two developments in particular are notable: (*a*) spreading of nasality and (*b*) stress-switching.

(*a*) *Distant spreading of vowel nasality*: certain words show nasality spreading away from the vowel segment to which it originally belonged and on to some other vowel segment which was previously oral. Instances of spreading affecting

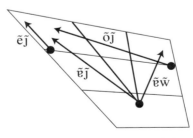

FIG. 4   Nasal diphthongs in Portuguese at the outset of the sixteenth century

adjacent vowels have been considered in 8.3.1.3(*b*); we consider here cases where spreading has occurred across intervening consonants. An example is the item *ontem* 'yesterday' whose pattern of evolution was: AD-NŎCTEM > [(ẽ)'õnte] > ['õntẽj̃], where nasality has been retained in the source stressed syllable.[21] In other forms, the nasal vowel of the source syllable has subsequently undergone denasalization, as in ANATEM > ['ãnde] > ['ãndẽj̃] > ['aðẽj̃] *adem* 'duck'. Two other words appear to share the same development, NŪBEM > ['nuvẽj̃] *nuvem* 'cloud' and MŪGILEM > ['muʒẽj̃] *mugem* 'mullet', but their final nasal vowels probably owe themselves to the analogical use of the quasi-suffix -*em*, rather than to nasal spreading from the stressed vowel to the unstressed vowel, the nasality having originally arisen by progressive nasalization. A reverse case is offered by the noun *pente* 'comb': PĔCTINE > ['pejtẽj̃] > ['pẽntẽj̃] (attested as *pentem* in sixteenth century) > ['pẽntə]. Here, nasality has spread to the stressed syllable, doubtless encouraged by the near-identity of the rhyme sequences in both syllables. However, despite the presence of the quasi-suffix -*em* the final syllable has denasalized.

(*b*) *Stress-switching*: this occurs in a small set of words, namely:

CAMPĀNA	>	kẽm'pẽɐ	>	'kẽmpɐ	*campa*	'handbell'
QUINTĀNA	>	kĩn'tẽɐ	>	'kĩntɐ	*quinta*	'farm'
VENTĀNA	>	vẽn'tẽɐ	>	'vẽntɐ	*venta*	'nostril'

Here, in all cases the final sequence evidently first developed to [-'ẽɐ]; cf. *canpãa* attested in 1382, *quintãa* in 1261, and the fourteenth-century *ventãa* (Machado 1977). However, the stress in these forms was moved back to the first syllable and the merged final sequence was denasalized. The reasons for this are far from clear. The presence of phonetically similar lexical items, *campa* 'tombstone', *quinta* 'fifth', *vento* 'wind', might have exerted some associative influence. However, the primary causation was doubtless phonological. A possible rationale for the change is that, as the final sequence [-ẽɐ] coalesced to [-ẽ], a constraint developed blocking disyllabic oxytonic words in which both vowels were nasal, unless the final vowel was transparently associated with a suffix (as with *canção*). A stress-shift occurred leading to the subsequent denasalization of the final (now unstressed) vowel. The later denasalization finds parallels in many Portuguese and Galician dialects (cf. 8.3.3, 8.4.4) and suggest possible dialectal influence in the forms affected.

8.3.2. POST-SIXTEENTH-CENTURY DEVELOPMENTS

By the end of the sixteenth century, the system of nasal vowels in the standard language has taken on a form which is similar to that found today. However, a limited but nonetheless significant number of changes have occurred within this system during the past four centuries.

8.3.2.1.   *Re-establishment of a Pre-Nasal Contrast* [ã] : [ẽ]

As a result of nasalization, the low vowel [ã] had been raised early on to [ẽ] particularly in eastern parts of the northern dialect area. This raising had also affected the stressed vowels in context (iii) forms such as *cana, cama, banho*, even though the nasality of such vowels was probably a good deal weaker. However, by the beginning of the sixteenth century at the latest, it became possible for a non-raised [ã] to appear once again in context (iii), so that a [ã] : [ẽ] contrast was introduced there. Non-raised [ã] arose in lexical items where there had been contraction of two hiatus vowels [ɐ] + [ẽ]. An example of this appears in forms derived from the Germanic verb *waidanjan* 'to forage' where the main stress fell on the stem, as in *ganho* ['gãɲo] (nowadays ['gãɲu]) < ['gɐ-ẽɲo] 'I earn; (deverbal noun) profit, gain' which was written *gaanho, gaaanho* in thirteenth-century documents.[22]   The resulting stressed vowel of *ganho* ['gãɲo] thus contrasted with that of *banho* ['bẽɲo] < BĂLNEUM 'bath'.

The scope of the opposition [ã] : [ẽ] in context (iii) forms evidently remained very limited in the sixteenth century. But subsequently it has been exploited to mark the distinction between 1st plural present and preterite forms of the first conjugation, as in present-day Portuguese *falamos* 'we speak' [fɐ'lẽmuʃ] vs. *falámos* 'we spoke' [fɐ'lãmuʃ]. The earliest clear indication of the establishment of this opposition in standard usage comes in the work of the eighteenth-century grammarian Caetano de Lima (1736). Previously, both verb forms appear to have had [ẽ] as the stressed vowel.

Various explanations have been proposed for this development. The fact that northern dialects of Portugal have [ã] in both these inflexional endings, while southern dialects widely have [ẽ] for both, is suggestive. It points to the possibility that in the dialects of the central dialect area there were conflicting tendencies so that a good deal of unpredictability existed in the use of [ã] or [ẽ] in individual word-forms. The standard language, which itself originated from the central area, could then exploit the variation for morphological reasons. A number of internal structural factors, phonological and morphophonological, might also be seen as having fostered the change. The existence of a parallel contrast in oral vowels between [a] and [ɐ] which occurred in unstressed syllables, e.g. [ɐ] 'the (f. sg.), to' vs. [a] < [ɐ] + [ɐ] 'to the (f. sg.)', orthographically distinguished as *a* and *á* respectively, may have acted as a model. Possible factors promoting the use of [ã] in the preterite ending *-ámos* include analogical influence from other preterite forms where stressed [a] is regular (e.g. *falaste* 'you (sg.) spoke'), and the desire to generalize the scope of the rule operative in *diss*[ɛ]*mos, pud*[ɛ]*mos*, etc., which blocked the raising of low(-mid) stem-final vowels in 1st plural preterites (cf. Xove 1988: esp. 488–90).

As a result of the reappearance of [ã], the range of contrasting vowel types in the system of allophonically nasal, context (iii) vowels in the modern standard language has been increased to six: [ĩ ẽ ɛ̃ ã õ ũ].

8.3.2.2. *Appearance of the New Diphthong* [ũj̃]

In modern Portuguese, the diphthong [ũj̃] is found almost exclusively in the lexical item *muito* < MŬLTUM 'much, very' and its inflexional variants. In addition, there is the rarely occurring variant of *muito*, namely *mui*, which has the same diphthong. The adjective *ruim* 'wretched' has a phonetically similar vowel, but the usual pronunciation is disyllabic [ru'ĩ] or monosyllabic [rwĩ].[23]

The presence of nasality in the stressed vowel of *muito* owes itself to the effect of progressive nasalization possibly encouraged by affective factors. The adoption of a nasal diphthong in this word came slowly and by no means in all areas of Galician-Portuguese. Galician in fact typically has the form *moito* with an oral stressed vowel. In standard Portuguese, the establishment of the nasal pronunciation [ũj̃] appears to date at the earliest from the late sixteenth or the seventeenth century and it may only have gained general acceptance as the norm pronunciation a good deal later.[24] In this way, the new nasal diphthong [ũj̃] represents the outcome of a very small-scale and slow development in Portuguese.

8.3.2.3. *The Merger of* [ẽj̃] *and* [ɛ̃j̃]

In the sixteenth century, a clear distinction was made in the standard variety between the nasal diphthong in *bens* 'possessions' and that in *cães* 'dogs'. The former was realized with a high-mid front vowel as its starting point while the latter [ɛ̃j] was initiated with a low-mid central vowel. This pattern where the two diphthongs were systematically distinguished has been preserved in many varieties of Portuguese to this day, in northern and southern dialects of Portugal and also in Brazil, although the precise realization of the former diphthong does vary regionally now and presumably also varied in the sixteenth century.[25]

However, beginning as a feature of lower-class speech in the nineteenth or possibly the later eighteenth century, an important development got underway in the Lisbon area. The initial element of the [ẽj̃] diphthong was centralized to [ɐ̃] and the resulting diphthong rapidly coalesced with the existing diphthong [ɐ̃j̃] occurring in words like *cães*. Already by the middle of the nineteenth century this novelty had gained acceptance amongst educated speakers and it established itself as the norm thereafter. Confirmation of this comes in a letter which the Brazilian poet Gonçalves Dias wrote to a friend during a stay in

Lisbon in 1857. He observes, with some consternation, that even good poets from Lisbon permitted rhymes between words such as *mãe* and *também*.[26]

This development ran directly in parallel with a change affecting the oral high-mid front vowel [e]. At the same period in the Lisbon area, this likewise took on a centralized pronunciation [ɐ] when it was stressed and followed by a palatal consonant [ʃ ʒ ɲ ʎ j], as in *peixe, beijo, lenha, orelha, meio*. Both developments are clearly interrelated, and although it is not certain whether it was initiated by the oral or the nasal vowel, dialectal patterns point to the oral vowel leading the way. Thus, northern dialects notably of the Minho commonly show a similar centralizing tendency for oral [e] (Silva 1961: 311–12). In southern dialects, there has usually been no centralization.

A further structural consideration existed which promoted centralization in the initial element of the nasal diphthong [ẽj]. Given the presence within the nasal diphthong system of [ẽw̃], the change of [ẽj] to [ɐ̃j] would result in a more compact and symmetrical arrangement, with two diphthongs sharing a common starting point and rising towards a front or back target position.

In this way, the system of nasal vowel phonemes which has emerged in the modern standard language is the following:

	front		*back*	
high	ĩ		ũ	
	ẽ		õ	
		ɐ̃		
low			ẽj ẽw̃ õj ũj	
			diphthongs	

8.3.3.   REGIONAL VARIATION IN CENTRE-SOUTH DIALECTS

There is a good deal of variation in the linguistic patterns found in different parts of Portugal. Already in the earliest writings on the Portuguese language by sixteenth-century grammarians there is a recognition of the existence of regional differences, which have only been partly attenuated in more recent times by the influence of the standard language. Unfortunately, we still do not have a detailed linguistic atlas of Portugal to provide information on present-day regional differences. Instead, the principal sources of data are general sketches of dialectal patterns, such as those by Vasconcellos (1970) and Boléo (1974) or more detailed monographs on the usage of specific localities or regions (e.g. Maia 1975, 1977; Delgado 1983). Consequently, a good deal of uncertainty still surrounds the incidence and distribution of particular linguistic features including the pattern of nasal vowels in many parts of Portugal. However, some indication of the diversity in the realization of vowel nasality dialectally may be given by a brief look at the circumstances in the southern dialects of the

Algarve, using as a basis the descriptions of Hammarström (1953) and Maia (1975).

Underlying all the modern dialects of the Algarve is a five-way system of nasal monophthongs directly comparable with that of the standard language, namely /ĩ ẽ ã õ ũ/. However, there are significant differences in their typical realization. The mid vowels /ẽ õ/ very generally have an open pronunciation, emerging as [ɛ̃ ɔ̃]. The high back vowel /ũ/ shows a strong tendency to front towards [ỹ], particularly in western varieties of the Algarve. Lastly, the low vowel /ã/ evidently varies a good deal in its realization both regionally and contextually. In context (i) forms like *campo*, western dialects in particular may have a velarized [ɑ̃] (Hammarström 1953: 158), though Maia cites [ẽw̃] for the western dialect of Marmelete, a realization which resembles that found in the northern dialects of the Minho. In context (iii) forms, velarization of the low vowel is very common, e.g. ['ʃɑ̃mɐ] and even ['ʃɔ̃mɐ] *chama*.

By way of résumé, therefore, we have:

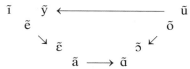

The movement seen here largely replicates what appears to be happening in the system of oral vowels where a general push-chain has been detected to be at work in dialects of the Algarve, e > ɛ > a > ɑ > ɔ > o > u > y (Lüdtke 1956: 194–9). The only exception concerns /õ/ which, unlike its oral counterpart, is tending to lower rather than raise.

So far, we have mainly realizational differences between the standard language and dialects of the Algarve. However, a much more significant variation concerns the reflex of the original [ã-a] sequence in early Portuguese. This gives [ẽ] in the standard variety, e.g. *lã* (< LĀNA). But it appears that the typical outcome in the Algarve has been diphthongal, [ãw̃] or [ɑ̃w̃]. This is found in many peripheral varieties of the west, north, and south of the Algarve to this day, although in the central area the pressure from the standard language has led to [ẽ] becoming established. Given that the same diphthong is the normal reflex of the early Portuguese sequences [ã-o] and [ã/ãw̃], as in ['mã-o] 'hand' and [kã/kãw̃] 'dog', respectively, it would seem that the hiatus in [ã-a] was resolved fairly quickly in the Algarve and the result identified with the latter diphthongs.

Looking further at nasal diphthongs, we find some striking divergences from the standard variety in the way these are realized in the varieties of the Algarve. Most have a diphthongal form corresponding to standard *ão*, although in general the first element is, predictably, realized velarized. In far western areas, the off-glide may be slight however, as in [kɑ̃ʷ] [mɑ̃ʷ] 'dog, hand' in Sagres

(Hammarström 1953: 54–5) and in dialects spoken near Faro [põ̃ʷ] [meˈlõ̃ʷ] 'bread, melon' and sometimes even full levelling [feˈʒõ] 'haricot' (Maia 1975: 70). Evidently, there has been an even stronger levelling tendency in diphthongs ending in [j̃], with the sole exception of the stable diphthong [ũj̃] found just in *muito*. The levelling tendency is especially strong in preconsonantal contexts. Thus, the final sequences [õj̃ʃ] [ãj̃ʃ] have commonly been levelled to [õʃ] [ãʃ].[27] In this way, the diphthong [õj] in particular has very limited incidence indeed. Finally, it may be noted that the medieval diphthong [ẽj̃] has also been levelled, so that the realization of *bem* is typically [bẽ]. This has prevented the possible merger of the vowel here with that of *mãe*, as in the standard language. *Mãe* appears widely as [mãj̃].

In this way, it seems that the general drift in the dialects of the Algarve has been towards the levelling of nasal diphthongs, particularly when these occur preconsonantally.

Another widespread, though weaker, tendency has been for nasal vowels in post-stress syllables to denasalize. Thus, in central and northern Algarve dialects, the counterpart to standard Portuguese [ẽw̃] in final unstressed syllables is [u] in verbal forms, as in [ˈtɔku] *tocam* 'they touch' (Maia 1975: 70). In non-verbal forms, a similar tendency to denasalize also commonly appears. The place name *Faro* was originally *Fárão*, while the form *orfão* is realized as [ˈɔɾfu] in many dialects. Final unstressed -*em* is also widely denasalized, emerging as [a], e.g [ˈɔma] 'man', [ˈkõma] 'they eat'. The pattern thus appears to be that nasality in vowels has been increasingly associated with the main stressed syllable, except for pre-stress syllables where the nasal vowel was covered by a following oral consonant, i.e. in context (i) forms .

8.4.   Nasal Vowel Evolution in Northern Portugal and Galicia

8.4.1.   HISTORICAL BACKGROUND

The establishment of an independent Portugal in the twelfth century had major linguistic repercussions on the north-western area of the peninsula. Already by the later thirteenth century, a rift was gradually beginning to appear between the usage found in the areas north and south of the political border separating Galicia from Portugal.

The varieties of Entre-Douro-e-Minho and Trás-os-Montes in the north of the Portuguese state became orientated southward to the central region which formed the administrative and political heart of the kingdom. Even so, these northern varieties retained many of their original features and already in the earliest descriptions of Portuguese, dating from the sixteenth century, attention was being drawn to certain northern 'peculiarities' some of which concerned the pronunciation of nasal vowels.

In contrast, when Galicia was definitively incorporated into the Kingdom of Castile during the reign of Ferdinand III (1217–52), its orientation was to be increasingly towards the east. Ferdinand established Castilian as the official language of Galicia, and in texts dating from the latter part of that century indications of Castilian influence are already discernible (Maia 1986: 901). A dynastic civil war in the following century was to hasten the process of Castilianization. Having supported the ultimate loser in this conflict, the Galician nobility found itself dispossessed by the victorious Henry II of Castile (1369–79). The result was that a new, and predominantly Castilian, nobility was installed which undermined the existing institutions and promoted the diffusion of Castilian. By the end of the fifteenth century, Castilian was clearly the language of power and authority, while Galician was retreating to the status of a local language. There are references in the sixteenth century to the increasingly marginal status of Galician as a result of the systematic Castilianization of the upper sectors of society in Galicia (Monteagudo and Santamarina 1993). The last known notarial documents in Galician, albeit significantly Castilianized, date from 1532 (Maia 1986: 905). Since the sixteenth century, Galician has remained in local usage, fragmenting progressively. Only in the nineteenth century was Galician cultivated once again as a literary language, most notably in the poetry of Rosalía de Castro (1837–85). Subsequently, a written norm (*gallego común* / *galego común*) has been developed and generalized, especially following its recognition as a co-official language in the 1978 Constitution. This is a consensus language based on majority patterns of usage found in the various dialects (Carballo Calero 1968: 13–18).

8.4.2.   LINGUISTIC SITUATION IN THE THIRTEENTH CENTURY

At the outset of the literary period in the thirteenth century, it would appear that most if not all the linguistic varieties of Galicia and northern Portugal had undergone the same early developments already identified for the central and southern Portuguese dialects. Thus, intervocalic /n/ had been deleted in context (iii) forms, leaving sequences of nasal vowel + oral vowel [-$\tilde{V}$V-]. Context (ii) forms had arisen as a result of the apocope of final /-e/, and in these the word-final nasal consonant had undergone weakening to [$\tilde{V}^n$] and was finally deleted leaving behind a trace of nasality in the preceding vowel, as in [fĩ] < [fĩ^n] < FĪNEM 'end'. In context (i) forms, we may assume that the vowel preceding the coda nasal consonant had become more heavily nasalized, although some trace of that coda nasal doubtless was still retained. Finally, it seems probable that in all nasalizing contexts the contrast between mid vowels had been neutralized, leaving five distinct vowel types [ĩ ẽ ã õ ũ].

From this basis we may briefly sketch the fate of nasal vowels in the dialects of North Portugal and in Galician.

8.4.3. NASAL VOWEL EVOLUTION IN NORTHERN DIALECTS OF PORTUGUESE

A certain amount of variation exists in the way nasal vowels have developed from one area to another in northern Portugal. In particular, the dialects of Entre-Douro-e-Minho in north-western Portugal have tended to follow more individual patterns of change.

One common feature, shared with dialects spoken further south in the rest of Portugal, was the tendency for the conditioning nasal consonant in nasalizing contexts to be progressively weakened to leave unconditioned nasal vowel phonemes. In context (i) forms the weakening has gone least far. Here, some trace of the coda nasal has usually remained but its weakening has given rise to substantial levels of nasality in the preceding vowel. In context (ii) forms, the conditioning nasal was lost. In some northern dialects spoken close to the frontier with Galicia, the resulting nasal vowel has remained unchanged, but in other dialects the nasal vowel has generally developed an off-glide. In context (iii) forms, the hiatus [Ṽ-V] resulting from the regular deletion of intervocalic /n/ was resolved in various ways. Coalescence has commonly occurred leaving a single syllabic element, which may be monophthongal or diphthongal. However, epenthesis of a velar nasal [ŋ] is occasionally found, particularly in dialects of the far north where it is bound up with developments in Galician.[28]

Despite these similarities with the centre-south, the northern dialects of Portugal show a number of characteristic patterns of evolution. First, in many dialects of Entre-Douro-e-Minho, mid vowels in nasalizing contexts appear to have adopted a low-mid point of articulation, [ɛ̃] and [ɔ̃], as in context (i) forms such as *nascente, fonte* and context (iii) forms like *menos, nome* which have low-mid nasal vowels in numerous Minhoto dialects (Silva 1961: 312, 313). Though this may at first sight seem to be little more than a minor phonetic variation, it was to have some significance in shaping the later evolution of nasal vowels in the dialects concerned.

A further development also concerned the Entre-Douro-e-Minho area, and in particular the western half. Here, the low vowel [ã] did not undergo the raising which occurred in the eleventh–twelfth centuries in other dialects including the one destined to give the standard language. Instead, it remained low and was increasingly retracted, passing in many dialects to [ɑ̃].

The movement of [ã] to [ɑ̃] was to have significant ramifications in some dialects during the later medieval period, especially in context (ii) forms. The back vowel [ã] remained unchanged in areas of the far north of Entre-Douro-e-Minho,[29] but in many other areas further south it rounded to [õ]. The result was that [ãw̃] (< -ANEM) and [õw̃] (< -ŌNEM) began widely to coalesce as [õw̃]. Signs of this having taken place date from the mid-fifteenth century.[30] Grammarians of the sixteenth century also confirm the existence of this dialectal trait. Duarte Nunes de Liao, for instance, remarked in 1576 that people in Entre-Douro-e-Minho and in Galicia said *capitom* 'captain' (and indeed *cidadom* < CIVITAT-ĀNUM 'citizen') with the same final vowel as *amarom, apelaçom* 'they loved, appellation'.

Looking more closely at context (ii) forms, we have noted that the conditioning nasal consonant was lost. Thereafter, the pattern of evolution was quite similar to that of the standard language. An off-glide was regularly formed after non-high vowels, but after high vowels any off-glide that may have developed was rapidly absorbed, as in [fĩ] < FĪNEM. Regarding non-high vowels, an off-glide appeared after [ẽ] to give [ɛ̃j] and, as we have seen, the reflexes of -ANEM and -ŌNEM also generally merged as in the standard variety, although their common outcome in central and southern parts of Entre-Douro-e-Minho was [õw̃] rather than [ẽw̃]. Subsequently, there was growing interplay between this diphthong and the diphthong [ãw̃] which derived from the sequence [ã-o] < -ANUM. The outcome in certain dialects was the merger between [õw] and [ãw̃], perhaps hastened by the influence of the standard language, where a comparable three-way merger had also occurred but along a different route. But in a number of Minhoto dialects, the sequence [ãw̃] < -ANUM has remained distinct from [õw̃], e.g. Viana do Castelo at the mouth of the River Lima [tru'βõw̃ põw̃] 'thunder, bread' < TURB-ŌNEM PĀNEM vs. [be'rãw̃ mãw̃] 'summer, hand' < VERĀNUM MĂNUM (Silva 1961: 316).

A further point may be made on the reflexes of context (iii) forms such as LĀNA and BŎNUM, in which the deletion of -N- left [Ṽ-V] sequences containing vowels of the same tongue position. Such sequences did not consistently contract to give [Ṽ] as in the standard language. In some dialects, the emerging pattern of terminating non-high final nasal vowels with an off-glide resulted in these forms also adopting an off-glide, hence LĀNA > 'lãa > lã > lãw̃, BŎNUM > 'bõo > bõ > bõw̃ with the former off-gliding diphthong being much more widespread (Silva 1961: 311, 313). Thus, some areas show common reflexes for -ONEM -ANEM and -ONUM, unlike the situation in the standard language.

In Trás-os-Montes in north-eastern Portugal, the development of nasal vowels in all but the most northern dialects close to the frontier have been comparable to those of the standard language in context (ii) forms. Thus, the reflexes of -ANEM and -ONEM have generally merged with -ANUM as [ẽw̃]. In northern frontier dialects, however, no merger has taken place with

-ANEM -ONEM, e.g. in the dialects of Rio de Onor and Deilão which have such present-day forms as [pẽ] < PĀNEM 'bread' and [rẽ'zõ] < RATIŌNEM 'reason' (Santos 1964–5). In these dialects, -ANUM gives [ẽ], presumably via the stages [ẽo > ẽw̃ > ẽ]. As regards other hiatus sequences which arose in context (iii) forms, their resolution has been broadly similar to that seen in the standard language. However, it seems that the sequence [ẽ-ɐ] < -ANA at first commonly followed the path seen in central and southern Entre-Douro-e-Minho to emerge as [ẽw̃], e.g. LĀNA > [lẽw̃] (Santos 1964: 152–3). But the influence of the standard language in more recent times has established [ẽ] as the predominant realization today.

The appearance of off-glides in word-final nasal vowels has been extended in certain areas to nasal vowels in context (i) forms. Thus, we have a diphthong [ɑ̃w] reported for the stressed vowel of branco and cántaro in many localities of western Entre-Douro-e-Minho.[31]   Also, a diphthongal realization [ɛ̃j̃] is indicated in the same area for vento, novembro (Silva 1961: 312; Vasconcellos 1970: 81). This contrasts with the tendency further east in the Alto Douro for original /e/ to lower through [ɛ̃] to [ɑ̃]. Comparable off-gliding with /õ/ in context (i) forms seems less widespread, although the ALPI (map 20) cites a diphthongal pronunciation for the stressed vowel of ontem at four points in the centre and south of Entre-Douro-e-Minho, typically ['ɔ̃w̃ntə].

Finally, as with many other regional varieties of Portuguese, the dialects of the north show a widespread tendency to denasalize nasal vowels in final unstressed syllables. In Entre-Douro-e-Minho, corresponding to standard sótão and chegam the forms ['sɔtu] and ['ʃeɣu] are widely found, and similarly ['birʒə] and ['ɔmə] are reported as the counterparts of standard virgem, homem (Silva 1961). Parallel changes are noted in Alta Beira (Maia 1977: 169, 174) and in Trás-os-Montes (Santos 1964: 195). In the latter area, morphological influences have also been at work, since denasalization is much more advanced in nominals than in verbal forms. Thus, beside denasalized ['bjaʒə 'ɔrfu] 'journey, orphan', we find ['fuʒẽ 'forũ] 'they flee, they went'.

8.4.4. GALICIAN

The fate of nasal vowels has been somewhat different from that found in varieties used within Portugal. The most important characteristic has undoubt-edly been that in Galicia unconditioned nasal vowel phonemes have never become established. Nasal vowels certainly occur but the nasality is allophonic as the vowels are typically accompanied by a following, tautosyllabic nasal consonant.[32]   Where the conditioning nasal consonant is not followed by another consonant, it is normally realized as the velar [ŋ], e.g. [mĩŋ mɑ̃ŋ bõŋ] 'me, hand, good (m. sg.)'. Where the nasal consonant is pre-consonantal it may be homorganic with the following consonant, e.g. ['tẽmpo 'kõnto] 'time, bill', or it may be uniformly realized as [ŋ] here too (Alvarez, Regueira, and Monteagudo 1986: 34).[33] Although variable in its surface form, the conditioning nasal consonant is always present. Nasality in vowels is consequently never more than an allophonic feature.

The intensity of vowel nasality used by Galician speakers may be influenced by sociolinguistic factors, notably their degree of education and familiarity with Castilian. According to Porto Dapena (1977: 23), the less educated and the less familiar with Castilian a speaker is, the greater the use and intensity of vowel nasality will be when speaking Galician.

Finally, bound up with the reduction of nasal vowels to the status of allophones of oral vowel phonemes has been the restoration of the same range of contrasts for nasal vowels as for vowels in oral contexts. Hence, we find that, matching the seven-way oral vowel system /i e ɛ a ɔ o u/ found in all Galician dialects, a sub-system of seven nasal vowels with a contrast between high-mid and low-mid vowels has been developed in western dialects in particular. However, as we shall see, the new contrasts [ẽ] vs. [ɛ̃] and [õ] vs. [ɔ̃] have remained of limited incidence in Galician.

8.4.4.1. *Historical Development of Vowel Nasality in Galician*

In contexts (i) and (ii), it seems likely that high-level vowel nasalization took place in the pre-literary period (up to the thirteenth century) and unconditioned nasal vowels probably developed, especially in context (ii) forms. Subsequently, however, levels of vowel nasality were systematically reduced and unconditioned nasal vowels were restructured into sequences of nasal vowel + conditioning nasal (cf. parallel change in northern Italian dialects, 10.4.4.2). In context (ii) forms, the 'default' nasal consonant [ŋ] was adopted; in context (i) forms, the restored nasal consonant was either [ŋ] or a nasal homorganic with the following oral consonant.

context (i)	NŬMQUAM	>	'nũŋka	>	'nũ$^{(ŋ)}$ka	>	'nũŋka	'never'
	VIGĬNTI	>	'bĩnte	>	'bĩ$^{(n)}$te	>	'bĩnte/'bĩŋte[34]	'twenty'
context (ii)	COMMŪNEM	>	ko'mũ$^{(n)}$	>	ko'mũ	>	ko'mũŋ	'common (sg.)'
	FĪNEM	>	fĩ$^{(n)}$	>	fĩ	>	fĩŋ	'end'

The chronology of this restructuring process doubtless varied regionally and hence is difficult to determine. If restructuring was related to the increasing Castilianization of Galicia, it seems likely that the process began to operate from about the fourteenth century.

Associated with the increasing vowel nasalization in these context types during the pre-literary period, there was neutralization of mid-vowel contrasts in all varieties of Galician. The dialects of the eastern half of the area have preserved the neutralization of contrasts. The neutralized mid vowel usually has an open quality [ɛ̃ ɔ̃] rather that [ẽ õ], e.g. ['dɛ̃nte], ['bɛ̃nda], [kɛ̃ŋ] < DĚNTEM VĒNDITA QUĚM 'tooth, sale, who'; ['fɔ̃nte], [re'ðɔ̃ndo], [sɔ̃ŋ] < FŎNTEM ROTŬNDUM SŬNT 'fountain, round, they are'. However, the adoption of [ɔ̃] rather than [õ] is less geographically widespread than [ɛ̃] instead of [ẽ] and is more typical of the far eastern area (Fernández Rei 1985: 489).

In western dialects of Galician, a high-mid value [ẽ õ] has remained normal for the neutralized vowel. More importantly, the contrast between high-mid and low-mid vowels has been restored as a result of the reappearance of [ɛ̃ ɔ̃] in certain forms. Four main sources for these can be distinguished:

(a) metaphonically determined verb-forms of -er, -ir conjugations:

['bɛ̃nde]	'he sells'	(vs. ['bẽnde]	'sell!')
[bɛ̃ŋ]	'he comes'	(vs. [bẽŋ]	'come!')
[re'spɔ̃nde]	'he answers'	(vs. [re'spõnde]	'answer!')
[pɔ̃ŋ]	'he puts'	(vs. [põŋ]	'put!')

(cf. ALGa, maps 73, 82, 318, 332, 372, 377)

(b) certain grammatical words:

['ɔ̃nte(s)] 'yesterday' and its derivatives, [bɛ̃ŋ] 'well', [ta'mɛ̃ŋ] 'also'.

(c) certain loanwords:

['mɔ̃nʃe] 'monk', [a'mɛ̃ŋ] 'amen'

(d) forms with contracted vowels (only [ɛ̃] is concerned):

['kɛ̃nte] 'hot' (< [ka'ẽnte] < CALĚNTEM)

Curiously, a parallel development is not found here with the back vowel [ɔ̃]; hence, PALŬMBUM > ['pombo] 'pigeon' rather than **['pɔ̃mbo].

In context (iii) forms, original intervocalic -N- was deleted in all varieties of Galician to leave diverse sequences of the form [ṼV]. Such sequences remain largely intact in the highly conservative dialect of Ancares (see 8.4.5 below) but in Galicia proper they have been modified in complex ways. The modifications vary somewhat according to the precise linguistic environment of the sequences and according to region, but two broad types may be distinguished:

(a) denasalization; and

(b) restructuring of [Ṽ] to [ṼN] (where 'N' is some type of nasal consonant).

Both types of modification share an important common characteristic, namely that they all result in the *loss of unconditioned nasality in vowels*.

In the sequence [Ṽ'V] where the nasal vowel preceded the main-stressed vowel, both patterns of change can be found, just as in Portuguese. Denasalization is seen in GENĔSTA > ['ʃɛsta] 'broom' and MINŪTUM > ['mjuðo] 'tiny'. On the other hand, in PANĪCIUM > [pa'ĩnθo] 'millet' and CANAL-ĪCULA > ['kẽnʎa] 'alley' there has first been spreading of nasality on to the main-stressed vowel and then restructuring of that vowel, [Ṽ'V > V'Ṽ > (V)'ṼN]. The incidence of one or other pattern varies from region to region, but it is notable that the latter pattern has been more widely used than in standard Portuguese, as is indicated by the last example cited (cf. Port. *quelha*) and other cases such as GENŪCULUM > ['ʃjõnʎo] 'knee', CUNĪCULUM > [ko'ẽnʎo] 'rabbit', and (Germ.) gan-ĀTUM > ['gãndo] 'cattle' (as against Port. *joelho, coelho, gado*).

Unstressed and in final position, the sequence [-ṼV] uniformly loses its nasality in modern Galician just as in many non-standard varieties of Portuguese: ŎRPHANUM > ['ɔrfão] > ['ɔrfo] 'orphan', HŎMINEM > ['ɔmẽe] > ['ɔme] 'man', etc. (cf. 8.4.3). Textual evidence suggests that locally denasalization here may well have been underway already in the thirteenth century (Börner 1976: 133–4; Maia 1986: 592).

In the sequence ['ṼV] where the nasal vowel carried primary stress, the unconditioned vowel nasality has once again been systematically eliminated, although the strategy used can differ for certain sequences from one area to another. In ['ṼV] sequences containing the high vowels [ĩ ũ] or the high-mid vowel [ẽ], all varieties of Galician share the same strategy (except in the sequence [-ẽes]). But sequences with the remaining vowel types [õ] and [ã] as their initial segment show regionally diverging patterns of change. Effectively, dialects of the centre and east of Galicia have typically made use of the first strategy (denasalization), while those of the western third of the region exploit the second strategy more widely. The main lines of evolution are summarized below:

ĩV > iɲV : VĪNUM > ['biɲo] 'wine'

Restructuring with the appearance of [ɲ] is attested from the mid-thirteenth century.

ũV > uV : LŪNA > ['lua] 'moon'

Denasalization of [ũ] is indicated textually from the late thirteenth century but may well have only been carried through in the fourteenth or fifteenth century. Except in certain eastern dialects, this change did not apply to the small set of grammatical forms consisting of ŪNA 'a (f. sg.)' and its derivatives ALIC-ŪNA 'some (f. sg.)', NEC-ŪNA 'none (f. sg.)'. These developed an anti-hiatic nasal consonant [ŋ] (cf. the parallel appearance of [m] in the same forms in Portuguese, see 8.3.1.3(*a*) above). The date when [ŋ] became established is uncertain. Since its appearance, intervocalic [ŋ] has shown a tendency to attach itself to the preceding vowel as a syllable-coda consonant (García de Diego 1909: 106; Carballo Calero 1968: 65; Alonso 1972*b*); indeed, in an apparent attempt to hypercharacterize its syllable-coda status, some speakers may introduce a non-nasal consonantal segment at the release stage, to give a sequence [Ṽŋ-C], where C may be either a glottal constriction or a velar plosive. However, for certain Galician speakers the [ŋ] of *unha* and related forms attaches to the following vowel as a syllable onset (Alvarez, Regueira, and Monteagudo 1986: 34).

ēV > eV : PLĒNUM, -A > ['tʃeo], ['tʃea] 'full (m. sg. / f. sg.)'

Denasalization is attested from the later thirteenth century. No anti-hiatus glide [j] develops as in Portuguese. The special case of [ẽes] figures below along with the other vowel sequences beginning with non-high nasal vowels.

			West Galician		East Galician	
	-one(s) > -õe(s) >		-õŋ	-õŋs	-õŋ	-os
õ V	-ona(s) > -õa(s) >		-oa	-oas	-oa	-oas
	-ono(s) > -õo(s) >		-õŋ	-õŋs	-o	-os
	-ane(s) > -ãe(s) >		-ãŋ	-ãŋs	-ãŋ	-as
ã V	-ana(s) > -ãa(s) >		-ãŋ	-ãŋs	-a	-as
	-ano(s) > -ão(s) >		-ãŋ	-ãŋs	-aw	-aws
ẽes	-enes > -ẽes >			-ẽŋs		-es/-ɛs

(Here, as in Portuguese, the reflexes of -ANEM -ONEM (in italics) represent context (ii) forms and are included here merely to complete the schematic table presented.)

In the sole case of this set where the second segment has a lower tongue position, in [õa], denasalization takes place in all dialects, this being indicated in texts of the mid-thirteenth century. In those sequences where denasalization has only occurred in some varieties, notably in central and eastern areas, the earliest signs begin to become apparent in the fourteenth century (Maia 1986: 584, 588, 590, 606).

The phonetic stages of development of ['ṼV] sequences are uncertain. In the western area of Galicia there has evidently been a systematic move to reduce the second element to the status of a nasalized off-glide, except where it had a lower tongue position (as in [õa(s)]). The resulting off-glide then consonantalized to emerge as [ŋ]. The rationale behind this change was perhaps the aim to extend and generalize the pattern already seen in context (i) and context (ii) forms where nasal vowels are always anchored to, and motivated by, the presence of a following nasal consonantal element.

In the eastern area of Galicia, it would appear that a comparable reduction to off-glide status also occurred with the second element. But, perhaps partly on account of the growing linguistic influence from central dialects of the peninsula especially Castilian, this second segment following the nasal vowel did not undergo full consonantalization and consequently did not pass to [ŋ]. The nasality of the stressed vowel thus lacked the presence of a following conditioning nasal consonant which it required for its maintenance. The result was the progressive abandonment of nasality. In sequences of identical vowels, this was followed by contraction:

$$-\tilde{o}o(s) \quad > \quad -oo(s) \quad > \quad -o(s)$$
$$-\tilde{a}a(s) \quad > \quad -aa(s) \quad > \quad -a(s)$$
$$-\tilde{e}es \quad > \quad -ees \quad > \quad -es \ / \ -\varepsilon s\,^{35}$$

The distinction between the evolution of these context (iii) sequences and of the phonetically close context (ii) shapes -ANEM -ONEM is notable, since items such as CĂNEM or RATIŌNEM appear everywhere in Galicia with a final sequence [-Ṽŋ] and never with an oral vowel. This suggests that, in eastern dialects, denasalization very probably preceded contraction, since the reverse would have created the final nasal vowels [-õ(s) -ã(s) -ẽ(s)] which would almost inevitably have been restructured with the addition of a following [ŋ] (Carvalho 1988*b*). Textual evidence suggests that denasalization began to operate from the fourteenth century (Maia 1986: 584).

In [ṼV] sequences where the second segment had a different tongue position, i.e. [ões] and [ães], it underwent assimilation to the first segment and subsequently there was the same contraction. Assimilated forms with <-oos> from earlier [-ões] are attested from the fifteenth century, and forms with <-aas> from earlier [-ães] already appear in the mid-fourteenth century (Maia 1986: 588, 608).

8.4.5. ANCARES

To the east of the political area of Galicia proper, there exist a number of linguistic varieties showing characteristically Galician traits. Examples of so-called *galego exterior* are found in localities in western Asturias (to just east of the River Navia), north-western León, and north-western Zamora.

The Galician of these areas has generally been influenced by more central varieties of Ibero-Romance, as one might predict. Consequently, it might be expected that the effect of vowel nasalization would be somewhat limited. In general, this is the case, such that at most allophonic nasality is found in vowels as a result of the conditioning nasal consonant segment regularly being strengthened or restored. In this way, the pattern which typically emerges is not dissimilar to that seen in the varieties of Galicia.

There is one notable exception, however. This concerns the variety found in

the Ancares valley area in north-western León, which was first described
systematically in the pioneering study of Alonso and Yebra (1972) and more
recently by Fernández González (1978, 1981). Here, various Galician features
appear, often in a highly archaic stage of development, the most interesting
aspect for our purposes being the preservation of phonemic vowel
nasality.[36]

In the dialect of Ancares the patterns of evolution in contexts (i) and (ii)
correspond fairly directly with those found further west in Galicia. Thus, in
context (i), there is some evidence that heightened allophonic nasalization
occurred but the conditioning coda nasal has been uniformly maintained:

> IŬNCTUM   >   ['ʃũnto]   'together, joined'
> CĂMPUM   >   ['kãmpo]   'field'

Context (ii) forms arose, as in the rest of Galician, from the apocope of /-e/
after original intervocalic -N-. But word-final /n/ also appears as a result of the
apocope in the final sequence deriving from -ĪNUM, this being a typical
Asturian development which has migrated southward. Some trace of the final
nasal remains in the form of a consonantal off-glide which we represent as [ŋ];
the question of the phonetic nature of this final off-glide is considered below.
The preceding (stressed) vowel is characterized by a high degree of nasality.
Thus:

> COMMŪNEM   >   [kuˈmũŋ]   'common (m. sg.)'
> PĀNEM   >   [pãŋ]   'bread'
> CAMĪNUM   >   [kaˈmĩŋ]   'way'

Neutralization of the contrast between mid vowels in context (i) and context
(ii) forms has taken place. For both front and back vowels, the outcome is a
high-mid vowel, as in DĔNTEM > ['dẽnte] 'tooth', BĔNE > [bẽŋ] 'well', and
PŎNTEM > ['põnte] 'bridge' (Fernández González 1981: 23). But where
contraction has occurred after the deletion of intervocalic -L-, a low-mid value
[ɛ̃] is found in the front series, ['kɛ̃nda] < CALĔNDA(E) 'period of duty'. In
the back series, however, a high-mid quality emerged as in ['põmba]
< PALŬMBA 'pigeon'.

The unusualness of the Ancares variety lies particularly in the outcome of
context (iii) forms. Here, the regular deletion of intervocalic -N- left behind a
trace of nasality in the preceding vowel, which later spread to an immediately
following vowel segment. The resulting nasal vowels in the forms concerned
have been preserved to the present day, and they may stand in surface contrast
with oral vowels, e.g. MĔOS > ['mews] 'my (m. pl.)' vs. MĬNUS > ['mẽw̃s]
'less', BŬL(L)A > ['boa] 'ball' vs. BŎNA > ['bõã] 'good (f. sg.)'. The following examples may be cited to illustrate the evolution of nasal vowels in context
(iii) forms in Ancares:

(VĪCĪNUM	>	[be'θĩŋ])	VICĪNOS	>	[be'θĩw̃s]
VICĪNA	>	[be'θĩã]	VICĪNAS	>	[be'θĩãs]
			RĒNES	>*	['rines] > [rĩs] 'kidneys'
PLĒNUM	>	[tʃẽw̃]	PLĒNOS	>	[tʃẽw̃s]
PLĒNA	>	['tʃẽã]	PLĒNAS	>	['tʃẽã]
			TĒNES	>	[tẽj̃s]
PLĀNUM	>	[tʃãw̃ŋ]	PLĀNOS	>	[tʃãw̃s]
PLĀNA	>	[tʃãã / tʃã:]	PLĀNAS	>	[tʃãas / tʃã:s]

(where the sequence ['ãa] may contract to give a long vowel)[37]

(PĀNEM	>	[pãŋ])	PĀNES	>	['pãj̃s]
BŎNUM	>	[bõŋ]	BŎNOS	>	[bõj̃s]
BŎNA	>	['bõã]	BŎNAS	>	['bõãs]
(PULMŌNEM	>	[pol'mõŋ])	PULMŌNES	>	[pol'mõj̃s]
ŪNUM	>	[ũŋ]	ŪNOS	>	[ũj̃s]
ŪNA	>	['ũã]	ŪNAS	>	['ũãs]
LŪNA	>	['lũã]	LŪNAS	>	[lũãs]
			LŪNAE-S	>	[lũj̃s] 'Monday'

(Alonso and Yebra 1972; Fernández González 1981)

Phonetically, the scope of nasality has spread from a stressed [Ṽ] to include the following vowel segment. Where the following segment was originally not low, it became some form of nasal off-glide [w̃] or [j̃]. A low final vowel segment was absorbed when the preceding vowel was also low, otherwise it remained unchanged except in respect of nasality. More recently, non-low nasal vowels occurring in absolute word-final position appear to have developed some sort of nasal consonantal off-glide, perhaps by analogy with context (ii) forms. This is apparent from the reflexes of PLĒNUM PLĀNUM BŎNUM and ŪNUM. The phonetic nature of this off-glide is elusive. Alonso and Yebra (1972) describe all such final nasal elements, be they in context (ii) and (iii) forms, as having a velar articulation [ŋ] (as in our transcriptions). However, Fernández González (1981: 72) identifies this word-final element with Castilian final /-n/ implying it is coronal [n]. The difference in interpretation may simply reflect the perceptual weakness of the sound or the increasing influence of Castilian on the speakers of this dialect.

Unstressed vowels which have been nasalized through the loss of -N- retained their nasality when they occurred in pre-stress syllables. They usually appear either in hiatus with a following vowel or have absorbed this vowel as an off-glide; thus, GENĒSTA > [ʃĩ'ɛsta] 'broom', BENEDĬCTUM > [bĩ'ẽj̃to] 'blessed', AD-MANESCĒRE > [amẽj̃'seɾ] 'to dawn'. In both cases, the nasality of the original nasalized vowel has been extended to the following element. However, unstressed vowels in final syllables have lost their nasality, e.g. HŎMINEM > ['ɔme], TURB-ŌNEM > ['tɾɔβo] 'bee hive'

Finally, it may be noted that the stock of nasal vowels has been increased, as in other varieties of Galician, by the effect of progressive assimilation. Thus, MĒ > [mĩŋ] 'me' (and by analogy TĒ > [tĩŋ] 'you'), NŎCTEM > ['nõĩte] 'night', etc.

Inevitably, pressures from Castilian have increased in recent years and most inhabitants are able to operate in diglossic fashion between 'pure' dialect and speech patterns showing various degrees of Castilianization. As far as vowel nasality is concerned, its non-standard nature is recognized. In partially Castilianized usage however, speakers from Ancares usually maintain nasal vowels, whereas the *geada* (the phenomenon whereby /g/ is realized as a voiceless fricative similar to the Spanish jota) is more strongly stigmatized and abandoned more quickly. In fully Castilianized usage, nasal vowels are denasalized, but usually without compensatory insertion of /n/ (Fernández González 1978: 42, 44).

NOTES

1. Such is the view of Barbosa (1962, 1983: 81–104) who uses a Prague School framework (though Tláskal 1980 adopting the same framework concludes that Portuguese does have phonemic nasal vowels), and also Mateus (1975: 43–71) who operates with a generative approach. Madonia (1969) advances an idiosyncratic view where nasal vowels are treated as /Ṽ/ or /VN/ depending on their precise environment. Parkinson (1983) proposes yet another interpretation, where all types of nasal vowel (monophthong or diphthong) are seen at a less abstract level as phonological diphthongs /VṼ/, the latter segment of which is 'a nasalized vocalic segment unmarked for vowel quality' (p. 174). At a deeper level however, they are viewed as tautosyllabic /VN/ sequences, cf. also Parkinson (1982: 23). More recently, Carvalho (1988*a*) has put forward a non-linear analysis whereby nasal vowels are represented by a syllabic nucleus /VN/ which is realized at a segmental level either by /Ṽ/ or /V/ + /N/. The syllabic element /N/ is of indeterminate nature and appears to function in a similar way to the 'focus' of a Firthian-style nasal prosody extending over syllable rimes.

2. Cf. J. Inês Louro, talking of the nasal consonantal element following a nasal vowel, 'No entanto, estas consoantes nasais, à semelhança do que se passa em francês, devem-se considerar meramente gráficas, quer sejam seguidas de consoante oclusiva, quer de constritiva. É que, embora escrevendo-se na actual ortografia, em nenhum caso há a consciência de se pronunciarem e, na realidade, também não lhes correspondem quaisquer movimentos articulatórios activos, próprios.' Cited in Lorenzo (1988: 290).

3. A further possible case is the reduced form of *muito*, namely *mui* 'very'. However, this item is now archaic.

4. This pattern is not found with all affective suffixes however. A notable exception is the augmentative suffix -*zarrão*, which likewise carries strong affectivity and also has a comparable formal structure (it bears the main stress and has an initial [z]). Infor-

mants from Lisbon indicate that the plural of items such as *leãozarrão* 'large lion' and *cãozarrão* 'large dog' would be *leãozarrãos* and *cãozarrãos*, rather than **leõezarrãos and **cãezarrãos.

5. Parkinson (1983: 174) offers a detailed description of the delicately varied realizations found in one informant's usage for the transition between a nasal vowel and a following oral consonant. For the nasal vowel /ĩ/ for example, such sequences as [ĩmb ĩ^{n}d ĩz] are noted.

6. Some measure of the graphic variability may be seen, for instance, in poem 116 of the *Cancioneiro da Ajuda*, where *cofonda* and *confonda* co-occur, the former appearing three times and the latter once. Both forms also occur in other poems of this collection.

7. Carvalho (1989*b*) has argued that in -VnV- sequences the nasal consonant was slow in disappearing and lingered on as the velar [ŋ], i.e. VnV > VŋV > ṼV. No indication is given of when the total deletion of [ŋ] might have occurred, but presumably it must be pre-fourteenth century. The evidence for this hypothesis is modest. Its central motivation seems to lie in the desire to equate the development of intervocalic [-n-] and final [-n] (after apocope), treating them both as coda segments which weakened via velarization. However, there is little to suggest that intervocalic [-n-] was ever interpreted as a coda consonant. Galician might appear to offer some support to this view, since the sequence VnV has given VŋV in some words, as in *unha* where *nh* indicates [ŋ] (cf. 8.4.4). But the velar nasal here probably represents a later anti-hiatic consonant. Also, it is not without interest that this intervocalic nasal [ŋ] < -n- is reported by some scholars at least (though by no means all) to be not a coda but an onset consonant, e.g. *ningunha* is [nĩŋ'gu-ŋã] (cf. Porto Dapena 1976; Alvarez, Regueira, and Monteagudo 1986: 33).

8. The two most reliable early texts using Portuguese orthography do not show the deletion of intervocalic [n] graphically but do indicate the parallel deletion of intervocalic [l]; cf. *uno, bona, irmana* but *taes, casaes, auoo* (< ŪNUM BŎNA GERMĀNA TĀLES CASĀLES AVIŎLA) in the early thirteenth-century *Notícia de torto*, and *sano, raina, manus* but *uoontade* (< SĀNUM REGĪNA MĂNUS VOLUNTĀTEM) in the 1214 Will of Afonso II. In the latter text, however, place names provide limited evidence of the deletion; *Coibria* (< CONIMBRIGA) beside *Lixbona* (< OLISIPONA), where post-stress [-n-] is retained.

9. The forms MŪGILEM > *mugem* 'mullet', NŪBEM > *nuvem* 'cloud' also apparently show progressive nasalization, but probably they underwent early suffixal restructuring to *MŪG-INE, *NŪB-INE from which a final nasal vowel regularly developed.

10. Earlier thirteenth-century forms *madre, mai* are found. *Mãe* is attested from the middle of that century (s.v. *mãe* in Machado 1977).

11. The non-survival (or non-formation) of an off-glide after high vowels may find a partial explanation in the familiar phonetic fact that higher vowels are typically relatively shorter than lower vowels (Lehiste 1970: 20). If off-gliding in Portuguese word-final nasal vowels is bound up with the presence of greater duration, it is to be expected that any vowels failing to develop off-glides will be high vowels.

12. For want of clear proof of added duration, we omit any indication of its possible presence here and in transcriptions elsewhere.

13. However, realizations of nasal *a* which appear to reflect speech habits of Minho are reported for some localities of Castelo Branco and Alentejo (*manhã* [mɐˈɲẽw̃]), and most widely in the Algarve, especially western dialects there (Boléo and Silva 1974). In the Algarve, widespread cases of velarization of /a/ context (iii) forms are also found, e.g. *chama* [ˈʃɑmɐ] (cf. 8.3.3). It is debatable whether such velarized reflexes reflect the presence of immigrants from Minho or whether they represent later independent developments.

14. There is a directly parallel coalescence with oral vowels, as in VĪLES >[ˈvi-es]>[viʃ] *vis* 'vile, base (pl.)', CŪLUM >[ˈku-o]>[ku] *cu* 'arse'.

15. An alternative explanation is that in the sequence [ˈẽ-es] the second element was closed to [i] as a result of regular phonetic change and then it passed to [j] before nasalizing to give [j̃]. Such an explanation is problematic. In particular, it would conflict with the development of the counterpart sequence [õ-o] where the second element did not close and become an off-glide. Thus, [ˈbõ-o] > **[ˈbõ-u] > **[ˈbõw̃]. Had this occurred, the resulting diphthong would have merged with that which arose from [õ] in context (ii) forms (e.g. [rɐˈzõw̃]) and the outcome would have been **bão*. The fate of TĔNERUM and ĞENERUM is interesting as -N- deletion might have yielded a sequence [ẽ-e]. However, syncope occurred beforehand, resulting in *tenro* (attested in the thirteenth century) and *genro* (first found in a document of 973).

16. The fifteenth-century *Vida e Feitos de Júlio César* has *comuũes* (Machado 1977: s.v. *comum*), but the *Cancioneiro Geral* contains *comuũs* (poem 28, l. 146 in rhyme with *huũs* < ŪNOS) which suggests that the sequence [ũ-e] had coalesced to [ũ] by the end of the fifteenth century, either through analogical influence from the singular form or, less plausibly, as a result of a general tendency to reduce [uj] oral or nasal to [u] (Williams 1962: § 38). For another possible source of final [-ũe(s)] in Old Portuguese, see below in the present section.

17. Epenthesis of [m] was evidently a localized development. Vasconcellos (1970: 105) notes the form *ũa* as being 'very frequent' in Portuguese dialects, as later studies have borne out (cf. Maia 1977: 213), and he also cites *ũɲa* for northern dialects of Portugal, this being the usual form in Galician.

18. Other possible sequences are only rarely encountered. Thus, [õ-e] appears to have existed in the reflex of DAEMONES which evidently had variable stress location (singular [ˈdemõ] and [deˈmõ] are both attested in the thirteenth-century *Cantigas de Santa Maria*). Reduction of the final vowel to an off-glide in the plural form, attested in the thirteenth century as *demõees*, is plausible.

19. The development of *geral* < GENERĀLEM 'general' is notable here. Unlike its congener *geração*, the initial vowel typically shows reduction to give [ʒəˈral]. However, Vasconcellos (1970: 140) notes that a pronunciation [ʒɛˈral] was formerly current and 'is still heard in some areas' (this remark referring to usage at the beginning of the century). The latter probably was the earlier pronunciation and the usual modern form with vowel reduction represents a recent development.

20. That specifically high vowels are affected by this development is clear from deriva-

tions such as gan-ĀTUM > [gẽ'ado] > *gado* 'cattle', PANĀTA > [pẽ'adɐ] > *pada* 'small loaf', where nasality has been lost after contraction because the receiving vowel was non-high.

21. Machado (1977: s.v. *ontem*) points to the variability in the realization of this word from earliest recorded times: *oonte* (thirteenth century), *oontem* (fourteenth century), *ootem* (fifteenth century). The *ALPI* (map 20) indicates for this word a pronunciation with nasal vowels in both syllables in virtually all Portugal south of the Douro, with the exception of a compact area in the Lower Douro region. To the north of the Douro, as well as in Galicia, only the first syllable contains a nasal vowel.

22. In poetry, the possibility nonetheless existed of rhyming the two types of vowel, cf. poem 457 by João Rodriguez de Saa in the *Cancioneiro Geral* (1516) where *Alemanha*: *Espanha*: *ganha* rhyme.

23. The diphthongal realization [wĩ] in *ruim* represents a more recent development. The word, which derives ultimately from RUĪNA 'ruin', originally had a disyllabic stem.

24. In the *Orthografia* (1576) of Duarte Nunes de Lião, no mention is made of a nasal diphthong [ũj]. The word *muito* figures alongside *ruivo* and *cuidado*, suggesting that in the norm variety a realization [uj] was usual. A nasal diphthong is still not indicated for *muito* in the *Verdadeiro método de estudar* (1746) of Luís António Verney, although cases of progressive nasality are noted since these of course are not predictable from the standard orthography (e.g. for *mãe* it is observed 'deve escrever-se *Maen*'). But whether this silence means that the nasal realization of the diphthong was still not yet accepted in standard pronunciation is uncertain.

25. Thus, in the Algarve the most common realization is a monophthong [ẽ] (Maia 1975: 69), whereas in northern and especially central dialects of Portuguese the diphthong has sometimes widened to [ɛ̃j], just as the oral diphthong [ej] > [ɛj]. In Brazil, [ẽj] seems to predominate.

26. The relevant comment was, 'e a prova é que não há brasileiro, nem mesmo surdo, que tolere a rima de *mãe* com *também*, como aqui [= Lisbon] fazem os bons rimadores, ou que admitisse um *tambãim* impossível, como a gente culta de Lisboa' (cited in Silva Neto 1963: 177).

27. For the distribution of the levelling of final [õjʃ] > [õʃ] in nominals, see map 10 in Maia (1975: 90).

28. Vasconcellos (1970: 84) reports ['lãŋa] (< LĀNA) in S. Julião in the far north-east of Portugal, noting however that at the turn of this century this pronunciation was virtually moribund. However, Santos (1964: 218, 222–4) found the same phenomenon still in the speech of two villages, Petisqueira and Deilão, situated a few kilometres north of S. Julião; e.g. ['uŋɐ 'lɐŋɐ] < ŪNA LĀNA. Nevertheless, [ŋ] < intervocalic -N- is evidently limited here to reflexes of -ANA and derivatives of ŪNUS.

29. For example, in the dialects of Monção and Melgaço on the Minho at the border between Entre-Douro-e-Minho and Galicia, the forms *cã*, *cãs* and *pã*, *pãs* 'dog(s); loaf, loaves' are reported by Vasconcellos (1928: 304, 310). Maia (1986: 586 n. 4) cites further references.

30. A form *pom* 'bread' (< PĀNEM) occurs in a document dated 1448 from Douro

Litoral alongside *condiçam* 'condition', suggesting that crossing and merger between /ã/ and /õ/ was underway in the fifteenth century (Maia 1986: 586).

31. For the former item, map 25 of the *ALPI* shows a nasal diphthong at nine points (201, 203, 206–9, 214–16) plus one isolated case further south (pt. 242) on the coast at W. Aveiro, while map 34 indicates a diphthong at six points (203, 207–9, 213, 215) for the latter item.

32. Lorenzo (1988: 293, § 3.4) asserts that phonetically nasal vowels are only really found between nasal consonants, as in *mundo* ['mũndo] 'world'. However, Alvarez, Regueira, and Monteagudo (1986) report phonetically nasal vowels not only in the contexts mentioned but also following the consonant [ŋ], e.g. ['uŋã] 'a (f. sg.)'.

33. Our description here is limited to the level of the word. Within tightly knit word groups, an internal word-final nasal is normally realized homorganic with a following word-initial consonant, as in [nõm'bɛβe] 'he does not drink'. Where the following word is vowel initial, the realization of the word-final nasal evidently depends on the degree of bonding between the words in the group; Alvarez, Regueira, and Monteagudo cite as typical of 'a pronuncia corrente': ['kɔmẽŋ'ɑz'ðuas] 'they eat at two', ['kɔmẽno'pɑ̃ŋ] 'they are eating the bread'.

34. For convenience, subsequent transcriptions give only one variant, that containing a homorganic nasal consonant.

35. The quality of the mid vowel in all of the few forms concerned has been affected by analogy or patterns of vowel inflexion. Thus, the plural form ['bɛs] 'goods' has been influenced by the singular [bẽŋ], while the verbal forms [bɛs] 'you (sg.) come', [tɛs] 'you (sg.) have' share the low-mid vowel of [bẽŋ] 'he comes' and [tẽŋ] 'he has' in conformity with the vowel inflexion pattern found in other *-er* verbs with stems containing a high-mid vowel (cf. *c*[o]*so c*[ɔ]*ses c*[ɔ]*se* 'to sew' present tense).

36. Interestingly, the inhabitants of Ancares seem fully aware of the isolation of their particular dialect; cf. 'Para ellos [= the inhabitants used as informants] el ancarés no es ni gallego, ni asturiano, ni castellano. Se consideran viviendo en el último rincón del mundo y tienen una clara conciencia de su aislamiento' (Fernández González 1978: 40).

37. According to Alonso and Yebra (1972), 'Esta *ā* es larga, como corresponde a la fusión de las dos vocales puestas en contacto', but in the transcriptions of Fernández González (1978, 1981) a disyllabic value is clearly suggested ['āā].

9

Rheto-Romance

9.1. Introduction

The term 'Rheto-Romance' (R-R) conventionally covers a heterogeneous grouping of Romance varieties spoken in south-eastern Switzerland and parts of north-eastern Italy.[1] Three main branches are customarily recognized. In the West, there are the various Swiss dialects spoken in the canton known in R-R as *Grischun*, in French as *Grisons,* and in German as *Graubünden.* No single standard variety exists, nor indeed is there a convenient unambiguous term to designate all the different varieties, since the commonly used label 'Romansh' (in R-R *rumantsch*) properly refers to one variety in particular, namely Surselvan, which is spoken in the west of the canton. We will use the French form 'Grisons' in referring to the area of R-R speech in Switzerland.

The two other branches are found in Italy. On the one hand, there is Ladin or Dolomitish, which is spoken on the north-east border area of Trentino, and, on the other hand, in the far north-east of Italy there is Friulan. Ladin does not possess a standard variety, but a widely accepted standard form has developed more recently for Friulan, based on usage in the central area and particularly that of the regional capital Udine.

The lack of strong historical and political bonds both between and within these three areas explains their high level of linguistic diversity. In more recent times, varying degrees of influence from outside languages enjoying greater prestige, notably German and Italian, have led to further diversification. Given all this, it may be expected that individual linguistic features such as vowel nasalization will at times show fluctuating patterns.

9.2. Vowel Nasality in Modern Rheto-Romance

Descriptions of contemporary R-R varieties suggest that phonemically nasal vowels are very seldom to be found. Isolated cases are reported but the vowel nasality usually has a somewhat marginal status at best. One instance is the Subselvan dialect of Rothenbrunnen in the central Grisons (see Map 12), where forms such as [pãw̃] 'bread' and ['lãw̃a]² 'wool' appear in superficial contrast with ['awa] 'water' and [tçawlt] 'hot' (Gartner 1883: § 200). However, phonemic nasality subsequently arose in contexts (ii) and (iii), although not in context (i), cf. [ku'rawnta] 'forty' < QUADRĀ(GI)NTA. It is notable that nasality affected almost exclusively the low vowel /a/, cf. 9.4.3 below. The nasalization of /a/ may be compared with the non-nasalizing development of other types of vowel appearing in the same nasalizing contexts: [baɲ] 'well', ['biæn] 'good (m. sg.)', ['tʃaɲa] 'dinner' (< BĚNE BŎNUM CĒNA).

The absence of such vowel nasalization in the dialects spoken in surrounding areas is significant and suggests that nasalization in Rothenbrunnen represents a recent, highly localized development. The fact that phonemic vowel nasalization has affected forms containing stressed /a/ not only in context (ii) but also context (iii) is noteworthy and indicates that the [w̃] element arising in both contexts represents an off-glide which developed from the second mora of an originally long nasal vowel (cf. 9.3.4). Thus, the likely evolution in context (ii) forms was as in PĀNEM > [pãːn > pãw̃ⁿ > pãw̃], while in context (iii) forms like ['lãw̃a] the developmental stages may have been LĀNA > ['lãːna > 'lãw̃na > 'lãw̃ⁿa > 'lãw̃a] with absorption of the nasal occlusive segment in both cases.

Elsewhere, the typical pattern has been for vowels to undergo at most allophonic nasalization. There are indications that allophonic nasalization has occurred fairly widely, and today significant levels of vowel nasality have been noted for many varieties of R-R, although detailed experimental evidence to support these observations is still regrettably lacking. In many modern varieties of Friulan, vowels occurring before word-final [ŋ] are reported to be fairly strongly nasalized especially when they are stressed, as in [mãŋ] 'hand' and [cas'trõŋ] 'castrated lamb' (Iliescu 1972: 96; Frau 1984: 50).³ In Ladin, the dialect of Fassa provides another case of high-level allophonic vowel nasalization. Here, vowels are described as being strongly nasalized when preceding a nasal consonant followed by a sibilant fricative, e.g. in ['õŋzer] 'to grease'. In such contexts, the nasal is realized as [ŋ] or may be weakened to the point of disappearing altogether (Elwert 1972: § 166). In Grisons varieties, it appears that allophonic nasality in vowels generally reaches only low levels.

In earlier times vowel nasality was doubtless a good deal more intense in many areas than it is now. Evidence for this comes principally from the distinct patterns of evolution which vowels may show when they appear in contexts containing nasal consonants. The broad lines of these patterns are considered for the different varieties of R-R in the following sections.

9.3.   History of Vowel Nasalization

9.3.1.   BACKGROUND DEVELOPMENTS

The vowel systems of all varieties of R-R derive from the seven-way system /i e ɛ a ɔ o u/ which arose in many other parts of the Empire in late Imperial times. In unstressed syllables, the contrast between mid vowels was neutralized leaving just high-mid vowels /e/ and /o/.

A further development, shared with northern French (*langue d'oïl*) and Italian dialects, was the lengthening of vowels in free stressed syllables. Thus,

$$\text{VĒNA} \quad > \quad \text{'ve-na} \quad > \quad \text{(early R-R)} \quad \text{'veːna 'vein'}$$
$$\text{VĒNDAM} \quad > \quad \text{'ven-da} \quad > \quad \text{(early R-R)} \quad \text{'venda 'I sell (subj.)'}$$

R-R also underwent extensive apocope. This operated on all final vowels except Late Latin /-a/ which has either remained as [-a] or partially weakened to give a central vowel of some sort. An important consequence of apocope was that long vowels now became able to appear in blocked syllables, as in [seːn] < ['seːn(u)] < SĬNUM 'bosom'. As regards the chronology of apocope, it is only possible to say that it occurred at some stage in the pre-literary period after the lengthening of free stressed vowels had taken place. It is certainly completed by the beginning of the fourteenth century in Friulan, when the earliest texts written in vernacular orthography appear, e.g. *timp* < TĔMPUS 'time'. In the Grisons, the first surviving vernacular texts of any substance date only from the sixteenth century, at which stage apocope is similarly well established.

9.3.2.   THE NASALIZING CONTEXT

Vowel nasalization in R-R has typically come about as a result of regressive assimilation by a nasal consonant. All types of nasal consonant have brought about vowel nasalization and there is evidence that heterosyllabic as well as tautosyllabic nasal consonants have led to heightened nasalization in a preceding vowel.

All three basic types of nasalizing contexts are found in R-R. Types (i) and (iii) were inherited in large numbers from Latin, as in items like PLĂNTA and LĀNA, respectively. And as a result of the action of apocope a substantial set of forms containing context (ii) came into being to add to the small tally of items already in Latin, e.g. NŌN.

9.3.3. IMPLEMENTATION OF VOWEL NASALIZATION

It is unclear at what stage levels of allophonic nasality in R-R were increased but there are a number of indications that the process is of some antiquity in most regions. One suggestive piece of evidence is provided by the widespread neutralization of the contrast in stressed syllables between mid vowels /ɔ/ vs. /o/ and /ɛ/ vs. /e/ specifically in a nasalizing context, this development finding a direct parallel in Gallo-Romance (4.2.3(a), 5.1.1, 6.2.1.2), Portuguese (8.2.3), and Italo-Romance (10.2.2.2, 10.5.1). When they appeared in such a context, the low-mid vowels /ɛ/ and /ɔ/ typically raised and merged with the high-mid vowels /o/ and /e/. In view of the fact that the change was associated with the presence of a following nasal consonant, it seems reasonable to assume that vowel nasalization took place. Neutralization of mid-vowel contrasts was usual in dialects of the Grisons and in Ladin, although occasional cases appear where it was not fully carried through. In Friulan, however, there was no neutralization. The following examples may be cited for Grisons and Ladin:

	Bergün (C. Grisons)	*Fassa* (Ladin)	
TĔNDERE/EXPĔNDERE	'tɛndər	'ʃpener	'to tend, spend'
VĒNDERE	'vɛndər	'venər	'to sell'
RESPŎNDERE	re'ʃpwøndər	re'ʃponer	'to answer'
ABŬNDE/TŬNDERE	a'wønda	'toner	'enough, to cut'
BĔNE	bɛːŋ	bɛŋ	'well'
PLĒNUM	pleːŋ	pjeŋ	'full (m. sg.)'
BŎNUM	(buŋ)[4]	boŋ	'good (m. sg.)'
-ŌNEM	-uŋ[5]	-oŋ	nominal suffix
TŎNAT	'toŋa	'tona	'it thunders'
CORŌNA	ka'roŋa	ko'rona	'rack, crown'

(Lutta 1923; Elwert 1972)

As we have noted, Friulan showed no parallel move to neutralize the contrast between mid vowels in nasalizing contexts. Contrasts have in fact been preserved in contexts (i) and (iii) to the present day. However, mid vowels did come to merge in context (ii). This may indicate that vowel nasalization only began to operate rather later on at a time after apocope had occurred, by when the original mid vowels of context (i) and (iii) forms had already developed along distinct paths. Significantly, the Friulan pattern of vowel nasalization resembles what is found in numerous northern Italian dialects, where context (ii) is likewise the preferred environment for nasalization (10.4.3). This suggests a common basis to vowel nasalization in these adjacent Romance areas. Examples are:

context (i)

TĔNDERE	>	'tindi	'to tend'	*vs.*	'vɛndi	< VĒNDERE	'to sell'
ABSCŎNDERE	>	'ʃkwindi	'to hide'	*vs.*	a'vɔnde	< ABŬNDE	'enough'

context (iii)

BŎNA	>	'bwine	'good (f. sg.)'	*vs.*	ko'rɔne	< CORŌNA	'crown'
but							

context (ii)

BĔNE	>	bɛ̃ŋ	'well'	=	sɛ̃ŋ	< SĬNUM	'bosom'
BŎNUM	>	bɔ̃ŋ	'good (m. sg.)'	=	dɔ̃ŋ	< DŌNUM	'gift'

9.3.4. FATE OF THE CONDITIONING NASAL CONSONANT

The conditioning nasal consonant in nasalizing contexts has undergone some weakening in most varieties of R-R but has almost invariably been retained as a nasal consonant segment of some sort. The dialect of Rothenbrunnen, where nasal vowel phonemes have developed, forms a notable exception (see above, 9.2).

9.3.4.1. *Context (i)*

The nasal coda consonant here was already homorganic with the following consonant in Latin and this pattern has widely been preserved. However, depending on the nature of the consonant which followed, the conditioning nasal consonant underwent major weakening at an early stage in a number of dialects and developed into some type of nasal off-glide to the preceding vowel. Later on, the nasal off-glide was usually strengthened and restored to full consonantal status as [ŋ], accompanied by some reduction in levels of vowel nasality. However, in very rare cases the weakening process could lead to the deletion of the nasal consonant and the appearance of unconditioned nasal vowels. The evolution may be summarized:

$$ \bar{V}NC > \tilde{V}\bar{G}C > \tilde{V}ŋC/VŋC/(rarely) \tilde{V}C $$

(where 'Ḡ' indicates a nasal glide)

As mentioned, the weakening process is directly conditioned by the nature of the consonant following the nasal (indicated above by 'C'), and the precise nature of this conditioning varies somewhat regionally.

In Friulan, weakening occurred most widely when the nasal was followed by a fricative or a palatal consonant, as in ['paɲse] < PĂNTICEM 'belly', [zgloɲf] < EX-CONFL-UM 'swollen', [diɲc] < DĔNTES 'teeth' as against

[dint] < DĔNTEM 'tooth' (Frau 1984).[6] In Ladin, the development was generally limited to environments where the following consonant was a *sibilant fricative*, ['ŏ̃ŋzer] < ŬNGERE 'to grease', ['vẽŋzer] < VĬNCERE 'to conquer'. In such items, an unconditioned nasal vowel can sometimes be found, ['ŏ̃zer] (Elwert 1972: § 166). The Friulan and Ladin data may be compared with developments in Old French (4.2.5(*b*)), Portuguese (8.2.4), and northern Italian dialects (10.4.3.3).

Comparable signs of major weakening of the conditioning nasal are less widespread in the Grisons, but occasional cases occur. Thus, in the dialect of Bergün the coda nasal was weakened when it preceded a voiceless consonant. Subsequently, the resultant nasal off-glide was restored to full consonantal status as [ŋ], as in [dɛːŋt] < ['dẽj̃(n)t] (attested in seventeenth-century texts as *deint*) < DĔNTEM 'tooth' and ['sɛːŋmpəl] < *['sẽj̃(m)pəl] < SĬMPLUM 'simple' (Lutta 1923). This development finds parallels in northern Italian dialects (10.4.3.3), suggesting that there may have been a broad tendency in north Italy and the Alpine area to favour vowel nasalization before sequences of nasal + voiceless consonant.

9.3.4.2.   *Context (ii)*

In this context, weakening and associated vowel nasalization have been more general. Where weakening was most intense, the word-final nasal consonant probably gave a nasal off-glide or even underwent deletion leaving an unconditioned nasal vowel. Where either process has occurred, there has been restructuring, whereby the second mora of the long nasal vowel is consonantalized to [ŋ] and the first mora may be downgraded in its level of nasality, [ṼG̃/Ṽː > Ṽŋ]. The weakening process has been carried furthest in the east of the R-R area and becomes progressively less significant the further west the dialect lies.

In the Grisons, weakening of word-final nasals has been slight except with final [-n] < simplex -N-, although in peripheral dialects this nasal too has remained unmodified. For example, in western (Surselvan) varieties and in those of the far south-east (Münster Valley), we find [pawn] < PĀNEM 'bread'. Elsewhere, weakening of final [n] < -N- was evidently considerable before a countertendency got underway to restore a coda nasal deriving from the second mora of the nasal vowel. This development was evidently accompanied by substantial vowel denasalization. In many dialects, the restored coda nasal was realized as a palatal [ɲ] when a front vowel preceded and a velar [ŋ] when a back vowel preceded. Thus, [veɲ plæɲ øɲ] < VĪNUM PLĒNUM ŪNUM 'wine, full (m. sg.), one (m. sg.)' but [caŋ buŋ] < CĂNEM BŎNUM 'dog, good (m. sg.)' in the southern Engadinish dialect of Bivio (*AIS*, pt. 35). Less commonly, [ŋ] has become established as the coda nasal irrespective of the quality of the preceding vowel. All other types of original nasal consonant which came to appear in word-final position have generally been preserved intact so that a range of contrasting nasals have continued to exist in this context. This can be illustrated with data from one of the more innovating dialects, that of Bergün (Lutta 1923):

	-n	PĀNEM	>	paŋ	'bread'
	but				
	-ɲ	BĂLNEUM	>	bwøɲ	'bath'
(geminate -NN- >)	-ñ	ĂNNUM	>	ɔn	'year'
(in proparoxytons)	-n	ŎRPHANUM	>	'ɔːərfən	'orphan'
	-m	FĀMEM	>	fɔm	'hunger'

A stronger trend towards weakening is found in Ladin dialects. Geographically it got underway first in the east and is still very gradually and slowly gaining ground westwards. The preferential order here amongst nasals for weakening with later vowel restructuring to vowel + [ŋ] may be represented as a parameter:

-n   (proparoxytonic) -n   -ŋ   -ñ (< -NN-)   -m

most widespread   *least widespread*

Thus, all dialects show [-ŋ] in forms originally containing final [-n] < simplex -N-, except with original proparoxytons where modern reflexes in [-ŋ] are found in some dialects only. Late Latin forms ending in [-ɲ] after apocope has taken place appear with final [-ŋ] in certain dialects only. Forms containing geminate -NN- that becomes word-final surface with reflexes in [-ŋ] solely in the Fassa valley, and in this innovating locality final [-m] undergoes weakening and allows the appearance of final [-ŋ] in just a subset of linguistic items, e.g. [fuŋ] < FŪMUM 'smoke' but [pom] < PŌMUM 'apple' (Elwert 1972). This pattern may be compared with that found in north Italian dialects (10.4.4.1.).

In Friulan, weakening has gone further still and some varieties show total neutralization as in:

	-n	PĀNEM	>	pãŋ	'bread'
	-ɲ	LĬGNUM	>	lẽŋ	'wood'
(geminate -NN- >)	-ñ	ĂNNUM	>	ãŋ	'year'
(in proparoxytons)	-n	ŎRPHANUM	>	'vwarfĩŋ	'orphan'
	-m	FĀMEM	>	fãŋ	'hunger'

However, in most dialects, the nasals [m] and [ɲ] show greater resistance to weakening and preserve their consonantal status. This would suggest a slightly different parameter of weakening from that seen for Ladin, namely:

-n   -ñ (< -NN-)/(proparoxytonic) -n   -ɲ/-m

most widespread   least widespread

Also, there has been considerable lexical diffusion in the implementation of weakening in the nasal. Thus, the reflex of FĀMEM 'hunger' is reported as [faŋ] in 24 out of the 32 localities recorded in *ASLEF* (map 2897), although the comparable item AERĀMEN 'copper' gives [raŋ] in only 5 out of 27 localities (map 2928). The palatal nasal of ARĀNEUM 'spider' also resists weakening in many areas, the reflexes ['raj/'raːj] appearing in 27 of 55 localities (map 894).

9.3.4.3. *Context (iii)*

The conditioning nasal here has been stable in most varieties of R-R. However, simplex -N- evidently underwent substantial weakening in certain dialects of the Grisons, especially those of the central area which had seen major weakening in context (ii) forms. Here, just as with context (ii) forms a process of restoration took place to re-establish a full nasal consonant from the second mora of long nasal vowels. The restored nasal had the same quality as the restored nasal in context (ii) forms, and in the resulting nasal consonant sequence it assimilated and absorbed the weakened reflex of original -N-, as has happened in the dialects of Genoa and Turin in north-western Italy (10.4.4.2.) Thus, the dialect of Bivio has: [gaˈeɲa kaˈdæɲa ʎøːɲa] < GALLĪNA, CATĒNA, LŪNA 'hen, chain, moon' but ['laɲa] < LĀNA 'wool'. However, in the dialect of Bergün, where [ŋ] developed from simplex -N- in all context (ii) forms, the corresponding forms are [djiˈʎeŋa tçaˈdeːŋa 'ʎeŋa 'ʎaŋa], a further example being [kaˈroŋa] < CORŌNA 'rack, top of door frame'. The likely phonetic paths for the changes here were:

$$\tilde{V}:nV > \begin{cases} \tilde{V}jnV > \tilde{V}ɲ^nV > VɲV \text{ (where } [\tilde{V}] \text{ is a front vowel)} \\ \tilde{V}wnV > \tilde{V}ŋ^nV > VŋV \end{cases}$$

It is striking that the weakening of simplex -N- in R-R also occurred in dialects where original geminate -NN- and -MM- were very slow to simplify, unlike in the rest of western Romance. Traces of them as slightly lengthened consonants have indeed survived up to the present day in a number of varieties of the Grisons.[7] The facts thus suggest that weakening of simplex -N- in this area may not have been triggered initially as a direct response to the simplification of geminates.

9.4.   Later Developments

From the early Middle Ages onward, there has been increasing phonological divergence in the varieties of R-R. The resulting diversity obliges us to deal with each of the three linguistic zones separately.

9.4.1.   FRIULAN

In the course of the medieval period, vowels occurring before nasal consonants began to undergo increasing and substantial nasalization. Two pieces of evidence argue for this.

(*a*) Certain types of mid vowel have developed differently depending upon whether they were or were not in a nasalizing context. Thus, following the regular diphthongization of /ɔ/ in blocked syllables, the fate of the diphthong in a nasalizing context has diverged from that of its oral counterpart as in:

	CŎNTRA	>	'kwintri	'against'
but	CŎSTA	>	'kweste	'rib'

(*b*) The distinctive tensing (reflected in raising and the preservation of length) which operated on free stressed vowels in oxytonic forms deriving from paroxytons affected by apocope did not take place when the vowels were pre-nasal, for example

NĬVEM > [neːf] 'snow' *but* FĒNUM > [fẽŋ] 'hay',
FŎCUM > [fuːk] 'fire' *but* BŎNUM > [bõŋ] 'good (m. sg.)'.

The consequences of the increased levels of nasality on tongue position in vowels have not been significant however. Original low and high vowels show no height changes when in nasalizing contexts, as the following examples demonstrate:

context (i)			*context (ii)*			*context (iii)*		
*CĪNQUE	>	tʃiŋk	VĪNUM	>	vĩŋ	GALLĪNA	>	ɟa'line
ŪNDECIM	>	'undiʃ	ŪNUM	>	ũŋ	ŪNA	>	'une
TĂNTUM	>	tant	MĂNUM	>	mãŋ	LĀNA	>	'lane

(respectively, 'five, wine, hen, eleven, one (m.), one (f.), so much, hand, wool')

The effect of nasality on mid-vowel evolution however has been more complex, as the following examples indicate:

	context (i)			*context (ii)*			*context (iii)*		
/ɛ/	TĔNDERE	>	'tinde	BĔNE	>	bẽŋ	—		
/e/	VĒNDERE	>	'vɛndi	SĬNUM	>	sẽŋ	POENA	>	'pɛne

/ɔ/   PŎNTEM > pwint   BŎNUM > bɔ̃ŋ   BŎNA   > 'bwine
/o/   ŬNGULA > 'ɔŋgule   -ŌNEM > ɔ̃ŋ   CORŌNA > ko'rɔne

(respectively, 'to tend, well, to sell, bosom, suffering, bridge, good (m. sg.), good (f. sg.), nail, (augmentative suffix), crown')

Vowel nasalization appears to have begun to operate after the regular diphthongization of /ɛ ɔ/ > /iɛ uɔ/ in free or blocked syllables. In context (i) and (iii) forms, nasality caused raising of the second element so that it emerged as a high vowel, [iɛ > ĩɛ̃ > ĩĩ > ĩ] and [uɔ > uɛ > ũɛ̃ > ũĩ > wĩ] (the early differentiation of [uɔ] to [uɛ] affects oral and nasal vowels alike, cf. FŎSSA > ['fwɛse] 'ditch'). It is notable that comparable raising did not affect the [ẽ] < nasalized /e/ in words like VĒNDERE > ['vɛndi] 'to sell' or TĬNCA > ['tɛnce] 'tench'. This was presumably due to the fact that at the time when raising began to operate as a result of nasalization the relevant vowels were level or perhaps even falling diphthongs rather than rising diphthongs, i.e. [ĩẽ ũẽ] or [ĩɛ̝̃ ũɛ̝̃] rather than [jẽ wẽ]. Consequently, no direct association was made between the second element of these sequences and the main stressed segment [ẽ] in VĒNDERE etc. The process of raising in forms such as ['tinde pwint] was completed in pre-literary times, i.e. before the fourteenth century.

In context (ii) forms, vowel nasalization was particularly intense. Diphthongization operated on words containing /ɛ ɔ/ but after apocope took place the high levels of nasality which developed resulted in the diphthongs /iɛ uɔ/ undergoing nasalization throughout their span and subsequently being levelled as the long nasal monophthongs [ẽː õː]. These vowels thus merged with [ẽː õː] < stressed /e o/ in context (ii) words. Later, in both cases there was restoration of a conditioning nasal consonant as the second mora was restructured into [ŋ]. Thus:

BĔNE   > 'biɛne > biɛn > bĩẽn > bẽːn > bẽː([n]) > bẽŋ > bẽŋ
SĬNUM > 'seːnu > seːn > sẽːn   > sẽː([n]) > sẽŋ > sẽŋ
BŎNUM > 'buɔnu > buɔn > būõn > bõːn > bõː([n]) > bõŋ > bɔ̃ŋ
DŌNUM > 'doːnu > doːn > dõːn   > dõː([n]) > dõŋ > dɔ̃ŋ

The systematic shortening of the formerly long stressed vowels in context (ii) forms, [vĩŋ sẽŋ bẽŋ pãŋ bɔ̃ŋ dɔ̃ŋ uŋ] < VĪNUM SĬNUM BĔNE PĀNEM BŎNUM DŌNUM ŪNUM 'wine, bosom, well, bread, good (m. sg.), gift, one (m.)', is typical of many northern Italian dialects and may indeed represent a phonetic change diffused from North Italy into the more peripheral Alpine varieties of Romance (cf. 10.5.2 and also Ladin below).

9.4.2.   LADIN

After the regular merger of high-mid and low-mid vowels, there have been few subsequent changes caused by the influence of nasality. The precise quality of the mid nasal vowels may vary from variety to variety, and within individual varieties there may be differences in the realization of a given nasal vowel type depending upon the nature of the context in which it appears. Thus, DĒNTEM LĬNGUA 'tooth, tongue' emerge with a high-mid vowel in the dialect of Livinallongo [dent 'leŋga] but with a low-mid vowel in the dialect of Fassa [dɛnt 'lɛŋga]. However, in the latter dialect a high-mid variant [e] is also found in certain contexts, namely in open syllables (as in ['vena] < VĒNA 'vein') and in verb-forms with final [-m] as in [ʒem] 'I groan' where analogy has doubtless operated from other forms of the paradigm where [e] is expected, e.g. the infinitive ['ʒemer]. Levels of vowel nasality appear to be generally modest.

The evolution of the stressed vowels of context (ii) forms that arose from the action of apocope pose a problem however. The present-day realization is a short vowel and followed by the velar nasal [ŋ]. The development of those words which originally contained mid vowels is of particular interest. Stressed free /e o/ in non-nasal contexts regularly underwent diphthongization to [ej ow] in the medieval period as in:

	Livinallongo	Marebbe	
PĒ(N)SUM	pejs	pejs	'weight'
CRŬCEM	krowʃ	kruːʃ (with [ow > uː])	'cross'

However it is not clear whether this diphthongization (which is known to post-date that of the low mid vowels /ɛ ɔ/) also affected the directly comparable nasal vowels appearing in context (ii) forms such as [feŋ] [veŋ], [te'moŋ/to'muŋ] < FĒNUM VĔNIT, TEMŌNEM 'hay, he comes, shaft/rudder' which appear in the same dialects (Kramer 1977). The present-day realization [feŋ], for example, could therefore represent the restructured version of either [fẽː(^{n})], with nasalization blocking the implementation of diphthongization, or [fẽj(^{n})], where diphthongization followed by strong nasalization has taken place. The possibility that high-level nasality could obstruct diphthongization here finds some support from a later development affecting free (and hence long) stressed /aː/. In Ladin, this was regularly fronted to /ɛː/ probably during the fifteenth–sixteenth centuries, as in NĀSUM > [nɛs nɛːs neːs] 'nose'. However, the nasal vowel counterpart remained unaffected, as in MĂNUM > [maŋ] 'hand'. This may have been due to the vowel having already become short as a result of restructuring or because the presence of high-level nasality blocked any association between this vowel and oral /aː/.

There are no signs of significant tongue height changes in vowels appearing in nasalizing contexts. Thus, high vowels typically remain high. The odd cases of lowering of Ū >[y] > [ø] which appear pre-nasally are paralleled by lowering before certain oral consonants as well, e.g. CŪNA > ['køna] 'cradle' just as CŪRA > ['køra] 'care' in Marebbe dialect. Likewise, the low vowel /a/ normally remains low in nasalizing contexts. The only notable exception is found in the dialect of Livinallongo where in contexts (i) and (ii) there is raising to [ə], e.g. [mən] 'hand', [səŋk] 'blood'. But in context (iii) forms, no such raising is indicated ['rana] 'frog', suggesting lower levels of nasality before heterosyllabic nasals at the period of raising. Curiously, in precisely this context but not in the others, the mid front vowel /e/ has retracted and lowered to give [ə] also, e.g. ['vəna pəna] (< VĒNA PĬNNA) 'vein, feather'. In this way, the vowel [ə] emerges in a full range of nasalizing contexts, albeit from differing sources. However, the developments in Livinallongo represent a geographically quite localized and a chronologically late phenomenon.

9.4.3.   GRISONS

In the Grisons, the impact of nasalization on vowel evolution has again been fairly limited. Following the widespread neutralization of the contrast between mid vowels in nasalizing contexts as a result of the raising of low-mid vowels, there have subsequently been few other instances of quality change due to nasal influence.

One apparent case concerns central dialects spoken south of Chur (Surmeiran and adjacent dialects of southern Engadinish), where high vowels preceding a nasal consonant are regularly lowered, whether in contexts (i), (ii), or (iii). Thus: VĪNUM, FŪMUM give [veŋ fem] and [veɲ fem] in the dialects of Bergün and Filisur, respectively (Lutta 1923: § 68), while the *AIS* indicates regular lowering in the reflexes of VĪNUM, *CĪNQUE, GALLĪNA; ŪNUM, ŪNDECIM, LŪNA at points 14 (Dalin), 15 (Mathon), 16 (Scharans), and 17 (Lenz), and there is vowel lowering in a majority though not all the reflexes of these six items at points 5 (Ems), 27 (Latsch) and 35 (Bivio). Outside this central zone, high vowels have usually preserved their tongue position in nasalizing contexts.

Although the vowel lowering seen here appears to owe itself specifically to nasal influence, in reality it forms part of a general lowering movement affecting high vowels in all blocked syllables. Thus, parallel to the data cited above for Bergün and Filisur we find developments such as: (Bergün) FĪLIUM > [feʎ], FRŪCTUM > [frets]; (Filisur) DĪCTUM > [zet], EXSŪCTUM > [sets] 'dry'. The implication is thus that high vowels in nasalizing contexts were interpreted as blocked vowels. In the case of vowels in context (iii), this interpretation presumably came about as a result of the lengthening of the intervocalic nasal, which in turn caused a compensatory shortening of the preceding stressed vowel, cf. ['ʎinna 'ʎynna] < LŪNA reported for various dialects of the Grisons in the *AIS* (pts. 7, 13, 47, etc.). Later, however, the vowel could regain length as a result of the shortening of the lengthened consonant, so that a good deal of interplay existed between the sequences V:CV and VCCV.

As regards the chronology of the lowering, texts in the dialects concerned dating from the sixteenth and seventeenth centuries still regularly show forms with high vowels, *emprim* (< IN-PRĪMUM), *fim* (< FŪMUM) (Stimm and Linder 1989: 765). The generalization of a lowered pronunciation for high vowels is thus evidently of comparatively recent date.

A more significant change has been mid-vowel lengthening. In context (i) forms, the front mid-vowel [e] has regularly undergone lengthening in most dialects. The corresponding back vowel, however, has not been affected in parallel fashion and neither has the high vowel /i/. Lengthening has been most generalized when the conditioning nasal consonant was followed by a voiceless consonant, i.e. in the context/___ NÇ. A comparable pattern is found in northern Italian dialects and it seems likely that both developments are linked (10.4.3.3.). The lengthening has commonly led to the formation of an off-glide, resulting most often in a diphthong ending in [j]. Thus:

		Tavetsch	*Bergün*	*Münster*
lengthening				
ĬNTUS	'within'	æ:jn	ɛ:ŋt	ajnt
TĔMPUS	'time'	tjams	tɛ:ŋmp	tajmp
no lengthening				
VĒNDERE	'to sell'	'vendɐr	'vendər	'vendər
MĔMBRA	'limb'	'membrɐ	'membrɐ	'membrɐ
PŎNTEM	'bridge'	pun	puŋt	punt
RŬMPERE	'to break'	'rumpɐr	'rompər	'rumpər
TŬNDERE	'to cut'	'tundɐr	'tondər	'tondər
*CĪNQUE	'five'	tʃun	tʃeɲtç	ciɲc

(cf. parallel development of /e/ in a non-nasalizing context)

| CRĒSCERE | 'to grow' | 'krɛʃɐr | 'krɛʃər | 'krɛʃər |

The incidence of this development suggests that it may well have arisen first in central areas before spreading incompletely to western and eastern parts of the Grisons. Already in the sixteenth century, the southern Engadinish writers Gian Travers (from Zuoz) and Jakob Bifrun (from Samedan) use forms such as *aint* (< ĬNTUS) and *saimpels* (< SĬMPL-OS). In the dialect of Bergün, the appearance of the velar nasal [ŋ] represents a fairly recent localized development whereby the nasalized off-glide has been consonantalized. The seventeenth-century work *Susanna* composed in Bergün dialect still has graphies such as *seimpel, teimp* showing the off-glide intact.

Nasality has also had an impact on the evolution of the low vowel /a/ (De Poerck 1962). In non-nasalizing contexts, stressed /a/ typically remained unchanged when blocked, whereas in originally free syllables it was regularly lengthened and in a number of dialects, especially Upper Engadinish, it later fronted to [ɛː] or [eː]. However, in all types of nasalizing context, a back off-glide [w] very commonly developed, the resulting diphthong often being levelled later on to a back rounded vowel [ɔ]. The modification of /a/ in nasalizing contexts is not confined to dialects showing changes to /a/ in oral contexts, however. Specimen examples are:

		Tavetsch	*Bergün*	*Münster*
PLĂNTA	'plant'	'plɔntɐ	'plaŋtɐ	'plawntɐ
INFĂNTEM	'child'	uˈfawn	umˈfaŋt	uˈfawnt
PĀNEM	'bread'	pawn	paŋ	pawn
LANA	'wool'	'lawnɐ	'laŋɐ	'lawnɐ
PĂNNUM	'cloth'	pɔn	pɔn	pɔn
FLĂMMA	'flame'	'flɔmɐ	'flɔmmɐ	'flɔmɐ
FĀMEM	'hunger'	fɔm	fɔm	fɔm

These derivations may be compared with the following in non-nasalizing contexts:

NĀSUM	'nose'	naːs	neːs	naːs
BĂRBA	'beard'	'barbɐ	'baːrbɐ	'barbɐ

The precise details of historical evolution here are fairly complex and show a good deal of variation regionally and even intra-dialectally (cf. ['plɔntɐ] but [uˈfawn] in the dialect of Tavetsch). In brief, during the medieval period, /a/ in nasalizing contexts diphthongized to [ãw̃] in most dialects of the Grisons, presumably after lengthening in context (i) forms (cf. a comparable development in Norman French and Anglo-Norman dialects 4.3.10, 5.3). This diphthongal stage has sometimes been preserved but principally in contexts where the following nasal consonant segment goes back to a simplex coronal -N- which remained coronal, e.g. in PĀNEM LĀNA, or in the velar sequences [ŋk] and [ŋg]. In other nasalizing contexts, the diphthong was widely reduced to a monophthong [ɔ], or, in Upper Engadinish dialects, to the monophthong [a] (cf. Celerina dialect: PĂNNUM > [pan], GRĂNDEM > [grant], CAL-CĀNEUM > [tçalˈtçaɲ], FLĂMMA > ['flamɐ]). No modern dialect and no surviving text present a diphthong in the reflexes of PĂNNUM FĀMEM etc. (De Poerck 1962: 80). In all varieties of Engadinish, the following consonant group /nt/ also had the effect of preserving the diphthong stage and obstructing monophthongization, probably because of the lengthening effect which sequences of /n/ + voiceless consonant had on a preceding vowel (see above). Texts of the sixteenth century reflect this situation with forms such as:

Old Surselvan   *maun, aungel;*   *plonta, grond, fom, flomma*
Old Engadinish   *maun, aungel, plaunta;*   *fom, flomma*

(Stimm and Linder 1989: 766)

Subsequently, various developments have taken place. The sequence [ãw̃(^{n})] in particular has undergone much local adaptation. In the Upper Engadine, fronting of the nuclear vowel occurred, accompanied by a consonantalization of the bilabial nasal glide [w̃] to give [ɛːm]. The outcome has been pronunciations such as [cɛːm] < CĂNEM and ['lɛːmɐ] < LĀNA (e.g. at *AIS*, pts. 28 (Zuoz), 47 (Sils)). In the lateral dialects of Lower Engadinish (in the East) and Surselvan (in the West), no such fronting took place and the sequence [ãw̃(^{n})] has either had the weak nasal consonant segment restored to give [awn] or [əwn], or the off-glide has consonantalized as [ŋ] giving [aŋ]. Thus, we find Tavetsch (Surselvan) and Münster Valley with [mawn], ['lawnɐ], while Ardez (= *AIS*, pt. 7) has [maŋ], ['laŋɐ], just as the transitional dialects of Bergün and Bivio (*AIS*, pt. 35). In the Lower Engadinish dialects between Zernez and Lavin which are near the Münster Valley, [aŋ] has progressively passed to [an] from the seventeenth century on. The possibilities may be summarized:

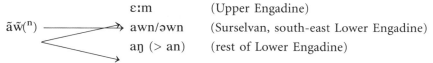

	ɛːm	(Upper Engadine)
ãw̃(^{n})	awn/əwn	(Surselvan, south-east Lower Engadine)
	aŋ (> an)	(rest of Lower Engadine)

Despite the complexity of phonetic development, it is significant that the reflex of original stressed /a/ has not come to coalesce with the reflexes of other vowel types. Phonologically, the developments encountered are therefore of limited significance for the overall vowel systems of the dialects concerned.

NOTES

1. It has long been a tradition to use a single label 'Rheto-Romance' to designate the Romance varieties treated in this chapter, as though they form some sort of linguistic unity or closely related language complex. However, this viewpoint has been challenged, with justification, by various linguists, cf. Pellegrini (1991); Haiman and Benincà (1992: 1–27). Although acknowledging the validity of the arguments made, we will use R-R as a convenient classificatory term for two reasons. The varieties involved are geographically fairly compact and may helpfully be dealt with together

and, more importantly for our purposes, they share certain common characteristics in the way vowel nasalization has affected them.

2. In his transcriptions, Gartner (1883) does not indicate the presence of nasality in the approximant [w], but in view of the likely history of this element and its function here as an off-glide to a fully nasal vowel, the presence of nasality seems very probable.

3. In the light of this, it is curious that in the extensive dialect atlas of Friulan, *ASLEF*, no indication is given of the presence of vowel nasality, phonemic or allophonic, in any of the forms cited.

4. The present-day form [buŋ] probably represents a remodelling based on the feminine ['buɲa]. The form [bʎoŋ] < [bjoŋ] < [bjuŋ] (attested as *biun* in the seventeenth century) is arguably the direct reflex of BŎNUM but it is only found now as an adverb.

5. Lutta (1923) in fact cites three possible outcomes, [-oŋ -ʊŋ -uŋ], whose distribution appears unpredictable, e.g. [tçar'voŋ tçan'tsʊŋ tça'puŋ] < CARBŌNEM CANTIŌNEM CAPPŌNEM 'coal, song, capon'.

6. Here, as elsewhere, we reproduce the transcriptions provided in the linguistic descriptions provided. The absence of a symbol indicating nasality may not necessarily mean however that the vowel concerned is accompanied by no more than universal phonetic nasality (cf. 1.2).

7. For the dialect of Bergün, Lutta (1923: § 309) reports that the main legacy of original geminates is the brevity of the preceding vowel, but when the preceding vowel is stressed, the reflex of geminate consonants still have a perceptibly greater duration in their articulation than that of originally simplex consonants. However, Lutta admits that this extra duration ceases to be perceptible, to him at least, in allegro speech styles or when the word concerned does not carry any sentential stress. Examples of the nasal geminates include ['flɔmma dɔnn brɛnn 'pɛnna] 'flame, damage, bran, feather' < FLĂMMA DĂMNUM BRĔNNUM PĬNNA. Schorta (1938: §§ 207–10) reports long intervocalic nasals for the south-eastern Grisons dialect of the Münster Valley, ['flɔmma 'pɛnna] 'flame, feather'. Strengthening of original simplex -M- and -N- also occurred sometimes, LĪMA > ['limma] 'file', CŪNA > ['cynna] 'cradle', in a development reminiscent of changes found in parts of northern Italy (cf. 10.4.4.2).

Italo-Romance

10.1. Introduction

The impact of vowel nasalization in Italo-Romance has been varied. In the standard language and in non-standard varieties of the centre and south, vowel evolution has scarcely been influenced at all by the effect of nasality. However, a very different picture presents itself in northern dialects. Here high-level nasalization has occurred widely and in some cases nasal vowel phonemes were created. The main developments in northern dialects are considered in section 10.4 after a brief look at circumstances in the standard language (10.2) and central and southern dialects (10.3).

10.1.1. HISTORICAL BACKGROUND

The collapse of the Empire in the fifth century AD had profound political and linguistic consequences for Italy. In the following centuries, unity was succeeded by fragmentation as invasions and the rise of internal power bases at local or regional level changed the political landscape, leading to the broad three-way division in Italy which is reflected in the linguistic patterns of Italo-Romance.

Of major importance early on was the invasion in 568 from north of the Alps by the Langobards. This profoundly changed the political and social conditions, particularly in northern Italy. The Langobards established a kingdom which unified Piedmont, Lombardy, Emilia, Romagna (at a later stage after the fall of Ravenna in 751), much of the Veneto though not Venice itself, and also Tuscany. After the overthrow of Langobardic power by Charlemagne in 774, all North Italy became exposed increasingly to social and linguistic influences from over the Alps. However, the influence from France was exerted against a background of increasing political disunity in this area. A complex of small, independent fiefs and states developed during the ninth and tenth centuries and these interacted variously amongst themselves throughout the remainder of the Middle Ages and after. By the later Middle Ages and the Renaissance, some major centres of influence and authority had arisen, notably the Republic of Genoa and the Duchy of Savoy in the West, the Republic of Venice in the East, and, in the central area, the Duchy of Milan. The different centres of political authority exercised growing, and often overlapping, cultural and linguistic influence on the surrounding areas. Venice and Milan in particular have been of especial importance within their respective provinces.

The central area, which includes Umbria, Lazio, and the Marche, had remained free of Langobard domination and instead came under the political authority of the Church to form the Papal States. After 774, Romagna was also incorporated, although in part it maintained its earlier northern orientation. As for Tuscany, the collapse of Langobard power left it free to develop in some degree of isolation.

In the south, a picture of growing diversity presents itself. Here, the political and social fragmentation was particularly acute, fostered amongst other things by the influence over just parts of the area by outside peoples, Byzantine Greeks, Langobards (forming two enclaves, the Duchies of Benevento and Spoleto, separated from the main northern power base), Arabs, and Normans. The result was the relative isolation of many local communities and their growing linguistic differentiation.

The prolonged political disunity was only resolved with the belated unification of Italy in the second half of the nineteenth century. It has had considerable linguistic consequences. The fact that a single sovereign state was late in developing has meant that local or regional forces have given rise to considerable dialectalization, with the result that Italy today shows a dialectal variety which is unmatched elsewhere within the domain of Romance. A fledgeling standard language, based on a refined form of Florentine, had already taken root in the fourteenth century, but it was pre-eminently a literary medium whose impact would have been limited to more cultivated urban dwellers.[1] Its diffusion amongst the illiterate and rural mass of the population of Italy, and particularly those living outside Tuscany, was therefore slight until modern times. Indeed, it has been calculated that even in 1861, when the unification of Italy was almost complete, less than 3% of the population were able to speak what was recognized to be the standard language (De Mauro 1972: 43).[2] It is only recently, following unification, that various bonding forces of a political and social nature have enabled standard Italian to become familiar to a majority of Italians. In particular, we may note the rise of mass literacy through education, the introduction of national military service, and the spectacular growth of the mass media. Even so, the use of non-standard varieties of Italian still remains widespread today and many speakers are in a real sense bilingual or plurilingual. Pellegrini (1975) in fact recognizes no fewer than four linguistic levels, *italiano comune, italiano regionale, dialetto regionale, dialetto locale*, and notes that, according to situation, many speakers are able to operate with most or all of these levels.

Beneath the superposed standard Florentine-based language, therefore, there is a wide diversity of non-standard varieties whose vitality has been and still is considerable. As far as dialects are concerned, these are conventionally divided into three main groups, northern, central, and southern, whose territorial spread reflects with a fair degree of accuracy earlier political and social divisions in Italy which we have seen.

10.1.2. VOWEL SYSTEMS AND NASALIZATION PATTERNS IN ITALY

The complex external linguistic history of Italy is reflected in the varied structural patterns found in the dialects of different areas. One example of this variation concerns the vowel systems which underlie the dialects of Italo-Romance. The dialects of northern and central Italy (including the standard language) have proceeded from the same vowel system which forms the basis of all varieties of Gallo-Romance and Ibero-Romance. This was a seven–way vowel system /i e ɛ a ɔ o u/ with neutralization of the contrast between /e/ and /ɛ/ and between /o/ and /ɔ/ in unstressed syllables. In the south, however, in dialects of Basilicata, Apulia, Calabria, and Sicily, different vowel systems developed in early Romance containing five or six distinctive vowel-types (cf. Rohlfs 1966: §§ 1–4; Tekavčić 1974: 20–33).

The different basis to the vowel systems used in Italo-Romance poses a potential difficulty in comparing patterns of vowel nasalization in this Romance area. However, it happens that nasalization has played a minimal role in shaping vowel evolution in southern dialects, and its significance has also been limited for vowel change in central dialects. Only in the dialects of North Italy has it been a notable determinant of change and these dialects all build on the seven–way system /i e ɛ a ɔ o u/.

In our review of Italo-Romance, we will begin by considering the effect of vowel nasalization in standard Italian. Then, after a brief outline of the circumstances in central and southern dialects, our attention will turn to the area of greatest interest, northern Italy.

10.2. Standard Italian

10.2.1. VOWEL NASALITY IN MODERN ITALIAN

In the contemporary standard language, nasality is not phonemically relevant for vowels. However, a number of phoneticians have called attention to the presence of notable levels of allophonic nasality in vowels which appear adjacent to a nasal consonant. In the earliest substantial study of the language using experimental evidence, it was found that in comparable contexts nasality levels were greater in low vowels than in high vowels, vowels showed higher levels of nasality when they were unstressed or in a blocked syllable, and vowels took on a nasal quality not only when a nasal consonant followed but also when one preceded, the nasal quality being especially strong if the vowel had a nasal consonant on either side, e.g. in *nome* (Josselyn 1900: 127–45).

Later phoneticians have largely corroborated these claims (e.g. Chapallaz 1979: 60–1), although the particular context vowel + nasal coda is often highlighted as the most characteristic site for conditioned vowel nasality. Thus, Tagliavini (1965: 2) cites *tonfo, ronfo, tondo* as examples of words containing nasal vowels, even claiming that the pronunciation of these words is typically ['tõːfo 'rõːfo 'tõːdo], and Castellani (1956: 445) asserts that nasality in blocked vowels is more intense when the blocking nasal consonant is followed specifically by a fricative, as in *pensare, inverno*.

Finally, one other special case of vowel nasality is reported to be found in casual styles of speech especially amongst younger people from Florence. This involves the spontaneous nasalization of vowels occurring adjacent to a glottal fricative which has arisen from an original intervocalic plosive, as in *quelle cose* ['kwellẽ'hõse] 'those things', *il sugo* [i'ssũfiõ] 'the sauce', *che fate?* [i'kke vu 'ffãːhẽ] 'what are you doing?', where the voiceless glottal fricative [h] and its voiced counterpart [ɦ] are also accompanied by nasality (Giannelli and Savoia 1978: 50). This pronunciation feature finds a parallel in certain varieties of Spanish (7.4.2). The rationale behind the appearance of nasality in such contexts is considered in 1.3.

10.2.2. VOWEL NASALIZATION IN THE HISTORY OF STANDARD ITALIAN

In the historical evolution of what was to become the standard variety, nasality has not exercised a great deal of influence on vowel change. Phonemically nasal vowels never appear to have developed at any stage, but two changes have occurred which may well have involved significant allophonic nasalization having operated in certain contexts at earlier stages of the language. In both changes, there has been mid-vowel raising leading to the neutralization of vowel contrasts in the contexts affected. Suggestively, both changes also have as the major conditioning factor the presence of a following coda nasal consonant, indicating the possibility that vowel nasalization acted as the key trigger for raising. In the first change, high-mid vowels raise to become high vowels and in the second there is vowel raising from low-mid to high-mid.

10.2.2.1.   *High-Mid Vowel Raising (Anaphonesis)*

In blocked syllables of a special type, high-mid vowels raise to become high in a development known as anaphonesis (*anafonesi*). In many cases, the coda element in these syllables is formed by a nasal consonant, i.e. context (i) forms are involved. Two types of anaphonesis may be distinguished, one occurring in syllables with the velar nasal [ŋ] as their original coda and the other with a palatal sonorant as coda.[3] Examples:

Velar nasal consonant coda

[e] > [i]			[o] > [u]		
VĬNCO	> *vinco*	'I win'	ŬNGO	> *ungo*	'I grease'
CĬNGULA	> *cinghia*	'belt'	ŬNGULA	> *unghia*	'nail'
TĬNCA	> *tinca*	'tench'	ADŬNCUM	> *adunco*	'hooked'
-ĬNG	(e.g. *casal-ingo*) adjectival suffix		FŬNGUM	> *fungo*	'mushroom'
LĬNGUA	> *lingua*	'tongue'	SPŎNGIA	> *spugna*	'sponge'

(cf. CĬRCO > *cerco* 'I try' and MŬLTUM > *molto* 'much, very' where the stressed vowels show the expected outcomes [e] and [o], respectively)

Palatal sonorant coda

[e] > [i]					
CONSĬLIUM	> *consiglio*	'advice'	TĬNEA	> *tigna*	'ringworm'
FAMĬLIA	> *famiglia*	'family'	POSTCĒNIUM	> (OIt.) *pusigno*	'night snack'

Geographically, anaphonesis primarily affected the central zone including Florence as well as the western area embracing Pisa, Prato, Pistoia, and Lucca.[4] The southern area of Tuscany, including Siena and Arezzo, did not undergo the change. However, in more recent times the Florentine pattern with raising has been diffused in Tuscany, although in more isolated communities forms without raising are still preserved, such as *lengua, penta* (= *spinta*) (Giannelli 1988: 595).

The action of anaphonesis was subject to certain constraints. It is notable that forms in which the palatal nasal derives from -GN- were not affected, as with *legno, segno, degno* < LĬGNUM SĬGNUM DĬGNUM 'wood, sign, worthy', as against forms with original -NJ-, *tigna* < TĬNEA. In this respect, *pugno* < PŬGNUM 'fist' is problematic, since the form **pogno would be expected. But, as *pugno* is found in the earliest texts from non-anaphonetic areas, the existence of a variant Latin form *PŪGNUM with a long vowel in Tuscany, and in other Romance areas, seems likely.

With the other type of anaphonesis (preceding a velar nasal coda), the need for a specifically velar nasal is decisive, cf. RŬMPO > *rompo* 'I break', LĬMBUM > *lembo* 'hem'; FŬNDUM > *fondo* 'bottom', DE-ĬNTRO > *dentro* 'within', etc. without raising. Also, [o] > [u] does not normally occur when [ŋ] is followed by a voiceless consonant, i.e. /k/. Thus, we have *tronco, spelonca* (beside OIt. *spilonca*) < TRŬNCUM SPELŬNCA 'trunk, cave', and this is the case even if a palatal element came to follow, cf. *carbonchio, centonchio* < CARBŬNCULUM CENTŬNCULUM 'carbuncle, chickweed'.[5]

Anaphonesis appears to be a change of some antiquity. Preceding palatal sonorants, it was presumably implemented before -GN- had developed into [ɲɲ]. Textual evidence suggests that this change was completed by the eighth century in Tuscany, but it was probably generalized long before in the spoken language of the region. In the light of this, Castellani (1980: 87) speculatively dates this type of anaphonesis to the third–fourth centuries. As for the other type (i.e. raising before a coda [ŋ]), an important consideration is its regular occurrence in forms such as VĬNCERE > *vincere* 'to win', SPŌNGIA > *spugna*, where palatalization has operated on the post-nasal consonant causing the nasal consonant to lose its velarity (pre-consonantal nasals are always homorganic with the consonant following). This indicates that it pre-dates or is at the latest broadly contemporaneous with the palatalization of velar plosives, since this would result in the preceding nasal ceasing to be velar because of the rule of homorganicity (for example, [ŋk] would become [ɲc]). Furthermore, the similarity with the mid-vowel raising before the [ŋ] + consonant sequence which occurred in pre-literary Latin is striking (3.2.1), suggesting the possibility that the Tuscan development may represent the final stages of this Latin change. Anaphonesis before a coda [ŋ] remained productive into the period when the Germanic suffix -ING of Langobard origin entered the language, yielding forms such as *casalingo, guardingo* 'domestic, cautious' (Aebischer 1941). This change in the Latin of Tuscany therefore is certainly productive from about the third century (if it is not older) and continued to be productive until at least the sixth–seventh centuries. Indeed, it appears to underlie a morpheme structure condition to this day in popular Florentine speech. Giannelli (1976: 18) notes that words containing /e o/ in anaphonetic contexts are not permissible, but rather than raising these vowels to /i u/ native speakers will normally lower them to /ɛ ɔ/. Thus, the proper names *Longo, Girardengo*, which might be expected to have high-mid vowels, are assigned low-mid vowels.

The motivation of anaphonesis remains unclear. Rohlfs (1966: § 49) views the whole phenomenon as a single process involving a special sort of metaphony.[6] But it seems more likely that the two types of anaphonesis indicated above represent originally separate developments, even if their outcomes are similar.[7] A good case can be made for recognizing the action of a type of metaphony to explain the anaphonesis of forms like *famiglia, tigna* (cf. Franceschini 1991;

Maiden 1995: 42). However, the influence of nasality has seemingly been the key factor in the other type of anaphonesis triggered by a following coda [ŋ]. This point we take up again below.

10.2.2.2. *Low-Mid Vowel Raising*

The other change suggesting the action of vowel nasalization also operated in syllables containing a nasal coda. Its effect was to raise the stressed low-mid vowels [ɛ ɔ] to [e o] (we omit any indication of nasality), thereby causing the neutralization of mid vowels which is found in many other varieties of Romance in nasalizing contexts. Examples are:

[ɛ]	> [e]			[ɔ]	> [o]	
MĔNTUM	> *mento*	'chin'		PŎNTEM	> *ponte*	'bridge'
-MĔNTE	> -*mente*	(adv. suff.)		CŎNCHA	> *conca*	'basin'
-MĔNTUM	> -*mento*	(nom. suff.)		RESPŎNDET	> *risponde*	'he
						answers'
INGĔNIUM	> *ingegno*	'talent'		SŎMNIUM	> *sogno*	'dream'
CONVĔNIUM	> *convegno*	'meeting'		ŎMNI	> *ogni*	'every'

Raising before the palatal nasal [ɲɲ] is entirely consistent, so that [ɛ ɔ] are impermissible in modern Florentine before this consonant.[8] But whilst [ɔ] > [o] occurred regularly in all syllables with a nasal coda, raising of [ɛ] > [e] is subject to limitations. It has occurred before the palatal nasal as in *ing*[e]*gno*, whereas no such raising is found before other types of palatal, *m*[ɛ]*glio*, *s*[ɔ]*glio* < MĔLIUS SŎLIUM 'better, seat'. Raising has also occurred in the noun *mento* and the suffixes -*mento*, -*mente*, where nasals precede and follow the vowel, but forms such as *comm*[ɛ]*nda*, *m*[ɛ]*mbro* < COMMĔNDA MĔMBRUM 'title, member' show that the change is subject to complex constraints.[9]

The raising here is problematic to date. It is later than anaphonesis since forms like INGĔNIUM would have emerged as **ingigno if the raising of low-mid vowels had pre-dated it; cf. POSTCĒNIUM > OIt. *pusigno* discussed above. However, the lack of a clear distinction of graphy between low-mid and high-mid vowels means that changes from one quality to the other are difficult to infer, particularly as poetic conventions permitted poets to rhyme low-mid and high-mid vowels, as with *volto* 'face': *volto* 'turned', *era* 'I was': *sera* 'evening' (*Inferno*, i. 34, 36; xv. 38, 42). On the basis of parallel developments elsewhere in *Romania* (4.2.3, 8.2.3), it may plausibly be dated however to the early Middle Ages.

Finally, the key question remains of the extent to which nasalization has contributed to the vowel changes at issue here. In the type of anaphonesis seen in *tigna*, raising probably owes itself primarily to the palatal quality rather than the nasality of the following nasal sonorant. But in the other type of anaphonesis (affecting vowels before a velar nasal coda), some increased level of nasality may be inferred as a contributory factor in raising, since a velar non-nasal coda has had no such raising effect. Thus, we have *secco* < SĬCCUM and in particular forms like *legno* < LĬGNUM, where presumably there was an oral velar coda in the stressed syllable for much or all the Empire period, the pronunciation being ['leɡnu] or ['leɣnu]. The developments in Tuscan, where it is the velar nasal [ŋ] in particular which has triggered raising, replicate in a striking way what happened in pre-Classical Latin, for here it was precisely the group [ŋn] which evidently exerted a more powerful raising effect than other nasal groups with a non-velar initial segment (cf. section 3.2.1). The similarity with developments in Ibero-Romance is also notable (cf. 7.3.1.2, 7.4.1.2, 8.2.3).

The later raising of low-mid vowels causing the neutralization of /e/ : /ɛ/ and /o/ : /ɔ/ is also consistent with heightened vowel nasalization by the tautosyllabic nasal. However, the patchy nature of the raising and the fact that the only context in which it was carried through completely was before a palatal nasal, where the raising influence of palatality assisted, indicate that levels of vowel nasality are unlikely to have been intense.

10.3.   Central and Southern Dialects

In the dialects of the centre and south of Italy, there are few indications that nasalization played any significant role in shaping vowel evolution. In general, vowels in potentially nasalizing contexts such as syllables with a nasal consonant coda have developed in the same way as their counterparts in non-nasal contexts. And certainly, if at some historical stage there was nasalization of some sort, its action was not strong enough to disturb in any serious way the operation of other factors affecting vowels. The most notable of these other factors in the centre-south of Italy has undoubtedly been metaphony (see n. 6) which has worked upon all dialects except those of the Province of Reggio in South Calabria, the southern tip of the Salento peninsula to a line running between Lecce and Brindisi, and western and much of eastern Sicily.[10] It appears that vowels located in potentially nasalizing contexts regularly undergo the same metaphonic changes as vowels in non-nasal contexts. This may be illustrated by items containing a stressed mid vowel followed by a nasal coda consonant (i.e. context (i) forms) as against comparable items with an oral coda. Three specimen dialects may be taken, those of Servigliano in the Marche, Altamura in Puglia, and Matera in Basilicata (Lucania).[11] (See Map 11.)

			Servigliano	Altamura	Matera
/e/					
VIGĬNTI	(+ uml)	'twenty'	'vinti	vɪnd	'vyndə
*MĬTT-ĪS	(+ uml)	'you send'	'mitti	mɪtt	'ddzyssə (<GῨPSUM)
LĬNGUA	(− uml)	'tongue'	'leŋgwa	lɛɲɲ	'leŋgwə
PĬSCEM	(− uml)	'fish'	'peʃʃo	pɛʃʃ	'peʃʃə
/ɛ/					
TĔMPUS	(+ uml)	'time'	'tempu	tɪmb	'timbə
LĔCTUM	(+ uml)	'bed'	'lettu	lɪtt	'littə
DĔNTEM	(− uml)	'tooth'	'dɛnte	dend	'dændə
SĔPTEM	(− uml)	'seven'	'sɛtte	sett	'sættə
/o/					
MŬNDUM	(+ uml)	'world'	'munnu	munn	'miənnə
CŬRTUM	(+ uml)	'short'	'kurto	kurt	'kiətə
ŬNGERE	(− uml)	'to grease'	'vonne	jɔndz	'ondzə
BŬCCA	(− uml)	'mouth'	'bokka	wɔkk	'vokkə
/ɔ/					
LŎNGUM	(+ uml)	'long'	'loŋgu	leɲɲ	'luɲɲə
NŎSTRUM	(+ uml)	'our (m. sg.)'	'nostru	nest	'nustə
FRŎNTEM	(− uml)	'forehead'	—[12]	pwond	'frondə
				(< PŎNTEM)	
FŎRTEM	(− uml)	'strong'	'fɔrte	fwort	'fɛərdə

(Camilli 1929; Loporcaro 1988; Festa 1917 and *AIS*, pt. 736)

The only sign of disturbance attributable to the possible presence of heightened nasality occurs with the vowel /ɔ/ in syllables containing a nasal coda, as in the items FRŎNTEM vs. FŎRTEM in the dialect of Matera. For Servigliano, the plural form *munti* is cited suggesting a singular form ['monte] < MŎNTEM 'mountain' with raising and this perhaps applies to all other words with Ŏ + coda nasal (see also n. 12). However, it appears that such raising is by no means typical of all central and southern dialects, as the highly representative evidence from Altamura demonstrates. Stehl (1980: § 27) confirms the non-raising of original Ŏ in Apulian dialects, with the one marginal anomaly of the dialect of Trinitapoli where the much later fronting of low-mid [ɔ] to [ø] is impeded when a coda nasal is present, [frɔnt] vs. [nøtt]. The raising of Latin Ŏ may thus have been limited to certain regions of the Centre and, less commonly, the south. Further, it may recalled that a number of context (i) forms containing -ŎNT- were noted by Latin grammarians to have a variant realization in -ŬNT- with a high vowel, e.g. FRUNTEM (3.2.1), so that it is not inconceivable that ['fronte] and ['frɔnte], possibly with heightened vowel nasality, continued to exist side by side as variants in different dialects from earliest times.

Other cases where vowel nasalization has apparently operated can occasionally be found. Usually these involve the vowel /a/, and the presence of nasalization is inferred from the different pattern of evolution followed by the vowel in nasalizing contexts. Three instances may be cited.

1. In various Apulian dialects of the coastal area to the south and especially the north of Bari, stressed /a/ evolves in a special way when adjacent to a nasal consonant. Thus, in Molfetta free or blocked /a/ passes to /ɛ/ in a nasal environment, CĂNEM > ['kɛːnə], ĂNNUM > ['ɛnnə], NĀSUM > ['nɛːsə], MĂRTIUM > ['mɛrtsə], whilst elsewhere it remains a low vowel (Rohlfs 1966: § 23). In a similar way, in the dialect of the nearby town of Bisceglie, stressed blocked /a/ > [ɛ] and free /a/ > [øː] when adjacent to a nasal, but elsewhere they give [a] and [ɔ], respectively (De Gregorio 1939: 35). Melillo (1986: 34–5, 49) reports similar phenomena at Bari and Monopoli, as well as in some inland towns to which the pattern has spread (Corato, Castellana Grotte, Cisternino). The degree of nasality in the vowels concerned is unfortunately not reported. The very localized nature of the developments here and their often far from regular implementation except in Molfetta[13] suggest that this is a fairly recent development. The unusual pattern of nasalization, both progressive and regressive, also mark it off as rather atypical in the general context of Romance.

2. In Calabria, a number of dialects of the Sila area lying to the east and the south-east of Cosenza likewise show the influence of nasal consonants on the evolution of the vowel /a/. In Mangone (= *AIS*, pt. 761), a village situated some 18 km. south-east of Cosenza, stressed /a/ gives a low centralized nasal vowel[14] when adjacent to a nasal consonant and [ɑ] elsewhere, e.g. ['mẽrti 'pẽne 'ẽnni] 'Tuesday, bread, years' vs. [pur'tɑre] 'to carry'. It seems difficult to believe that this allophonic splitting has a common basis with that found in Puglia, since the two areas have not historically been in direct social or political contact and furthermore they are separated geographically by the linguistically wholly distinct Basilicata region. Instead, we apparently have an independent development in each case, in which the inherently greater degree of articulatory-acoustic nasality in the open vowel /a/ has for uncertain reasons been locally hypercharacterized. Having developed nasal allophones, some Calabrian dialects have later gone on to extend them to non-nasal contexts, as in [dẽtu 'kẽsa 'stẽri] 'given, house, to stand' in the rustic dialect of Acri, where the earlier motivation for the allophonic variation has evidently been completely lost (Rohlfs 1977: 20).

3. It is reported that in some Campanian dialects stressed /a/ can be nasalized when it appears word-finally, particularly as a result of apocope as in the infinitive *fa* [fã] 'to do' (Radtke 1988: 654). Tatò (1981) indicates the same

phenomenon for the dialect of Bari in central Apulia, although the outcome here is not a retracted nasal vowel but a very low-mid front nasal vowel, as in [al'dzæ̃ vəl'dæ̃] 'to raise, to turn', and Bigalke (1980) reports a slightly nasal vowel of similar tongue position in the single lexical item [kræ̃j(ə)] < CRAS 'tomorrow' in the dialect of Albano Lucano in Basilicata. In these cases, the inherent slight nasality of the open vowel [a] may have been exaggerated so that it could serve as a boundary marker in these oxytonic lexical items (cf. a comparable case in Gallo-Romance 5.2.2).

10.3.1.   VOWEL NASALIZATION IN THE 'GALLO-ITALIAN COLONIES'

In contrast to the usually restricted incidences of vowel nasalization in central and southern dialects, some striking examples of systematic nasalization occur in a small number of dialects in Sicily and Basilicata. The dialects concerned are the so-called Gallo-Italian colonies which were established in the course of the twelfth or thirteenth centuries, when settlers from north-west Italy, especially S. Piedmont and Liguria, founded communities in central and eastern Sicily and on the mainland around Potenza in central Basilicata and Trecchina (near Maratea) in south Basilicata (Rohlfs 1931, 1941, 1972). In view of their quite different linguistic background, these dialects stand apart from the rest of the central and southern dialect area.

In the mainland dialects, nasal vowels are no longer generally found nowadays, but there are signs that strong vowel nasalization operated in earlier times. In particular, simplex -N- in context (ii) forms has been weakened and lost in a parallel way to that found in northern Italian dialects, e.g. [pa fɛ sa'vɔ] 'bread, hay, soap' < PĀNEM FĒNUM SAPŌNEM (Rohlfs 1972: 209). An oral vowel is now found in these forms, but it seems likely that highly nasal vowel allophones and even nasal vowel phonemes formerly appeared as the conditioning nasal consonant weakened and was deleted, PĀNEM > [paːn] > [pãːⁿ] > [pãː] > [pa(ː)].

In Sicily, the surviving Gallo-Italian dialects likewise clearly show the presence of vowel nasalization. Four of the eighteen survey points of the *AIS* in Sicily were Gallo-Italian colonies, San Fratello, Novara, Sperlinga, and Aidone (pts. 817, 818, 836, 865, respectively), and the dialects spoken in each of them offer evidence of vowel nasalization, particularly in contexts (ii). Here, the likely path of development has been the same as in many northern Italian dialects (10.4.4), namely [Ṽːn > Ṽː > ṼG̃ > Ṽŋ], where after the loss of the reflex of final -N- a long unconditioned nasal vowel appears (which may shorten at some later stage). A further possible development is that the second mora of the long nasal vowel can become a glide which later hardens to [ŋ]. The dialects of San Fratello and Aidone show this secondary evolution, e.g. San

Fratello [kxæŋ] 'dog', [kar'baŋ] 'coal' as against Aidone [kãŋ, kar'būŋ]. The presence of stronger allophonic nasality is reported for the latter dialect. The more central dialects of Novara and Sperlinga have only followed the earlier stages of evolution and continue to have phonemically nasal vowels, as in [kɛ̃ kar'bɔ̃] in the dialect of Novara and [kã kar'bõ] in Sperlinga.

As regards context (iii), the dialect of Novara has undergone the deletion of intervocalic -N- so that it has unconditioned nasal vowels in context (iii) forms as well, e.g. [la 'lũːa] 'the moon', ['spĩːa] 'thorn', [ka'dẽːa] 'chain'. The other dialects have uniformly preserved the nasal and significant vowel nasalization is not indicated, e.g. Sperlinga has [a ɖ'ɖuːnᵃ] ['spiːnᵃ] and [ka'deːnᵃ]. In context (i) items, vowel nasality is not indicated in any of these dialects, although this may not necessarily mean that it is not present. Unfortunately, there is no systematic indication in the *AIS* of the levels of nasality in vowels occurring in context (i) forms. Relevant context (i) forms appearing in the dialect of Novara include ['dentu] 'tooth' and ['frunti] 'forehead'. It is clear that nasal codas in such forms have been consistently preserved suggesting that at most limited allophonic nasalization has operated.

In view of the strong impact of vowel nasalization in northern Italy and the Gallo-Italian colonies, its relative lack of effect in central and southern dialects is striking. The implication is that nasal consonants in the latter dialects successfully preserved their full articulation rather than weakening and being increasingly co-articulated with the vowel which preceded them. Why this should have been so is mysterious, but there is no doubting that nasal consonants in this area of Italy retained their articulatory strength. This fact is borne out by two independent pieces of phonetic evidence. First, nasal geminates (like all other geminate consonants) have been preserved as geminates and have not been simplified to become single segments as elsewhere in Romania. It is notable that the southern limit of geminate simplification in Italy runs through the North of the Marche and the northern boundary of Tuscany, along a line almost identical with the southern limit of vowel nasalization (see Map 6).

The other indicator of the strength of nasal consonants concerns their behaviour in clusters when followed by an obstruent. Here the nasal consonant regularly causes progressive assimilation. South of a line from the southern boundary of Tuscany across to Ancona in the Marche, there is full nasal assimilation in nasal + voiced obstruent sequences, -MB- > [-mm-], -ND- > [-nn-], and from a line slightly further south, crossing Lazio south of Rome and passing through the south of Umbria and central Marche over once more to Ancona, there is voicing assimilation in nasal + voiceless obstruent sequences, -MP- > [-mb-], -NT- > [-nd-], -NK- > [-ŋg-]. The non-Romance nature of progressive assimilation, rather than the normal regressive type, lends some credence to the view that it may represent a feature promoted by the Osco-

Umbrian substratum, cf. Oscan *úpsannam* = Latin OPERANDAM 'to be worked (acc. f. sg.)'. But irrespective of its origins, the assimilation points to the complete absence of a tendency to weaken word-medial nasal codas, this commonly being the prelude to vowel nasalization elsewhere in Romance.

10.4.   Northern Dialects

The dialects of the north of Italy are no less structurally diverse than those of the south.[15] As far as vowel nasalization is concerned, nasal vowels are to be found as surface phonemes in a wide range of dialects, running from northern and eastern Piedmont through western and central Lombardy and down to the south-eastern area of Emilia-Romagna (see Map 7). Significant vowel nasalization in the south-east ceases in the area of Pesaro in the northern Marches (Schürr 1919: 131).[16] Elsewhere, though nasality may not be phonemic in vowels, it may reach high levels phonetically and its presence is frequently associated with special types of phonological patterning.

Historically, there is good evidence for believing that nasal vowels (phonemic and strongly allophonic) were much more widespread in earlier times than nowadays. Indeed, not only has the general trend towards vowel nasalization lost impetus but in many dialects there has been a reverse movement whereby vowels have undergone partial or complete denasalization. An important factor in limiting vowel nasalization and encouraging denasalization has undoubtedly been the influence of the emerging standard language based on Florentine, in which vowel nasality was never phonemic and heightened allophonic nasality has only been of limited scope (cf. 10.2.1, 10.2.2). Already from the later Middle Ages, the standard language variety provided the model for the influential, educated milieux of the large cities of the North, such as Milan and Venice, and this model has gradually diffused amongst more and more speakers. Nonetheless native patterns have often continued to survive although sometimes, but not always, in an attenuated form.

It is tempting to speculate what might have happened if the social and political history of Italy had taken a different turn and, say, Lombardy with Milan as its main city, rather than Tuscany with Florence as its main city, had become the politico-cultural and hence linguistic centre of Italy. The standard Italian which emerged might well have been based upon the native Milanese dialect in which nasal vowel phonemes are still found today, as in [bũː] 'good (m. sg.)' and [bẽ̞ː] 'well' < BŎNUM BĔNE (Nicoli 1983). Standard Italian would then have resembled French in containing nasal vowel phonemes, thereby changing to some extent the perception among linguists of the 'naturalness' of nasal vowels in languages in general and in the Romance languages in particular. This did not happen, though, and the result has been the checking of vowel nasalization as an ongoing historical process and, increasingly, its reversal through the restructuring seen in the dialect of Bologna, as speakers increasingly gravitate away from local dialect towards the use of a *dialetto italianizzato* or further to an *italiano regionale* (de Mauro 1972: ch. 4; Foresti 1988: 577).

The effects of standardization in North Italy run precisely counter to what is found in the Occitan dialect area in southern France. In the former the prevailing pattern has been for speakers to restructure nasal vowels into sequences of (decreasingly nasal) vowel + [ŋ] in order to approximate to the standard variety. However, amongst non-standard speakers from southern France using *français régional*, the tendency has been for them to adapt their pronunciation in the opposite direction so that sequences of (more or less nasal) vowel + coda nasal [VN/ṼN] are restructured to varying degrees to give [Ṽᴺ] and even [Ṽ], in order to conform with the more prestigious norm variety.[17] A common motivating factor, namely conformity with the norm variety, thus yields directly opposite results.

To help trace the complex history of vowel nasalization in northern dialects, we have at our disposal vernacular texts which begin to appear in Italy in substantial numbers from the thirteenth century. However, these can sometimes be rather less revealing than might be expected because they have been subject to influence from the Florentine-based standard language. Such influence is detectable in northern writings of a literary character even in the thirteenth century. Later, in the sixteenth century, there is a move toward the conscious use of dialect as a medium for literary composition, which offers a fuller picture of certain non-standard varieties, even if it is far from complete. It is not until the nineteenth and twentieth centuries when reliable linguistic descriptions of individual dialects start to become available that a more precise knowledge of non-standard varieties in North Italy can be obtained. Unfortunately, therefore, for most varieties of this area no substantial textual continuity exists to underpin reconstructions of patterns of vowel nasalization.

10.4.1. BACKGROUND DEVELOPMENTS

All the dialects of North Italy derive their vowel systems from the seven–way arrangement found in many other varieties of Romance, namely /i e ɛ a ɔ o u/. In unstressed syllables, the mid-vowel contrasts /e/ : /ɛ/ and /o/ : /ɔ/ were neutralized to give /e/ and /o/, respectively.

An early important development was that vowels in stressed syllables came to vary in length depending upon whether the syllable was free or blocked. In free stressed syllables, vowels were lengthened whilst they remained unchanged in length in blocked syllables. Thus:

(free)   VĒNA   > ['ve-na] > (early medieval) ['veː-na] 'vein'
(blocked) VĒNDAM > ['ven-da] > (early medieval) ['ven-da] 'I sell (subj.)'

This syllabically conditioned length differentiation in vowels is found in other areas of Italo-Romance as well as in Rheto-Romance and much of Gallo-Romance.

Subsequently, in the early medieval period, a further change got underway which was of major importance for vowel nasalization. This was apocope, which brought about the progressive deletion of all word-final vowels except /a/ and substantially increased the number of forms showing nasalizing context (ii), see 10.4.2 below. Unlike in Gallo-Romance where a parallel process of apocope systematically operated in almost all areas, it was only incompletely carried through across North Italy as a result of varying phonological and morphological constraints. However, all northern dialects show some evidence of apocope of final vowels, in contrast to the dialects of Tuscany and of the rest of central Italy where apocope has not occurred. The central and western area comprising Emilia-Romagna, Lombardy, and Piedmont shows regular loss of non-low vowels, but in the peripheral areas of Liguria and the Veneto systematic apocope is limited to forms in which final non-low vowels originally followed the intervocalic simplex consonants -L- -R- -N- but not necessarily -M-.[18] In fact, in certain dialects of central Veneto, apocope occurs solely after -N-. This is the case in the Paduan dialect, both today and from the time of the earliest texts of the fourteenth century (Ineichen 1957: 82).[19] The implication for northern Italy as a whole is thus that apocope initially operated on non-low final vowels which followed original simplex -N-, before it went on in most areas to affect vowels following other simplex sonorant consonants, first -L- and -R- and then -M-. At a still later stage and in certain dialects only, it came to affect vowels following geminates and obstruent consonants. A simple parameter showing the preferential environment for apocope in northern Italian dialects may therefore be identified (cf. Tuttle 1981–2; Mayerthaler 1982: 246):

after -N- > after -L- and -R- > after -M- > after geminates and obstruents

$$\longrightarrow$$

most favoured   *least favoured*

where loss in a given context type implies loss in contexts indicated further to the left. The pattern here corresponds well with the pattern of apocope seen from eastern to western Ibero-Romance; in the east there is generalized apocope in Catalan, but in the centre and west it is limited to vowels following simplex coronal consonants although these include obstruent consonants (cf. 7.3.1.1, 7.4.1.1, 8.2.1).

As regards chronology, it is clear that apocope post-dates vowel lengthening in stressed free syllables, since long vowels could, and still can, appear in syllables which became blocked after final-vowel deletion, cf. Bolognese [aˈmiːg muːr] < [aˈmiːgu ˈmuːru] < AMĪCUM MŪRUM 'friend, wall' (Coco 1970). Nonetheless, it is an early change. Even in very conservative areas experiencing limited apocope like the Veneto, there is clear evidence that this change has already operated by the thirteenth century when vernacular texts begin to appear in significant numbers. In the earliest Venetian text appearing in Stussi (1965), dating from 1253, apocopated forms such as *canal, senter, man, raxon* 'canal, path, hand, reason' < CANĀLEM SEMITĀRIUM MĂNUM RATIŌNEM are found, contrasting with forms such as *ano, mese* 'year, month' < ĂNNUM MĒ(N)SEM. Elsewhere, some even earlier evidence from vernacular texts is available, e.g. twelfth-century Piedmontese sermons showing *temp, carn, munt, gardem,* 'time, flesh, world, we take care (subj.)', etc. (Förster 1879–80). Indeed, the range of contexts admitting apocope in the earliest extant texts is so extensive that for some regions the beginnings of this change may well be broadly contemporaneous with similar developments in Gallo-Romance, i.e. pre-ninth century.

10.4.2.   THE NASALIZING CONTEXT

Where vowel nasalization has occurred, it owes itself almost exclusively to the effect of regressive assimilation. The main environments for vowel nasalization have been syllables where the vowel was followed by a nasal coda consonant, i.e. in context (i) and (ii) forms. Context (i) forms had been inherited directly from Latin in large numbers, for example VĒNDERE CĂMPUM. Context (ii) forms developed primarily as a result of the action of apocope which was discussed in the previous section, e.g. CĂN(EM) BŎN(UM). These supplemented the small number of original Latin monosyllabic items which also satisfied this context type, e.g. NŌN.

Significant vowel nasalization has been less widespread in context (iii) forms like LĀNA, where the conditioning nasal formed the onset of the following syllable, although it is clearly indicated in dialects of Emilia-Romagna and many parts of north-western Italy. Vowel nasalization in context (iii) has occurred almost exclusively where the conditioning nasal was an original simplex Latin -N-.

10.4.3.   MAJOR CONDITIONING FACTORS IN VOWEL NASALIZATION

The patterns of vowel nasalization show a good deal of variation across the different dialects of northern Italy. This is due to the fact that a number of distinct factors have governed the process of nasalization, and these factors have each operated with varying degrees of importance from dialect to dialect. Four structural factors may be identified as being of especial importance in determining the implementation of vowel nasalization. These are: *length, stress, the nature of the segment following the conditioning nasal consonant,* and *vowel quality.* Each may be briefly considered in turn.

10.4.3.1. *Length*

It will be recalled that from early times significant vowel length differences have existed in stressed syllables within all varieties of Italo-Romance, these differences being conditioned by syllabic structure (10.4.1). The observed patterns of evolution in northern Italian dialects indicate that these contextually determined length variations in vowels have played an important part in determining the incidence of nasalization. As Hajek (1997) demonstrates, nasalization has typically operated on vowels that were *long.*[20] Thus, vowels in context (ii) and context (iii) would have been more susceptible to being nasalized than vowels in context (i), since in this context-type the original vowel was short. Nasalization of vowels in context (i) has occurred in certain northern Italian dialects, but it is noticeable that nasalization is always associated with lengthening of the vowel. This link between length and nasalization is in keeping with the findings of experimental studies which indicate the desirability of added duration to enable the hearer more readily to perceive a vowel as nasal and to discriminate its oral quality (cf. 1.1 on perceptual correlates of nasality). More is said on length as a conditioning factor in section 10.5.2 below (see also Ch. 13).

10.4.3.2. *Stress*

In dialects where significant vowel nasalization has taken place, it has typically affected *stressed* syllables. Vowel nasalization in unstressed syllables has generally been much less in evidence. Even in dialects which develop phonemically nasal vowels there may only be relatively slight nasalization in unstressed syllables; in such dialects the nasal vowel phonemes are confined to stressed syllables. The dialects of Romagna and Lombardy in particular offer striking examples of such a disparity. Thus, the dialect of Imola (C. Romagna) has [sẽ:kw] < *CĪNQUE 'five' with full nasalization yielding a phonemic nasal vowel as against [siŋ'kwẽ:ta] < *CINQUAGĬNTA 'fifty' whose first syllable is comparable to that of the previous item but as a result of not carrying the main stress it shows minimal nasalization (Schürr 1919). Likewise, in syllables following the main stress there has been no significant vowel nasalization in this dialect. Thus, in the handful of Latin proparoxytons where a post-stress vowel has been preserved in a nasalizing context, such as HŎMINEM 'man' and IŬVENEM 'young', the modern reflexes show no sign of vowel nasalization ['oᵊmən] ['dzovən]. For Lombardy, we may cite from the dialect of Bergamo the forms [for'meːt] < FRUMĔNTUM 'corn' and its suffixal derivative [formen'tu] 'maize', where the stressed vowel of the former item underwent full phonemic nasalization with the loss of the conditioning nasal [n] before denasalization subsequently took place (see 10.5.5 for denasalization). However, the pre-stress vowel of the latter item evidently experienced no nasalization. Comparable non-nasalization occurred with post-stress vowels, as in ['zuen] and ['pɛten] < IŬVENEM PĔCTINE 'young, comb' (Sanga 1987).

An inference which can be drawn from such data as these is that vowel nasalization in northern Italian dialects may well have operated at first in stressed syllables and that nasalization in unstressed syllables represents a later development generalizing the original scope of vowel nasalization (Tuttle 1991: 51–5). If this is true, the following simple parameter would represent the preferential operation of vowel nasalization in northern Italian dialects with respect to stress:

main stressed	>	unstressed
more favoured		*less favoured*

Hajek (1997) goes further and notes that amongst unstressed vowels there is some evidence to suggest that pre-stressed vowels may have been more susceptible to nasalization than post-stressed vowels. Thus, in the dialect of Milan the level of nasality in the pre-stress syllable of forms such as [mũn'tãɲa] or [mũ'tãɲa] (with optional nasal consonant deletion) < MONTĀNEA 'mountain' is reportedly greater than that in the post-stress syllable of forms such as ['aːzen] < ĂSINUM 'donkey'. On the basis of this and some other pieces of comparable evidence, the following preferential order for vowel nasalization is proposed:

main stressed	>	pre-stress	>	post-stress
more favoured				*less favoured*

However, the validity of the right-hand side of such a parameter is questionable in view of the limited amount of confirming evidence.

A rather different factor connected to stress can also be noted, highlighted by Hajek (1997: § 4.3). This relates to the rhythm structure of the word. Differing patterns of vowel nasalization may sometimes be found in stressed syllables depending upon their location relative to other syllables within the word at the time when vowel nasalization operated. Three possibilities existed. The stressed syllable could be: (*a*) word-final, i.e. in *oxytons* such as NŌN or PĀN(EM); (*b*) next to final, i.e. in *paroxytons* such as CĂNTA(T); (*c*) located two syllables away from final, i.e. in *proparoxytons* such as CĬNCTULA. Thus, in the dialect of Bergamo, vowel nasalization (and later denasalization) regularly affected the stressed vowels of oxytons [paˈ], but not paroxytons [ˈteŋka ˈkanta] 'tench, (s)he sings' < TĬNCA CĂNTA(T)[21] nor proparoxytons [ˈsɛntola ˈlampada] 'belt, lamp' < CĬNCTULA LĂMPADA. The Ligurian dialect of Val Graveglia, however, differentiates between paroxytons and proparoxytons, showing nasalization in the former but not the latter: [ˈlaɲa] 'wool' (< [ˈlaɲna]) < LĀNA but [ˈmaneɡa] 'sleeve' < MĂNICA (Plomteux 1981). These data suggest the following parameter of preferential vowel nasalization for stressed vowels of the form:

oxytonic   >   paroxytonic   >   proparoxytonic

more favoured   *less favoured*

For both these parameters which relate vowel nasalization to stress, it appears that vowel length is the key consideration. Experimental observation has revealed that vowels are typically longer phonetically when they are stressed than when they are unstressed (Vogel 1982: 39, for Italian; Navarro Tomás 1968: 199–204, for Spanish).[22] Also, stressed vowels are longer the closer they are to the end of a word; that is, all other things being equal the stressed vowel of a paroxyton will be shorter than the stressed vowel of an oxyton, and similarly the stressed vowel of a proparoxyton will be shorter than that of a paroxyton or an oxyton (Fowler 1981). The degree of influence which such fine differences in vowel length have had in shaping the patterns of vowel nasalization adopted by speakers of northern Italian dialects is remarkable and unparalleled elsewhere in Romance.[23]

10.4.3.3.   *Nature of the Segment Following the Conditioning Nasal Consonant*

In context (i) forms, where the conditioning nasal consonant is followed by another consonantal segment, patterns of vowel nasalization can vary significantly in certain dialects according to the nature of the post-nasal consonant. Nasalization may be promoted by the presence of two types of such consonant: (i) a *fricative*, and (ii) a *voiceless* consonant.

Heightened nasalization of vowels followed by a conditioning nasal consonant + fricative has occurred in a number of Alpine dialects of Italian (cf. 10.4.4). Here the process has usually been accompanied by the weakening and even loss of the nasal consonant. It may be noted that speakers of standard Italian have also been reported to show vowel nasalization particularly in this context (10.2.1). Elsewhere, similar examples can be found where pre-fricative nasals have been weakened and deleted suggesting the operation of vowel nasalization, e.g. Latin (3.2.2) and French (4.2.5).[24]

Turning to the other environment favouring vowel nasalization, nasal consonant + voiceless consonant, we find that certain dialects of Lombardy and Emilia-Romagna have only experienced vowel nasalization in forms originally of this type, as in the Romagnolo dialect of Imola where we find vowel nasalization in VĔNTUM > [vẽːt] 'wind' but not in VĒNDIT > [vent] 'he sells'. It appears that this divergent pattern of evolution is once again bound up with considerations of length. Cross-linguistic experimental evidence indicates that nasals are typically somewhat shorter when they precede a voiceless consonant than when they are followed by a voiced consonant (Raphael et al. 1975; Hajek 1997: § 6.4.1.3). The preferential adoption of nasalization in vowels preceding the shorter nasal and the subsequent weakening and deletion of that nasal in these northern Italian dialects suggest that speakers were able to discriminate remarkably fine length differences sufficiently well for them to be used as a basis for determining distinct paths of phonetic evolution.

10.4.3.4. *Vowel Quality*

There is some limited evidence to suggest that *low* vowels are more susceptible to nasalization than non-low vowels. Thus, in the Piedmontese dialect of Piverone at the turn of the century only low nasal vowels were reportedly found, e.g. [ˈlãⁿna] 'wool' but [kaˈdeːna] 'chain', [ˈluːna] 'moon' < LĀNA CATĒNA LŪNA. (Flechia 1898, cited in Tuttle 1991: 49 n. 64). Also, in the dialect of Imola secondary lengthened stressed low [aː] has undergone some (allophonic) nasalization whereas the lengthened low-mid vowel [ɔː] has not, as in CANNA > [ˈkẽːna] 'reed' vs. NŎNNA > [ˈnɔːna] 'grandmother' (Schürr 1919).[25] The difference in the pattern of nasalization here, however, may have been conditioned by other factors. Nasalization crucially depends on the vowel first undergoing lengthening, and the evidence from surrounding dialects clearly indicates that the lengthening of [aː] took place some time before that of [ɔː]. Vowel nasalization may therefore have been productive after [a] > [aː] occurred but have ceased to be so prior to the lengthening of [ɔ] > [ɔː], in which case chronology rather than vowel quality would have been decisive. Other data which have been adduced in support of a low > high parameter of receptivity to vowel nasalization tend to be based on observed patterns of denasalization, where the order high > low has been identified in certain dialects and the conclusion drawn that nasalization must operate in reverse fashion. Of the few clear cases that have been found we may cite the Alpine dialect of Teglio in northern Lombardy. Here the high vowels of [viŋ] 'wine' < VĪNUM, [neˈgyŋ] 'nobody' < NEC-ŪNUM have been denasalized and restructured, but other vowel types have not [fẽː] 'hay', [būː] 'good (m. sg.)', [kã̃ː] 'dog' < FĒNUM BŎNUM CĂNEM (Merlo 1951, cited in Tuttle 1991: 51).

There is very little evidence that vowel nasalization in the dialects of North

Italy was governed by a *front–back* parameter. In the Romagnolo dialects of Faenza and Forlì, some data are available which indicate that nasalization has preferentially affected back rounded vowels in oxytons ending in [-m]: thus, NŌMEN > [noːm] > [nõː] 'name', LŪMEN > [luːm] > [lũː] 'light', as against RĒMUM > [reːm] > [rem] 'oar', PRĪMUM > [priːm] > [prem] 'first' (Schürr 1919). However, it is also possible to detect dissimilatory action at work here rather than preferential patterns of vowel nasalization (i.e. [-m] spread its nasality to the preceding vowel and was deleted to avoid a sequence of two word-final labial segments). Furthermore we shall see below (10.4.4.1 and n. 31) that in this and certain other Romagnolo dialects the deletion of final [-m] and associated vowel nasalization represent a lexically sensitive phenomenon betraying likely influence from outside dialects.

10.4.4. THE FATE OF THE CONDITIONING NASAL CONSONANT

The intense vowel nasalization which occurred in many parts of North Italy has widely been associated with weakening of the conditioning nasal consonant. In its most extreme form, the weakening led to the total loss of the nasal consonant and the creation of unconditioned nasal vowel phonemes, i.e. [ṼN] > [Ṽː]. Where this occurred in stressed syllables the resulting nasal vowel was usually long (cf. 10.5.2). The loss of conditioning nasals was a development which evidently affected large numbers of dialects at some stage of their history, and it took place particularly when the nasal was in coda position, i.e. in contexts (i) and (ii). In certain dialects, however, the degree of nasal consonant weakening was more limited and led to just variable amounts of articulatory reduction only.[26]

The trend towards the weakening and ultimately the possible deletion of conditioning nasals has widely undergone reversal in more recent times. Many dialects have seen the *restoration* of some sort of nasal consonantal segment in coda position, so that unconditioned nasal vowels have once again become overtly conditioned. Commonly too, the degree of nasality in such vowels may be reduced. Thus, a widespread pattern of evolution has been [ṼN] > [Ṽː] > [ṼN]/[VN] (with variable levels of vowel nasality). In the majority of cases, restoration has come about largely as a result of influence from the standard language and has been increasingly in evidence from the later nineteenth century onward. It has tended to gain ground more rapidly in urban dialects than in rural dialects and in more formal, educated registers rather than in informal, colloquial usage.

Two opposing tendencies have thus been at work across northern Italy and each has operated to varying degrees from dialect to dialect, creating a complex and diverse picture. The main characteristics may be briefly outlined.

10.4.4.1. *Weakening*

In context (i) forms, the nasal coda has very widely undergone weakening associated with heightened nasalization of the preceding vowel. Weakening possibly leading to deletion may be selective (i.e. limited to certain environments only) or generalized. In selective weakening, various determining factors can be distinguished. Much more usually, however, the key determining factor has been the nature of the consonant which follows the nasal consonant (see 10.4.3.3 above). One type is found in various peripheral dialects spoken in the Alpine area. Here, coda nasals have been deleted when the consonant following the nasal was a fricative, the result of which is the creation of phonemically nasal vowels. Thus, in the far north-west in the dialects of the Antrona valley we find [fũːʃ ʃũːʒa mũːs] 'mushroom, grease, milked (past part.)' < FŪNGUM AXŬNGIA *MŬNSUM 'milked (past part.)', although before labial fricatives it seems that deletion was less consistently carried through, hence ['bamfa] 'he blows' < banf (*REW* 932) as against [rãːf] 'crayfish' < rampf (*REW* 7032) (Nicolet 1929).[27]   Similarly, in the dialect of Erto, forms with comparable deletion were reported at the end of the nineteenth century, [ĩˈfɛr ĩˈvɛr ʃeˈmɛ̃iθa ˈðɛ̃iðre põʃ ˈðɛ̃iç] 'hell, winter, seed, son-in-law, apples, teeth' < INFĚRNUM IN-HIBĚRNUM SEMĚNTIA GĚNERUM PŌMOS DĚNTES (Gartner 1892).[28] The process of weakening and possible deletion of nasal consonants specifically before fricatives has operated on a limited geographical scale, however, and seems often to be of comparatively recent date, as the conditioning fricatives may represent later Romance creations. Much more widespread has been the selective weakening and loss which occurred when a voiceless consonant followed the nasal coda. This pattern is found in most of Emilia-Romagna and in central and eastern Lombardy; thus, the dialect of Imola in central Romagna has [vɛ̃ːt ˈkɔ̃ːprə] 'wind, he buys' < VĚNTUM CŎMPARAT as against [vent klomp] 'he sells, dove' < VĒNDIT COLŬMBUM.[29] Such is its geographical spread that it may well represent a chronologically earlier pattern of weakening or deletion which various dialects have later adapted by generalizing its scope to all context (i) forms. Generalized weakening appears, for example, in the extreme west of Emilia south of Piacenza where phonemic nasality is still found, as in [mõːt mõːd bjãːk pjõːb] 'mountain, world, white, lead' < MŎNTEM, MŬNDUM, (Germ.) blank, PLŬMBUM in the dialect of Travo (Zörner 1986).[30]

Two final observations may be made. First, notwithstanding the data from the Antrona valley dialects seen above, it seems that the criterion of place of articulation of the coda nasal in context (i) forms has not normally acted as a significant determinant for vowel nasalization.   Secondly, nasal consonants which only become pre-consonantal later on in Romance as a result of syncope are normally not subject to weakening. Thus, in the dialect of Bologna where original coda nasals were regularly lost (though with restoration taking place in recent times), there are examples such as ['maːndga] 'sleeve' and ['tsemza] 'bedbug' < MĂNICA CĪMICEM in which coda nasals have been fully preserved (Coco 1970).

In context (ii) forms, word-final nasals arising from apocope show very varied outcomes in northern Italian dialects. On the one hand, the differences reflect variation over the scope and chronology of apocope from dialect to dialect. On the other hand, structural considerations have played a part, certain nasal consonants being more susceptible to triggering vowel nasalization and subsequently undergoing weakening and possible loss.

Original simplex -N- in particular has been the nasal consonant type most subject to change in northern Italy. After nasalizing the preceding stressed vowel, it weakened and was then widely deleted to leave behind nasal vowel phonemes. Numerous dialects have preserved such vowels to this day, especially in Lombardy and Emilia-Romagna. However, later restoration has operated in many areas to re-establish sequences of vowel + nasal consonant. Other types of nasal consonant which became word-final through apocope have generally not undergone major modification except that original geminate nasals have become simplex as part of a general trend of geminate simplification. The dialect of Milan offers an example of the pattern widely found in the central part of northern Italy:

	simplex	-N-	>	-Ø	[pãː]	< PĀNEM	'bread'
but							
	geminate	-NN-	>	-n	[pan]	< PĂNNUM	'cloth'
	post-stress syllable	-N-	>	-n	['aːzen]	< ĂSINUM	'donkey'
	palatal	-ɲɲ	>	-ɲ	[baɲ]	< BĂLNEUM	'bath'
	simplex/geminate	-M(M)-	>	-m	[ram]	< RĀMUM	'branch'

(Nicoli 1983)

In dialect areas further away from the Po valley, cases of weakening in nasals other than -N- may be found. Geminate -NN- and simplex -N- in proparoxytons were affected in dialects of northern Veneto and the Lunigiana; modern forms usually show a word-final velar [-ŋ] which points to deletion and later restoration. For example, the dialect of Feltre (Veneto) has [soŋ daŋ] 'sleep, harm' < SŎMNUM DĂMNUM (Migliorini and Pellegrini 1971), and Pontremolese (Lunigiana) [aŋ daŋ] 'year, harm' and ['aːzuŋ 'ɔːmuŋ] 'donkey, man' < ĂSINUM HŎMINEM (Maffei Bellucci 1977). Word-final simplex and geminate -M(M)- have undergone weakening and deletion with later restoration of [ŋ] in dialects of northern Veneto, i.e. adjacent to the Friulan region where weakening and later restoration are regular (cf. 9.3.4), and in far western Piedmont dialects exposed to Gallo-Romance influence; cf. [fãː]

'hunger' < FAMEM (*AIS* 1015, pt. 140, Rochemolles). Some central and eastern Romagnolo dialects have also been affected so that nasal vowel phonemes have resulted, as in the dialect of Forlì [fū: fã: nõ: in'sẽ:] 'smoke, hunger, name, together' < FŪMUM, FĀMEM, NŌMEN, *IN-SĚMEL. However, in this dialect other forms also appear in which final [-m] is apparently preserved intact, such as [prem ram om rem] 'first/I squeeze, branch/copper, man, oar' < PRĪMUM/PRĚMO RĀMUM/AERĀMEN HOMO RĒMUM. The implication is that weakening of -M(M)- was probably the native development in this area, but that there was was later piecemeal restoration by lexical diffusion as a result of outside influences, especially from Bologna (where word-final [-m] was preserved) and the standard language (cf. Schürr 1919: esp. 124–8).[31] Lastly, the word-final palatal nasal [-ɲ] appears to remain unchanged in all dialects.

The data thus point to there being a parameter of nasal weakening/deletion operating in context (ii) forms of northern Italian dialects, representable as:

(simplex) -N-   -M(M)-   (in proparoxytons)-N-   -NN-   ɲ

more favoured   *less favoured*

Synchronically, the differences may be noted between the present parameter and that proposed for Rheto-Romance (9.3.4.2). Also, the gradience of weakening/deletion in northern Italian dialects may be compared with the systematic deletion found in northern French (cf. 4.2.4).

Comparing the fate of coda nasals in contexts (i) and (ii), we find that in certain dialects the patterns of weakening appear to be broadly comparable between the two contexts. Thus, in the dialect of Imola, deletion has occurred and nasal vowel phonemes created in both context (ii) forms and in context (i) forms where a voiceless consonant followed the original conditioning nasal consonant, e.g. [dẽ:t pɔ̃:t] 'tooth, bridge' vs. [fɛ̃: bɔ̃:] 'hay, good (m. sg.)' < DĚNTEM PŎNTEM FĒNUM BŎNUM. However, this does not hold true throughout northern Italy. There are numerous dialects where coda nasals have been more subject to weakening in context (ii) than in context (i), such a pattern being in conformity with the observations on the link between length and nasalization which were made earlier (10.4.3.1). Thus, in the Emilian dialect of Piacenza, Gorra (1890) reported full nasal consonant deletion in context (ii), PĀNEM > [pã:], BŎNUM > [bõ:] (the description of there being a 'semplice strascico nasale' (p. 149) implies the vowel to have been long, though this is not explicitly indicated). But in context (i) there is just some consonantal weakening with partial vowel nasalization, which moreover 'va col tempo sempre più affievolandosi' (p. 149), SĂNCTUM > [sãnt], PRŌMPTUM > [prõnt]. Likewise, the Lombard dialect of Milan shows [bẽ: bũ:] as against [vẽ:nt pjũ:mp], and in the latter context (i) items the coda nasal is reported to be fully present and, as Nicoli (1983: 58–9) observes, nasality in the preceding vowel is 'meno evidente'. Context (ii) therefore is the more likely of the two to experience nasal coda weakening and associated vowel nasalization.

Chronologically, it is often difficult to date cases of weakening and deletion of nasal codas in individual dialects. Textual evidence points to weakening in context (i) forms being well advanced by the thirteenth century in the dialect of Bergamo (east Lombardy) and the early seventeenth century description of Milanese by Biffi indicates that original simplex -N- in context (ii) forms was very weak and close to deletion (cf. below 10.5.3). However, in the absence of textual materials any attempts at dating changes for most dialects can only be speculative.

In context (iii) forms, significant weakening of conditioning nasals is unusual but is found in dialects of far western Liguria, western Piedmont, and in the Val d'Aosta. It is closely associated with parallel developments in the nearby Franco-Provençal area (cf. 5.4(b)). In both areas, only the reflex of simplex -N- is affected. In Ligurian dialects, such as those of Triora and Perinaldo, this nasal consonant has weakened to become a vestigial glide or tap often preceded by a nasal vowel (Forner 1988: 462; Petracco Sicardi and Azaretti 1989: 36). Sometimes the nasal tap [r̃] has undergone denasalization to emerge as a weak oral tap [r]. For example, the dialect of Pigna has ['seːra] 'supper' < CĒNA and [meˈrɛstra] 'soup' < MENĒSTRA, although nasality was preserved when stressed [i] preceded giving a palatal nasal [ɲ]; e.g. [ˈɟaˈliɲa ˈliɲa] < GALLĪNA LŪNA 'hen, moon' (Merlo 1959). The tap [r], which is described by Merlo as 'poco o punto apicale, debole, palatale' ('slightly or not at all apical, weak, palatal'), has emerged as the reflex not only of -N- but also of simplex -R- and -L- (cf. CĒRA > ['seːra] 'wax', TĒLA > ['teːra] 'cloth'). This development may be compared with the rhotacism found in Romanian dialects (12.2.4).

In certain dialects of western Piedmont and the Val d'Aosta, the weakening process was taken further such that the nasal consonant was deleted altogether and phonemically nasal vowels emerged. Thus, in the dialect of Rhême-St.-Georges (Val d'Aosta) there are such forms as [ɛˈpẽːa ˈtsẽːa ˈbũːå] 'thorn, chain, good (f. sg.)' < SPĪNA CATĒNA BŎNA[32] (AIS, pt. 121); similarly in the dialect of Prali (Val Germanasca, west Piedmont) we have [ˈsĩːõ ˈlãːõ ˈly̆ːõ] 'dinner, wool, moon' < CĒNA LĀNA LŪNA (Genre 1992).[33] This development was evidently already well advanced by the twelfth century, since it was taken by emigrants who established settlements in Sicily at that time (cf. 10.3 above). Unconditioned nasal vowels are still found in the dialect of Novara (AIS, pt. 818).[34]

10.4.4.2.   Restoration

In many dialects across northern Italy there has been a growing counter-tendency in more recent times to restructure unconditioned nasal vowels into sequences of vowel plus nasal coda. Typically the nasal coda appears as a velar [ŋ]/[ⁿ] of variable duration and degree of occlusion, as in PĀNEM > [pãːn] > [pãː] > [pãŋ]/[pãⁿ]/[paŋ] 'bread' (where the vowel itself shows variable degrees of nasality at the final stage).[35]   In such sequences, the velar nasal [ŋ] would thus not represent a direct continuer of the original nasal but rather the result of the 'hardening' of the second mora of an earlier long nasal vowel. This process of nasal consonant regeneration [Ṽː] > [Ṽŋ] we refer to as *restoration*. The appeal to restoration as the source of the velar nasal in forms like [paŋ] was initially made for northern Italian by Rohlfs (1966: § 305) and has been more fully expounded by Hajek (1991a, 1991b, 1997: § 8.1.8.1). Such an interpretation seems preferable to the view whereby [ŋ] arose through phonetic weakening of a coda nasal associated with vowel nasalization, e.g. [Ṽn] > [Ṽⁿ] > [Ṽŋ] (Chen 1972a: 102 and 1973b: 913; Ruhlen 1978: 225; Tuttle 1991: 50). Support for a restoration-based view comes from textual evidence showing that modern [Ṽŋ] sequences may earlier have been realized as long nasal vowels (or nasal vowel + off-glide);[36]   the evidence of more conservative rural dialects still possessing unconditioned nasal vowels alongside urban dialects with hardening;[37]   and evolutionary plausibility, as with forms such as ['tẽːŋp] 'time' < TĔMPUS (in Novellara dialect, northern Emilia; Malagoli 1910–13) in which any direct progression from [m] to [ŋ] would be phonetically unlikely.

The effect of restoration has been to enlarge the distribution and range of coda nasals in contexts where vowel nasalization had operated selectively, by establishing (restored) velar [ŋ] along with the preserved nasal types. Thus, the dialect of Alpago (north-east Veneto) has context (i) forms such as ['viŋθer 'peŋsa] 'to win, (s)he thinks' < VĬNCERE PĒNSAT as against [kamp dɛnt 'vɛnde] 'field, (s)he sings, (s)he sells' < CĂMPUM DĔNTEM VĒNDIT, where high-level vowel nasalization has evidently only affected vowels followed by a nasal + fricative sequence and later restoration has established [ŋ] before non-velar consonants (Zörner 1997). For context (ii) forms, the reintroduction of word-final [ŋ] by restoration enlarged the range of permissible word-final nasal consonants in a number of dialects; e.g. Novellara (northern Emilia) has [pãːŋ] 'bread' < PĀNEM alongside [paːn raːm] 'cloth, branch' < PĂNNUM RĀMUM (Malagoli 1910–13).

The precise diachronic stages by which restoration has taken place in the dialects concerned was doubtless variable, but one pattern which appears to have operated widely is [VN > Ṽᴺ > Ṽː > Ṽᴳ > Ṽ(ː)ŋ], where 'G' is an off-glide. Here the second mora of the long unconditioned nasal vowel has developed into an off-glide which subsequently hardened into a full nasal consonant (Hajek 1991b). When hardening occurs, the new nasal consonant which results has usually been a velar [ŋ], as our historical schema and earlier examples indicate. However, other possibilities are occasionally found. In dialects of the far north and north-west of Italy, the restored nasal in context

(ii) forms often has its place of articulation determined by the quality of the preceding vowel. Thus, in the Antrona Valley (northern Piedmont) bilabial [m] arose after rounded vowels and palatal [ɲ] after unrounded vowels, as in [kanˈtum] 'corner' vs. [piɲ fɔɲ paɲ] 'pine, hay, bread' < CANTŌNEM; PĪNUM FĒNUM PĀNEM (Nicolet 1929), while in Legnano which lies just north-west of Milan a similar distinction is found, this time between [m] after rounded vowels and [ŋ] after unrounded vowels, [bum] 'good (m. sg.)' vs. [fiŋ] 'end' < BǑNUM FĪNEM (Tuttle 1991: 43).[38] Exceptionally, restoration may re-establish the etymologically appropriate coda nasal as in the dialect of Cremona, e.g. [vɛːnt kaːmp bɛːn paːn] 'wind, field, well, bread' < VĔNTUM CǍMPUM BĔNE PĀNEM, even though surrounding dialects have final [ŋ] (Heilmann 1976).

Restoration has also operated in context (iii) forms such as LŪNA. In such forms, the stressed vowel was of course long because it was in a free syllable and it too underwent hardening of the second mora, especially in dialects of Piedmont and Liguria in the west but also further east in dialects of western Lombardy and Emilia-Romagna. The general pattern has been [Ṽː-nV] > [Ṽ$^{\tilde{G}}$-nV] > [Ṽŋ-nV] > [Vŋ-V]. One of the earliest reliable indications of this development comes in an eighteenth-century description of Genoese where the sequence [ŋn] is seemingly identified.[39] Such a sequence remains in dialects of Monferrato in south-eastern Piedmont and in southern Canavese, e.g. [gaˈliŋna] 'hen' < GALLĪNA, but in most of Piedmont [ŋn] has fairly recently simplified to [ŋ] probably via a stage [ŋŋ] which is still found occasionally, e.g. in the dialect of Antagnod in the Val d'Aosta (Berruto 1974: 37–41; Tuttle 1991: 38–9). Similarly, intervocalic [ŋ] appears in Ligurian, except in some western dialects and the transitional dialect of Ormea where intervocalic [n] is found with no restoration (Parodi 1907). Simplification to [ŋ] began to take place in Genoese during the later eighteenth century although educated speakers preserved older [ŋn] until the mid-nineteenth century (Forner 1988: 459). As regards the dialects of Parma and Bologna, the sequence [ŋn] has arisen in modern times. For Parma, in the 1930s forms such as [faˈreŋnᵉ ˈloŋnᵉ] < FARĪNA LŪNA are recorded as characteristic of the city centre as against outlying areas where no nasal hardening has occurred (Tuttle 1991: 36 n. 32), while for Bologna the use of comparable hardened forms [faˈreŋna ˈloŋna] appears in the 1960s to be characteristic of middle and younger generations of speakers (cf. Coco 1970: esp. 19 n. 31).

Other outcomes are sometimes found. A sequence [nn] appears in odd parts of southern Piedmont, for instance in the dialect of Murazzano which has [ˈlynna] < LŪNA, and it also presents itself in dialects spoken in rural and especially mountain areas around Bologna, e.g. in [gaˈlenna furˈtonna] 'hen, fortune' < GALLĪNA FORTŪNA (Tuttle 1991: 36 n. 32; Canepari and Vitali 1995: 143, 147). Other dialects have a simplex [n] but with the preceding stressed vowel realized short. This is found notably in a cluster of dialects in south-western and western Lombardy, including Milanese: e.g. dialect of Voghera (south-west Lombardy) [fɐ'renɐ 'venɐ 'lænɐ 'lønɐ] 'flour, vein, wool, moon' < FARĪNA VĒNA LĀNA LŪNA (Maragliano 1976) and Milanese [fa'rina ka'dɛna 'lana 'lyna] 'flour, chain, wool, moon' < FARĪNA CATĒNA LĀNA LŪNA. Some controversy exists over the evolution of these forms with short stressed vowels:[40] either they owe themselves to specially conditioned vowel shortening with later possible nasal consonant lengthening [Ṽːn > Vn (> Vnn)] (Hajek 1997: § 7.2.0),[41] or they arose from restoration and later assimilation [Ṽːn > Ṽŋn > Vnn > Vn] (Tuttle 1991: 38). Crucial is the interpretation of forms appearing in later medieval Milanese texts such as *penna* < POENA 'pain' and *vanna* < VĀNA 'vain (f. sg.)'. If the graphy *nn* merely indicates a short stressed vowel, as Hajek plausibly contends, an evolution without restoration may be hypothesized. This in turn would mean that the forms with apparent off-glides which Maragliano (1976) cites from eighteenth-century texts from Voghera, e.g. *medseina fortöina* (< MEDI-ĪNA, FORTŪNA), would probably not be the direct ancestors of the modern forms. Instead, displacement by the Milanese pattern would be indicated.

10.5.   Evolution of Nasal Vowels in Northern Dialects

Although vowel nasalization has affected dialects throughout northern Italy, its consequences have been varied from region to region. Nasal vowel phonemes developed in many dialects but, as we have seen (10.4.4), recent restoration of a conditioning nasal consonant has often occurred reducing vowel nasality to allophonic status only and also typically diminishing phonetic levels of nasality. Nasalization has usually not affected the tongue position of vowels to the extent found in French, although adjustments causing neutralization have occurred in most dialects. However, vowel length has widely undergone significant changes associated with nasalization. Finally, we may note that tracing the chronology of the various developments which have occurred is frequently problematic. Many dialects lack documentary evidence until this century, and where textual materials are available they are usually unclear as to the presence of vowel nasality. Historical accounts therefore must be somewhat tentative.

10.5.1.   NEUTRALIZATION OF MID-VOWEL CONTRASTS

As has already been noted, all North Italian dialects have vowel systems based upon the original seven–way arrangement /i e ɛ a ɔ o u/. An early indicator of possible nasalization has been the neutralization of the contrast between the mid vowels /e ɛ/ and /o ɔ/ when they occurred specifically in syllables with a nasal coda, i.e. in context (i) forms. The low-mid vowel types were raised to leave just /e/ and /o/ in this context (cf. Rohlfs 1966: §§ 98, 119).[42] Usually, the resulting high-mid vowels have followed the same patterns of metaphonically conditioned change as original Late Latin /e/ and /o/.[43]

In the varieties of some peripheral areas of North Italy, the general tendency to neutralize mid vowels in context (i) forms did not take place. In certain dialects of the far west of Liguria, /o ɔ/ and /e ɛ/ have remained distinct even though the presence of restoration indicates that significant levels of vowel nasalization formerly occurred. For example, from the dialect of Olivetta may be cited [hɛŋt] 'hundred' < CĔNTUM but ['treŋta] 'thirty' < TRIGĬNTA, [tɛŋp]/pl. ['tɛŋpi] 'time(s)' < TĔMPUS/*TĔMP-I but ['preŋdi] 'I take' < PRĒ(HE)NDO (Petracco Sicardi and Azaretti 1989). The lack of neutralization here may well reflect the influence of the adjacent Provençal speech-area which has regularly preserved the contrast between mid vowels in context (i) forms (cf. section 6.2.1.2). Romagna too was only partly affected. Western Romagnolo dialects such as that of Bologna clearly show neutralization, but the evidence of early Romagnolan texts of the sixteenth century suggests that in the peripheral dialects of the south-east of this region the process of neutralization was slower in being carried through. The evidence for this comes from the evolution of mid vowels appearing in metaphonic environments, i.e. in forms containing final -ī. Metaphony regularly caused diphthongization of low-mid /ɛ ɔ/ but caused raising with high-mid /e o/ (cf. n. 6). Now, in the anonymous late sixteenth-century poem *Pulon Matt* composed in the dialect of Cesena, original /ɔ/ in a nasalizing context displays raising in metaphonic environments just like original /o/ implying that the neutralization of mid back vowels as /o/ pre-dated metaphonic diphthongization. In contrast, original /ɛ/ in a nasalizing context has undergone diphthongization in metaphonic environments suggesting that neutralization of mid front vowels post-dated metaphonic diphthongization; thus, *cunt* 'accounts' < CŎMPUT-Ī = *urs* 'bears' < ŬRSĪ as against oral /ɔ/ in *nuost* 'our (m. pl.)' < NŎSTRĪ, but *dient* 'teeth' < DĔNT-Ī = *ier* 'you (sg.) were' < ĔR-ĪS as against *quist* 'these (m. pl.)' < ECCU-ĬSTĪ (Schürr 1919: 119). Elsewhere however, even in other peripheral zones such as the Lunigiana area in the northern spur of Tuscany itself, /ɛ ɔ/ in syllables with a coda nasal share the fate of original /e o/ (Maffei Bellucci 1977). The implication of this development is that in syllables with a nasal coda some significant enhancement of the nasality of the vowel took place very widely, sufficient in almost all areas to blur the rather fine distinction between mid vowels.

Dating this change is problematic. The philological evidence from Late Latin texts of the area from Ravenna (Carlton 1973) and from the Langobardic laws promulgated by King Rothari (643) is inconclusive. Some apparent cases of pre-nasal raising are to be found in the latter, e.g. *prehindere, ascinderit, infiscintur, contimpserit* (Löfstedt 1961: 30) but no examples have been found for back vowels.[44] Nonetheless, in view of the widespread occurrence of the change in northern Italian dialects and its appearance in many other varieties of Romance, it is likely to be a development of some antiquity (cf. 3.2.1). Furthermore, as we have seen, there has been interaction between this change and metaphonic diphthongization triggered by final -ī. Given the probable antiquity of the latter development, the neutralization caused by nasalization would appear to be a very early change.

A final consideration relates to mid vowels in context (ii) forms. After apocope had operated, the vowels /e ɛ/ and /o ɔ/ found themselves before a nasal coda, i.e. in a context comparable to nasalizing context (i) where the contrast between these mid vowels had been neutralized. As a result, a tendency arose in many dialects to extend neutralization to mid vowels in context (ii) forms as well. Thus, Milanese has [bẽː] and [pjẽː][45] 'well, full (m. sg.)' < BĚNE PLĒNUM, just as [būː] and [karˈbūː] 'good (m. sg.), coal' < BŎNUM CARBŌNEM. However, dialects which preserved the contrast between mid vowels in context (i) have also done so in context (ii), e.g. dialect of Olivetta (Liguria) [bɛŋ] vs. [tʃeŋ] 'well, full (m. sg.)' < BĚNE PLĒNUM and [boŋ] vs. [kanˈtuŋ] 'good, corner' < BŎNUM CANTŌNEM.

10.5.2. VOWEL LENGTH ADJUSTMENTS

Northern Italian dialects have been very sensitive to vowel length differences in the way nasalization was implemented. As already noted, there is strong evidence from many modern dialects to indicate that nasalization took place preferentially in vowels which were long. This suggests that heightened nasalization would have first affected the vowels in contexts (ii) and (iii), since these vowels were already systematically long by the end of Imperial times thanks to being stressed (only stressed vowels could be long) and appearing in a free syllable. It will be recalled that the syllabic pattern V̆C-CV/V̄-CV (i.e. short vowel in blocked stressed syllables and long vowel in free stressed syllables) became general in Italy and other areas of central *Romania* (cf. 10.4.1).

In context (i) forms, the vowel appeared in a blocked syllable and was therefore systematically short in Late Latin. Given the evidence for the preferential nasalization of long vowels, it seems likely that the short vowels in context (i) forms may have only undergone heightened nasalization at some later stage in many areas of northern Italy. Precisely how this came about is, however, rather unclear. A notable point is that in modern dialects the available evidence indicates that nasalized vowels in context (i) forms have typically been lengthened. Thus, the Emilian dialect of Novellara [vẽːŋt tẽːŋp ˈkõːŋpra] 'wind, time, (s)he buys' < VĚNTUM TĚMPUS CŎMPARAT (Malagoli

1910–13) has systematically long vowels. Elsewhere a diphthong may appear which betrays an originally lengthened vowel, as in Rimini [deᶦnt] 'tooth' < DĔNTEM, Parma [veᶦnt] 'wind' < VĔNTUM (both these forms showing just slight vowel nasality), and Tizzano [vẽjnt] 'wind' (*AIS*, pt. 443) where there is strong nasality. The question thus arises whether the lengthening preceded, accompanied, or was a consequence of, vowel nasalization. Hajek (1997) argues strongly for the first possibility, but no less acceptable is the view that the adoption of increased levels of nasality was accompanied by the use of greater duration by speakers in order to ensure that the vowel's nasality was readily perceptible (cf. 1.1 and Ch. 13).

The long vowels which emerged after nasalization in the various nasalizing contexts have in some cases emerged as short vowels in modern dialects. This has typically come about as a result of restoration by which the second mora of a long nasal vowel developed into a glide and hardened into a nasal consonant, usually [ŋ], as in PĀNEM > [pãː] > [paŋ] (see above, 10.4.4). The characteristic short vowel which is now usually found in forms affected by restoration does not therefore reflect a simple shortening of the vowel, [Ṽː] > [Ṽ], but rather the reflex of the first mora of the original vowel. However, sporadic cases of shortening are occasionally reported, for instance with the low vowel in dialects of eastern Lombardy. This is apparently a recent change affecting only certain lexical items, to give forms such as [pa] < PĀNEM as against long [beː buː] etc. < BĔNE BŎNUM in the dialects of Bergamo and Bagolino. Only context (ii) forms are involved, these having first undergone regular vowel denasalization.

10.5.3.   RISE OF PHONEMIC NASAL VOWELS

In many parts of northern Italy, nasal consonants which had brought about the conditioned nasalization of a preceding vowel were eventually deleted. The result was that the nasality in such vowels was no longer overtly conditioned so that phonemic nasal vowels were created. They probably arose at varying periods in different dialects, and it is almost certain that they were found much more widely in earlier times than they are today, the reduction in their incidence being caused primarily by the growing counter-tendency towards restoration (10.4.4.2). In modern times, phonemic nasal vowels have been reported patchily in Piedmont, in western and central Lombardy and especially in Emilia-Romagna (see Map 7).

Normally, the nasal vowel phonemes which have been created are only able to contrast with their oral counterparts when word-final or preceding an oral consonant, as in the Romagnolo dialect of Faenza [vẽː] 'wine' vs. [seː] 'thirst' < VĪNUM SĬTEM and [põːt] 'bridge' vs. [tot] 'all' < PŎNTEM *TŬTTUM.

However, in a few Romagnolo dialects, contrasts have also arisen between oral and nasal vowels before nasal consonants. This has come about as a result of two sound changes affecting stressed vowels: (*a*) nasalization of (long) vowels appearing before simplex -N- (but not before geminate -NN-) and (*b*) later secondary lengthening of (short) low vowels; thus, in the dialect of Imola, [ˈbõːnɐ] 'good (f. sg.)' vs. [ˈnɔːnɐ] 'grandmother' < BŎNA NŎNNA (Schürr 1919).

The chronology of the deletion of conditioning nasal consonants that gave rise to phonemic nasal vowels in the northern Italian dialects affected is uncertain. The main problem is that for most dialects textual evidence from earlier periods is either lacking or inconclusive. For the dialect of Bergamo, however, there is a fourteenth-century glossary translating Latin words into the local dialect. This offers items such as *vi, fe, pa, carbo* < VĪNUM FĒNUM PĀNEM CARBŌNEM as against *pan* < PĂNNUM *lum* < LŪMEN *leng* < LĬGNUM, and *zoven* < IŬVENEM where deletion of original simplex -N- in context (ii) forms is apparently indicated. But the glossary shows little evidence that comparable deletion has occurred yet in context (i) forms, for example *argent, bianch, dent, campo* < ARGĔNTUM blank DĔNTEM CĂMPUM. Only from the sixteenth century do texts appear from Bergamo which consistently contain context (i) forms such as *cap tep* < CĂMPUM TĔMPUS indicating nasal deletion (Lorck 1893). Such data are in conformity with the assumption that nasal vowel phonemes arose earlier in context (ii) forms than in context (i) forms (10.4.3.2 and 10.4.4).

A rather different source of information is provided by contemporary descriptions of earlier stages of dialects where nasal vowel phonemes have developed. For Milanese, a brief but precious example is the *Prissian da Milan della parnonzia milanesa* (The Milan 'Priscian' of Milanese Pronunciation) by G. A. Biffi, published in 1606 (Lepschy 1978). Under the paragraph devoted to the consonant N, it is stated that in words such as *son, pan, fen* the nasal consonant is pronounced 'meza morta', and a comparison is made with the dull sound of a cord striking into cotton wadding.[46] The value intended is not entirely clear. Does Biffi mean [ŋ] or some weak nasal off-glide, or, less plausibly perhaps, is he indicating the presence of simple nasality in the preceding vowel? The author's difficulty in capturing the nature of this nasal element is reminiscent of that experienced by the Parisian grammarian Bèze writing about French just two decades earlier (cf. 4.2.4). It may be that in both cases the word-final nasal consonant was in the very last stages of disappearing. Certainly, two centuries later the first major dictionary of Milanese by Cherubini (1839) clearly indicates the existence of unconditioned nasal vowels.[47]

10.5.4. LOWERING OF HIGH NASAL VOWELS

In a development finding a parallel in the history of northern varieties of French including the standard language, high nasal vowels have lowered to take on a mid point of articulation in a number of dialects of Emilia-Romagna and southern Lombardy (see Map 8). Lowering operated on vowels in contexts (i), (ii), and (iii). Thus, in the central Romagnolo dialect of Imola there are forms such as [sẽːkw ɔ̃ː 'vzẽːna 'lɔ̃ːna prem lom] 'five, one (m. sg.), neighbour (f. sg.), moon, first (m. sg.), light' < *CĪNQUE, ŪNUM, VICĪNA LŪNA PRĪMUM LŪMEN (Schürr 1919). The dialect of Bologna has [zeŋkv vzeŋ oŋ ga'leŋna 'loŋna 'pjoma lom] 'five, neighbour (m. sg.), one (m. sg.), hen, moon, feather, light' < *CĪNQUE VICĪNUM ŪNUM GALLĪNA LŪNA PLŪMA LŪMEN (Coco 1970) and from the dialect of Voghera in south-western Lombardy may be cited the following items ['øndes feŋ øŋ fa'rena 'løna] 'eleven, end, one, flour, moon' < ŪNDECIM FĪNEM ŪNUM FARĪNA LŪNA (Maragliano 1976). Lowering of [ī] is found more widely in modern dialects of Emilia-Romagna than that of [ū] or [ỹ], so that [ī] > [ẽ] may represent the first stage of the development (cf. the comparable situation in standard French, 4.3.3).

The lowering of high nasal vowels may be related to the lowering of the blocked oral vowels [i u y] which occurred principally in Emilia-Romagna. If the changes are linked, the explanation for the association between the two types of vowel might lie in the widespread tendency for nasal vowels to be realized phonetically long initially but for them later to develop off-glides (and in many cases these glides have subsequently been modified by hardening to [ŋ], cf. above 10.4.4.2). The creation of such off-glides may have led to the nucleus of the nasal vowels [ĩj ũw̃ ỹj̃] (< [ĩː ũː ỹː]) being interpreted as short segments which were then identified with the short blocked oral vowels [i u y]. Lowering would thus have operated systematically on short high vowels, oral or nasal.

The disparity in the present-day geographical spread of oral and nasal vowel lowering poses some difficulties for such an interpretation. Lowering of oral [i] has occurred in an area forming just a part of the zone where nasal [ī] lowering is found. Similarly, lowering of nasal [ū] is more widespread than that of oral [u] in Romagna. In south-eastern Lombardy, lowering appears to have been a later development which only affected oral high vowels, whereas in most of Emilia only nasalized vowels have been subject to lowering. It is problematic to reconcile these facts with the suggestion that nasal and oral high vowel lowering were associated processes. However, one possible interpretation might be that there was a general tendency for short high vowels to lower but that it was implemented more rapidly with the nasal vowels in the focal area of change, Romagna. Two factors may have promoted the speedier acceptance of lowering in the nasal vowels: (*a*) the desire to differentiate two adjacent high nasal segments, hence [ĩj̃ > ẽj̃ ũw̃ > õw̃ ỹj̃ > œ̃j̃]; (*b*) the action of general background perceptual forces identified by phonetic theory (cf. 1.1). Once a mid target pronunciation for these nasal vowels became established in Romagna, it may have spread as a borrowed feature into those dialects of Emilia which had not been affected by any tendency to lower short high vowels.

Dating this change is problematic. It certainly post-dates the fronting of /u/ > /y/ in view of forms such as [œ̃ː] [võː] [võːŋ] < ŪNUM appearing in western Emilia (*AIS*, pts. 454, 443, 423). The change /u/ > /y/ spread from the west into Lombardy and south of the Po it gradually extended into western Emilia as far as the River Taro (i.e. a little to the west of Parma) and in the Apennines as far east as Modena. A fully front pronunciation /y/ probably only became established in Lombardy and Emilia at the earliest in the twelfth–thirteenth centuries, so that the lowering of high vowels in western Emilian dialects presumably dates from the end of the Middle Ages or even later (Rohlfs 1966: § 35, Tekavčić 1974: §§ 79–81). As regards those areas where the fronting of /u/ never took place, there are occasional glimpses of the lowering of the high vowels /i u/ already in texts of the thirteenth century. In a work completed *c.*1243, the Bolognese writer Guido Fava uses *deçonio* 'fasting' < DE-IŪNIUM, *legome* 'vegetable' < LEGŪMEN, *conoscoda* 'known (past part., f. sg.) < COGNOSC-ŪTA, and in a Bolognese document dated 1289 there is the form *negono* 'no (one)' < NEC-ŪNUM (Rohlfs 1966: § 34). Yet lowering is not consistently indicated for nasal or oral high vowels in texts from central and eastern Romagna until the end of the eighteenth century (Schürr 1919: 131). There are very few clear examples in early texts to indicate lowering of /i/. A Bolognese poem of *c.*1280 has *dex* 'he said' < DĪXIT, and Bertoni (1925: 23) cites one example with lowering of /i/ in a nasalizing context, *mesquelén* 'sulkiness', which appears in a Modenese text of the sixteenth century. But it is only towards the end of the eighteenth century that central and eastern Romagnolan texts regularly show the graphy /e/ for original oral or nasal /i/. Thus, moves to lower high vowels may sporadically have occurred in the late medieval period but the development appears only to have gained ground in more modern times.

Finally, the widespread raising of nasalized [õ] > [ũ] in Lombardy offers an apparent contrast to the lowering development just considered. It operated regularly in all three nasalizing context types in eastern Lombardy, as in Bergamasco [muːt buː kuˈruːna] 'mountain, good, crown' < MŎNTEM BŎNUM CORŌNA (with later denasalization, see below 10.5.5). But raising was limited to contexts (i) and (ii) in Milanese, [mũːnt bũː] as against [kuˈrɔna]. In all these cases, the raising can be seen to form part of a drag chain in which oral or nasal allophones of /o/ raised to /u/ after original /u/ was fronted to /y/.

10.5.5.   RETREAT FROM VOWEL NASALITY

As we have noted, it is likely that almost all northern Italian dialects experienced high-level vowel nasalization at some stage of their history and some went on to develop phonemic nasal vowels in certain contexts. However in more recent times there has been a growing counter-tendency, fostered in large part by influence from the standard language, to downgrade nasality in vowels. Its effect has been twofold: (*a*) phonemic nasal vowels have tended to be eliminated, and (*b*) levels of nasality have been reduced in allophonically nasal vowels.

Where phonemic nasal vowels have been eliminated, it has been achieved either through *vowel denasalization* or through *restoration*. Denasalization of unconditioned nasal vowels has operated systematically in dialects of central and eastern Lombardy as well as in adjacent dialects of western Veneto, leaving behind long oral vowels; e.g. the dialect of Bagolino in east Lombardy shows uniform denasalization of the nasal vowel phonemes which arose in contexts (i) and (ii) and later shortening of the low vowel [aː], as in [siːk teːp kap muːt (v)iː beː pa buː nedzyː] 'five, time, field, mountain, wine, well, bread, good (m. sg.), no (one)' < *CĪNQUE TĔMPUS CĂMPUM MŎNTEM VĪNUM BĔNE PĀNEM BŎNUM NEC-ŪNUM (Bazzani and Melzani 1988).[48] Similarly, the nearby dialect of Bergamo has [beː buː teːp muːt] 'well, good (m. sg.), time, mountain' (Sanga 1987). The chronology of this change is uncertain. However, textual evidence suggests that the process was well under way in the sixteenth century (10.5.3).

Much more widespread has been the alternative strategy of eliminating phonemic nasal vowels through restoration, whereby the vowels are restructured into sequences of vowel + nasal coda consonant such that vowel nasality becomes allophonic. For example, from Genoa we have ['dɛŋte 'kaŋpo 'fruŋte piŋ paŋ buŋ yŋ] 'tooth, field, forehead, pine tree, bread, good, one (m. sg.)' (*AIS*, pt. 178; Parodi 1902). Here, in each item there was doubtless once a phonemic nasal vowel which has undergone later restructuring with the restoration of the most typical conditioning nasal consonant [ŋ]; cf. 10.4.4.2.

Alongside the downgrading of phonemic vowel nasality there has been a widespread phonetic tendency to reduce levels of (conditioned) nasality in vowels. This tendency affected all allophonically nasal vowels, whether these had arisen through restoration from earlier nasal vowel phonemes or whether they had always had only conditioned nasality, as for instance in context (iii) forms. The reduction of levels of vowel nasality however has not occurred in a uniform way across northern Italy. Instead, different and competing sociolinguistic factors have operated, giving rise to delicate variations. One important variable distinguishes urban from rural dialects: urban dialects have generally been in the vanguard in retreating from the use of vowel nasality, while rural dialects have tended to be more tenacious in preserving it. Thus, in the Veneto high levels of vowel nasality are reported in some 'rustic' dialects, especially those of the provinces of Padua, Vicenza, and Rovigo. These appear in rapid, casual styles of speech and are followed by a conditioning nasal consonant which may be a nasal approximant, as in ['gã^{ɣ}ba 'dẽ^{ɣ}te 'bã:ɟo] = *gamba, dente, bagno*, where [ɣ̃] is an unrounded velar nasal approximant (Canepari 1979: 66–7, and 1984: 95). However, dialects of the Veneto more generally present forms in which there has been a greater degree of restoration with the nasal glide hardened into a velar nasal of varying duration and occlusion [ŋ]/[ⁿ] while the preceding vowel may show reduced levels of nasality, e.g. ['tẽⁿpo 'gãⁿba 'dẽⁿte] 'time, leg, tooth' < TĔMPUS GĂMBA DĔNTEM (Canepari 1979: 67; Zamboni 1988: 534). The influence of the prestigious variety based on educated usage in Venice where vowel nasality has been less intense has also played a significant role here.[49]   This variety has increasingly provided the linguistic model for the Veneto forming the basis of the regional *koine* and its influence would doubtless be felt more strongly in urban rather than rural communities of the region. Elsewhere, Malagoli (1910–13: § 29) notes the retention of strongly nasal vowels specifically in country dialects around Novellara (Emilia). Likewise for Bologna and the surrounding area, it is in the rural and mountain dialects rather than the urban dialect that the use of significantly nasal vowels is reported by Canepari and Vitali (1995: 139).

For certain dialects, documentation is available from earlier periods so that some idea of the chronology and tempo of downgrading in phonetic levels of vowel nasality can be inferred. Gorra (1890) revealingly says of usage in Piacenza at his time that nasality in context (i) forms was less strong than in other context types and that its intensity was diminishing as time went by. For the dialect of Parma, the same scholar in 1892 reported high-level conditioned nasality in context (iii) forms, as in ['kõ:na lõ:na] 'cradle, moon' < CŪNA LŪNA. However, more recent surveys from this century point to reduced levels of nasality establishing themselves (Tuttle 1991: 36 n. 32 and *AIS*, pt. 423). A similarly rapid denasalizing trend is indicated for the dialect of Bologna (Coco 1970: 61 n. 115). In this retreat from vowel nasality, sociolinguistic perceptions of 'good speaking' have evidently played some part. Thus for the dialect of Genoa, Forner (1975: 163) suggestively reports the increasing tendency amongst speakers to view the use of nasal vowels negatively as signs of 'plebeian' or 'rustic' speech.

10.6.   Modern Nasal Vowel Systems

In modern dialects where phonemic nasal vowels are found they regularly form a smaller set than that of oral vowels. The early neutralization of mid-vowel contrasts in nasalizing contexts is a major contributory factor, although later neutralizations have further reduced the stock of nasal vowel types in individual varieties.

Milanese still shows a five-way system of nasal vowels which are realized long in stressed syllables:

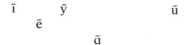

as in [vĩː fẽː pãː būː vỹː] 'wine, hay, bread, good (m. sg.), one (m. sg.)'
< VĪNUM FĒNUM PĀNEM BŎNUM ŪNUM.

However, in the dialects of Emilia-Romagna where high nasal vowels have lowered (10.5.4), there have been further neutralizations. Where the high back vowel /u/ had fronted to /y/, the nasal vowel allophone [ỹ] (which either remained allophonic or went on to become a phoneme) has usually preserved its separate identity despite lowering. But the lowering of [ĩ] has resulted in its merging with the existing mid vowel [ẽ]. In dialects where nasal vowels became phonemic, a four-way system emerged. For example, the variety of Tizzano in Emilia (*AIS*, pt. 443) has the following pattern in which the monophthongal vowels are long in stressed syllables:

as in [vɛ̃j fɛ̃j pãː bɔ̃ː vœ̃ː] < VĪNUM FĒNUM PĀNEM BŎNUM ŪNUM.

The dialects of Romagna have not undergone the fronting of /u/. Lowering has therefore commonly led to the merger of earlier [ĩ] with [ẽ], and [ũ] with [õ]. Thus, the dialect of Ravenna tended towards a three-vowel system of nasal vowels. However, a later independent development which will be considered below came to reintroduce a high nasal vowel phoneme /ĩ/. A four-way system is therefore found today:

ĩ

ẽ   õ

ẽ

As in other Romagnolan dialects, these nasal vowels are semi-long according to Schürr (1919), with the exception of /ẽ/ which is normally phonetically long. However, they are all systematically indicated as being long in the *AIS* (pt. 459). Examples with modern non-high vowels are [vẽː fẽː pẽː bõː õː] < VĪNUM FĒNUM PĀNEM BŎNUM ŪNUM.

A rare case of further neutralization appears in the Romagnolan dialect of Meldola where the fronting and raising of earlier nasal [ã] has resulted in a merger between it and [ẽ]. A new high vowel phoneme /ĩ/ has also become established here, so that a three-way system has developed:

$$ĩ$$

$$ẽ \qquad õ$$

Examples of the non-high nasal vowels are [avzẽː vẽː pẽː bõː võː] 'neighbour (m. sg.), he comes, bread, good, one' < VICINUM VĔNIT PĀNEM BŎNUM ŪNUM. It may be noted that the neutralizations between nasal vowels do not reflect a general feature of vowel development. Amongst oral vowels in originally blocked syllables (only blocked high vowels undergo the same lowering as high nasal vowels), neutralization has only occurred with the original /i/ : /e/ and /u/ : /o/ contrasts to give a five-way pattern with oral blocked vowels [e ɛː ɑː ɔː o] (Schürr 1919).

Where lowering of original high vowels took place, occasionally new instances of high nasal vowels arose as a result of later raising of mid vowels through the influence of a preceding high palatal segment. Thus, in forms such as PLĒNUM the mid vowel appearing at the stage [pjẽː] has been raised to give [pjĩː] in a number of dialects of Emilia-Romagna, and particularly in Romagna this may simplify to [pĩː]. For example, the dialect of Piacenza has [pjĩː dzĩːnt] < PLĒNUM GĔNTEM (Gorra 1890), and the reduced form [pĩː] appears in the dialects of south-eastern Romagna including those of Ravenna and Meldola discussed above and also in western Romagnolan dialects, e.g. those of Concordia and Albineo (*AIS*, pts. 415, 444). As to the chronology of the appearance of high [ĩ], it is already indicated for south-eastern Romagnolo in the sixteenth-century poem *Pulon Matt* where the form *pin* 'full (m. sg.)' is found (Schürr 1919: 187). It must be assumed that the palatal element [j] in this word and others like it was retained until the rule lowering [ĩ] > [ẽ] had ceased to be productive.

10.7. Nasal Vowel Evolution in Selected Northern Italian Dialects

By way of conclusion, the patterns of vowel nasalization in four dialects of northern Italy may be briefly outlined. These dialects all lie in the major nasalizing area and are of particular interest in that they have all developed unconditioned nasal vowels in at least one type of nasalizing context.

	MILAN (W. Lombardy)	COLI (W. Emilia)	NONANTOLA (E. Emilia)	MELDOLA (SE Romagna)
Context (i)				
*CĪNQUE	tʃĩːŋk	'siŋkɐv	siːŋk	sẽːkw[50]
LĬNGUA	'lɛŋgwa	'liŋgwa	'leŋgwa	'leŋgwɐ

VĔNTUM	vẽːnt	vẽːt	vẽːnt	sẽːt[51]
CĂMPUM	kaːmp[52]	kaːp		kẽːp
FRŎNTEM	frũnt	frɔ̃ːt	frõːnta	reˈkoːt[53]
PLŬMBUM	pjũːmp	pjɔ̃ːp	pjoːmp	pjomp
ŪNDECIM	ˈvyndɛs	ˈvõːdas	ˈundeʃ	ont͡s[54]

Context (ii)

VĪNUM	vĩː	vɛŋ	vẽː	ɐvˈzẽː[55]
PLĒNUM	pjẽː	pɛŋ	pĩː	pĩː[56]
BĔNE	bẽː	bɛŋ	bẽː	vẽː[57]
PĀNEM	pãː	paŋ	pãː	pẽː
BŎNUM	bũː	bɔŋ	bɔ̃ː	bõː[58]
CARBŌNEM	karˈbũː	karˈbɔŋ	karˈbɔ̃ː	pɐˈdrõː
ŪNUM	vỹː	jɔŋ	ũː	õː

Context (iii)

FARĪNA	faˈrina	faˈrẽːna	faˈrẽːna	mɐˈtẽːnɐ[59]
CATĒNA	kaˈdɛna	kaˈdẽːna	kaˈdẽːna	ˈsẽːnɐ[60]
LĀNA	ˈlana	ˈlãːna	ˈlãːna	lunˈtẽːnɐ[61]
BŎNA	ˈbona	ˈbõːna	ˈbõːna	ˈbõːnɐ
CORŌNA	kuˈrɔna			pɐrˈdõːnɐ[62]
LŪNA	ˈlyna	ˈlõːna	ˈlũːna	ˈlõːnɐ

(For Milan, *AIS*, pt. 261 and Nicoli (1983); for Coli, *AIS*, pt. 420; for Nonantola, *AIS*, pt. 436; for Meldola, Schürr (1919) and *AIS*, pt. 478.

Notes

(*a*) Milan

Nasalization has affected stressed vowels much more than unstressed vowels. Hence, the level of vowel nasality in [frũnt] < FRŎNTEM is much higher than in the first syllable of [fũnˈtana] < FONTĀNA.

Phonemically nasal vowels are confined to context (ii) forms. Here, a five-way system has developed maintaining the status quo which arose after the neutralization of mid-vowel contrasts, /e ɛ/ > /e/ and /o ɔ/ > /o/, in medieval times. The non-occurring nasal vowel types **/ɛ̃ ɔ̃ ø̃/ identified by Nicoli (1983: 57) are precisely the expected outcomes of Late Latin /ɛ/ and /ɔ/ (> /ø/ in diphthongizing contexts) if they had not been eliminated by raising caused by nasalization.

When context (ii) forms appear within a phonetic phrase, a pattern comparable with Modern French *liaison* is found. Only pre-noun modifiers appear to be affected. When preceding a vowel-initial word, the final nasal vowel of the modifier is changed to a sequence of oral vowel + [n], hence [bũː] 'good' but [el bunˈɔm] 'the good man'. Elsewhere, the nasal vowel is maintained without a liaison consonant appearing; for example, in coordinate structures there appear forms such as [pãː e ˈvĩː] 'bread and wine' and [aˈvỹː aˈvỹː] 'one by one'.

In context (i), nasalization has been less intense so that only allophonic vowel nasality has resulted. Nicoli (1983: 58) characterizes it as being less apparent than in context (ii) forms but nonetheless more conspicuous than in standard Italian. As the forms cited from the *AIS* show, its presence is not consistently indicated. In context (iii), nasalization has been slight and has left no perceptible nasality in the vowel.

(*b*) Coli

Phonemic nasalization has been confined to context (i), where it has operated both when the consonant following the original conditioning nasal was voiceless and voiced. The reflex of *CĪNQUE presumably represents a form borrowed from some outside source. Context (iii) shows some increase in allophonic nasalization, but there has been restructuring in context (ii) forms suggesting that phonemic vowel nasalization once occurred, as in PĀNEM > [pãː] > [paŋ].

(*c*) Nonantola

As with the dialect of Milan, vowels in context (ii) have undergone phonemic nasalization at some stage after the neutralization of /e ɛ/ and /o ɔ/. In the other context types, there has been significant vowel nasalization; in context (i), it has characteristically operated when the conditioning nasal consonant was followed originally by a voiceless consonant.

(*d*) Meldola

Phonemic nasalization has occurred with vowels in context (ii) with subsequent neutralizations between the nasal vowels in more recent times. The much reduced nasal vowel system tended towards just two types /ẽ/ and /õ/, but a new member /ĩ/ has appeared from earlier [jẽ]. In context (i), phonemic nasalization has taken place when a voiceless consonant followed the conditioning nasal consonant. Parallel neutralizations to those in context (ii) have affected the result nasal vowels. In context (iii), nasalization has been slight.

The very varied contemporary situation in these four dialects may be summarized as follows:

dialect	context (i)	context (ii)	context (iii)
MILAN	(+)	+	−
COLI	+	−	(+)
NONANTOLA	(+)	+	(+)
MELDOLA	+	+	(+)

(where '+' = phonemic nasality, '(+)' = high-level allophonic nasality, and '−' = low-level allophonic nasality)

NOTES

1. For instance, Lurati (1988: 499) detects influence from the standard variety on pronunciation patterns in Milan already from the thirteenth century, 'Almeno dal Duecento il milanese non ha cessato di avvicinarsi al modello fonetico italiano, abbandonando progressivamente tratti locali'.

2. This often quoted statistic has been challenged. Castellani (1982) estimates that the number of Italophones at the time of unification was approximately 10% of the population.

3. One other context for anaphonesis is sometimes cited, namely preceding [-skj-], as in *mischio, fischio, vischio* < MĬSC(U)LO FĬST(U)LO *VĬSC(U)LUM 'I mix, I whistle, mistletoe'. Raising here, however, would seem to be more recent and hence not directly related. The non-raised form *veschio* is used by Petrarch, and *meschiare* and derivatives in *meschi-* still appear widely in later medieval Florentine texts.

4. The original geographical scope of anaphonesis is disputed. Rohlfs (1966: § 49) suggests that Lucca and Pistoia were not systematically affected by anaphonesis, whereas Bertoni (1916: § 78) claims that Lucca, Pistoia, and Pisa only failed to undergo back vowel anaphonesis, /o/ > /u/. Castellani (1980: 73–87) presents a powerful case for the geographical distribution which we have indicated. However, regarding the Lucca region, he notes a discrepancy between the city itself and the surrounding area; early texts from the city consistently show anaphonesis but in the immediate hinterland the change has been more fitful, suggesting that anaphonesis radiated out as an urban influence.

5. Two anomalies with vowel raising stand out: *giunco* 'reed' < IŬNCUM, and *-unque* '-ever' < ŬMQUAM and its congener *dunque* 'therefore' < DUNC + UMQUAM. However, *onque, ovonque*, etc. without raising are found in early Florentine texts and *donque/donqua* appears in sundry texts from anaphonetic areas, though not apparently in Florentine texts (Castellani 1980: nn. 24, 43). The initial palatal of *giunco* may have helped to cause vowel raising.

6. Metaphony is a special type of harmonizing process causing vowels to raise or (for /ɛ ɔ/) to diphthongize. In Italo-Romance and other Romance areas, metaphony typically operates on non-high stressed vowels and is triggered by the presence of a high vowel /i/ or /u/ in the final syllable or following palatal sound (these also being phonetically high). For an overview of Italian metaphony, see Maiden and Parry (1997: 15–25), and for more detailed discussion Rohlfs (1966: §§ 20, 53, 74, 96, 117); Tekavčić (1974: §§ 82–94); Maiden (1991, 1995). For metaphony in Romance, see Leonard (1978). See also 10.3 and 10.5.1 for the interplay of vowel nasalization and metaphony in, respectively, southern and northern Italian dialects.

7. This is suggested by the fact that whereas both the front and back vowels /e o/ are affected by the first, nasal type, the second type operates on the front vowel /e/ only. Hence, *cotogno, cicogna, vergogna* < COTŌNEUM CICŌNIA VERECŬNDIA 'quince, stork, shame', and *moglie*, OIt. *doglio* < MŬLIER DŌLIUM 'wife, vat'. Also, it is not easy to understand how metaphonic conditioning triggered by a following *palatal* consonant could have operated on cases like *lingua, tinca* < LĬNGUA TĬNCA where no palatal consonant is present.

8. One exception is the verb *spegnere* 'to extinguish' for which both /ɛ/ and /e/ are found as the stressed vowel, s.v. *spegnere* in the *DOP*. For Rohlfs (1966: § 49), the irregular outcome is due to the desire to avoid homonymic clash with *spingere/spignere*. Originally probably a loan from the dialects of Arezzo (Rohlfs) or Siena (Meyer-Lübke 1927: 45, and *REW* 3049), the form *spegnere* had its anomalous stressed vowel /e/ (rather than anaphonetic /i/) modified later to /ɛ/ by Florentine speakers, perhaps through hypercharacterization.

9. In regional varieties of the standard language, the incidence of /ɛ/ raising in stressed syllables with a nasal coda is greater. In Rome various lexical items show /e/ against Florentine /ɛ/, *attento, centro, esempio, membro*. In North Italy, standard speakers normally use /e/ in all syllables with a nasal consonant coda. Poggi Salani (1976: 253) reports this for the influential variant of the standard used in Milan, citing as normal such pronunciations as *part*[e]*nza, sorg*[e]*nte, v*[e]*nto*. In this variety, a pattern of near-complementary distribution with stressed mid-front vowels is found: [ɛ] is systematically used in blocked syllables with an oral consonant coda, and [e] is found elsewhere.

10. Pellegrini (1977*a*) provides useful maps; for the individual areas, see *LRL*, iii. 665, 727 and Mancarella (1975: 19).

11. The dialect of Matera builds on the same original seven-way vowel system as the other dialects presented. However, the dialects of southern and central Basilicata have evolved from different base vowel systems in Latin. Even so, the same lack of influence of nasalization on vowel evolution is to be found in these dialects. Thus, in the 'Mittelzone' dialect of Nova Siri, which originally had a Sardinian-style vowel system where Latin long and short vowels simply merged (Ī Ĭ > /i/, etc.; cf. 11.1), we find for the mid vowels /e/ and /o/ that would be most likely to show nasal influence: PĔRDO > [pɛrd] = DĔNTEM > [ðɛnd], SĒRA > [seːra] = CATĒNA > [kaˈteːn], PŎRTA > [pɔrt] = PŎNTEM > [pɔnd], NEPŌTEM > [nəˈpoːt] = FULLŌNEM > [fudˈɖoːn] (Lausberg 1939: §§ 99–100).

12. Camilli gives no indication of the reflex of FRŎNTEM. The dialects immediately surrounding it in the *AIS* (Servigliano is not itself covered) show /o/ as the stressed vowel whereas Ascoli Piceno a little further south and Grottammare to the southeast, points 578 and 569, have the open vowels /ɔ/ and /a/, respectively (*AIS*, i. 99).

13. Even here, since the time of Merlo's 1916 article, there has been considerable influence from the standard language affecting the degree of consistency with which this nasally conditioned variation is used by modern speakers of the dialect (Melillo 1986: 54 n. 10).

14. Falcone (1976: 16) describes this vowel as being articulated with the tongue lying flat in the mouth and with spread lips and lowered velum. Rohlfs, following his earlier rather unclear attempt at a description (1966: § 23), indicates in a later work that the vowel concerned is slightly nasal and the tongue position is located somewhere between that of oral [a] and [œ] (1977: 20).

15. Even within individual regions there can be considerable variation. Some measure of this can be seen, for instance, in Lombardy where: 'un milanese "medio" può incontrare le medesime difficoltà nel capire un bergamasco/bresciano/mantovano che parli il suo dialetto, che nell'intendere, ad esempio, un siciliano o un calabrese

che si esprimano nella loro parlata familiare', cited from E. Banfi et al., *Pedagogia del linguaggio adulto* (Milan, 1970), by Massariello Merzagora (1988: 7). The varied incidence and effect of vowel nasalization contributes to this diversity.

16. This geographical demarcation shows some similarity to the patterns of Celtic settlement in North Italy in the fifth and fourth centuries BC. Neither the Veneto in the north-east nor Liguria and Piedmont in the north-west appear to have been occupied to any significant extent by Celts (Pellegrini 1977a: 19; Devoto and Giacomelli 1972: 2, 10). Their main centre of colonization was the Po valley reaching down to the northern limits of modern-day Tuscany in the west and in the east down to the River Esino, near Ancona in the Marche (cf. AB ANCONA GALLICA ORA INCIPIT 'the region of the Gauls starts from Ancona', Pliny the Elder, *Nat. Hist.*, iii. 112). Whether the Celtic substratum actively fostered the tendency to weaken coda nasals and nasalize vowels is difficult to demonstrate, but even so the Celtic basis of vowel nasalization has had a number of proponents (Meyer-Lübke 1920: 234; Bolelli 1940: 193–7). Certainly, such a tendency was already present in Latin before Roman conquest brought Latin to northern Italy so there is no suggestion of Celtic influence introducing an entirely novel phonetic pattern (cf. 3.2). Nonetheless the possibility remains that Celtic may have reinforced a pre-existing tendency in the language, but this is unconfirmable.

17. A detailed account of contemporary usage in the *français régional* of Aix-en-Provence appears in Taylor (1996: esp. 43–53).

18. Hence, the Venetian forms [gra mjɛl po'der] 'grain, honey, to be able' < GRĀNUM MĚLE *POTĒRE but ['ano 'vae 'karo 'meze] 'year, valley, cart, month' < ĂNNUM VĂLLEM CĂRRUM MĒ(N)SEM etc. without apocope (Zamboni 1977: esp. 26). For western Ligurian, the dialect of Pigna has [kaŋ mɛːʳ koːʳ] 'dog, honey, heart' < CĂNEM MĚLE CŎR-E but ['lime 'anu 'karu a'vale] 'light, year, cart, down' < LŪMEN ĂNNUM CĂRRUM AD-VĂLLEM with no apocope (Merlo 1959).

19. However, this conservative area is skirted by areas where final vowel loss is more far-reaching. Thus, in Bellunese we find [val] < VĂLLEM and [an] < ĂNNUM where apocope clearly operates after /l/ and also after geminates, and southern Veneto dialects near the Po show forms such as [raŋ agr] as against Venetian ['rame 'agro] (Zamboni 1977: 42–3, 1988: 525).

20. The delicacy with which length distinctions have governed vowel nasalization may be seen in the Romagnolo dialect of Imola, with such forms as BŎNA > ['bõːna] 'good (f. sg.)' vs. NŎNNA > ['nɔn(n)a] > ['nɔːna] 'grandmother' (Schürr 1919). These indicate that when vowel nasalization operated it only affected long vowels present in the early medieval period, and that the later vowel lengthening which operated on forms like ['nɔːna] post-dated the period of productivity of vowel nasalization in this dialect.

21. One apparent counterexample (cited by Hajek) is TANTA > ['taːta] 'so much (f. sg.)'. This form doubtless represents an analogical formation based on the masculine ['taːt] where nasalization is regular.

22. Spanish is unusual, however, in that unstressed vowels in word-final syllables are

reported to be as long as or even longer than stressed vowels. In other types of unstressed syllable, vowels are systematically shorter than in stressed syllables.

23. Cf. Hajek (1997: § 9.3), 'Speakers of Northern Italian dialects, as those in other parts of Italy, seem to have been particularly sensitive to phonetically determined vowel length differences before /m/ and /n/'.

24. The case of certain Sardinian dialects stands apart (11.2.2). Here sequences of nasal consonant + fricative have regularly emerged as geminate fricatives, suggesting assimilation rather than weakening of the nasal. In the dialects concerned there is no sign of vowel nasalization having occurred. Less clear is the situation in Spanish (7.4.1.2). In those instances where there has been nasal consonant deletion, it is unclear whether it was accompanied by heightened vowel nasalization.

25. High-mid and high stressed vowels have not undergone lengthening in this dialect and have never nasalized, as in ['pena] 'feather' < PĬNNA.

26. For example, in the dialects of south-east Romagna which abut onto the non-nasalizing area of northern Marche, coda nasals have been preserved in a reduced form: e.g. Cesena [bẽːⁿ tẽːᵐp mõːⁿt] 'well, time, mountain' < BĚNE TĔMPUS MŎNTEM with limited but clearly perceptible vowel nasality (Schürr 1919).

27. More recently, there has been a tendency to restore a conditioning nasal consonant in Antrona dialects, hence variant forms such as [rãːᵐf ʃũːⁿʒa], etc. are found (Nicolet 1929: § 102). The association of vowel nasality with a following fricative has also led to the creation of forms such as ['gãjⁿza ʃa'rẽːʒ/ʃa'rẽːʃ] 'magpie, cherries' < Ital. gazza CERĔSIAE 'cherries', where an unetymological nasal vowel or vowel + nasal consonant has appeared (cf. also Tuttle 1991: 34 n. 27). Such forms may be due to hypercorrection, but an additional factor may well be that they arose through spontaneous nasalization caused by the presence of a high airflow fricative appearing adjacent to the vowel (cf. 1.1.2 and parallel cases from Ibero-Romance (7.4.2) and Florentine 10.2.1).

28. Nasal consonant deletion in the Erto dialect led to the creation of regular morphophonemic alternations between oral vowel + nasal consonant and nasal vowel, e.g. [poŋ] 'apple' vs. [põʃ] (no indication given for vowel length) 'apples' < PŌMUM/-OS, [pont] 'bridge' vs. [põʃ] 'bridges' < PŎNTEM/-ES, [ont] 'beef fat' vs. ['õðe] 'to grease' < ŬNCTUM/ŬNGERE (Gartner 1892). However, more recent descriptions of this dialect point to regular restoration of a conditioning nasal consonant, e.g. [poŋ] 'apple(s)', with an identical form for singular and plural, and [pont] vs. [ponθ] 'bridge' 'bridges' (ASLEF, pt. 38, v. 3441/3442 and i. 189/190, respectively).

29. For Lombardy, the central dialect of Bergamo has [siːk tɛːp] 'five, time' < *CĪNQUE TĔMPUS, but [saŋgw 'pjomp] 'blood, lead' < SĂNGUINEM PLŬMBUM. Here, although vowels have later undergone denasalization (see 10.5.5), it is clear that nasal coda deletion (associated originally with vowel nasalization) occurred only before voiceless consonants as in the first pair of forms.

30. Cf. the dialect of the nearby village of Coli (AIS, pt. 420) where the following forms appear [kãːp sẽːt pjõːp vẽːt] 'field, hundred, lead, to sell' < CĂMPUM CĔNTUM PLŬMBUM VĒNDERE with the same generalized deletion of coda nasals.

31. The sense of volatility here is increased by the conflicting data given for specific

dialects. For the nearby town of Meldola, the *AIS* (pt. 478) reports the forms [fæ̃ᵉ] and [flɔ̃] (< FĀMEM, FLŪMEN) whereas Schürr (1919) cites [femə] and [fjom], respectively. The *AIS* forms date from a 1923 survey, while those of Schürr are based on extensive investigations conducted just before World War I. Both used just one informant, but Schürr's was in fact twenty years younger. The data seem thus to lend some support to the idea of there being a trend amongst successive generations to reverse an uncompleted move to delete final /m/.

32. In this dialect, forms containing back vowels can also show a competing pattern of development with nasal strengthening, [kɔˈrɔnna ˈlənna] < CORŌNA LŪNA. This pattern is also found in neighbouring dialects.

33. The phonemic status of these vowels is supported by the existence of minimal pairs contrasting nasal and oral vowels. Thus, from the dialect of Prali may be cited [ˈȳːõ] 'a (f. sg.)' vs [ˈyːo] 'grape', [ˈsĩːõ] 'dinner' vs [ˈsiːo] 'sickle', [ˈsũːõ] 'it sounds' vs [ˈsuːo] 'his (f. sg.)', [ˈtʃãːso] 'chance' vs [ˈtʃaːso] 'hunt' (Genre 1992). Genre also reports the results of a test he carried out on native speakers which indicate that they are aware that nasal and oral vowels 'are not the same thing' and that, for instance, rhyming them in verse would sound 'cobbled together'.

34. Examples for Novara are SPĪNA > [ˈspĩːa], LŪNA > [ˈlũːa], VĒNA > [ˈvĩːa], and with an unstressed vowel FENĒSTRA > [fĩˈɛʃˠa]. See also Tuttle (1991: 73–6).

35. Malagoli (1910–13: § 29) provides a detailed description of the coda nasal found in the dialect of Novellara (northern Emilia), 'la punta della lingua non tocca i denti superiori, ma s'appoggia alla base degl'inferiori, e l'avvicinamento avviene nel palato molle: l'occlusione non vi è completa e si ha così . . . un suono intermedio fra vocale e consonante', and he adds that accompanying this velar sound is 'un aumento ossia un doppio grado di nasalizzazione della vocale precedente, più spiccata nella campagna che nell'interno del paese'. Elsewhere, the velar coda can be much more energetic; for example, Canepari and Vitali (1995) describe the restored velar in Bolognese as being lengthened and intense, and propose the transcription [ŋː].

36. As we have already seen, the dialect of Bologna offers a clear example. Bolognese is clearly reported to have had unconditioned nasal vowels 'alla francese' in the early nineteenth century by Ferrari (1835), but the urban dialect of today systematically presents sequences of [Vŋ] (Canepari and Vitali 1995).

37. Thus, in a survey of the dialect of Parma conducted in 1938 by Ugo Pellis, the central urban dialect was found to have undergone hardening [ˈloŋnᵉ ˈpjeŋnᵉ] 'moon, full (f. sg.)' < LŪNA PLĒNA, whereas outlying districts had preserved the earlier stage [ˈlojnᵉ ˈpjejnᵉ] (data from Tuttle 1991: 36 n. 32). Parry (1984: ch. 4) reports a complex transitional picture for the dialect of Cairo Montenotte on the Liguria–Piedmont border: hardened and non-hardened forms co-exist in the same community and even in the usage of a single speaker. For instance, one informant used the variants [kamˈpajna] and [kamˈpaɲna] 'bell' < CAMPĀNA during the same conversation.

38. The diachronic variability of the quality of restored nasal codas within a single variety is seen in the dialect of Trieste. Textual evidence suggests that in the first half of the nineteenth century there has been restoration in context (ii) forms and

the restored nasal was [m], e.g. *um bocom de pam* 'a morsel of bread' in a transcription made prior to 1842. But transcriptions from the early twentieth century already indicate that a velar realization is normal, just as in the modern dialect (Doria 1978: 10, 120–1).

39. The preface of the 1745 edition of *Çittara Zeneize* contains the following description of a sound written *ñ* 'si pronunzia in guisa, che alla vocale antecedente lascia attaccato il suono di una *n* vocale Francese, e poi essa suona come *n* Toscana innanzi alla vocale seguente. Così nella voce *peña* si pronunzia come se fosse *pen* colla *n* Francese, e poi *na* Toscana, *pen-na*', cited by Parodi (1902: § 176) who concludes that a pronunciation ['pẽŋna] is indicated.

40. We may note that a good deal of variation is found in the length of the stressed vowel in these forms amongst native Milanese speakers. The two Milanese informants used for the *AIS* (pt. 261) both had a short vowel in [ka'dɛna] but differed with ['lana]/ ['laːna]. Hajek's three informants showed striking variation, one consistently using short vowels, one using long vowels, and the third with standard Italian-style length variation (1997: § 2.2.3.1, n. 49).

41. Hajek (1997) claims that the short vowel in forms like ['lana] arose by analogy with the geographically much more widespread shortening which affected stressed vowels before the nasal /m/, as in FŪMUM > ['fuːmo] > ['fumo] 'smoke'.

42. In a number of dialects, the high-mid vowel /e/ < /ɛ/ yielded by neutralization has regularly lowered to /ɛ/ in blocked syllables, e.g. in Turinese [tɛmp dɛŋt] < TĔMPUS DĔNTEM. But forms such as ['vɛŋde 'tɛŋze] < VĒNDERE TĬNGERE confirm the earlier merger of original /e/ and /ɛ/ in context (i) forms.

43. Metaphony operated very widely in northern Italian dialects and its effect on high-mid vowels was to cause raising. The trigger was the presence of original or analogical final unstressed -Ī. See also n. 6.

44. Forms such as *munte, muntibus* (= CL MONTE, MONTIBUS, inflected forms of MONS 'mountain') do appear in Latin texts composed in northern Italy later in the medieval period (Stotz 1996: 50).

45. Nicoli (1983) clearly describes this vowel as being high-mid in quality, as does Sanga (1988). However, *AIS*, pt. 261 has both [pjẽː] and [pjẽ̞ː] from the informants used and just [bẽː] for the other form (*AIS*, vii. 1335 and v. 920).

46. We may note that specifically context (ii) forms are discussed here. In modern Milanese, only context (ii) forms show nasal vowel phonemes, cf. 10.7.

47. In fact, a three-way distinction is drawn for low vowels between *san* 'healthy (m. sg.)' < SĀNUM, *sann* 'healthy (f. pl.)' < SĀNAE (f. pl.), and *san* 'they know' < SĂPIUNT ('tre suoni affatto diversi', p. 268). The value of the first two is probably [sãː] and [san], but the pronunciation of the final item is less obvious. Cherubini identifies here an 'N strascicata' which is only found in 3rd plural verb endings, *san, stan, cantaran*, where the 'strascico' goes with 'una quasi compagnia di E muta'. The reference to mute E is evidently an allusion to French, and since this final vowel in French triggered lengthening in the preceding stressed vowel in the French of the period, the pronunciation of *san* ('they know') indicated here was perhaps [sãːn]. Such a pronunciation has not survived and the modern pronunciation is [san] (now spelt *sann*), identical with that of the fem. pl. adjectival form *sann*.

48. In this dialect, nasal vowel phonemes in context (i) developed only when the original nasal coda consonant preceded a voiceless consonant. When it preceded a voiced consonant, vowel nasalization was slight with no nasal vowel phonemes resulting and an oral vowel is still found, e.g. [plomp 'undɐs 'lɛŋgwɐ] 'lead, eleven, tongue' < PLŬMBUM ŬNDECIM LĬNGUA. In context (iii) forms, the downgrading of nasality has led to reduced levels of allophonic nasality, as in [fɐ'rinɐ 'lanɐ 'lynɐ] < FARĪNA LĀNA LŪNA.

49. In his description of the Venetian dialect, Lepscky (1963: 62) reports that coda nasals in context (i) forms are usually realized homorganic with the following consonant, suggesting that vowel nasalization and associated nasal consonant weakening have been at best limited.

50. *AIS*, pt. 420 gives [sãɟŋkw].

51. Form derived from SĔNTIT; cf. also [tẽ:p] < TĔMPUS. The entry of *AIS*, pt. 478 indicates a diphthongal form [vãɛ̃t] < VĔNTUM, such diphthongal realizations as against the monophthongs recorded by Schürr appearing widely in the *AIS*.

52. In the adjacent dialect of Vigevano (pt. 271), the form [kã:ᵐp] with a nasal vowel is reported.

53. Form derived from RE-CŎMPUTO 'I recount'.

54. *AIS*, pt. 478 indicates [ont͡ʃ].

55. Form derived from VICĪNUM. As reflexes of this word and VĪNUM, the *AIS* gives diphthongal forms [bʒæ̃ᵉ] and [vã̄ᵉ], respectively.

56. Length is not indicated in the *AIS* for this item, presumably by inadvertent omission.

57. Form derived from VĔNIT, no reflex for BĔNE being provided by Schürr. As with other items, the *AIS* reports a diphthongal form [bæĩ] (cf. above). Adjacent dialects of Santa Lucia and Forlì have the expected outcome [bẽ:] < BĔNE (Schürr 1919).

58. The *AIS* records a low-mid back vowel for this item and also for the reflex of LŪNA. Our transcription follows Schürr (1919).

59. Form derived from MATUTĪNA 'morning'.

60. Form derived from CĒNA 'dinner'.

61. Form derived from LONGITĀNUM 'far'.

62. Form derived from PERDŌNAT '(he) pardons'.

11

Sardinian and Corsican

11.1. Introduction

The islands of Sardinia and Corsica have undergone rather special linguistic evolution. Sardinia fell under Roman control comparatively early, from 238 BC, but after a lengthy period of romanization lasting two centuries which established the use of Latin, the island remained socially and linguistically somewhat isolated. The result has been that a distinctive and often archaic form of Romance has developed. As far as vowel evolution is concerned, the long/short vowel-length contrast in Latin has been lost but without the qualitative adaptations of short vowels which are commonly found elsewhere in Romance. A simple five-vowel system has thus arisen:[1]

$$
\begin{array}{lllll}
\bar{\text{I}} \; \ddot{\text{I}} > & \text{i} & & \text{u} & < \bar{\text{U}} \; \ddot{\text{U}} \\
\bar{\text{E}} \; \ddot{\text{E}} > & \text{e} & & \text{o} & < \bar{\text{O}} \; \ddot{\text{O}} \\
& & \text{a} \; < \bar{\text{A}} \; \ddot{\text{A}} & &
\end{array}
$$

Unstressed vowels have been widely preserved. In particular apocope has not occurred, although significant weakening (but never systematic deletion) of final vowels has taken place in many southern Corsican dialects.[2] An important consequence of this is that nasalizing context type (ii) never developed in either Sardinian or Corsican.

Underlying the dialects of Corsica there is a rather complex vowel pattern. In southern dialects, the same five-way vowel system as that found in Sardinia arose and this is still operative as far north as the area around the town of Lévie, or Livía (Rohlfs 1966: § 3). The speech of the area in and near the town of Bonifacio in the very south of the island stands apart. Here, influence from Genoese due to political and commercial contacts during the Middle Ages has led to a distinct Ligurian-style dialect becoming established (Bertoni 1915–17). In central and northern Corsica, it may well be that the same five-vowel system as that found in southern dialects and in Sardinia was initially used (cf. Schmeck 1952: 61, Nesi 1988: 824). However, the familiar seven-way system /i e ɛ a ɔ o u/ of most types of Italo-Romance and indeed most other forms of Romance has supplanted it.[3] A powerful factor in this has undoubtedly been the influence from Tuscany, and in particular from Pisa which had authority over the island from 1077 to 1284. Although the Genoese exercised control officially from 1284 to 1768, the principal commercial and cultural influences in the north and centre continued to radiate from Tuscany.

In both islands, vowel nasalization has operated in a significant way. In Sardinia, instances of high-level nasalization are of comparatively recent date and are confined to certain dialects only. In Corsica, the action of vowel nasalization is discernible over a wide geographical area but there is some uncertainty as to when it began to operate. Contributing to this uncertainty has been the fact that a basic five-vowel system developed in Sardinia and also in much, if not all, of Corsica originally. Since the rise of such a system resulted in only one type of mid vowel /e/ and /o/ coming into being, the tell-tale merger of mid-vowel contrasts in nasalizing contexts cannot be exploited as an indicator of nasalization.

11.2. Sardinian

Evidence of substantial vowel nasalization appears in a broad band of territory cutting diagonally across the Campidanese dialect area in southern Sardinia (see Map 9). Unconditioned nasal vowels have arisen here, as in ['lũːã 'bĩːũ 'mãːũ] < LŪNA VĪNUM MĂNUM 'moon, wine, hand', the long vowels here reflecting the general rule that stressed vowels are lengthened in free syllables (Contini 1987). Elsewhere to the north and south of this zone, there is little sign of anything but minor allophonic nasalization of vowels. Our discussion will focus on developments in the dialects which have experienced nasalization.

11.2.1. THE NASALIZING CONTEXT

Significant vowel nasalization has taken place in context (iii) forms only. There are no context (ii) forms as apocope has not occurred in any Sardinian dialect, and in context (i) forms vowel nasalization has evidently been slight. Typically vowel nasalization has arisen through the action of regressive assimilation. However, other processes have occasionally provoked vowel nasalization. These special cases are considered in 11.2.3.

11.2.2. EVOLUTION OF NASAL VOWELS

In context (iii), original intervocalic simplex -N- weakened and was finally deleted, and the preceding vowel was fully nasalized. The vowel originally following the nasal consonant has also been affected. After the deletion of the consonant, this vowel became adjacent to the nasalized vowel and was itself nasalized to some degree; for example, LŪNA > ['lū:(n)a] > ['lū:ã] 'moon'.[4]

In the area of Sárrabus in the south-east and also in the central Campidanese dialect of Isili, intervocalic -N- was similarly deleted after having caused vowel nasalization, but a glottal stop subsequently developed separating the vowels which were brought together, as in LŪNA > ['lū:ʔa]. This development is not specific to the nasal consonant /n/ however. It reflects a general tendency in many Sardinian dialects to introduce a glottal stop to prevent hiatus between vowels which became adjacent as a result of the deletion of a consonant. Thus, in dialects of Sárrabus, the regular deletion of intervocalic /l/ has also triggered the appearance of a glottal stop, SŌLEM > ['sɔ:(l)i] > ['sɔ:ʔi] 'sun', and to the north of the nasalizing area, in the region just south of Nuoro, loss of intervocalic /k/ has had the same effect (Wolf 1985).

Nasalization has not resulted in any change in vowel height. High and low vowels remain unmodified, and the height of mid nasal vowels is metaphonically conditioned in the same way as that of mid oral vowels (high-mid quality when the original vowel of the following syllable is high, low-mid quality elsewhere). Thus:

VĪNUM	> ['bī:ū] 'wine'	LŪNA	> ['lū:ã]	'moon'
CĒNA	> ['kẽ:ã] 'supper'	PULL-IŌNEM	> [pil'lõ:ĩ]	'bird'
		SŎNUM	> ['sõ:ũ]	'sound'
CĂNEM	> ['kã:ĩ] 'dog'			

(data from Contini 1987)

Vowel nasalization has not operated in a uniform way in all context (iii) forms however. It has regularly occurred in paroxytonic forms where the original simplex intervocalic -N- followed the stressed vowel, as in LŪNA and MĂNUM. In paroxytons where the -N- followed a secondary stressed vowel, deletion of -N- and associated vowel nasalization were also regular. Thus, the outcome of CAN-ICĔLLUM 'little dog' has been [kãĩ'ɣeɖɖu], via a stage ["kani'ɣeɖɖu] where ["] and ['] mark secondary and primary stress, respectively. However, in forms where -N- followed an unstressed syllable, deletion of the nasal consonant and vowel nasalization are uncommon. A metrically based pattern has tended to operate therefore, in which a preceding strong, stressed syllable triggers -N- deletion and nasalization and a preceding weak syllable does not. Such a pattern can lead to the creation of stress-conditioned [Ṽ]/[Vn] alternations in morphologically related forms, for example:

nasal vowel [Ṽ]	['sõ:ũ]	'sound',	["sõã'ziɖɖu]	'sound it to him'
oral vowel + /n/	[sɔ'naɖɖu]	'sound it',	[sɔ'nai]	'to sound'

We may briefly outline developments when -N- appears in environments other than those already considered.[5]

(*a*) In forms where -N- immediately follows a weak unstressed syllable, nasalization has not usually occurred, as already noted; for instance FENŬCULUM FENĚSTRA > [fe'nuːɣu frɔ'nɛsta] 'fennel, window' in dialects of the Oristano area. However, in a few varieties nasalization has operated here too, as in [frɔ̃'ɛ̃sta] 'window' in the dialects of Milis and Cabras and [fĩ'ʔũːɣu] 'fennel' in the glottalizing dialect of Isili.[6]

(*b*) In proparoxytons, forms like ĂCINA 'grape' where -N- did not immediately follow the primary-stressed syllable but instead was preceded by an intervening weak syllable have not usually undergone nasalization, as in the dialect of Riola: FĒMINA > ['femmina] 'woman'. However, a few dialects have experienced -N- deletion and associated nasalization of the surrounding vowels, although the nasality is reported to be less intense than in primary-stressed syllables, e.g. ĂCINA > ['aːʒĩã] 'grape', FĒMINA > ['femĩã] 'woman' (dialects of Mógoro and Villacidro). Vowel nasality here is less strong and occasionally denasalization has subsequently occurred, ['aːɣia 'femmja] (dialect of Tramatza).[7]

(*c*) In proparoxytons where -N- immediately follows the strong stressed syllable, deletion and associated vowel nasalization may take place, as in the dialects of Mógoro and Villacidro, MĂNICA > ['mãːɣia] and ['mãːĩɣa] 'sheaf of corn', respectively. However, such a development conflicted with a general rule in Sardinian dialects whereby simplex post-stress intervocalic consonants were strengthened and often geminated in proparoxytons.[8] Many dialects evidently operated this rule with -N- also, thereby blocking deletion and associated vowel nasalization, although certain dialects did implement nasalization. Individual dialects typically either underwent nasalization in a parallel way in both environments (*b*) and (*c*), as in Mógoro and Villacidro, or in neither, as in Riola where ['maːniɣa] parallels ['femmina]. However, as a result of cross-dialectal influence, conflicting outcomes can occasionally arise; thus ['sambini] 'blood' < SĂNGUINEM without vowel nasalization but ['mãːĩɣa] 'sheaf of corn' < MĂNICA with nasalization, in the dialect of Baratili.

As regards context (i) forms, it is notable that there has been at most fairly weak allophonic vowel nasalization. (It will be recalled that context (ii) forms do not appear in Sardinian dialects since apocope never took place.) Thus, in nasalizing dialects we find forms such as ['kampu 'bentu 'kɔŋka] < CĂMPUM VĔNTUM CŎNCHA 'field, wind, head' where there is no appreciable vowel nasality present. Possible indications of significant nasalization having occurred in context (i) are to be found in some areas of Sardinia in forms where a nasal coda directly preceded a voiceless fricative, e.g. [i(f)'ferru 'laθθa kus'sɛrβa] < INFERNUM LANCEA (Ital.) conserva 'hell, spear, preserve'. However, although this development has occurred widely in Sardinian dialects, it did not take place in the nasalizing area of Sardinia. The changes [nf ns] > [(f)f ss] appear mainly in Logudorese and northern dialects, and [nθ] > [θθ] is characteristic of central dialects. All three changes form part of a general tendency to assimilate consonant clusters. Thus, in the dialects where [nθ] > [θθ], the cluster [rθ] likewise gives [θθ], and the assimilations [rs] > [ss] and [lf] > [ff] are widely found in northern and central Sardinia. It is questionable therefore whether nasal consonant loss in the dialects concerned was accompanied at any stage by vowel nasalization.

The patterns of vowel nasalization in Campidanese are striking and do not find direct counterparts elsewhere in Romance. The contrast between the development of phonemic nasal vowels in context (iii) forms as against the very slight impact of nasalization in context (i) forms is particularly notable. Other Romance varieties showing -N- deletion and the rise of unconditioned nasal vowels have also experienced high-level vowel nasalization in other context types, cf. Galician Portuguese (8.2.3), Gascon (6.3), and dialects spoken on the Franco-Provençal/Piedmontese frontier (5.4, 10.4.4). The developments in Campidanese are also of a more general significance in that they suggest that vowel nasalization in context (iii) forms can operate independently from nasalization in other context types (see also Ch. 13).

11.2.3. OTHER TYPES OF VOWEL NASALIZATION

Within the nasalizing area of Sardinia two other instances of vowel nasalization present themselves, each of a very special nature. First, there has been progressive nasalization involving /n-/ and especially /m-/ followed by a stressed vowel, as in ['mã:u 'nĩ:u] < MĀIUM NĪDUM in the dialects of Milis and Villacidro (Wagner 1941: § 94). The other case concerns spontaneous nasalization which has occurred in the stressed vowel of the infinitival ending -ARE in a few dialects to give [-ãĩ], e.g. [pi'γãĩ] < PICĀRE 'to take' in the dialect of Milis. The nasalization here, which finds a parallel in certain dialects of southern Italy (10.3), appears to have arisen from the enhancement of the low-level nasality which naturally occurs in low vowels so that it could serve as a word-boundary marker.

11.2.4. CHRONOLOGY AND MOTIVATION OF VOWEL NASALIZATION

Vowel nasalization in southern Sardinian has been directly bound up with weakening and deletion of intervocalic -N-. The latter change appears to be of fairly recent date. In early texts emanating from the area concerned, the nasal is always indicated, even as late as the *Comedia de la Pasión de Nuestro Señor Christo* (containing Sardinian text) of 1688. This would suggest a dating from the end of the seventeenth century and into the eighteenth century. However, the use of graphies with <n> in such late texts may merely reflect a conservative orthographical tradition. If the deletion of -N- is broadly contemporaneous with the parallel weakening of intervocalic -L- (which develops variously to [w], [ʀ], [ø] and in Sárrabus it gives [ʔ] just as -N- does), then it may well go back a little further to the sixteenth and early seventeenth century when the latter change occurred (Contini 1987: i. 136).

The motivation of -N- deletion is not entirely clear. Elsewhere in Romance, cases of deletion of intervocalic -N- can be understood in structural terms as a response to the simplification of geminate -NN-. As geminate -NN- simplifies to -N-, the earlier contrast between -NN-/-N- is replaced by a new contrast -N-/Ø with possible vowel nasalization in the latter case. However, Sardinian dialects have shown no sign whatever of simplifying geminate consonants. Indeed, just as in central and southern dialects of Italy the stock of original geminates has been preserved, as in ['annu] < ĂNNUM 'year', and has actually been significantly increased particularly as a result of assimilation, cf. ['janna 'linna 'sonnu] < IĀNUA LĬGNUM SŎMNUM 'door, wood, sleep'. Perhaps the most plausible rationale for the weakening of simplex -N- is that it represents a later extension of the more general process of lenition which systematically affected simplex obstruents in Sardinian. In the dialects concerned, all simplex sonorants except -M- were affected, particularly when they immediately follow the stressed vowel. Thus, in the dialect of Milis, just as LŪNA > ['lũːã] 'moon', so too QUAERIT FĪLUM > ['kɛːið, 'fiːu] 'he asks, thread'.[9] In contrast, -M- is strengthened in this dialect: LĪMA > ['limma] 'file', FŪMUM > ['fummu] 'smoke'.

11.2.5.   SUBSEQUENT DEVELOPMENTS

In certain dialects, additional developments have taken place further to -N-deletion and vowel nasalization. As we have seen, in some areas there has been denasalization of nasalized vowels, notably in post-primary-stress syllables. Examples are found in the dialects of Cabras and Ruinas, e.g. *CĂNIPA > *CAPINA > ['kaːvũã] > ['kaːvua][10] 'billhook', ĂCINA > ['aːɣĩã] > ['aːɣia] 'grape'. Such denasalizations find parallels in Portuguese dialects (8.3.3, 8.4.3).

An alternative pattern of change appears in dialects lying on the northern border of the nasalizing zone. Here, seemingly in some sort of reaction to the threatened deletion of intervocalic -N- and also of intervocalic -L-, these two sonorants have been strengthened and reinterpreted as geminates. Thus, MĂNUM > ['maːnu] > ['mannu] just as MĒLA > ['mɛːla] > ['mɛlla]

'apple'. The dialects of Fordongianus and Allai in particular show such gemination as a regular phenomenon (Contini 1974, 1987: i. 137). A further remarkable
aspect of the gemination here, which is a fairly recent phenomenon going back
at most three centuries, is that it has also come to operate across word-
boundaries, as in [sa 'nuːra] > [san'nuːra] 'the daughter-in-law'. In fact, the
original weakening of simplex -N- had never affected word-initial N- even
when it lay in intervocalic position within a phrase, so that sequences such as
**[sã'ūːra] (< IPSA NŪRA) evidently never developed (Contini 1987: 457).
Accordingly, we have in forms such as [san'nuːra] a notable extension in the
scope of gemination.

11.3.   Corsican

Significant levels of vowel nasality are found in many if not all Corsican
dialects.[11] However, the degree varies a good deal depending on the nature of
the nasalizing context and also on geographical and social factors. Geographically, the dialects of the northern area of the island in particular have
been claimed by a number of scholars to show high levels of vowel nasality
(Nesi 1988: 804), although sporadic cases of dialects with highly nasal vowels are
reported from central Corsica and as far south as Sartène (see Map 9). Socially,
the use of nasal vowels has acquired a clear symbolic status and become more
widespread amongst younger dialect-speakers in recent times. The presence of
vowel nasality is seen as an emblem of Corsican identity which serves to mark
the linguistic varieties of the island off from those of mainland Italy from which
Corsican ultimately derives (Dalbera-Stefanaggi 1989).

    The task of establishing the nature and extent of vowel nasality in Corsican
has unfortunately been complicated by the conflicting standpoints adopted by
the French and Italian linguists who have addressed the question. From the
time of the earliest systematic investigation, the incomplete *ALF Corse* which
appeared in 1914–15, French linguists have consistently indicated the existence
of nasal vowels. On the other hand, Italian linguists have sought to ignore them
or at least to minimize their importance. The extensive dialect atlas of
Bottiglioni, the *ALEIC* which was published between 1933 and 1942, never at
any stage notes the presence of nasal vowels, while Melillo in his study of
Corsican makes just fleeting reference to such vowels and rather dismissively
attributes them to French influence (1977: esp. 30). The different native
linguistic background of the scholars involved doubtless helps to explain the
divergent interpretations. Also, the historical circumstances surrounding the
passing of Corsica from Italian, or more precisely Genoese, control into French
hands in 1768 and the turbulent aftermath of this are perhaps not without
importance in explaining the difference of perspective.[12]

Tracing the historical background to the already complex modern situation is further complicated by the paucity of old texts in Corsican. Official writings from early on tended to be in Italian, influenced to a greater or lesser extent by Corsican. French only takes over here in the nineteenth century, with the result that the birth certificate of Corsica's most famous son, Napoleon Bonaparte, who was born in 1769, is in Italian. Literary activity in Corsican only gets underway in the nineteenth century.

11.3.1. THE NASALIZING CONTEXT

Only context types (i) and (iii) have been affected by vowel nasalization. Since final unstressed vowels have generally been retained despite isolated instances of apocope, context (ii) forms are rarely encountered.

In context (i), vowel nasalization has occurred with varying degrees of intensity in all varieties of Corsican (Dalbera-Stefanaggi 1991: 80). In context (iii), the rise in vowel nasalization has been accompanied by progressive weakening of the nasal consonant with the result that in certain dialects, e.g. that of Galéria, there has been total deletion of the nasal consonant so that phonemic nasal vowels are created (Dalbera-Stefanaggi 1989). Full deletion of the conditioning nasal consonant in context (i) forms however appears to take place only rarely.

11.3.2. EVOLUTION OF NASAL VOWELS

In context (i) forms there has been significant vowel nasalization. Nasality has usually remained just allophonic, however, although it may be of high intensity in dialects of the northern area. Only isolated cases are reported in which the conditioning nasal consonant has been deleted. For instance the dialect of Corti, which lies in the north-centre of the island, reportedly has the form ['tãːtu] < TĂNTUM 'so (much)' (Dalbera-Stefanaggi 1991: 81).[13]

Various pieces of evidence point to the antiquity of vowel nasalization in context (i). First and foremost, we find that in all northern and central dialects there has been neutralization of contrasts between the mid vowels /e/:/ɛ/ and /o/:/ɔ/ in this context type. The outcome is a low-mid vowel in each case, as in the central dialect of Veru ['dẽnti 'vẽnda 'frɔ̃nti 'rɔ̃mpa] < DĔNTEM VĒNDERE FRŎNTEM RŬMPERE 'tooth, to sell, forehead, to break'. In fact, the sequences **/eNC/ and **/oNC/ with stressed high-mid vowels in context (i) are still impermissible (Dalbera-Stefanaggi 1978: 50). Also implicated in this development was the palatal nasal which was originally long intervocalically; hence, ['lɛ̃ɲu var'gɔ̃ɲa] < LĬGNUM VERECŬNDIA 'wood, shame'.

The appearance of a low-mid vowel [ɛ̃ ɔ̃] in this nasalizing context does not owe itself to any lowering influence caused by nasalization. Rather it is due to the regular 'flip-flop' pattern of evolution which is found in stressed mid vowels in these dialects, such that original high-mid vowels emerge as low-mid and vice versa. Thus, Late Latin /e o/ > /ɛ ɔ/ and Late Latin /ɛ ɔ/ > /e o/, as in ['krɛsta 'ɔlmu] < CRĬSTA ŬLMUM 'peak, elm' vs. ['festa 'porta] < FĔSTA PŎRTA 'celebration, door'. The implication is therefore that in context (i) forms vowel nasalization led to the neutralization of mid-vowel contrasts, leaving just the high-mid vowels [ẽ õ]. Later, like the other allophones of the high-mid phonemes /e o/, they underwent lowering to a low-mid point of articulation.

In the southern dialects, where it will be recalled that the original five-way Sardinian-style vowel system was preserved, the same phonetic outcome [ɛ̃ ɔ̃] is found. In these dialects, the regular pattern of vowel evolution has been for original stressed /e o/ to develop a high-mid allophone [e o] in free syllables and a low-mid allophone [ɛ ɔ] in blocked syllables. The typical forms found ['dɛ̃nti 'vɛ̃nda 'frɔ̃nti] therefore represent regular outcomes, since the stressed vowels are of course blocked here. Though they resemble their counterparts in northern and central dialects, in reality their path of evolution has been quite different, as we have seen. Nowhere does nasalization bring about any change in the tongue position of the high vowels /i u/ and the low vowel /a/.

Occasional pieces of textual information suggest that the presence of substantial levels of nasality in vowels in this context goes back at least several centuries. Thus, in his sixteenth-century *Historia di Corsica*, the Bishop of Aléria, A. P. Filippini, uses a tilde in items such as *lũnga*. As the nasal consonant is also written in, the tilde may indicate the presence of strong vowel nasality. Interestingly, this scribal practice is not adopted to mark possible nasality in the other type of nasalizing context to which we now turn (Nesi 1988: 825).

Stressed vowels in context (iii) forms were nasalized widely throughout Corsica. In northern and central dialects this result was that the /e ɛ/ contrast was neutralized leaving just [ɛ̃]. Thus, for example, in the central dialect of Veru we find the following forms today:[14]

CATĒNA	>	ka'tɛ̃ːna	'chain'
HABĒMUS	>	a'wɛ̃ːmi	'we have'
BĔNE	>	'bɛ̃ːni	'well'
TĔNET	>	'tɛ̃ːni	'he holds'

(Dalbera-Stefanaggi 1978)

However, the situation with the back vowels /o ɔ/ is rather different as the expected neutralization has not systematically occurred. All northern and central dialects show /o/ > [ɔ̃], but the low-mid vowel /ɔ/ emerges in three lexical items as [õ] (in a development paralleling that of oral vowels) or as [ɔ̃]. For instance, the dialect of Veru has:

MELŌNEM	>	mi'lɔ̃:ni	'melon'
NŌMEN	>	'nɔ̃:mi	'name'
SŎNUM	>	'sɔ̃:nu	'sound'
TŎNUM	>	't ɔ̃:nu	'thunder'
but	BŎNUM	>	'bõ:nu	'good'
HŎMO	>	'õ:mu	'man'
DŎMINA	>	'dõ:na	'woman'

In other dialects, similar variation in the outcome of nasalized /ɔ/ is also found; cf. ['bõ:nu õ:mu] beside ['tɔ̃:nu] in the north-eastern dialect of Bastia (Melillo 1977: 38).

In southern dialects, the evolution of the mid vowels /e o/ in context (iii) is no less anomalous. Usually, the oral variants of these vowels in free syllables emerge with a high-mid value [e o], but when they are nasalized in context (iii) forms the outcome is uniformly low-mid [ɛ̃ ɔ̃]. Typical forms are: [ka'tɛ̃:na a'wɛ̃:mu 'bɛ̃:ne kan'dzɔ̃:na 'nɔ̃:mu 'bɔ̃:nu 'ɔ̃mmu] < CATĒNA HABĒMUS BĔNE CANTIŌNEM NŌMEN BŎNUM HŎMO 'chain, we have, well; song, name, good (m. sg.), man'.

The precise details of the evolution of nasalized mid vowels in context (iii) are thus somewhat unclear. As far as the southern dialects are concerned, if we assume that vowel nasalization was implemented later in context (iii) than in context (i), one possible interpretation is that the nasal vowels which gradually arose in the former context type came to be aligned with those already present in context (i). Accordingly, just as the blocked mid vowels of context (i) forms regularly adopted a low-mid point of articulation (see above), so too the new set of nasalized vowels appearing in context (iii) forms came to be pronounced with a low-mid value.

In central and northern dialects, once again we might assume that vowels in context (iii) followed the same pattern of evolution as that seen in context (i). That is, the contrast between mid vowels was at first neutralized as a result of nasalization so that just high-mid nasal vowels emerged and these subsequently gave [ɛ̃ ɔ̃] by regular sound change. The forms ['tɔ̃:nu 'sɔ̃:nu] would therefore represent the regular pattern of evolution, and ['bõ:nu] and ['õ(m)mu] are anomalies requiring some explanation.[15] As yet, no satisfactory account has been provided.[16]

11.3.3. LATER DEVELOPMENTS

The changes considered so far probably took place at a comparatively early stage in the history of Corsican. Subsequently, further developments with nasal vowels and vowel nasalization have also taken place. Two in particular may be noted: (*a*) the split of the mid front vowel [ɛ̃]; and (*b*) the weakening of the simplex nasal -N- in context (iii) forms. The chronology of these changes is uncertain, although the former may be comparatively recent in origin.

11.3.3.1. *Split of the Mid Front Nasalized Vowel*

The contrast between mid front vowels was neutralized in nasalizing contexts to give a low-mid vowel [ɛ̃] as the normal outcome. However, in a large spread of dialects there have been moves towards a split of this vowel. In one area running from the centre of Corsica up to the Balagna region in the north-west, this is realized by the use of different levels of nasality, as in central dialect of Noceta: [u 'vɛ̃ːⁿu] < (ILLU) FĒNUM 'hay' with strong nasality vs. [a 'βɛ̃ːna] < (ILLA) AVĒNA 'oats' with weaker nasality. In north-eastern dialects however, a qualitative distinction has arisen, as between ['fæːnu] 'hay' ['læːnɛ] < LĒNEM 'gentle' vs. ['beːna] 'oats' ['meːnu] < MĬNUS 'less' in the dialect of Loretu di Casinca (Dalbera-Stefanaggi 1991: 486–7). The distribution of one or other variant is not predictable on formal grounds but appears to be mainly lexically determined.

A further aspect is that in north-eastern dialects where a qualitative distinction arose ([e] vs. [æ]), the latter vowel has come into the orbit of a fronted variant of the low vowel /a/ which has developed through lexical diffusion in certain context (i) forms. Thus, in the same dialect of Loretu di Casinca, where we find the variants [ã]:[æ̃] for nasalized /a/, the fronted variant [æ̃] has become identified with the lowered variant of the mid front vowel. The following examples illustrate the arrangement:

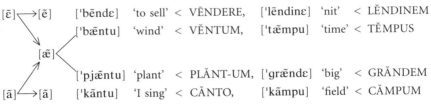

[ɛ̃]⟶[ẽ]   ['bẽndɛ] 'to sell' < VĒNDERE,   ['lẽndinɛ] 'nit' < LĔNDINEM
           ['bæ̃ntu] 'wind' < VĔNTUM,   ['tæ̃mpu] 'time' < TĔMPUS

    [æ̃]

           ['pjæ̃ntu] 'plant' < PLĂNT-UM, ['græ̃ndɛ] 'big' < GRĂNDEM
[ã]⟶[ã]   ['kãntu] 'I sing' < CĂNTO,   ['kãmpu] 'field' < CĂMPUM

It remains to be seen whether this is the first stage in a complete merger between the two nasal vowels in this dialect. The resemblance between this development and what occurred in standard French many centuries ago is notable (cf. 4.3.2.1).

11.3.3.2. *Weakening of Simplex -N- in Context (iii) Forms*

In dialects spoken in a band of territory running from the north-west across to the east-centre of the island, the reflex of simplex intervocalic -N- has undergone major articulatory weakening. This development appears to form part of a more general process of lenition which has restructured the whole consonant system including sonorants in the dialects of the centre and north of Corsica. With sonorants the results have been very varied from dialect to dialect. The broad pattern has been that the original geminates have tended to simplify and the original simplex sonorants have tended either to weaken further, possibly to be deleted, or to undergo articulatory repositioning. As far as the coronal nasals -NN-/-N- are concerned, weakening of -N- in particular has been associated with heightened nasalization of a preceding stressed vowel. Unstressed vowels appear not to have been significantly affected.

Although the weakening of simplex -N- has given rise to vowel nasalization, sometimes of high intensity, it has usually remained allophonic. However, phonemic nasal vowels have developed in a limited number of dialects. This has occurred when the nasal consonant deriving from -N- has been weakened and ultimately deleted altogether, so that the vowel nasality became unconditioned. Some dialects have maintained unconditioned nasal vowels, but others appear to have subsequently restored a brief nasal consonantal interlude [^{n}] after a nasal vowel in a development reminiscent of that found in northern Italian dialects (10.4.4.2). Some measure of the fluctuation in the weakening, deletion, and restoration of conditioning nasal consonants across dialects can be seen in the following:

	Lozzi[17] (north-western)	San Gavino (east-centre)	Galéria (north-west coast)	
VĪNUM	'bīː^{n}u	'vĩː$^{\tilde{}}$	'bĩːu	'wine'
PĀNEM	pãːnɛ	'pãː^{n}ɛ	'pãːɛ	'bread'
PŌNERE	põːnɛ	'põː^{n}a	'põːɛ	'to put, plant'
brún	'brũː^{n}u	'brũː$^{\tilde{}}$	'brũː(u)	'brown'

(Dalbera-Stefanaggi 1991: 249, 449)

In Lozzi, the conditioning nasal remains more in evidence when the following vowel is not [-u]. In forms ending in [-u], complete deletion evidently occurred with full accompanying vowel nasality but some marginal restoration of the conditioning nasal has taken place. San Gavino shows incomplete deletion of the nasal with retention/restoration in the environment where the dialect of Lozzi has more fully preserved a conditioning nasal. In Galéria, generalized deletion has taken place, the phonemic status of nasal vowels being assured by the presence of minimal or near-minimal pairs for all five vowel types:

['fiːu]	'thread'	vs.	[fĩːu]	'fine (m. sg.)'	< FĪLUM,	FĪNUM
['bɛːɛ]	'to see'	vs.	['bɛ̃ːɛ]	'to come'	< VIDĒRE,	VENĪRE with stress shift
['paːɛ]	'canes'	vs.	['pãːɛ]	'bread'	< PĀLAE,	PĀNEM
['kɔːɛ]	'tails'	vs.	['põːɛ]	'to put down'	< CAUDAE,	PŌNERE
['kruːɛ]	'raw (f. pl.)'	vs.	['krũːɛ]	'eyes of a needle'	< CRŪDAE,	CORŌNAE

The appearance of vowel nasality through the weakening and ultimate deletion of the reflex of simplex -N- in Corsican has obvious parallels with developments already seen in Sardinian (11.2.2). A further similarity is that word-initial /n-/ is not affected when it is found phrase-medial in intervocalic position, e.g. [a 'noːra] 'the daughter-in-law' (and not **[ã oːra]) (11.2.5). However, there appears to be no direct link between the Corsican and Sardinian changes.

Nasal vowels with a near-phonemic status have also sometimes arisen by a quite separate path of evolution. In certain areas, there has been simplification of the geminate nasal -NN-, but the simplex nasal -N- has not undergone significant weakening. As a result, the reflexes of these two consonants have merged. However, at some earlier stage vowel nasalization had occurred before simplex -N- so that near-contrasts have been created between nasal and oral vowels before [n]. For example, in the north-western dialect of Lozzi, the following forms appear:

-NN- >	[n]	PĬNNA	>	'pɛna	'feather'
		CĂNNA	>	'kana	'reed'
-N- >	[n]	AVĒNA	>	'bɛ̃ːna	'hand'
		LĀNA	>	'lãːna	'wool'

(Dalbera-Stefanaggi 1991)

Although Dalbera-Stefanaggi's transcription does not make clear whether the stressed vowel in the last two items is long or short, it appears from remarks which she makes elsewhere (e.g. 1978: 23) that the original length of the free stressed vowel has been preserved in forms such as these where a simplex -N- had formerly occurred. If the vowel is long, we would not have nasal vowel phonemes here as the nasality could be seen to be conditioned by length and the following nasal. Some dialects have gone on to generalize the use of nasality to vowels preceding the reflex of -NN-. Thus, in the east-central Corsican dialect of Chisà there regularly appear forms such as ['pɛ̃nna] 'feather' ['kãnna] 'reed' beside ['pɛ̃ːna] 'suffering' ['lãːna] 'wool'. Here, the fact that there is no sign of lenition in the simplex or geminate nasal consonant suggests that vowel nasalization in this dialect may well represent a feature which was originally taken over from dialects further north. The occurrence of vowel nasalization before a geminate [nn] is noteworthy as it contrasts with the situation in northern Italy where such a change is almost unknown despite the widespread incidence of vowel nasalization (cf. 10.4.3.4). Also, the fact that a short vowel has been nasalized without associated lengthening is striking in view of the northern Italian pattern (see 10.4.3.1 and 13.3).

11.3.4. VOWEL NASALIZATION AS A FRENCH-BASED PHENOMENON

Despite the initial and obvious temptation to attribute vowel nasalization in Corsican to French influence (and some linguists have succumbed to it), there is little reason to doubt that this was a native development and that French has at most encouraged the wider use of nasal vowels. Diachronic and synchronic evidence is available to demonstrate the independent origin of vowel nasalization in Corsica.

The diachronic developments which have been outlined indicate that certain cases of vowel nasalization pre-date by a considerable margin the arrival of French influence on the island in the later eighteenth century. Indeed, even the recent change in context (iii) forms whereby intervocalic [n] is deleted with resultant vowel nasalization appears to have little obvious basis in French influence. In the standard French of the later eighteenth century and later, vowels occurring before a nasal consonant were non-nasal so that French can hardly have provided a model for Corsican.

Synchronically, vowel nasalization is reported over a wide geographical area and is especially prominent in rural parts where direct French influence has only been marginal until very recently. Indeed, the most evolved cases of vowel nasalization, where phonemically nasal vowels have arisen through the deletion of intervocalic [n], are to be found in the more isolated varieties. Furthermore, the use of this evolved style of pronunciation appears to be more widespread amongst older speakers whose exposure to French has been slight, a fact which again suggests that it represents a native Corsican phenomenon. It is true that under French influence younger speakers have in recent times extended the use of enhanced (allophonic) vowel nasality for the sociolinguistic purpose of emphasizing their Corsican identity and marking themselves off as different from Italians. However, this tendency is quite separate from the long-running indigenous patterns of vowel nasalization.

NOTES

1. The Sassarese variety used in the north-west area forms the only exception. Here, there has been restructuring as a result of influence from mainland dialects, probably via Corsica, and a seven-vowel system has been established: Ī > /i/, Ĭ > /ɛ/, Ē Ĕ > /e/, Ā Ă > /a/, Ŏ > /o/, Ō Ŭ > /ɔ/, Ū > /u/.

2. According to Dalbera-Stefanaggi (1991: 509–10), the general evolution of final vowels in the different varieties of Corsican 'se caractérise . . . par une diminution sensible du pouvoir distinctif des voyelles dans cette position et se manifeste concrètement, dans un premier temps, par une fermeture des voyelles moyennes, dans un second temps, par une réduction de toute voyelle à une sorte de [ə].' Thereafter, morphological pressures are claimed to have helped to save these vowels from effacement.

3. The seven-vowel system was adopted in two distinct ways. In most dialects, the system which became established shows exactly the same historical basis as that found in Tuscany and elsewhere in northern and central Italy, with Ī > /i/; Ĭ, Ē > /e/; Ĕ > /ɛ/; Ă Ā > /a/; Ŏ > /ɔ/; Ō, Ŭ > /o/; Ū > /u/. However, Dalbera-Stefanaggi (1991: 474–80) has found that in the south-central dialects of Taravu the seven-vowel system that arose has a quite different basis, which seems to have no counterpart anywhere else in Romance: Ī > /i/; Ĭ > /ɛ/; Ē, Ĕ > /e/; Ă Ā > /a/; Ŏ Ō > /o/; Ŭ> /ɔ/; Ū > /u/.

4. Parallel cases of the spreading of vowel nasality are found elsewhere in Romance, as in the Piedmontese dialect of Prali in north-western Italy, cf. ['lỹːõ] < LŪNA 'moon', ['lãːõ] < LĀNA 'wool' (Genre 1992).

5. Data are drawn from Contini (1987), Wagner (1941: 62–4), and the *AIS*. Contini and Boë (1972) provide an acoustic phonetic and phonological description of present-day nasal vowels in Sardinian.

6. Nasalization evidently operated by lexical diffusion in these dialects and some words have never been affected. Thus, CENA-PURA 'Friday', which developed early on into a proparoxyton, is reported to have retained its nasal consonant in all dialects, e.g. Milis [kaˈnaːβara] (Wagner 1941: § 93).

7. In the Sárrabus area, it may be noted that denasalization has not led to the elimination of the glottal stop. Thus, forms such as [ˈaʒiʔa] < ĀCINA appear in several varieties.

8. Cf. PŌNERE > [ˈpɔnnere] 'to place' TENĒRE > [ˈtɛnnere] 'to hold' (with stress shift) in the non-nasalizing dialects of Logudoro.

9. Blasco Ferrer (1984*b*: 204) detects in the weakening of -L- in Campidanese a possible Catalan-based development arising from the lengthy period of Catalan and then Spanish occupation of Sardinia. Weakening of the nasal -N- would thus represent an independent Sardinian generalization of a trend initiated for laterals by Catalan. However, there is no solid evidence for this hypothesis.

10. The etymology of this word is highly uncertain. *REW* 1591 proposes the etymon *CĂNIPA and derives various dialectal forms in Sardinian from it, meaning either 'billhook' or 'cheek'. Wagner (1960–4) is sceptical and offers no etymon.

11. Cf. 'il reste clair que des voyelles nasalisées, apparaissant devant une consonne nasale implosive plus ou moins nettement articulée, figurent sans conteste dans la totalité des parlers corses' (Dalbera-Stefanaggi 1989: 149).

12. For a review of the differing descriptive attitudes to vowel nasality in Corsican, see Dalbera-Stefanaggi (1991: 79–81).

13. We assume that a long stressed vowel appears here. Unfortunately, vowel length is not marked in the transcriptions of Dalbera-Stefanaggi, but elsewhere (1978: 23) it is indicated that stressed vowels are normally phonetically long unless they precede a

strong consonant (these deriving usually from former geminates). Regarding vowel nasalization in the dialect of Corti, it is not clear whether unconditioned nasal vowels have developed systematically in context (i) forms or whether it has only occurred in specific environments or lexical items.

14. Nasality in context (iii) forms has now evidently become very slight in this dialect, perhaps as a result of influence from the dialect of Ajaccio (Dalbera-Stefanaggi 1991: 449, 486). We cite here forms from the Veru dialect in particular as it has been the subject of a detailed study by Dalbera-Stefanaggi (1978). Other present-day dialects show higher and sometimes even intense degrees of conditioned nasality, as in the central dialect of Venacu [ka'dɛ̃:^{n}a, 'tɛ̃:^{n}ɛ] 'chain, he holds' (Dalbera-Stefanaggi 1991: 486). However, as Dalbera-Stefanaggi notes elsewhere (1991: 544, n. 445), there are strong grounds for believing that nasalization in context (iii) forms was once known throughout the island, even if its presence today is much less apparent.

15. Exceptionally, a low-mid vowel is found in the former item but only when it is proclitic in set phrases, e.g. [bɔ̃na'zɛːra] 'good evening' (Dalbera-Stefanaggi 1991: 491).

16. Dalbera-Stefanaggi (1991: 541 n. 439) advances a rather unconvincing proposal whereby the present-day form developed from a phono-syntactically conditioned alternant which subsequently underwent reinterpretation.

17. The data for Lozzi appearing in Dalbera-Stefanaggi (1989: 151) indicate the systematic presence of a weak velar nasal consonant after every nasal vowel. We assume that the fuller discussion in her 1991 work represents a revised and more accurate description.

12

Romanian (Balkan Romance)

12.1. Introduction

In the Balkans, two forms of Romance survived up to modern times. These are Romanian and Dalmatian. Romanian is spoken by about 25 million people and is conventionally divided up into four main sub-groups: (*a*) *Daco-romanian* (DR), which is spoken in the state of Romania by over 20 million people and divided regionally into a number of sub-types, notably Transylvanian (north and west), Moldavian (north-east and east), and Wallachian (south), the standard language being a cultivated variety of Wallachian based on the usage of Bucharest; (*b*) *Istro-romanian* (IR) which is closely linked to western types of DR and only split off at some stage before the end of the thirteenth century as a result of the westward migration of its speakers to what used to be north-western Yugoslavia; (*c*) *Aromanian* (AR) which is spoken by up to half a million people living mainly in migrant pastoral communities in northern Greece, Bulgaria, Albania, and former Yugoslavia; (*d*) *Megleno-romanian* (MR) which is a variant of AR used by a small community living north of the Gulf of Salonica.

The other form of Romance is, or more precisely was, Dalmatian. It derived from the Latin spoken in Illyricum, approximately former Yugoslavia. But after the invasions and settlement of the Balkans by the Slavs, its use steadily became confined to the Adriatic seaboard where the rise of the Venetian Republic further undermined it. The last known speaker, who lived on the island of Krk (formerly Veglia), died in 1898. Before his death however, his mother tongue (also known as Vegliote) was analysed and described in some detail by the Italian linguist Bartoli (1906).

12.1.1.   HISTORICAL BACKGROUND

The imposition of Roman authority in the Balkans extended over a number of centuries. Illyricum in the western area became a Roman province already in 167 BC, but it was not until the campaigns of AD 101–2 and 105 under Trajan that the province of Dacia was established north of the Danube in the territory which was later to emerge as Romania. A century and a half later, in 271, the emperor Aurelian ordered the withdrawal of Roman troops from Dacia to south of the River Danube. The subsequent fate of the Latin language in Dacia has aroused much controversy amongst scholars. Did it continue to be used in uninterrupted fashion by a community of speakers north of the Danube through the following centuries to give the Romanian language of today, or did the use of Latin gradually die out in this area only for it to be reintroduced by speakers migrating up from south of the Danube during the Middle Ages? It is not possible to prove either of these views, and in fact a combination of both seems attractive: a doubtless fragmented speech-community using an evolving form of Latin continued to exist north of the Danube after the Slavic conquest and occupation of the area, but during the medieval period this was reinforced by Latin-Romance speakers migrating up from south of the Danube.

It is likely that as a result of its closer proximity to Italy and the longer period it enjoyed as a Roman province, Illyricum was more intensely romanized than Dacia. There was some urbanization in Dacia which helped to diffuse Latin, but no major cultural centres developed and there is no evidence of schools like those in Gaul and Spain. The division between western and eastern areas of the Balkans was reinforced under the emperor Gratian (375–83) who brought Illyricum under the ecclesiastical and administrative jurisdiction of Italy, whereas the areas in the east of the Balkans were assigned to the Eastern Empire (Niculescu 1981: 9).

The irruption of the Slavs en masse into the Balkans was a major factor in shaping the linguistic history of the area. The first significant incursions are traditionally dated to 602 when internal divisions in Byzantium left the Danube exposed. Thereafter, the Slavs began on the systematic conquest and settlement of Thrace and Illyricum, cutting Dacia off from contact with other Romance areas. A further influx of invaders came with the Bulgars, an Asiatic people, who were slavicized already by the tenth century. They took over control of Dacia by the beginning of the ninth century and a prolonged process of Romance and Slavonic interpenetration began.

Looking more specifically at the area that was to become Romania, we find that a variety of later political and social influences have left their mark but none had an effect as momentous as that of the Slavs. In the tenth century, the Magyars conquered and settled Transylvania in the north-west, but elsewhere they exercised little or no control. The presence of numerous loanwords in DR but not in IR and AR reflects the limited geographical extent of their authority. Then, from the fourteenth century the influence of the Turks began to be felt. In the following century, two of the three major principalities north of the Danube, Wallachia and Moldavia, had to accept Turkish rule, although the third, Transylvania, was able to remain relatively independent. The Turks continued to control the destiny of Romania until recent times. With the decline of Turkish power, the principalities of Wallachia and Moldavia were finally able to unite into an independent state in 1878 and Transylvania joined them in 1918 to form modern Romania.

The linguistic backcloth to these developments is complex and frequently uncertain. The latest surviving texts from the Balkan area written in Latin date from the sixth century (Mihăescu 1978) and it is not until the early sixteenth century that we have the first running text in Romanian. Written texts are found in the intervening period but these are composed in Slavonic, which was only to disappear from official and ecclesiastical use during the seventeenth century and early eighteenth century.[1] The earliest known grammar of Romanian is the *Gramatică rumânească* (Romanian Grammar) of 1757 by Dimitrie Eustatievici, which survives in manuscript form only. There is therefore a span of roughly one thousand years when our direct knowledge of early Romanian is effectively nil. As regards the other varieties of Romanian, AR first appears documented in the eighteenth century, and direct knowledge of IR and MR dates only from the nineteenth century.

In the sixteenth century, the earliest written Romanian texts show clear signs of dialectal variation. However, by the end of the century the usage of the southern principality of Wallachia was already gaining prestige. The influence of the important printing press in Braşov founded *c*.1560 by the Deacon Coresi was considerable in this connection; the many religious works which he published followed Wallachian speech habits. Subsequently, the identification of Wallachian as the most prestigious variety of DR has been confirmed and the norm today is based on the educated usage of the capital of Wallachia and also of the state of Romania, Bucharest.

12.1.1.1. *Periodization*

The complex historical circumstances which have been outlined pose some practical difficulties for our review of vowel nasalization. In particular, there is the question of the chronological framework that should be used. Given the lack of documentary evidence over much of the history of Romanian, it seems wise to operate with a fairly simple framework containing just two broad chronological divisions.[2] The first (Period I) covers the period from the introduction of Latin into Dacia, the second century AD, up to the time when the Romance-speaking peoples of the lower Danube area were beginning to develop widespread bilingualism with their new masters, the Slavs. This we may place in the ninth–tenth centuries.

The second period (Period II) runs from the ninth–tenth centuries to the present day. During this span of time the relative unity of the Romance-speaking community of the lower Danube is progressively broken up as a result of changing social and political circumstances, leading to the establishment of the four sub-groups of Romanian found today.

12.1.2. VOWEL NASALIZATION IN BALKAN ROMANCE: GENERAL
COMMENTS

Vowel nasalization has played a very different role in the two types of Balkan
Romance. In Dalmatian, a seven-vowel system arose in the early stages of the
language, identical to that which developed in central and northern Italy and in
Gallo-Romance and Ibero-Romance, namely /i e ɛ a ɔ o u/. There is no
evidence at all that nasality exercised an influence on its subsequent evolution:
vowels develop in an identical way irrespective of whether they occur in a
potentially nasalizing context or not. The evolution of forms containing the
low-mid stressed vowels /ɛ ɔ/ may be cited by way of illustration, for it is
usually the case that if significant vowel nasalization does take place, then it is
these vowels in particular which are the ones most likely to indicate it by
following distinct patterns of evolution from those found in oral contexts.
Such is certainly the case for example in Romanian and French, but not in
Dalmatian where the following is found:

/ɛ/	BĔNE	>	'bine	/ɔ/	BŎNUM	>	bun
	DĔCEM	>	dik		LŎCUM	>	luk
	DĔNTEM	>	djant		LŎNGA	>	'lwaŋga
	FĔSTA	>	'fjasta		CŎRPUS	>	kwarp

(Data from Hadlich 1965)

The data suggest that even if allophonically nasal vowels may have developed in
certain contexts, the nasality remained fairly low-level. Such vowels continued
to be readily associated with their oral counterparts so that they evolved in a
uniform way. Vowel nasalization has therefore played no significant role in
Dalmatian and we take no further account of this variety of Romance.

Turning to Romanian, we find another situation altogether. Here, there is
clear evidence from all modern varieties of the language that nasality has played
a major role in shaping vowel change. This emerges from such data as the
following, drawn from DR:

Latin vowel	nasalized				non-nasalized			
Ĭ	SĬNUM	>	sîn	'bosom'	SĬTEM	>	sete	'thirst'
Ē	CĒNA	>	cină	'supper'	CĒRA	>	ceară	'wax'
Ĕ	BĔNE	>	bine	'well'	DĔCEM	>	zece	'ten'
A	CĂNEM	>	cîine	'dog'	CĀSEUM	>	caş	'cheese'
Ŏ	BŎNUM	>	bun	'good'	LŎCUM	>	loc	'place'
Ō	PŌNIT	>	pune	'he puts'	TŌTUM	>	tot	'all'

The stressed vowels of these examples have developed in quite distinct ways
depending on whether or not they were nasalized by a following nasal

consonant. Broadly, nasalized vowels have developed a higher point of articulation than their oral counterparts. Indeed, in almost all modern varieties of Romanian only the high vowels /i ɨ u/ are now found as the reflexes of originally nasalized vowels. The historical circumstances of vowel nasalization which created this pattern in Romanian are highly complex however and will be explored from section 12.2 onward.

12.1.3. VOWEL NASALITY IN MODERN ROMANIAN

Relatively little attention has been paid to the nature and incidence of vowel nasality in Romanian. This is doubtless because nasal vowels are not phonemic in any modern variety of Romanian.[3]

However, the presence of sometimes high levels of allophonic vowel nasality has been widely recognized. In IR, all vowels preceding a tautosyllabic nasal, especially [n] and less noticeably [m] and [ŋ], are reported to show high-level nasality (Kovačec 1971: 34). For standard DR, the classic study by Petrovici (1930) offers detailed information based on instrumental and perceptual data. This revealed some variation in the intensity of vowel nasality depending on the precise context of the vowel. Greater nasality appears in vowels preceding tautosyllabic nasal consonants or lying between nasal consonants. As to the conditioning tautosyllabic nasal consonant which follows a nasal vowel, its articulation is weakened although some trace of it usually remains. However, it typically takes on the place and manner of articulation of the consonant which it precedes and where this consonant is a continuant, especially one of the fricatives /s z ʃ ʒ/, the nasal consonant may disappear altogether, as in *pensulă* 'brush'.

Yet, although surface unconditioned nasal vowels can exist in certain special contexts, Romanian speakers are evidently accustomed to realize and perceive them as sequences of (oral) vowel + nasal consonant. Thus, on the articulatory side it seems that in principle 'une bouche roumaine est incapable de prononcer une voyelle purement nasale sans la faire suivre d'une consonne nasale quelconque' (Petrovici 1930: 67). With regard to the perception of nasal vowels, Lombard (1935: 133–4) found that Romanian speakers are generally unaware of the existence of nasality in vowels even though it may be of high level and the conditioning nasal consonant may be scarcely present.

12.2. Early Developments: Period I (up to the Tenth Century)

Whereas the vowel systems of most varieties of Romance have developed from a seven-way system /i e ɛ a ɔ o u/ which arose in late Imperial times, a different base underlies the vowel systems of all types of Romanian. This was an

asymmetrical system of six vowel-types which had evolved from the Latin of the
Classical period in the following way:

Classical Latin   Ī   Ĭ Ē   Ĕ   Ā Ă   Ŏ Ō   Ŭ Ū   AU

Late Imperial Latin of the Balkans i   e   ɛ   a   o   u   au

The full six-way system, plus one diphthong, was probably found in stressed
syllables only. Unlike in central *Romania* (4.2.1, 9.3.1, 10.4.1), there is no evidence
that a systematic length distinction developed in stressed vowels, conditioned by
syllabic structure. In unstressed syllables, it seems likely that by the end of the
Empire certain contrasts were neutralized. The mid-vowels /e/ and /ɛ/ in particular
never seem to have been systematically distinguished in any Romance variety when
they were unstressed, so the loss of this contrast in the Balkans too is probable. Also,
the contrast between the back vowels /o/ and /u/ was neutralized as /u/ at an early
stage, especially in final unstressed syllables, although in non-final unstressed
syllables analogical factors occasionally intervened to preserve /o/. In this way,
we can envisage a basically four-way unstressed vowel system becoming increasingly generalized in late Balkan Latin, with the form:

$$
\begin{array}{ccc}
i & & u \\
e & & (o) \\
& a &
\end{array}
$$

12.2.1. CHRONOLOGY OF VOWEL NASALIZATION

Vowel nasalization appears to have begun operating early on in the history of
Balkan-Romance. Whether it had been brought as an incipient feature with the
colonists who came to Dacia after its conquest under Trajan in the campaigns of
AD 101–2 and 105–6[4] or it subsequently arose as a specifically local feature is
impossible to establish. At all events three pieces of evidence, each involving the
characteristic raising of vowel height, suggest that high levels of nasality in
vowels may have been found even at the end of the Imperial period.

(*a*) All varieties of Romanian show very similar patterns of raising with
vowels preceding nasal consonants (for details of nasalizing contexts, see
12.2.3 below). Since it can be shown on independent grounds[5] that links
between the major varieties of Romanian were more or less broken from about
the eleventh century onwards, the common phenomenon of vowel raising
through nasalization presumably got underway in the period when the
Balkan-Romance speech community hung together. The processes of vowel
nasalization and consequent raising would thus at least date to before the
eleventh century.

(*b*) Inscriptional and textual evidence from Imperial times points to a tendency amongst some speakers of the Balkans to raise vowels which are followed by nasal consonants. The following forms from the Balkan area may be cited: ACI(NTE) [= AGĔNTE] *CIL*, iii. 10637, SINECA [= SĔNECA] *CIL*, iii. 10434, CINER [= GĔNER] *CIL*, iii. 1595, VINTUM [= VĔNTUM] Iordanes *Rom.* 252 (Mihăescu 1978: 172).

In all these cases, an original stressed Ĕ has been graphied as <I>. Now, the use of the graphy <I> for words containing original long Ē is understandable given that Ĭ and Ē regularly merged as /e/ so that some confusion between <I> and <E> graphies in words with /e/ is to be expected. However, original Ĕ normally remained a low-mid front vowel at this stage. So the use of the graphy <I> in forms such as VINTUM implies that the stressed vowel here was articulated, by some speakers at least, with a high-mid value [e] and the likely explanation for this is that nasalization had operated causing raising.

Similarly, there are cases of apparent raising of the mid back vowel /o/. Examples from inscriptions include: CUNTRA [= CŎNTRA] Dalmatia, FRUN(TE) [= FRŎNTE] *CIL*, iii. 9722, PUNERE [= PŌNERE] *CIL*, iii. 9585, NUN [= NŌN] *CIL*, iii. 8277 (Mihăescu 1978: 178). However, parallel graphies with <U> for expected <O> are also found in non-nasal contexts, so that the examples cited are less conclusive of a tendency for vowel raising due to nasalization. Evidence of a different type comes in the writings of the grammarian Priscian (flor. early sixth century) who, having cited the variant forms ACHERUNTE, FRUNDES, FUNTES, comments that they are rejected by younger speakers as 'rustic' pronunciations (K., ii. 27). Priscian was writing in Byzantium, so that the raising before nasals indicated by him may well have been a feature of the regional pronunciation of the eastern part of the Latin-speaking world, but not necessarily exclusively here of course (see 3.2.1).

Given that known Latin inscriptions from the Balkans do not date from later than the fourth century and that the latest textual references are from the sixth century (cf. Mihăescu 1978; Arvinte 1980: 20), vowel nasalization appears already to be underway in late Imperial times in Balkan Latin.

(*c*) Finally, some internal evidence is provided by patterns of sound change in certain words in Romanian. The key case concerns the interplay of vowel nasalization and diphthongization in words containing stressed /ɛ/ < Ĕ. This vowel regularly diphthongizes in late Balkan Latin to give [je], as in MĔLE > (DR) *miere* 'honey', PĔCTUS > (DR) *piept* 'chest'. However, in forms where /ɛ/ preceded a tautosyllabic nasal consonant, diphthongization has not occurred. For example:

pre-nasal			*elsewhere*			
TĔMPUS	>	(DR) *timp* 'time'	ANNO TĔRTIO	>	(DR) *anţărţ* 'two years ago'
DĔNTEM	>	(DR) *dinte* 'tooth'	DĔXTRAE	>	(DR) *zestre* 'dowry'

The items in the second column have undergone regular diphthongization, and subsequently the palatal on-glide of the resulting diphthong has palatalized the preceding dental plosive, /t/ > /t͡s/ (spelt 'ț' in the standard orthography) and /d/ > /d͡z/ > /z/. The absence of such palatalization in the items of the first column suggests that no diphthongization of /ɛ/ occurred with them, and the obvious explanation for this is that /ɛ/ was raised to /e/ under the effect of nasalization before diphthongization applied.

Now the date when /ɛ/ diphthongization began to operate is uncertain, though there is no doubt that it represents a fairly early development in Romance. On the basis of various factors it has been dated in Balkan-Romance to the fifth–sixth centuries, and it is certainly unlikely to be much later than this (Sampson 1985). Given then that raising of /ɛ/ to /e/ in forms like TĔMPUS pre-dated the diphthongization of /ɛ/, the implication is that levels of vowel nasality capable of causing changes in perceived vowel height were already found in late Balkan Latin.

12.2.2. THE NASALIZING CONTEXT

Vowel nasalization arose in Romanian, as in most other varieties of Romance, typically as a result of the effect of regressive assimilation from some nasal consonant. However, the precise circumstances under which nasalization occurred are fairly complex and show interesting differences from the patterns seen elsewhere in Romance.

First, it may be noted that nasalizing context type (ii) is not relevant for Romanian. This is because the action of apocope has been very limited in the overall history of all varieties of Romanian. Of the four vowel types found in final unstressed syllables in late Balkan Latin [-i -e -a -u], the non-high types [-e -a] have shown no tendency to disappear at any stage. The two other types [-i -u] remained until quite recent times, albeit progressively weakened in many areas. Today, most varieties of DR (including the standard language) still have a final non-syllabic off-glide [ⁱ] for the former. Word-final [-u] has been lost in all save a few special environments (for example when immediately following the stressed vowel as in *rîu* 'river', *ou* 'egg', *rău* 'bad'), but it is a relatively recent change which was probably still in progress during the sixteenth century.[6]

However, the two other types of potentially nasalizing context are well represented, context (i) as in forms such as QUĂNDO and context (iii) as in words like LŪNA. Vowels in both types of nasalizing context began to undergo high levels of nasalization at an early stage. However, nasalization did not systematically affect all vowels in these contexts. Instead, rather delicate constraints arose determining the precise circumstances under which vowels were nasalized.

In context (i) forms, nasalization occurred only when the consonant following the conditioning coda nasal was oral, e.g. in the stressed vowels of Balkan Latin ['dɛnte 'kampu 'loŋgu] < DĔNTEM CĂMPUM LŎNGUM. The presence of nasality is revealed by the tell-tale raising which gives modern DR *dinte, cîmp, lung* ['dinte kɨmp luŋ] 'tooth, field, long'. If the following consonant was nasal, then vowel nasalization did not take place, as in ['annu 'leŋnu 'somnu] < ĂNNUM LĬGNUM SŎMNUM where no subsequent raising appears in the modern DR forms *an, lemn, somn* [an lemn somn] 'year, wood, sleep'.

Romanian linguists have generally sought to account for the failure of nasal + nasal clusters (including geminate nasals) to trigger vowel nasalization by appealing to syllabic considerations. The assumption has been that if vowel nasalization has not occurred, the reason must be that, at the critical period for nasalization, the vowel concerned was not followed by a coda nasal consonant. Thus, whilst DĔNTEM was syllabified as ['dɛn-te] and hence [ɛ] was nasalized, SŎMNUM was re-syllabified as ['so-mnu] and ĂNNUM developed a 'tense' simplex [ñ] to give ['a-ñu] so that in neither case was there a nasal coda and therefore nasalization did not operate (cf. Sala 1976: 81–3, 98; Rosetti 1978: 251; Avram 1990: 20–4). The rather ad hoc nature of this account is clear, however, particularly with the proposed syllabification of forms like ['so-mnu].

A somewhat more plausible explanation is available here if we assume that it was the strength of the nasal coda consonant which prevented vowel nasalization from operating. As far as nasal geminates are concerned, these are typically strong consonants and hence unlikely to promote vowel nasalization. More importantly, if they were simplified very early in Balkan Romance to give tense simplex consonants (as seems possible), then the resultant forms like ['a-ñu] < ĂNNUM with regular resyllabification would no longer fall under the scope of context (i). As regards the nasal clusters, the phonological distinctiveness of the coda nasal seems to have been of key significance. In Latin clusters of nasal consonant + oral consonant (which did cause vowel nasalization), it will be recalled that the nasal was always realized homorganic with the following consonant, as in [mp mb] [nt nd] [ŋk ŋg]. We have therefore a nasal archiphoneme, the only distinctive feature of which is [+ nasal]. This means that weakening of the nasal with vowel nasalization could occur without communicational loss, since just the presence of nasality was needed to ensure the word was communicated. Thus, /'kampu/ could be realized as ['kã^{m}pu] and even ['kãpu] but still be readily interpretable as /'kampu/.[7] However, in clusters of nasal consonant + *nasal* consonant, the place of articulation of the first nasal was not predictable from that of the following segment. In fact, contrasts could be found, as in AMNI ['amni:] 'river (dat. sg.)' vs. ANNI ['anni:] 'years (nom. pl.)' vs. AGNI ['aŋni:] 'lambs (nom. pl.)', and such contrasts continued to be possible in the Balkan area throughout the Imperial period and beyond.

The maintenance of contrasts between the coda nasals [m n ŋ] was doubtless important in preventing the weakening of these consonants and the associated nasalization of the vowel which preceded.

As regards context (iii) forms, these too have brought about vowel nasalization in certain circumstances only. In early Balkan Romance, three types of nasal consonant could appear intervocalically: /m n ɲ/. Of these, the first two already appeared in the Classical period, but the palatal /ɲ/ only developed during later Imperial times or perhaps later. Taking /m/ and /n/ first, the characteristic sign of vowel nasalization, raising of tongue height, presents itself regularly in stressed vowels followed by -N- but not by -M-. Examples are:

	Latin		Early Balkan Romance		DR		
	PLĒNUM	>	'plēnu	>	plin	[plin]	'full (m. sg.)'
	VĚNIT	>	'vjēne	>	vine	['vine]	'he comes'
	LĀNA	>	'lāna	>	lînă	['linə]	'moon'
	BŎNUM	>	'bɔ̃nu	>	bun	[bun]	'good (m. sg.)'
but							
	TĬMET	>	'teme	>	teme	['teme]	'he fears'
	GĚMIT	>	'ǵeme	>	geme	['d͡ʒeme]	'he groans'
	SQUĀMA	>	'sk(w)ama	>	scamă	['skamə]	'lint'
	PŌMUM	>	'pōmu	>	pom	[pom]	'tree'

The differing treatment here in respect of vowel nasalization is bound up with the general development of intervocalic sonorants. The widespread Romance tendency to simplify geminates, which was especially rapid and intense in Balkan-Romance, resulted in notable restructuring of sonorants in intervocalic position in the early medieval period. Geminates regularly simplified (-LL- > [l] etc.), while simplex sonorants preserved their distinctiveness by reducing to become brief, flap articulations. The pattern which emerged with simplex sonorants may be represented as follows:

		example					
-L-	⟍		QUĀLEM	>	['k(w)are]	>	care	'who, which'
	⟩ -ɾ-						
-R-	⟋		MĀRE	>	['mare]	>	mare	'sea'
-N-	> -r̃-		CĂNEM	>	['kãr̃e]	>	cîine	'dog'

(where [ɾ] represents an oral alveolar flap and [r̃] its nasal counterpart)

Intervocalic -M-, however, did not remain distinct from its corresponding geminate -MM- but evidently merged with it at an early stage as [m]. The lack of weakening in simplex -M-, which led to its ready coalescence with the simplifying geminate -MM-, may be attributed to the greater inherent duration and consequent strength which generally characterizes the articulation of a bilabial nasal as compared with the coronal type (cf. Italo-Romance 10.4.41, and Rohlfs 1966: § 222).[8]

The nasal flap [r̃] < -N- and the oral flap [r] contrasted with each other (cf. the examples ['kãr̃e] vs. ['kare] above), and both consonant types evidently had very brief articulations. The extension of the distinctive nasality of [r̃] to the preceding vowel segment to ensure its ready perception and identification is therefore understandable. (The difference between the pronunciation of the third and fourth segments of *twenty* and *sweaty* in many varieties of American English, as [-ẽr̃-] vs. [-er-], respectively, may well replicate the situation in Balkan-Romance.) In this way, the reflex of CĂNEM probably came to be realized as ['kãr̃e] with an increasingly nasalized vowel from the time when the reduction of simplex -N- occurred.

12.2.2.1. *The Palatal Nasal*

The palatal nasal /ɲ/ developed in the Balkans from the sequence [nj], for instance in ARĀNEA, and was typically found intervocalically.[9] In Romance, it was generally realized geminate in intervocalic position, and indeed in those varieties which have preserved geminate consonants (notably central and southern Italo-Romance including standard Italian) the palatal nasal is still pronounced geminate.

Now, if the palatal nasal was geminate in early Balkan-Romance, we would expect it to function like other nasal geminates and not cause vowel nasalization. However, there is clear evidence that vowels preceding the palatal nasal could be nasalized. Thus, the forms ARĀNEA > (DR) *rîie* ['rɨje] 'itch, scab' and CALCĀNEUM > (DR) *călcîi* 'heel' show the characteristic raising of /a/ to /ɨ/ seen in *cîmp* 'field' *lînă* 'wool' < CĀMPUM LĀNA, and comparable raising is found with mid vowels, VĔNIO > (DR) *viu* ['viju] 'I come', *PŌN(I)O > (DR) *pui* 'I put', COTŌNEUM > (DR) *gutui* 'quince'.[10] To account for the presence of vowel nasalization here, we must assume that at the period in early Balkan-Romance when nasalization began to operate, the palatal nasal /ɲ/ had not yet developed. Instead, the sequence [nj] (or perhaps more precisely [ɲj]) which was to develop into the palatal nasal still retained its sequential structure and was consequently syllabified as [n-j] so that it fell under the scope of nasalizing context (i), cf. Sampson (1995). The same process of vowel nasalization therefore occurred in [a'ran-ja] and in ['kam-pu].

12.2.2.2. *Further Considerations on Nasalizing Contexts*

Two final points remain to be considered on nasalizing contexts. The first concerns a further, rather special nasalizing context which was identified by Avram (1969). When followed by a nasal consonant or nasal sequence which would not otherwise have triggered nasalization (e.g. simplex intervocalic -M- or a nasal geminate), vowels were nasalized if in addition there was a nasal consonant preceding. Examples:

NŌMEN   > *nume*   'name',
NŎNNUM   > *nun*   'man who gives away the bride'
NĒMINEM   > *nimeni* 'nobody'

Here, vowel nasalization has evidently come about as a result of the cumulative influence of the surrounding nasal consonants.[11]

The other point concerns the significance of *stress* in determining whether a given vowel undergoes nasalization. Not all the nasalizing contexts identified caused nasalization uniformly with stressed and unstressed vowels. Instead, certain operate with stressed vowels only. Thus, in context type (iii), vowels have nasalized and raised if they were stressed but not if they were unstressed. Similarly, only stressed vowels were nasalized in the special 'inter-nasal' context just considered above. Examples:

CĒNA   > (DR) *cină*   *but* CINŪSIA   > (DR) *cenuşă* 'ash'   (not **cinuşă*)

NĒMINEM > (DR) *nimeni but* GĂLBINUM > (DR) *galben* 'yellow' (not **galbin*)

ANIMĀLIA > (Banat) *nămaie* 'cattle' (not **nimaie*)[12]

LĀNA   > (DR) *lină*   *but* MANŬCULUM > (DR) *mănunchi* 'bunch' (not **mînunchi*)

In contrast, vowels in context (i) forms underwent nasalization whether stressed or unstressed. This difference in treatment between contexts (i) and (iii) points to the likely chronological priority of the former. We return to this point below in section 12.2.3.

To summarize, the range of nasalizing contexts in early Balkan-Romance (where 'N' indicates any nasal consonant) were the following:

context   *vowels affected*

1. ____ N-C   stressed or unstressed
   context type (i),
   provided that the consonant 'C' was oral

2. ____ -r̃ V   stressed only
   context type (iii),
   where [r̃] < simplex -N-

3. N ____ X   stressed only
   where 'X' includes any simplex
   nasal or nasal cluster unable by itself
   to trigger vowel nasalization

12.2.3.   VOWEL NASALIZATION: UNITARY OR STAGED PROCESS?

As we have seen, high-level vowel nasalization in early Romanian occurred in a number of different contexts. Of these, the third type (as in *nun* < NŎNNUM) represents a special case where nasalization came about for cumulative reasons. The two remaining types of nasalizing context however show clear similarities. It is tempting therefore to assume that they share a common basis and operated at broadly the same time in a unitary process of vowel nasalization. Nonetheless, despite appearances, there is good reason for believing that vowel nasalization was not a unitary process. Instead, two stages were probably involved. First, vowel nasalization occurred in context (i) forms (e.g. in the forms deriving from CĂMPUM DĔNTEM etc.) and only later on did vowels become nasalized in other contexts (e.g. in the reflex of LĀNA) .

Two pieces of evidence point to this. On the one hand, only in context (i) forms do both stressed and unstressed vowels undergo nasalization. This implies that the nasalization process in this context type was not identical with that of vowels in other contexts. It was probably earlier and thus had time to be generalized to all vowels, irrespective of their degree of stress.

On the other hand, there is the evidence offered by the interplay between nasalization and the diphthongization of stressed /ɛ/.[13]   Taking the items TĔMPUS > (DR) *timp* 'time', DĔNTEM > (DR) *dinte* 'tooth', and TĔNET > (DR) *ține* 'he holds', we see that in all of them there is the tell-tale sign of raising which indicates nasalization. However, in the first two items the nasalization and vowel raising of /ɛ/ evidently occurred before the regular diphthongization of /ɛ/ operated, since the resulting diphthong /je/ would have caused the preceding dentals /t d/ to palatalize to /t͡s d͡z/. Now, such palatalization has occurred with *ține*, indicating that in this item the diphthongization of /ɛ/ must have taken place before nasalization affected the stressed vowel and caused it to raise. Thus, the evolution of TĔMPUS and TĔNET in early Balkan-Romance apparently proceeded in the following way (where the columns represent successive chronological stages):

TĔMPUS > 'tɛmpu(s) > 'tẽmpu > 'tẽmpu > 'tẽmpu > 'tẽmpu
TĔNET   > 'tɛne(t)   > 'tɛne   > 'tjɛne > 'tjẽ̃r̃e > 'ts(j)ẽ̃r̃e

A special problem relates to proparoxytonic forms containing original stressed /ɛ/ such as:

VĔNERIS   > (DR) *vineri* 'Friday'
TĔNERUM   > (DR) *tînăr*, (pl.) *tineri* 'young'
VĔNETUM   > (DR) *vînăt*, (pl.) *vineți* 'violet-blue, pallid'

Here, it is curious that stressed /ɛ/ has not undergone regular diphthongization, hence the modern DR outcome *tînăr* rather than palatalized ***ţînăr.[14] The development of these forms remains unclear.[15]

It therefore appears that nasalization was a two-staged process in early Romanian. Initially, applying to vowels preceding nasal codas, i.e. in context (i) forms, it was only later extended for special reasons to context (iii) forms of a particular type, namely those in which the vowel was stressed and followed by the heterosyllabic alveolar nasal flap [r̃] < -N-. As regards the third of the nasalizing contexts relevant for Romanian, seen in NŎNNUM > (DR) *nun*, its chronology is uncertain, but given its application to stressed vowels only, it is perhaps more likely to have formed part of the later wave of vowel nasalization.

12.2.4. FATE OF THE CONDITIONING NASAL CONSONANT

The appearance of higher levels of vowel nasalization during Period I was evidently accompanied by the weakening of the conditioning nasal. In context (i) forms, the result was a weak nasal coda whose place and manner of articulation was probably identical with that of the consonant which followed it. Such indeed is still the arrangement in modern standard DR. In context (iii) forms, the only intervocalic nasal which was relevant, simplex -N-, had weakened to give the nasal flap [r̃].

In Period II, the process of nasal consonant weakening was gradually halted. In context (i) forms, the conditioning nasal consonant was never systematically deleted so that a consonantal segment of some sort has usually been preserved into the modern language, accompanied by variable degrees of nasality in the preceding vowel. The only exception concerns those cases where the nasal precedes a fricative. Here, there may be deletion of the nasal in some varieties (12.1.3).

There is even some evidence of strengthening taking place in nasal codas, at least in certain types of context (i) form. This relates to the appearance of contrasts between coda nasals before coronal consonants so that the long-established rule of homorganicity in nasal + oral consonant sequences was undermined. Examples of the new contrasts in DR are *simt* 'I feel' vs. *mint* 'I lie' and *simţi* 'to feel' vs. *dinţi* 'teeth'. In other varieties of Romanian, the range of contrasting nasals is even wider. In IR, all three nasals /m n ɲ/ can occur before the coronals /t͡s/ and /s/, as in ['nimt͡si] 'Germans' vs. [se'mint͡sə] 'seed' vs. ['muɲt͡si] 'inhabitant of Mune' (Kovačec 1971: 64), while in AR the incidence of /m/ as well as /n/ before coronals is considerable, ['vimtu] 'wind' ['timsu] 'spread out', etc. Of these non-homorganic nasal + oral consonant sequences, [mt] is the most frequent and doubtless the earliest chronologically, for it is well attested in the earliest DR texts of the sixteenth century. Its origins have been much debated, but the most likely explanation is that it goes back to the

Latin sequence [ŋkt] which was found in past participles such as ŬNCTUM 'greased' and, by analogy, FRĂ(N)CTUM STRĬ(N)CTUM 'broken, squeezed' (Hamp 1981).[16] Subsequently, [ŋkt] regularly developed to [mpt] (just as [kt] > [pt]) and later simplified to [mt]. The new sequence [mt] (and [mt͡s] in plural forms) then provided the model for past participles in [ns], adapting them to [ms] (cf. AR *timsu* 'spread out' < TĒNSUM), and also influenced non-participial verb-forms and nominals in [nt(s)], as in DR *simt*, AR *simtu* < SĔNT(I)O 'I feel', AR *vimtu, sîmtu* 'wind, holy' < VĔNTUM SĀNCTUM. Subsequently, other sound changes sporadically capitalized on the possibility of having non-homorganic coda nasals, as in the syncopated derivatives of *frumos* such as *frîmsete* 'beauty' *înfrîmsa înfrumsa* 'to embellish' which appear in sixteenth-century texts (Densusianu 1975: 455). Loanwords such as *neamţ* 'German' further established the new pattern. The significance of all these changes is considerable. When the rule of homorganicity in nasal + oral consonant sequences was abandoned, one likely consequence was that nasals in this environment took on a strengthened articulation as speakers sought to characterize them more clearly so that they could be discriminated. Any such strengthening may in turn be expected to have had direct repercussions leading to some downgrading of levels of nasality in the vowels preceding the nasal consonants.

12.2.4.1.   *The Conditioning Nasal [r̃]*

The nasal [r̃] had arisen as the reflex of simplex -N- in context (iii) forms. However, this was the only context where it appeared in early Balkan Romance. Its phonological isolation and its lack of any counterpart in Slavonic probably helped to bring about its progressive elimination during Period II (cf. 12.2.5). This was achieved by adapting it into some other more widely distributed consonant type. In the standard variety of DR and most other central and southern varieties, as well as AR and MR, [r̃] was strengthened to become identical with [n] < -NN- The consequence has been some corresponding decrease in the degree of nasality in the preceding vowel; thus, LŪNA > ['lũr̃ə] > ['lunə]. Some nasality remains in the preceding vowel but the strong heterosyllabic [n] now exercises a much more limited nasalizing influence than tautosyllabic nasals (Petrovici 1930: 76).

Elsewhere, in many northern varieties of DR and in IR, the nasal flap [r̃] developed into a nasal trill [r̃] which in almost all areas later denasalized to give an oral trill [r]: LŪNA > ['lũr̃ə] > ['lūr̃ə] > ['lurə] *lură* 'moon'. This development of original simplex -N- to become a trill is known as *rhotacism*.[17] The earliest evidence of rhotacism comes from isolated Romance material appearing in fifteenth-century Moldavian texts written in Slavonic, *Žireapă(n)* (1410), *Neburešti* (1448), cf. modern DR *jneapăn* 'juniper' *nebunești* 'mad

(m. pl.)' (Rosetti 1978: 472; Bolocan 1981). By the sixteenth century, when running texts in Romanian first appear, rhotacizing forms occur in northern Transylvania and northern Moldavia. Rosetti (1978: 252) sees the source area of the phenomenon as lying in the north-west, from where it spread into Moldavia probably via north-eastern Transylvania and Bucovina. Occasional dialects still preserve the likely phonetic structure of the late medieval and sixteenth-century rhotacized forms (i.e. with nasality maintained), notably in the Apuşeni Mountains of Crişana in north-west Romania. In one dialect of the Ţara Moţilor region, for instance, the forms ['lũr̃ə] 'moon' and ['mĩr̃ə] 'hand' (< MAN-A) are reported (Mocanu 1972).[18]   However, the phonetic facts can be fairly complex, so that even in individual rhotacizing dialects of the Apuşeni Mountains, different outcomes of original [Ṽr̃V] sequences may occur in different lexical items, [VnV] [VrV] [ṼrV] [Ṽr̃V] (Rosetti 1947: 209). Sociolinguistic pressures, arising notably from the low prestige of rhotacized forms, have hastened the retreat of this feature in recent years.

In IR, rhotacism is general. In the modern form of this Romanian variety, all trace of nasality has been lost and a sequence of oral vowel + oral trill appears, hence ['bire vir sir 'lurə bur 'lərə] < BĔNE VĪNUM SĬNUM LŪNA BŎNUM LĀNA 'well, wine, bosom, moon, good (m. sg.), wool'. Rhotacism has meant that the reflexes of -N- -L- -R- and -RR- have merged, as in ['burə 'ɣurə 'sɛrə fʎer] < BŎNA GŬLA SĒRA FĔRRUM 'good (f. sg.), mouth, evening, iron' (Kovačec 1971). It seems unlikely that the development of rhotacism in IR is independent of the parallel change in the north and north-west area of DR. As IR separated from DR during or before the thirteenth century (Rosetti 1978: 655), we may assume that at least the initial stages of rhotacism had begun by that time.

The changes to early Romanian [r̃], all of which involve some strengthening, parallel the development of the corresponding oral flap [ɾ] < -R- -L-, which is strengthened to give a trill [r]. Both consonant types had limited distributions and found no counterpart in Slavonic or other languages that Romanian closely interacted with. It is therefore understandable that they were gradually equated with the consonants /n/ or /r/ which were widely distributed.

12.2.4.2. *Further Changes Involving the Nasal Flap* [r̃]

Before disappearing, [r̃] was involved in two further changes: *nasal spreading*, and various cases of *assimilation and dissimilation* in which oral [ɾ] was also implicated.

In forms where [r̃] occurred before the stressed vowel, e.g. in early Romanian [mə'r̃utu] < MINŪTUM 'small', there has regularly been spreading of the nasality from its original location in the pre-stress syllable to the stressed syllable (cf. Gascon, 6.3, and Portuguese, 8.3.1.5). Two further conditions were that the stressed vowel was high and followed by a non-continuant.[19] Examples are:

MINŪTUM	>	mɔ̃'ɾutu	>	DR	*mărunt*	'small'
CANŪTUM	>	kɔ̃'ɾutu	>	DR	*cărunt*	'grey'
GENŬCULUM	>	dzẽ'ɾukʎu	>	DR	*genunchi*	'knee'
AD-MINĀCIAT	>	amẽ'ɾatsə	>	DR	*ameninţă*	'he threatens'
GRANŪCEUM	>	grɔ̃'ɾutsu	>	DR	*grăunte*	'grain'

In all these cases, nasality spread to the following stressed vowel and subsequently was lost on the unstressed vowel. Since nasal vowels could not appear without a following nasal consonantal segment, a nasal homorganic with the following oral consonant was created. If this had the effect of establishing two coronal nasals [ɾ̃ . . . n] in the stressed syllable, the first nasal usually dissimilated to give oral [ɾ] which later strengthened to emerge as [r]. Regarding the last two items, the expected form *amerinţă* is attested in the sixteenth century (Rosetti 1978: 532), while *grăunte* (which represents a remodelled singular from the regular plural *grăunţi*) probably lost the expected medial [r] through dissimilation from the preceding [r].

A quite separate development is found in AR. Here, the flap [ɾ̃] evidently strengthened early to [n] and thereby reduced levels of nasality in the pre-stress vowel sufficiently to block spreading, hence the corresponding forms *minut cănut dzinucliu*. The variation observable between different varieties of Romanian reflects the delicacy of spreading and also its relative lateness. For instance, *genuchiu* (as against present-day *genunchi*) is still by far the more common variant found in sixteenth-century DR texts (Densusianu 1975: 491).

There has also been nasal spreading to the stressed vowel from a post-stress nasal vowel. This took place in DR but is less evident in AR. Examples are:

PETĪGINEM	>	[pe'tʃidʒẽɾe]	>	[pe'tʃĩdʒẽɾe]	>	DR *pecingine*	'herpes'
FULĪGINEM	>	[fu'ridʒẽɾe]	>	[fu'ɾ̃ĩdʒẽɾe]	>	DR *funingine*	'soot'
						cf. AR *furidzină*	

Regional variation is also evident in the fate of forms where the phonetically similar consonants [ɾ̃] and [r] came to co-occur. Such forms experienced variable assimilation or dissimilation. The following cases may be cited:

early Romance consonants

[ɾ̃ . . . ɾ̃]	VENĒNUM	>	DR	*venin*	AR *virin*	'poison'
[r . . . ɾ̃]	CORŌNA	>	DR	*cununā*	AR *curună*	'wreath'
	SERĒNUM	>	DR	*senin*	AR *sirin*	'clear'
	ARĒNA	>	DR	*anină*	AR *arină*	'sand'
				(sixteenth century)		
	FARĪNA	>	DR	*făină*	AR *fărină*	'flour'
[ɾ̃ . . . r]	FENĔSTRA	>	DR	*fereastră*	AR *fireast(r)ă*	'window'

AR tends to generalize a dissimilated arrangement with [r . . . n] in that order, while DR opts for an assimilated arrangement with [n . . . n]. Sixteenth-century DR texts have the expected *făninǎ* (Rosetti 1978: 533). For the final item, the same dissimilatory (in AR) or assimilatory (in DR) target is achieved by a different route.

Finally, one much-debated set of words may be mentioned:

FRĒNUM	>	DR	*frîu*	AR	*frîn*	'rein'
BRĒNUM	>	DR	*brîu*			'belt'
GRĀNUM	>	DR	*grîu*	AR	*grîn*	'wheat'

In these items, the deletion of [r̃] in DR does not appear to have come about as a result of regular phonetic change (cf. VETERĀNUM > *bǎtrîn* 'old') but because of the dissimilatory deletion of the second flap in the plural forms ['fr̃ɘ(r̃)uri] etc. The stem of the plural form containing no [r̃] was then seemingly generalized to the singular. In those varieties where the plural suffix *-uri* did not develop, no such dissimilation occurred; the relevant plural forms in AR, it may be noted, are *frîne grîne*.

12.2.5. EVOLUTION OF NASALIZED VOWELS IN PERIOD I

Although the lack of direct textual evidence makes it difficult to determine the path of development of nasalized vowels in the period up to the tenth century, it is possible to infer the broad pattern of evolution from later stages of Romanian. There is certainly no evidence that unconditioned nasal vowels existed but allophonically nasalized vowels undoubtedly did, and it is very likely that all the stressed vowels of early Balkan-Romance had strongly nasal allophones.

ĩ	'vĩr̃u	<	VĪNUM	'wine'
ẽ	'tẽmpu	<	TĚMPUS	'time'
jẽ	'tjẽr̃e	<	TĚNET	'he holds'
ã	'kãmpu	<	CĂMPUM	'field'
õ	'põnte	<	PŎNTEM	'bridge'
ũ	'ũr̃u	<	ŪNUM	'one'

Subsequently, the tendency for nasalized vowels to raise, seen early on in the development of TĚMPUS ([ɛ̃] > [ẽ]), probably continued to operate. The presence of just high vowels in nasalizing contexts in virtually all modern varieties of Romanian suggests this. However, it is uncertain whether the raising tendency had led to any non-high vowels becoming high already by the end of Period I. Even so, some scholars have claimed that the raising of mid vowels [ẽ] > [ĩ] and [õ] > [ũ] did take place as early as this (Nandriş 1963: 21, 213; Sala 1976: 218, 224; Avram 1990: 35, 56). The main supporting argument centres upon the relationship between this change and another quite independent development, namely the metaphonic diphthongization of stressed /e o/. Briefly, the latter caused /e o/ to move to [ea ɔa], respectively, when a non-high vowel appeared in the following syllable (at this stage the only unstressed non-high vowels were [e ə] < Latin /e a/). Examples are: SĒRA > ['sera] > ['seara] *seară* 'evening', SŌLEM > ['sore] > ['soare] *soare* 'sun'. Now, the nasalized mid vowels were not affected by this diphthongization and instead emerged with high vowels: hence, PLĒNA > ['plẽr̃ə] > *plină* 'full (f. sg.)', TITIŌNEM > [te'cõr̃e] > *tăciune* [tə'tʃune] 'firebrand' rather than **pleană > **pleînă, **tăcioane > **tăcioîne. To explain the absence of metaphonic diphthongization here, the assumption has been that it only began to operate after the raising of [ẽ õ], and as metaphonic diphthongization almost certainly goes back to before the tenth century,[20] raising must have occurred well before the tenth century.

Despite its initial attractions, this idea that nasal [ẽ õ] underwent raising early on creates a number of difficulties in accounting for other sound changes, especially with the front vowel [ẽ].[21] Accordingly, it seems wiser to assume that [ẽ] was maintained as a mid vowel up to at least the tenth century. The raising of the back vowel [õ] to [ũ], however, may have begun to take place by this time, as Vasiliu (1968: 72–3) believes. The earliest recorded example of [ũ] appears to be in a Slavonic document dated between 1222 and 1228, where *Bun'* occurs as a proper name (Mihăilă 1974: s.v. *bun*). It is possible that this reflects a pronunciation feature going back a few centuries earlier, but this remains unprovable.

If [ẽ] and [õ] did remain as mid vowels, distinct from [ĩ] and [ũ], in Balkan-Romance of the tenth century, their non-participation in metaphonic diphthongization requires explanation. The answer would seem to be that although these vowels were allophones of /e/ and /o/, their nasality caused them to be realized with a relatively high tongue position. In languages which have just single front-mid and back-mid vowel phonemes, there is often a good deal of variation in the way the allophones of these are realized, depending principally on phonetic context.[22] Assuming then that [ẽ] and [õ] remained high-mid vowels, still distinct from [ĩ] and [ũ], the lack of metaphonic diphthongization in *plină*, *tăciune*, etc. could be attributed to the closer articulation of these nasalized vowels and their tendency to raise (induced by nasality) which ran directly counter to the *lowering* or *opening* harmonizing effect which motivated the metaphonic diphthongization of /e o/.[23]

The remaining nasalized vowels [ã] and [jẽ] may well have undergone some raising by the tenth century. The diphthong [jẽ] has given a high outcome [ĩ] or [i] everywhere in modern varieties of Romanian, as in DR *bine* < BĚNE 'well'. As there is no evidence of anything but a high articulation in the earliest texts of the sixteenth century, even in the special contexts where [ẽ] with no preceding off-glide [j] remained non-high (Densusianu 1975: 434), a rapid and general shift [jẽ] > [jĩ] is not unlikely, prompted by the assimilatory influence of the initial high element [j]. Later on in the pre-literary period, there was contraction of [jĩ] to [ĩ] but it is not clear when this became generalized.[24]

The low vowel [ã] in unstressed syllables doubtless shared the fate of all unstressed allophones of /a/, and raised to become a shwa. In stressed syllables, some raising is likely too in view of the fact that all varieties of Romanian show evidence of raising from earliest recorded times. The first textual examples of the raising of [ã] do not come until the mid-fifteenth century when a number of Slavonic documents include proper names deriving from FONTĀNA which show raising. These are *Fǎntǎnele* and *Fîntîrěle* (Mihǎilǎ 1974: s.v. *fîntînǎ*; Rosetti 1978: 472), with some scribal variation in the Cyrillic symbol used to represent the vowel. Given the universality of [ã]-raising across the different varieties of Romanian and the fact that raising would not threaten any phonemic contrasts, it is not unlikely that raising to [ẽ] or [ɔ̃] had occurred with some speakers by the tenth century.[25]

To sum up, we may envisage the following possible pattern for nasal vowels at the end of Period I in the tenth century:

	stressed			*unstressed*	
(j)ĩ		ũ	ĩ		ũ
ẽ	ɔ̃	õ	ẽ	ɔ̃	
	(ã)				

All of these vowel types were allophones only. There is no evidence to suggest the development of nasal vowel phonemes.

12.2.6.   THE SLAVONIC CONNECTION

The transitional phase between the two periods which we have identified is marked by the settlement of the Slavs in the Balkans. Apart from its political and social significance, this led to the introduction of much linguistic material from Slavonic in the resulting period of widespread and prolonged bilingualism. The influence of the Slavs in the Balkans begins with the mass invasions of the early seventh century and such was their political and social domination that Slavonic provided the written medium of communication for most literate Romanians until as late as the sixteenth century, and it remained even later in ecclesiastical usage surviving into the beginning of the eighteenth century in the liturgy of the Orthodox Church (Coteanu 1981: 88).

By a curious chance, the Slavs brought with them a language which evidently also possessed nasal vowels.[26] The creation of these vowels was the result of a general 'conspiracy' to establish free syllable structure (Nandriş 1965: 11; Lunt 1974: 29). In sequences of the form VN-C and VN #, there was complete or near-complete deletion of the coda nasal accompanied by nasalization of the preceding vowel so that these sequences emerged as Ṽ-C and Ṽ #, respectively.[27] In some cases, alternations between Ṽ and V-N in morphologically related forms could be found, as in Old Church Slavonic (OCS) *klęti* ['klɛ̃ːti] 'to curse' vs. *klinǫ* ['klinõ] 'I curse' which show the alternating stems *klę-* and *klin-* (Lunt 1974: 40).

Four types of nasal vowel had arisen in Slavonic, namely [ĩ ɛ̃ õ ũ]; the original vowel /a/ had already merged with /o/ in primitive Slavonic prior to the appearance of nasal vowels. By the time of the earliest texts in OCS, the nasal sub-system had been further simplified to just two members [ɛ̃] (< [ĩ ɛ̃]) and [õ] (< [õ ũ]).[28] When Slavs first began to come into contact with Romance-speaking peoples from the seventh century on, it is likely that they were using this two-way nasal vowel arrangement. Much lexical material was assimilated into the evolving Balkan-Romance of the ninth century onward, and a fair number of loanwords contained nasal vowels.

In all Romance borrowings from Slavonic which contained nasal vowels, the nasal vowel was stressed and it was followed by an oral heterosyllabic consonant. There were no Slavonic borrowings of the form nasal vowel + nasal consonant and none containing a word-final nasal vowel. Thus, the typical form in borrowed items was 'Ṽ-C whereas there is no trace of the sequences **Ṽ-N (impossible in Slavonic) and **Ṽ# (possible in Slavonic but never adopted in Romance). The borrowed items were aligned with context (i) forms already in the language, such as ['vɛ̃n-tu] < VĔNTUM. The main features of the incorporation of Slavonic loans with nasal vowels may be outlined.

The front nasal vowel type had a fairly open mid quality, approximately [ɛ̃] or even [æ̃] (Shevelov 1964: 329; Rosetti 1978: 345). Though lower than early Romanian [ẽ], it was nonetheless similar enough to it to be readily associated with it. Hence:

OCS		Early Romanian		Modern DR	
gręda	>	'grɛ̃ndə	>	*grindă*	'beam'
pętino	>	'pɛ̃ntenu	>	*pinten*	'spur'
cęta	>	'tsɛ̃ntə	>	*ţintă*	'nail'

Slavonic loanwords also shared the fate of native early Romanian [ẽ] in those contexts where it centralized to [ə̃] and subsequently raised to [ɨ̃] (this occurs when a labial consonant or /r/ precedes and a back vowel follows in the next syllable). Thus, (OCS) *rędu* > ['rẽndu] > (DR) *rînd* 'row, line', *svętu* > ['sfẽntu] > (DR) *sfînt* 'holy' evolve just as Latin RĒN-A > ['rẽr̃ə] > (DR) *rînă* 'side, flank' and VĔNTUM > ['vẽntu] > (DR) *vînt* 'wind'.

For the back vowel, two patterns of adaptation are discernible. In certain loans, Slavonic [õ] was identified with early Romanian [õ] whilst in others it was aligned with the central nasal vowel [ə̃] which developed from [ã]. In both cases, the nasal vowel underwent regular sound change thereafter in Romanian.[29] Examples:

OCS		Early Romanian		Modern DR	
dǫga	>	'dõŋgu	>	*dungă*	'streak'
prǫdu	>	'prõndu	>	*prund*	'gravel'
kǫpona	>	'kõmpənə	>	*cumpună*	'scales'
tǫpu	>	'tõmpu	>	*tîmp*	'blunt'
trǫba	>	'trõmbə	>	*trîmbă*	'cylinder'
oblǫku	>	o'blõŋku	>	*oblînc*	'saddle bow'

The explanation for this double treatment is generally held to lie in the chronology of the borrowing. Earlier Slavonic loans had [õ] rendered as [õ] in early Romanian, but later borrowings were assigned the central vowel [ə̃] (Densusianu 1975: 258; Rosetti 1978: 346; Avram 1990: 73). The prime source for loanwords into Romanian was early Bulgarian, and for a long time this language remained unaffected by the general tendency in Slavonic languages for nasal vowels to be denasalized. Nasal vowels were preserved until well after the eleventh century, probably remaining until as late as the thirteenth century (Shevelov 1964: 329). However, before denasalization began to operate in Bulgarian, the quality of [õ] had been changed through centralization to [ə̃] (hence modern Bulgarian [rə'ka] < OCS *rǫka* 'hand', after denasalization and later regular stress switch).

12.2.6.1.   *Impact of Slavonic on Romanian Vowel Nasalization*

The overall effect of Slavonic on the nasal vowel sub-system of early Romanian seems at first to have been slight. The number of loanwords containing nasal vowels was considerable, but they did not cause any change in the nasal vowel sub-system itself. The five types of nasal vowel previously present still remained.

However, a couple of significant changes may be attributed, in part at least, to Slavonic influence. The first relates to the range of nasalizing contexts. As we have seen, even though Slavonic itself had developed vowel nasality in context-type (i) and (ii) forms, all the borrowings into Romanian belonged exclusively to context-type (i). Consequently, the presence of nasal vowels in other sorts of context in early Romanian, notably context (iii), as in LĀNA > ['lə̃r̃ə], would have become somewhat anomalous to both bilingual and monolingual Slavonic speakers, since vowels preceding an intervocalic nasal consonant were always only oral in Slavonic. Certainly, in the numerous borrowings from Slavonic containing the sequence *vowel + nasal consonant + vowel*, the first vowel segment is always rendered by an oral vowel in Romanian,[30] as in:

zvonu > ['zvonu] > DR *zvon*   'rumour'   (cf. BŎNUM > *bun*)
mrena > ['mreanə] > DR *mreană* 'barbel fish' (cf. CĒNA > *cină*)
rana   > ['ranə]   > DR *rană*   'wound'   (cf. LĀNA > *lînă*)

The Slavonic sound sequences were simply identified with sequences already present in native Latin-based words in which there had originally been a geminate -NN-. In such words, a sequence of oral vowel + /n/ emerged with no associated raising, as in ĂNNUM > ['anu] (> DR *an*) and PĬNNA > ['pęanə] (> DR *pană*). The new batch of Slavonic loans such as ['zvonu] thus reinforced the oral vowel + nasal consonant pattern, while marginalizing the sequence nasal vowel + [r̃].

There is a further indication of the resistance to identifying a stressed vowel as being nasal in Slavonic loans if the following nasal consonant was hetero-syllabic. In native Latin forms, vowel nasalization occurred when a stressed vowel was both preceded and followed by any sort of nasal consonant (cf. 12.2.2 above). However, comparable vowel nasalization did not occur in Slavonic loans:

> izmena   > [iz'męanə] > DR *izmană* 'underpants'
> pomenu / -a > [po'męanə] > DR *pomană* 'alms'
> rumenu   > [ru'menu]   > DR *rumen*   'rosy red'

The systematic failure to implement vowel nasalization in Slavonic loanwords containing vowel + [n] + vowel was important. It doubtless helped to isolate the native Romance forms with the structure nasal vowel + nasal consonant + vowel (for example, the forms deriving from LĀNA BĔNE) and thereby undermine the productivity of nasalizing context (iii). Certainly, borrowings into DR from Hungarian which probably date from the eleventh-twelfth centuries onward (Rosetti 1978: 429) suggest that nasalization is effectively confined to vowels in context (i) forms. Examples:

raising			*no raising*			
(indicating vowel nasalization)						
gyenges >	DR	*gingaş* 'frail'	ban >	(Old DR) *banu*	> *ban*	'coin'
gond >	DR	*gînd* 'idea'	hitlen >	(Old DR) *hicleanu*	> *viclean*	'cunning'

The other consequence of Slavonic influence relates to the nasal flap [r̃] which derived from Latin simplex -N-. This consonant was already unusual in early Romanian, being found only in intervocalic position. Also, it had no counterpart at all in Slavonic, and the practice of regularly identifying Slavonic intervocalic /n/ with early Romanian 'strong' [n] which derived from geminate Latin -NN- must have highlighted the isolated and anomalous status of [r̃]. The rise of widespread Romance-Slavonic bilingualism may therefore have acted as a major factor in encouraging moves to eliminate this sound from the consonant system.[31] However, the disappearance of the nasal flap as a distinctive consonant type was a change which took some time to be carried through, and the results vary from one variety of Romanian to another (cf. 12.2.4).

12.3. Developments in Period II (from Tenth Century)

12.3.1. EVOLUTION OF STRESSED NASAL VOWELS

At the outset of Period II, there was probably a five-way sub-system of stressed nasal vowels:

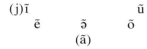

The nasal vowels subsequently underwent a number of developments. These have notably involved raising and their effect has been to neutralize certain distinctions between nasal vowels. In most but not all varieties of Romanian, the modern reflexes of the medieval nasal vowels are high vowels [ī ɨ ū]. However, at no stage do nasal vowels establish themselves as separate phonemes. Nasality has exercised a great influence in redistributing vowel types but it has failed to become a genuinely distinctive feature for vowels.

We may review the main developments in stressed nasal vowels (for unstressed nasal vowels, see 12.3.3 below). First, high nasal vowels have not changed in respect of vowel height. Cases of repositioning on the front–back axis have occurred however (see 12.3.2). The simplification of [jĩ] > [ĩ] may be noted, as in ['bjĩr̃e] > DR *bine* 'well'. This could still have been incomplete in some varieties during, and for some time after, the tenth century.

Amongst the three non-high nasal vowels there have been more significant changes. The different vowel types may be considered in turn.

[õ]

It seems likely that [õ] underwent raising to [ū] early on in Period II. All modern varieties of Romanian have a high vowel and in the texts of the sixteenth century the Cyrillic graphy corresponding to <u> is always used. Furthermore, there are isolated cases of forms with <u> graphies in Romance forms appearing in Slavonic texts from as early as the thirteenth century. It may therefore be that in some varieties a high articulation was already established by the tenth century (cf. 12.2.5).

[ə̃]

The mid central vowel [ə̃] < [ã] developed in different ways depending on the variety of Romanian concerned. Three possibilities exist:

   (*a*) in IR and in one subtype of AR (*fărşerotesc*, spoken by a small community in Albania), [ə̃] has remained a mid central vowel; e.g. IR *lâră* ['lərə] 'wool', *sâr* [sər] 'healthy (m. sg.)';

   (*b*) in MR, just as stressed oral [ə] passes to [ɔ] so too nasal [ə̃] has given [ɔ̃], e.g. ['lɔ̃nə] 'wool', [kɔ̃mp] 'field';

   (*c*) in DR and in the great majority of varieties of AR, [ə̃] has closed to [ɨ̃], e.g. *lînă* ['lɨ̃nə] 'wool', *cîmp* [kɨ̃mp] 'field'.

The dating of the change in (*b*) is uncertain given the lack of documentation for MR until very recent times, but Ivănescu (1980: 591) proposes sometime between the sixteenth and eighteenth centuries. A little more is known of (*c*), at least as far as DR is concerned, although the picture is confused by the complex situation with central vowel phonemes. In the sixteenth century, it appears that no phonemic opposition had as yet arisen between /ə/ and /ɨ/ (Avram 1964: 265–94).[32] Instead, there was just one central vowel phoneme which varied a good deal in its realization, not only from one dialect of DR to another but also from context to context within individual dialects. Interdialectally, Rosetti (1978: 461) claims to detect one broad characteristic: Moldavian dialects in the east generally used [ə] and Wallachian dialects in the south opted for [ɨ]. The date of the creation of two distinct central vowel phonemes /ə/ and /ɨ/ is not certain, but it could go back to the seventeenth century in Wallachian (from which the standard language derives). In 1683 the Bishop Dosoftei in his *Faptele Apostolilor* (The Acts of the Apostles) makes clear and systematic use of two distinct Cyrillic symbols to express central vowels, suggesting the /ə/ : /ɨ/ distinction of today (Suteu 1976: 148). As far as the nasal vowel [ə̃] is concerned, it is probable that, during the later medieval period, it gradually took on a higher tongue position [ɨ̃] in most varieties of DR and this realization was general by the sixteenth century. While just one central vowel phoneme existed, the nasal allophone figured amongst the variants with a high tongue position. When two central vowel phonemes subsequently became established, the high articulatory position [ɨ̃] of the nasal vowel led it to be interpreted as a member of the high central /ɨ/ phoneme.

[ẽ]

The remaining non-high nasal vowel [ẽ] has also regularly undergone raising. In IR, AR, and MR dialects, the change was completed before the appearance of the earliest records of these, i.e. prior to the eighteenth century. Modern forms are IR *mire, vinde, virer* ['mire 'vinde 'virer], AR *mine, vinde, viniri* ['mine 'vinde 'vinir[i]], MR *mini, vindi* ['mini 'vindi] 'me, (he) sells, Friday' (Kovačec 1971; Papahagi 1974; Caragiu Marioțeanu 1977).

However, in DR the process of raising was a long and complex one. In the sixteenth century when Romanian texts become available, the process was evidently still not complete, as is indicated by attested forms such as *cuvente, sfente* (= modern DR *cuvinte, sfinte*) 'words, holy (f. pl.)'. Indeed, some modern dialects of the mountainous area of central and south-eastern Transylvania are reported to have preserved forms with a non-raised vowel, e.g. *mene, mente* as against standard DR *mine, minte* (Ivănescu 1980: 403).

For the attested DR varieties of the sixteenth century, the available phonetic facts are far from clear. One problem lies in scribal inconsistency. Fluctuating representations as <e> or <i> appear from text to text and from form to form within individual texts. Further complicating factors also exist. It appears that stress exerted some influence, the raising of [ē] occurring more rapidly in stressed syllables than in unstressed syllables (Avram 1990: 45). And there is strong evidence that raising was retarded when [ē] was immediately preceded by a labial consonant and followed in the next syllable by a front vowel, as in attested forms such as *veneri* (= mod. DR *vineri*) 'Friday' and *mene* (= mod. DR *mine*) 'me'. Analogical influence may also come into play. For example, attested forms such as *cene, tene* (= mod. DR *cine, tine*) 'who, you', where there is no preceding labial consonant, seem to owe their non-raised vowel to influence from the pronoun *mene* 'me'.

The presence of such variation has led to much debate amongst historians of the language about the value which early Romanian [ē] had acquired by the sixteenth century. Various lines of interpretation have emerged. Rosetti (1970 and 1978: 506–9) claims that the maintenance of the <e> graphy was a purely scribal feature and that, phonetically, both <e> and <i> graphies in forms like *mene/mine* reflected just the pronunciation [ī] which was already established by the sixteenth century. The more general view, however, has been that the pronunciation [ē] was still found in certain words at the beginning of the sixteenth century depending on phonetic context, although some difference of opinion exists over the precise identity of the relevant phonetic contexts.[33]

The raising of [ē] > [ī] was thus a prolonged process which probably remained uncompleted by the sixteenth century in many varieties of DR, and occasional traces of non-raised [ē] lingered on into more recent times. The form *cuvente* (= mod. DR *cuvinte*) 'words' is found in DR texts as late as the eighteenth century (Avram 1990: 47), though this may simply represent a conservative graphy. And one relic word with a non-raised vowel survives in the standard language to the present day. This is the preposition *pentru* 'for' (< **PER ÎNTRO**), to which the dialectal forms *pintru, pîntru* correspond. Also, as noted earlier, certain dialects of Transylvania still have [ē] in the forms which showed fluctuation in the sixteenth century (*mene, mente,* etc.).

As a result of the raising of [ẽ] and the two other non-high nasal vowels, a sub-system [ĩ ɨ̃ ũ] emerged in almost all varieties of DR, including the standard language, and in AR. However, in more recent times non-high allophonically nasal vowels have reappeared in the sound structure of all varieties of Romanian. This is due principally to the borrowing of a number of items containing the sequence of non-high vowel + nasal + fricative, where the productive rule of nasal consonant weakening before a fricative gives rise to heightened vowel nasality, e.g. in *pensulă* 'brush', *revanşă* 'response', *conjugal* 'conjugal'.

12.3.2. DISTURBING FACTORS

In the history of Romanian, the expected pattern of evolution of nasal vowels has been modified by various special factors. Their effect has not been to create new types of nasal vowel but to cause redistribution along the front–back axis. Three cases may be identified: (*a*) retraction of front vowels, (*b*) fronting of central vowels, (*c*) fronting of back vowels. Finally, the special case of word-initial nasal vowels requires consideration.

12.3.2.1. *Retraction of Early Romanian Front Vowels*

In all four sub-groups of Romanian, front vowels have been retracted to become central vowels under certain circumstances. All instances of retraction normally applied to oral and nasal allophones alike. This reflects the fact that nasalization itself usually exercised no influence over the front/back dimension of vowel articulation: if nasalization modifies the tongue position of a vowel in Romanian, it is the dimension of height which is affected. The changes affected Slavonic loanwords and native words.

Two sorts of front vowel retraction may be distinguished: one occurred when a *coronal* consonant preceded, and the other involved presence of a preceding *labial* consonant.

The first type operated on both /i/ and /e/ and was triggered specifically when an oral coronal consonant preceded and when there was a back vowel in the following syllable. This change affected all types of Romanian, although we will focus on the details in DR only. Both oral and nasal vowels were subject to retraction. Thus, oral vowel retraction has occurred in AD-TĪTIAT > DR *aţîţă* 'he stirs up' and RĔUM > DR *rău* 'bad', and the following are examples with nasal vowels:

		early DR	mod. DR	
TĚMPLA	'tẽmplə	'tə̃mplə	*tîmplă*	'temple'
*RĒN-A	'rẽr̃ə	'rə̃r̃ə	*rînă*	'hip'
*CAPITĪNA	kəpə'tsĩr̃ə	kəpə'tsĩnə	*căpăţînă*	'head'
(OCS) rędu	'rẽndu	'rə̃ndu	*rînd*	'row, line'

The implementation of this change has not been entirely consistent in respect of either nasal or oral vowels. Analogical pressures have intervened, especially with verbal forms (e.g. STRĬNGO > *strîng* 'I squeeze' vs. PRĒNDO > *prind* 'I take' with a non-retracted vowel through paradigmatic analogy). Also, individual coronal consonants vary in their retracting strength: word-initial trilled /r-/ is the strongest while the others have exercised a more sporadic retracting influence, cf. TĚMPLA > DR *tîmplă* 'temple' but TĚMPUS > DR *timp* 'time'. Finally, there is a good deal of regional variation in the degree of strength of individual retracting influences.[34]

As regards the chronology of this retraction, a number of linguists have concluded from its uneven implementation that it represents a later development occurring after 'Common Romanian', i.e. some time after the eleventh century (Vasiliu 1968: 55; Sala 1976: 190–1). However, this must remain rather speculative.

The effect which this complex change had on nasal vowels was twofold. A new high central type [ɨ̃] was created, in forms like *căpăţînă* 'head'. Nonetheless, this vowel was still an allophone of /i/. The other effect was to cause a merger between [ə̃] deriving from [ã] and the retracted variant [ə̃] from [ẽ]. Thus, the stressed vowels of LĀNA > ['lə̃r̃ə] and *RĒN-A > ['rə̃r̃ə] became identical and later developed in a uniform way to give DR *lînă* 'wool', *rînă* 'hip'.

The other retracting context only affected the mid front vowel /e/. It operated when this vowel was preceded by a *labial* consonant and when there was no palatal element, consonantal or vocalic, in the following syllable. It therefore helped to generalize the vowel harmonizing pattern just considered in which central rather than front stressed vowels are adopted in word-forms containing a non-front vowel in the following syllable. The change applied equally to oral and nasal allophones of /e/. Examples with nasal vowels are:

		Period I	*Period II*	*mod. DR*	
	VĒNA	'vẽr̃ə	'və̃r̃ə	*vînă*	'vein'
but	VĒNAE	'vẽr̃e	'vẽr̃e	*vine*	'veins'
	PAVIMĚNTUM	pə'mẽntu	pə'mə̃ntu	*pămînt*	'earth'
but	MĚNTEM	'mẽnte	'mẽnte	*minte*	'mind'

Retraction after labials has occurred exclusively in dialects of DR. In the other types of Romanian, [ẽ] has remained a front vowel and subsequently underwent regular raising to [ĩ]. Compare:

	AR	MR	IR	DR
VĒNA	*vină*	*vină*	*viră*	*vînă*
PAVIMĔNTUM	*pimintu*	*pimint*	*pemint*	*pămînt*

In DR too, certain varieties did not adopt this rule of change. It is absent in dialects of north-eastern Banat and eastern Crişana in the west and in parts of Maramureş in the north (Sala 1976: 111; Caragiu Marioţeanu 1977: 154, 160). In view of its limited geographical incidence, we may see this type of retraction as a development of the later Middle Ages which post-dated retraction after coronals by some time.

The effect of retraction after labials was to create further cases of the mid central nasal vowel [ə̃], which subsequently underwent regular raising to [ɨ̃].

A final aspect of this change is that, unlike with the previous type of retraction, it set up alternations between front and central high vowels which have been preserved into contemporary standard DR. This applies particularly to nominals, as in *vînă* : *vine* 'vein : veins' and *vînăt* : *vineţi* 'violet-blue (m. sg.): (m. pl.)', since alternation in verbs has been almost totally eradicated in recent centuries through paradigmatic levelling. In modern usage, it is only in the verb *a vinde* that the alternation remains, in *vînd* : *vinde* 'I sell, he sells' (Irimia 1976); all other verbs undergo levelling with the generalization of /i/ forms.[35] Indeed, even *a vinde* has gone the same way in some DR dialects; in Banat, for instance, there has been levelling, once again in favour of the /i/ alternant (cf. *ALR*, maps 1926, 1927).

12.3.2.2. *Fronting of* [ə̃/ɨ̃]

Nasalized central vowels have been fronted at various stages in the history of Romanian. As already noted (12.3.1), it was probably only in the later seventeenth century that two separate central vowel phonemes /ə/ and /ɨ/ came into existence. Before then, there was just one central vowel phoneme and indeed this is still the case in some dialects of Romanian. The phonetic quality of the nasal allophones of this phoneme in later medieval times is uncertain, either mid [ə̃] or possibly [ɨ̃] in certain contexts. Either variant could be affected by fronting so that [ə̃] > [ẽ] (which later closed to [ĩ]) or [ɨ̃] > [ĩ]. Both developments therefore would give the same result and the particular path of change followed would depend on the chronology of the change and its regional basis. Fronting takes place in three types of context.

1. When a palatal consonant immediately preceded [ə̃], its frontness caused [ə̃] to pass to [ẽ] by assimilation, and later [ẽ] > [ĩ]. Thus:

GLĂNDA	>	DR	*ghindă*	'acorn'
CHRISTIĀNUM	>	DR	*creştin*	'Christian'

| MEDIĀNUM | > | DR | *mezin* | 'youngest child' |
| FILIĀNUM | > | DR | *fin* | 'godchild' |

To these may be added EXCĀMBIO > DR *schimb* 'I change' where fronting has evidently been caused by a following yod which arose as a result of metathesis ['skɔmbju > 'skɔjmbu]. Usually, yod metathesis occurs only when there is one intervening consonant present, cf. RŬBEUM > *roib* 'sorrel' but ĀLVEA > *albie* 'river bed'. The implication is therefore that the reflex of /m/ in EX-CĀMBIO was very weak so that it failed to block metathesis, a point further confirming the weakened articulation of nasals in context (i) forms in late Balkan Latin and early Romanian.

2. Related to the previous change is the fronting of stressed [ɔ̃] to [ẽ] (> [ĩ]) when a front vowel, especially [i], followed in the next syllable. This development is somewhat sporadic in its implementation. Examples:

GRĂNDINEM	>	DR	*grindină*	'hail'
EX-PĂNTICO	>	DR	*spintec*	'I cut apart'
IN-AB-ĂNTE	>	DR	*înainte*	'before'

Fronting in forms of this type is found in DR only, cf. the comparable AR forms *grîndină, spîntic, nînte*. Furthermore, even in DR itself we find cases where fronted forms have not become established, e.g. *pîntece, sînge, cîntec* 'belly, blood, song' < PĂNTICEM SĂNGU(IN)EM CĂNTICUM. Finally, there seem to be no examples of fronting when [ɔ̃] preceded [r̃] < -N-. As we shall see in the next paragraph, the results were rather different in this context. This suggests that either the nature or intensity of the nasality was different in the contexts [ɔ̃] + coda nasal and [ɔ̃] + [r̃], or that the fronting assimilation here took place at different stages. The latter is perhaps more likely.

3. When preceding a syllable containing word-final [i], [ɔ̃] diphthongized to [ɔ̃i] which then gave [ĩi] by regular raising. The change only affected [ɔ̃] preceding [r̃], and owes itself to partial metaphony, the stressed vowel adopting a fronted articulation in anticipation of the following front vowel. Examples are:

CĂN-Ī	>	DR	*cîini*	'dogs'
PĀN-Ī	>	DR	*pîini*	'loaves'
MĂNI	>	DR	*mîini*	'hands'
MĂNE	>	DR	*mîine*	'tomorrow'

It appears that this development applied at first just to forms whose word-final front vowel was specifically high. Accordingly, we must assume that the singular forms *cîine, pîine* 'dog, loaf' developed their diphthong by analogy with the plural (Lambrior 1880: 100–1; Rosetti 1978: 521). Analogy did not operate with the singular *mînă* 'hand' because the final unstressed vowel was not front.

The form *mîine* 'tomorrow' presumably acquired its diphthong by analogy. However, a number of exceptions to this change are found in DR: SEPTI-MĀN-Ī > *săptămîni* 'weeks', LĀN-Ī > *lîni* 'quantities of wool', TATĀN-Ī > *tătîni* 'fathers', and MĬN-ĪS > *mîni* 'you drive on', SĬN-Ī > *sîni* 'bosoms', though the last two may only have developed their [ɔ̃] (via retraction from [ẽ]) when diphthongization had ceased to be productive. The reasons for the absence of *îi* in the other items are less obvious. For the first two, it is possible that the modern plurals in -*i* only established themselves in place of the expected plural marker -*e* after diphthongization had occurred. Another aspect is that given the patchy implementation of the change [ɔ̃] > [ɔ̃i], we may suspect that, after it got underway and gained ground, it may have been halted for social or other reasons, leaving a residue in just certain high-frequency items.

Geographically, this development was ·confined principally to Wallachian dialects of DR, from which standard DR proceeds (Caragiu Marioțeanu 1977: 164). Outside DR, it is also found in other varieties too. In northern AR, the forms *cîine*, *mîini* are reported (Papahagi 1974: s.v. *cîine*, *mîna*), and in MR the forms ['kɔjni 'pɔjni mɔjn] 'dog, bread, hands' are indicated as variants used by some speakers beside the more general variant with non-diphthongal [ɔ] (Atanasov 1990).

As to chronology, the existence of a fronting diphthong is already attested in sixteenth-century texts; *caine*, *paine*, etc. (Rosetti 1978: 521). However, it is uncertain how far back its origins lie in the medieval period. Also, its presence in DR and south of the Danube may well reflect independent developments.

12.3.2.3. *Centralization of Back Nasal Vowels*

In a significant number of lexical items, there has been an unexpected centralization of back nasal vowels. Examples are:

PULMŌNEM	>	plə'mõr̃u	>	DR	*plămîn*	'lung'
FLAMMABŬNDUM	>	flə'mũndu	>	DR	*flămînd*	'hungry'
					(IR *flămund*, MR *flămund*)	
ADŬNCUM	>	a'dũŋku	>	DR	*adînc* (AR *adînc*)	'deep'
AXŬNGIA	>	o'sũndzə	>	DR	*osînză*	'lard'
FRŎNTEM	>	'frõnte	>	AR	*frîmte*	'forehead'
			but DR	*frunte*	

In DR dialects other items may also be affected, e.g. *părîmbă* < PALŬMBA 'dove' as against standard DR *porumbă* (Nandriș 1963: 42). Even so, this has never become established as a regular sound change. Instead, it appears to reflect a weak background tendency which operates sporadically in many varieties of Romanian. It is unclear whether it is related to the shift in Slavonic from [õ] to [ɔ̃], a development which left its mark on Romanian (see 12.2.5), but given the pervasive and long-lasting Slavonic-Romanian bilingualism the possibility cannot be excluded.

12.3.2.4. *Modifications to Word-Initial Non-high Nasal Vowels*

When in absolute word-initial position, non-high nasal vowels may show a different pattern of evolution from that found elsewhere. The special significance of word-initial position for determining vowel change applies to oral vowels too, it may be noted; for instance, unstressed /a/ usually gives [ə], but word-initial unstressed /a/ regularly remains as [a] (hence *amar* 'bitter', *aşa* 'thus').

The total number of lexical items with a stressed non-high nasal vowel in word-initial position in early Romanian was small. The following is a more or less complete list:

ĬMPL(E)O	>	'ẽmplu	(DR *umplu*)	'I fill'
ĬNFLO	>	'ẽnflu	(DR *umflu*)	'I inflate'
ĬNTRO	>	'ẽntru	(DR *intru*)	'I enter'
ĬPSUM	>	'ẽnsu	(DR *îns / ins*)	'he, him'
ĂMBULO	>	'ɔ̃mblu	(DR *umblu*)	'I walk'
ĂMBI	>	'ɔ̃mbi	(DR *îmbi*)	'both'
ĂNGULUM	>	'ɔ̃ŋɡʎu	(DR *unghi*)	'angle'
ĂNGELUM	>	'ɔ̃ndzeɾu	(DR *înger*)	'angel'
ĂNIMA	>	'ɔ̃ɾemə	(DR *inimă*)	'heart'

In medieval times these forms suffered competing phonological pressures. On the one hand, by normal evolution the mid vowels [ẽ ɔ̃] would raise to [ĩ ɨ̃], respectively. On the other hand, the developments with unstressed word-initial nasal vowels prompted a different path of change. Unstressed vowels typically coalesced with a following nasal consonant so as to leave just a syllabic nasal consonant word-initially. Such was evidently the realization for many sixteenth-century speakers, and indeed it is still found in contemporary DR pronunciation. Thus, Petrovici (1930: 71) observes, 'La vraie prononciation du mot *împărat* est [m̩pərat] . . . ce qu'on désigne par [î] initial nasal n'est le plus souvent qu'une consonne nasale syllabique.'[36]

As a result of the existence of verbs with initial nasal vowels which could be stressed or unstressed depending upon the inflexional form concerned, the possibility of having syllabic nasals spread to stressed syllables too. Thus, just as a syllabic nasal developed in AMBULĀTUM (past part.) > [m̩'blat] and INTRĀTUM > [n̩'trat], it also developed in ĂMBULO > ['ɔ̃mblu] > ['m̩blu], ĬNTRO > ['entru] > ['n̩tru]. And by extension, other words possessing stressed word-initial nasal vowels also came to develop syllabic nasals, even if they had no alternants with unstressed initial nasal vowels.

In the literary period (since the sixteenth century), there has been a general move in DR to restructure initial syllabic nasal consonants as sequences of vowel + nasal consonant, particularly where the initial syllable was stressed.[37] The vowel segment created, however, often did not reflect the original initial vowel. Its quality was determined by the phonetic context and by a morpho-phonemic constraint to the effect that stressed central vowels may not occur word-initial in open-set lexical items.

The broad pattern for Wallachian dialects, and hence standard DR, was:

stressed syllabic nasal   >

[um-], [uŋ] /___ labial or velar consonant

[in-] /___ coronal consonant

hence *umblu, umflu, umplu, unghi* 'I walk, I inflate, I fill, angle', and *intru* 'I enter'.

One or two items are problematic. Of the grammatical forms *îns/ins* and *îmbi*, the vowel of the latter probably reflects the generalization of the unstressed variant, while the evolution of the former item has been much affected by its syntactic context. It was typically used in prepositional phrases and the quality of its vowel (front or central) increasingly reflected that of the preceding preposition, hence *dens(u), dins(u)* < DE-ÎPSUM but *cătrăns(u)* < CONTRA-ÎPSUM in sixteenth-century texts. But subsequently the latter, centralized alternant was progressively generalized (cf. Avram 1990: 86–9). Amongst lexical items, ĂNIMA would be expected to give ['ṇimə] but the following front vowel guided the restructuring to ['inimə]. However, the form *înger* < ĂNGELUM is curious and may well reflect the vocalism of another DR dialect where different restructuring patterns operated.[38]

For unstressed initial syllabic nasals, if a sequence of vowel + nasal is pronounced, the vowel segment is typically [ɨ], as in *împărat, întreg, îngust, înalt* 'emperor, whole, narrow, high' < IMPERĂTOR INTĔGRUM ANGŬ-STUM IN-ĂLTUM. In all such forms the initial syllabic nasal doubtless came to be taken as a prefix. This was scarcely feasible for the form [ṇ'elu] 'ring' < ANĔLLUM, and hence phonological forces have acted leading to restructuring as [in-] *inel* under the fronting influence of the stressed vowel.

Outside DR, different patterns are found. Just to consider the facts of AR, we find that no AR word has initial stressed [ɨ-] and only northern dialects have initial unstressed [ɨ-] (Papahagi 1974: s.v. *î-*). Southern dialects have generally no vowel, e.g. *ntreb* 'I ask', or a prothetic [a-] *angustu* (beside *ngustu*) 'narrow'. Corresponding AR reflexes for the items considered above are: *umplu, umflu, intru, inima, ntreg, analt(u)*.

12.3.3. UNSTRESSED NASAL VOWELS

At the outset of period II, the range of unstressed nasal vowels was probably

$$ \tilde{\imath} \qquad\qquad \tilde{u} $$
$$ \tilde{e} \quad \tilde{ə} $$

Examples of the vowel [ĩ] appear only in derived forms and this vowel shows no subsequent change, e.g. VINĀRIUM > AR [ɣĩ'nar] 'wineseller'. The other front vowel [ẽ] has regularly raised to [ĩ] when in context (i) forms:

MENTIŌNEM > mẽn't͡ʃõ͡r̃e > DR *minciună* AR *minciună* 'falsehood'
GINGĪVA   > d͡ʒẽn'd͡ʒie   > DR *gingie* AR *dzindzie* 'gum'

But in context (iii) forms, raising has been less regular so that [ẽ] may be retained in some varieties. Examples:

CINŪSIA   > t͡ʃẽ'r̃uʃe   > DR *cenuşe* AR *cinuşe* 'ash'
GENŬCULUM > d͡ʒẽ'r̃ukʎu > DR *genunchi* AR *dzinucliu* 'knee'
HŎMIN-Ī   > 'ǫamẽr̃i   > DR *oameni* AR *oamini* 'men'

The non-raising in this context-type is typical of Wallachian dialects and hence standard DR. However, in dialects of Transylvania and some Moldavian varieties a high vowel is found in post-stress syllables, for example in HŎMIN-Ī > ['ǫaminⁱ] (*ALR* 6, 1582; *TDR*: 361). Elsewhere, IR has a pattern similar to Transylvanian and Moldavian dialects, ['omir] but [ʒe'ruŋkʎu], but AR and MR have generalized a high vowel in all unstressed syllables.

The central vowel [ə̃] developed from unstressed nasalized [ã], and in DR it also evolved from [ẽ] which was centralized when a labial consonant preceded and a non-front vowel appeared in the following syllable (cf. 12.3.2.1). Subsequently, this vowel raised to [ɨ̃] in context (i) forms:

LANGUŌREM > lə̃ŋ'gǫare > DR *lîngoare* AR *lîngoare* 'typhus'

In context (iii) forms, there is no raising except in transparently derived forms such as *lînos* 'woolly' from *lînă* < LĀNA 'wool'. Examples:

MINŪTUM   > mə̃'r̃utu   > DR *mărunt* AR *minut* 'small'
PANĪCUM   > pə̃'r̃iku   > DR *părînc, părinc*   'millet'

The unstressed prepositional phrase PAENE AD > pẽr̃(e) a > DR *pînă*, AR *pînă* 'up to' probably owes its high vowel to the influence of other prepositions such as *în, lîngă* 'in, near to'.

The evolution of the back nasal vowel [ũ] is more complex. It is very probable that Late Balkan Latin unstressed [õ] had raised to merge with original [ũ] already by the end of Period I. But in context (i) forms this vowel has frequently centralized to give [ɨ̃]. Examples:

FONTĀNA	> *fîntînă* 'well'	IN-CONFLĀRE	> *îngîmfa*
			'to put on airs'
RHONCHĪZO	> *rînchez* 'I snore'	HIRUNDINĚLLA	> *rîndunea*
			'swallow'
LONGUM AD (phrasal prep.)	> *lîngă* 'near to'		

These contrast with context (iii) forms where [ū] remained a back vowel, *bunătate, cunosc, uni* < BONITĀTEM COGNŌSCO UNĪRE 'goodness, I know, to join'.

Earlier scholars claimed that there was a general rule of centralization, whereby unstressed [u] passed to [ɨ] (e.g. Densusianu 1975: 400–1). However, this view has been contested (Rosetti 1978: 402; Avram 1990: 63), the assumption being that each case of centralization is due to special and individual circumstances. Yet, the clear centralizing tendency in context (i) forms is striking, and exceptions to it may in their turn be seen as due to special circumstances; for example, *muncel* < MONTICĚLLUM 'hillock' could well be analogically influenced by *munte* 'hill'. The variable phonetic development here shows interesting parallels with that found in stressed word-initial position in different dialects, as in *umplu* vs. *împlu* (cf. 12.3.2.4).

12.3.4.   UNDERMINING OF POSSIBLE PHONEMIC VOWEL NASALITY

Despite the apparent intensity of vowel nasalization in early Romanian, the resulting nasal vowels never went on to gain full phonemic status. Though it is impossible to know for sure what prevented such a development from going through, a number of factors can be identified which may have helped to block the rise of phonemically nasal vowels.

First, in context (i) forms the partial restoration of contrasts between coda nasals in the later medieval period, as in DR *strîmt* vs. *frînt*, doubtless served to strengthen nasals somewhat in this environment (12.2.4). In fact, coda nasals which are homorganic with a following oral consonant have generally continued to be phonetically weakly articulated in DR, since their identity is readily inferable from the following oral consonant. However, the appearance of non-homorganic nasal consonants in coda position, as in *strîmt*, may be expected to lead to some strengthening of coda nasals to ensure their discrimination by hearers, and as a result the purely conditioned status of the nasality in the preceding vowel would be reinforced.

Secondly, in context (iii) forms the reflex of -N- was weakened but never deleted, unlike in Galician-Portuguese (8.2.4), Gascon (6.3), and certain other Romance areas (10.4.4.1, 11.2.2). Unconditioned nasal vowels never arose here therefore. Furthermore, in the later medieval period the phonologically isolated nature of the early Romanian reflex [r̃] resulted in its restructuring to [n] in most varieties of Romanian. The associated strengthening involved here appears to have been accompanied by some denasalization of the preceding vowel.

Thirdly, no context (ii) forms developed in Romanian until the end of the Middle Ages. By then the developments just noted had effectively blocked moves toward vowel nasalization. The word-final nasal consonants which arose after apocope have shown no sign of losing their contrastiveness or of significantly nasalizing the preceding vowel.

Forming a backcloth to these structural developments was the sustained and widespread presence of Slavonic-Romanian bilingualism. Bulgarian was the key Slavonic language and it almost certainly had nasal vowels until the thirteenth century when denasalization occurred (Rosetti 1978: 453). The effect which the abandonment of vowel nasalization in Bulgarian had on Romanian is difficult to assess, but it may well have added some impetus to structural developments within Romanian which were tending to keep nasality in vowels as a purely allophonic feature.

The treatment of loanwords into Romanian points to the chronological stages at which the raising triggered by vowel nasalization gradually lost productivity. There are already signs of this in Hungarian loans, which date from the eleventh to twelfth centuries in the main. In the most productive nasalizing context, type (i), mid vowels are subject to nasalization and raising, hence *gyenges* > DR *gingaș* 'fragile' and *gond* > DR *gînd* 'idea'. However, the low vowel /a/ is not, e.g. *hang* > DR *hang* (not **hîng*) 'accompaniment'. Later loans from other sources confirm the non-productivity of nasal vowel raising for /a/ and the spread of non-productivity to other vowel types. Greek borrowings attested in the fifteenth century include *trandafir* 'rose' (stressed on the final syllable), and Turkish loans dating from the sixteenth century onward include *renghi* 'hoax', *pezevenchi* 'swindler' (< *renç, pezevenk*) where there has been no raising effect on mid vowels. Henceforth, vowels in nasalizing contexts may be nasalized but their height remains unmodified.

12.3.5. CONCLUSION

Vowel nasalization in Romanian shows a number of individual characteristics which mark it off from comparable developments in other Romance varieties. The original rule of vowel nasalization in late Balkan Latin consists in reality of two separate and successive rules, and their effect has been progressively to raise non-high vowels to a high tongue position. Nasal vowels, however, never became established as independent phonemes, as a result of various developments in the period from about the tenth century on. The absence of any clear divorce between nasal and oral vowels is borne out by the fact that, at various stages in the history of Romanian, major processes which affected oral vowel evolution, such as retraction and fronting, also operated on nasal vowels.

NOTES

1. In the chancellery of Moldavia, the use of Slavonic was abandoned in the reign of Peter the Lame (1574–89) and in the chancellery of Wallachia it was in the reign of Michael the Brave (1593–1601). The Orthodox Church continued to issue liturgical works in Slavonic up until the end of the seventeenth century, and the liturgy of the Church continued to use Slavonic until the early eighteenth century (Coteanu 1981: 88).

2. In the standard reference manual for the history of Romanian, Rosetti (1978) distinguishes no fewer than five divisions: second–seventh/eighth centuries; tenth–thirteenth centuries; thirteenth–seventeenth centuries; seventeenth century–now.

3. Occasionally there have been claims that Romanian has phonemic nasal vowels, e.g. E. Tănase (1972) and A.-M. Tănase (1984), but these have found little favour.

4. The much-quoted assertion of the fourth-century historian Eutropius (VIII. vi. 21), 'On the conquest of Dacia, Trajan had moved huge numbers of men to it from all over the Roman world to till the fields and build up the towns' suggests very diverse origins for the colonists. However, linguistic considerations point to a substantial proportion of the new settlers in Dacia probably coming from southern and particularly south-eastern Italy.

5. These are mainly lexical in nature and relate to the incidence of borrowings from outside languages whose geographical and social spheres of influence can be dated fairly precisely. Notable here is the impact of Hungarian from the eleventh–twelfth centuries, which has affected DR considerably but has scarcely been felt in IR, AR, and MR.

6. Cf. Densusianu (1975: 465–9). In contrast, Rosetti (1978: 511–15) argues that the apparent retention of final -u in sixteenth-century forms such as loc(u) 'place' is purely scribal, and that the deletion of the final vowel was already underway in the thirteenth century and completed by the sixteenth century. However, it seems likely that especially after consonant clusters, e.g. in cîmp, some residue of the original final vowel still existed in the sixteenth century in many DR dialects although deletion after simplex consonants was widespread, cf. Avram (1964: 160–9). Today, traces of final -u in forms where the standard language has long deleted them are still to be found in south-east, central and north-west dialects of DR (Caragiu Marioțeanu 1977: maps 7, 8 for tînăr(u) stîngaci(u)).

7. The same neutralization between nasals preceding oral consonants is still found in modern Romanian; cf. 'il y a peu de Roumains qui se rendent compte que, dans împăca, ils prononcent une consonne nasale différente de celle de îndesa' (Pușcariu 1937: 128–9).

8. The greater duration of [m] as opposed to [n] ceteris paribus has been demonstrated instrumentally for a number of Romance varieties. Navarro Tomás (1918), Sampson (1981), Borzone and Signorini (1983), and Ayuso (1991) all report intervocalic [m] to

be realized anything from 14% to 65% longer than [n], depending on the variety and the precise location of the nasal relative to the primary stressed vowel. See also Tuttle (1991: 55–8) for the 'strong *m*' of northern Italian dialects.

9. In Western Romance the sequence -GN- also evolved to give /ɲ/. In Balkan Latin the pronunciation [ŋn] for -GN-, which was widespread in Classical times, was at first retained but later the first segment labialized and the sequence emerged as [mn] in all varieties of Romanian, LĬGNUM > (DR) *lemn* 'wood', COGNĀTUM > (DR) *cumnat* 'brother-in-law'. This sequence did not operate as a nasalizing context.

10. Apparent counterexamples exist such as *VULP-ŌNEUM > (DR) *vulpoi* 'male fox'. Here, the stressed vowel lies in a suffix, and it is likely that the non-raising is due to influence from other suffixes designating male beings which also contain stressed /o/ such as -*tor* < -TŌREM, as in *cumpărător* 'buyer'.

11. Parallels to this are not unknown elsewhere in Romance. For example, in standard Italian, [ɛ] is commonly raised to [e] when surrounded by nasal consonants but there is no raising if it is merely followed by a nasal, cf. MĔNTEM > *m*[e]*nte* but SĔNTIT > *s*[ɛ]*nte* (cf. 10.2.2).

12. In DR, this word which means 'smaller horned livestock' is confined to the dialect of Banat; cf. Puşcariu (1976: 224) and Rosetti (1978: 386). A variant form, *nămaliu* 'small wool-bearing livestock', is also found in AR and the *REW* 476 also notes a form in MR meaning 'a steer'.

13. It will be recalled that the interplay between these two changes has also served to demonstrate the early implementation of vowel nasalization in Romanian, cf. 12.1.2.

14. In AR, where labial consonants also regularly palatalize, further proof of non-diphthongization is forthcoming. The following forms may be compared: VĔSPEM > ɣ*easpe* 'wasp', VĒRUM > *ver* 'cousin', where [ɣ] derives from an earlier sequence [vj-]; VĔNTUM > *vimtu* 'wind' with raising of [ɛ] > [e] *before* diphthongization was able to occur, as against VĔNIT > ɣ*ine* 'he comes' where raising took place *after* diphthongization had operated. The proparoxytons VĔNERIS > *viniri* ['vinir[i]] 'Friday', VĔNETUM > *vinit* 'purple, dark grey' evolved like *vimtu* with no diphthongization (Papahagi 1974).

15. Few explanations have been advanced, and none is tenable. Sampson (forthcoming) reviews these and advances another proposal according to which the unusual treatment of nasalization in proparoxytons may reflect the adaptation of a pronunciation feature borrowed for prestige reasons from Southern Italy.

16. Usually, the sequence [ŋkt] in Latin developed to [nt] (cf. SĀNCTUM > Old and regional DR *sînt* 'holy'). Also, the creation of past participle forms in [ŋkt] is more extensive in some varieties than others; thus, DR has *strîmt* but *unt frînt*, whereas in AR past participles in [ŋkt] were more widespread, hence *strimtu umtu frîmtu*.

17. The literature on rhotacism in Romanian is extensive. The early study by Rosetti (1924) provides a clear overview, and all standard manuals of the history of Romanian have subsequently addressed the question. Avram (1990: 114–53) usefully reviews previous work.

18. Some indeterminacy surrounds the transcriptions used for these rhotacized sequences. Some writers assign the nasality to the trill, others to the preceding vowel, i.e. ['lur̃ə] or ['lūrə]. However, it seems rather likely that in such forms

nasality was present over both segments as a sort of prosody, as [ˈlūr̃ə], although the focus for the prosody was doubtless the trill.

19. Very rarely, cases of migration are found where a continuant is involved. Thus, CINŪSIA has given [tʃeˈnūʃə / tʃeˈrūʃə] 'ash' in the conservative dialects of the Apuşeni Mountains.

20. Rosetti (1978: 704) places the likely period of productivity of metaphonic diphthongization to between the sixth and eighth centuries.

21. The main problem concerns forms such as VĔNTUM > (DR) vînt 'wind' and VĒNA > (DR) vînă 'vein'. These have undergone the regular retraction of [e] to [ə] caused by the presence of a preceding labial consonant and a following back vowel. This change affected oral and nasal vowels alike, cf. PĬLUM > (DR) păr [pər] 'hair', although nasal vowels underwent raising later on. Now, because the retraction of /e/ is a specifically Daco-Romanian development and hence presumably post-dates the tenth century, the implication is that forms like VĔNTUM kept a mid vowel until after the tenth century to be able to participate in the change. Recognizing this, Avram (1990) is obliged to hypothesize a rather unconvincing three-stage scenario for [e] raising.

22. The /e/ and /o/ phonemes of Castilian Spanish provide a clear example. These have relatively high realizations (as in pero and cosa) and relatively low realizations (as in perro and hoja), determined by syllable structure and segmental environment; cf. Navarro Tomás (1968: §§ 51, 52, 58, 59).

23. A similar view is proposed in an earlier work by Avram (1964: 156) though it was evidently abandoned by him more recently, cf. supra n. 21. Comparable instances of resistance to (originally) metaphonically conditioned change in vowel height are found elsewhere in Romance involving nasal vowels. Thus, in Portuguese, the 1st and 3rd person singular present tense verb forms v[e]rto : v[ɛ]rte d[e]vo: d[ɛ]ve < VĔRTO VĔRTIT, DĒBEO DĒBET show an [e] : [ɛ] alternation which occurs regularly in -er verbs, as part of a wide-ranging pattern of mid-vowel metaphony in -er and -ir verbs. However, the alternation is overridden in nasal contexts, although not with verbs containing nasalizing context (iii) in European Portuguese. Hence, the verb vender 'to sell' has the present tense forms v[ẽ]ndo : v[ẽ]nde not **v[ẽ]nde < VĒNDO VĒNDIT (Parkinson 1982).

24. Avram (1990: 51) dates the raising to [j̃ĩ] and simplification to [ĩ] to 'Common Romanian', i.e. by the tenth century, though of course such dating can only be speculative.

25. Certain linguists, e.g. Vasiliu (1968: 76) and Sala (1976: 223), assume that [ã] had already raised to [ə̃] by the eighth century. There is of course no direct evidence for this assumption.

26. Some uncertainty surrounds this question, since no direct knowledge exists of Slavonic at the time of the invasion of the Balkans (seventh century) and the early period of occupation. The first extant running texts in Slavonic were composed in the ninth century by two Greek missionaries from Byzantium, Constantine (later called Cyril) (d. 869) and Methodius (d. 885). These were written in Old Church Slavonic, a language apparently devised artificially on the basis of Macedonian dialects (Shevelov 1964: 1). The originals no longer exist and

the earliest extant manuscripts in Slavonic go back to the late tenth or early eleventh centuries only.

27. At the time when this development occurred, there appear to have been no sequences of the form VN-N. This was because all geminates had already been simplified and intervocalic /mn/ and /nm/ sequences had had their first segment deleted (Shevelov 1964: 323–4; Lunt 1974: 29).

28. Cf. Marti (1984: 140) who concludes from a detailed study of the earliest Slavonic texts in Glagolitic characters that 'the phonological system of Proto-OCS as represented by the original *glagolica* distinguished two true nasal vowels'.

29. Other results are occasionally found as well, for instance in rostǫpu > (DR) *răstimp* 'interval, duration' where the outcome is a front vowel [i]. The unexpected vowel probably reflects interference from the native item *timp* < TĔMPUS 'time'. Other exceptional developments likewise seem to result from special causes.

30. One group of anomalous forms stands out: županu > DR *jupîn* 'boyar, master', stopanu > DR *stăpîn* 'master', sumętana > DR *smîntînă* 'sour cream', (?) stanu > DR *stînă* 'sheep pen'. Their background has been much discussed; Petrovici 1966; Mihăilă 1971: 360–3; Sala 1976: 92; Densusianu 1975: 259; Rosetti 1978: 344. All these words must have entered early Romanian at a time when /VnV/ was still a productive nasalizing context and Latin geminate -NN- was still unsimplified, so that the simplex /n/ of these loanwords was identified with Latin simplex -N-. They must therefore all be early loans. Similarly, Greek borrowings such as *spîn* 'beardless' (< σπανος) must have entered Romanian early on since later context type (iii) Hellenisms show the same non-nasalization as Slavonic loans, e.g. *litanie* [li'tanije] 'litany' (< λιτανια).

31. In the same way, Slavonic influence was doubtless involved in the abandonment of the oral flap [ɾ] < simplex -L- -R- as a distinctive sound. Slavonic intervocalic /r/ was systematically identified with the reflex of Latin geminate -RR- rather than of simplex -R- in early Romanian.

32. It may be noted that oral [ɨ] had developed as a positional variant of [i] at some stage in the later Middle Ages, for example after strong [r], e.g. *rîu* 'river' < RĪVUM (Sala 1976: 190). Some scholars have claimed that the high central vowel /ɨ/ arose in Romanian as a borrowing from Slavonic, but Petrucci (1995) argues strongly that the vowel represents a native Romanian creation. As far as /ɨ/ in nasalizing contexts is concerned, there can be little doubt that the latter view is correct and that all cases of [ɨ] reflect the result of native Romanian changes.

33. For a helpful and more detailed review, see Avram (1990: 33–47).

34. For instance, the DR dialects of central and east Wallachia (including the standard language) resisted retraction after /(d)z/ and only patchily adopted it after /t͡s/ and /s/, hence standard *zic, țin, simt* 'I say, I hold, I feel' as against [(d)zɨk t͡sɨn sɨmt/ sɨmt͡s] which appear in all other DR dialects (*ALR* 1928, 1942, 1953).

35. In sixteenth-century texts, there is clear evidence of more widespread alternation, as in *învînc, învîncă* 'I defeat; defeat (pres. subj.)' < INVĬNCO INVĬNCAM/-S/-T) beside *(în)vence, învenge, vinge* 'defeats (3rd sg. pres.) < INVĬNCIT (Densusianu 1975: 436, 551).

36. In the process of developing to a syllabic nasal, it has been suggested that the

unstressed nasal vowel [ẽ-] in the initial sequences [ẽm-/ẽn-/ẽŋ-] may first have undergone lowering to [ã-], just as ERĪCIUM > DR *arici* 'hedgehog' (Avram 1990: 101–2).

37. Nandriş (1963: 168) attributes this to an attempt to avoid major consonant clusters in connected speech following the regular deletion of word-final [-u] and [-i] at the end of the medieval period. Thus, in sequences such as *un om prost mblă* 'a foolish man is walking along', the lengthy cluster [stm̩bl] which would arise as *prostu* lost its final vowel could be avoided by restructuring the syllabic [m̩] as vowel + [m].

38. Outside Wallachia, there is in fact a good deal of variation. In Banat and Transylvania, the typical outcome of ĬNTRO is *întru*, whereas it appears as *untru* in parts of N. Crişana (*ALR*, vii. 1900). Beside standard *umflu* and *umplu*, there is *îmflu* and *împlu* in W. Banat, Maramureş, and parts of N. Moldavia (*ALR*, vii. 1903, 1904). Restructuring thus followed differing regional lines, where the two guiding forces identified above and possibly others besides operated variously.

13

Conclusion: Retrospect and Prospects

The picture which has emerged from our review of Romance nasal vowel evolution has been a varied one. That there should be variation is of course predictable given that the developments which have been considered extend over a span of two thousand years and relate to a vast geographical area encompassing a host of separate communities. Yet it is possible to detect certain common characteristics for vowel nasalization in Romance in a similar way to what Chen (1972a, 1975) has sought to do for Chinese dialects. A number of shared characteristics have in fact presented themselves fairly clearly in the course of our coverage. Some of these may be directly compared with patterns of nasalization identified by linguists working on data from outside Romance also. In this way, our findings will serve to confirm or qualify claims that these patterns may have general validity in language. Others, however, are less readily reconciled with general assumptions which have been made about vowel nasalization and signal areas where further investigation is needed. In this final chapter these broader issues are considered as we briefly evaluate the data which have emerged from our review.

13.1. 'Universal' Patterns of Nasalization and Romance

Amongst the findings from Romance, several may first be considered which relate to the process of implementation in vowel nasalization.

1. High-level allophonic (phonologized) and phonemic vowel nasalization in Romance have typically arisen from the action of regressive assimilation, whereas nasalization is much rarer as a result of progressive assimilation and has normally occurred in dialects already knowing regressive assimilation (cf. 4.2.2, 5.4, and 8.2.4). Spontaneous nasalization is perhaps best seen as an independent 'maverick' phenomenon (cf. 5.2, 5.4, 7.4.2, and 10.2.1). Romance data here accord well with observations from other languages (e.g. Chen 1972a, 1975 for Chinese) and the conclusions drawn from general cross-linguistic

studies (Schourup 1972, 1973 and Ruhlen 1978: 223), and they suggest the existence of a general directionality parameter for vowel nasalization: regressive assimilation > progressive assimilation (signifying that the presence of progressive assimilation implies that of regressive assimilation, but not vice versa).

2. Stressed vowels have tended to be more receptive to vowel nasalization than unstressed vowels (cf. especially 10.4.3.2), although in a number of Romance varieties the data are indeterminate as stressed and unstressed vowels show similar receptivity only (e.g. 4.3.1).[1] Attempts to go further and grade types of unstressed vowels (pre-stress vs. post-stress, etc.) into a hierarchy of receptivity to nasalization may be unwise for want of sufficient data (10.4.3.2). The findings for stressed vs. unstressed vowels are in line with the results of cross-linguistic surveys (Schourup 1973: 192–3), and point to the appropriateness of identifying a parameter of vowel nasalization: stressed vowels > unstressed vowels.

3. Long vowels are more receptive to nasalization than short vowels. This finding correlates with the preceding one in that stressed vowels are typically longer than unstressed vowels. The greater receptivity of long vowels to nasalization is more clearly in evidence for some varieties of Romance (10.4.3) than others, but nowhere are the data incompatible. This finding accords with Hombert (1986), Hajek (1997), and suggests a vowel-length parameter for nasalization: long vowels > short vowels. The nature of the relationship between length and vowel nasalization is problematic, however, and is taken up again below in 13.3.

4. Height or backness variations have not played any clear and consistent role in determining the receptiveness of a vowel to nasalization in Romance. As regards the relevance of height variation, the available data are somewhat conflicting. There are cases offering some indication of low vowels being more receptive to nasalization than high vowels (9.2, 10.2.1, 10.4.3.4) but certain instances appear where high vowels rather than low vowels have been nasalized, e.g. in the dialect of Aniane in Hérault (6.2.2.4). The variation here may in part reflect the use of different criteria (articulatory vs. perceptual) in determining whether a vowel is described as 'nasal'. Most conspicuously, the classic example of standard French was found to provide no clear evidence of low vowels having been more receptive to nasalization than high vowels (4.2.3). The findings from Romance thus provide muted support for the widespread assumption amongst non-Romanists that there is a low > high parameter operative in vowel nasalization, this assumption ironically drawing strongly on French as a paradigm case (Chen 1972a, 1973a, 1973b; Schourup 1973; Ruhlen 1978).

The other property of vowels sometimes postulated as having relevance in governing the process of nasalization relates to the front/back dimension. The history of Romance offers occasional indications of a back > front parameter operating (4.2.3, and Tuttle 1991: 50–1), but evidence for a front > back parameter may also be encountered (6.2.2.4). The variability here finds a counterpart in the conflicting claims made by certain non-Romanists. For instance, Schourup (1973) posits a back > front parameter whereas Chen (1972*a*, 1973*a*, 1973*b*) and Ruhlen (1978) postulate the reverse. Romance data thus provide no strong support for identifying a parameter of vowel nasalization based on either the front/back axis or height variation.

5. Regarding the conditioning nasal consonant and its involvement with vowel nasalization, more than one finding may be distinguished.

(*a*) There is evidence that the receptivity to nasalization in a vowel is determined by the place of articulation of the conditioning nasal consonant. This is especially the case in contexts where place of articulation was distinctive. The coronal nasal [n] has been the strongest trigger of vowel nasalization. Its precedence in context (ii) is clear in Romance (6.2.1.3, 7.3.1.3, 9.3.4, 10.4.4.1), and it is the nasal par excellence involved in vowel nasalization in context (iii) forms (8.2.4, 10.4.4, 11.2.2, 12.2.4), although in section 13.2 below we shall see that nasalization in this context type may involve other considerations. The other types of nasal have shown a locally variable propensity to nasalize vowels which precludes any general Romance statement of precedence being made for these. A simple parameter of the following type is all that can safely be proposed therefore: n (deriving from -N-) > m ɲ ñ (from -NN-). In context (i) forms, there is no clear parametrization. This can be attributed to the fact that in this context type the place of articulation of the nasal consonant was not distinctive and a nasal archiphoneme was usually found. However, there have been cases of vowel raising apparently due to nasalization where the trigger was a velar nasal (3.2.1, 7.3.1.2, 8.2.3, 10.2.2). A highly tentative parameter might therefore be proposed for context (i): ŋ > n m. The parameter for contexts (ii) and (iii) is compatible with that posited by Hajek (1997) for northern Italian, but is at odds with the proposal m > n > ŋ of Chen (1972*a*, 1975) working on Chinese data in which just context type (ii) forms are found.

A preferential order is also found in the relative susceptibility of conditioning nasal consonants to deletion and the consequent creation of nasal vowel phonemes. Predictably perhaps, the same parameter for nasal deletion emerges in Romance as that which has just been seen above for vowel nasalization. This may be contrasted with the rather speculative parameter advanced for nasal consonant deletion by Foley (1975: 200), namely: ŋ > n > m.

(*b*) When conditioning nasal consonants undergo weakening and are deleted to give nasal vowel phonemes, they do not necessarily pass through a velar stage [ŋ] prior to deletion. Although a number of linguists have assumed that velarization is the normal precursor to deletion of a nasal consonant (Chen 1972*a*, 1973*a*; Ruhlen 1978 with one reservation; Tuttle 1991), the evidence from Romance is not supportive. Weakening led to the neutralization of place of articulation contrasts between nasals in context (ii) forms to give coronal [n] in almost all Gallo-Romance (4.2.4, 6.2.2.4), while in northern Italy weakening had no regular effect on place of articulation. In other context types, place of articulation changes have normally not occurred amongst conditioning nasals prior to deletion. Confusing the interpretation of the available data from Romance has been the phenomenon of restoration whereby an unconditioned nasal vowel has been restructured into a sequence of nasal vowel + conditioning nasal consonant, $\tilde{V} > \tilde{V}N$, the typical value of the restored nasal consonant being velar [ŋ] (6.2.2.4, 6.3, 7.4.2, 8.4.4, 9.3.4, 10.4.4.2).

Further findings relate to repercussions of the implementation of vowel nasalization.

6. When high-level allophonic or phonemic vowel nasalization has occurred, the resulting nasal vowel system will never be larger than the corresponding oral vowel system. This is in accordance with statement XI in Ferguson (1966) and reflects an uncontroversial universal of human languages. An additional finding has been that if the oral vowel system contains more than five members, the nasal vowel system will be smaller. A comparable disparity in the size of oral and nasal systems is widely found amongst non-Romance languages also (Maddieson 1991). The reduction in the relative size of the nasal system has usually come about through neutralization having taken place. Most affected by neutralization have been mid-vowel contrasts (4.2.3, 6.2.1, 8.2.3, 9.3.3, 10.5.1). The experimental data reported by Wright (1980, 1986) on the basis of perception tests offer some rationale for the reduction in nasal vowel contrastivity (cf. 1.1).

7. There is no safe evidence that nasalization has directly caused lowering of (high or high-mid) nasal vowels. Experimental investigation has indicated that there is a tendency for nasality to have the perceptual effect of lowering high or high-mid vowels (cf. 1.1), but the findings from Romance do not provide clear support that nasal vowels have a special predisposition to lowering. Certainly the notorious claim of Straka (1955: 248) that 'dès qu'une voyelle se nasalise, elle tend aussitôt à s'ouvrir', which was essentially based on the history of French, is unsustainable. Lowering has occurred in a number of Romance varieties (4.3.3, 5.2.4, 6.2.2.3, 9.4.3, 10.5.4), but by no means in all (6.3, 8.1.2, 11.2.2, 11.3.3.2). Furthermore, there are cases where (non-high) nasalized vowels have undergone systematic raising to a high tongue position with no discernible lowering tendency affecting them thereafter (10.5.4 and especially 12.3.1). Similarly contradictory evidence about the effect of nasality on vowel height (raising or lowering) is found in non-Romance languages. Working on data from a cross-linguistic survey, Schourup (1973) has attempted to reconcile the disparate facts by postulating that there is a tendency for *conditioned* nasal vowels to raise but that nasal vowels tend to lower when the conditioning nasal consonant is deleted,[2] and Ohala (1981) offers a speculative acoustic-perceptual rationale

for this alleged double tendency. It is proposed that, in the absence of a conditioning nasal consonant, speaker-hearers would be more likely to adopt the perceptually lower quality of a (high) vowel as the target position. But when the conditioning nasal is present, hearers may attribute any apparent perceptual lowering to the influence of the consonant and, in an attempt to compensate for this when acting as speakers, a target articulation may be adopted which is higher than that used in producing the original. More circumspectly, Ruhlen (1975) finds no real evidence for any lowering tendency with unconditioned nasal vowels (cf. 1.2 also), although he accepts that there is a raising tendency with the conditioned type. Some Romance evidence for the latter alleged tendency may be seen in the widespread neutralization of nasalized mid-vowel contrasts, typically in favour of a high-mid realization [ẽ õ] (4.2.3, 6.2.1, 8.2.3, 9.3.3, 10.5.1), but on the other hand, there are examples of lowering in conditioned high or high-mid nasal vowels (4.3.2.1, 9.4.3, 10.5.4). The variability of the data suggests that nasalization in Romance has typically acted as a fairly weak background factor in shaping vowel height change, sometimes serving to reinforce independently motivated tendencies in the language concerned (4.3.3) but at other times capable of being overridden by opposing structural forces within the sound system of the language.

13.2.   Nasalizing Mechanisms

Rather more at variance with previous characterizations of vowel nasalization in Romance or other languages has been our recognition of two separate though related nasalizing 'mechanisms' whereby nasal vowels can be created. The syllabic relationship between the nasalizing vowel and the (following) conditioning nasal consonant is of central importance to the distinction between the two mechanisms, in particular whether the nasal consonant forms the coda to the syllable in which the vowel occurs or whether it belongs to the following syllable, i.e. whether the syllable structure was VN- or V-N (where '-' indicates a syllable boundary). Diachronic evidence from Romance indicates that patterns of vowel nasalization may be quite different in these two types of syllabic environment. Thus, in certain Romance varieties phonemic vowel nasalization has been confined to the first type of context whereas the second context type has only undergone limited allophonic vowel nasalization But in other varieties a quite different pattern presents itself in which phonemic nasalization has taken place in the second type only whereas in the first context type only limited allophonic vowel nasalization has occurred. The incidence of phonemic nasalization may be represented diagrammatically as in Figure 5.

The implication of such data is that any characterization of vowel nasalization which systematically unifies contexts containing a coda conditioning nasal

	VN-	V-NV
Milan (Lombardy)	-/+	-
Meldola (Romagna)	+	-
St. French	+	-
Ancares (NW León)	-	+
Galeria (Corsica)	-	+
Milis (Sardinia)	-	+

(where '-/+' indicates phonemic nasalization in a major subset of environments)

FIG. 5 Patterns of nasalization
Sources: (respectively) *AIS*, pt. 261 and Nicoli (1983), *AIS*, pt. 478, personal knowledge; Alonso and Yebra (1972) and Fernández González (1981), Dalbera-Stefanaggi (1989, 1991), Contini (1987).

(= context-types (i) and (ii)) and those where the conditioning nasal is an onset (= context-type (iii)) within a single parameter would appear to be ill-founded. This view thus conflicts with the proposals of Ruhlen (1973), Schourup (1973), and Hajek (1997), all of whom hypothesize a single unified parameter in this connection.[3]

A principled basis underpinning the distinction between the two mechanisms can be identified. With the first mechanism, the operative factor is nasalization through the assimilatory influence of a following nasal consonant. This mechanism usually operates more intensively where the conditioning nasal consonant is tautosyllabic with the vowel, but it may go on to operate secondarily where the conditioning nasal is heterosyllabic. In some varieties therefore, such as medieval French, context (iii) forms can also be affected by this mechanism in the same way as context (i) and (ii) forms. However, a single principle is at work, namely the enhancement of a feature present because of anticipatory co-articulation. It is to this mechanism alone that the parameters proposed by other scholars relate.

The other mechanism has a motivation which lies in paradigmatic rather than syntagmatic factors. It only involves context (iii) forms and has only operated where the conditioning nasal was intervocalic -N-. Basic to the mechanism are the weakening and possible loss of -N-. This usually forms part of a more general leniting tendency affecting simplex intervocalic sonorants, a tendency which is often associated with the simplification of their geminate counterparts. The different rationale of the mechanisms means that they may in principle operate independently of one another, and this possibility is confirmed by the data above. It is also possible that both mechanisms may operate at various stages in the history of a given Romance variety, as has happened for instance in Gascon (6.3).

The significance of paradigmatic factors in determining the path of vowel nasalization has perhaps been undervalued at times by scholars. In addition to underpinning the second nasalizing mechanism, they have guided vowel nasalization in at least one other way. In many Romance varieties, environments in which there was contrastivity between the conditioning nasal consonants, i.e. in nasalizing context types (ii) and (iii) in particular, show different patterns of vowel nasalization from environments where no such contrastivity existed, namely in context (i). In the former context types, vowel nasalization has commonly been sensitive to the quality of the conditioning nasal, the coronal /n/ being the nasal which has exerted the greatest nasalizing influence and also been the most susceptible to deletion, as we have seen. In context (i), however, vowel nasalization has usually operated in uniform fashion without consideration of the phonetic quality of the non-contrastive conditioning nasal. This suggests that the absence of contrastivity typically overrides the possible impact of phonetic distinctions between the types of conditioning nasal. Additional evidence for this comes from the evolution of Romanian, where vowel nasalization has regularly occurred in context (i) forms but exceptionally it has not done so in a special subset of forms in which the conditioning nasal could form paradigmatic contrasts (12.2.2). Paradigmatic considerations thus seem to have played a significant role in determining patterns of vowel nasalization, but the relationship between these and syntagmatic factors in nasalization is not a clear one and awaits further investigation inside and outside Romance. In particular it would be desirable to know how widespread the two mechanisms of vowel nasalization are and how great the degree of independence is which holds between them.

13.3.   Further Problem Areas

Two other aspects of vowel nasalization which have been in evidence in this study are deserving of closer examination in the future. These are the relationship between vowel nasalization and *length* and the problem of how *denasalization* fits together with nasalization.

As we have already seen, a relationship between vowel nasalization and length can be recognized for Romance, pointing to the existence of a long vowel > short vowel parameter of vowel nasalization (13.1). However, having identified such a parameter on the basis of his detailed study of northern Italian dialects, Hajek (1997) is led to make the strong empirical claim that in dialects with a phonologized long/short vowel distinction a vowel must have phonologized length as a prerequisite for nasalization.[4] This means that in dialects with long/short vowel distinctions the vowels in context (i) forms would necessarily trace the following path when undergoing vowel nasalization: VN-C > V:N-C > Ṽ:N-C.[5] Such a claim is controversial however and faces at least two problems. First, as short vowels in blocked syllables have not normally lengthened unless there is a special factor at work, it is difficult to see what could have caused the lengthening in the second stage if it was not the effect of nasalization. Yet, in this scenario, lengthening is being taken to be the necessary *precursor* to vowel nasalization rather than its concomitant or consequence. Second, in varieties of Romance showing significant vowel nasalization there has regularly been neutralization of mid-vowel contrasts in context (i) forms. However, in many of these varieties there has been no neutralization with originally long mid vowels, as found in context (ii) forms. For instance, in French we find *plein* 'full (m. sg.)' vs. *bien* 'well' (< PLĒNUM BĔNE) with no neutralization, as against *vente* 'sale' and *lente* 'nit' (< VĒNDITA *LĔNDITEM) where neutralization has taken place. It may therefore be wondered how it came about that the lengthened mid vowels in context (i) forms were systematically neutralized whereas originally long mid vowels were maintained distinct. If neutralization in context (i) forms is assumed to have taken place before lengthening when the vowels were still oral, this would conflict with the usual lack of mid-vowel neutralization in non-nasalizing blocked syllables of the Romance varieties concerned. Neutralization after lengthening would also be curious given the widespread maintenance of contrasts in nasalized, originally long vowels. That there is a relationship between vowel length and nasalization seems unarguable (cf. 1.1), but the claim that the former is a necessary and absolute precondition to the latter is difficult to sustain. Indeed, there are even some rare cases where Romance varieties containing a long/short vowel length distinction have undergone nasalization of short vowels without there being any associated lengthening, these concerning short vowels specifically occurring before geminate [nn] (11.3.3).

In the light of all these considerations, an alternative view might be preferable of the link between nasalization and short vowels as found in context (i) forms. This is that nasalization can become phonologized without prior lengthening but that in dialects where this begins to take place speakers will usually extend the length of the vowel to ensure ready discrimination of the nasality. The two features of length and nasality would thus be concomitants rather than one serving as a necessary precondition to the other. This question is however highly problematic and more evidence is required from experimental, dialectological, and diachronic investigation for its resolution.

We may turn to denasalization. A number of cases have appeared in this study, involving either the loss of nasality in nasal vowel phonemes so that nasality is no longer a distinctive feature in vowels, or the downgrading of high-level allophonic nasality so that the vowels concerned adopt an oral target pronunciation. The process of denasalization may implicate just the nasal vowel segment concerned, but it may also result in the restoration or strengthening of a following nasal consonant, as in:

(a) $\tilde{V}$ >   V/VN
(b) $\tilde{V}N/\tilde{V}^n$ >   VN

The nature of the relationship between denasalization and nasalization remains far from clear. A number of linguists have claimed that, when denasalization takes place, there is a preferred order in which vowels are affected. Some assume that denasalization operates in reverse order to that found with nasalization, in line with a 'first in, last out' principle, e.g. Pope (1952: § 440), while others argue for a 'first in, first out' principle, e.g. Chen (1972a: 163). Either view of course presupposes that there is an established preferred order for nasalization in the first place, and, as we have seen, this is by no means certain. Furthermore, the data reveal apparent counterexamples for both. The former claim finds problems with certain French evidence (4.3.10) suggesting that denasalization has operated preferentially with stressed vowels rather than unstressed vowels despite finding (2) above (13.1). Opposing the latter claim there are various cases showing unstressed vowels denasalizing more readily than stressed vowels (8.3.3, 8.4.3, 11.2.2). In view of the diversity of developments in Romance, the safest conclusion to be drawn is perhaps that there is no necessary and direct link between patterns of nasalization and denasalization, although a direct relationship between the two may be found in individual dialects.

A more general query might also be raised as to why, given the widespread tendency for vowels to undergo nasalization in Romance, the opposite process of denasalization should also be so well represented. Do the two processes form part of a unified tendency in Romance whereby vowels under appropriate conditions are first nasalized and later denasalized, as Meyer-Lübke (1890: § 389) proposed over a century ago? Or does denasalization constitute a distinct process which only arises under special circumstances in individual linguistic varieties? It seems likely that the phonologically marked status of nasal vowels in relation of oral vowels might act as a determinant factor in eliminating them. To that extent, denasalization in Romance could be seen as an expected corollary to nasalization (Ruhlen 1978: 228–9). However, a number of the actual cases of denasalization which have occurred in Romance can be attributed to special factors which may not relate to the internal dynamics of the variety concerned. An obvious example has been the influence of standard Italian in bringing about increasing denasalization in northern dialects of Italy. In view of this, denasalization may be viewed as a possible but by no means necessary process following vowel nasalization.

The reference to northern Italian dialects leads on to a final observation. Cross-cutting the action of the various formal factors in guiding the implementation of vowel nasalization, there has been the impact of sociolinguistic forces. In Romance, socio-political events such as invasions and population displacements and politico-cultural movements such as standardization and the rise of literacy have had significant consequences on linguistic patterns. Such phenomena may often show certain broad similarities in their effect within the individual areas where they occur, but their precise timing and the details of their consequences in any given area show a familiar but nonetheless disconcerting unpredictability. Account has been taken as far as space permits of this determinant of linguistic change in the coverage of each area considered. However, full justice can scarcely be done to it. The future effects of the growth in communications and state centralization on linguistic usage will doubtless be considerable, fostering increased convergence and complex patterns of dialect mixing. The fortunes of vowel nasalization will form a fascinating chapter against this changing background.

NOTES

1. Isolated examples may be found in Romance where vowel nasalization has occurred preferentially in unstressed syllables, as in Franco-Provençal dialects (5.2, 5.4). However, the nasalization here is of the spontaneous type and consequently this may be seen as a special and exceptional case. It appears that other examples likewise proceed from special circumstances and hence do not constitute valid counterexamples

2. Schourup's views conflate two claims in fact, as Beddor (1983: 8) correctly notes. A lowering tendency is recognized for nasal vowels which lose their conditioning nasal consonant, but he adds that 'vowels with apparent phonemic nasalization do not show clear directional tendencies' (1973: 203). In this way, the actual loss of the conditioning nasal consonant is being seen as a crucial factor in triggering the lowering tendency. The relationship between this diachronic consideration and the essentially synchronic statement which we have cited is not clear. Certainly, there is no obvious reason why the deletion of the conditioning nasal as such should promote lowering, as is implied. The following discussion relates just to the hypothesis of raising/lowering determined respectively by the unconditioned/conditioned nasality of the vowel concerned.

3. The following parameters are proposed. Ruhlen (1973) suggests VNC > VN#C > VN#V > VNV. The parameter of Schourup (1973: 213) is VN# > VNCont > VNObstr > VNV, and Hajek (1997: § 6.1.2) offers Vːn# > VNFric > VNStop [- vce] > VːnV > VNStop [+ vce] > Vn#, VnV > Vnn(V).

4. By 'phonologized', Hajek does not mean 'phonemic' or 'phonological' (cf. above, 1.2). Rather, the term designates a language-specific phenomenon of speech for which the speaker-hearer has a non-default value in his/her internalized grammar. Thus, for example, if high-level vowel nasality is used in VN sequences instead of just the low-level nasality which is universally present in such an environment, the vowel nasality would be said to be phonologized. However, it is notable that a number of the parameters in Hajek (1997) appear to be founded less on phonologized than *universal* length phenomena. Thus, the Foot Parameter (§ 4.3.4 and above, 10.4.3.2) and the Nasalization Contextual Parameter (§ 6.1.2 and above, 10.4.3.3) both relate to areas where the observed vowel length variation is seemingly universal rather than grammaticalized language-specific.

5. Hajek does however acknowledge that vowels preceding a nasal followed by a fricative may undergo nasalization without phonologized vowel lengthening taking place (1997: § 6.4.1.1 and n. 22).

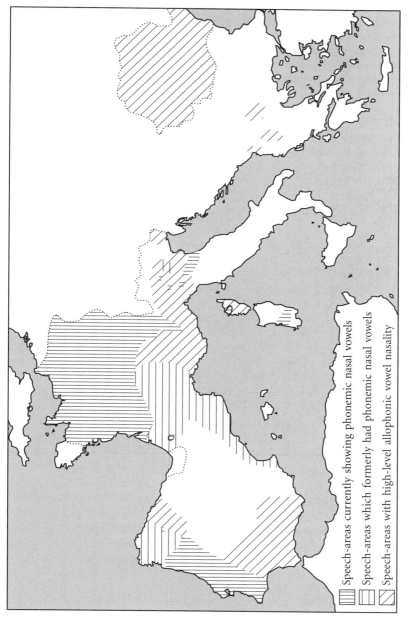

Speech-areas currently showing phonemic nasal vowels

Speech-areas which formerly had phonemic nasal vowels

Speech-areas with high-level allophonic vowel nasality

MAP 1.   General patterns of vowel nasality in Romance

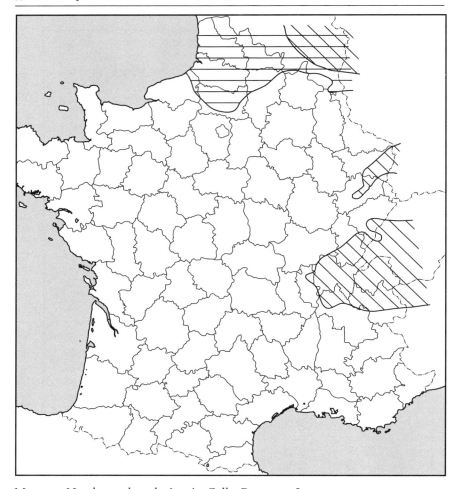

MAP 2.   Nasal vowel evolution in Gallo-Romance I

Areas where [ū] has not fronted to [ȳ]
    (based on *ALF* 220 *chacun* and 787 *lundi*)
Area of the *langue d'oïl* where [ẽ] has not lowered to [ã]
    (based on *ALF* 551 *fente* and 1369 *vent*)

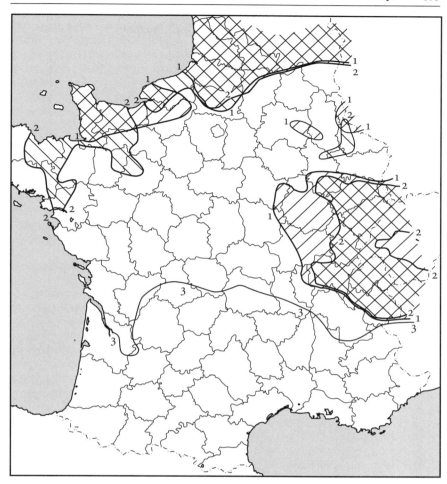

MAP 3.   Nasal vowel evolution in Gallo-Romance II

1 ⬜ Areas where [ĩ] has lowered before intervocalic -N-
    (based on *ALF* 476 *épine* and 1126 *racine*)
2 ⬜ Areas where [ỹ]/[ũ] has lowered before intervocalic -N-
    (based on *ALF* 788 *lune*)
3   Schematic indication of southern limit of lowering of high nasal vowels preceding
    asyllable-coda nasal
    (based on *ALF* 182 *brun*, 287 *lundi*, 772 *lin*, 289 *cinq*)

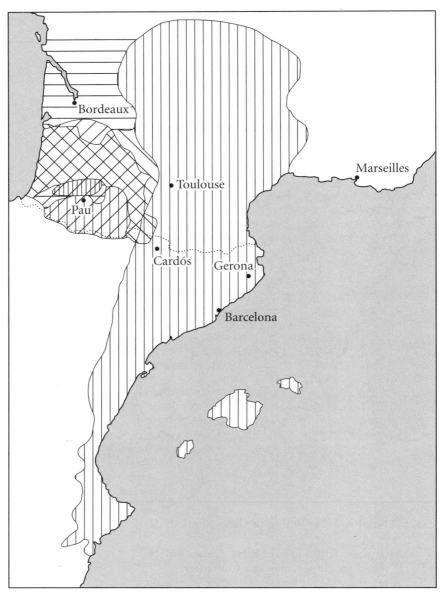

MAP 4. Nasal vowel evolution in south-west France and north-east Spain

Area of loss of intervocalic -N-
(based on *ALG* 1010 *lune*)

Area in which unconditioned nasal vowels still appear in forms deriving from -VN#
and from -N- (based on *ALG* 975 *pain* and 1010 *lune*)

Area in which -N# has been lost leaving a word-final oral vowel
(based on *ALG* 975 *pain*, *ALF* 791 *maçon* and 1411 *voisin*, *ALLor* 808 *grain*, *ALPI*
crin, *ALEANR* 822 *tizón*)

Area in which nasality in forms deriving from -VN# has remained conditioned,
typically [-Ṽŋ] (based on *ALG* 2170)

Area in which -VN# has emerged as an unconditioned nasal vowel
(based on *ALG* 323 *vin* and 975 *pain*)

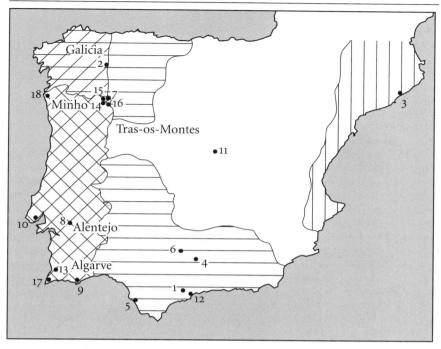

MAP 5.   Nasal vowel evolution in Ibero-Romance

Numbered localities

 1 Almogia
 2 Ancares
 3 Barcelona
 4 Cabra
 5 Cadiz
 6 Cordoba
 7 Deilão
 8 Evora
 9 Faro
10 Lisbon
11 Madrid
12 Malaga
13 Marmalete
14 Petisqueira
15 Rio d'Onor
16 S. Julião
17 Sagres
18 Viana do Castelo

Area in which phonemic nasal vowels have developed and been maintained

Area of loss of intervocalic -N-

Area in which forms formerly in -VN# are now realized as [-Ṽŋ] (based on *ALPI* 11 *aguijón* and 53 *crin*, *ALEA* 258 *pan*)

Area in which -N# has been lost, leaving a word-final oral vowel

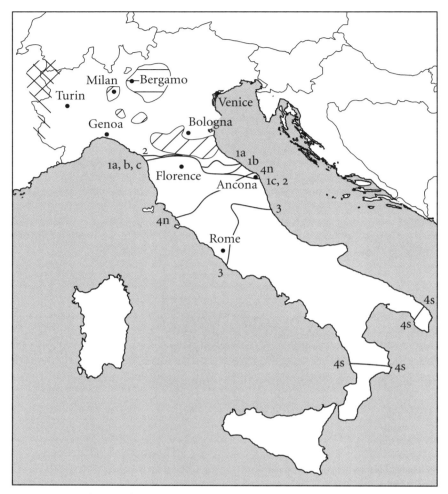

MAP 6. Incidence of vowel nasalization and other phonological processes in Italo-Romance

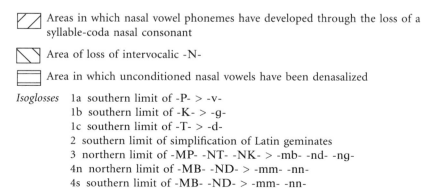

▨ Areas in which nasal vowel phonemes have developed through the loss of a syllable-coda nasal consonant

◩ Area of loss of intervocalic -N-

▤ Area in which unconditioned nasal vowels have been denasalized

Isoglosses   1a southern limit of -P- > -v-
1b southern limit of -K- > -g-
1c southern limit of -T- > -d-
2 southern limit of simplification of Latin geminates
3 northern limit of -MP- -NT- -NK- > -mb- -nd- -ng-
4n northern limit of -MB- -ND- > -mm- -nn-
4s southern limit of -MB- -ND- > -mm- -nn-
(based on Pellegrini 1977*b*)

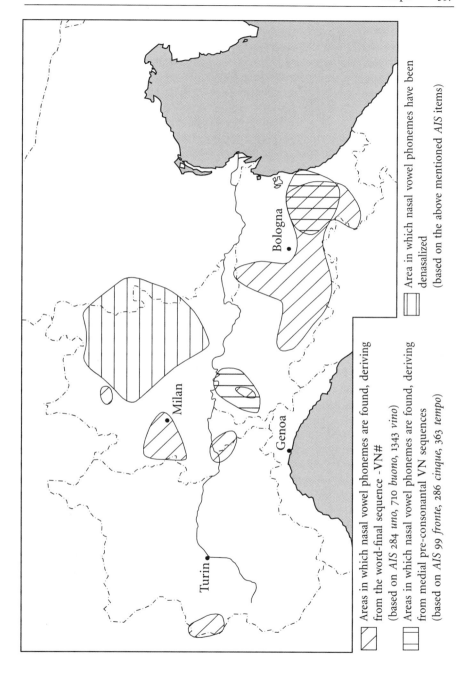

MAP 7. Incidence of nasal vowel phonemes in northern Italian dialects

Areas in which nasal vowel phonemes are found, deriving from the word-final sequence -VN# (based on AIS 284 *uno*, 710 *buono*, 1343 *vino*)

Areas in which nasal vowel phonemes are found, deriving from medial pre-consonantal VN sequences (based on AIS 99 *fronte*, 286 *cinque*, 363 *tempo*)

Area in which nasal vowel phonemes have been denasalized (based on the above mentioned AIS items)

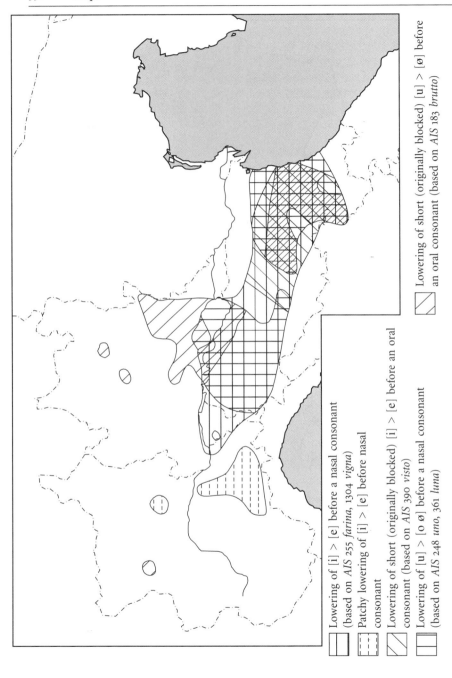

Lowering of [i] > [e] before a nasal consonant
(based on *AIS* 255 *farina*, 1304 *vigna*)

Patchy lowering of [i] > [e] before nasal
consonant

Lowering of short (originally blocked) [i] > [e] before an oral
consonant (based on *AIS* 390 *visto*)

Lowering of [u] > [o ø] before a nasal consonant
(based on *AIS* 248 *uno*, 361 *luna*)

Lowering of short (originally blocked) [u] > [ø] before
an oral consonant (based on *AIS* 183 *brutto*)

MAP 8.   High nasal vowel lowering in northern Italian dialects

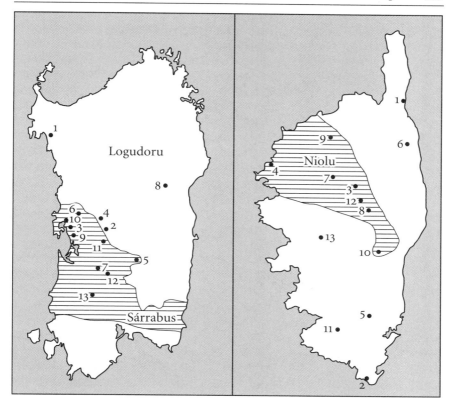

MAP 9.   Vowel nasality in Sardinia and Corsica

Sardinia
 1 Alghero
 2 Allai
 3 Cabras
 4 Fordongianus
 5 Isili
 6 Milis
 7 Mógoro
 8 Nuoro
 9 Orestano
10 Riola
11 Ruinas
12 Tramatza
13 Villacidro

Corsica
 1 Bastia
 2 Bonifaciu
 3 Corti
 4 Galeria
 5 Livia
 6 Loretu di Casinca
 7 Lozzi
 8 Noceta
 9 Pioggiola
10 San Gavino
11 Sartène
12 Venacu
13 Veru

Sardinia: area in which nasal vowel developed (based on Wagner (1941: 292)

Corsica: principal area in which phonemic and high-level allophonic nasal vowels have developed (based on data in Dalbera-Stefanaggi 1978, 1991)

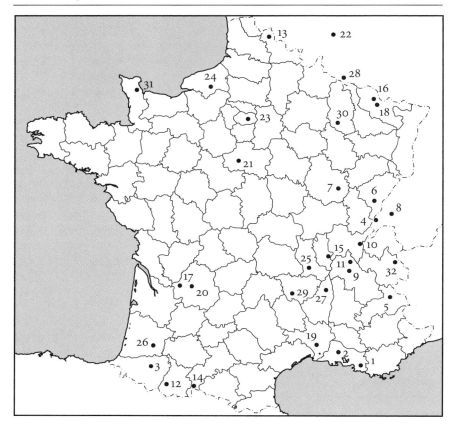

Map 10.   Localities in France

1	Aix	17	Mussidan
2	Arles	18	Nied
3	Artix	19	Nîmes
4	Bagnes	20	Notre-Dame-de-Sanilhac
5	Briançon	21	Orleans
6	Damprichard	22	Oreye
7	Dijon	23	Paris
8	Dompierre	24	Rouen
9	Eydoche	25	Saint-Jean-de-Soleimieux
10	Hauteville	26	Saint-Sever
11	Le Rivier d'Allemont	27	Saint-Victor
12	Lescun	28	Saint-Vincent
13	Lille	29	Saugues
14	Luchon	30	Tannois
15	Lyon	31	Val de Saire
16	Messin	32	Valezan

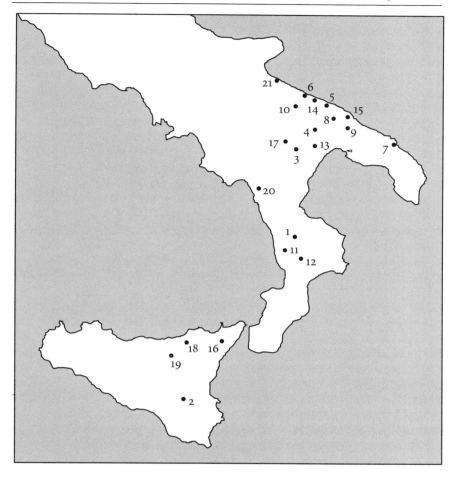

MAP 11.   Localities in southern Italy

1 Acri
2 Aidone
3 Albano Lucano
4 Altamura
5 Bari
6 Bisceglie
7 Brindisi
8 Castellana Grotte
9 Cisternino
10 Corato
11 Cosenza

12 Mangone
13 Matera
14 Molfetta
15 Monopoli
16 Novara
17 Potenza
18 San Fratello
19 Sperlinga
20 Trecchina
21 Trinitapoli

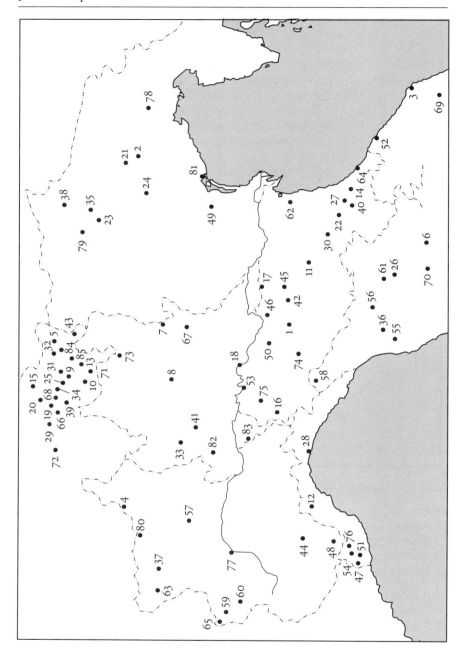

MAP 12.   (*Opposite*) Localities in Switzerland and northern and central Italy

KEY

1	Albineo	44	Murazzano
2	Alpago	45	Nonantola
3	Ancona	46	Novellara
4	Antrona Valley	47	Olivetta
5	Ardez	48	Ormea
6	Arezzo	49	Padua
7	Bagolino	50	Parma
8	Bergamo	51	Perinaldo
9	Bergün	52	Pesaro
10	Bivio	53	Piacenza
11	Bologna	54	Pigna
12	Cairo Montenotte	55	Pisa
13	Celerina	56	Pistoia
14	Cesena	57	Piverone
15	Chur	58	Pontremoli
16	Coli	59	Pragelas (Pragelato)
17	Concordia	60	Prali
18	Cremona	61	Prato
19	Dalin	62	Ravenna
20	Ems	63	Rhêmes-St-George
21	Erto	64	Rimini
22	Faenza	65	Rochemolles
23	Fassa	66	Rothenbrunnen
24	Feltre	67	Salò
25	Filisur	68	Scharans
26	Florence	69	Servigliano
27	Forlì	70	Siena
28	Genoa	71	Sils
29	Gruob	72	Tavetsch
30	Imola	73	Teglio
31	Latsch	74	Tizzano
32	Lavin	75	Travo
33	Legnano	76	Triora
34	Lenz	77	Turin
35	Livinallongo	78	Udine
36	Lucca	79	Val Gardena
37	Maisonasse	80	Valtournanche
38	Marebbe	81	Venice
39	Mathon	82	Vigevano
40	Meldola	83	Voghera
41	Milan	84	Zernez
42	Modena	85	Zuoz
43	Münster Valley		

Bibliography

ABBREVIATIONS

AGI	*Archivio Glottologico Italiano*
AFLS	Association for French Language Studies
AR	*Archivum Romanicum*
BF	*Boletim de Filologia*
BSRLR	*Bulletin de la Société Roumaine de Linguistique Romane*
CEC	Centre Educatif et Culturel
CJL	*Canadian Journal of Linguistics*
CL	*Cercetări de Lingvistică*
CLEUP	Cooperative Libraria Editrice dell'Università di Padova
CLUEB	Cooperative Libraria Universitaria Editrice Bologna
CNRS	Centre National de Recherche Scientifique
CSIC	Consejo Superior de Investigaciones Científicas
CUP	Cambridge University Press
ESRI	European Studies Research Institute
FL	*Foundations of Language*
FM	*Le Français Moderne*
HSMS	Hispanic Seminary of Medieval Studies
ID	*L'Italia Dialettale*
INIC	Instituo Nacional de Investigação Científica
JASA	*Journal of the Acoustical Society of America*
JFLS	*Journal for French Language Studies*
JL	*Journal of Linguistics*
JPh	*Journal of Phonetics*
Lang	*Language*
LIn	
LRL	Holtus, G., Metzeltin, M., Schmitt, C. (eds.). 1988– . *Lexikon der romanistischen Linguistik.* Tübingen: Niemeyer.

    ii/1 Latein und Romanisch: historisch-vergleichende Grammatik der romanischen Sprachen (1996)

    ii/2 Die einzelnen romanischen Sprachen und Sprachgebiete vom Mittelalter bis zur Renaissance (1995)

    iii. Romanian, Dalmatian, Rheto-Romance (1989)

    iv. Italian, Corsican, Sardinian (1988)

    v/1 French (1990)

    v/2 Occitan, Catalan (1991)

    vi/1 Aragonese-Navarrese, Spanish, Asturo-Leonese (1992)

	vi/2 Galician, Portuguese (1994)
LS	Chicago Linguistic Society
MSL	*Mémoires de la Société de Linguistique de Paris*
NM	*Neuphilologische Mitteilungen*
NS	*Die Neueren Sprachen*
OUP	Oxford University Press
PUF	Presses Universitaires de France
RFE	*Revista de Filología Española*
RID	*Rivista Italiana di Dialettologia*
RLiR	*Revue de Linguistique Romane*
RPF	*Revista Portuguesa de Filologia*
RPh	*Romance Philology*
RRL	*Revue Roumaine de Linguistique*
SCL	*Studii şi cercetări lingvistice*
SEER	*The Slavonic and East European Review*
SL	*Studii Lingvistice (Timişoara)*
TraLiLi	*Travaux de Linguistique et de Littérature*
VR	*Vox Romanica*
ZrP	*Zeitschrift für romanische Philologie*
ZrP Beih.	*Beiheft zur Zeitschrift für romanische Philologie*

BIBLIOGRAPHY

Adams, J. N. 1977. *The Vulgar Latin of the Letters of Claudius Terentianus*. Manchester: Manchester UP.

Aebischer, P. 1941. 'Pour l'histoire du suffixe d'origine lombarde *-ing* dans l'Italie centrale'. *ZrP* 61: 114–21.

Akamatsu, T. 1967. 'Quelques statistiques sur la fréquence d'utilisation des voyelles nasales françaises'. *La Linguistique*, 1: 75–80.

Al-Bamerni, A. 1983. 'Oral, Velic and Laryngeal Coarticulation across Languages'. D.Phil. diss., University of Oxford.

Alex, P. 1965. *Le Patois de Naisey, canton de Roulans, arrondissement de Besançon*. Paris: Voisin.

Allen, W. S. 1978. *Vox latina*. 2nd ed. Cambridge: CUP.

Almeida, A. 1976. 'The Portuguese nasal vowels: phonetics and phonemics'. In J. Schmidt-Radefeldt (ed.), *Readings in Portuguese Linguistics*. Amsterdam: North Holland, pp. 349–96.

Alonso, D. 1972a. *Obras completas*. Vol. 1. Madrid: Gredos.

—— 1972b. 'Gallego-asturiano engalar "volar"'. In Alonso (1972a), pp. 457–64.

—— and Yebra, V. G. 1972. 'El gallego-leonés de Ancares y su interés para la dialectología portuguesa'. In Alonso (1972a), pp. 315–57.

Alvar, M. 1959. *El español hablado en Tenerife*. [*RFE* Anejo, 69]. Madrid: CSIC.

Alvarez, R., Regueira, X. L., and Monteagudo, H. 1986. *Gramática galega*. Vigo: Ed. Galaxia.

Anderson, S. R. 1975. 'The description of nasal consonants and the internal structure of segments'. In Ferguson et al. (1975), pp. 1–25; also in *Lang* 52 (1976), 326–44.

Andolf, S. (ed.). 1941. *Floovant, chanson de geste du XII siècle*. Uppsala: Almqvist and Wiksell.

Anglade, J. 1921. *Grammaire de l'ancien provençal*. Paris: Klincksieck.

d'Arbois de Jubainville, H. 1872. 'La Phonétique latine de l'époque mérovingienne et la phonétique du XIe siècle dans le Saint Alexis'. *Romania*, 1: 318–27.

Arvinte, V. 1980. *Die Rumänen. Ursprung, Volks- und Landesnahme*. Tübingen: Narr.

Atanasov, P. 1990. *Le Mégléno-roumain de nos jours*. Hamburg: Buske.

Avram, A. 1964. 'Contribuţii la interpretarea grafiei chirilice a primelor texte românești'. *SCL* 15: 15–37, 147–67, 265–94, 471–95, 575–614.

—— 1968. 'Sur le rapport entre les voyelles neutres et la nasalité'. *RRL 13*: 567–73.

—— 1969. 'Sur le traitement roumain des voyelles latines accentuées précédées et suivies de consonnes nasales'. *BSRLR 6*: 7–17.

—— 1990. *Nazalitatea şi rotacismul în limba română*. Bucharest: Ed. Acad. Rom.

Ayres-Bennett, W. 1990. 'Variation and change in the pronunciation of French in the seventeenth century'. In J. N. Green and W. Ayres-Bennett (eds.), *Variation and Change in French*. London: Routledge, pp. 151–79.

Ayuso, M. J. M. 1991. 'Acoustic description of Spanish nasal consonants in continuous speech'. *Papers of the XII International Congress of Phonetic Sciences*, vol. 2: 414–17.

Balcke, C. 1912. *Der anorganische Nasallaut im Französichen*. [*ZrP Beih.* 39]. Halle: Niemeyer.

Barbosa, J. M. 1962. 'Les Voyelles nasales portugaises: interprétation phonologique'. In *Proceedings of 4th Int. Congress of Phonetic Sciences*. The Hague: Mouton, pp. 691–709.

—— 1983. *Etudes de phonologie portugaise*. 2nd ed. Evora: Universidade de Evora.

Bartoli, M. G. 1906. *Das Dalmatische. Altromanische Sprachreste von Veglia bis Ragusa und ihre Stellung in der apennino-balkanischen Romania*. 2 vols. Vienna: Hölder.

Bassols de Climent, M. 1981. *Fonética latina*. 5th repr. Madrid: CSIC.

Bauche, H. 1920. *Le Langage populaire*. Paris: Payot.

Bazzani, F. and Melzani, G. 1988. *Il dialetto di Bagolino*. Brescia: Grafo Ed.

Beaulieux, C. 1967 [1927]. *Histoire de l'orthographe française*. I. *Formation de l'orthographe des origines au milieu du XVIe siècle*. Repr. Paris: Champion.

Bec, P. 1968. *Les Interférences linguistiques entre gascon et languedocien dans les parlers du Comminge et du Couserans*. Paris: PUF.

Beddor, P. S. 1983. *Phonological and Phonetic Effects of Nasalization on Vowel Height*. Bloomington: Indiana Univ. Ling. Club.

—— 1991. 'Predicting the structure of phonological systems'. *Phonetica*, 48: 83–107.

—— 1993. 'The perception of nasal vowels'. In Huffman and Krakow (1993), pp. 171–96.

—— Krakow, R. A., Goldstein, L. M. 1986. 'Perceptual constraints and phonological change: a study of nasal vowel height'. *Phonology Yearbook*, 3: 197–217.

Bédier, J. 1927. *La Chanson de Roland*. Paris: Ed. d'Art.

Bell-Berti, F. 1993. 'Understanding velic movement control: studies of segmental context'. In Huffman and Krakow (1993), pp. 63–85.

Bendor-Samuel, J. T. 1970. 'Some problems of segmentation in the phonological analysis of Terena'. In F. R. Palmer (ed.), *Prosodic Analysis*. London: OUP, pp. 214–21.

Benguerel, A.-P., and Lafargue, A. 1981. 'Perception of vowel nasalization in French'. *JPh* 9: 309–21.

—— Hirose, H., Sawashima, M., Ushijima, T. 1977. 'Velar co-articulation in French: an electromyographic study'. *JPh* 5: 159–67.

Berruto, G. 1974. *Piemonte e Valle d'Aosta.* [Profilo dei dialetti italiani 1]. Pisa: Pacini.

Bertoni, G. 1915–17. 'Nota sul dialetto di Bonifacio (Corsica)'. *Romania,* 44: 268–73.

—— 1916. *Italia dialettale.* Milan: Hoepli.

—— 1925. *Profilo del dialetto di Modena.* Geneva: L. Olschki.

Bèze, T. 1584. *De francicae linguae recta pronuntiatione.* Geneva, 1584. Repr. Geneva: Slatkine, 1972.

Bigalke, R. 1980. *Dizionario dialettale della Basilicata.* Heidelberg: Winter.

Bjerrome, G. 1957. *Le Patois de Bagnes (Valais).* Stockholm: Almqvist & Wiksell.

Björk, L. 1961. *Velopharyngeal Function in Connected Speech.* Acta Radiologica, Supplementum 202. Stockholm.

Blasco Ferrer, E. 1984*a. Grammatica storica del catalano e dei suoi dialetti con speciale riguardo all'algherese.* Tübingen: Narr.

—— 1984*b. Storia linguistica della Sardegna.* [*ZrP Beih.* 202]. Tübingen: Niemeyer.

Bloomfield, L. 1935. *Language.* London: Allen & Unwin.

Bolelli, T. 1940. 'Contributo allo studio dell'elemento celtico nella fonetica romanza'. *AR* 24: 188–205.

Boléo, M. de Paiva. 1974. *Estudos de lingüística portuguesa e românica.* Vol. I. Coimbra: Universidade de Coimbra.

—— and Silva, M. H. S. 1974. 'O "Mapa dos dialectos e falares de Portugal continental"'. In M. de Paiva Boléo, *Estudos de lingüística portuguêsa e românica.* vol. I, pp. 311–52.

Bolocan, G. 1981. *Dicţionarul elementelor româneşti din documentele slavo-române 1374–1600.* Bucharest: Ed. Acad.

Bond, Z. S. 1976. 'Identification of vowels excerpted from neutral nasal contexts'. *JASA* 59: 1229–32.

Börner, W. 1976. *Schriftstruktur und Lautstruktur. Studien zur altgalicischen Skripta.* Tübingen: Niemeyer.

Borzone de Manrique, A. M. de M., and Signorini, A. 1983. 'Segmental duration and rhythm in Spanish' *JPh* 11: 117–28.

Bourciez, E. 1956. *Eléments de linguistique romane.* 4th ed. Paris: Klincksieck.

Bouvier, J.-C. 1976. *Les Parlers provençaux de la Drôme.* Paris: Klincksieck.

Brandenstein, W. 1951. 'Kurze Phonologie des Lateinischen'. In F. Altheim, *Geschichte der lateinischen Sprache.* Frankfurt: Klostermann, pp. 481–98.

Brichler-Labaeye, C. 1970. *Les Voyelles Françaises: Mouvement et positions articulatoires à la lumière de la radiocinématographie.* Paris: Klincksiek.

Buben, V. 1935. *Influence de l'orthographe sur la prononciation du français moderne.* Bratislava: Univ. of Bratislava.

Burger, M. 1964. 'La Nasalisation spontanée dans les dialectes de la plaine vaudoise et fribourgeoise: conditions et extension du phénomène'. *RLiR* 28: 290–306.

Bussche, H. van den. 1984. 'L'Ouverture de la voyelle (e) issue de (e) roman entravé (Ē, Ĭ latins) en ancien français. Essai de dation et de localisation'. *Folia Linguistica Historica,* 5: 41–90.

Caduff, L. 1952. *Essai sur la phonétique du parler rhétoroman de la Vallée de Tavetsch.* Berne: Francke.

Calvet, M. 1969. *Le Système phonétique et phonologique du parler provençal de Saint-Victor en Vivarais.* Grenoble: Faculté des Lettres et Sciences Humaines.

Camilli, A. 1929. 'Il dialetto di Servigliano'. *AR* 13: 220–71.

*Cancioneiro Geral de Garcia de Resende.*1516. Edited by A. J. da Costa Pimpão and A. F. Dias. 2 vols. Coimbra: Centro de Estudos Românicos, 1973–5.

Canepari, L. 1979. 'I suoni dialettali e il problema della loro trascrizione'. In M. Cortelazzo (ed.), *Guida ai dialetti veneti.* Padua: CLEUP, pp. 45–81.

—— 1984. *Lingua italiana nel Veneto.* Padua: CLEUP.

—— and Vitali, D. 1995. 'Pronuncia e grafia del bolognese'. *RID* 19: 119–64.

Caragiu Marioțeanu, M. 1989. 'Areallinguistik. I. Dakorumänisch/*Les Aires linguistiques I. Dacoroumain*'. *LRL*, iii. 405–23.

—— Giosu, S., Ionescu-Ruxandoiu, L., Todoran, R. 1977. *Dialectologie română.* Bucharest: Ed. didactică și pedagogică.

Carballo Calero, R. 1968. *Gramática elemental del gallego común.* 2nd ed. Vigo: Ed. Galaxia.

Carlton, C. M. 1973. *A Linguistic Analysis of a Collection of Late Latin Documents Composed in Ravenna between A.D. 445–700.* The Hague: Mouton.

Carnoy, A. J. 1906. *Le Latin d'Espagne d'après les inscriptions.* 2nd ed. Brussels. Repr. Hildesheim–Zurich–New York: G. Olms, 1983.

Carter, H. H. 1941. *Cancioneiro da Ajuda. A Diplomatic Edition.* New York–Oxford: Modern Language Association of America–OUP.

Carton, F. 1990. 'Areallinguistik. I. Nördliche Dialekte, (b) Pikardie/*Les Aires linguistiques I. Dialectes du Nord, (b) Picardie*'. *LRL*, v/1, 605–15.

Carvalho, J. Brandão de. 1988*a*. 'Nasalité syllabique en portugais et en galicien: approche non-linéaire et panchronique d'un problème phonologique'. *Verba*, 15: 237–63.

—— 1988*b*. 'Evolution phonologique, interférences grammaticales et aréologie: à propos des résultats de -ANU/-ANA en galicien'. *VR* 47: 184–98.

—— 1989*a*. 'L'Origine de la terminaison -*ão* du portugais'. *ZrP* 105: 148–60.

—— 1989*b*. 'L'Évolution des sonantes ibéro-romanes et la chute de -N-, -L- en gallaïco-portugais'. *RLiR* 53: 159–88.

Castellani, A. 1956. 'Fonotipi e fonemi in italiano'. *Studi di Filologia Italiana*, 14: 435–53.

—— 1980. 'Sulla formazione del tipo fonetico italiano'. In id., *Saggi di linguistica e filologia italiana e romanza (1946–76).* Vol. I. Rome: Salerno Ed., pp. 73–122.

—— 1982. 'Quanti erano gl'italofoni nel 1861?'. *Studi Linguistici Italiani.* 8: 3–26.

Catalán, D. 1989. *El español. Orígenes de su diversidad.* Madrid: Ed. Paraninfo.

Chapallaz, M. 1979. *The Pronunciation of Italian.* London: Bell and Hyman.

Chen, M. 1972*a*. 'Nasals and Nasalization in Chinese: Explorations in Phonological Universals'. Ph.D. diss., University of California.

—— 1972*b*. 'The time dimension: contribution towards a theory of sound change'. *FL* 8: 457–98

—— 1973*a*. 'On the formal expression of natural rules in phonology'. *JL* 9: 223–49.

—— 1973*b*. 'Metarules and universal constraints in phonological theory'. *Project on Linguistic Analysis* (Univ. of Calif., Berkeley), 13: 909–24.

—— 1975. 'An areal study of nasalization in Chinese'. In Ferguson, Hyman, and Ohala (1975), pp. 81–123.

Cherubini, F. 1839. *Vocabolario milanese-italiano*. Milan: Regia Stamperia. Repr. Milan: Milan SAS, 1978.

Chiflet, L. 1659. *Essay d'une parfaite grammaire de la langue françoise*. Antwerp: van Meurs. Repr. Geneva: Slatkine, 1973.

Chomsky, N., and Halle, M. 1968. *The Sound Pattern of English*. New York: Harper & Row.

Christ, K. 1984. *The Romans*. London: Chatto and Windus.

Cintra, L. F. Lindley. 1984. *A linguagem dos foros de Castelo Rodrigo*. Lisbon: Imprensa Nacional–Casa da Moeda.

Clumeck, H. 1976. 'Patterns of soft palate movement in six languages'. *JPh* 4: 337–51.

Coco, F. 1970. *Il dialetto di Bologna: fonetica storica e analisi strutturale*. Bologna: Forni.

Cohn, A. C. 1988. 'Phonetic rules of nasalization in French'. *UCLA Working Papers in Phonetics*, 69: 60–7.

—— 1990. 'Phonetic and Phonological Rules of Nasalization'. Ph.D. diss., UCLA. Ann Arbor: UMI.

—— 1993. 'Nasalisation in English: phonology or phonetics?'. *Phonology*, 10: 43–81.

Contini, M. 1974. 'Un phénomène de réaction à la frontière du campidanien: le passage -l- > -ll- et -n- > -nn-'. *RLiR* 38: 106–12.

—— 1987. *Etude de géographie phonétique et de phonétique instrumentale du sarde*. 2 vols. Alessandria: Ed. dell'Orso.

—— and Boë, L. J. 1972. 'Voyelles orales et nasales du sarde campidanien'. *Phonetica*, 25: 165–91.

Cornu, J. 1877. 'Phonologie du bagnard'. *Romania*, 6: 369–427.

Coromines, J. 1971. *Lleures i converses d'un filòleg*. Barcelona: Club Editor.

—— 1976–7. *Entre dos llenguatges*. 3 vols. Barcelona: Curial.

—— 1990. *El parlar de la Vall d'Aran*. Barcelona: Curial.

Costa Pimpão, A. J. da, and Dias, A. F. (eds.). 1973–5. *Cancioneiro Geral de Garcia de Resende*. 1516. 2 vols. Coimbra: Centro de Estudos Românicos.

Coteanu, I. 1981. *Structura şi evoluţia limbii române*. Bucharest: Ed. Acad.

Coustenoble, H. N. 1945. *La Phonétique du provençal moderne en terre d'Arles*. Hertford: S. Austin & Sons.

Crothers, J. 1978. 'Typology and universals of vowel systems'. In J. H. Greenberg (ed.), *Universals of Human Language*. 2. Phonology. Stanford, Calif.: Stanford UP, pp. 93–152.

Dagenais, L. 1991. 'De la phonologie du français vers 1700'. *La Linguistique*, 27: 75–89.

Dalbera-Stefanaggi, M.-J. 1978. *Langue corse. Une approche linguistique*. Paris: Klincksieck.

—— 1989. 'La Nasalisation en corse'. *RLiR* 53: 145–58.

—— 1991. *Unité et diversité des parlers corses*. Alessandria: Ed. dell'Orso.

Damourette, J., and Pichon, E. 1911–50. *Des Mots à la pensée. Essai de grammaire française*. 7 vols. Paris: d'Artrey.

Dangeau, Abbé de 1694. *Essais de grammaire*. In *Opuscules sur la langue française, par divers académiciens*. Paris: B. Brunet, 1759. Repr. Geneva: Slatkine, 1969.

Debrock, M. 1974. 'La Structure spectrale des voyelles nasales'. *Rev. de Phon. Appliquée*, 21: 15–31.

Dees, A. 1980. *Atlas des formes et des constructions des chartes françaises du* 13e siècle [*ZrP Beih.* 178]. Tübingen: Niemeyer.

—— 1987. *Atlas des formes linguistiques des textes littéraires de l'ancien français*. [*ZrP Beih.* 212]. Tübingen: Niemeyer.

De Gregorio, I. 1939. 'Contributo alla conoscenza del dialetto di Bisceglio (Bari)'. *ID* 15: 31–52.

Delattre, P. 1947. 'La Liaison en français, tendances et classification'. *French Review*, 21: 148–57. Also in Delattre (1966).

—— 1954. 'Les Attributs acoustiques de la nasalité vocalique et consonantique'. *Studia linguistica*, 8: 103–9. Also in Delattre (1966).

—— 1955. 'Les Facteurs de la liaison facultative en français'. *French Review*, 29: 42–9. Also in Delattre (1966).

—— 1956. 'La Fréquence des liaisons facultatives en français'. *French Review*, 30: 48–54. Also in Delattre (1966).

—— 1965. 'La Nasalité vocalique en français et en anglais'. *French Review*, 39: 92–109.

—— 1966. *Studies in French and Comparative Phonetics*. The Hague: Mouton.

—— 1968. 'Divergences entre nasalités vocalique et consonantique en français'. *Word*, 24: 64–72.

—— and Monnot, M. 1981. 'The role of duration in the identification of French nasal vowels'. In P. Delattre, *Studies in Comparative Phonetics*. Heidelberg: J. Groos, pp. 17–38.

—— Liberman, A. M., Cooper, F. S., Gerstman, L. J. 1952. 'An experimental study of the acoustic determinants of vowel color; observations on one- and two-formant vowels synthesized from spectrographic patterns'. *Word*, 8: 195–210.

Delgado, M. J. 1983. *A linguagem popular do Baixo Alentejo e o dialecto barranquenho*. 2nd ed. Beja: Ed. da Assembleia Distrital de Beja.

Dell, F. 1973. *Les Règles et les sons: Introduction à la phonologie générative*. Paris: Hermann.

Deloffre, F. 1961. *Agréables conférences de deux paysans de Saint-Ouen et de Montmorency sur les affaires du temps*. Paris: Les Belles Lettres.

De Mauro, T. 1972. *Storia linguistica dell'Italia unita*. 3rd ed. Bari: Laterza.

Densusianu, O. 1975 [1901–38]. *Histoire de la langue roumaine*. 2 vols. Repr. in 1 vol. Bucharest: Ed. Minerva.

De Poerck, G. 1962. 'Le *a* tonique devant nasale dans les parlers rhéto-romans'. *VR* 21: 57–82.

Desgranges, J.-C.-L.-P. 1821. *Petit dictionnaire du peuple à l'usage des quatre cinquièmes de la France*. Paris: Chaumerot Jeune.

Devoto, G., and Giacomelli, G. 1972. *I dialetti delle regioni d'Italia*. Florence: Sansoni.

Deyhime, G. 1967. 'Enquête sur la phonologie du français contemporain'. *La Linguistique*, 1: 97–108, 2: 57–84.

Diehl, E. 1924–31. *Inscriptiones Latinae Christianae Veteres*. 3 vols. Berlin: Weidmann.

Dinguirard, J.-C. 1979. 'Observations sur le gascon des plus anciennes chartes'. *Annales de la Faculté des Lettres de Toulouse-Le Mirail*, 15: 9–46.

Domergues, U. 1797. *La Prononciation française determinée par des signes invariables*. Paris: Barret.

Dondaine, C. 1972. *Les Parlers comtois d'oïl*. Paris: Klincksieck.

Doria, M. 1978. *Storia del dialetto triestino*. Trieste: Ed. 'Italo Svevo'.

Droixhe, D., and Dutilleul, T. 1990. 'Externe Sprachgeschichte/*Histoire externe de la langue*'. *LRL*, v/1, 437–71.

Duarte i Montserrat, C., and Alsina i Keith, A. 1984. *Gramàtica històrica del català*. 2 vols. Barcelona: Curial.

Duraffour, A. 1932. 'Phénomènes généraux d'évolution phonétique dans les dialectes franco-provençaux étudiés d'après le parler de la commune de Vaux (Ain)'. *RLiR* 8: 1–280.

Durand, M. 1953. 'De la formation des voyelles nasales'. *Studia Ling.* 7: 33–53.

Elwert, W. T. 1965. *Traité de versification française*. Paris: Klincksieck.

—— 1972. *Die Mundart des Fassa-Tals*. Wiesbaden: F. Steiner.

Encrevé, P. 1988. *La Liaison avec et sans enchaînement*. Paris: Du Seuil.

Entenman, G. L. 1976. 'The Development of Nasal Vowels'. Ph.D. thesis, University of Texas.

Entwistle, W. J. 1962. *The Spanish Language together with Catalan, Portuguese and Basque*. 2nd ed. London: Faber.

Ernst, G. 1985. *Gesprochenes Französisch zu Beginn des 17. Jahrhunderts* [*ZrP Beih.* 204]. Tübingen: Niemeyer.

Fagan, D. S. 1988. 'Notes on diachronic nasalization in Portuguese'. *Diachronica*, 5: 141–57.

—— 1990. 'Nasal elision and universals: evidence from Romance'. *CJL* 35: 225–36.

Falcone, G. 1976. *Calabria*. [Profilo dei dialetti italiani, 18]. Pisa: Pacini.

Fant, G. 1960. *Acoustic Theory of Speech Production*. The Hague: Mouton.

Feng, G. 1987. 'Etude articulatori-acoustique des voyelles nasales'. *Bulletin de l'Institut de Phonétique de Grenoble*, 16: 1–102.

Féraud, Abbé J.-F. 1787. *Dictionaire critique de la langue française*. 3 vols. 3rd ed. Marseille: Mossy. Facsimile in P. Caron and T. E. Woolridge (eds.). 1994. Tübingen: Niemeyer.

Ferguson, C. A. 1966. 'Assumptions about nasals: a sample study in phonological universals'. In J. H. Greenberg (ed.) *Universals of Language*. 2nd ed. Cambridge, Mass.: MIT Press, pp. 53–60.

—— Hyman, L. M., and Ohala, J. J. (eds.). 1975. *Nasálfest*. Stanford, Calif.: Stanford Univ. Press.

Fernández González, J. R. 1978. *Etnografía del Valle de Ancares. Estudio lingüístico según el método 'Palabras y Cosas'* [*Verba* Anejo, 10]. Univ. de Santiago de Compostela.

—— 1981. *El habla de Ancares (León). Estudio fonético, morfosintáctico y léxico*. Univ. de Oviedo.

Fernández Rei, F. 1985. 'Areas lingüísticas do galego actual'. In F. de Moll (ed.), *Actes XVI Congrès Int. de Ling. i Filol. Rom.* Vol. 2 Palma, pp. 485–97.

Fernández-Sevilla, J. 1980. 'Los fonemas implosivos en español'. *Thesaurus*, 35: 456–505.

Ferrari, C. E. 1835. *Vocabolario bolognese-italiano colle voci francesi correspondenti*. 2nd ed. Bologna: Tipografia della Volpe.

Festa, G. B. 1917. 'Il dialetto di Matera'. *ZrP* 38: 129–62, 257–80.

Flechia, G. 1898. 'Atone finali, determinate dalla tonica, nel dialetto piveronese'. *AGI* 14: 111–20.

Flutre, L.-F. 1977. *Du moyen picard au picard moderne*. Amiens: Musée de Picardie.

Foley, J. 1975. 'Nasalization as a universal phonological process'. In Ferguson, Hyman, and Ohala (1975), pp. 197–212.

Fonagy, I. 1989. 'Le Français change de visage?' *Revue Romane*, 24: 225–54.

Foresti, F. 1988. 'Areallinguistik. V. Emilia-Romagna/*Aree linguistiche. V. Emilia e Romagna*'. *LRL*, iv. 569–93.

Forner, W. 1975. *Generative Phonologie des Dialekts von Genua*. Hamburg: Buske.

—— 1988. 'Areallingustik. I. Ligurien/*Aree linguistiche. I. Liguria*'. *LRL*, iv. 453–69.

Förster, W. 1879–80. 'Galloitalische Predigten'. *Romanische Studien*, 4: 1–92.

Fouché, P. 1959. *Traité de prononciation française*. 2nd ed. Paris: Klincksieck.

—— 1966. *Phonétique historique du français. I. Les Consonnes*. Paris: Klincksieck.

—— 1969. *Phonétique historique du français. II. Les Voyelles*. 2nd ed. Paris: Klincksieck.

Fowler, C. 1981. 'A relationship between coarticulation and compensatory shortening'. *Phonetica*, 38: 35–50.

Franceschini, F. 1991. 'Note sull'anafonesi in Toscana occidentale'. In L. Giannelli et al. (1991), pp. 259–72.

Frau, G. 1984. *I dialetti del Friuli*. Udine: Società filologica friulana.

Gaeng, P. 1968. *An Inquiry into Local Variations in Vulgar Latin as Reflected in the Vocalism of Christian Inscriptions*. Chapel Hill: Univ. of North Carolina Press.

Galmés de Fuentes, A. 1983. *Dialectología mozárabe*. Madrid: Gredos.

García de Diego, V. 1909. *Elementos de gramática histórica gallega* [Burgos, 1909] Repr. in *Verba* Anejo, 23. Univ. de Santiago de Compostela, 1984.

Gartner, T. 1883. *Raetoromanische Grammatik*. Heilbronn: Gebr. Henninger.

—— 1892. 'Die Mundart von Erto'. *ZrP* 16: 183–209, 308–71.

Gauchat, L. 1890. 'Le Patois de Dompierre (Broyard)'. *ZrP* 14: 397–466.

Genre, A. 1992. 'Nasali e nasalizzate in Val Germanasca'. *RID* 16: 181–224.

Geschiere, L. 1968. 'L'Introduction des phonèmes vocaliques nasaux en français et le témoignage de Jehan Palsgrave'. *Word*, 24: 175–92.

Giannelli, L. 1976. *Toscana*. [Profilo dei dialetti italiani, 9]. Pisa: Pacini.

—— 1988. 'Areallinguistik. VI. Toskana/*Aree linguistiche. VI. Toscana*'. *LRL*, iv. 594–606.

—— and Savoia, L. M. 1978. 'L'Indebolimento consonantico in Toscana. I'. *RID* 2: 23–58.

—— Maraschio, N., Poggi Salani, T., Vedovelli, M. (eds.). 1991. *Tra Rinascimento e strutture attuali*. Turin: Rosenberg and Sellier.

Gorra, E. 1890. 'Fonetica del dialetto di Piacenza'. *ZrP* 14: 133–58.

—— 1892. 'Il dialetto di Parma'. *ZrP* 16: 372–9.

Gossen, C. T. 1970. *Grammaire de l'ancien picard*. Paris: Klincksieck.

Gougenheim, G. 1935. *Eléments de phonologie française*. Strasbourg: Univ. de Strasbourg.

Grammont, M. 1892–8. 'Le Patois de la Franche-Montagne et en particulier de Damprichard (Franche-Comté)'. *MSL* 7 (1892): 461–77; 8 (1894): 52–90; 10 (1898): 167–206, 290–323.

Guth, G. 1975. *Contribution expérimentale à l'étude des attributs acoustiques de la nasalité*. Algiers: Société nationale d'édition et de diffusion.

Hadlich, R. L. 1965. *The Phonological History of Vegliote*. Chapel Hill: Univ. of North Carolina Press.

Hagège, C., and Haudricourt, A. 1978. *La Phonologie panchronique*. Paris: PUF.

Haiman, J., and Benincà, P. 1992. *The Rhaeto-Romance Languages*. London: Routledge.

Hajek, J. 1991a. 'La Nasalizzazione ed il bolognese: aspetti fonologici'. In Giannelli et al. (1991), pp. 273–7.

—— 1991b. 'The hardening of nasalized glides in Bolognese'. In P. M. Bertinetto, M. Kenstowicz, and M. Loporcaro (eds.), *Certamen Phonologicum II. Papers from the 1990 Cortona Phonology Meeting*. Turin: Rosenberg & Sellier, pp. 259–78.

—— 1993. 'Old French nasalization and universals of sound change'. *JFLS* 3: 145–64.

—— 1997. *Universals of Sound Change in Nasalization*. Publications of the Philological Society, 31. Oxford: Blackwell.

Halle, M., and Stevens, K. 1979. 'Some reflections on the theoretical bases of phonetics'. In B. Lindblom and S. Öhman (eds.), *Frontiers of Speech Communication Research*. New York: Academic Press, pp. 335–49.

Hammarström, G. 1953. *Etude de phonétique auditive sur les parlers de l'Algarve*. Uppsala: Almqvist and Wiksell.

Hamp, E. P. 1981. 'The chronology of a cluster type in Romanian'. *RRL* 26: 405–9.

Hansen, A. B. 1998. *Les Voyelles nasales du français parisien moderne*. Copenhagen Museum Tusculanum Press, University of Copenhagen.

Hardcastle, W. 1976. *Physiology of Speech Production: An Introduction for Speech Scientists*. London: Academic Press.

Harms, R. T. 1968. *Introduction to Phonological Theory*. Englewood Cliffs, NJ: Prentice Hall.

Harris, W. V. 1989. *Ancient Literacy*. Cambridge, Mass.: Harvard UP.

Hattori, S., Yakamoto, K., Fujimura, O. 1958. 'Nasalization of vowels in relation to nasals'. *JASA* 30: 267–74.

Hatzfeld, A., and Darmesteter, A. 1926. *Dictionnaire général de la langue française*. 2 vols. 8th ed. Paris: Delagrave.

Haudricourt, A. G. 1947. 'En/an en français'. *Word*, 3: 39–47.

—— 1948. 'Problèmes de phonologie diachronique (français ei > oi)'. *Lingua*, 1: 209–18.

Hawkins, R. 1993. 'Regional variation in France'. In C. Sanders (ed.), *French Today*. Cambridge: CUP, pp. 55–84.

Hawkins, S., and Stevens, K. 1985. 'Acoustic and perceptual correlates of the non-nasal–nasal distinction for vowels', *JASA* 77: 1560–75.

Heilmann, L. 1976. *Dizionario del dialetto cremonese*. Cremona: Libreria del Convegno.

Hempel, C. G. 1965. *Aspects of Scientific Explanation and Other Essays in the Philosophy of Science*. New York: Free Press.

Henderson, J. B. 1984. 'Velopharyngeal Function in Oral and Nasal Vowels: A Cross-Language Study'. Ph.D. diss., University of Connecticut.

Hindret, J. 1687. *L'Art de bien prononcer et de bien parler la langue française*. Paris: Laurent d'Houry. Repr. Geneva: Slatkine, 1973.

Hockett, C. F. 1955. *A Manual of Phonology*. Baltimore: Indiana University–International Journal of American Linguistics.

Holtus, G. 1990. 'Französisch: Gliederung der Sprachräume/*Les Aires linguistiques*'. *LRL*, v/1: 571–95.

Hombert, J.-M. 1986. 'The development of nasalized vowels in the Teke language group (Bantu)'. In K. Bogers and H. van der Hulst (eds.), *The Phonological Representation of Suprasegmentals*. Dordrecht: Foris, pp. 359–79.

Horning, G. 1890. 'Zur Lautgeschichte der ostfranzösischen Mundarten'. *ZrP* 14: 376–96.

House, A. 1957. 'Analog studies of nasal consonants'. *Journal of Speech and Hearing Disorders*, 22: 190–204.

—— and Stevens, K. 1956. 'Analog studies of the nasalization of vowels', *Journal of Speech and Hearing Disorders*, 21: 218–32.

Huffman, M. K., and Krakow, R. A. (eds.). 1993. *Nasals, Nasalization, and the Velum*. San Diego: Academic Press.

Hug, M. 1979. *La Distribution des phonèmes en français*. Geneva: Slatkine.

Iliescu, M. 1972. *Le Frioulan, à partir des dialectes parlés en Roumanie*. The Hague: Mouton.

Ineichen, G. 1957. 'Die paduanische Mundart am Ende des 14. Jahrhunderts auf Grunde des Erbario Carrarese'. *ZrP* 73: 38–123.

Inês Louro, J. 1952. 'Origem e flexão dalguns nomes portugueses em -ão'. *BF 13*: 37–65.

Irimia, D. 1976. *Structura gramaticală a limbii române. Verbul*. Iaşi: Junimea.

Ivănescu, G. 1980. *Istoria limbii române*. Iaşi: Junimea.

Jakobson, R., and Halle, M. 1956. *Fundamentals of Language*. The Hague: Mouton.

James, E. 1982. *The Origins of France from Clovis to the Capetians, 500–1000*. London: Macmillan.

Joos, M. 1948. *Acoustic Phonetics*. Baltimore: Linguistic Society of America.

Josselyn, F. M. 1900. *Etude sur la phonétique italienne*. Paris: A. Fontemoing.

Jungemann, F. 1955. *La teoría del sustrato y los dialectos hispano-romances y gascones*. Madrid: Gredos.

Kasten, L., and Nitti, J. (eds.). 1978. *Concordances and Texts of the Royal Scriptorium Manuscripts of Alfonso X, El Sabio*. Madison, Wis.: HSMS.

Kaye, J. D. 1971. 'Nasal harmony in Desano'. *Linguistic Inquiry* 2: 37–56.

Keil, H. 1855–80. *Grammatici latini*. 8 vols. Leipzig: Teubner.

Kent, R. G. 1945. *The Sounds of Latin: A Descriptive and Historical Phonology*. 3rd ed. Baltimore: Publications of the Linguistic Society of America.

Kovačec, A. 1971. *Descrierea istroromânei actuale*. Bucharest: Ed. Acad.

Krakow, R. A., and Huffman, M. K. 1993. 'Instruments and techniques for investigating velopharyngeal function in the laboratory: an introduction'. In Huffman and Krakow (1993), pp. 3–59.

Kramer, J. 1977. *Historische Grammatik des Dolomitenladinischen. Lautlehre*. Gerbrunn bei Würzburg: Verlag Lehmann.

—— 1989. 'Ladinisch: Grammatikographie und Lexikographie/*Ladino: Grammaticografia e lessicografia*'. *LRL*, iii. 757–63.

Kremer, D. (ed.). 1988. *Homenagem a Joseph M. Piel por ocasião do seu 85.o aniversário*. Tübingen: Niemeyer.

Kremnitz, G. 1991. 'Okzitanisch. Soziolinguistik/*L'Occitan. Sociolinguistique*'. *LRL*, v/2: 33–45.

Kröll, H. 1994. 'Dialektale und regionale Varianten in Portugal/*Dialectos e variedades regionais em Portugal*'. *LRL*, vi/2: 545–59.

Lacerda, A. de, and Head, B. F. 1966. 'Análise de sons nasais e sons nasalizados do português'. *Revista do Lab. de Fonética Experimental* (Coimbra), 6: 5–71.

Ladefoged, P. 1971. *Preliminaries to Linguistic Phonetics*. Chicago: Chicago UP.

—— and Maddieson, I. 1990. 'Vowels of the world's languages'. *JPh* 18: 93–122.

—— 1996. *The Sounds of the World's Languages*. Blackwell: Oxford.

Lafon, J.-Cl. 1961. *Message et phonétique*. Paris: PUF.

Lafont, R. 1991. 'Okzitanisch. Interne Sprachgeschichte. I. Grammatik/*L'Occitan. Histoire interne de la langue. I. Grammaire*'. *LRL*, v/2: 1–18.

Lahti, I. 1953. 'La Dénasalisation en français'. *NM* 44: 1–33.

Lambrior, A. 1880. 'Essai de phonétique roumaine. Voyelles toniques: A'. *Romania*, 9: 99–116, 366–76.

Lanoue, P. de 1596. *Le Grand Dictionnaire de rimes françoises*. Geneva: Berjon. Repr. of 2nd ed. of 1623. Geneva: Slatkine, 1972.

Lapesa, R. 1951. 'La Apócope de la vocal en castellano antiguo: intento de explicación histórica'. In *Estudios dedicados a Menéndez Pidal*. Vol. 2. Madrid: CSIC, pp. 185–226.

—— 1975. 'De nuevo sobre la apócope vocálica en castellano medieval'. *Nueva Revista de Filología Hispánica*, 24: 13–23.

Lartigaut, A. 1669. *Les Progrés de la véritable orthografe*. Paris: Ravenau. Repr. Geneva: Slatkine, 1972.

Lass, R. 1980. *On Explaining Language Change*. Cambridge: CUP.

Lausberg, H. 1939. *Die Mundart Südlukaniens*. [*ZrP Beih.* 90]. Halle: Niemeyer.

—— 1963. *Romanische Sprachwissenschaft. I. Einleitung und Vokalismus* 2nd. ed. Berlin: De Gruyter.

Laver, J. 1980. *The Phonetic Description of Voice Quality*. Cambridge: CUP.

—— 1991. *The Gift of Speech*. Edinburgh: Edinburgh UP.

Lehiste, I. 1970. *Suprasegmentals*. Cambridge, Mass.: MIT Press.

Léon, P. R. 1973. 'Modèle standard et système vocalique du français populaire de jeunes Parisiens'. In G. Rondeaux (ed.), *Contributions canadiennes à la linguistique appliquée*. Montreal: CEC.

—— 1979. 'Standardisation vs. diversification dans la prononciation du français contemporain'. In H. and P. Hollien (eds.), *Current Issues in the Phonetic Sciences*. Vol. I. Amsterdam: Benjamins, pp. 541–9.

—— 1992. *Phonétisme et prononciations du français*. Paris: Nathan.

Leonard, C. S. 1978. *Umlaut in Romance: An Essay in Linguistic Archaeology*. Grossen–Linden: Hoffman.

Lepelley, R. 1974. *Le Parler normand du Val de Saire (Manche)*. Caen: Musée de Normandie.

Lepschy, G. C. 1963. 'The segmental phonemes of Venetian and their classification'. *Word*, 19: 53–66.

—— 1978. 'Una fonologia milanese del 1606: il *Prissian de Milan della parnonzia milanesa*'. In id., *Saggi di linguistica italiana*. Bologna: Il Mulino, pp. 177–215.

Lieberman, P., and Blumstein, S. E. 1988. *Speech Physiology, Speech Perception, and Acoustic Phonetics*. Cambridge: CUP.

Lindqvist, J., and Sundberg, J. 1976. 'Acoustic properties of the nasal tract'. *Phonetica*, 33: 161–8.

Linthorst, P. 1973. *Les Voyelles nasales du français. Etude phonétique et phonologique*. Groningen: V.R.B. Offsetdrukkerij.

Lipski, J. M. 1973. 'On the evolution of Portuguese "-ão"'. *VR 32*: 95–107.

—— 1992. 'Spontaneous nasalization in the development of Afro-Hispanic language'. *Journal of Pidgin and Creole Languages*, 7: 261–305.

Littré, E. 1863–73. *Dictionnaire de la langue française. 4* vols. Paris: Hachette.

Lloyd, P. M. 1987. *From Latin to Spanish.* I. *Historical Phonology and Morphology of the Spanish Language.* Philadelphia: American Philosophical Society.

Lodge, R. A. 1993. *French: From Dialect to Standard.* London: Routledge.

Löfstedt, B. 1961. *Studien über die Sprache der langobardischen Gesetze.* Uppsala: Almqvist and Wiksell.

Lombard, A. 1935. *La Prononciation du roumain.* [= *Uppsala Universitets Årsskrift* fasc., 10; *Språkvetenskapliga sällskapets i Uppsala förhandlingar,* 1934–6]. Uppsala: A.-B. Lundeqvist.

Lonchamp, F. 1979. 'Analyse acoustique des voyelles nasales françaises'. *Verbum* (Univ. of Nancy II), 2: 9–54.

Loporcaro, M. 1988. *Grammatica storica del dialetto di Altamura.* Pisa: Giardini.

Lorck, J. E. 1893. *Altbergamaskische Sprachdenkmäler (IX.–XV. Jahrhundert).* Halle: Niemeyer.

Lorenz-Gonzalez, D. 1985. 'A Phonemic Description of the Andalusian Dialect Spoken in Almogia, Malaga, Spain'. Ph.D. diss., UCLA.

Lorenzo, R. 1988. 'Consideracións sobre as vocais nasais e o ditongo *-ão* en portugués'. In Kremer (1988), pp. 289–326.

Lote, G. 1949. *Histoire du vers français.* I. *Les Origines du vers français.* Paris: Boivin.

Lüdtke, H. 1956. *Die strukturelle Entwicklung des romanischen Vokalismus.* Bonn: Rom. Seminar an der Universität Bonn.

Lunt, H. G. 1973. 'Remarks on nasality: the case of Guaraní'. In S. R. Anderson and P. Kiparsky (eds.), *A Festschrift for Morris Halle.* New York: Holt, Rinehart and Winston, pp. 131–9.

—— 1974. *Old Church Slavonic Grammar.* 6th ed. The Hague: Mouton.

Lurati, O. 1988. ' Areallinguistik. III. Lombardei und Tessin/*Aree linguistiche. III. Lombardia e Ticino'. LRL,* iv. 485–516.

Lutta, C. M. 1923. *Der Dialekt von Bergün.* [*ZrP Beih.* 71]. Halle: Niemeyer.

Machado, J. P. 1977. *Dicionário etimológico da língua portuguesa.* 5 vols. 3rd ed. Lisbon: Livros Horizonte.

McMahon, A. 1994. *Understanding Language Change.* Cambridge: CUP.

Maddieson, I. 1984. *Patterns of Sounds.* Cambridge: CUP.

—— 1991. 'Testing the universality of phonological generalizations with a phonetically specified database: results and limitations'. *Phonetica,* 48: 193–206.

—— and Ladefoged, P. 1993. 'Phonetics of partially nasal consonants'. In Huffman and Krakow (1993), pp. 251–301.

Madonia, G. 1969. 'Les Diphtongues décroissantes et les voyelles nasales du portugais'. *Linguistique,* 1: 129–32.

Maffei Bellucci, P. 1977. *Lunigiana.* [Profilo dei dialetti italiani, 9, 1]. Pisa: Pacini.

Maia, C. de Azevedo. 1975. 'Os falares do Algarve'. *RPF* 17: 37–205.

—— 1977. *Os falares fronteiriços do concelho do Sabugal e da vizinha região de Xalma e Alamedilla.* Suplemento IV da *Revista Portuguesa de Filologia.* Coimbra: Faculdade de Letras da Universidade de Coimbra.

—— 1986. *História do Galego-Português. Estudo lingüístico da Galiza e do Noroeste de Portugal desde o século XIII ao século XVI.* Coimbra: INIC.

Maiden, M. 1991. *Interactive Morphonology: Metaphony in Italy.* London: Routledge.

—— 1995. *A Linguistic History of Italian.* London: Longman.

—— and Parry, M. 1997. *The Dialects of Italy.* London: Routledge.

Malagoli, G. 1910–13. 'Studi sui dialetti reggiani'. *AGI* 17: 29–146, 147–97.

Malécot, A. 1960. 'Vowel nasality as a distinctive feature in American English'. *Language* 36: 222–9.

—— 1975. 'French liaison as a function of grammatical, phonetic and paralinguistic variables'. *Phonetica,* 32: 65–88.

—— and Lindsay, P. 1976. 'The neutralization of /ɛ̃/-/œ̃/ in French'. *Phonetica,* 33: 45–61.

Malkiel, Y. 1990. 'Six categories of nasal epenthesis: their place in the evolution from Latin into Romance'. In id., *Diachronic Problems in Phonosymbolism. Edita and Inedita, 1979–88.* Amsterdam: Benjamins, pp. 231–49.

Malmberg. B. 1969. *Phonétique française.* Malmö: Hermods.

Mancarella, G. B. 1975. *Puglia.* [Profilo dei dialetti italiani, 15–16]. Pisa: Pacini.

Maniet, A. 1975. *La Phonétique historique du latin dans le cadre des langues indo-européennes.* 5th ed. Paris: Klincksieck.

Maragliano, A. 1976. *Dizionario dialettale vogherese.* Bologna: Patron.

Marchello-Nizia, C. 1979. *Histoire de la langue française aux XIVe et XVe siècles.* Paris: Bordas.

Mariner Bigorra, S. 1962. 'Fonemática latina'. In M. Bassols de Climent, *Fonética latina.* Madrid: CSIC, pp. 249–71.

Marshall, J. H. (ed.). 1969. *The 'Donatz Proensals' of Uc Faidit.* London: OUP.

Marshall, M. M. 1984. *The Dialect of Notre-Dame-de-Sanilhac.* Saratoga, Calif.: ANMA Libri.

Marti, R.W. 1984. 'Old Church Slavonic nasal vowels: Ѫ or VN?'. *New Zealand Slavonic Journal,* (no number): 119–52.

Martin, J.-B. 1990. 'Frankoprovenzalisch/Francoprovençal'. *LRL,* v. 671–85.

Martinet, A. 1945. *La Prononciation du français contemporain.* Geneva–Paris: Droz.

—— 1955. *Economie des changements phonétiques. Traité de phonologie diachronique.* Berne: Francke.

—— 1956. *La Description phonologique avec application au parler franco-provençal d'Hauteville (Savoie).* Paris: Droz.

—— 1969*a*. 'Les Voyelles nasales du français'. In A. Martinet, *Le français sans fard.* Paris: PUF, pp. 144–54.

—— 1969*b*. 'C'est jeuli, le Mareuc!'. In A. Martinet, *Le Français sans fard.* Paris: PUF, pp. 191–208.

—— 1980. 'Peut-on prévoir les modifications à venir d'un système phonologique?'. In H. Izzo (ed.), *Italic and Romance* [Festschrift Pulgram]. Amsterdam: Benjamins, pp. 219–31.

—— 1985. 'La Prononciation du français entre 1880 et 1914'. In G. Antoine and R. Martin (eds.), *Histoire de la langue française 1880–1914.* Paris: CNRS, pp. 25–40.

—— and Walter, H. 1973. *Dictionnaire de la prononciation française dans son usage réel.* Paris: France-Expansion.

Martinon, P. 1929. *Comment on prononce le français.* 3rd ed. Paris: Larousse.

Martins, A. M. 1995. 'A evolução das vogais nasais finais ã, õ, no português'. In C. da Cunha Pereira (ed.), *Miscelânea de estudos lingüísticos, filológicos e literários In Memoriam Celso Cunha.* Rio de Janeiro: Nova Fronteira, pp. 617–46.

Massariello Merzagora, G. 1988. *Lombardia.* [Profilo dei dialetti italiani, 3]. Pisa: Pacini.

Mateus, M. H. Mira. 1975. *Aspectos da fonologia portuguesa.* Lisbon: Publ. Centro de Estudos Filológicos.

Matisoff, J. 1975. 'Rhinoglottophilia: the mysterious connection between nasality and glottality'. In Ferguson, Hyman, and Ohala (1975), pp. 265–88.

Matte, E. J. 1982. *Histoire des modes phonétiques du français.* Geneva: Droz.

—— 1984. 'Réexamen de la doctrine traditionnelle sur les voyelles nasales du français'. *RPh* 38: 15–31.

Mayerthaler, E. 1982. *Unbetonter Vokalismus und Silbenstruktur im Romanischen. Beiträge zu einer dynamischen Prozesstypologie.* Tübingen: Niemeyer.

Melillo, A.M. 1977. *Corsica.* [Profilo dei dialetti italiani, 21]. Pisa: Pacini.

Melillo, M. 1986. *Prosodia e vocalismo tonico dei dialetti di Puglia.* Bari: Univ. d. Studi di Bari.

Menéndez Pidal, R. 1940. *Manual de gramática histórica española.* 6th ed. Madrid: Espasa-Calpe.

Merlo, C. 1934. 'Note fonetiche sul dialetto francoprovenzale di Valtournanche (Aosta)'. *ID* 10: 1–62.

—— 1951. 'Profilo fonetico dei dialetti della Valtellina'. *Abhandlungen der Akademie der Wissenschaften (Mainz), Geistes- und Socialwissenschaften* [Wiesbaden: Steiner] 15: 1369–98.

—— 1959. 'Contributi alla conoscenza dei dialetti della Liguria odierna'. In id., *Saggi linguistici.* Pisa: Pacini–Mariotti, pp. 127–60.

Meyer-Lübke, W. 1890. *Grammaire des langues romanes. I. Phonétique.* Tr. E. Rabiet. Paris: Welter.

—— 1920. *Einführung in das Studium der romanischen Sprachwissenschaft.* 3rd ed. Heidelberg: Winter.

—— 1927. *Grammatica storica della lingua italiana e dei dialetti toscani.* 2nd ed. Turin: Loescher.

Michaëlsson, K. 1934–5. 'Alternances -*ien*/-*ian* en ancien français'. *Studia Neophilologica,* 7: 18–29.

—— 1958. *Le Livre de la taille de Paris de l'an 1296* [Romanica Gothoburgensia, 7]. Gothenburg: Almqvist and Wiksell.

Migliorini, B., and Pellegrini, G. B. 1971. *Dizionario del feltrino rustico.* Padua: Liviana.

Mihăescu, H. 1978. *La Langue latine dans le sud-est de l'Europe.* Bucharest–Paris: Ed. Acad.–Les Belles Lettres.

Mihăilă, G. 1971. 'Criteriile delimitării împrumuturilor slave în limba română'. *SCL* 22: 351–66.

—— 1974. *Dicţionar al limbii române vechi (sfîrşitul sec. X – începutul sec. XVI).* Bucharest: Editura enciclopedică.

Mocanu, N. 1972. 'Asupra rotacismului dacoromân. Situaţie actuală în Ţara Moţilor (comunele Scărişoara, Gîrda, şi Arieşeni, jud. Alba)'. *CL* 17: 81–97.

Mombello, G. 1976. *Les Avatars de 'Talentum': Recherches sur l'origine et les variations des acceptions romanes et non-romanes de ce terme*. Turin: Soc. Ed. Internazionale.

Monteagudo, H., and Santamarina, A. 1993. 'Galician and Castilian in contact: historical, social and linguistic aspects'. In R. Posner and J. N. Green (eds.), *Trends in Romance Linguistics and Philology*. 5. *Bilingualism and Linguistic Conflict in Romance*. Berlin–New York: Mouton–De Gruyter, pp. 117–73.

Moraes, J. A. de, and Wetzels, W. L. 1992. 'Sobre a duração dos segmentos vocálicos nasais e nasalizados em português'. *Cadernos de Estudos Lingüísticos*, 23: 153–66.

Morin, Y.-C. 1977. 'Nasalization and diphthongization in Marais Vendéen French'. In M. P. Hagiwara (ed.), *Studies in Romance Linguistics. Proceedings of the 5th Linguistic Symposium on Romance Linguistics*. Rowley, Mass.: Newbury House, pp. 125–44.

—— 1994. 'Quelques réflexions sur la formation des voyelles nasales en français'. *Communication & Cognition*, 27: 27–110.

—— and Kaye, J. 1982. 'The syntactic bases for French liaison'. *Journal of Linguistics*, 18: 291–330.

Muljacic, Z. 1965. 'Per un'analisi binaria dei fonemi latini'. In *Omagiu lui A. Rosetti la 70 de ani*. Bucharest: Ed. Acad., pp. 599–605.

Nandriş, G. 1965. *Handbook of Old Church Slavonic. I. Old Church Slavonic Grammar*. Rev. ed. London: Athlone.

Nandriş, O. 1963. *Phonétique historique du roumain*. Paris: Klincksieck.

Nauton, P. 1974. *Géographie phonétique de la Haute-Loire*. Paris: Les Belles Lettres.

Navarro Tomás, T. 1918. 'Diferencias de duración entre las consonantes españolas'. *RFE* 5: 367–93.

—— 1968. *Manual de pronunciación española*. 14th ed. Madrid: CSIC.

Nesi, A. 1988. 'Interne Sprachgeschichte/*Evoluzione del sistema grammaticale*'. *LRL*, iv. 799–808.

Neto, S. da Silva. 1963. *Introdução ao estudo da língua portuguêsa no Brasil*. Rio de Janeiro: Inst. Nac. do Livro.

Nève de Mévergnies, F.-X. 1984. '"Auquin doute: un parfum brun s'en va . . . " La disparition du phonème /œ̃/ en français contemporain'. *FM* 52: 98–219.

Nicolet, N. 1929. *Der Dialekt des Antronatales*. [*ZrP Beih*. 79]. Halle: Niemeyer.

Nicoli, F. 1983. *Grammatica milanese*. Busto Arsizio: Bramante Ed.

Niculescu, A. 1981. *Outline History of the Romanian Language*. Bucharest: Ed. ştiintifică şi enciclopedică.

Niedermann, M. 1953. *Historische Lautlehre des Lateinischen*. 3rd ed. Heidelberg: Winter.

Nobiling, O. 1903. 'Die Nasalvokale im Portugiesischen'. *NS* 11: 129–53.

Nolan, F. 1982. 'The role of Action Theory in the description of speech production'. *Linguistics*, 20: 287–308.

Nunes, J. J. 1960. *Compêndio de gramática histórica portuguesa*. 6th ed. Lisbon: Livraria Clássica.

Ohala, J. 1975. 'Phonetic explanations for nasal sound patterns'. In Ferguson, Hyman, and Ohala (1975), pp. 289–316.

—— 1981. 'The listener as a source of sound change'. In M. Miller et al., *Papers from the Parasession in Language and Behaviour*. Chicago: Chicago LS, pp. 178–203.

—— 1987. 'Explanation in phonology: opinions and examples'. In W. U. Dressler et al. (eds.), *Phonologica 1984*. Cambridge: CUP, pp. 215–25.

d'Olivet, Abbé P. J. T. 1736. *Traité de la prosodie française*. Paris: Barbou. Repr. Geneva: Slatkine, 1968.

Omeltchenko, S. 1977. *A Quantitative and Comparative Study of the Vocalism of the Latin Inscriptions of North Africa, Britain, Dalmatia, and the Balkans*. Chapel Hill: Univ. of N. Carolina Press.

O'Shaughnessy, D. 1981. 'A study of French vowel and consonant durations'. *JPh* 9: 385–406.

Palmer, L. R. 1954. *The Latin Language*. London: Faber.

Palsgrave, J. 1530. *Lesclarcissement de la langue françoyse*. London: Haukyns. Repr. in F. Génin (ed.), *Documents inédits sur l'histoire de France*. Paris: Imprimerie Nationale, 1852.

Papahagi, T. 1974. *Dicţionarul dialectului aromân*. Bucharest: Ed. Acad.

Paris, G. 1878. Rev. of G. Lücking, *Die ältesten französischen Mundarten* (1877). *Romania*, 7: 111–40.

—— 1898. Review of Uschakoff (1897). *Romania*, 27: 300–4.

—— and Pannier, L. (eds.). 1872. *La Vie de St. Alexis, poème du XIe siècle et renouvellements des XIIe, XIIIe et XIVe siècles*. Paris: Champion.

Parkinson, S. 1982. 'Phonology versus morphology in the Portuguese verb'. In N. Vincent and M. Harris (eds.), *Studies in the Romance Verb*. London: Croom Helm, pp. 19–41.

—— 1983. 'Portuguese nasal vowels as phonological diphthongs'. *Lingua*, 61: 157–77.

—— 1993. 'Final nasals in the Galician-Portuguese *cancioneiros*'. In D. Mackenzie and I. Michael (eds.), *Hispanic Studies in Honour of F. W. Hodcroft*. Llangrannog: Dolphin, pp. 51–62.

—— 1997. 'Aspectos teóricos da história das vogais nasais portuguesas'. In *Actas do XII Encontro Nacional da Associação Portuguesa de Lingüística*. Vol. 2 Lisbon: APL, pp. 253–72.

Parodi, E. 1902. 'Studj liguri. Il dialetto di Genova dal secolo XVI ai nostri giorni'. *AGI* 16: 105–61, 333–65.

—— 1907. 'Intorno al dialetto d'Ormea'. *Studj Romanzi*, 5: 89–122.

Parry, M. M. 1984. 'The Dialect of Cairo Montenotte'. Ph.D. diss., Univ. of Wales at Aberystwyth.

Passy, P. 1914. *The Sounds of the French Language*. 2nd ed. Oxford: Clarendon.

Payán Sotomayor, P. M. 1988. *La pronunciación del español en Cádiz*. Cadiz: Univ. of Cadiz.

Pellegrini, G. B. 1975. *Saggi di linguistica italiana*. Turin: Boringhieri.

—— 1977a. *Studi di dialettologia e filologia veneta*. Pisa: Pacini.

—— 1977b. *Carta dei dialetti d'Italia*. Pisa: Pacini.

—— 1991. *La genesi del retoromanzo (o ladino)*. [*ZrP Beih.* 238]. Tübingen: Niemeyer.

Penny, R. 1990. 'Labiodental /f/, aspiration and /h/-dropping in Spanish: the evolving phonemic value of the graphs *f* and *h*'. In D. Hook and B. Taylor (eds.), *Cultures in Contact in Medieval Spain*. King's College London Medieval Studies III, 157–82.

—— 1991a. *A History of the Spanish Language*. Cambridge: CUP.

—— 1991b. 'El origen astur-leonés de algunos fenómenos andaluces y americanos'. *Lletres asturianes*, 39: 33–40.

Pensado Ruiz, C. 1984. *Cronología relativa del castellano*. Salamanca: Univ. de Salamanca.

Pereira dos Santos, C. J. 1958. 'Os falares portugueses nos séculos XVII e XVIII'. Diss., Univ. of Coimbra: Coimbra.

Petracco Sicardi, G., and Azaretti, E. 1989. *Studi linguistici sull'anfizona Liguria-Provenza*. Alessandria: Ed. dell'Orso.

Petrovici, E. 1930. *De la nasalité en roumain. Recherches expérimentales*. Cluj: Institutul de arte grafică 'Ardealul'.

—— 1966. 'Le Latin oriental possédait-il des éléments slaves?'. *RRL* 11: 313–21.

Petrucci, P. R. 1995. 'The historical development of Rumanian /ɨ/'. In J. Amastae, G. Goodall, M. Montalbetti, M. Phinney (eds.), *Contemporary Research in Romance Linguistics*. Amsterdam: Benjamins, pp. 167–76.

Philipon, E. 1910. 'Les Parlers du Duché de Bourgogne aux XIIIe et XIVe siècles'. *Romania*, 39: 476–531.

Pignon, J. 1960. *L'Évolution phonétique des parlers du Poitou (Vienne et Deux-Sèvres)*. Paris: Bibl. du 'Français Moderne'.

Pittau, M. 1972. *Grammatica del sardo-nuorese*. 2nd ed. Bologna: Patron.

Plénat, M. 1987. 'On the structure of rime in French'. *Linguistics*, 25: 867–87.

Plomteux, H. 1981. *I dialetti delle Liguria orientale odierna, la val Graveglia*. Repr. of 1975 ed. in 2 vols. Bologna: Patron.

Poggi Salani, T. 1976. 'Note sull'italiano di Milano'. In R. Simone, U. Vignuzzi, G. Ruggiero (eds.), *Studi di fonetica e fonologia*. Rome: Bulzoni, pp. 245–60.

Pope, M. K. 1932. 'a, ã, ɑ, ɑ̃n in French and Anglo-Norman'. In M. Williams and J. A. de Rothschild (eds.), *A Miscellany of Studies in Romance Languages and Literatures Presented to Leon E. Kastner*. Cambridge: Heffer, pp. 396–402.

—— 1952. *From Latin to Modern French*. 2nd ed. Manchester: Manchester UP.

Porto Dapena, J. A. 1976. 'Fonología de la N velar gallega'. *Revista de Dialectología y Tradiciones Populares*, 32: 467–77.

—— 1977. *El gallego hablado en la comarca ferrolana*. [*Verba* Anejo, 9]. Santiago de Compostela: Univ. de Santiago.

Posner, R. 1971. 'On synchronic and diachronic rules: French nasalization'. *Lingua*, 27: 184–97.

Postal, P. M. 1968. *Aspects of Phonological Theory*. New York: Harper and Row.

Price, G. 1971. *The French Language: Present and Past*. London: Arnold.

—— 1991. *An Introduction to French Pronunciation*. Oxford: Blackwell.

Pulgram, E. 1958. *The Tongues of Italy*. Cambridge, Mass.: Harvard UP.

Puşcariu, S. 1937. *Etudes de linguistique roumaine*. Cluj–Bucharest: Monitorul oficial şi imprimeriile statului.

—— 1976 [1940]. *Limba română*. I. *Privire generală*. Bucharest: Ed. Minerva.

Quilis, A. 1992. 'Spanisch. Phonetik und Phonemik/*Español. Fonética y fonemática*'. *LRL*, vi/1: 55–62.

Radtke, E. 1988. 'Areallinguistik. IX. Kampanien, Kalabrien/*Aree linguistische. IX. Campania*'. *LRL*, iv. 652–68.

Raphael, L. J., Dorman, M. F., Freeman, F., Tobin, C. 1975. 'Vowel and nasal duration as cues to voicing in word-final stop consonants: spectrographic and perceptual studies'. *Journal of Speech and Hearing Research*, 18: 389–400.

Rasico, P. D. 1981. 'El tractament català dels grups de nasal e líquida més oclusiva, a la llum de la documentació medieval: precisions filològiques'. *Estudis de llengua i literatura*. Vol. 3. Montserrat: Publ. de l'Abadia de Montserrat, pp. 9–25.

—— 1982. *Estudis sobre la fonologia del català preliterari*. Montserrat: Curial.

—— 1985. 'La conservació de la -N' etimològica a l'antiga diòcesi de Girona'. In *Actes del Quart Col.loqui d'Estudis Catalans a Nord-Amèrica*. Montserrat: Publ. de l'Abadia de Montserrat, pp. 41–56.

—— 1986. 'Consideracions fonològiques sobre el parlar de l'Alt Urgell a l'Edat Mitjana'. In J. Veny and J. M. Pujals (eds.), *Actes del Setè Col.loqui Internacional de Llengua i Literatura Catalanes*. Montserrat: Publ. de l'Abadia de Montserrat, pp. 441–65.

Ravier, X. 1991. 'Okzitanisch. Areallinguistik/*L'Occitan. Les aires linguistiques*'. *LRL*, v/2: 80–105.

Recasens i Vives, D. 1991. *Fonètica descriptiva del català*. Barcelona: Inst. d'estudis catalans.

Reenen, P. van. 1982a. *Phonetic Feature Definitions: Their Integration into Phonology and their Relation to Speech. A Case Study of the Feature NASAL*. Dordrecht: Foris.

—— 1982b. 'Voyelles nasales en ancien français non suivies de consonne nasale'. *Rapports. Het Franse Boek*, 52: 132–43.

—— 1985. 'La Fiabilité des donnés linguistiques (A propos de la formation des voyelles nasales en ancien français)'. In *XVI Congrés Internacional de Lingüística i Filologia Romàniques. Actes*. Vol. II. Palma: Ed. Moll, pp. 37–51.

—— 1987. 'La Formation des voyelles nasales en ancien français d'après le témoignage des assonances'. In B. Kampers-Mahne and C. Vet (eds.), *Etudes de linguistique française*. Amsterdam: Rodopi, pp. 127–41.

—— 1994. 'Les Premières (?) voyelles nasales en ancien français et le rapport avec la non-prononciation du *r*, -*ss*- intervocalique dans *pensser* et *perssonne*'. *Communication & Cognition*, 27: 111–21.

Reichstein, R. 1960. 'Etude des variations sociales et géographiques des faits linguistiques'. *Word*, 16: 55–95.

Remacle, L. 1948. *Le Problème de l'ancien wallon*. Liège: Bibl. Fac. de Phil. et Lettres, Univ. Liège.

Rheinfelder, H. 1968. *Altfranzösische Grammatik*. I. *Lautlehre*. 4th ed. Munich: Hueber.

Richter, E. 1934. *Beiträge zur Geschichte der Romanismen*. I. *Chronologische Phonetik des Französischen bis zum Ende des 8. Jahrhunderts*. [*ZrP Beih*. 82]. Halle: Niemeyer.

Rizzi, E. 1987. 'Fonologia'. In E. Rizzi and G. C. Vincenzi, *L'italiano parlato a Bologna: fonologia e morfosintassi*. Bologna: CLUEB, pp. 13–29.

Robe, S. L. 1960. *The Spanish of Rural Panama: Major Dialectal Features*. Berkeley: Univ. of California Press.

Rochet, B. L. 1974. 'A morphologically-determined sound change in Old French'. *Linguistics*, 135: 43–56.

—— 1976. *The Formation and the Evolution of the French Nasal Vowels*. [*ZrP Beih*. 153]. Tübingen: Niemeyer.

Rohlfs, G. 1931. 'Galloitalienische Sprachkolonien in der Basilikata'. *ZrP* 51: 249–79. It. trans. in Rohlfs (1988), pp. 9–37.

—— 1941. 'Galloitalienische Sprachkolonien am Golf von Policastro'. *ZrP* 61: 79–113. It. trans. in Rohlfs (1988), pp. 41–76.

—— 1966–9. *Grammatica storica della lingua italiana e dei suoi dialetti. 3* vols. [I. *Fonetica* (1966), II. *Morfologia* (1968), III. *Sintassi e formazione delle parole* (1969)]. Turin: Einaudi.

—— 1970. *Le gascon. Etudes de philologie pyrénéenne* [*ZrP Beih.* 85]. 2nd ed. Tübingen: Niemeyer.

—— 1972. 'Colonie galloitaliche in Lucania'. In id., *Studi e ricerche su lingua e dialetti d'Italia*. Florence: Sansoni, pp. 203–19.

—— 1977. *Nuovo dizionario dialettale della Calabria*. Rev. ed. Ravenna: Longo.

—— 1988. *Studi linguistici sulla Lucania e sul Cilento*. Galatina: Congedo Ed.

Rosetti, A. 1924. *Etude sur le rhotacisme en roumain*. Paris: Champion.

—— 1947. *Mélanges de linguistique et de philologie*. Bucharest–Copenhagen: Inst. de Ling.Rom.–Munksgaard.

—— 1970. 'Despre *den* şi *din*'. *SCL* 21: 693–4. Also in Rosetti (1978), pp. 735–6.

—— 1978. *Istoria limbii române*. 2nd ed. Bucharest: Ed. şt.şi encicl.

Rosset, T. 1911. *Les Origines de la prononciation moderne, étudiée au XVIIe siècle d'après les remarques des grammairiens et les textes en patois de la banlieue parisienne*. 2 vols. Paris: A. Colin.

Rothe, W. 1972. *Phonologie des Französischen*. Berlin: Schmidt.

Rousselot, Abbé J.-P., and Laclotte, F. 1903. *Précis de prononciation française*. Paris: Welter.

Ruhlen, M. 1973. 'Nasal vowels'. *Working Papers on Language Universals* 12: 1–36.

—— 1975. 'Patterning of nasal vowels'. In Ferguson, Hyman, and Ohala (1975), pp. 333–51.

—— 1978. 'Nasal vowels'. In J. H. Greenberg (ed.), *Universals of Human Language*. 2. *Phonology*. Stanford, Calif.: Stanford UP, pp. 203–41.

—— 1979. 'On the origin and evolution of French nasal vowels'. *RPh* 32: 321–35.

Safarewicz, J. 1974. *Linguistic Studies*. The Hague: Mouton.

Sainliens, C. de [C. Holyband]. 1576. *The French Littelton*. Repr. of 1609 edition, M. St. Clare Byrne ed. Cambridge: CUP, 1953.

Sala, M. 1976. *Contributions à la phonétique historique du roumain*. Paris: Klincksieck.

Samaran, C., and Laborde, Comte A. de. 1933. *La Chanson de Roland: Reproduction phototypique du manuscrit Digby 23 de la Bodleian Library d'Oxford*. Paris: Société des Anciens Textes Français.

Sampson, G. 1980. *Schools of Linguistics*. London: Hutchinson.

Sampson, R. 1981. 'Subphonemic length variation in Italian consonants'. *Word* 32: 35–44.

—— 1983. 'The origin of Portuguese -*ão*'. *ZrP* 99: 33–68.

—— 1985. 'The pattern of evolution of Balkan Latin /ɛ/'. *RRL* 30: 327–59.

—— 1989. 'Vowel nasalization and its implementation in Romanian'. *NM* 90: 185–93.

—— 1993. 'La nasalización vocálica en las hablas iberorromances'. In R. Penny (ed.), *Actas del Primer Congreso Anglo-Hispano*. I. *Lingüística*. pp. 171–80.

—— 1995. 'Romanian vowel nasalization and the palatal nasal /ɲ/'. *SEER* 17: 601–12..

—— (forthcoming) 'Diphthongization and nasalization of /ɛ/ in Romanian proparoxytons'.

Sanga, G. 1987. *Lingua e dialetti di Bergamo e delle valli*. 3 vols [I. *Il dialetto di Bergamo*, II.

I dialetti delle valli, III. *L'italiano regionale bergamasco*]. Bergamo: Fondo Emma Giudici Lubrina.

—— 1988. 'La lunghezza vocalica nel milanese e la coscienza fonologica dei parlanti'. *RPh* 41: 290–7.

Santos, M. J. de Moura. 1962–8. 'Os falares fronteiriços de Trás-os-Montes'. *RPF* 12 (1962– 3), 509–65; 13 (1964–5), 65–261; 14 (1966–8), 213–415.

Sauzet, P. 1988. 'L'Occitan: langue immolée'. In G. Vermes (ed.), *Vingt-cinq communautés linguistiques de la France*. I. *Langues régionales et langues non-territorialisées*. Paris: L'Harmattan, pp. 208–60.

Schane, S. 1968. *French Phonology and Morphology*. Cambridge, Mass.: MIT Press.

Schlieben-Lange, B. 1991. 'Okzitanisch: Grammatikographie und Lexikographie/ *L'Occitan. Grammaticographie et lexicographie*'. *LRL*, v/2, 105–26.

Schlösser, R. 1985. *Historische Lautlehre des Aromunischen von Metsovon*. Hamburg: Buske.

Schmeck, H. 1952. 'Probleme des korsischen Konsonantismus. Phonologische Darstellung'. *ZrP* 68: 49–72.

Schorta, A. 1938. *Lautlehre der Mundart von Müstair*. Paris–Zürich, Leipzig: Droz– Niehans.

Schourup, L. C. 1972. 'Characteristics of vowel nasalization'. *Papers in Linguistics*, 5: 530– 48.

—— 1973. 'A cross-linguistic study of vowel nasalization'. *Working Papers in Linguistics (Ohio State University)*, 15: 190–221.

Schürr, F. 1918–19. *Romagnolische Dialektstudien*. 2 vols. [I. *Lautlehre alter Texte* (1918), II. *Lautlehre lebender Mundarten* (1919)]. Vienna: Akad. d. Wissenschaften.

Schwartz, M. F. 1968. 'The acoustics of normal and nasal vowel production'. *Cleft Palate Journal*, 5: 125–37.

Scullen, M. E. 1994. 'On using moras to analyze liaison and vowel nasalization'. In C. Lyche (ed.), *French Generative Phonology: Retrospective and Perspectives*. Univ. of Salford, Salford: AFLS and ESRI, pp. 259–75.

Shaffer, M. 1981. 'Portuguese *-idão*, Spanish *-(ed)umbre* and their Romance cognates. A critical survey of a century of philological gropings'. *RPh* 35: 37–62.

Shevelov, G. Y. 1964. *A Prehistory of Slavic. The Historical Phonology of Common Slavic*. Heidelberg: Winter.

Silva, M. H. Santo. 1961. 'Características fonéticas do falar minhoto'. *BF* 20: 309–21.

Silva Neto, S. 1963. *Introdução ao estudo da língua portuguêsa no Brasil*. Rio de Janeiro: Inst. Nac. do Livro.

Sletsjøe, L. 1959. *Le Développement de l et n en ancien portugais*. Oslo: Oslo Univ. Press.

Solé, M.-J. 1992. 'Phonetic and phonological processes: the case of nasalization'. *Language and Speech*, 35: 29–43.

—— 1995. 'Spatio-temporal patterns of velopharyngeal action in phonetic and phono-logical nasalization'. *Language and Speech*, 38: 1–23.

Sommer, F. 1977. *Handbuch der lateinischen Laut- und Formenlehre*. I. *Einleitung und Lautlehre*. 4th ed. Heidelberg: Winter.

Spence, N. C. W. 1960. *A Glossary of Jersey French*. Oxford: Blackwell.

Stehl, T. 1980. *Die Mundarten Apuliens: Historische und strukturelle Beiträge*. Münster: Aschendorff.

Stevens, K. N., Fant, G., Hawkins, S. 1987. 'Some acoustical and perceptual correlates of nasal vowels'. In R. Channon and L. Shockey (eds.), *In Honor of Ilse Lehiste*. Dordrecht: Foris, pp. 241–54.

Stimm, H., and Linder, K. P. 1989. 'Bündnerromanisch. Interne Sprachgeschichte. I. Grammatik/*Le Romanche. Histoire linguistique interne. I. Grammaire*'. *LRL*, iii. 764–85.

Stotz, P. 1996. *Handbuch zur lateinischen Sprache des Mittelalters*. 3. *Lautlehre*. Munich: C. H. Beck'sche Verlagsbuchhandlung.

Straka, G. 1955. 'Remarques sur les voyelles nasales, leur origine et leur évolution en français' *RLiR* 19: 245–74.

—— 1981. 'Sur la formation de la prononciation française d'aujourd'hui'. *TraLiLi* 19: 161–248.

—— 1985. 'Les Rimes classiques et la prononciation française de l'époque'. *TraLiLi* 23: 61–138.

—— 1987. 'Sur le traitement de l'*e* devant nasale en syllabe initiale: *fener–faner*, mais *fenouil, fenaison*'. In G. Lüdi et al. (eds.), '*Romania ingeniosa*' *Festschrift Hilty*. Bern–Frankfurt: Lang, pp. 237–59.

—— 1990. 'Phonetik und Phonemik/*Phonétique et phonématique*'. *LRL*, v/I. 1–33.

Sturtevant, E. H. 1968. *The Pronunciation of Greek and Latin*. 2nd ed. Bouma: Groningen.

Stussi, A. 1965. *Testi veneziani del Duecento e dei primi del Trecento*. Pisa: Nistri–Lischi.

Suchier, H. 1893. *Altfranzösische Grammatik. I. Die Schriftsprache*. Halle: Niemeyer.

Şuteu, F. 1976. *Influenţa ortografiei asupra pronunţării literare românesti*. Bucharest: Ed. Acad.

Svenson, L.-O. 1959. *Les Parlers du Marais vendéen*. Göteborg: Elanders Aktiebolag.

Szabo, R.K. 1973. 'The proper underlying interpretation for nasalized vowels'. *Glossa*, 7: 130–40.

Tagliavini, C. 1965. *La corretta pronuncia italiana*. Bologna: Casa Editrice Libraria Capitol.

Tănase, E. 1972. 'Nazalizarea vocalică în limba romấnă'. *SL*: 9–14.

Tănase, A.-M. 1984. 'Correspondances phonologiques franco-roumaines en diachronie'. *RRL* 29: 139–46.

Tatò, P. 1981. 'Romance phonological evidence for the noncontinuant status of /l/'. In W. W. Cressey and D. J. Napoli (eds.), *Linguistic Symposium on Romance Languages: 9*, pp. 69–82.

Taylor, J. 1996. *Sound Evidence. Speech Communities and Social Accents in Aix-en-Provence*. Berne: Peter Lang.

Tekavčić, P. 1972. *Grammatica storica dell'italiano*. 3 vols. [I. *Fonematica*. 2nd ed. (1974)]. Bologna: Il Mulino.

Teyssier, P. 1980. *Histoire de la langue portugaise*. Paris: PUF.

Tilander, G. 1959. 'Porque -*am*, -*om* se tornaram -*ão* em português'. *Revista de Portugal Série A, Língua portuguesa*, 24: 292–303.

Tláskal J. 1980. 'Remarques sur les voyelles nasales en portugais'. *Zeitschrift für Phonetik*, 33: 562–70.

Traina, A. 1953. *L'alfabeto e la pronunzia del latino*. 4th ed. 1973. Bologna: Patron.

Tranel, B. 1981. *Concreteness in Generative Phonology: Evidence from French*. Berkeley: Univ. of California Press.

—— 1987. *The Sounds of French*. Cambridge: CUP.

—— 1992. 'On suppletion and French liaison'. In P. Hirschbühler and K. Koerner (eds.), *Romance Languages and Modern Linguistic Theory*. Amsterdam: Benjamins, pp. 269–308.

Tuaillon, G. 1994. 'Le Français a-t-il quatre voyelles nasales?'. *Communication & Cognition*, 27: 123–32.

Turculeţ, A. 1989. 'Rumänisch: Grammatikographie/*Le Roumain. Grammaticographie*' *LRL*, iii. 481–91.

Tuttle, E. F. 1981–2. 'Un mutamento linguistico e il suo inverso: l'apocope nell'alto veneto'. *RID* 5–6: 15–35.

—— 1991. 'Nasalization in northern Italy: syllabic constraints and strength scales as developmental parameters'. *Rivista di linguistica*, 3: 23–92.

Uschakoff, I. 1897. 'Zur Frage von den nasalierten Vokalen im Altfranzösischen'. *Mémoires de la Société Néophilologique à Helsingfors*, 2: 19–50.

Väänänen, V. 1966. *Le Latin vulgaire des inscriptions pompéiennes*. 3rd ed. Berlin: Akademie-Verlag.

—— 1967. *Introduction au latin vulgaire*. 2nd ed. Paris: Klincksieck.

Vasconcellos, J. Leite de. 1928. *Opúsculos. II. Dialectologia*. Coimbra: Imprensa da Universidade.

—— 1970. *Esquisse d'une dialectologie portugaise*. Repr. of 1901 ed. Lisbon: Centro de Estudos Filológicos.

Vasiliu, E. 1968. *Fonologia istorică a dialectelor dacoromâne*. Bucharest: Ed. Acad.

Vaudelin, G. 1713–15. *Nouvelle manière d'écrire comme on parle en France* and *Instructions crétiennes*. Paris: Cot & Lamisle. Repr. Geneva: Slatkine, 1973.

Vaugelas, C. F. de. 1647. *Remarques sur la langue françoise*. Facsimile edition, ed. J. Streicher. Paris: Droz, 1934.

Veny, J. 1991. 'Katalanisch: Areallinguistik'/*Le Catalan. Areas lingüísticas. LRL* ,v/2, 243–61.

Vielliard, J. 1927. *Le Latin des diplômes royaux et chartes privées de l'époque mérovingienne*. Paris: Bibl. de l'Ecole des Hautes Etudes.

Villena Ponsoda, J. A. 1987. *El vocalismo del español andaluz. Forma y sustancia*. Malaga: Univ. of Malaga.

Vincent, N. 1989. 'Latin'. In M. Harris and N. Vincent (eds.), *The Romance Languages*. London: Routledge, pp. 26–77.

Vogel, I. 1982. *La sillaba come unità fonologica*. Bologna: Zanichelli.

Wacker, G. 1916. *Über das Verhältnis von Dialekt und Schriftsprache im Altfranzösischen*. Halle: Niemeyer.

Wagner, M. L. 1941. *Historische Lautlehre des Sardischen*. [*ZrP Beih*. 93]. Halle: Niemeyer.

—— 1960–4. *Dizionario etimologico sardo*. 3 vols. Heidelberg: Winter.

Wailly, M. de. 1786. *Principes généraux et particuliers de la langue française*. 10th ed. Paris: Barbou.

Walter, H. 1982. *Enquête phonologique et variétés régionales du français*. Paris: PUF.

—— 1988. *Le Français dans tous les sens*. Paris: Laffont.

—— 1989. 'Prononciation et phonologie du français à la fin du XVIIe siècle d'après le corpus de Gile Vaudelin'. In *La Variation dans la langue en France du XVIe au XIXe siècle.* Ed. du CNRS, pp. 73–86.

Warnant, L. 1956. *La Constitution du mot en wallon.* Paris: Société d'Edition 'Les Belles Lettres'.

Weinrich, H. 1969. *Phonologische Studien zur romanischen Sprachgeschichte.* 2nd ed. Münster: Aschendorff.

Wells, J. C. 1982. *Accents of English.* 2 *The British Isles.* Cambridge: CUP.

Whalen, D. H., and Beddor, P. S. 1989. 'Connections betwen nasality and vowel duration and height: elucidation of the Eastern Algonquian intrusive nasal'. *Language,* 65: 457–86.

Williams, E. B. 1962. *From Latin to Portuguese.* 2nd ed. Philadelphia: Univ. of Philadelphia Press.

Wolf, H. 1985. 'Knacklaut in Orgosolo'. *ZrP* 101: 269–311.

Wright, J. T 1975. 'Effects of vowel nasalization on the perception of vowel height'. In Ferguson, Hyman, and Ohala (1975), pp. 373–88.

—— 1980. 'The behavior of nasalized vowels in the perceptual vowel space'. *Report of the Phonology Laboratory (Univ. of Calif., Berkeley),* 5: 127–63.

—— 1986. 'The behavior of nasalized vowels in the perceptual vowel space'. In J. J. Ohala and J. J. Jaeger (eds.), *Experimental Phonology.* Orlando, Fla.: Academic Press, pp. 45–67.

Wüest, J. 1979. *La Dialectalisation de la Gallo-Romania.* Berne: Francke.

Xove, X. 1988. 'Notas sobre a orixe da oposición /a/-/ɐ/ en portugués'. In Kremer (1988), pp. 461–96.

Zamboni, A. 1977. *Veneto.* [Profilo dei dialetti italiani, 5]. Pisa: Pacini.

—— 1988. 'Areallinguistik. IV. Venezien/*Aree linguistiche. IV. Veneto'. LRL,* iv. 517–38.

Zamora Vicente, A. 1967. *Dialectología española.* 2nd ed. Madrid: Gredos.

Zaun, A. 1917. *Mundart von Aniane.* [*ZrP Beih.* 51]. Halle: Niemeyer.

Zéliqzon, L. 1924. *Dictionnaire des patois romans de la Moselle.* Strasbourg: Fac. des Lettres de l'Univ. de Strasbourg.

Zerling, J.-P. 1984. 'Phénomènes de nasalité et de nasalization vocaliques: étude cinéradiographique pour deux locuteurs'. *Travaux de l'Institut de Phonétique de Strasbourg,* 16: 241–66.

Zörner, L. 1986. 'Caratteristiche liguri nei dialetti di montagna della provincia di Piacenza'. *RLiR* 50: 67–118.

—— 1989. *Die Dialekte von Travo und Groppallo: diachrone und synchrone Studien zum Piacentinischen.* Vienna: Verlag der Österreichischen Akademie der Wissenschaft.

—— 1997. *Il Pagotto. Dialetto dell'Alpago.* [Quaderni Patavini di Linguistica Monografie, 16]. Padua: Unipress.

Subject index

Word index

Langue d'oïl (including standard French and Old French)

Spanish

Galician-Portuguese

Italo-romance (including standard Italian)

OTHER

English

Index of localities

DATE DUE

DEMCO 38-297